THE HANDBOOK OF STRATEGIC PUBLIC RELATIONS & INTEGRATED COMMUNICATIONS

CLARKE L. CAYWOOD, Ph.D.

*Department of Integrated Marketing
and Communications
Medill School of Journalism
Northwestern University*

Boston, Massachusetts   Burr Ridge, Illinois
Dubuque, Iowa   Madison, Wisconsin   New York, New York
San Francisco, California   St. Louis, Missouri

Library of Congress Cataloging-in-Publication Data

Handbook of strategic ublic relations & integrated communications /
  [edited by] Clarke L. Caywood.
      p.   cm.
    Includes index.
    ISBN 0-7863-1131-2
    1. Public relations. 2. Communication in management.
  3. Communication in marketing.   I. Caywood, Clarke L., 1947–   .
  HM263.H317   1997
  658.4'5—dc20   96–36234

McGraw-Hill

A Division of The McGraw·Hill Companies

7 8 9   BKM BKM   9 0 9 8 7 6 5 4 3 2 1 0

ISBN 0-7863-1131-2

This publication is designed to provide accurate and
authoritative information in regard to the subject matter
covered. It is sold with the understanding that neither the
author nor the publisher is engaged in rendering legal, accounting,
or other professional service. If legal advice or other expert
assistance is required, the services of a competent professional
person should be sought.

   —From a Declaration of Principles jointly adopted by a Committee
   of the American Bar Association and a Committee of Publishers.

Dramatic change characterized public relations during the last four decades. As in many fields and disciplines, public relations has grown up since World War II. Change has been the hallmark of the growing-up process. Despite constant barbs, criticisms, lambastings, and crises, public relations has not only survived, but flourished and prospered with ever-increasing success and value, becoming more sophisticated, professional, and productive. Today, corporations and nonprofit institutions are staffed with competent and experienced public relations professionals. Many public relations agencies and consultants get high marks for their services. Despite their frequent denials, even the media must often rely on the help and services of public relations professionals.

In attempting to put in perspective my over 40 years of experience in public relations, I see not a revolution, but an evolution encompassing three periods of growth and development. First, in the 1950s and 1960s, the field was characterized by relatively simple and traditional activities, including new personnel announcements, modest new product marketing efforts, trade magazine bylined articles, annual reports and quarterly financial statements, annual shareholder meetings, modest community relations programs, and occasional executive speeches before Rotary and Chamber of Commerce groups. Public relations was becoming more businesslike as more and more capable young people came into the business.

The second period evolved in the 1970s and 1980s as the spectrum of public relations activities and responsibilities broadened. Public relations professionals with corporations or agencies were not only former newspaper reporters, but now came from a variety of backgrounds, including finance, marketing, government, law, and education. The acceptance of corporate communications and public relations rose. By the 1980s, many top public relations executives reported directly to the CEO. Public relations agencies diversified, and many of the larger firms offered management services which brought them into direct competition with general consulting firms. The corporate senior communications officer often became an integral part of the top executive group. A few were even put on the board of directors.

Public relations practioners not only provided advice on how to communicate, but increasingly on what to say. Specialists in public affairs, community relations, investor relations, media relations, and speechwriting all became key parts of public relations staffs. Increasingly, all of the publics—customers, shareholders, employees, consumer activists, environmental groups, the financial community, and local, state, and federal government— required specific communications groups. My former associate and partner, Harold Burson, summarized brilliantly the "maturation of public relations." Here are Harold Burson's reflections:

> Over this half-century I have been in public relations, the evolution has been something like this:
> In the early days of public relations as a formal business discipline, roughly the first half of the 20th century, the question the CEO asked his (in those days it was always "his") senior public relations officer was "How do I say it?" The question inevitably followed a management decision. There was a desire or a need to communicate a decision or an action, invariably via a press release. The problem was putting it in the right words. Doing that and getting it to the

right media outlets was the job of the senior public relations officer. Ergo, the "How do I say it?" era of public relations.

But along came the decade of the 1960s and with it lots of situations new to even the most farsighted and sophisticated business executives. That was the decade when civil rights emerged as a corporate issue. That was the decade of the "consumer's right to know." That was the decade when the environment surfaced visibly and forcefully.

Civil rights issues manifested themselves in protest marches and meetings, in confrontations at annual meetings, in sit-ins at public lunch counters, in boycotts against specific products. For corporate management, these were totally new experiences not included in the MBA curriculum, experiences CEOs were facing for the first time.

Since all of them involved interaction with the public and with the media, it was natural for the CEO to turn to his senior public relations officer. On these occasions, however, the question went beyond "How do I say it?" The question became "What do I say?" For public relations, that was a major upward step.

Public pressures on business continued to intensify through the decades of the 1970s and 1980s and into the 1990s. Such issues included not only the by-now-mature issues of minority rights, consumer's right to know, and the environment, but new challenges brought about by global competitive forces that added to the business lexicon such new words and terms as "downsizing" and "restructuring" and "hostile takeovers" and "corporate governance."

Starting in the 1970s, business news began moving from the business page to the front page. But the fact most significant of all, in terms of audience, was that television news directors discovered business as a new source, the actions and behavior of which attracted audiences. They learned to dramatize business news and, eventually, to sensationalize it. Business news became a staple on the network evening news and has been a subject of continuing interest for the producers of the television "news magazines," as well as the more sensational investigative and exposé shows.

Dealing with public perceptions, once low on the list of CEO priorities, became a subject of primary concern. How the corporation communicated and how the public perceived it conducted its business assumed new importance in the executive suite. Public relations, the function that many CEOs took for granted as necessary but not important, took on a new significance. The CEO as well as the corporation would be evaluated on how well it could explain itself to its many audiences.

It was then that public relations entered its third stage, the "What do I do?" stage, having advanced from "How do I say it?" and "What do I say?" At long last, public relations has become a recognized part of the corporate decision-making process, to an extent undreamed of as recently as 20 years ago.

Harold Burson's "maturation of public relations" characterizes succinctly the progress and current status of the field.

This brings us to the third period which will be marked by the movement toward integrated communications. Increasingly, corporations will use database marketing with customer-driven practices which will lead to an integration of all of its marketing communications. Professionals in advertising, direct marketing, sales promotion, and certainly public relations will work together in a manner that will help ensure business effectiveness, efficiency, and social responsibility. In the long-term integration process, public relations will thrive. An increasing number of companies will give the top public relations executives the responsibility and authority for managing internal and external integrated communications. Such executives will most often report directly to the CEO, whose support and belief in integration will be essential.

To date, very few companies have fully implemented the integrated concept, but there are a significant number of firms studying and analyzing how it can be applied. By the year 2000, most successful organizations will have integrated their communications programs.

It is interesting to note that, as early as the mid-1950s my company, Marsteller, Inc. (Marsteller Advertising and Burson-Marsteller PR), was practicing marketing integration. We called it "total communications." Indeed, almost 50 percent of our clients used our advertising, sales promotion, and public relations services, integrating them against common objectives and customer/prospect groups. And in the mid-1990s we added direct marketing to provide an additional tool of communications integration.

This book illustrates not only the three stages of the public relations evolution, but also documents Harold Burson's "maturation of public relations."

This is a book you will like. This is a book you will use. Whether you are an experienced, sophisticated public relations executive, a young, inexperienced executive, a public relations educator, or a student, there is something for everybody. And that "something" gives the reader insights, ideas, solutions, and rewards.

Richard C. Christian
Associate Dean
Medill School of Journalism
Northwestern University

ACKNOWLEDGMENTS

University careers are often team efforts given the unusual hours, uneven demands, lack of organizational support, and economic pressures. A great deal of credit for the completion of this book is due to Mary Westing Caywood. Her diligence as proofreader and editor was absolutely crucial given the complexity and size of the book project. Her personal and professional patience with the named editor goes beyond any level of reasonableness, but reflects on her own determined character and intellectual strengths. The fact that her graduate degree in foreign languages permits her to understand the grammar of several languages qualifies her to be a first rate editor.

Four books, book length monographs, and many articles and individual book chapters later, the evidence of career sharing is evident in this family. Matthew who left for college in the middle of the project, Emily who moved from junior high to high school, and Graham who grew several inches taller made their contribution of family time, energy, and hard drive space on the home computer to the project.

The book was reinforced by the stability of the editing team from the publisher even though the publication company's ownership changed hands twice. Beginning with Jim McNeil who saw the idea as a contribution to the field and to business and continuing with Kevin Thornton who became the constant contact and source of reinforcement to complete the book. Judy Brown provided clear typing and design skills from the uneven formats on many disks submitted by the authors. Jim Labeots provided well-timed and well thought-out notes to the authors in the final throes of the editing.

The most important contribution must be credited to the 44 authors who must have taken many hours of valuable time from their personal and professional lives to write to a waiting audience of readers. In writing their chapters, the authors were compelled to share their ideas with a discipline rarely experienced in formal or informal verbal communications. The written word still reflects the best forum for efficient and effective description, explanation, and predictions. The authors of this book demonstrate that intellectual and practical discipline.

If the book is a project *and* work of ideas that makes any sense it is due to the thoughtful contribution of the team of professionals and authors who helped to carry the project to its logical conclusion. If the project and book have any failings then they are appropriately addressed (literally and figuratively) to me as the named editor at c-caywood@nwu.edu or through the book's internet web site at http://www.medill.nuw.edu/imc/html/book_6.html.

Clarke L. Caywood, Ph.D.
Chairman
Department of Integrated Marketing
    and Communications
Medill School of Journalism
Northwestern University
Evanston, IL

LIST OF CONTRIBUTORS

John A. Bace, APR
Principal
J. A. Bace Communications, Inc.

Brent Baker
Dean
College of Communication
Boston University

Ray Boyer
Associate Vice President, Communications
The John D. and Catherine T. MacArthur
*   Foundation*

Jean Cardwell
President
Cardwell Enterprises, Inc.

Clarke L. Caywood, Ph.D.
Chairman, Department of Integrated Marketing
*   and Communications*
Medill School of Journalism
Northwestern University

Kevin A. Clark
Director, Communications
Networked Applications Services Division
International Business Machines Corporation

Richard T. Cole, Ph.D.
Vice President
Corporate Communications
Blue Cross and Blue Shield of Michigan

Scott M. Cutlip, Fellow, PRSA
Dean Emeritus
College of Journalism and
*   Mass Communication*
University of Georgia

David R. Drobis, APR
Chairman and Chief Executive Officer
Ketchum Public Relations Worldwide

James M. Dudas
Director of Corporate Relations
Allstate Insurance Company

Raymond P. Ewing, APR
Professor of Corporate Relations (Retired)
Medill School of Journalism
Northwestern University

Lisa Fortini-Campbell, Ph.D.
Associate Professor
Medill School of Journalism
Northwestern University, and
President, Fortini-Campbell Company

Terence Franklin
President
Franklin Associates

Matthew P. Gonring
Vice President, Corporate Communication
USG Corporation

Robert Gorman
Associate
Callahan Group

John D. Graham
Chairman and Chief Executive Officer
Fleishman-Hillard, Inc.

Anders Gronstedt
Assistant Professor
Department of Journalism
University of Colorado,
and Senior Advisor to
Kraeb/Strategy XXI Group

Larissa A. Grunig, Ph.D.
Associate Professor
University of Maryland College
*   of Journalism*

Richard L. Hanneman
President
Salt Institute

George Harmon
Associate Professor
Medill School of Journalism
Northwestern University

Thomas L. Harris, APR
Managing Partner
Thomas L. Harris & Company

Nancy A. Hobor, Ph.D.
Vice President, Communications and
*   Investor Relations*
Morton International

Lee W. Huebner, Ph.D.
Professor, Communications Studies and
 Journalism
Medill School of Journalism
Northwestern University

Susan Croce Kelly, APR
Executive Vice President
The Cresta Group

John A. Koten
President
The Wordsworth Group

Leah Landolfi
Vice President (Formerly)
Ogilvy Adams & Rhinehart

Marilyn Laurie
Executive Vice President, Public Relations
AT&T

Steven H. Lesnik, APR
Chief Executive Officer
Kemper Lesnik Communications

Sandra E. Moriarty, Ph.D.
Professor
School of Journalism
 and Mass Communication
University of Colorado–Boulder

Mary C. Moster
Vice President, Corporate Communications
Comdisco, Inc.

James E. Murphy
Managing Director of Worldwide Marketing
 and Communications
Andersen Consulting
and President, Murphy & Company

Richard L. Nelson
Vice President, Public Affairs
The NutraSweet Kelco Company

Larry Nuffer
Executive Vice President
Nuffer, Smith, Tucker, Inc.

Cornelius B. Pratt, Ph.D., APR
Professor
College of Communication Arts and Sciences
Michigan State University

Stan Sauerhaft, Fellow, PRSA
Vice Chairman, Burson-Marsteller
Managing Director, Global Mergers and
 Acquisitions Practice

Jackie Saunders Goettsch, APR
Staff Vice President–Corporate Relations
Meredith Corporation

Howard Schacter
Vice President
Kemper Lesnik Communications

Elliot S. Schrieber, Ph.D.
Senior Vice President, Communications
Northern Telecom

Kihyun Shin
Manager of Programming Team
Arirang, Korea World Network
The Korea International Broadcasting
 Foundation

Michael Shore
Manager, Media Relations
IBM Corporation

Kurt P. Stocker
Associate Professor, Integrated Marketing
 Communications
Northwestern University
and Principal, Stocker & Associates

Kerry D. Tucker
President
Nuffer, Smith, Tucker, Inc.

John W. Tysse
Vice President of Public Affairs
DOW North America

John Wallis
Vice President, Sales and Marketing
Hyatt International Corporation

CONTENTS

PART FOUR

ADVANCED PUBLIC RELATIONS PRACTICE IN KEY INDUSTRIES

PART FIVE

SPECIAL TACTICS FOR PUBLIC RELATIONS AND
CORPORATE COMMUNICATIONS

Twenty-First Century Public Relations:

The Strategic Stages of Integrated Communications

Clarke L. Caywood, Ph.D.
Chairman
Department of Integrated Marketing
and Communications
Medill School of Journalism
Northwestern University

Entering the twenty-first century, public relations will lead business and other complex organizations. Its leadership will be defined by the public relations professionals' ability to integrate at several levels of business and society and create more integrated management processes. The value of integration as a public relations contribution emerges from the self-defined role of public relations building "relations" or integrating relationships between an organization and its publics.

DEFINITION

Emerging from the work by the authors in this book is an understanding of the role and definition of public relations that suggests that PR provides a new level of leadership for management to integrate relationships inside as well as outside an organization using a wide range of management strategies and tactics including communications.

RELATIONSHIP INTEGRATION

First, PR will lead corporations and other organizations on several levels including the integration of relationships with various stakeholders, the integration of management functions, the integration of corporate and organizational structures, and finally the integration with society. These first contributions to the integration of complex organizations will demonstrate the range of leadership that public relations professionals can offer from a macro level of interaction with society to a more micro level of individual stakeholders.

> Public relations is the profitable integration of an organization's new and continuing relationships with stakeholders including customers by managing all communications contacts with the organization that create and protect the brand and reputation of the organization.

STAKEHOLDER RELATIONSHIP INTEGRATION

The first level of integration relies on the intellectual- and skill-based advantage of the public relations professional to foster new relationships with valuable stakeholders and maintain and enhance the reputations of his or her organization with stakeholders and audiences who are familiar with the organization. Stakeholders include individuals and organizations that have a "stake" in the failure or success of another organization. The leadership role open to public relations is the ability and management charge to work with many groups, audiences, publics, and stakeholders. As the name suggests, public relations manages relations with various publics. Rather than focusing on the more narrow relationships of marketing with customers, for example, public relations is expected to manage the corporation's or organization's relationships and reputation with many groups. More than other professions, public relations strengthens the outside-in perspective of an organization through its managed relationships with many stakeholder groups inside and outside the organizational boundaries.

PUBLIC RELATIONS MACRO/MICRO INTEGRATION

- Societal Integration
- Corporate Structure Integration
- Management Function Integration
- Stakeholder Relationships Integration

MANAGEMENT FUNCTION INTEGRATION

The second level of integration of public relations is with other management functions including marketing, finance, accounting, human resources, and general management. PR also integrates its role with the legal profession.

The interaction of public relations with other managers will provide the men and women in this field the opportunity to assume a leadership role. A force driving this development is the downsizing of organizations which has increased the expectation that all members of the organization are members of a management team rather than staff. The lines between line and staff have blurred to the degree that projects must be managed by qualified individuals rather than by people with job titles or historical job credentials. Public relations has earned a "place at the management table" over the past decade and through the growth of professional management level education of public relations professionals in universities, through professional societies, from corporate educational efforts, and through individual commitments to learning (Graham, chapter 18).

This level of integrated leadership of public relations is also demonstrated by its perceived and real advantage as experts in the managing of communications. Public relations still offers its organizations the greatest experience and skill using various communications-based strategies and tactics. Other management fields represented by the educational curriculum of the master's in business administration for finance, management, marketing, human resources, production, and accounting do not receive any serious level of communications knowledge or training. While PR does not use only communications to accomplish its goals, the practitioners in this field have built their careers using, testing, and recommending all forms of communications including written, oral, and nonverbal. PR has used and refined all channels of communications, including advertising, speeches, press releases, internet and intranet, direct mail, events, displays, etc. The experience and skill of public relations with various communications tactics will permit PR to lead the integration of the communications of an organization or corporation with its customers in integrated marketing communication programs or with other stakeholders including the press, government, employees, community, and others.

CORPORATE STRUCTURE INTEGRATION

The third level of integration emerges from the changes in the restructuring and design of organizations. Corporations and other complex organizations are also forcing public relations into the role of potential leadership. With the need to integrate the increasingly diversified corporate structures where profit and management responsibility have been given to strategic business units (SBUs) and separate profit centers, public relations must examine its role in all areas of management. The "flattening" of the corporate hierarchy will force public relations managers to examine the role of PR in the management of divisions and at the corporate level.

While corporate PR has played a significant role at the traditional headquarters level, the movement of power and responsibility to the divisions will compel PR to examine its contribution to the marketing function, the ability to create employee communications and relationships at a more local level and other diversified management issues. Building relationships with the general media for a division president, strengthening specific trade press relationships for the products and services of the division, local community relations, and other contacts must be moved from the corporate level to the SBU level.

The ability of the PR professionals to integrate the communications, product and corporate branding strategies, and unified message to investors increases the operational level role of PR versus its traditional staff or even high level counselor role. Again, the ability to manage current issues and anticipate future demands on corporate resources provides well-trained and educated public relations professionals to demonstrate and take leadership roles.

SOCIETAL INTEGRATION

Finally, public relations managers will lead their organizations' relationships with society. From the micro relationship built with many stakeholder groups, the corporate and organizational public relations professional will guide the corporate values that permit organizations to operate in society at a macro level.

Again, the education and training of the PR professional may equip him or her to reflect the dynamics between the legal–political and social expectations of society of corporations and other organizations. From years of listening, speaking to, and building relationships with various publics and stakeholder groups, PR professionals have the experience to manage the corporate response to society and societal changes.

The boundary spanning role of public relations in which the managers operate at the porous boundary of the organization permits the PR professional to interact with a wide range of stakeholders, but it also creates the expectation that PR is fully aware of the changing expectations of society and the matching of corporate purposes with societal goals. The ability of the PR professional to describe, explain, and predict the societal pressures on the firm provides general management with a risk assessment and interpretation necessary to operate in a complex social setting. Having one more manager at the table with a vision of ethical and value-driven purpose and actions gives PR one more reason to be recognized for its leadership (Pratt, chapter 17).

PUBLIC RELATIONS PROCESS INTEGRATION

While the first analysis of public relations expects it to integrate various levels of business and society, the second dimension of the management of PR is the development of a more integrated process. One of the fastest growing strategies associated with public relations and public relations communications tactics is integrated marketing communications (IMC). Pioneered by the faculty in my Department of Integrated Marketing Communications in Northwestern University's Medill School of Journalism, the field has flourished for the past six years in theoretical development and in practice. The definition of IMC developed for a national study for industry at Northwestern was:

> [IMC is a] concept of marketing communications planning that represents the added value of a comprehensive plan that evaluates the strategic roles of a variety of communications disciplines—general advertising, direct response, sales promotion, and public relations—and combines these disciplines to provide clarity, consistency, and maximum communication impact.

> *(Caywood et al. 1991)*

Emerging from an academic department that for several decades had been recognized as the number one advertising program in the country and perhaps internationally, the department had also redefined public relations and direct marketing education with a strong managerial approach to traditional staff functions. The coursework included many of the core elements of a master's in business administration to position the students to "sit at the management table" with financial, organizational, marketing, and general management knowledge and skills.

The leadership of the school was again demonstrated when the faculty, administration, and students integrated the existing power of the advertising, sales promotions, direct marketing, and public relations courses and knowledge. The combination of the fields provided businesses and organizations who hired the graduate students, interacted with the faculty, and read the research of the faculty with a competitive advantage over the traditionally nonintegrated and functionally separate operations of these business and organizational activities.

The distinctions were important signals of the new direction that the academic team was taking the traditional elements of advertising, direct marketing, and public relations education. The distinct elements were also what provided corporations and other organizations with compelling reasons to reexamine their business processes. The reinvention and reengineering of marketing, public relations, and direct marketing as a more fully integrated process has offered public relations professionals the most significant opportunity for advancing the influence of the profession. Integrated marketing communications and integrated communications will permit PR to take the leadership role it deserves based upon the range and depth of the field, its attention to multiple stakeholder groups, and its experience and strength using communications as an important management tool (Gonring, chapter 4).

STAGES OF INTEGRATED COMMUNICATIONS

Most organizations facing changing markets and societal expectations reexamine their organizational structure and processes. Many companies and organizations undertake some form of reengineering, restructuring, transformation, or realignment to better equip the organization to respond to the changes. The following approach to corporate and organizational integration takes an evolutionary approach. The process assumes that corporations can integrate their marketing, public relations, advertising, sales promotions, and direct marketing function over a period of time. The process also assumes that the managers will gain experience at each stage, permitting them to increase the level of performance.

The stages of integration are not always precise. Some organizations attain different levels of integration with a different mix of factors. But, in general, the companies and organizations that address the issues of integration proceed in a logical way.

The stages of integration include:

1. Awareness.
2. Image integration.
3. Functional integration.
4. Consumer-based integration.
5. Stakeholder integration.
6. Utopian integration.

The stages begin with a recognition that the environment for an organization has changed enough to demand a new approach to the market and to various stakeholders. Each stage contains the seeds of a more advanced management process which expects a greater degree of integration of managers, goals, messages, targeted customers and other stakeholders, strategies, and tactics including communications tactics.

Each stage increasingly demands a greater contribution of leadership from public relations. But even in the early stages of integration in which the focus is on the market and marketing, the role of public relations is clear. Each stage logically has conditions of change that lead to that stage. Each stage also has distinct management activities characteristic of that stage.

Stage 1 – Awareness

The first stage of integration is awareness. Awareness of the changes in the marketplace, environment, government policy, community, employees, technology, and other issues will often awaken a company or organization to the need to change. The "wake-up call" of a failed product, a change in fashions, new laws, a crisis threatening the reputation of the organization, or the loss of key employees to competitors may harshly remind management of the volatile market and environment.

While most managers admonish their consultants and program speakers: "Don't tell me that the market has changed; tell me what to do about it", companies and organizations can still be blindsided by specific changes in the market or trends they did not recognize. For example, the dairy industry has been notoriously slow to create packaging that fits the needs and lifestyles of the consumer. While the makers of the newest mini-vans fight for who can create the greatest number of cupholders in their products and even the heralded Mercedes-Benz finally conceded to create cupholders for its luxury car products, the dairy industry has not responded with packaging that fits in the cupholders or performs satisfactorily (stays cold) under traveling situations. Literally having square pegs for round holes, the industry is now playing catch-up with juice beverages and others. Similarly, when IBM Corporation created a strategy of large-scale downsizing in the 1980s it took some time to recognize that the remaining employees would require more advanced processes and programs to be motivated and managed. The company took some time to recognize that it would take a more integrated "go to market" strategy to replace the thousands of sales representatives and staff personnel who had left the company under various offers.

This stage of integrated communications and management forces the assessment of the changes in the environment and provides the motivation for a more integrated approach. For example, the increasing number of media alternatives from cable, direct video, CD, audio tape, internet, interactive point of purchase coupons, and still traditional print and video must be constantly assessed for their possible contribution to the management and communication programs of an organization. (See Clark, chapter 14; Shore, chapter 27; Bace, chapter 5.)

Once the pressures to change have been identified, labeled, and discussed, the manager can prepare the firm for continuing change with action designed to institutionalize the organization's ability to "spot" change and move more quickly to respond to it.

For example, the corporate planning process, if conceived from the "outside-in" rather than the "inside-out," can prepare a firm to be more adaptive. Articulating and committing to paper (or the intranet) the corporate values, corporate mission, and specific goals and objectives before budgeting can help to align the company with trends. This traditional business process, if thought of as a means to respond to the changing market, can be more productive than its traditional role as a bureaucratic requirement for complex organizations.

A second process of "benchmarking" the best practices of competitors and of noteworthy noncompetitors can help an organization to understand how other successful organizations responded to changes in their environments. By focusing on the processes of management rather than the products, a company can find out which organizations are being most responsive to the environment. For example, Southwest Airline's study of the auto racetrack team's ability to "turn around" a car from the pit provided ideas for arriving at and exiting an expensive airport gate site rather than simply comparing their performance to that of larger competitors. Examining how another company satisfies its customers and stakeholders can also be a refreshing way to benchmark (Gruning, chapter 19).

A third action might be to use "zero-based" planning and budgeting. The practice, long recognized in state and even federal government, permits the managers to assume that last year's program is not necessarily going to be supported in the forthcoming budget. While it is dangerous to try to zero-base the budget too widely since an organization finds it difficult to rethink all its activities at once, the selective zero-basing of a program can be productive. The challenge to the management team is to permit fresh ideas, new strategies, and certainly new tactics to be recommended.

Using selectively the traditional notion of "zero-based" planning and budgeting with selective programs can mentally challenge an organization's team not to think incrementally. While many organizations operate on a year to year basis with budget increases or decreases of "plus or minuses" of a small percent (2 to 5 percent) such common incrementalism does not provide a manager with the courage to totally reexamine the reason for the program, expenditure, or objective. "Just because we did it last year," as the saying goes, does not mean the conditions of the market or environment are correct for the same program or tactic in the coming year. A fresh, zero-based, view of the program gives permission to the management team to make new assumptions, use new developments to plan totally new programs.

For example, Dairy Management, Inc. (DMI), as the largest national dairy food marketer for its farmer members, initiated under the direction of its CEO, Tom Gallagher, a "no sacred cows" planning effort to create a zero-based attitude among it managers and members. The effort was symbolized by an image of a dairy cow with a halo over its head and within a circle with the international symbol of a diagonal bar meaning "no". Used on printed planning materials and naturally on the ever present baseball or corn seed style cap, the symbol sent the signal to the organization that the future might not necessarily look like the past for DMI.

Finally, during this stage toward a more comprehensive integrated communications and management program, an issues management system with scanning can be used. Such systems (see Ewing, chapter 11) can create a formal program for an organization to track emerging trends and issues that will affect an organization in the three- to five-year time period. Using tracking systems for identifying relevant trends in research, obscure publications, opinion leaders, and other sources of ideas, an organization can be more anticipatory in its management. The existence of the formal process of issues management is unknown to many organizations partly because of the lack of education in business schools about the process despite a well-developed history and literature.

Stage 2—Image Integration

The second stage toward a more completely integrated organization is the integration of the image of the company or organization. Several conditions contribute to the need for this stage and the careful attention to communications.

First, the change in an organization's name, its acquisition by another firm, its acquisition of new product or service lines not historically compatible with the company's communications, may confuse customers, investors, and even employees. The "flattening" of many organizations from steep bureaucratic hierarchies or pyramids and the creation of SBUs has created an organizational environment in which managers with profit responsibility may unravel many years of consistent and carefully planned communications. The corporate name and image may be jeopardized by one division, department, or wholly owned subsidiary using different messages, logos, and communications objectives.

For example, the 3-M Corporation celebrates its managerial complexity and innovation with thousands of products. But to communicate an integrated message to those who see 3-M as a single organization (investors, employees, the media, and customers who trust the 3-M brand) the firm has created in the mid-90s a more cohesive message for corporate branding that links the product branding efforts. Using the "1,2, 3-M" creative message in national general business and trade publications and the creation of a set of standards for the use of the 3-M logo, the firm tries to use the corporate brand to signal a more integrated company and message.

A second pressure on companies at this stage of integrated communications is the recognition of brand value to the firm. Branding of products and companies is a powerful communications activity that only can be successful if it is both strategic and tactically integrated. While image integration does not necessarily mean "one voice, one look, one message," the look and feel of all communications at this stage must be strategically examined. If the messages are not consistent or creatively connected, the management team examining the level of integration needs to ask if there is a good reason for the apparent "disintegration."

Various tactics and actions can help the management team to determine if the organization is fully integrated at this stage. It is an easy test of the disheveled nature of many organizational messages that a "table-top audit" can reveal the inconsistency of messages and images. The exercise is to place all the printed materials and related communications including audio and video on a conference table in a firm to examine the degree of inconsistency. The exercise has revealed cases in which the company's former name (even of several years before) is still being used on printed materials. The exercise also reveals an astounding (but not necessarily good) range of creative efforts to establish a message about the organization. For example, in a hospital-based healthcare company in suburban Chicago, the marketing communications team is inspired to constantly create new messages and new printed materials more out of boredom with their work (and the need to be constantly creating new images).

While the organization might celebrate the creative variety of the marketing and public relations team, the integrated strategy of the organization can be "undone" with inconsistent messages being seen by various stakeholders (Moriarity, chapter 37). However, if the purpose of the creative work, a particular message or program is intentionally different from the overall corporate message, then the decision can be noted and the exception understood in the overall marketing and communications program. For example, the Sara Lee Company wholly owns such highly distinct brands and companies such as Hanes, Coach Leather, and, of course, the Sara Lee Bakeries. The products are so diverse with their own branded image and identity that they do not try to link the separate brands together (except for the investor relations program). Unlike the failed effort of Beatrice which tried to link, with a short musical note at the end of ads, such diverse products as Stiffel Lamps and Fisher Nuts, Sara Lee has made a concerted strategic decision not to have a consistent message to the general consumer from its subsidiaries.

Various traditional communications research methods (Gronstedt, chapter 3) can test for message content and consistency. In addition, the use of brand valuation studies may help the firm to determine the need to protect in a more integrated way the product and corporate name.

For many years IBM Corporation and other national and global firms spent inordinate amounts of money and management time to "protect" the brand from the company perspective. During this stage toward integration, the role of all communications professionals should open discussion where the brand is seen by the customer and other stakeholders as an inconsistent message. This level of integration creates the possibility that the various communications managers in public relations, advertising, sales, sales promotions, direct marketing, and other areas must cooperate.

Stage 3—Functional Integration

The integrated stage that seems to be most controversial with the professionals who manage the still separated activities of advertising, public relations, marketing, sales, and even direct marketing and sales promotions is functional integration. A national study commissioned by the American Association of National Advertising Agencies (4As) and the Association of National Advertisers (ANA) in 1990 found that one of the significant barriers to integrated marketing and communications were so-called functional silos. The separate career paths, education, and training of professionals in these areas contributed to their continued separate actions in organizations. A common reaction with presidents or CEOs of firms could be articulated as "What do you mean my PR (or advertising, or sales, etc.) people don't talk to my marketing managers?" The unspoken threat had not been enough to compel these business functions to work together. The not-so-subtle threat of a more integrated strategy was the pressure to join strategies, programs, and budget for the overall benefit of the company and its stakeholders and shareholders (Caywood, Schultz, and Wang 1991).

The more positive condition at this stage is the increasing recognition by fully trained and educated professionals with a strategic orientation that some degree of cooperation is necessary in a world of limited resources. The label of "MARCOM" taught at the undergraduate and graduate level in schools of business suggests that various elements of communications can be coordinated. Of course, the existence of small- and medium-sized advertising and public relations agencies practicing their own form of marketing communications and integration validated the logic of the advertising program, reinforcing the public relations and direct mail tactics in areas such as sports marketing and PR (Lesnik and Schacter, chapter 28).

Additional support for the pressure to integrate at this level came from the success of direct marketing and mail as a marketing tactic adopted by a wide range of for-profit and not-for-profit organizations. The need to have consistency in the second stage of integration compelled firms and their agencies to figure out how to work together.

For example, the efforts of the IBM-Midwestern Area to run more local campaigns to reach highly segmented business-to-business segments required the IBM managers to force local vendors of PR services, video, telemarketing, and direct mail to work closely together (Caywood in Kaatz 1995). The same efforts to understand the contributions of each element of marketing communications lead the companies to use more strategic marketing tools including syndicated databases such as Dow-Jones, industry directories for business to business, and scanner data and related services for consumer goods.

A significant contribution to integration at this point was the recognition by marketers that public relations, and especially marketing PR (Harris, chapter 6) added great value to the marketing programs. PR in its broadest definition was also seen as important in "risk marketing" companies (Duncan and Caywood in Thorson and Moore 1996) where marketing of healthcare products (Schrieber, chapter 23; Cole, chapter 30) and food (Nelson, chapter 21) required a more complete contribution by those who understood regulatory issues, activism, and environmentalism (Croce Kelly, chapter 13). In short, marketing was discovering the value of public relations from a marketer's perspective (Landolfi, chapter 24).

Actions at this stage of integration include a more organized planning process to coordinate and integrate the efforts of the traditional functions. Still widely understood and used by business are planning models using acronyms such as SWOT (strength, weaknesses, opportunities, and threats) an exercise in which managers participate in planning meetings to identify from instinct and data both the internal (strength and weaknesses) and more external (opportunities and threats) dynamics of the marketplace and environment. One lesson learned by IBM, Advocate Healthcare, and others including Golin/Harris public relations is the value of diagnosing the company from the outside-in by discussing the threats and opportunities first and then the more internal strengths and weaknesses as part of the planning session. The acronym TOWS (threats, opportunities, weaknesses, strengths) is a more accurate representation of the outside-in thinking evident in a more integrated process (Caywood in Kaatz 1995).

Organizations such as the Wisconsin Milk Marketing Board have found the power of a more integrated strategy useful for their efforts to promote Wisconsin cheese products. Rather than relying entirely on national advertising to sell a product manufactured by 100+ cheese producers in the state, their integrated team of PR and marketing experts have created programs that promote the use of cheese to chefs who then create recipes and menus featuring the "Wisconsin" branded cheeses seen in national nutrition, cooking, and women's magazines. Joint programs with the California wine industry also offer creative alternatives using tactics that do not rely on only paid media. Their use of a database (called Chainlink) collected from the menus of chain restaurants all over the United States also helps them to identify the level of cheese use and branded labeling on popular menus. An absence of cheese-based foods or listing of "Wisconsin Cheese" provides an opportunity for more targeted messages to those restaurants and to food brokers.

Andersen Consulting (Murphy, chapter 25) has also overcome the barriers to a more integrated corporate effort with a carefully planned strategy discussed in detail in the chapter to focus the business development efforts and professional promotion of the firm. Using a model of integration designed to integrate media relations, advertising, event planning, and business development or sales, the firm pulled the separate tactics together in a more strategic marketing and communications program.

Higher Degrees of Integrated Communications

At the more advanced levels of integration a new definition of integrated marketing and communications may be necessary to move the organization to more advanced management and communications processes and to expand the range of audiences from customers to all stakeholders. Once again, public relations offers new sources of strategies, tactics, and general experience that marketing or other organizational functions alone cannot provide.

A more advanced definition of integration includes the notion that the organization must manage all the brand contact points that the consumer and other stakeholders come into contact with for the firm (Fortini-Campbell, chapter 9). See sidebar.

INTEGRATED MARKETING COMMUNICATIONS VER. 2

The process of managing all sources of information about a product/service to which a consumer, prospect, or stakeholder is exposed which behaviorally moves them toward a sale and/or relationship and maintains consumer/stakeholder loyalty.

(Adapted from Schultz, Tannenbaum and Lauterborn, 1992)

Stage 4 – Consumer and Databased Integration

This stage of integration focuses most intently on the customer and the consumer and increases the level of management measurement. The condition for change at this level includes the likelihood that the firm might have reengineered the organization including the sales function. The firm will have adopted various forms of customer and consumer orientations such as measurement of consumer satisfaction.

The company or organization will have managed a number of communications-led marketing programs that used existing databases for targeting and then collected data as part of the campaign. For example, in the IBM Corporation, the direct marketing managers created campaigns that used communications requiring some form of response by the targeted customer. Operating under the "rule of engagement" that all communications must contain a response mechanism, the direct mail, telemarketing, advertising, events, and media story reprints contained an offer for the customer to respond to the company. This ensured that the marketing and communications team then could enter in the database what the consumer's response was to a particular offer, when they interacted with the firm, what channel of message delivery was as most effective (mail, phone, event, etc.), and what response the customer expected in the future.

This higher level of integrated marketing and communications permits for the first time, a more advanced level of research (Gronstedt, chapter 3). In some areas of direct marketing, including catalogues, subscription products, magazines, and insurance industry (Gorman, chapter 22), the notion of "life-time customer value" permits the organization to estimate the cash flow of revenue from the customer over a stated period of time ("life-time" being relative). A company might expect several thousand dollars discounted for its net present value over a period of five years from a customer.

Rather than planning marketing and communications efforts on shorter annual or even quarterly cycles, the company can "invest" more of its communication dollars to build a relationship with the customer, expecting a higher return over a period of years. While there is some risk with this calculation, catalogue and direct mail companies have relied for many years on such estimates (Saunders, chapter 29). Parenthetically, the author's work with the Internal Revenue Service found that this agency used a similar calculation. Clearly the meaning of "lifetime value" may have even greater meaning to the mission of the IRS than other organizations.

At this level of development of an integrated program companies are estimating the return-on-investment of each element of the communications mix. For example, they try to calculate the return on PR media coverage, the sales leads generated from an event, the response tracked from direct marketing or telemarketing contacts, and the sales results tracked to a particular customer from any of the leads or contacts generated in an integrated communications program.

Agencies, such as Targetbase Marketing in Dallas, Texas, use an ROI approach to help their clients estimate the payoff of a particular set of communications tactics. They report in industry presentations that a standard of expectation is 120 percent return with results up to 400 percent on some programs. The PR service known as ADI PressTrac from Ft. Myers, Florida also has estimated the ROI of public relations media programs. The model works in their formulation by placing advertising cost value on PR and then weighing the results. IBM managers have used a simple spreadsheet model generated by Professors Don Schultz and Paul Wang at Northwestern University's IMC department with some success. The general direction of determining the contribution of the costs and the profits of a marketing or communications program is an indication of the level of expectation at this stage of integration.

Finally, at this stage the companies and organizations are able to concern themselves with the level of success from programs both to acquire and retain customers and other stakeholder groups including employees (Laurie, chapter 15; Moster, chapter 8). The distinction between programs designed to increase market share by acquiring new customers and programs designed to retain current customers or cross sell to them is evident in the new language of business.

As some industries describe their role, it is to increase the "share of wallet" (in banking), "share of stomach" (in the fast food industry) and "share of garage" (for the automotive and power equipment industry) by working to retain and develop sales from existing customers. The message differences in each case are logically different. In addition, the campaigns and programs designed to speak to each market in an interactive way are quite different.

For example, using a simple decile analysis and customer value scoring model, Hyatt International (Wallis, chapter 26) determines which of its current guests are most profitable. It then creates specific communications and relations programs which build a continuing and profitable relationship with the customer. One of the challenges facing companies and especially not-for-profit organizations is the determination of which audience, customers, or stakeholders are most valuable to the organization and which audiences can be "ignored."

In business, the two "e" goals of *efficiency* (meaning less cost or use of resources per sale) and *effectiveness* (meaning successful completion of a stated goal) are paramount. For example, while it might be cheaper (efficient) to *not* provide room flowers or other luxuries in preferred guest rooms it might be more effective since the goal is to create a customer relationship that encourages return business. Most businesses have developed a clear understanding of the value of both efficient and effective business strategies and tactics. However, in government and not-for-profit organizations including healthcare and welfare services there is a strong tendency to want to be sure that all possible prospects for services receive an equal opportunity for the service, thereby adding the element of a third "e" for *equity* (Baker, chapter 31). The challenge in applying the standards of advanced communications programs which deliberately communicate with some audiences more than others based upon the return on investment and profitability is a difficult one (see Boyer, chapter 32, Hanneman, chapter 33, and Koten, chapter 10).

While the standards of profitability can be redefined in terms of who is helped the most rather than who happens to see or hear about undirected information about the agency's services, the logic of more targeted and "profitable" messages must be factored into the strategy. However, under conditions of increasingly limited resources, the lessons of an integrated communications program suggest that organizations must allocate the contacts with patrons, patients, and service users in the most efficient, effective, and equitable way.

Stage 5– Stakeholder Integration

On the advanced levels of integration, the world of public relations opens widely. While the attention to stakeholders other than customers or consumers is practiced at many levels of integration, the full benefit of a mature integrated process can be applied here (Sauerhaft, chapter 20).

The concept of stakeholder management is an advanced approach in management and public relations to understanding how an organization relates to a rich mix of individuals and groups (Caywood and Ewing 1992). Those organizations and individuals can be approached with the same level of targeted intensity as customers were targeted using database systems previously built for marketing.

For example, the ability to reach investors (Hobor, chapter 7) quickly under conditions of a takeover or bid for a company can be more easily accomplished with data from firms such as Georgeson. The firm provides subscription or list services of shareholders with or without the street name designation for ease of appealing directly to shareholders.

Many not-for-profit organizations including universities know the benefit of maintaining up-to-date alumni or donor lists and databases with advanced information on targeted individuals, their previous contacts, and fields of relevant data useful for communication programs. Most advanced practitioners in public relations use printed, CD-ROM, or on-line directories of general and trade press. Such lists including Burrelle's, the Bulldog Reporter, and various local and state directories contain details of contact information on members of the press with general assignments, fax numbers, e-mail addresses, and accurate information on preferred methods of contact.

Each company must build its own proprietary database of media and other stakeholders. Under conditions of a crisis, for example, it is probably too late to begin to locate the contact names and numbers of media relevant to the crisis (Stocker, chapter 12). In each case a relevant database can be designed, built, and maintained for more effective communications. For example, a new advertising campaign, direct mail, or trade show event can be augmented with pinpoint targeting of the media, community leaders, and other influentials in the geographic area of the marketing program or in the area of influence of the media.

Stage 6– Utopian Integration

In the best of worlds the methods and processes practiced at the highest level will advance with new technologies and new thinking. While it is always difficult to predict the future (see many of the book's chapter conclusions), the future of integration must contain the elements of any advanced, information-based and probably digital system.

Over twenty-five years ago my first graduate degree program at the University of Texas-Austin offered the power (at a very simple level) of some new computer languages for purposes of building "intelligent" decision-making processes. I was intrigued then with the potential for machine-based augmentation to the ability of man to make increasingly complex choices in high-risk decision situations. As early as 1967, at the University of Wisconsin-Madison I worked on a project that was a precursor to the current full text Lexis/Nexis and West Law systems. A decade later I would use Lexis/Nexis and West Law to complete my doctoral dissertation on First Amendment law and political advertising.

The idea of automated systems for decision making even for simple word and concepts search has expanded widely with the adoption of the various search engines for the World Wide Web. According to my son, Matthew, a Harvard College sophomore whose major is cognitive sciences, the future may, at last, be here with alternative models permitting more advanced man and machine interface. Beyond the expert decision systems used for reporting retail sales and inventory choices on a near real-time basis and beyond the work done at Northwestern University by the Institute for Learning Sciences, the future holds some help for integrated communications managers.

SELECTED STAKE-HOLDER LIST

- Employees, prospective employees, and retired employees
- Local, state, regional, and national governments
- Global, national, local, and trade media
- Institutional and individual investors
- Donors and members
- Industry, general business, and professional associations
- Educational institutions
- Community members and leaders
- Corporate office, plant, and retail site neighbors
- Business partners selling products/services relying on the company
- Vendors and suppliers
- Financial institutions
- Taxing authorities and districts
- Environmental interest groups
- Unions and related labor interest groups
- Others

The ability to manage increasingly complex communications programs with hundreds of alternative messages, dozens of delivery systems, hundreds and hundreds of thousands of current customers, and thousands and even millions of prospects suggests that automated marketing processes will need to be developed. The greater the degree of segmentation and targeting of a customer or stakeholder, the greater the need for new technology delivery systems. My son tells me the future for the cognitive sciences is bright; I always put my faith in areas of new science and technology in the next generation.

The implementation of utopia, like any advanced goal or objective, is always left to the assumption that as you move toward attaining a serious goal, the next objective or goal should be set farther out in the future. So, the utopian strategies and tactics will be constantly moving stages of integration and achievable stages of integration on the way to utopia. The stages will have their own labels, conditions, strategies, and tactics to accomplish each higher and higher level of integrated communications.

CONCLUSION

This book explores the power, the depth, and the breadth of the field of public relations as a professional field of study and practice, as a highly applied discipline in the wide range of businesses and other organizations. The book's authors have recognized, with the newest generation of public relations practitioners and a previous generation, that public relations does not operate in a vacuum.

In fact, the power of public relations is its ability to "relate" and develop productive relationships with other business functions and with multiple stakeholders. PR has not been introduced to the notion of integration in the last decade. It has defined the concept and practice over many decades of leadership. If the future of public relations is *not* integrated then the future could not be as bright as the authors will tell you in this volume in the following pages.

". . . all of the authors are people you would want to spend hours with talking about the topic they have generously summarized for this book."

As the editor of this book, I promise you that all of the authors are individuals you would want to spend hours with talking about the topic they have generously summarized for this book. If you remember conversations about important subjects with your favorite teacher, professor, peer, boss, or brightest friend, you will realize that these authors reflect the very highest levels of thought, trust, and ability to recommend. If they were readily available, you would want to ask their opinions before making a decision.

As an editor, my objective was to permit the "voice" of each author as a leader in the field to speak with her own point of view or in his own style. Even with editing, the book tries to maintain the tone of each person's work and its detail. Collectively, their chapters, then, represent their willingness to share with you their experience and current thinking about how to manage, work, and think now and in the future. It is not their cumulative experience that makes their ideas so powerful (though the total years of experience is significant); instead it is the vitality and currency of their ideas that has permitted them to be successful their entire lives through change after change in the environment, market, and society.

The book is organized around several principles: (1) The areas of professional practice in public relations and corporate communications that focus on specific stakeholder groups or publics important to an organization including investors, media, labor, community, and others. (2) A large number of chapters provide an extraordinary view of the practice of corporate communications and public relations in numerous industries and businesses including hospitality, technology, healthcare, consulting, and others. (3) The book also includes several chapters related to career development, the history of the profession, and good writing (Cardwell, chapter 1; Cutlip, chapter 2; Tucker, chapter 34; Huebner, chapter 35; Harmon, chapter 36).

This book was designed as both a professional project and a work of art and social science. The project dimensions were clear to the original publishers as we discussed the depth and breath of the field and the range of experts necessary to define the field. The coordination of 46 authors on over 37 topics was a management challenge.

GENERAL CHAPTER OUTLINE

- Introduction to Topic
- Definition
- Strategies
- Tactics
- Case Examples
- The Future

Based upon an agreed structure for each chapter, the authors were asked to use their experience and knowledge of the field to produce chapters that (1) defined the area of PR; (2) described the strategic approach that their company and other organizations had taken to the field; (3) discussed and listed tactics that had usefully implemented the strategies; (4) described in some detail case studies illustrating the best practices in public relations; and (5) discussed the future relevant to their industry or area of expertise in PR. The format proves useful to the reader searching for specific ideas across industries, a sense of the future from a wide range of authors, and a wide selection of case examples illustrating the practice of PR.

The book also proves to be a resource for general knowledge about public relations. The authors, time and time again, demonstrate their depth and breadth of knowledge about the field of PR. Seen as personal essays from individuals with experience and credentials, the chapters provide an extraordinary insight to a wide range of organizations and PR practices. The chapters are highly credible sources of information about their topics. In addition, many of the authors have relied on research from their organizations and others to document specific issues. The book serves as a source of personal insight, research, and parallel discussion of key issues, industries, and activities in public relations and management.

Without over promising, I know that you will learn from the authors and enjoy their insightful perspectives on the field of integrated public relations now and for your career in the twenty-first century.

REFERENCES

Caywood, Clarke L., Schultz, Don E. and Paul Wang. *A Survey of Consumer Goods Manufacturers.* American Association of Advertising Agencies, NY, 1992.

Wang, Paul. "Measuring ROI." *Integrated Marketing Communications Symposium.* Ron Kaatz, (Editor). NTC Business Books, Lincolnwood, IL, 1995.

Caywood, Clarke. "Integrated Marketing Campaigns." *Integrated Marketing Communications Symposium.* Ron Kaatz, (Editor). NTC Business Books, Lincolnwood, IL, 1995.

Duncan, Thomas and Caywood, Clarke. "The Concept, Process and Evolution of Integrated Marketing
    Communications." *Integrated Communication: Synergy of Persuasive Voices.* Esther Thorson
    and Jeri Moore, (Editors). Lawrence Erlbaum Associates, Mahwah, NJ, 1995.

## PART ONE

Introduction

## CHAPTER 1

Career Paths in Public Relations

Jean Cardwell
President
Cardwell Enterprises, Inc.

Welcome to the brave new world of careers in public relations!

This decade has created a Darwinian marketplace for communications professionals, one in which survival of the fittest reigns. The old career path no longer exists. There are new rules and new dynamics to follow that virtually obliterate the 25-year-tenure, gold-watch corporate "lifer." Says Abraham Zaleznik, psychoanalyst and professor emeritus at Harvard Business School, "We're all up against a relentless, impersonal reality called the marketplace, which will reward those who do good jobs and punish those who don't."[1]

Those new rules and the nature of communications careers in the 21st century depend heavily on the acceptance of two frameworks: an understanding of professional paths before and during the 1990s, and a view of public relations as a microcosm of the business world. "What's past is prologue" reads the inscription above the entrance to the National Archives. What's past, in short, provides us insight into many of today's career assumptions and trends and supplies a base on which to predict the future.

Public relations is seen best as a miniature version of the workplace since, after all, communicators support and promote the goals of their specific institutions or clients. While little of the professional literature deals with career paths, business magazines, newspapers, and nonfiction books supply plenty of relevant information. And, to track career paths in *any* profession, we need to adopt the mantle of a Faith Popcorn or a John Naisbitt and self-confidently gaze into our own futures. Without being able to interpret and predict trends based on a comprehension of history and of the larger world in which we operate, any discussion of public relations career paths will prove futile and, ultimately, of little use.

THE PAST

Traditionally, journalism, even in the post-1970s' Woodward-Bernstein investigative era, was the feeder profession of choice for public relations. Both corporations and agencies embraced ex-newsgatherers who, they felt, would not only bring new viewpoints and ideas but also would be able to effect more cordial alliances with the Fourth Estate. Harold Burson and Dan Edelman, founders of agencies that bear their names, began as newspaper reporters.

So did Jim Dowling, now chairman emeritus of Burson-Marsteller. In fact, this career switch goes back to the days of John Hill of Hill & Knowlton fame and is still an accepted entrée into the profession.

Much of the allure of journalists to public relations employers had to do with the previous nature of the business. Communications was defined narrowly. For the most part, before the mid-1980s, many agencies and some corporations practiced what was known then as product publicity. There also were media relations experts, employee communicators (usually ex-magazine editors who published newsletters and other internal print vehicles), and speechwriters, as well as product publicists at the corporate division level and in agencies.

A background in politics and government also drew talent into communications. Intimacy with D.C. ways of doing business was especially pertinent in the 1970s to the oil and energy companies, which were being portrayed by the media (and, hence, perceived by the public) as "the bad guys." Government specialists adroit in managing issues were recruited to handle—and change—the industry's image. This was truly the golden era of the behind-the-scenes wordsmith, with CEOs such as Walter Wriston at Citibank actively promoting social responsibility and the notion of corporate "do-goodism." Now, though the demand for in-house speechwriters is low, experience in the ways and means of government remains attractive: Tod Hullin, senior vice president of communications and public affairs at Time Warner Inc., for example, originally worked for the Secretary of Defense.

The initial round of public and media attention to Ralph Nader in the 1960s and the subsequent questioning of product viability led many corporations to create consumer affairs departments, staffed with knowledgeable experts who could respond with empathy to public interest groups. In both the food and consumer durables industries, those professionals were recruited from the ranks of dietitians, nutritionists, and home economists. That trend is almost moribund today, having been replaced by environmental and/or total quality management (TQM) communicators.

After years of practicing public relations, professionals found that, if they stayed for a while in corporate or agency or association or nonprofit life, they would be stereotyped as area-specific communicators. Certainly, there was movement within the field: agency folks jumped to other agencies and corporate communicators to new jobs in other companies. Yet rarely was there any cross-fertilization at the middle or senior manager level. Only in the 1980s did America's businesses begin to recognize the value of agency experience (Bill Neilsen, vice president at Johnson & Johnson, for example, was once at Carl Byoir; Fidelity Executive Vice President Peter Dowd worked at Hill & Knowlton). And the same held true for agencies, associations, and nonprofits. But hiring powers still are reluctant to recruit from different sectors of the communications business.

The "business of the business" broadened quite considerably in the 1970s and 1980s, thanks to aggressive agency growth and corporate raiders. Public relations became a segmented profession. To employee communications, media relations, and product publicity were added integrated marketing communications (IMC), public affairs, editorial services, and investor and financial relations. The specialization of the practice first gained impetus from agency executives who anticipated and responded to client needs. Pure and simple, acquisitions were required to provide multinational clients with a wider range of expertise and offices. Burson-Marsteller bought Cohn & Wolfe; Porter/Novelli, the Public Relations Board; and Edelman, a number of small firms here and overseas. Ogilvy & Mather acquired Adams & Rinehart, and WPP swallowed Hill & Knowlton, among others.

Corporate raiders were responsible, in part, for the emergence of the investor relations professional, one of the two anomalies in the field (the other is the speechwriter; see the box on "The Invisible Profession" at the end of this chapter). Unlike his/her colleagues, the IR specialist was lured from the ranks of accountants, security analysts, and business reporters. The traditional reporting structure, then and now, is to the corporation's chief financial officer, but many eventually moved beyond that position.

Somewhere, sometime, somehow, the enormous growth in the number of practitioners and the power of communications—best evidenced by former President Reagan's nickname of "The Great Communicator"—had to stop. It did so with the advent of the 1990s and with a seemingly never-ending recession.

THE PRESENT

It doesn't require the abilities of a Daniel Yankelovich or George Gallup to predict that the primary issue today among all workers is how to cope with constant change. Yet change itself causes a number of other trends, variables of great importance to the communications business. The most obvious are reductions in force (RIFs), downsizing, rightsizing, re-engineering, and transformation. All are by now old terms that mean loss of jobs for public relations professionals. "Lean and mean" is still the operative phrase of the decade, as once-huge corporate staffs struggle to keep up with business needs and demands and farm out work to a growing number of consultants and boutiques. Agencies, too, have continued to offer early retirement packages or to simply slash staff when billings drop.

What can explain the cause of this industry contraction? Definitely, the mergers and acquisitions of the 1970s and 1980s extracted a penalty. Communications positions, among others, were duplicated in the merger of two companies; obviously, one had to be sacrificed. But the other reason for the decline in communications positions goes to the root of the profession itself. People in this business perceive themselves as "creative professionals." There's an ivory tower mentality among many communicators who say: "I don't want to play politics." "I don't want to be a manager or develop people." "I don't need to be concerned about operations, profit/loss, or business." Lest that seem an exaggeration, a 1993 International Association of Business Communicators (IABC) survey buttresses that attitude. "As a profession, we need to perform a reality check if we are going to continue to make decisions based on any of the following assumptions about communicators' career preferences: (1) communicators enjoy working with top management; (2) most have high-level corporate career goals; (3) most communicators don't enjoy the 'technician' aspect of the job. At least based on the responses of 188 people responding to this fax poll, any such assumptions would appear to be in serious doubt."[2] Clearly, 188 responses may not be conclusive, but the indications seem to underscore that this "I'm creative" attitude undermines the vitality and visibility of the profession.

Unexpected layoffs and the dearth of positions have forced many to reexamine career paths, if not career choices. Those unwilling or unable to move from a particular city or region either take lower-paying technician jobs or exit the business altogether. Real estate, sales, teaching, and the nonprofit arenas—even owning a franchise or resort-area restaurant—continue to attract many whose skills are transferable to those careers.

On the other hand, some choose—without much hesitation and with good reasons—the path of independent consultancies and specialty agencies or mini-boutiques. Many new refugees from the agency and Washington worlds had, over the years, carved out excellent reputations in specific specialties such as corporate speechwriting, crisis, and audits. They now parlay expertise to major businesses and associations. The success of these ventures is not even: Those who persevere and excel are those with exceptional understanding of client needs and an ability to subsume egos to the greater corporate cause, *in addition* to possessing excellent communications skills. The types of assignments these independents are garnering were once and almost exclusively the province of agencies. Public relations firms used to count on the million-dollar-plus retainers from global corporations. Now project work—assignments with definite beginnings and endings—is the order of business for agencies. And more and more corporations, searching for the best expertise at a lesser cost, are hiring consultants and boutiques.

Demographics and psychographics play a large role in the formation of new career paths during this recession and recovery, especially for two large groups: the baby boomers and the baby busters. Obviously, many boomers, in terms of sheer numbers, are blocked from senior-level communications positions because other colleagues have grabbed the brass ring first and top managers ensconced in their jobs just aren't letting go. The lack of suitable career-step positions forces an incredibly large pool of talent to consider other options.

> Baby boomers, having won the White House, will soon move into other centers of power. Financially, boomers have barely kept their heads above water by maintaining two-income families, but now their generation is poised to inherit enormous wealth from parents. On the job, boomers are fast transforming their unconventional career choices—working more at home, for example—into a new status quo.[3]
>
> *John Kotter*
> *Harvard Business School*

Those attitudes are remarkably dissimilar from those held by the busters, 80 million of them born between 1961 and 1981: disillusioned, cynical, and seemingly aware only of themselves and how fast they're moving up. Opinion researchers and other trend watchers confirm these differences. Says Dr. Sylvia Wagonheim, director of the Center for the New American Workforce:

> [The young women now joining large corporations] want a balanced lifestyle early on. While the [older] women . . . most of whom started work in the early '70s, had to wait until they had achieved very senior levels before demanding lifestyle changes, the new workforce wants them early. It's not that the fire in the belly is missing now, but it's been tempered.[4]

These are future public relations executives. And though not all maintain an "I've been slighted and I deserve more" mindset, statistics underscore their dilemma: People under 35 are earning 20 to 30 percent less than their counterparts did in the 1970s.[5]

Quality of life, then, for both boomers and busters, has become more than a slogan. A 1989 survey of 1,000 professionals showed the average workload had increased 10 hours since the mid-1970s, up to 51 hours weekly. Yet two-thirds were willing to take a salary cut averaging 13 percent in exchange for more family/personal time.[6] The impact on public relations careers is—and will be—phenomenal. Midlife crisis professionals will opt out or change the nature of the business. Taught that corporate loyalty no longer exists, young communicators will job-hop whenever opportunities appear and, generally, be more ambitious and competitive than their predecessors.

The rise of communications as a vital business resource in the 1980s sparked an increase in the number of public relations programs at both the undergraduate and graduate levels. No longer are communicators culled solely from journalism and government, or those degreed in the social sciences and the humanities or liberal arts. Young careerists can now enter the business armed with a degree in their chosen field. And some, already in mid-career, are choosing graduate studies in communications, figuring that more education will only help their career progression—a much-debated option among employers and academia.[7] In my opinion, the most successful programs expose students to all parts of business—and to real life—not just teach the tools and philosophies of public relations. Because professionals in the highest positions sit on executive committees and in the board room, they must understand finance, law, operations and human resources in addition to communications. Will a major in public relations or a graduate degree in communications ensure career success? The jury is still out.

As leaders of the profession in their 1950s and 1960s select early retirement or are eased out, another unfortunate trend is occurring: The communications function is disbanded or parceled out to different departments, or talent is recruited from the outside. Why? There was—and still is—a tremendous reluctance among senior professionals to appoint a strong successor because of competition or simply the mistaken notion of individual indispensability. Such occurrences have downgraded the communications function at many a corporation, leaving survivors to report to human resources (HR), marketing, or administration, instead of to the CEO. It's a loss to the continuing viability of public relations and, yes, to management.

We need to learn from business: Both the late Michael Walsh at Tenneco and Ken Pontikes at Comdisco deliberately appointed strong No. 2s. Unless we all cultivate and encourage the rising young stars, challenge them, and mentor them, the potential power of public relations never will be realized. Mentoring, once in vogue, also has passed into the lean-and-mean graveyards: "It's a good idea, but there's no time." Its death has been noticed not only in public relations. *Creativity*, a sister publication of *Advertising Age*, commented recently:

> Advertising agencies have become insecure and defensive places, some say, and the art of mentorship could be in jeopardy . . . Part of the problem is the insecurity bred by absentee ownership and huge holding companies. Individuals just don't seem important anymore . . . For those who do seek out the stars for guidance, chances are the stars are on the road pitching business or trying to keep it. Even though they claim mentorship is still possible, and at their agencies they try to hire and groom young talent, everyone is worried about having time to do it right.[8]

Mentoring, as practiced by Harold Burson, still occasionally crops up in the corporate world and, more infrequently, in agencies. In the close of this century and the beginning of the next, if time is not spent passing on skills and knowledge sets, careers of promising professionals will be stalled or aborted. The very valuable contributions top-level managers can make are not limited solely to one-on-one coaching; opportunities for guidance appear in teaching and in nonprofit volunteer work.

In a sense, mentoring goes hand in hand with two more issues that not only have dogged the communications business for two decades but also have bewitched, bothered, and bewildered the entire management structure of the American workplace: diversity (aka affirmative action) and women/the glass ceiling. First, some rather astounding statistics: From 1983 to 1993, the percentage of white, male professionals and managers in the workforce dropped 8 percent (from 55 to 47 percent), while the same group of white women increased from 37 to 42 percent.[9] That diversification will only speed up. The U.S. Department of Labor estimates that, through the year 2005, half of all workforce entrants will be women and more than one-third will be Hispanics, blacks, or representatives of other ethnic groups.[10] Add to that the results of a just-completed study with great significance for communications: U.S. companies implementing quality affirmative action programs benefit economically—through a higher evaluation of company stock held by investors.[11]

Corporate cultures that currently embrace all employees equally can, most probably, be counted on fingers and toes: Corning, Honeywell, and IBM are among those behemoths trying to make the transition. Surprisingly, the high voluntary turnover of women and minorities in business is not due to discrimination, sexual harassment, or lack of day care. Informal surveys show that these employees leave companies because of slow career progress, boring assignments, and a general feeling of not fitting in.[12] Yet isn't it of interest that neither the communications profession nor its members have spearheaded that change or even encouraged, via specific programs, the development of minority professionals? If we believe, according to a 1993 survey, that companies are addressing affirmative action barriers primarily by promoting awareness of diverse cultures through internal communication,[13] then we should be seeing an accompanying growth in the number of employee communicators and other trained professionals ready to spread the word. It just isn't so. Either the responsibility for diversity awareness is being handled by other departments—HR, for one—or we're only paying lip service to this need. Agencies and association communicators, too, are equally as slow as corporate managers to adopt the education and training necessary to ensure that a diverse workforce is not an oxymoron.

Women, an affirmative action subset in the general business world, become even more of an issue in the public relations profession simply because of their large numbers. Within agencies, there is no doubt that women have and will continue to climb career ladders. However, unless they have launched their own firms, few women currently direct the business of global agencies. Female corporate communicators in top positions are yet another story. Yes, there are a handful—Joan Walker at Ameritech; Betty Hudson at Reader's Digest; Marilyn Laurie at AT&T; Mary Moster at Comdisco; and Karen Rugen at Boston Market, among others. The same frustrations other minorities experience—lack of career progress, for one—are seen in the dropout rate of women from the profession or, at least, from conventional agency and corporate communications life. Though no statistics currently exist for public relations, generic studies of women at work indicate that three-fourths of female executives, compared with 30 percent of the men, want to opt out of the corporate treadmill well before retirement.[14]

The numbers of female communications executives will most likely remain the same over the next few decades. The reason is primarily because women in public relations have not been adequately prepared to be managers. *Business Week*'s comment on how to break the glass ceiling is revealing:

> Companies also must review the assignments that are essential to advancement and begin placing more women in them. These are usually the "line positions" responsible for profits and losses: marketing, in a consumer-products company, or plant management, in a manufacturing company. Currently, female managers may rise high—but usually it's in the areas of communications and of human resources, which rarely lead to the senior jobs.[15]

It's a slightly different spin on the old refrain: Communicators are unwilling or unable to continue career paths because of the perception of communications as a nonmanagement function and because they perceive themselves as creative technicians. Second, the mentoring system is dead or just barely breathing. How can a young female communicator learn about strategic thinking and positioning, crisis and audits, unless she attaches herself to a senior professional, male *or* female, who's willing to guide, to lead, to teach? And third, there's not much of an "old girls' network," though Women in Communications, Inc. (WICI) has tried to promote female communicators. Contrast that to the male versions— alive and well and working at full speed.

THE FUTURE

What do all of these present trends—diversity, succession planning, demographics, consultants/boutiques, and a pared-down workforce—foretell for future career paths?

No question, this marks the beginning of the best of times and the worst of times. And change, lots of it. Labor Secretary Robert Reich says it best: "Job security is a thing of the past. People are going to have to get used to the idea of involuntary separations—sometimes four, five, or six times during a career." [16] Adopting a flexible mindset will be critical in the years ahead. But the other breaks in the profession, I predict, will be as follows:

New Specialties, New Firms

Agencies will continue to grow, albeit at a much smaller pace than in the 1980s. The growth will come through two avenues: mergers and acquisitions of consultancies/boutiques, and by the offering of new expertise. Burson-Marsteller, for instance, is starting to incorporate advertising professionals into its staff, marking the beginnings of truly integrated marketing communications. Other specialties to be added at the agency level will include benefits, labor relations, TQM, reengineering, and employee relations. Many firms are beginning to realize that communications expertise knows no boundaries . . . and has many competitors. These include the big benefits consultants who, as part of their package, routinely offer communications services; management consultants promoting TQM which, as a customer-focused process, demands only the best in communications thinking and execution; and labor relations professionals who, as exemplified by the United Airlines employee buyout, will be crucial to the success of many businesses today. These experts will be recruited from outside the firm and outside of the profession unless more risk-embracing men and women within public relations decide to expand their educations and horizons. Bottom line, communicators inside agencies and inside corporations must adopt a new attitude—that all parts of the company are potential clients, not just the CEO or the marketing department. For example, they must add value to the explanation of a new employee benefits package, become an expert in interactive technology and volunteer to train other departments, or go on sales calls. The learning possibilities are almost endless, as is the potential to gain stature and visibility within the corporation or agency. In the end, it will be the responsibility of the top professional to educate each sector of the company about communications and its promise and possibilities.

The Rebirth of Employee Communications

Despite some new studies showing that downsizing and reengineering efforts might be misguided,[17] RIFs will continue. To survivors as well as to those laid-off managers and workers who find new positions and jobs, communications in the new work environment is key. Loyalty to an institution is dead. To cite the findings of a 1993 national survey conducted by Northwestern University's J. L. Kellogg Graduate School of Management and Loyola

University's Department of Management, 64 percent of middle managers feel less loyalty to their companies today than they did five years ago. And 57 percent of American corporations feel less loyalty to their employees.[18] Those feelings need to be dealt with, openly and honestly, to forge new employer–employee alliances. And what better agent to encourage the formation of that new partnership than communications—or, more specifically, employee communications? The employee communications experience of one Fortune 500 corporation should be instructive:

> Though profitability is up sharply, Chevron decided that isn't enough. The company has bravely posted the results of employee morale surveys in company bulletins and in the lobby of headquarters in San Francisco, and has vowed to improve them by developing a new relationship with workers. "It's not easy," Vice Chairman James Sullivan says candidly. "Until you try to write about it or talk about it, you don't realize how inept you are." Nonetheless candor and communication are essential, he has found.[19]

Now we enter the era of employee communications—a much-neglected and often ignored stepchild of public relations. Until now, this area has been relegated to the bottom of communicators' top-ten priorities list and delegated to excellent writers and editors who usually are *not* strategically, management, or bottom-line oriented. It's about time that changed, as well as the focus of employee communications beyond newsletter production— if for no other reason than CEOs and other experts now recognize the need. "Employees don't expect the impossible," says Robert Levering, coauthor of *The 100 Best Companies to Work for in America*, "but they do demand the possible. And good, two-way communication is probably the most important thing companies can do."[20]

Think Globally, Act Locally . . . For Now

The global revolution has turned into an evolution for communicators for several reasons. One, the European Community is more an aggregate of nations than one solid union. Two, with the exception of the United States and Asia, many corporations in Europe and the Americas simply do not understand the value of public relations, or that their perceptions of communications are far different than ours.[21] Third, because of U.S. downsizings, more corporations are reluctant to commit staffers overseas, believing that responsibilities can be handled from headquarters here, with some travel. Certainly, that conviction has impacted both corporate and agency communicators. Opportunities to practice the profession outside the U.S. are limited; no longer is an overseas corporate communications posting considered a good career move. Also, agencies that staffed up or bought offices in various parts of the world are finding that client business is, once again, in the form of project work or is awarded to local firms best versed in that country's culture. "After a huge build-up in worldwide office networks in the 1980s, big operations like WPP Group's Hill & Knowlton and Young & Rubicam's Burson-Marsteller are finding major corporate customers no longer need or want global campaigns from a single agency." [22] So the opportunity that global public relations presents is a limited one, at least until the next century.

IMC: Is It Real . . .?

Integrated marketing communications, once considered solely the bailiwick of advertising agencies, will begin to gain momentum in both the corporate and public relations agency sectors. For the first time in its history, giant Leo Burnett is offering full public relations services to its clients. To some extent, IMC is still an embattled discipline. At the beginning of the 1990s, ad agencies like DDB Needham Worldwide created plans to embrace the entire marketing mix; their particular umbrella, called "Total Creativity/Guaranteed Results," seems to have been received with mixed emotions.[23] Clients, on the other hand, are asserting their rights of first refusal on the IMC initiative.[24] Major barriers to success include egos and fear of budget loss.[25] However, those stumbling blocks can—and should—be overcome in the next few years. Is it too much to ask that public relations smooth out issues and lead the way?

Then, there are the type of crystal-ball predictions that may or may not occur. To come true, they depend on the espousal of certain assumptions and attitudes—one, that professionals rely on self-confidence to take risks. Here, then, is a wish list of forecasts for career opportunities in public relations:

1. That the development of top-notch communications managers be considered among the highest of priorities in agencies, corporations, associations, and other nonprofit organizations.

2. That the breaking down of perceptual barriers occur between "agency" and "corporate" communicators. Agency-trained professionals can make the segue to corporate jobs; they understand client needs and bring a fresh, creative perspective to the responsibilities of communications. On the other hand, some corporate professionals also can switch to an agency; their sensitivity to nuances and politics and their involvement in executive suite matters are two of many valuable assets to be plumbed.

3. That communications professionals of all kinds be willing to take on responsibilities outside their designated areas of expertise. Then, and only then, will public relations realize its ultimate goal of becoming a management function and regain its seat at the policy-making table. In fact, that assumption of other duties may happen sooner than we think: Consider the very recent phenomenon of broad banding, wherein employees are loosely grouped into a few broad job categories rather than the two-dozen-plus traditional classifications.[26] Even though only six percent of companies surveyed in 1993 have implemented this new structure,[27] chances are great that more corporations will institute broad banding, thus giving managers more flexibility in determining compensation and employees more skill-developing opportunities.

4. Finally, that communicators take responsibility for their own careers, a point that essentially spells out the new career paths in public relations. What does that entail?

   a. An acceptance that job security is a creature of the past and that, says *Fortune* magazine, there's a new work contract:

      There will never be job security. You will be employed by us as long as you add value to the organization, and *you* are continuously responsible for finding ways to add value. In return, you have the right to demand interesting and important work, the freedom and resources to perform it well, pay that reflects your contribution, and the experience and training needed to be employable here or elsewhere.[28]

   b. A commitment to lifelong learning. Workers will be rewarded for their knowledge and flexibility. Eighty-five percent of 851 companies surveyed in 1993 by Hewitt Associates reimbursed employees for tuition expenses toward *any* job-related course; 67 percent toward a master's degree in business; 48 percent toward other graduate courses.[29] Take advantage of it—whether you pursue formal or informal education. Emory University management professor Jeffrey A. Sonnenfeld discovered startling responses in a 1991 study he conducted of 300 midcareer executives in the financial services field. About 20 percent believed they lacked the skills to meet the expectations of their bosses, and another 75 percent replied they'd probably be behind the curve within five years.[30]

c. The psychological ability to *objectively* assess career opportunities, based on chemistry and learning. More often than not, professionals eager to snag the next upwardly mobile position hear only what they want, while hiring managers feed into that proclivity. Evaluate any and all positions offered by listening between the lines and through copious research. Is the culture comfortable? Will challenge and learning be integral to the job? Make sure that the environment fits, that the annexation of responsibilities is not just a paper promise, and that all commitments are fully understood—in writing, if at all possible.

d. And, finally, some tips from Vicky Farrow, director of executive and workforce development at Sun Microsystems:

(1) The overarching principle: Think of yourself as a business.

(2) Define your product or service. What is your area of expertise?

(3) Know your target market. To whom are you going to sell this?

(4) Be clear on why your customer buys from you. What is "value proposition"—what are you offering that causes him to use you?

(5) As in any business, drive for quality and customer satisfaction, even if your customer is just someone else in your organization—like your boss.

(6) Know your profession or field and what's going on there. What is "best of breed" in your area? Is your profession, just possibly, becoming obsolete?

(7) Invest in your own growth and development, the way a company invests in R&D. What new products or services will you be able to provide?

(8) Be willing to consider changing your business or starting a new one. Says Farrow: "I don't think it's possible anymore to have one career for your whole life."[31]

The brave new world of career paths in public relations, in short, is of your making.

BOX 1–1

THE INVISIBLE PROFESSION

One of the few highly specialized professions rarely aspired to by either public relations practitioners or the public at large is speechwriting.

Of the 2,000 or so now wielding their craft full-time at corporations, nonprofits, and associations (note the omission of agencies), most entered speechwriting through the back door. Journalists, English majors, government press secretaries, and teachers are prime recruits for the speechwriting business.

The job is much more difficult than it seems, demanding a composite of psychologist, political strategist, professor, and, of course, top-notch writer and communicator. A good view of the actual—and often arduous—process of crafting the right remarks comes from no less a source than *The Wall Street Journal*:

> . . . it was another compromise in the often tortuous process of getting a corporate speech from draft to delivery. Typically, that process involves battling layers of cautious bureaucrats intent on "dulling up" a speech. It means learning to cope with conflicting suggestions from various departments, and fending off subordinates who want to influence corporate policy. It means reasoning with engineers, scientists, and technical specialists who love streams of numbers and jargons. And it requires getting through to busy—and sometimes uncooperative—executives.[1]

This is, of course, where the true "creative technician" shines, and where career paths lead to independent consultancies or, very infrequently, to management. It *is* a burn-out business; most speechwriters last about two to seven years in any one position, then either move on or out. Speechwriters who fill managerial slots in communications are exceptions, not the rule; many simply prefer to do the "writing thing" without having to deal with supervising, training, and managing subordinates. Unlike their colleagues in public relations, wordsmiths usually don't have or recognize the opportunity to align themselves with up-and-coming managers within their corporations.

The outlook for this specialty? Brighter than the past few years, when speechwriters have been chopped from payrolls. The new willingness of CEOs to speak out about issues and talk to employees more candidly should create job opportunities for a very undervalued, underpaid, and often anonymous segment of the profession: the speechwriter.

---

1. Larry Reibstein, "For Corporate Speech Writers, Life Is Seldom a Simple Matter of ABCs," *The Wall Street Journal*, June 30, 1987, p. 33.

E N D N O T E S

1. Sherman, Stratford, "A Brave New Darwinian Workplace," *Fortune* (January 25, 1993), pp. 50–56.

2. McGoon, Cliff, "Life's a Beach, for Communicators," *IABC Communication World*, (January-February 1993), pp. 12–15.

3. Sherman, op. cit.

4. Lyne, Barbara, "Women at the Top: Role Models or Relics?," *The New York Times* (September 27, 1992), p. 27.

5. Sherman, op. cit.

6. Paterau, Alan, "Slow Zone Ahead," *Chicago Tribune* (September 25, 1991).

7. Duncan, Tom, Clarke Caywood, and Doug Newsom, "Preparing Advertising and Public Relations Students for the Communications Industry in the 21st Century: A Report of the Task Force on Integrated Communications" (December 1993).

8. Madison, Cathy, "The Sorcerers' Apprentices," *Creativity* (July 1994), pp. 10ff.

9. Galen, Michele, "White, Male, and Worried," *Business Week* (January 31, 1994), pp. 50–55.

10. Ibid.

11. Kleiman, Carol, "Companies Taking Stock in Affirmative Action," *Chicago Tribune* (June 8, 1994), pp. 5–6.

12. Deutsch, Claudia H., "Listening to Women and Blacks," *The New York Times* (December 1, 1991), p. 25.

13. "Managing People," edited by Ellyn E. Spragins, *Inc.* magazine (January 1993), p. 33.

14. Noble, Barbara P., "Women Pay More for Success," *The New York Times* (July 4, 1993), p. 25.

15. Garland, Susan B., "How to Keep Women Managers on the Corporate Ladder," *Business Week* (September 2, 1991), p. 64.

16. Topolnickui, Denise, "Down and Out?," *Chicago Tribune* (May 5, 1994), pp. 1ff.

17. Noble, Barbara P., "Questioning Productivity Beliefs," *The New York Times* (July 10, 1994), p. 21.

18. Yates, Ronald E., "Downsizing's Bitter Pill," *Chicago Tribune Magazine* (November 21, 1993), pp. 14ff.

19. O'Reilly, Brian, "The New Deal," *Fortune* (June 13, 1994), pp. 44–52.

20. Ibid.

21. Bovet, Susan Fry, "Trends in the 'New' Europe," *Public Relations Journal* (September 1993), pp. 18–21.

22. Levin, Gary, "Global PR Efforts on the Wane," *Advertising Age* (May 16, 1994), p. 28.

23. *Public Relations Journal* (July 1990), p. 9ff.

24. Hume, Scott, "New Ideas, Old Barriers; Survey: 'Egos' Inhibit Integrated Marketing," *Advertising Age* (July 22, 1991), 6.

25. Ibid.

26. Rowland, Mary, "Sidestepping toward Success," *The New York Times* (January 24, 1993), p. 17.

27. Ibid.

28. O'Reilly, op. cit.

29. Rowland, Mary "Career Advance by Degrees," *The New York Times* (May 1, 1994), p. 13.

30. Labich, Kenneth, "Take Control of Your Career," *Fortune* (November 18, 1991), pp. 86ff.

31. Kiechell, Walter, III, "A Manager's Career in the New Economy," *Fortune* (April 4, 1994), pp. 68–72.

## CHAPTER 2

The Unseen Power: A Brief History of Public Relations

Scott M. Cutlip, Fellow, PRSA
Dean Emeritus
College of Journalism and
Mass Communication
University of Georgia

The way to get at the nature of an institution, as anything else that is alive, is to see how it has grown.

A. G. Keller

EARLY HISTORY OF PUBLIC RELATIONS

Modern public relations, today an essential management function in enterprises around the world, large and small, got its start in the United States in the sense that we describe it today. Public relations has evolved in response to the growth of democratic freedoms and free markets. Efforts go back to antiquity; only the tools, degree of specialization, breadth of knowledge required of counselors, costs and intensity of effort have escalated in the 20th century. Public relations truly began when men came to live together in tribal camps. To function, civilization requires communication, conciliation, cooperation, and consensus on common interests.

As far back as 1800 BC, Persian farmers were being instructed through bulletins how to deal with field mice and how to harvest their crops. Much of the literature and art of antiquity was designed to build support for kings, priests and other spiritual and secular leaders. Virgil's *Georgics* was written to get urban dwellers to return to the land so that they could produce food for a growing Rome. Rudimentary elements of public relations can be found in ancient India and in the English kings' Lords Chancellor, the keepers of the king's conscience and his intermediaries with the people. The concept of propaganda, now a major element of international public relations, was born in the Catholic Church in the 17th century when the church set up its *Congregation de Propaganda* to propagate the faith. The world's communication networks today are flooded with the propaganda of countries and causes.

Today, the function of public relations counseling is an essential element in management's dealing with a global economy and its competition for markets, causes that cross national borders, and nation states' efforts to achieve their political objectives in a volatile and interdependent world. The function's increased utilization has been compelled by today's instant global communication, the growth of free markets, and the spread of democracy and conflict around the globe. Truly, Marshall McLuhan's "global village" has come to pass, and with it the need for specialists in public opinion and communication to deal with a highly competitive and somewhat chaotic world in transition to the 21st century.

To understand how this function and its supporting corps of practitioners have evolved in democratic societies, one must comprehend the forces in the world that have coerced and compelled its development. I hold that a professional practice must be informed by its history. Surely we will be better able to deal with today and tomorrow if we understand our yesterdays. Experience will teach us if we are wise enough to learn its lessons. A concise history of public relations follows with the hope that it will be instructional to today's practitioners.

The utilization of publicity, puffery, and press agentry to promote causes, tout land ventures, and raise funds is older than the nation itself. American talent for hype can be traced back to the first settlements on the Atlantic Coast in the 16th century.

The need for foreign governments to explain themselves and to promote trade and tourism in the United States became apparent after the Spanish-American War caused the United States to shed its isolationism and move onto the world stage. These needs intensified through the 20th century as nations grew more interdependent and a fiercely competitive world economy, ethnic wars, and nationalism emerged in the wake of the Cold War. These needs are being met by a growing corps of public relations professionals in the United States specializing in the representation of foreign governments. These men and women serve variously the roles of promoters, propagandists, and lobbyists. There has been a similar exponential growth in the number of professionals employed in government information services around the world.

Hype for the Colonies

The exaggerated claims that today often characterize publicity began with Sir Walter Raleigh's ill-fated effort to settle Roanoke Island off the Virginia coast. When Captain Arthur Barlowe returned to England in 1584 from that desolate, swampy area, he reported to Raleigh that "the soile is the most plentiful, sweete, fruitful, and wholesome of all the worlde . . . they have those Okes that we have, but farre greater and better . . . the highest and reddest Cedars of the world and a great abundance of Pine or Pitch Trees." He even described the Indians as "most gentle, loving, and faithfull, voide of all guile or treason."

Even more glowing was the description of Raleigh's "lieutenant governor." Writing from Virginia is 1585, Ralph Lane trumpeted that the mainland had "the goodliest (s)oyle under the cope of heaven," and that "what commodities soever" France, Spain, Italy, or the East produced, "these parts doe abound with the growth of them all . . ."

Contrary to the accounts of bold settlers eagerly flocking to the newly-discovered America given in grade-school histories, it would appear that many came from Europe to the new land in response to exaggerated publicity claims. Historian Hugh Lefler observes: "The glorified advertising of every colony was the chief means of procuring money and men. The degree of success varied considerably from time to time and from place to place."[1]

Although it is not possible to assess the effectiveness of this promotional material, Lefler wrote that a tract published by a layman, Robert Johnson, entitled "Nova Brittania: Offering Most Excellent Fruites by Planting in Virginia," published in 1609, did produce "a great increase in investments in the Company and in the number of people migrating to Virginia." Virginia's early promotional efforts were matched varying degrees by the later colonies of the South Atlantic region. The promotion of Maryland began in 1622 with the Charles I edition of the "Charter of Maryland." Another tract, "Objections Answered concerning Maryland," was published in 1662. In Lefler's opinion, Carolina's publicity did not match Virginia in the variety of appeals or in media used. "There were no poems or officially inspired sermons, few broadsides, and only a minimum of prospectuses."

Georgia's promotion of its colony for the poor and the outcast was most intensive because Lord Oglethorpe's venture was a philanthropic one. Because of its dependence on charity and Parliamentary appropriations, the Georgia Colony mounted an intensive, broadscale campaign of promotion and persuasion unmatched by any other colony. In one scholar's opinion, the trustees' promotional activities paralleled many of today's promotions. Like many a propaganda campaign since, the high, unrealistic expectations created by Georgia's unprecedented public relations turned to bitter disillusionment. Up and down the Atlantic Coast, disappointment set in. In the exaggerated publicity hype of the new American colonial settlements on the Atlantic Coast, there is a basic lesson many practitioners have yet to learn: Building false hopes in hyping a product, service, or a candidate's message inevitably leads to disappointment, with the ultimate loss paid by the sponsor. No glowing accounts sent back to England from the malarial swamps of Jamestown and Savannah could alter the reality that would lead to hardship and heartache on the part of our intrepid forebears.

The first known systematic effort to raise funds on this continent was that sponsored by Harvard College in 1641 when the infant institution sent a trio of preachers to England on a "begging mission." Once the preachers got to England, they found what fund raisers know today—they needed a brochure making their case. In response to this request came *New England's First Fruits*, written in Massachusetts but printed in London in 1643, the first of countless public relations pamphlets and brochures.

Samuel Adams Brings on a Revolution

Employment of public relations skills to shape the course and impact of government is older that the United States Government itself. The tools and techniques of persuasive communication have long been utilized in the nation's political struggles. Political public relations practice dates back to the nation's pre-Revolution years, when a small and resourceful band of propagandists fed the fires of revolt, from 1763 to 1776, that brought the birth of the world's oldest constitutional government. These revolutionaries were among the first to demonstrate the power of an organized, articulate minority, carrying the day against the unorganized, apathetic majority of citizens. The small band of Whig propagandists were no match for Samuel Adams and his daring band. Little wonder Philip Davidson thought "The influence of the propagandists was out of all proportion of their number."

Today's public relations practice has been shaped far more than most practitioners realize by the innovations in mobilizing public opinion developed by Adams and his cohort. In fomenting revolt against Great Britain, the Revolutionaries developed and demonstrated the power of these techniques:

1. The necessity of organization, such as The Committees of Correspondence, to implement actions made possible by a propaganda campaign.
2. The use of symbols, such as the Liberty Tree, that are easily recognizable and arouse emotions.

3. The use of slogans, notably "Taxation without representation is tyranny," that compress complex issues in easy-to-remember stereotypes.

4. Staged events, for example, the Boston Tea Party, that catch public attention and thus crystallize public opinion.

5. The importance of getting your story to the public first so that your interpretation of events is the one accepted. An example is "The Horrid Boston Massacre" pamphlet that was spread swiftly throughout the colonies.

6. The necessity of a sustained, saturation campaign using these techniques through all available media to penetrate the public mind with a new conviction.

"Greatest Public Relations Work Ever Done"

The power of propaganda to mobilize public opinion was relied upon heavily in the history-making campaign that won ratification of the United States Constitution in 1787–1788. This campaign, ranking alongside the propaganda campaign for independence in shaping the United States, was praised by the late historian Allan Nevins as "the greatest work ever done in America in the field on public relations." Surely it was the most important one in United States history. The burden of the campaign to win quick ratification of the new Constitution, drafted in secrecy in Philadelphia in 1787, was carried by the Federalist Papers, which, like the Declaration of Independence, were written as propaganda documents. The Papers were the work of Alexander Hamilton, James Madison, and John Jay. A contemporary damned them as "the frankest, baldest, and boldest propaganda ever penned." The Hamilton-led campaign was strongly opposed by the Antifederalist forces, led by Virginia's Richard Henry Lee. In historian Frederick Jackson Main's opinion, at the outset public opinion seemed to favor the Antifederalists, who argued that America had just fought a war to throw off the shackles of a strong central government and should not return to such.

Historian Robert Rutland saw this political contest as "the seedtime of American politics." He puts this battle for public support in perspective:

> The political ordeal that produced the Constitution in 1787 and brought about its ratification in 1788 was unique in human history. Never before had the representatives of a whole nation discussed, planned, and implemented a new form of government in such a manner and in such a short time. In little more than a year, Americans established a political network which enlightened Europeans viewed with skepticism.

Surely this was the most important public relations campaign ever done.

Jackson and Kendall Reshape America's Democracy

The presidential election of 1828, in which war hero Andrew Jackson decisively defeated President John Quincy Adams, marked a watershed in American politics by bringing a shift in political power from the "Eastern Establishment" to the nation's expanding frontier, an enlargement of the Presidency and the genesis of the nation's second two-party political system. In these accomplishments, President Jackson had significant assistance from Amos Kendall, an astute political strategist and skilled publicist. Kendall served as Jackson's adviser for his two terms, devising his political strategy, publicizing his views and actions, and providing accurate assessments of prevailing public opinion. Kendall performed all the work that now requires a large White House public relations staff.

His work was significant. A biographer, Robert V. Remini, sees Jackson as a great democrat who changed "the pure republican character" of the political system as originally established by the Founding Fathers by insisting on greater representation of the people and a greater responsiveness to their will.

Kendall played a decisive role in the first great public relations battle between Big Business and Government—the Jackson-Biddle War that brought the end of the United States Bank, a contest that changed America's banking system forever. Directing the propaganda campaign for Nicholas Biddle's Bank of the United States was Mathew St. Clair Clarke, perhaps the first publicist to be employed by Big Business. The battle over the Bank was fully joined in July 1832, when Congress passed a bill rechartering the bank as of 1836, a move that had been requested by Biddle but that would prove a blunder.

Congress passed the reauthorization bill, but President Jackson, at Kendall's strong urging, decided to veto the bill and directed his aide to write the veto message. The only complete draft of Jackson's veto message in the Library of Congress is in Kendall's handwriting. Jackson's veto was upheld.

One of the by-products of the Biddle-Jackson political struggle was in the build-up of Davy Crockett, financed by Biddle and promoted by the Bank's publicists in a futile effort to counter Jackson's popularity along the Western Frontier. They portrayed Crockett as a "real frontiersman" who boasted that he wore "no collar labelled 'My Dog–Andrew Jackson.'" Clarke and Whig Party publicists went to great lengths to create the public image of Crockett as the bold, coonskin-capped frontier democrat with a lusty pioneer spirit. When Crockett was defeated in his bid to be re-elected to Congress, he told his constituents they could go to hell and he went off to die in the Battle of the Alamo. Such shirt-stuffing we see in today's celebrity world.

PRESS AGENTRY AND ADVERTISING IN THE 19TH CENTURY

Led by the American railroads in their effort to sell land and lure settlers to the West, press agentry, promotion, and advertising flowered in the 19th century. These fields, which often meld into one another, have the common purpose of attracting the public's attention for an entertainment, product, or service. Today the world is stuffed with the cascading messages of the press agent, promoter, and advertiser. The commercial value of publicity to sell books, circuses, stage shows, and patent medicines, discovered early in the 19th century, was put to wide and imaginative use. As early as 1809, Washington Irving used press agent gimmickry to promote his *Knickerbocker's History of New York.*

The circus—a fabulous development of the 19th century—did much to stimulate the growth of press agentry and display advertising. Today's patterns of promotion and press agentry in the world of show business were the innovations of Phineas Taylor Barnum, the greatest showman and press agent of all time, "The Prince of Humbug." One writer termed him ". . . the first great advertising genius and the greatest publicity exploiter the world has ever seen." Barnum once remarked, "Advertising is like learning: a little is a dangerous thing." Though he had no equal in dreaming up newsmaking stunts, Barnum employed a staff of press agents. Barnum was the first to use display advertising on a large scale to promote his circus.

The practice of press agentry became more pervasive as the businesses of book publishing, travelling theater productions, resorts, and professional sports developed in the last century. Near the end of 1898, *The Fourth Estate*, a newspaper trade journal, reported:

> Press agents have become a necessary adjunct to nearly all commercial enterprises. It was not so long ago when those energetic purveyors of publicity were confined in their efforts to the circus, theatrical, and operatic fields . . . But business methods have changed materially during the last few years. Advertising and plenty of it is now essential to the success of almost any undertaking that depends on a large public patronage.

Advertising and product promotion, today intertwined under the umbrella of marketing, have their roots in the post-Civil War industrialization in the United States. With the introduction of mass production methods, more and more businesses needed regional and national distribution of their mass-produced soaps, foods, and other products. For example, to break down a person's fear about meat that was slaughtered weeks earlier and far away, the meat packer Swift turned to advertising. By 1879, advertising revenue in newspapers totaled $21 million. The advertising agency was born at the end of the Civil War and became a vital part of the great expansion of industry and business that took place after the war and before the turn of the century. The oldest agency, J. Walter Thompson, was started in 1864, and N. W. Ayer & Son was founded in 1869. In March of 1877, Albert Frank opened a two-man agency in lower Manhattan. These agencies survive to this day, but other agencies started in those years have long since disappeared.

The railroads used publicity, tours, and advertising to the hilt to lure settlers west to buy land, and they provided settlements that would bring passenger and freight traffic to their lines. Charles Russell Lowell, who was employed as a publicist for the Burlington Railroad in the 1850s, wrote a friend in 1859: "We are beginning to find that he who buildeth a railroad west of the Mississippi must also find a population and build up business. We wish to blow as loud a trumpet as the merits of our position warrants." A sound principle for today's practitioner! Historian J. Valerie Fifer has concluded: "Together the transport, tourist, and information industries played a crucial role in Western development. All brought new settlement and investment into the West, demanded a new awareness of the environment, helped to define the new word, 'transcontinental,' and stimulated the growth of a new spirit of American nationalism." The legacies of the promoter and advertiser are many and significant.

The Era of "The Public Be Damned"

The final two decades of the 19th century brought the beginnings of today's public relations practice in the United States. Contemporary public relations, as a practice and as a management concept, was to emerge from the melée of opposing forces in this period of the nation's growth both in business and in politics. Eric Goldman, in his brief history, *Two-Way Street*, observed: "Shouldering aside agriculture, large-scale commerce and industry became dominant over the life of the nation. Big Business was committed to the doctrine that the less the public knew about its operations, the more efficient and profitable . . . operations would be." It was a day of business arrogance toward employee and citizen alike, a day when railroad magnate E. H. Harriman would boast, "I don't want anything on this railroad that I cannot control," a day when Marshall Field made $600 an hour each day while his clerks earned a maximum of $12 dollars a week.

It was truly the era of "The Public Be Damned," epitomized in the memorable phrase of William Henry Vanderbilt, owner of the New York Central Railroad. He was reported to have made the remark to a Chicago freelance reporter in an 1882 interview. Vanderbilt vehemently denied making the remark, but whether he did or not didn't matter. It summarized the contempt of Big Business for the public interest and thus stuck.

These industrialists, who were ruthlessly exploiting the nation's resources and their laborers, thought nothing beyond purchase for their selfish ends. They also knew the power of publicity as it had been demonstrated by the railroads. Buccaneer Jim Fisk employed a publicity man, George Crouch, to plant stories when he was trying to corner the gold market. Publicity was heavily used in the brawling insurance field. A Mutual Life Insurance Company historian describing this period wrote:

> To facilitate the labors of the sales force, the Mutual Life, like all similar institutions, endeavored to establish in the public mind not only its name, but also a favorable impression of its operations. Its chief vehicles of advertising were the insurance press and pamphlet literature. In the former the Company not only inserted bona fide advertisements, but it also paid editors to run its message as news articles or editorials. For the campaign against Jacob L. Greene of the Connecticut Mutual, the Mutual, along with the Equitable and New York Life, hired the services of C. C. Hine, editor of the *Insurance Monitor*, Stephen English of the *Insurance Times*, Charles J. (Dollar a Line) Smith of the *Insurance Record*. The editor of the *Insurance Monitor* had a fixed price for his Connecticut Mutual extras of $50 a thousand and boasted that he sold them "by the ton."

This obvious purchase of editorial content in these trade journals was expensive and had its risks. These mercenaries were for hire to all sides. The use of paid ads as news matter continued in public relations practice well into the 20th century. Mutual was one of the first to use this shady practice. It established a "species of a literary bureau" in 1888 under the direction of Charles J. Smith. Another large firm that was buying news space in this period was the Standard Oil Company of Ohio.

In James Playsted Wood's history *The Story of Advertising*, he writes: "Part of this impulse and impetus behind the force which burst into the eruption of advertising in the United States in the 1890s sprang from England. Much of this came from Thomas Lipton, a canny Scotsman with a great flair for publicity and a strong believer in advertising of all kinds. The world-renowned merchant used every publicity and advertising trick his innovative mind could dream up." His racing for yachting's American Cup was one of these.

There also came a realization to businessmen whose innovations were bringing rapid-fire changes in living to America's frontier. For example, the National Biscuit Company revolutionized marketing at the turn of the century when it took the cracker out of the grocer's barrel and put it in a sanitary package. The N. W. Ayer advertising agency had the National Biscuit account. Ayer's executives soon realized that advertising alone could not get the public to buy the Uneeda Biscuit in the sanitary package. They learned a fundamental of public relations—change requires long-term education. Ayer used the homier word "biscuit" instead of the old-fashioned word cracker, and introduced the use of symbols with the little boy in the yellow slicker. But it found the campaign needed publicity. Ayer developed a publicity department to supplement its advertising campaigns for National Biscuit and the Standard Oil Company. The agency found that "it was compelled to prepare publicity material as part of its regular work and also prepare news releases," according to its historian, Ralph W. Hower. The Ayer agency was the first to establish a publicity department in 1919.[2]

The Beginnings in Politics and Government

The modern political campaign, employing the talents of campaign consultants, publicists, poll takers, electronic mail experts, video producers, and writers, had its genesis in the last two decades of the 19th century. Employment of publicists by the federal government also got its start in those years. The political campaigns fashioned by Amos Kendall and Martin Van Buren in the 1820s and 1830s changed little until 1880. The Republican Party, which had dominated the nation's elections since the Civil War by waving "The Bloody Shirt," got a rude jolt in the Rutherford B. Hayes–Samuel Tilden squeaker of 1876. As a result, both parties laid out systematic efforts to win in 1880. Such plans were given impetus by improved printing presses, reduced cost of paper, and a growing awareness of the power of newspaper publicity.

The epochal 1896 campaign set the pattern for national presidential campaigns for the next 50 years, save for the innovation of radio in the 1928 campaign. This dramatic, hard-fought campaign between the conservative William McKinley and the populist William Jennings Bryan brought a marked increase in publicity and campaign management. The first step for both parties was to move the center of their campaign operations to Chicago, both sides realizing that the West would be a crucial battleground in this time of intense political and economic unrest. McKinley's front-porch campaign was implemented by large staffs in his hometown of Canton, Ohio as well as in New York and Chicago. It overlooked no detail and spared no expense. Bryan, on the other hand, possessing a rare oratorical talent and having little money, was forced to rely on cross-country tours that would take him to as many voters as money and time permitted. Thus was born "the campaign train," last used by President Harry Truman in 1948 so effectively.

GOP Campaign Chairman Charles G. Dawes hired Perry Heath, a Cincinnati reporter, to direct the Chicago-based Bureau of Publications and Printing early in July. The Bureau started sending out news releases, canned editorials, and editorial reprints in large numbers. More than 275 pamphlets and leaflets, a series of posters, sheets of cartoons, and other campaign materials were produced at a furious pace over the next four months. These were being sent to newspapers and GOP workers in carload lots. The scope of Heath's output can be seen in the total of $469,079 spent for printing—in a day when printing was inexpensive.

Another important innovation in the Chicago headquarters was the organization of specially staffed bureaus to mobilize special-interest groups on McKinley's behalf. Pamphlets were printed in German, French, Italian, Spanish, Swedish, Norwegian, Finnish, Dutch, and Hebrew in an effort to influence the tidal wave of immigrants who had come to the United States during the past two decades. Also created were a Colored Department, a Women's Department (even though women could not vote), and a German Department. Bicycling had become a popular pastime in the 1890s, so Dawes also set up a department for Wheelmen to woo bicyclists. No special-interest group was overlooked. Dawes also used a rudimentary public opinion poll to assess the electorate.

The Bryan campaign, by contrast, was pinched for money and not well organized. Campaigning by train was his only recourse. According to Bryan's figures, he traveled 18,009 miles in his whistle-stop campaign. This was no match for the intensive and expensive McKinley campaign, and McKinley won easily. The result of the GOP's massive publicity campaign can be seen in the fact that 2 million more voters voted Republican than had done so in any previous election.

This power of publicity did not go unnoticed in the executive branch of the federal government. Among the first of the bureaucrats to see the need for publicity was Major John

Wesley Powell, explorer of Colorado River and architect of the U.S. Geological Survey. Named to head the new agency by President James A. Garfield, Powell moved quickly to expand its size and concept. To build support in Congress and in the scientific community, Powell hired W. A. Croffut, an experienced journalist and editor who knew the ways of Washington. Two years later, in 1884, Powell set up a division of publications with John C. Filling as editor.

The Department of Agriculture led the way among the executive agencies in developing public relations as a tool of administration and education. In 1889, Jermiah Rusk of Wisconsin was named secretary of agriculture by incoming President Benjamin Harrison. Rusk, after observing that some 40,000 letters of inquiry reached the department during the first 10 months of 1889, decided that the public must get out agricultural information more promptly and in more readable form. Rusk ordered the development of farm bulletins to disseminate information in plain language. This work was first carried on in Rusk's office; in 1890 he established a Division of Records and Editing to increase the output of agricultural information. "Tama" Jim Wilson, appointed secretary by President McKinley in 1897, made many innovations in the department's expanding public information effort at the turn of the century.

Thus was born a large and effective public relations–education organization that would make American agriculture the envy of the world through the work of the nation's Land Grant colleges and county agents in the 20th century.

THE SEEDBED YEARS OF PUBLIC RELATIONS

The force setting the stage for the emergence of the pioneer public relations agencies in the early 1900s in the United States was the exploitive and bold development of industry, railroads, utilities, and banking in America's post-Civil War years. In 25 breathtaking years from 1875 to 1900, America doubled it population, moved its people into cities, developed mass production, and spanned the nation with rail and wire communications which, in turn, brought a news forum of national press associations and popular magazines. With what Vernon Parrington termed "A Huge Buccaneering Orgy" came large concentrations of wealth. By 1900, one-tenth of the population owned nine-tenths of the wealth. The rise of powerful monopolies, concentrations of wealth and power, and the roughshod tactics of The Robber Barons would inevitably bring a strong wave of protest and demands for reforms by government. Out of this melée of opposing political forces would come the infant vocation of public relations.

The muckraking journalists—David Graham Phillips, Lincoln Steffens, Upton Sinclair, Ida Tarbell, and others—were the catalysts that brought the popular revolt that manifested itself in political reforms championed by President Theodore Roosevelt—a master of publicity in his own right. Roosevelt forced the large corporations and railroads to adopt defensive publicity measures to defend themselves in the public forum. As Cutlip, Center, and Broom record: "Long accustomed to a veil of secrecy, business leaders felt the urge to speak out but did not know how. Their first instinct was to turn to their lawyers [long used to 'fix' legislatures] and their advertising men."[3] When this didn't prove effective, they came to see the need for newspapermen who had access to the nation's newspapers and muckraking magazines.

The first agency, the Publicity Bureau, was organized in mid-1900 in Boston by George V. S. Michaelis, Herbert Small, and Thomas Marvin, all former newspapermen. Its first client was Harvard University, which agreed to pay $200 a month for publicity services.

Two years later, President Eliot quit paying, saying the prestige of having Harvard as a client was "pay enough." The Bureau agreed and continued to serve Harvard, along with the competing Massachusetts Institute of Technology, the Fore River Shipyard, and the American Telephone Company.

As the waves of the Progressive Revolt began rising around Capitol Hill, it became apparent that conventional lobbying and legislative fixing would not prove adequate in a time when, in TR's words, there was "a condition of excitement and irritation in the public mind . . ." The first Washington newsman to sense this was William Wolf Smith, who opened a "publicity business" in the Capital in 1902. Later Congressional testimony asserted, "He used to solicit press-agent employment from anybody who had business before Congress . . . and the whole press-agent business sprung up from that." The third agency started was that of Parker & Lee. George F. Parker, veteran newsman and political publicist for President Grover Cleveland, had directed publicity for the Democrats' 1904 losing presidential campaign. He was assisted by a young New York journalist, Ivy Lee, who would go on to define this emerging vocation. After the campaign, they opened a publicity bureau at 20 Broad St., New York City. In 1906 Lee landed the Pennsylvania Railroad account, and two years later left the firm to work full-time for the Pennsy. The firm folded in 1913 when Parker took a full-time public relations job with the Protestant Episcopal Church.

Hamilton Wright was the first practitioner to see the need for American interests to explain themselves abroad, and an equal need for foreign nations to make their case before America's public opinion. His son and his grandson, both named Hamilton Wright, would follow in the elder Wright's footsteps in building a public relations agency that specialized in representation of foreign governments and institutions. The stakes involved in this representation are high and often crucial for the Israel seeking to maintain its support by the United States or a South Africa seeking aid and investment to shore up its new democratic government. Hamilton Wright was engaged by sugar interests to encourage support for and investment in the United States' newly acquired Philippine Islands. He also trumpeted the blessings of America's occupation of the Philippines with the encouragement of Major General Leonard Wood, who commanded the occupation forces. Wright's Philippine promotion culminated with publication of a book, *A Handbook of the Philippines*, which is still in circulation.

Wright formally opened his office in 1908 upon his return from the Philippines. His strong advocacy of the expansion of U.S. trade across the Pacific led to his being chosen editor-in-chief of the Pacific International Exposition, a position he held from 1915 to 1917. After completion of the exposition and a series of Latin American trips to promote travel in the Caribbean nations, Wright opened a publicity office in New York City later in 1917. The agency was closed by the third Hamilton Wright in the late 1960s. Wright was the first of a growing army of practitioners who represent foreign nations and interests in this country. As of August 1994, there were 735 primary registrants (usually lobbying firms) representing 1,350 foreign principals and 3,400 short-form registrants (individuals).

The fifth firm to be started in this century's first decade was opened by Pendleton Dudley in 1909 on Wall Street. Dudley, a reporter for *The Wall Street Journal*, did so at the urging of his friend, Ivy Lee. The Dudley name disappeared from the PR marque in November 1988 when his successor firm, DAY, purchased by Ogilvy and Mather in 1983, was renamed Ogilvy & Mather Public Relations.

The last known agency started in this period was that of Thomas Reed Shipp in 1914 in Washington, moving into the vacuum created when William Wolff Smith decided to quit and go to law school. Shipp had served his public relations apprenticeship under two masters, Theodore Roosevelt and Gifford Pinchot, who had made conservation a household word in the United States in the early 1900s. The TR–Pinchot campaign to promote conservation of our forests and create our national parks was one of the innovative public relations efforts of this period, later widely copied. Their campaign drew the first of many efforts by Congress to halt or hamstring public relations in the executive branch of the federal government. This emerging vocation was given a national boost in 1914 when John D. Rockefeller, Jr., appointed Ivy Lee as his personal advisor.

World War I Brings Large-Scale Propaganda

When America entered World War I in April 1917, public opinion was far from united. Soon after the U.S. declared war, President Woodrow Wilson, acting on the advice of Josephus Daniels, Raleigh publisher and Secretary of the Navy, created the Committee on Public Information to mobilize supportive public opinion at home and to make known our peace aims abroad. He appointed George Creel, a crusading journalist, to head the committee and, because of Creel's strong personality, the CPI became known as the Creel Committee. The formal committee seldom met. Creel's deputy, Carl Byoir, then 28, was the one who kept the store and the projects moving. In 1930, Byoir founded the public relations firm which was the nation's largest until the 1960s.

While early public relations emerged largely as a defensive measure on the part of Big Business, Creel converted it into a mighty offensive weapon, building a patriotic fervor for "the war to make the world safe for democracy" that ultimately led to public disillusionment and the corrosion of the word propaganda. The Liberty Loan drives were promoted by Guy Emerson, later a pioneer in bank public relations, and John Price Jones, who led the way in organized fund-raising after the war. During World War I, Ivy Lee directed public relations for the American Red Cross which raised $273,239,768 in two war drives, an unprecedented sum. When the war started, the Red Cross had a membership of 486,000; when it ended, membership had zoomed to nearly 19 million. Also coming to a successful close in this decade were the well-organized drives for women's suffrage and prohibition, both adopted in 1920. Little wonder that in the years after the war there emerged an overly optimistic belief in the power of propaganda, then the common term, or in today's terms, the power of public relations.

The Publicity Boom of the 1920s

The needs of World War I had brought about expansion of the nation's industrial capacity, new inventions and new ways of producing mass consumer products. By war's end there was an acute shortage of consumer goods and a need for experts in advertising, marketing, public relations, and fund-raising. Many war veterans who had been schooled in these skills in the war found a ready market for their talents in the 1920s.

Leo Rosten observed that there was a heightened consciousness of the importance of "a good press." The Creel Committee had been particularly influential in spreading the gospel of the magic of publicity.

Ivy Lee, who had pioneered the practice in the early 1900s, left his work with the American Red Cross and returned to New York to greatly enlarge his agency, now titled

Ivy Lee & Associates. In 1919, Lee hired Thomas J. Ross, just back from the Army. Ross would assume leadership of the firm after Lee died of a brain tumor in 1934. Edward L. Bernays, who died in March 1995, opened the nation's eighth agency in 1919. Bernays had been a Broadway press agent before the war, and in 1918 worked for the Creel Committee's New York office. Early in this period, Bernays began promoting the term "public relations counsel," and in 1923 wrote a landmark book, *Crystallizing Public Opinion*, which for the first time defined the function as a two-way street, asserting that it was the job of the counsel to interpret the public to the institution as well as interpret the institution to the public, a concept that took decades to be fully understood and accepted by management.

Other agencies quickly followed those of Lee and Bernays. John Price Jones, who had learned the art of fund-raising in World War I's Liberty Bond drives, opened a firm in November 1919 "to give counsel and service in organization and publicity to business houses, institutions of public, semi-public, and private character, and to meet the demand for highly specialized knowledge in these fields." Jones would make his mark in fund-raising more than in public relations. Harry Bruno and Richard Blythe, wartime fliers, formed a publicity agency in 1923. Their firm gained national prominence when they handled Charles A. Lindbergh's historic flight across the Atlantic in May 1927. Bruno, demonstrating one of the important tasks of public relations—gaining acceptance of change—did much to speed acceptance of commercial aviation. In 1926, William Baldwin III opened an agency "to serve corporate and civic clients." His firm folded in 1957 when he retired.

In 1927, John W. Hill, experienced in business writing, opened an office in Cleveland with Republic Steel and a bank as his first two clients. He later took in Don Knowlton as a partner in the Cleveland office. In 1933, Hill moved to New York to take a position with the American Iron and Steel Institute. A year or so later, he formed Hill & Knowlton, Inc., which in time would become one of the giant agencies. Don Knowlton had no role in the New York firm. Public relations growth from these uncertain early years was dramatically demonstrated when Hill & Knowlton, Inc., was sold in 1980 to J. Walter Thompson for $28 million. Both now are "profit centers" in the conglomerate WPP Group, based in London.

The Booming Twenties (1919–1929) brought a boom in public relations agencies and in corporate recognition. Terms like "public relations counsel," "specialized knowledge," and "the power of public opinion" became common parlance. The advertising field grew even faster than public relations.

But the Twenties ended on a sour note for this new vocation when Congress investigated the propaganda of Samuel Insull's creation, The National Electric Light Associa-

The first major corporate recognition of this new vocation came when Walter S. Gifford, president of American Telephone & Telegraph, hired his Harvard classmate Arthur W. Page in 1927 as vice president of public relations. In accepting the new position, Page made it clear that he would come in at the policy-making level, not as a publicist. Over the next 20 years Page built probably the most sophisticated corporate public relations program this nation has seen. He was an innovator; for example, he was the first in public relations to use opinion research as a guide in communicating with the public. Today the Arthur W. Page Society keeps Page's credo alive: "All business in a democratic country begins with public permission and exists by public approval."

tion. The Federal Trade Commission probers found that NELA, since 1922, had been carrying on a campaign of misinformation and bribery of educators. As Bernays noted: "The new profession received a bad name from which it did not free itself for years."

There were also significant advances in public relations in the 1920s. The National Publicity Council for Welfare Services was organized in 1922 by Evart G. Routzahn and Mary Swain Routzahn of the Russell Sage Foundation. In 1918, the National Lutheran Council started an extensive church publicity program. Later that same year, the Knights of Columbus, a Catholic organization, set up a publicity bureau. The first of many professional associations that would, in time, bring increased competence to the craft began to grow in numbers in this period. The Financial Advertisers Association, a bank group started in 1915, and the American College Publicity Association, organized in 1917, came alive in the 1920s. The New York-based National Association of Publicity Directors and the American Public Relations Council, started on the West Coast by pioneer Rex F. Harlow, were started in the late 1930s and early 1940s and formed the foundation stones for the 1947 emergence of the Public Relations Society of America.

Franklin Roosevelt and World War II

The Great Depression, which set in after the historic Stock Market Crash of 1929, and World War II, would bring substantial expansion of the practice and its concepts. President Franklin D. Roosevelt, a consummate practitioner who had been tutored in public relations by Louis McHenry Howe since 1912, would lead the way. He was elected president four times against the strong opposition of the majority of American newspapers by using his strong leadership and taking his message to the people on the nation's front pages and on radio. FDR's success in winning public support spurred the efforts of the conservative forces, particularly Big Business, to develop programs to counter his appeals. To bring the United States out of the Depression, President Roosevelt initiated a number of action agencies—the Agricultural Adjustment Administration, the Civilian Conservation Corps, and the Works Project Administration—that required extensive publicity in order to gain cooperation and acceptance. Thus, the public information function in the federal government was greatly enlarged in FDR's administration.

The years 1932–45 brought a tool that is today sine qua non in the practice of effective public relations—the scientific public opinion poll. The Roper and Gallup polls, born in the mid-1930s, gained great respect in predicting the outcome of the 1936 presidential election. This same election brought the demise of the unscientific *Liberty Digest* straw poll based on persons with telephones, a rare commodity in the Depression. In 1934, the first minority firm opened in Philadelphia when Joseph Varney Baker quit his job as city editor of the *Philadelphia Tribune* to provide counsel to the Pennsylvania Railroad.

This era also brought Whitaker & Baxter, the forerunner of today's army of campaign specialists who dominate the American political process. In 1933, Clem Whitaker and Leone Baxter, who later became his wife, opened an office in San Francisco to manage political campaigns. California, with its weak political party structure and its heavy reliance on initiatives and referendums to legislate, provided the propitious climate for this new specialty. From 1935 through 1958, the firm managed 80 political campaigns and won all but six. Today, political public relations is a major segment of the practice.

Just as World War I gave great impetus to the growth of public relations by demonstrating its efficacy and schooling hundreds in its techniques, so did World War II, but on a much larger scale. It is estimated that some 100,000 persons served in information posts—information was then the government euphemism for public relations. (Today public affairs is used generally in government.) In June 1943, President Roosevelt created, by executive order, the Office of War Information and appointed newsman Elmer Davis its director. The OWI set the pace for a great expansion of the practice in the armed forces, in industry, and in allied fields. OWI developed many new techniques of communication and trained many more practitioners than did the Creel Committee. Public relations in government and in the armed forces comprise large segments of the practice. The United States Information Agency, created in the post-war Cold War, is the successor to the OWI and employs some 10,000 persons to tell America's story around the world. The war also brought advertising to the fore as a major tool of public relations. The War Advertising Council, organized in 1942, combined the efforts of industry and government to get urgent war messages, such as the need for rationing, to the public. Today, advertising is heavily used as a major public relations tool.

The Post-War Boom

The greatest expansion of domestic public relations practice the field has known came between 1945 and 1980. Expanding world trade and political conflict spread the vocation around the world. Advances in communication and jet travel brought the closest contacts in the history of civilization. The same ecological forces that were operating in the United States to compel public relations' growth were now operating on a world scale. The advent of television as a powerful national and international medium—the most powerful communications medium man has known—brought vast new public relations opportunities and problems to institutions and their executives. The impact of television, now magnified by satellite communication, on the lives of all peoples is beyond calculation, beyond accurate measurement. One example: In the United States, it has demonstrably changed the nation's political process by weakening the party system and by requiring that candidates raise millions of dollars from special interests to be spent on meaningless TV sound bites.

These and like developments of the postwar decades of the late 1940s, 1950s, and 1960s brought rapid expansion, increased stability, and increased management acceptance. This era saw the number of practitioners pass the 100,000 mark. Today it is estimated that more than 150,000 practitioners serve business, education, government, health, and other fields. This period also saw the foundations for professionalism put in place by strong professional associations. In this period, the Public Relations Society of America initiated its accreditation program. These advances were undergirded by an increased number of strong educational programs in the nation's colleges and universities. Both these developments were spurred by more books and journals devoted to the practice. Today, public relations has an accepted body of knowledge and the most comprehensive bibliography of any field of mass communication to guide its growing body of researchers. The 1945–65 period was given impetus by these developments:[4]

1. Steady growth in the number of programs in industries, institutions, social agencies, government bureaus, and trade associations. Already-established programs tended to mature and to move beyond publicity.
2. Stabilization in the number of independent counseling firms, especially in the communication hubs of New York, Washington, Chicago, and Los Angeles.

3. A tremendous spurt in the number of books, articles, and journals devoted to the practice and its philosophy, problems, and techniques. The literature is voluminous, although somewhat repetitive.

4. Organization of new associations for practitioners and redirection or consolidation of those already established. Many of these are now mature.

5. Growth in the number of college courses and students and in the breadth and depth of the courses. Increased support for collegiate preparation from practitioners and great acceptance of young graduates in the job market.

6. Internationalization of the practice and its standards, reflected in the formation of the International Public Relations Association in 1955.

THE GLOBALIZATION OF PUBLIC RELATIONS

With the advent of the Information Age and its globe-girdling communications, and with world strife creating a more volatile public opinion environment, public relations practice grew more complex as it spread around the world. John Naisbett, keen student of society's trends, sets the beginnings of today's information society in 1956 and 1957. In 1956, the Russian Sputnik brought the world satellite communication. In 1957, the number of white-collar, high-technology jobs outnumbered industrial workers for the first time in U.S. history. From the mid-1960s, a time of turmoil in the United States and the Cold War, the public relations function increased markedly in importance and difficulty for executive officers. CEOs and their staffs faced a world made small and interdependent by the computer and the satellite. International trade, the turbulence of politics at home and abroad, and the resultant increased importance of public affairs forced management to take the public relations counselor more seriously. Although this new age of global public relations had its roots in earlier decades, as Naisbett observed, it really took off in the mid-1960s. Naisbett observed that, by the 1980s, the output of information was accelerating by some 40 percent annually. Surely computer technology is to this Age what the assembly line production was to the Industrial Age at the dawn of this century. Advances in computer technology are moving at almost an exponential rate as we near the next millennium.

Truly, this time of the Information Highway, Internets, satellites, faxes, and supersonic jet travel is the Information Age. We face a world glutted with a torrent of information in media and quantities far beyond the citizen's ability to consume or comprehend. Just one example: In 1994, the U.S. Postal Service delivered 171 billion pieces of mail, 580 million pieces every business day. To this add daily and weekly newspapers, network television, and cable television, which now reaches 80 percent of American homes with hundreds of channels. In 1993, the sale of CDs and cassettes totaled $8.9 billion dollars, motion pictures had their best year ever, and Americans spent $15.5 billion dollars on books. This glut of communication hammering our senses is truly awesome. And now comes the Information Superhighway!

How these technological advances have changed the ways of doing business abroad was succinctly stated by Frank Popoff, then president of Dow Chemical Company, to the 1989 graduating class of Alma College:

> Twenty years ago people talked in terms of air travel shrinking space and time, making it possible to move among nations and continents in hours instead of days. Today, with the advent of telecommunications, business people in Japan, Europe, and Midland, Michigan, can meet simultaneously without leaving their offices.

. . . Once people talked about industrialization, about nations developing the machinery and the skills to manufacture and distribute products on a large scale at affordable cost. Now we talk about globalization, about the world as a global community where nations and people can share one economy, one environment, one technology, and, at least in commerce, one language.

International public relations had its substantial beginnings in the wake of World War II. Today, the global market offers a challenging frontier for young persons with ability and a sense of adventure. As indicated at the outset of this chapter, the accelerating forces of interdependence, transportation, and communication contribute to the intense battles for political support and market share that face organizations at home and abroad. International public relations emerged in the 1950s, primarily as a marketing tool in Europe and Latin America. Most firms emphasized product publicity in these early years; the large extractive companies, understandably, were more concerned with public relations in the broad sense, born of fear of expropriation.

These substantial beginnings of international practice are reflected in the birth of the International Public Relations Association (IPRA), which brought about a developing esprit and exchanges of information among the world's practitioners. This association had its genesis in 1949 when a group of Netherlands industrialists invited some 20 public relations men from Western Europe and the United States to Holland to discuss informally their common interests. Out of this group's spirited shop talk came a provisional committee to study the feasibility of an international association. The committee was organized in 1950 with Odd Medbo of Scandinavian Airlines (SAS) as chairman and Tim Traverse-Healy, a London counselor, as secretary. The organizing group found wide support, but getting international agreement took time. IPRA was finally organized at a meeting in London in 1955, with Sir Tom Fife Clark, able director of Britain's Central Office of Information, as president. This is an association of individual members, not a superstructure over the national public relations associations that now circle the globe. IPRA's biennial conferences and its publications have contributed substantially to the advancement of the practice worldwide.

A Major Factor: Governments

Governments, too, employ thousands of practitioners to win world support for their foreign policy goals, to promote tourism, and to establish a nation's identity in the world community. Much of today's world newsflow is provided by governments and their public relations departments. As I wrote in *The Unseen Power: Public Relations*:

> The need for foreign governments to explain themselves and to promote trade, tourism, and political support in the United States increased after the turn of the century when America shed its isolation and became a world power in the wake of the Spanish-American War. These needs have grown over the course of the 20th century as nations grew more economically and politically interdependent in today's fiercely competitive world economy. Today, with the United States as the world's sole Super Power, caught in a highly competitive global economy and one torn by ethnic and religious wars, the demands for U.S. political and economic support are many and intense. This has led to a boom in public relations representing foreign governments, and enterprises pushing their claims in the halls of Congress and in the public opinion arena.[5]

For example, a powerful Iraq invades its smaller neighbor Kuwait to gain control of its rich oil supply. Kuwait's monarchs retain a U.S. public relations agency, Hill and Knowlton, Inc., to build public support in the United States for U.S. intervention to rescue Kuwait's kingdom and its oil.

In 1994, there were 4,135 persons or firms registered under the Foreign Agents Act with the Department of Justice. This Act had its origins in 1938 in the wake of Congressional hearings on Ivy Lee's serving I.G. Farben and, through it, the Nazi government, and Carl Byoir & Associates' representation of the German Railroads Tourist Bureau. On March 20, 1934, a resolution was passed by the House of Representative to provide appointment of a special committee to investigate the extent of Nazi propaganda in the United States. Rep. John McCormack of Massachusetts, later to be Speaker, was appointed chairman of this committee. The Ivy Lee & T.J. Ross and the Carl Byoir firms were caught in the crossfire of the committee's concern for "dangerous propaganda of foreign origin." This led, ultimately, to passage of the Foreign Agents Registration Act of 1938. Senator J. William Fulbright revisited this issue with a series of Senate hearings in 1963. Fulbright argued that the 1938 law was being skirted. The Hamilton Wright Organization, Selvage & Lee (now Manning, Selvage & Lee), Julius Klein, and Harry Klemfuss were brought before this Senate committee. The Wright agency took most of the beating, which became one of the factors that led to its closing in the late 1960s. Senators Fulbright and Bourke Hickenlooper introduced and got passed a bill strengthening the Act and moving its enforcement from the Department of State to the Department of Justice.

Public relations around our fast-shrinking world offers great opportunities for the expansion of public relations agencies here and abroad and for young persons entering this field in an exciting time. Public relations is being adapted to the needs of business firms, non-profit institutions, and nations of the world at breathtaking rate. In ever-growing numbers, as Dow's President Popoff indicated, U.S. companies are operating abroad through subsidiaries, branches, distributorship, and in partnership with local and multinational corporations. Firms doing business across national boundaries and in different cultures find public relations more imperative than at home. Corporations abroad have to buck the onus of absentee ownership, avert the threat of expropriation, combat the ethnic and religious hatreds of centuries, and deal sensitively with the cultures of other peoples.

In meeting these problems, there is increasing reliance on international public relations agencies and PR firms in foreign markets. Take just one example of doing business in today's interdependent, shrunken world: The far-flung operation of International Telephone and Telegraph Corporation, a diversified, worldwide industrial firm with 200 affiliates in 67 countries and 236,000 employees. It must transact its business in 12 languages and in widely varying cultures. I.T.T. employs more than 100 professionals to meet these formidable tasks. Growth of international trade had caused a number of U.S. public relations agencies to develop worldwide services.

U.S. Agencies Expand Overseas

Showing the courage and vision that led to his building Hill & Knowlton, Inc., into what for a time was the largest U.S. public relations firm, John Hill was first to see the burgeoning opportunities for international public relations. In September 1956, he established Hill & Knowlton International. He announced that the firm would have headquarters in The Hague, Netherlands, and offices in Dusseldorf, Germany, and would include the facilities of experienced nationals in Great Britain, France, Belgium, Holland, Sweden, Australia, New Zeland, Canada, Mexico, and Latin America. Hill chose an ally from his battles for Little Steel, J. Carlisle McDonald, as director of the new firm and its senior consultant in Europe, with offices in Paris. This was a bold, pioneering move on Hill's part, one that lost money its first several years, but eventually became profitable.[6]

Other agencies, in time, followed suit: Ruder & Finn, which in the 1960s represented Iran; Edelman International; Harry Bruno & Associates; and Burson-Marsteller, Inc. These agencies, which began developing overseas branches in the 1960s, saw, in Sylvan M. Barnet, Jr.'s, view, a shift in emphasis from marketing to nonmarketing problems in the world economy. Barnet, long active in international practice, summarized:

1. A new emphasis on nonmarketing problems.
2. Marked impact of the worldwide consumerism movement.
3. Development of new government-industry relationships.
4. Development of financial public relations as it is known in the United States.
5. Centralization in multinational public relations practice.
6. Movement to upgrade the public relations function within the corporate structure.

The globalization of public relations has been accompanied by the merger of advertising and public relations agencies on a global scale. WPP Group, P.L.C., the London-based advertising-public relations holding company, owns Hill & Knowlton, Inc., J. Walter Thompson, and Ogilvy & Mather—the latter two WPP's biggest advertising agencies. After years when its survival seemed threatened by bloated debt, WPP had its best year in 1994. Saatchi & Saatchi, P.L.C., also London-based, is another of the world's largest advertising and marketing conglomerates. It, too, was having a good year in 1994 after some lean ones.

Burson-Marsteller, Inc., is owned by Young and Rubicam, a major advertising agency. This merger of public relations and advertising agencies on a mega basis is a hotly debated issue among professionals.

An Example: Burson-Marsteller, Inc.

To demonstrate how this international practice has grown as we near the end of this century, let's take the operations of Burson-Marsteller, Inc., around the world as illustrative.

Approximately half of Burson-Marsteller's $200 million annual fee income is realized from operations outside the United States, and overseas growth is at a greater rate than its domestic business. Burson-Marsteller was one of the first public relations firms to make a major commitment overseas. While B-M established its first European office in 1961, its first office outside the U.S. was opened in Toronto in 1959. B-M entered the Asian market with offices in Hong Kong and Singapore in 1973, the Latin American market in 1978, and the Australian market in 1980.

Today, Burson-Marsteller has 60 offices in 32 countries. It is the largest public relations firm operating in both Europe and Asia. It has three offices in China, the first dating back to 1986, and it is the largest firm operating in the former Eastern Block countries. Abroad, Burson-Marsteller is managed and staffed by local nationals. Today, almost all B-M non-U.S. offices are managed by non-U.S. nationals, some who began their public relations careers with Burson-Marsteller as many as 25 years ago.

Thus, international public relations, which began in the 16th and 17th centuries as colonial hype to lure settlers to the new land of America, at the end of this 20th century has reached global dimensions and billions of dollars in agency business. Similarly, since the first U.S. agency, the Publicity Bureau founded in 1900, U.S. public relations has grown in like dimensions. It is now a vocation employing some 150,000 practitioner in agencies, corporations, government, colleges and universities, health services, and nonprofit enterprises. As a new century dawns, the need for public relations in successful enterprises becomes clearer; and as the need grows so do its opportunities.

E N D N O T E S

1. This account of Colonial hype is taken from my book, *Public Relations History, 17th to 20th Century* (Hillside, NJ: Lawrence Erlbaum Associates, Inc., 1995).

2. For a history of the Ayer agency, see Ralph M. Hower, *The History of an Advertising Agency* (Cambridge, MA: Harvard University Press, 1939).

3. Cutlip, Scott M., Allen H. Center, and Glen M. Broom, *Effective Public Relations,* 7th ed. (Englewood Cliffs, NJ: Prentice Hall, 1994).

4. Ibid.

5. Cutlip, Scott M., *The Unseen Power: Public Relations, a History* (Hillside, NJ: Lawrence Erlbaum Associates, Inc., 1994).

6. The story of Hill's pioneering venture is told in the John W. Hill papers, Mass Communications History Center, State Historical Society of Wisconsin, Madison.

## CHAPTER 3

The Role of Research in Public Relations Strategy and Planning

Anders Gronstedt
Assistant Professor
University of Colorado,
and Senior Advisor to
Kreab/Strategy XXI Group

The public relations profession is under intense pressure to justify its existence and demonstrate accountability. Nobody questions the need to have a sales, accounting, or manufacturing department. The senior vice president of sales can show up for top management meetings with sales statistics. The VP of manufacturing can bring productivity numbers, defect rates, and cycle time reduction data. The chief financial officer can dazzle senior management with budget forecasts and cash flow analyses. But most senior public relations/corporate communications directors do not have the hard data to demonstrate their value to the corporation. This is an important reason why only one of four public relations/corporate communications managers in the United States is a member of the senior management team, helping make the decisions that have a real impact on the organization.[1]

Demonstrating accountability through research is not only necessary to get behind the mahogany doors, but to avoid being out placed. Public relations has been a prime target for reduction and elimination during the cost-cutting and downsizing mandates of the 1980s and 1990s. To reaffirm the central, strategic role of public relations/corporate communications, we need to be vigorous and persistent in systematically capturing and analyzing information from key stakeholders and in keeping the organization informed and focused on the stakeholders' needs. We need to be the organizational radar, taking soundings and providing early warnings to help the senior management team steer clear of public relations problems and charting the course to building a desired corporate reputation.

The focus of this chapter is on developing public relations strategy and objectives based on insights from research, and on using research to evaluate progress towards predetermined objectives. In survey after survey, public relations professionals rank measurement and accountability as the number one priority of the profession.[2] But few public relations managers "walk the walk" and "talk the talk." Most public relations research decisions are still based on gut feelings, speculation, and hearsay. More that 50 percent of recently surveyed public relations managers rarely or never budget for research.[3] Experts in the industry recommend that at least 10 percent of the public relations budget should be allocated to research.

Lack of funding is the most frequently mentioned reason for not doing public relations research.[4] The more appropriate question is how anyone can afford *not* to do research. There are instances in which public relations departments have tripled the outcomes of their efforts as a result of research-based planning and implementation.

What little research most PR departments do is tactically rather than strategically oriented, and designed to legitimize decisions that have already been made rather than to get new insights. In the words of the advertising luminary David Ogilvy, research is used like the drunkard uses the lamppost, for support rather than illumination. Because public relations is largely intangible, there is a strong tendency to focus the research on what is most tangible and easy to count, like the number of print publication clips about the company. Two-thirds of all public relations managers in one survey listed "count clips and broadcast placements" as the research approach of "first importance."[5] Such research is not exactly the fabric that strategy-building insights are built on. It is like a VP of sales citing "initiated sales calls" as the number-one measure of success. Clip counting was a more important measure of success in the past when the number of media outlets was small and people still trusted media. Besides, there were few other research methods available in the 1950s and 1960s. Today, we have more sophisticated methods at our disposal.

Public relations professionals frequently bemoan that senior managers "don't understand public relations," when, in fact, the real problem is that many public relations professionals do not understand management. Our profession needs to develop tools and measures of accountability like our peers in other departments. When senior management asks, "what have you done for me lately," we need to have the hard data to support our answers.

Effective public relations should be practiced in four iterative steps, as illustrated in Figure 3–1: (1) planning and goal setting, (2) implementation and monitoring, (3) evaluation, and (4) acting on the evaluation to make improvements. This approach is analogous to the continual improvement cycle of "plan-do-check-act" prescribed by W. Edwards Deming and other total quality management proponents. We will briefly describe these steps and then give examples of how they are applied to research different stakeholders.

PLANNING

Every carpenter knows that you save time, aggravation, and money by measuring twice and cutting once. The same holds true for public relations and overall business planning. Research helps to frame issues, identify key stakeholders, and set the objectives that the public relations program can be measured against.

Public relations research should not only support planning of the public relations programs, but also the planning of the overall business strategy. Research can be used to redefine the organization's strategic direction in response to changing conditions in the environment. The researcher's involvement in strategic management processes ensures that public relations plans and objectives are aligned with overall business plans and objectives. In fact, one study indicated that 83 percent of public relations/corporate communications managers make no separation between corporate goals and public relations goals.[6]

F I G U R E 3–1

The Role of Research in the Four Interative Steps of Effective Public
Relations Practice

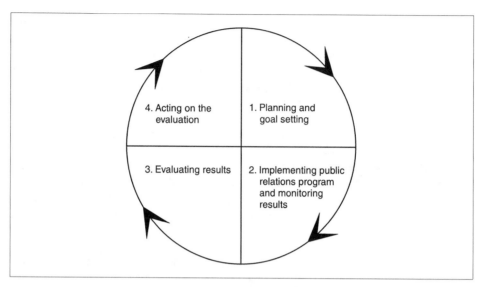

To support the strategic management and strategic public relations planning processes,
public relations professionals need to research the following issues:

What are our most significant strengths, weaknesses, opportunities, and threats?
The first step in any planning is an environmental scan, in which the researcher is charting
what is happening in the environment. One useful format is the "strengths, weaknesses,
opportunities, and threats (SWOT) analysis," which analyzes the company's *strengths* and
weaknesses in meeting the *opportunities* and *threats* in the external environment. The
opportunities and threats have to be prioritized, and strategies developed to leverage the
company's strengths and address its weaknesses.

The environmental scan needs to be ongoing. By monitoring issues, opinions, and
corporate reputation over time, the researcher uncovers "dynamic complexity,"[7] that is, recurring processes of change that the organization can act upon. In contrast, most research in the field
today consists of the occasional "snapshot" survey with hundreds of variables that create
"detailed complexity" without discerning any patterns. The research process needs to anticipate
and prepare for events that are likely to affect the organization in the future, such as evolving
debates over political issues or changes in customer preferences. Organizations that enter a
communication process at an early stage are more likely to affirmatively manage issues.

One approach to make the environmental scan ongoing is to set up an "issues
anticipation team" composed of employees from different parts of the organization who
meet on a regular basis to discuss emerging issues that will affect the organization.[8]

Who are our most important stakeholders? When the SWOT analysis is completed, it is important to identify the key stakeholders and rank their relative importance
to the organization. The stakeholders can first be ranked generically—customers, employees, investors, etc. The next step is to identify the specific groups and individuals that have
a stake in the organization's purpose. If at all possible, the stakeholders should be seg-

mented based on behavior. Examples of behavior segmentation among customers are nonusers, light users, and heavy users. News reporters can be divided into categories based on whether they have written negative stories about your organization, neutral stories, positive ones, or no stories.

The development of relational database technology makes behavior segmentation manageable. Companies in the airline, hotel, and mail order industries have massive amounts of individual consumer data, for instance. The relational database plays an important strategic role in public relations as well. The public relations department at Wal-Mart, for instance, uses a database to track individual journalists. To build a stakeholder database, start with internal sources: the rolodex, the Christmas card mailing list, the billing list from the accounting department, etc. Next, consider renting outside lists to enhance your database. The process of incorporating different databases with each other and deleting duplicates in called "merge/purge."

The database can identify the "critical few," the small number of stakeholders that cause most problems or accomplishments. For instance, 80 percent of sales usually come from 20 percent of the customers. This phenomenon is called the "Pareto effect," after the Italian economist Wilfredo Pareto who concluded that 80 percent of wealth was owned by 20 percent of the people. The Pareto effect is true for any stakeholder group. Most organizations will find, for instance, that 20 percent of all journalists account for 80 percent of the media coverage of the company, and 20 percent of all shareholders own 80 percent of the company. The critical few is, in most cases, the most cost-effective group to target with communications.

If behavioral data is not accessible, the segmentation can be based on demographic criteria such as sex, age, marriage status, race, education, income, or geographic region. Alternatively, segmentation can be based on psychographic criteria, such as opinion or lifestyle.

The researchers responsibility goes beyond just defining a target audience by sterile behavioral or demographic data (which will probably tell you that the average audience member has one testicle and 2.2 children). They need to bring the target audience member "to life" by describing that person in qualitative terms. Celestial Seasonings, the herbal tea manufacturer, has even given its target customer a name, Tracy Jones. Tracy is a 35-year-old professional woman who enjoys relaxing in the evening with a soothing cup of herbal tea. During any meeting, employees will ask, "What would Tracy Jones say?" or "Would Tracy like that?"

What are the most important needs of each of the stakeholder groups that our organization can address? For each prioritized stakeholder segment, the research must identify its most important needs. The critical questions to ask to identify these needs are:

Customers: Why should I buy from company X?

Employees: Why should I work for company X?

Investment community: Why is company X a good long-term investment for me?

Regulators: How will changes in regulatory policies and practices which favor company X also provide benefit to customers or the general public?

Local communities and public at large: What makes company X an asset to my community and my country?

When the critical needs are identified, the public relations function needs to collaborate with the departments responsible for respective stakeholders to address these. Employee needs are addressed in collaboration with the human resource department, customer needs with marketing, shareholder needs with the finance department. Thus, public relations research is not only supporting changed behavior by the stakeholder, but also changed behavior by the organization.

What are the behavioral and communication objectives? Based on the stakeholder needs analysis, behavioral objectives should be developed for each targeted stakeholder group. The behavior objective for a consumer segment of "brand switchers" can be to turn them into "loyal users," for employees it can be to recommend the company to a friend as a place to work, and for investors it can be to get the largest current shareholders to buy more shares in the company. When behavioral objectives for each stakeholder group are determined, communication objectives can be developed to support them.

What is the "personal media network" of a typical target audience member? The final step of the planning process is to develop a media plan for each target group. Research plays an important role in identifying the "personal media network" of a target audience member. By mapping a typical day in the life of such a person, the researcher can identify *when*—during the year, month, week, and day—and where the target audience member would be most receptive to your message. The advertising agency DDB Needham calls these windows of opportunities media "apertures" (which is the opening in an optical instrument that limits the amount of light passing through). The agency has, for instance, found that people are more susceptible to home mortgage offers on Monday mornings, and the best media aperture to advertise diapers is right after the birth of a new baby. Sophisticated companies ask its most important stakeholders when and how they want to receive information, to tailor the communication to each individual's need. New owners of a Lexus car, for instance, are asked how they want information from Lexus, if they like to get a call or a letter, if they want to be contacted at home or at work, etc. The next issue is what combination of media vehicles can be used to communicate with the target audience at the times and places when it is ready to hear it. This "zero-based media approach," where the media are selected from the target stakeholder's point of view, is dramatically different from traditional approaches where the planning team picks the tried-and-true media vehicles (like events and press releases) that have worked well in the past and that they are most comfortable with.

"Inside-Out" versus "Outside-In" Planning

The approach just described is an "outside-in" approach to strategic public relations planning, which can be contrasted with the traditional "inside-out" planning model.[9]

The "inside-out" approach starts with the organization's objectives, which determine cognitive objectives, which determine attitude objectives, which determine action objectives. This model builds on an almost 100-year-old communication model of cognitive, affective, and behavioral response from the target audience, or "think-feel-do."[10] That is, communication will put information in the consumers' minds, change their attitudes, and get them to act. There are endless variations of this learning hierarchy—"awareness-interest-desire-action" (AIDA), is one of the most commonly used. Every self-respecting research firm and public relations agency has its own in-house version of the model. There is only one little problem with this theory: the last 50 years of research indicate that the model is wrong![11]

The "think-feel-do" model is built on the assumption that communication is like injecting a hypodermic needle into someone; people will uncritically absorb messages, later develop a feel for them, and eventually act upon them. In reality, the different steps of the hierarchy might even be in conflict. United Color of Benetton's advertising, for instance, gets attention for reasons that make many consumers develop a negative attitude toward the brand; a different message focusing on an important product difference might be persuasive but fail to get the target audience attention in today's cluttered media environment.[12] Another problem with the approach is that it treats the action as the culmination of the communication process, instead of treating it as the beginning of an ongoing relationship. The model does not address the issue of how communication can support a relationship with customers, employees, shareholders, and other stakeholders, only how to attract new ones.

The traditional "inside-out" approach to public relations research is the product of a time when more than 90 percent of the U.S. population watched the three television networks and the rest of the world watched government-controlled TV stations. In today's world, people are actively seeking information they believe to be relevant. They are active, interactive, and equal participants of an ongoing communication process, rather than passive sponges. The role of the communicator is increasingly to make information available to stakeholders in a user-friendly way, rather than shoving it down their throats, and to support an ongoing relationship rather than transferring information. The purpose of communications is not necessarily to influence stakeholders, but to add value to them.

Rather than focus the research on *what communication does to the stakeholder*, we need to focus on *what the stakeholder does with the communicated messages*. This is the focus of the "outside-in" approach to research and planning. The "outside-in" approach begins with the key stakeholders' needs, then determines behavior objectives of the organization and the stakeholders. Research is essential in this process to determine what stakeholders value, monitor how well their needs are being met, and measure how their behaviors are changing.

Designing the Research Study

A number of sources should be drawn upon to answer the research questions. Every organization has internal sources of information such as records of customer service calls, market research, and product performance data that need to be tapped. Most importantly, it has internal databases that can be used.

In addition, there are a number of external sources of information that can be tapped at low cost and with little effort. Trade and popular press and academic journals are readily available through computer databases (like Lexus/Nexus in the United States). The World Wide Web is becoming a more accessible information source with search programs like Alta Vista. There are a number of syndicated research studies which companies can subscribe to. Examples of such studies in the U.S. are Simmons, MRI, and Nielsen for consumer information and media usage data, and the Yankelovich Monitor and Roper Report for public opinion data. In addition, external databases can be purchased and overlaid onto the company's own database.

The analysis of existing information inside and outside the organization will determine what new research information is needed. The type of information that is needed, as well as the budget and time frame, determine the design of the research study. The most effective research design in most situations is a combination of qualitative and quantitative methods.

Qualitative methods like focus group interviews, in-depth interviews, and observation are valuable to help determine the target audience, frame the issues, and develop key

BOX 3–1

QUALITATIVE RESEARCH METHODS

FOCUS GROUP

A focus group is a group of 8 to 12 people in a roundtable discussion, lead by a moderator (two moderators are preferred if resources allow). The discussion is typically videotaped and monitored by the client through a one-way mirror. The participants are screened to create homogenous groups. For instance, one focus group might consist of people 45 and older, another of people 30 to 44, and another of people under 30. The moderator(s) begin by asking easy and general questions about the topic, and get more and more specific as the discussion progresses. An important task for the moderator(s) is to avoid permitting a few individuals to dominate the discussion. The focus group is typically used in the early developmental stages of the planning process, but can also be used to test and hone in on messages and creative message executions.

ETHNOGRAPHY (OBSERVATION)

Ethnography, developed initially by anthropologists, is based on extensive field observations. The researchers leave their offices and immerse themselves in the lives of the people being studied. By living and breathing the lives of consumers, employees, or whoever form the focus of the study, the researcher will experience the problem from their perspective. The researcher can either observe people or act in the role of the people under study. "Mystery shopper" is a common application of ethnography in marketing research, where researchers will act as customers and report their experiences.

IN-DEPTH INTERVIEW

Personal in-depth interviews offer many of the advantages of a focus group without the negative side-effect of someone dominating the discussion. This format allows the researcher to use a questioning technique called "laddering," in which the interviewer asks "why" several times to discover underlying feelings and motives. Another situation that calls for personal in-depth interviews is when the subjects are opinion leaders and experts who are difficult to recruit to a focus group. In a crisis situation, when the researcher only has a few hours to get information, it can be valuable to do a "soft sounding," that is, in-depth interviews with a handful of opinion leaders over the phone.

messages. Box 3–1 briefly describes these methods. The aim of such research is to get insights into the hearts and minds of key stakeholders in order to formulate the public relations strategy.

A strength of the qualitative interview is that the interviewer can probe the underpinnings of the interviewees' standpoints. That is important because most people are *unable* to describe or are *unaware* of their underlying feelings and motives. There are various creative questions that can be used in an in-depth interview or focus group to make it easier for people to talk about their feelings, like "If company X were an animal, what animal would it be?" or "If it were a country . . ." When Apple did focus group studies in preparation for the launch of its Macintosh, it found that people associated IBM with Big Brother, which sparked the idea of the famous 1984 commercial in which IBM was portrayed as author George Orwell's "Big Brother." Such questions require a lot of creativity to interpret.

BOX 3-2

QUANTITATIVE RESEARCH METHODS

TELEPHONE SURVEY

The telephone survey is by far the most commonly used research method in public relations. It is a quick, inexpensive, and convenient way to reach people. With today's computer technology, the results can be tabulated immediately after the interviews are completed. The drawbacks are that the survey needs to be relatively short and the interviewer cannot show visuals.

OMNIBUS STUDY

A less expensive approach to telephone surveying is to piggyback some questions on a research company's omnibus poll.

MAIL SURVEY

So-called "self-administered" mail surveys are inexpensive, but usually take a lot of time and the response rate is low. The low response rate makes the findings less reliable because the people who responded might not be representative of the population. Another drawback is that people give more superficial answers than in personal interviews and telephone interviews.

FAX AND E-MAIL SURVEY

In recent years, fax and E-mail have emerged as alternative ways to distribute a survey. Fax surveys have a higher response rate than mail, but there are few comprehensive fax number databases available and the respondents cannot answer anonymously. E-mail is less expensive than mail, more environmentally correct because it does not use paper, the turn around time is short, and the results can be entered directly into a data bank for analysis. But we are probably still a few years away from using it in large scale because most people still do not have access to it and there are few adequate databases of E-mail addresses.

MALL-INTERCEPT STUDY

When the population is hard to reach by phone or mail or the budget is limited, people can be intercepted in a convenient public area. Employees can be surveyed in the lunchroom, doctors can be surveyed at a trade show, and children can be surveyed at a shopping center.[13] Caution should be used in analyzing results of such surveys because the sample is not random. Everyone in the population does not have the same probability of being selected. Some employees don't go to the lunchroom and some parents never take their children to the mall.

After insights have been developed, it is important to use quantitative survey research to verify the insights and get baseline data to measure progress. By repeating the survey after a public relations program, a researcher can measure the effect. The most commonly used quantitative, verification-oriented methods—telephone, mail, and mall-intercept surveys—are described in Box 3–2.

The advantage of the survey is that the results reflect the general population from which the sample is drawn. The logic is much the same as drawing a blood sample. You do not need to drain your entire body of blood to determine your blood type. Similarly, a small random sample of people can represent a larger population. The key is that the sample must be randomly selected. Every individual in the population should have the same probability of being selected. The margin of "random sampling error" can be calculated mathematically, based on the sample size and some other factors. The results of a survey might, for example, have a 95 percent chance of having a margin of error of +/–3 percent. It is important to keep in mind that there will also be "systematic errors" resulting from such factors as biased questions and poorly trained interviewers, which cannot be calculated.

Most questions in a quantitative survey are closed-ended. The answer alternatives can be dichotomous (yes-no), determinant ("pick one from the list"), frequency of occurrence ("how many bottles do you drink a day?"), or scale (good, fair, or poor?). Such forced choices make quantitative analysis possible. It is common to include a few open-ended questions as well, thus combining quantitative and qualitative analysis.

Quantitative research delivers hard data. It is rigid and formulaic and does not leave as much room for subjective interpretations as qualitative methods do. But if the quantitative survey is not grounded in qualitative research, it is likely to generate useless statistical artifacts. Do you remember Coca-Cola's change of formula for its soft drink in 1985, for example? The Coca-Cola Company spent $4 million on customer research, asking all the wrong questions. The questions were limited to the drink itself. Not once did it ask the critical question of whether consumers were willing to switch from the old formula to a new formula. Moreover, it never asked the bottlers, a key stakeholder group which organized the public protests against New Coke.

It is important to recognize that qualitative and quantitative research play different roles and can complement each other. Qualitative research stresses depth rather than breadth, and offers insights instead of numbers. Quantitative research, with a larger randomly selected sample, is important to verify the insights and measure what number of people hold certain attitudes and behaviors. The main differences between qualitative and quantitative methods are summarized in Box 3–3.

Unfortunately, many researchers get married to a particular research method and apply it to every situation, much like the carpenter who only has a hammer and thinks any problem can be fixed with a nail. Instead, it is important to use a combination of methods for each problem to "triangulate" findings. This is a metaphorical expression borrowed from the navigation technique by which an unknown point can be located by establishing the intersection of three vectors. In social science research, triangulation is the cross-checking of data and interpretations through the use of multiple methods and sources.

Implementation and Monitoring

When a strategy has been developed and the public relations plan is implemented, research plays an important role in monitoring its effectiveness and making adjustments. Telephone surveys of the targeted audiences and analyses of media coverage are quick ways to get an indication of how things are going.

Evaluation

After a public relations program is implemented, the effect should be measured against predetermined objectives. If this sounds like a truism, consider that more than 70 percent of the winners in the most prestigious American public relations award, the Public Relations

COMPARISON OF QUALITATIVE AND QUANTITATIVE RESEARCH METHODS

Qualitative, Discovery-Based Methods:

- Discovering new insights ←————→
- Small number of purposefully ←————→ selected participants
- Emphasizes *learning* from people ←————→
- Emerging and creative survey ←————→ design
- *Creative* skills are important in ←————→ analyzing results

Quantitative, Verification-Based Methods:

- Verifying the insights
- Large number of randomly selected participants
- Emphasizes *studying* people
- Fixed and rigid survey design
- *Analytical* skills are important in analyzing results

Society of America's Silver Anvil, did not measure how well the campaign met predetermined goals.[14]

Quantitative methods are most commonly used to evaluate public relations programs because they are replicable, i.e., the same question can be asked at a later time to measure change. But qualitative evaluations, like focus groups, are appropriate as well to identify improvements. The evaluation is not complete without measuring changes in behavior. Customer loyalty can be measured with recency, frequency, amount, retention and longevity of purchases, and life time customer value. Employee, shareholder, and customer loyalty can be measured with annual defection and retention rates and "half-life," the time it takes for half a class of entering customers, employees, or shareholders to leave the company.

"Benchmarking" is key to putting the evaluation in perspective. The evaluation of public relations programs can be benchmarked against other units in the same company, industry averages, or companies that are "best in class." Figure 3–2 shows examples of benchmarking in the area of employee relations from one of the 1994 winners of the European Quality Award, Design To Distribution (D2D), Ltd.

With all this said, it is important to acknowledge the limitations of public relations evaluations. There is a fundamental difficulty inherent in establishing cause-and-effect relationships between public relations programs and such bottom-line outcomes as increased sales, lower employee turnover, higher earnings per share, and more favorable legislative decisions. These outcomes are the results of a host of complex interactions, only a few of which are under the control of the public relations department or even a particular company. Public relations research will never be as precise a science as finance and manufacturing. The CFO can calculate return on investments in minute detail based on different assumptions of interest rates. The VP of operations can measure defect levels with the accuracy of a thousandth of a percentage point. Public relations is different. Many aspects of public relations' effects cannot be measured at all.

Consider the case of a company that is faced with an environmental accident and whose public relations department has prepared a crisis communication plan, conducted crisis simulation training with the senior managers, and developed strong relationships with environmental groups which are supporting the company in the crisis. You do not measure

F I G U R E 3–2

D2D Employee Satisfaction Compared to a Benchmark*

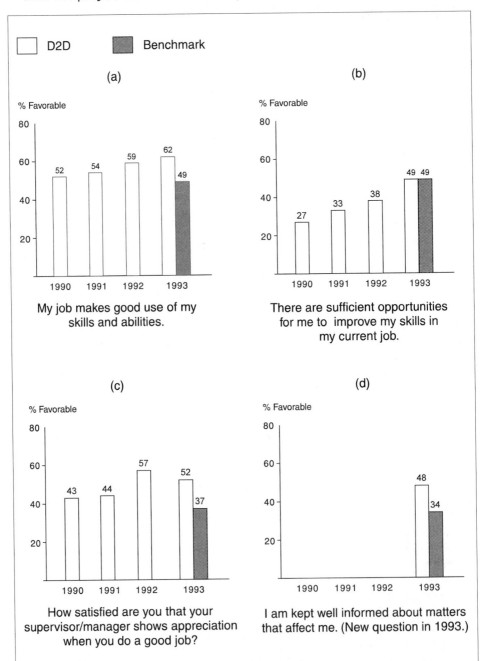

*The benchmark is an average from the "Benchmark Club," which has survey data from 18 questions that have been given to 24 million employees in 46 countries.

Source: Design To Distribution's 1994 European Quality Award submission.

the benefits of such actions, any more than you measure the benefits of putting on your pants in the morning. It is simply not possible to measure the outcome of every action by the public relations department. That does not make it less important. Even total quality management guru Edwards W. Deming argued that it is wrong to suppose that only what is measured can be managed.[15]

Acting on Findings

It is important to make research *actionable* and share it widely in the organization. Most public relations research gets relegated to the bookshelf when it is done. Information that is collected but not properly disseminated throughout the organization and acted upon is one of the largest sources of waste in any company. Approaches to making research findings "come alive" in a presentation include narrative description, role playing, videotaped interviews, and quotes. Tailoring a research presentation to different audiences is another key to making it actionable. Senior management needs an overall picture to develop strategy, and salaried employees need to know what they can do to improve stakeholder satisfaction. Yet another important factor in making research actionable is to present the research information in a timely fashion. One case in point is the Eurobarometer, a telephone survey conducted every day in 15 European countries. The telephone interviewers are on-line with a central computer which tabulates last night's results every day, allowing the EU Commission to track Europeans' opinions on a daily basis.

One of the problems with public relations research is that the people who learn most about the stakeholders under study are the researchers, who typically are outsiders. To make the research really actionable, the researcher needs to be a member of the public relations project team, rather than someone who is called on an as-needed basis to deliver statistical pronouncements from on high. Public relations staffs should look at advertising agencies for inspiration. They have thrown out the old research departments and replaced them with "account planners." The "planners" use qualitative research methods to immerse themselves in the lives of the customers and translate customer insights to the creative team. The planner works with the account team during the entire period an advertising campaign is under development to keep it focused on the final customer.

The most sophisticated companies have problems to involve all managers in firsthand interaction with stakeholders. For instance, Federal Express' managing directors and above are required to spend one day each month out in the field with a salesperson. Xerox offers a similar example of a formal program to make managers interact with customers. The top 25 managers at Xerox spend one day every five weeks taking customer complaint calls and following through until the complaints are resolved. These top managers are also assigned a few clients each, to whom they are responsible for sales and service. Another example of such personal contacts is the telephone systems manufacturer Ericsson. Its Great Britain subsidiary matches employees at all levels with a counterpart at its major client, British Telecom. For instance, each Ericsson secretary is responsible for keeping in touch with an assigned secretary at British Telecom, each engineer is responsible for a particular engineer at BT, and Ericsson's public relations director keeps in touch with the public relations director at BT. Ericsson finds that such personal communication is important to develop partnership with clients.

In addition to these programs for keeping in touch with customers, many companies go to great length to keep in touch with another high-priority stakeholder group, their own employees. At Saturn, for instance, every staff member has a partner in the union. When the media relations manager gives an interview, he will frequently bring his union partner. When Saturn was behind in production last year, it asked all administrative staff members to work Saturdays in the plant. Many of Saturn's retailers have experienced assembly line work as well. The day after a recent meeting with the retailers from the Midwest region, the car dealers went to work on the assembly line for a day.

Human beings learn best through firsthand experience. A Xerox manager who takes customer complaint calls and who is selling copy machines to clients on a regular basis can relate to clients in a unique way. Similarly, a Saturn manager who has a union worker as a partner and who has spent time on the plant floor assembling cars has a unique understanding of the importance of employee communications. When all communications professionals and other managers know their various stakeholders firsthand, instead of just as a set of demographic variables, communication with them is greatly improved.

CASE STUDIES

One of the challenges of research in public relations is that it addresses such a variety of audiences. The following examples show how the research process has been applied to different stakeholders.

Customer Satisfaction at Xerox

Customers are the *raison d'être* of any organization, including nonprofits for whom the customers are students, patients, inmates, or beneficiaries of charitable support. The customer needs to be put on a pedestal above every other stakeholder. Without customers, there would not be any other stakeholders. Surely, the customer focus needs to be balanced by the needs of other stakeholders. The stakes of the noncustomer stakeholders have never been higher, as evidenced during the last decade by the rise of business litigation, demise of employee moral, confrontations by interest groups, and shareholder activism. But the focus on the customer still needs to pervade the organization.

Customer information is gathered by a number of functions in the organization—the marketing department researches customer needs, the salesforce gets feedback from prospective customers, R&D anticipates future needs, customer service gets feedback from dissatisfied customers, managers get information from customer visits, and the quality department gathers customer satisfaction information. Surprisingly few companies have a systematic process to compile all this customer information and share it with everyone in the organization.

A case in point showing how information from customer surveys is shared broadly in the organization is Xerox's Customer Satisfaction Measurement System (CSMS). Xerox mails out a customer satisfaction survey to 55,000 customers every month! The survey asks customers to rate Xerox's equipment, sales, service, and customer administration performance. The survey results are sent to the customer relations representatives at the geographical sales district, who will make a call to every customer who has identified any dissatisfaction. It is also shared with the design and manufacturing departments for corrective actions.

Such sharing of research information so that people in the entire organization can add value to stakeholders is an important task of the communications function. Public relations and marketing have a unique role in setting up and running a customer database to capture information about individual customers and make the information available to the entire company. The role of the communication/public relations function is increasingly to manage such an integrated two-way process of communication between stakeholders and the organization as a whole.

Public relations has a particular responsibility for dissatisfied customers, who might turn into hostile publics if they are not treated appropriately. Many companies encourage customers and other stakeholders to call a toll-free number with complaints and concerns. This is unique information that needs to be shared broadly in the organization. Federal Express communications managers get reports regularly about what concerns and complaints have been expressed by hot-line callers. Saturn frequently involves customer service representatives as members of communications task-force teams. Celestial Seasonings has headsets by the copy and fax machines in its headquarters so that any employee can listen in on conversations between customer service representatives and customers (who have been informed that calls might be monitored). Eastman Chemical Company has a 24-hour hot line for citizens to voice concerns about environmental issues or anything else on their minds. Special "customer advocates" follow up and resolve complaints. Eastman's goal is to respond to 90 percent of the complaints with an acknowledgment to the customer within 24 hours, and to have 90 percent of complaints resolved within 30 days.

On-Line Surveys and Town Hall Meetings at Federal Express

Federal Express is an example of a company that is zealous about keeping in touch with employees. The company has a separate employee communication department of equal size and status as the public relations and marketing communication departments. FedEx's employees fill out on-line employee satisfaction forms every third month. A "leadership index" is calculated based on the survey. Eight of the ten items on the survey measure managers' communication activities with employees. All managers present their results to their employees and develop action plans together with their work groups to improve areas in which the managers' scores are low. If a manager's leadership index is below a certain level, he or she receives support to become a better leader and communicator. If the scores are below the accepted level for two consecutive years, the manager will be reassigned to a non-management position.

To create a dialogue between employees and senior management, Federal Express has regularly occurring television call-in shows on its internal satellite television network, so that any employee can pick up the phone and speak live on the air to the company's founder and CEO, Fred Smith. The calls are not screened. The format can be characterized as a *Larry King Live*-style show. The programs serve as corporate town hall meetings where problems get resolved on the spot. As a typical example, a customer service representative called in to tell her CEO that she did not know how to respond to a particular customer request. Smith suggested a response and told her that one of his colleagues would send out a memo the following day to all customer service representatives worldwide, explaining how to respond to the particular request.

The IPO of a Swedish Steel Company

Investor relations research played a key role in the initial public offering (IPO) by the Swedish government-owned steel manufacturer, SSAB, both in the strategic planning stage and in the course of the campaign. Initially, a telephone survey was conducted using a random sample of 1,200 people from the general public. The survey asked about perceptions of different approaches to savings and to privatization, knowledge about the privatization of SSAB, and how much the respondents were willing to invest in its stocks. Later in the planning stage, focus groups were used to test messages and specific advertising approaches. The participants were asked if they understood, had interest, and had trust in the company and the offering.

The campaign consisted of advertising and information pamphlets that were mailed to the clients of one of Sweden's largest banks and distributed at the bank's branch offices. During the course of the campaign, a telephone survey of the general public was conducted every third day to monitor progress. The survey asked about awareness of the campaign and intention to sign up to buy stock. Branch managers of 80 randomly selected bank offices that handled the applications were interviewed as well. The bank offices were asked how many applications they had received and how many they expected. These ongoing studies saved the company hundreds of thousands of dollars because the studies suggested that it could pull some of the ads that were planned. The studies predicted that 130,000 people would apply to get the 67,000 available stock option packages; in reality, 118,000 people applied.

Two telephone surveys were conducted after the public offering, one with the general public and one with the new shareholders. The studies identified improvement opportunities for the next time the government decided to privatize a company.

Taking the Pulse of Members of a Professional Association

Members are a key stakeholder of any association. An example of an association that conducts membership research is the Swedish Association for Certified Accountants. Every three months, in preparation for the association's board meeting, it commissions a telephone interview with 100 members. It is conducted during two evenings by five interviewers, and a report is prepared the following day. The survey addresses different issues every time. One of the studies, for instance, focused on the association's two membership publications. Over half of the respondents found that the publications needed improvement. The survey contained open-ended questions about what kinds of improvements the publications needed. The report listed the responses and discussed some of the most frequently mentioned suggestions.

The case shows that research does not have to be elaborate and time and cost consuming. A telephone survey with a combination of quantitative and qualitative questions asked of a hundred members over the course of a few days can help keep the board focused on the members' needs.

Customer Satisfaction Survey of State Legislatures

Eastman Chemical Company, a Tennessee-based chemical manufacturer, has a company-wide index called "key result areas" (KRA) which measures how well the company is achieving its mission of "creating superior value for customers, employees, investors, suppliers, and publics." Examples of how this measure applies to public affairs are the KRA score for the percent of bills in the Tennessee state legislature for which Eastman has lobbied successfully and the KRA score for the dollar value of these bills. In addition, the company has a KRA score based on a customer satisfaction survey of the Tennessee legislators in which they are asked about the service that the government relations department is providing them and how well Eastman Chemical Company performs as a corporate citizen. Another example of a public affairs KRA score is the company's philanthropy; Eastman tracks the time it takes for recipients to get contributions.

A Power Plant Measures Trust in the Community

An example of community relations research is a series of studies by a Swedish nuclear power plant, Forsmark. The community stakeholders are of paramount importance to the nuclear industry. The U.S. power industry's ignorance of the local community is a big reason why no nuclear power plant has been approved in this country for the last 25 years.

The Swedish power plant's management conducts a survey of local communities every year. It shows, for instance, that trust in the power plant has increased from 73 to 81 percent between 1990 and 1994. The results are tabulated separately for the "inner circle" of people living close to the power plant and an "outer circle" of people living further away. It shows that the increase of trust is particularly strong among the important "inner circle" community. The survey, moreover, asks how much trust people have in the information the power plant provides. The findings suggest that the "inner circle" of neighbors who receive a regular newsletter have more trust in the information from the power plant. A second study is conducted with opinion leaders in the entire country of Sweden. The opinion leaders were corporate executives, editorial page writers, city council members, and union leaders. The findings guide the power plant's public affairs strategy.

Intel's Cyberspace Relations

An increasingly important area of research is the discourse in cyberspace. Consider the debacle a few years ago of Intel's Pentium chip. A math professor initiated a discussion in 1994 about the bugs found on Intel's Pentium chip, which spurred discussions in over 20 Internet news groups. After several months of discussions and ridicule of Intel on the Net, CNN picked up the story on its *Headline News*. Later, IBM stopped shipping products with the Pentium chip, which made the issue explode in the media. If Intel had refuted the charges in the discussion groups and offered to replace the chip, the story would probably never had made it to the mainstream news.

Today, Intel, along with a number of other companies, has assigned staff members to the task of following discussions on Internet Usenet groups and commercial service forums. If someone is critical of Intel, the company representative will ask to get the person's phone number and call up and resolve the issue. Similar types of cyberspace research are being offered by an increasing number of research firms. One research company offers an "on-line image analysis," which includes information about the subject and tone of on-line postings about the client company, location and author of postings, positive and negative issues, and "share of voice" on particular Usenet groups and commercial service forums.[16] Figure 3–3 gives an example of such an analysis during the Republican party's primary election in 1996. Some firms keep track of issues and their progress and report daily to clients.

Another cyberspace area of research is web traffic analysis of companies' web sites. The area is still in its infancy and most of the measurements originate from advertising research, such as cost per thousand and exposures (hits). Such methods fail to account for the differences of the on-line communication medium—that a web site can lead a prospective

F I G U R E   3-3

Analysis of an Internet News Group During the Republican Primary
Elections, 1996

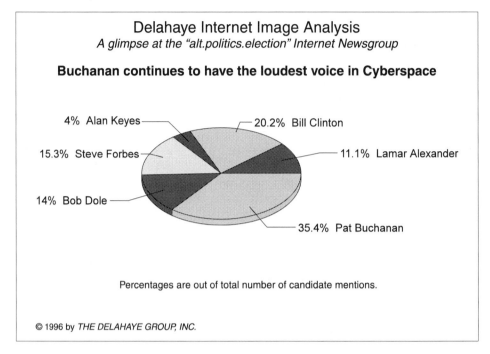

Delahaye Internet Image Analysis
A glimpse at the "alt.politics.election" Internet Newsgroup

Buchanan continues to have the loudest voice in Cyberspace

4% Alan Keyes
20.2% Bill Clinton
15.3% Steve Forbes
11.1% Lamar Alexander
14% Bob Dole
35.4% Pat Buchanan

Percentages are out of total number of candidate mentions.

© 1996 by *THE DELAHAYE GROUP, INC.*

buyer through the entire buying cycle, for instance, or that most visitors are more motivated
because they are self-selected, or that the web site can capture names, build a database, and
initiate and develop a relationship. A web site that attracts a few thousand loyal customers
who are engaged in a continuing dialogue with each other and the company can be much
more valuable than one where millions of people visit but never come back. In this sense,
counting the number of eyeballs the site attracts is not as relevant as measuring the quality
of the interaction. Box 3–4 gives examples of criteria in researching the effectiveness of
web sites. Research firms including Neilsen, I/Pro, Westrack, Audit Bureau of Circulation,
and others are entering this market with new methods to measure interaction quality.

Research to Get Publicity

Research information can have news value, and as such can be used for publicity purposes.
An example of an organization that skillfully used polling to get publicity is the Swedish
Employers Confederation. It wanted to move the focus of debate from short-term economic
cycles to long-term economic trends. To accomplish this goal, it surveyed business executives in each of Sweden's 24 regions, and publicized the research in a book. The study
showed distinct differences among the regions, which created a lot of regional and local
press coverage. The news media in every region wanted to know how their region stacked
up against the rest of the country. In addition, the employees and members of the association
got copies of the book and became more informed ambassadors of the organization.

B O X   3–4

HOW TO JUDGE THE EFFECTIVENESS OF A WEB SITE

- Ease of use/navigability.
- Key messages conveyed.
- Interactivity.
- Content.
- Integration with other communication programs.
- Number of names that are captured.

Caution is called for in interpreting studies designed for publicity purposes. Many such studies are designed to purposely skew the results with leading questions, skewed sample frames, and biased interpretations of results.

Researching Internal Clients

The public relations/corporate communications department serves "internal clients," such as the human resource, finance, and marketing departments, by offering counsel and by communicating with the internal clients' stakeholders (employees of the HR department, investors of the finance department, and customers of the marketing department). It is important to do research on these internal clients on an ongoing basis as well. This research is typically more informal and qualitative than the external stakeholder research. The senior communications managers at Eastman Chemical Company, for instance, meet once a year with all the senior managers to discuss what their communications needs are and what opportunities for improvement exist. They also determine how well the service provided by the communications department is adding value to the company.

Another example is AT&T's public relations department, which has established a standard client satisfaction survey for general managers. The survey asks how important the managers find different communications tasks to be and how well they find that the public relations departments perform them. The questions deal with the overall quality of the public relations counsel, the quality of the public relations professionals, and the quality of the communications service they offer to external stakeholders. The questionnaire also asks if the public relations function is worth its cost, if the overall service meets the general managers' expectations, and if public relations gives AT&T a competitive advantage. Aggregate top-line results of the survey are distributed to all communications professionals in the company every three months, broken down by business units.

Media Research

The traditional tallying of press clippings and broadcast placements is still the prevailing method of evaluating mass media coverage. Occasionally, PR professionals will compare what equivalent advertising space would cost. These are quick and dirty ways of measuring publicity that can be extremely misleading. There are easy ways to "get more ink"—set your plant on fire or kidnap your CEO, for example. The clip-counting approach assumes that more is better, when in fact the objective sometimes is to minimize the amount of press coverage.

Instead of simply counting the clips, public relations professionals are increasingly relying on content analysis. In the most simple format, the researcher distinguishes articles and television broadcasts that are negative, neutral, and positive to the client company. A more sophisticated form of content analysis measures the rate of articles in which the company was mentioned with its key message. Studies by one research firm show that, of all articles a particular company is mentioned in, on average, 30 percent of articles are positive, 6 percent are negative, and 29 percent contain key messages.[17] These figures can be used as a benchmark. Other variables to consider in a content analysis are:

- Circulation of the publication
- Quality of the publication. (Is it *Fortune* or *Mad Magazine*?)
- Prominence of the company in the story. (Is the company the main feature or just mentioned in passing, along with other companies in the same industry?)
- Prominence of the article in the publication. (Is it on the front page or hidden by the obituaries and birth announcements at the end of the paper?)
- Visual presentation. (Was there a favorable photo or graph?)
- Spokesperson. (Who gets quoted? What percentage of the CEO's quotes contain key messages?)

Public relations/research firms have developed scorecards on which articles are rated on these criteria.

In addition, public relations has borrowed tools from advertising to measure cost. One way to compare the cost of different forms of mass media publicity and to compare publicity with advertising is CPM, cost per thousand. The CPM is the cost of producing the press release, video news release, press conference, of whatever publicity vehicle is used, divided by the circulation number of each publication or program where it was featured, multiplied by a thousand.

These examples of media analysis are important because they show which messages are getting through and which are not, which media outlets and which reporters are favorable and which are unfavorable and why, which spokespeople are most successful at getting the key messages across, and which approaches are most cost effective. Keep in mind, however, that they are limited to the output of mass media relations. The true test of public relation's value comes from measuring the actual impact it had on the target audience.

HOW TO SELECT AND WORK WITH RESEARCH FIRMS

Most public relations research is conducted by outside firms. The choice of firm and the relationship with it are key success factors in public relations research. As with any professional service, it is not a straight transactional process in which the supplier delivers a product that is consumed by the client. The research is co-produced by the research firm and the client, so the success of the research depends as much on the client as on the research firm. Instead of shopping for lowest bids, it is important to evaluate the research firm's ability to be a good partner and add value to the research process.

Research firms come in all shapes and forms, ranging from full-service companies with in-house telephone interview and focus group facilities, to smaller consultants who contract out most of the work. Here is a list of specific considerations in hiring a research firm:

- Do you need a full-service firm that will contract for an entire project or just specialized firms that can do focus group interviews, field interviews, or data tabulation?

- If you choose a full-service firm, will the particular firm you are considering select the combination of methods that best suits your needs, or will they want to use particular methods that they have more expertise in or make more money on?

- Do you want to use a research firm that has developed a standardized method for researching a particular area, like content analysis of mass media coverage or advertising testing?

- Does the firm have any experience in your industry or with the particular group of stakeholders you will research?

- Will the firm provide a list of clients for whom it has provided similar service? What experiences did these past clients have with the firm?

Two directories of research firms in the U.S. are:

The Green Book, published by the American Marketing Association, New York Chapter, 310 Madison Avenue, New York, N.Y. 10017; and *The Blue Book*, published by the American Association for Public Opinion Research, P.O. Box 1248, Ann Arbor, Michigan 48106.

When the firm is selected, it is important to develop a written research plan detailing the responsibilities of the research firm and the client during every step of the research process. The plan should include a time frame and budget.

Most larger public relations agencies have their own research departments. Some agency clients feel that the agency researchers represent a conflict of interest. These clients do not find it appropriate for public relations agencies to evaluate their own performance. Instead, they turn to independent research firms that do not have any vested interest in the outcome of the research. The agencies, on the other hand, argue that the only way they can make research an integral part of the public relations process is to have their own in-house research department. The agency researchers assert that the emphasis of their research is on identifying areas of improvement and building continual learning into the research process, rather than on judging the quality of the agency.

RESEARCH TO SUPPORT INTEGRATED COMMUNICATIONS

Public relations cannot be managed independently from the rest of the business. The most powerful messages transmitted to stakeholders are not the annual report and brochures that the public relations department has direct control over, but the product or service offerings, the financial performance of the firm, and the environmental impact of its plants. We will now broaden the scope to describe how to set up an integrated communications research process that focuses not only on the communications functions, but on how the entire business communicates with key stakeholders. The first step is to evaluate and improve the

F I G U R E   3–4

Integrated Communications Research Added to the Stages of
Effective Public Relations

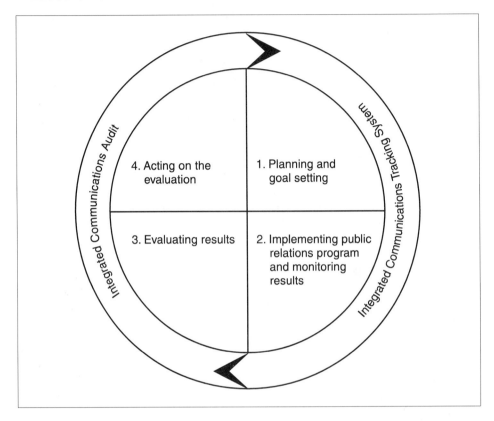

communication process with an integrated communications audit. The next step is to set up
a tracking system of integrated communications indicators. As illustrated in Figure 3–4,
these are the strategic research components of effective public relations.

Integrated Communications Audit

An audit is a good starting point to determine the extent to which communications are
integrated. Unlike traditional marketing and public relations research, which focus on the
outcome of the communications process such as attitude and behavior changes among
stakeholders, an integrated communications audit is designed to focus on the process leading
up to the results.

One approach to an integrated communications audit has been developed at the
University of Colorado at Boulder, as a class project in its master's program in integrated
marketing communications.[18] This audit has three parts: (1) interviews with managers in
marketing communications as well as in other functions to find out if there is a consensus
on objectives and key messages (there hardly ever is!); (2) content analysis of communications materials such as advertising, annual reports, and brochures to find out how well

integrated the messages are; and (3) review of existing stakeholder research and "mystery shopper" exercises where the researchers act in the role of customers who try to get refunds for merchandise, call and ask questions, etc.

The integrated communications audit can be conducted by an outside consultant or internally by senior management. The advantage of outsiders is that they bring a fresh perspective and can be more candid in their analysis. But consider these advantages of an internal audit by top management:

- The company's own managers, not an outsider, get the long-term benefit of the intimate knowledge of the organization that the audit process provides.
- It is a moral booster for employees to see that top management cares.
- It is not just a paper exercise. Senior management is committed to implementing suggestions.

Sometimes the term "audit" is intimidating. Other terms like "assessment" or "review" can be used. Procter & Gamble calls its quality management audits "visits." Whatever term is used, the audit is an opportunity to identify weaknesses that need improvement, as well as the best practices that can be duplicated throughout the organization. The audit should lead to an action plan to improve the integration and quality of the communications.

In one of the University of Colorado's audits of a large beverage company, the product and marketing service managers were asked to identify the marketing communications objective for the company's major brand on which they were all working. Ten different objectives were mentioned, ranging from "top quality" to "fun in the sun" and "refreshing." When all of the advertising and merchandising materials for the previous 12 months were analyzed, the student audit team found that less than a third executed the communications objective that was stated in the marketing plan.[19]

Integrated Communications Tracking System

Integrated communications calls for an integrated research system with key indicators that are linked to each other and monitored. The first steps in establishing an integrated communications research process are to define a single overall communication goal for the entire organization and to identify key stakeholders. Consider the case of American Telephone & Telegraph Co., AT&T. Its overall communication goal, or "brand objective," as the company put it, was to build the perception among stakeholders that AT&T was "the most helpful company." This objective was further defined as "offering the most helpful service, innovations that enhance people's lives, and being a company worthy of trust." Its priority stakeholders were customers, its own employees, and the investment community.

The next step is to identify the communications programs that have the biggest leverage on the goal. The theory of leverage suggests that small, well-focused processes can cause large-scale improvements if they are in the right place. In the case of AT&T, its public relations staff identified four communications programs, or "brand programs," which its corporate communications focused around.

1. Producing innovations that enhance people's capabilities.
2. Being a leader in protecting the environment.
3. Being a superior employer.
4. Improving education in America.

These are the leverage points that AT&T found to have the largest impact on its overall objective to be perceived as a "helpful" company.

The third step is to establish a comprehensive measurement process to track stakeholders' perceptions of the communication goal and the key messages on an ongoing basis. Such a measurement process helps to give all communication functions a shared understanding about the progress toward strengthening the corporate communication objective. Each measurement is plotted on a chart. By tracking processes of change, the research is used as a tool to direct long-term efforts.

After measurements are identified, it is important to link the items together in a system. Figure 3–5 summarizes the system of measurements at AT&T. It depicts the "process-result" or "means-end" relationships between the measurements. It can be described the following way. The senior VP or corporate communications at AT&T is accountable for the perceptions of AT&T as the "most helpful company" among its three priority stakeholder groups, customers, investors, and employees. That is her *end*, illustrated on top of Figure 3–5 by the charts for each of its priority stakeholder groups. Her *means* to achieve this end are the four key messages, the "brand programs." For the manager of the "innovation" brand program, the perceptions of AT&T as an "innovative company" among the prioritized stakeholders is the *end*, and the advertising campaign at the time, entitled "You Will," is one of the *means*. For the advertising manager of the "You Will" campaign, the *end* is how well the campaign changes stakeholders' perceptions of AT&T as an innovative company, and the *means* are the "recall" and "recognition" scores of the ad campaign. In this fashion, means become the ends for the next level of management, which in turn has to develop means to accomplish its ends. The process itself of setting up such a system facilitates important discussions between departments about how their processes relate to each other.

Such indicators are much better predictors of future success than financial information. Financial indices are lagging indicators that do not say anything about the future. Today's accounting practices are an anachronism, focusing on cost rather than value, precision rather than relevance, the past rather than the future, and material assets rather than relationships. The traditional controller, who focuses only on finance and accounting, needs to be replaced by a "relationship equity controller." The new job responsibility of the controller involves controlling, monitoring, and auditing the relationship equity. The controller is the proactive custodian of corporate reputation and relationships with key stakeholders—the assets that matter above all others in the post-industrial corporation.

THE CENTRAL ROLE OF RESEARCH IN THE FUTURE OF PUBLIC RELATIONS

American managers often complain that it is lonely at the top. That is probably because the people at the top have lost touch with the company and its stakeholders. The public relations/corporate communications function has a unique role in keeping senior management in touch with the external environment through research. They are the eyes and ears of senior management to the external and internal environment, the early warning system of emerging crises and opportunities. They use research to support overall strategic management planning, as well as the planning of the public relations function itself.

The public relations/corporate communications managers of the future not only have a finger on the pulse of their stakeholders, they have an intravenous tube connected to the stakeholders inserted into them. They track the perceptions of their key stakeholders and

An Example of AT&T's Integrated Tracking System of Leading Communication Indicators

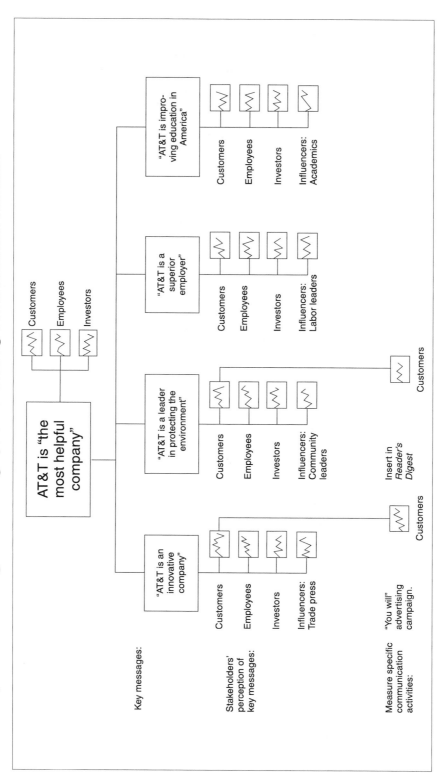

internal clients, and they leave their offices to go out to the field to live and breathe the lives of the stakeholders. They use research to systematically measure progress toward predetermined objectives, to identify areas of improvement, and to demonstrate accountability. This systematic use of research is the only way we can learn from experiences and grow as a profession. Most public relations programs have consequences that are neither immediate nor unambiguous. We cannot possibly learn from experiences if we never experience the consequences of our actions. By building in research in the public relations process through continual cycles of planning, monitoring, evaluating, and acting upon finds, we are building organizational learning, institutional memory, and continual improvements.

ACKNOWLEDGMENT

Special thanks are due to Per Hörnsten and Arne Modig, President and Senior Vice President of Sweden's leading public relations research firm, Demoskop, who provided all of the European case studies for this chapter. A warm thanks also for the valuable help from Professors Clarke Caywood, Frank Durham, and Bill Celis.

ENDNOTES

1. Barlow, Walter, *Establishing Public Relations Objectives and Assessing Public Relations Results* (New York: The Institute for Public Relations Research and Education, 1993).

2. 1995 "Survey on Measurement and Accountability, Results of a Poll of Public Relations Professionals," conducted by Schenkein/Sherman Public Relations and *PR News*, "demand for measurement/accountability" was ranked as the top issue in public relations by 44 percent of the respondents. In a 1992 survey by the Counselor's Academy of the Public Relations Society of America, "demand for measurement/accountability" was named the top industry challenge by 70 percent of the respondents.

3. Schenkein/Sherman Public Relations and *PR News*, "Survey on Measurement and Accountability."

4. Ibid.

5. Ibid.

6. Barlow, Walter, *Establishing Public Relations Objectives.*

7. Senge, P. M., *The Fifth Discipline: The Art and Practice of the Learning Organization* (New York: Doubleday/Currency, 1990), p. 71.

8. Suggested by Patrick Jackson, PRSA National Conference 1995.

9. Schultz, Don E., and Beth E. Barnes, *Strategic Advertising Campaigns*, 4th ed. (Lincolnwood, IL: NTC Publishing Group, 1995).

10. Preston, Ivan L., "The Association Model of the Advertising Communication Process, *Journal of Advertising* 11, no. 2 (1982), pp. 3–15.

11. Dozier, David M., and William P. Ehling, "Evaluation of Public Relations Programs: What the Literature Tells Us About Their Effects, in *Excellence in Public Relations and Communication Management*, James E. Grunig, ed. (Hillsdale, NJ: Erlbaum, 1992), pp. 159–184.

12. Stewart, D. W. "Speculations on the Future of Advertising Research," *Journal of Advertising* XXI, no. 3 (September 1992), pp. 1–18.

13. Lindenmann, Walter K., "A Brief Look at Public Relations Research at Ketchum," (New York: Ketchum Public Relations, 1995).

14. Fisher, Rick, "Control Construct Design in Evaluating Campaigns," *Public Relations Review* (1995).

15. For instance see the foreword to *Fourth Generation Management* by Brian Joiner (New York: McGraw-Hill, 1994).

16. The Delahaye Group, Inc., Portsmouth, New Hampshire.

17. Ibid.

18. Duncan, Thomas R., and Sandra E. Moriarty, *Driving Brand Value* (Burr Ridge, IL: Irwin, 1997).

19. Ibid.

## PART TWO

Organizational Chart of Public Relations

## CHAPTER 4

Global and Local Media Relations

Matthew P. Gonring
Vice President of Corporate Communication
USG Corporation

STRATEGY

MEDIA RELATIONS DEFINED

Balance. The word best summarizes the challenge for this particular area of public relations management and communications. From getting your message to key audiences to meeting the needs of reporters, media relations is an exercise in tightrope walking. In an era of global communications, the difficulty lies in practicing a worldwide strategy while keeping in mind local interests.

Media relations—communicating with the news media verbally or through assorted media—must also balance public opinion with business strategy. It does so by monitoring social and political trends, counseling management, and cultivating relationships both internally and externally. For today's global companies, media relations must also manage the convergence between emerging trends and the worldwide public's thirst for news. This broad perspective is one characteristic that differentiates media relations from publicity. Media relations professionals around the world use press releases and a broad array of publicity tactics. However, they are also learning to strategize and manage press coverage to shape the opinions of important constituents.

Who these audiences are varies depending on organizational objectives. The following factors also shape the media relations function:

- Type of organization.
- Public/private nature of the enterprise.
- Media interest in the products, services, or other organizational activities.
- Expectations of the organization.

Depending on media relations' role within the organization, its activities take one or more of the following approaches: reactive, proactive, or interactive.

Reactive media relations fields and responds to inquiries. Professionals should follow these general guidelines when the media come calling:

- Always avoid immediate comment and off-the-cuff remarks.
- Keep a file of issues likely to receive media attention.
- Understand deadlines.
- Always be available and return calls promptly.
- Be curious and ask questions.
- Place yourself in the reporter's shoes.
- Provide balance or know where to get it.
- Know what background information is helpful.
- Set internal expectations appropriately.
- Keep records of to whom you talked and what you said.
- Never lie.

Proactive media relations builds upon reactive steps and goes even further to promote and publicize the organization. It begins with answers to the following questions:

- Do you know the messages you want to deliver?
- Are your messages clear, concise, and straightforward?
- Which media do you want to reach in priority order?
- Which reporter/editor should you reach?
- What are the newsworthy elements to your message?
- How should you package or sell your item?
- Who are the key third parties, and what will they say?
- Have you listened for signs that reporters are busy or uninterested?
- Do they understand you will go elsewhere if they are uninterested?

Professionals who strive for interactive media relations go even deeper to develop relationships with the press. Their reasoning is that media interest and subsequent coverage evolve from positive, ongoing interactions. Here are some ways to reach this level:

- Discuss issues other than your news that may be of interest.
- Be a source; make yourself available for comment as an expert in your industry.
- Always think in terms of needs and deadlines; a few minutes of advance notice may make you a hero.
- Exclusivity should depend on the subject, organizational objectives, disclosure laws, and other ramifications.
- Converse in depth on timely news topics and industry trends.
- Talk about other publications and reporters and how they approach different issues.
- On articles they have written, be complimentary, not thankful. Reporters do not want to be accused of being a mouthpiece.
- Call to talk about relevant news and to keep in touch.
- Look for legitimate non-news reasons to interact with the news media.

- Avoid asking favors; only make suggestions.
- Adjust your message and conversation according to the reporter's time constraints and level of interest.

Taking an interactive approach to media relations is more easily said than done. Professionals who seek to develop their position within an organization can do so by developing a framework for successful communications based on the following:

- Knowledge of business.
- Knowledge of the subject matter.
- Understanding of what is news (news must be timely, relevant, and interesting to the audience).
- Extensive internal network for development of information support.
- Knowledge of third-party experts in the field for referral.
- Familiarity developed by being well read on world events and business news.
- An approach that is consistent with internal management expectations.
- Practical, hands-on experience in dealing with news media.
- Knowledge of each reporter's reputation and track record.
- Understanding of how particular news media outlets have covered news.
- Interpersonal skills.
- Relationships built over a professional lifetime.

Since the media are able to reach virtually every audience, these efforts can pay substantial dividends. The media also have the advantage of being perceived as independent, lending your message third-party credibility.

Effective media relations begins with understanding the inherent differences in the media's needs and approaches. Although unique characteristics exist among the world's media, many basics apply across the globe. The following examples describe general media:

- *Daily newspapers* structure their newsrooms around beats, assignment desks, and sections. They cover breaking news and features and need access to quotable sources, background information, and visuals. Usually on tight deadlines, editors of daily newspapers must weed through hundreds of press releases and are looking for the few that break through the clutter.

- *Weekly newspapers* operate with limited editorial staff. They generally take a feature or local focus. Many weekly newspapers demand a local focus and will not use information without it. Suburban papers frequently rely on mat releases—camera-ready copy and photographs.

MEDIA INFLUENCE

The media's influence with the general public is particularly strong, since most people rely heavily on the media for their information. However, there are no guarantees. The media retain their influence because they shape and control what information is disseminated, when, and in what form. Thus, media relations becomes a management practice without the influence of control.

- *Regional/national magazines* have varied resources, depending on the extent of their circulations and advertising revenues. Their editorial staffs are frequently dedicated to a specific subject focus or regional coverage. They want high-level access for photos and quotes.

- *Trade magazines* usually operate with skeleton editorial staffs and limited resources. They take a subject focus and rely heavily on freelancers and outside sources. Industry professionals often write articles and provide case studies.

- *Special-interest publications* target niche audiences, such as ethnic groups, sports enthusiasts, collectors, and other groups with distinct lifestyles or interests. These media seek information that can benefit their specific audiences, and they present this information in the language/jargon of their audience.

- *Newsletters* usually specialize in one subject area and tend to take a more detailed, in-depth approach. They generally assume previous knowledge of the subject.

- *Regional/national television stations* have a breaking-news and entertainment orientation and will sometimes present features. They need access for visuals and are always on tight deadlines.

- *Cable television stations* operate with limited resources and rely heavily on outside sources. They take a feature orientation and serve a specific purpose.

- *Regional/national radio stations* have limited staff support and focus on breaking news with occasional features. They need audio for on-air broadcast. (Radio news releases include localized interviews and are a good way to obtain a great deal of coverage in a short period.)

- *Wire services*—such as financial/investor research wires—track breaking or market-moving news with spot assignments. News wire services, including the Associated Press, cover the day's breaking news with occasional features. Wire services need accurate facts and data *fast*.

- *Internet/On-line services*—the World Wide Web and secure Intranets are rapidly growing in speed and sophistication. Increasingly relied upon for business communications, the technology offers companies a means of communicating instantaneously and interactively with customers, investors, and employees on a global basis. The company can gather database information and provide up-to-the-minute news, product information, and financial data.

TRENDS AND DEVELOPMENTS

The business community's perception of the media (and vice versa) has been characterized as everything from being starry-eyed to having mutual contempt. In the 1950s, for instance, public relations professionals viewed the media as targets for positive publicity. Reporters believed they were contributing to the economic system by reporting positive product and company news. That is not to say media attacks against business are new phenomena; they've been affecting American industry since the early 1900s. It is difficult, however, to pinpoint the moment when reporters began to see themselves as the drivers of business reform. Specific industries, companies, products, and business practices came under attack by critical reporters who opened a wave of investigative reporting.[1]

While this skepticism continues today, a new degree of personal respect is building between journalists and public relations practitioners. Both are beginning to realize that their relationship depends on mutual influence and dependence. Case in point: It is estimated that 25 to 95 percent of the editorial material contained in published or broadcast media either originates with, or involves, a public relations professional. Similarly, business relies on the media to get its story told and to help identify the potential impact of major decisions.

To develop relationships with the media, communications professionals should provide information designed and packaged to meet the needs of journalists. This is particularly important, as media staffs have been pared to the bone. Many of these individuals need outside help more than ever. At the same time, cutbacks in media staff, contracting newspapers, and less editorial space make it more difficult to get coverage. This requires you to "sell your story" by personalizing it to meet the journalist's needs.

As the journalists' friend, you can help them do their jobs and avoid their two greatest fears: missing the story and having their integrity challenged. Supply journalists with enough information to uncover all the angles and insights, but never allow them to become your mouthpiece. Instead, learn what approach the journalist is taking and offer the necessary information. The following are descriptions of common media approaches to reporting the news:

- *Hard or breaking news*—Reports facts and balances them.
- *Forward spin*—Looks ahead or analyzes future impact; used in features.
- *Point of view*—Draws a conclusion based on research.
- *Consumer interest*—Carries particular interest to buyers of products and services; uses surveys and research to provide information that the average shopper can use.
- *Opinion*—Represents reporter's or publication's view on a subject, supported by rationale and studies.
- *Entertainment*—Has novel or even sensational appeal and is favored by TV and tabloid media.
- *Profiles*—Take in-depth look at interesting personalities.
- *Introspective analysis*—Examines a subject through the eyes of an individual.
- *Historical*—Describes what has occurred before and its influence on today's events.
- *Tension*—Uses controversy or opposing viewpoints, often played up by reporters.

The media's mission to report the news is being made more difficult by the industry's fragmentation, which forces media to fight for market share and cut operating costs. The number of media options—cable news and programming, in particular—is proliferating. Technology is creating these new outlets, while it simultaneously changes the way the media covers the news.

Reporters are also catching the instant information wave as local stations begin to use satellite news gathering and interconnections with other local stations. Media relations professionals must tailor their approach to meet the information needs of this new breed of reporters while also fulfilling their own growing information needs. Fortunately, new products and services are enabling media relations professionals to easily store, organize, and use large amounts of media-related information.

This increasing media sophistication extends to local markets worldwide, particularly in Europe and to a lesser degree in the developing countries of Asia and Latin America. Italy boasts about 150 TV stations. Germany offers "N," an all-news station. And France is forging ahead with two-way communication, spurred by its Minitel interactive telephone information and automatic payment system.[2]

Media fragmentation can also be seen in the growing number of publications. France offers many national daily newspapers and magazines, 100 national weeklies, and numerous regional dailies, weeklies, and monthlies. Magazines are particularly well read and take a more educational approach. French trade publications cover topics ranging from high-tech to consumer interest, while insider newsletters give information on business trends.[3] In Great Britain, national dailies and tabloids are thriving. Local newspapers also abound and concentrate on business within their circulation area.[4]

To gather the news, European media are increasing their use of fax and other distribution methods employed by media relations professionals. Italy, for instance, is increasingly using more video news releases (VNRs). This is one indication that the greatest growth in public relations activities is taking place in the Mediterranean countries of Spain, Portugal, and Italy.[5]

Nonetheless, traditional media relations activities still predominate, with the recent Europe-wide recession tempering the industry's progress. Eastern Europe's erratic economic systems compound the challenge. Editors in these countries can sometimes be hard to reach, given limited telephone lines and underdeveloped distribution systems. But the effort may be worth your while: More than 80 percent of Eastern Europeans watch TV daily, and in Hungary and Czechoslovakia, two-thirds of the population read newspapers.[6]

New opportunities also abound in Asia, where living standards are rising and countries are adopting more flexible trading policies. Understanding the varying nuances between these countries is vital. The Japanese, for instance, already have a sophisticated press club system in place and rarely accept a news release at face value. In Hong Kong, however, a press release written in Cantonese will often be printed almost as is.[7] Controls on the media are a reality, however, with countries such as Singapore censoring foreign newspapers and banning direct satellite dishes. The same challenges of government-controlled media exist in Latin America, although Puerto Rico and Mexico are two Spanish-speaking markets where public relations has developed rapidly.[8]

Consumerism is spreading worldwide, fueling business growth and a demand for business communications. The section below explores business's immediate need for media relations.

CONTRIBUTION TO OVERALL CORPORATE GOALS

In an era of increased accountability, "contributing to corporate goals" often means showing your impact on the bottom line. More business executives are beginning to understand the interrelationship between responsible media relations, corporate image, and sales. According to *Public Relations Quarterly*, "CFOs and investor relations executives are eager for media coverage that builds public awareness of a company's fundamental strengths, value, and values. They realize that even a small drop in sales can mean a large drop in earnings."[9] In other words, media relations' credibility-building talents help companies to secure investors and lenders and strengthen supplier/customer relationships—all of which contribute to bottom-line sales. These considerations are particularly vital for companies operating overseas. By being seen as a credible, contributing member of the local community, a company can link the corporate name to its products—without seeming like a foreign invader.

Unifying the communications of local operations with those of the corporate office requires open, candid channels of information. Communication to the media must also be meaningful.

This requires top executives to be accessible—even in the midst of "bad news." Despite companies' conditioned fear of in-depth reporting, candid communication pays off in more objective coverage. The same theory applies to risk communication, which can be thought of as reporting on the hazards of everyday life.[10]

Bringing your management into the communication loop enables you to train them to proactively address potentially controversial issues. Media relations professionals must also work to make risk communications part of a larger risk management program.

Media and public relations should also be part of a larger business plan, with every communication directed at a specific audience. This, of course, requires a clear understanding of the company's goals and how it plans to achieve them. For a corporation's international companies, this means having individual business/communication plans based on local markets, issues, and products. A global communications strategy integrates these plans.

Media contacts within any local market must support the organization's mission, including its sales and marketing objectives, if media relations is to increase its stature within the organization. As mentioned before, accountability is the name of the game. By being friends, not foes, media relations and marketing can work together to build credibility that protects and increases sales of company products and services.

Media relations' credibility-building talents help companies to secure investors and lenders and strengthen supplier/customer relationships— all of which contribute to bottom-line sales.

With both functions trying to learn new ways of operating overseas, they can benefit from each other's experiences. By reviewing marketing plans, strategies, white papers, and research, media relations professionals can gain an understanding of local markets. Similarly, media relations helps marketing to identify the broader issues that can affect its sales efforts. By keeping a pulse on the marketplace, media relations guards against marketing ideas that just won't fly in a local market. Marketing executives also turn to media relations for creative ideas that compensate for the high cost of advertising and help to reach disenchanted audiences.

The advice to "think global act local" has become cliché. Media relations professionals have learned that the question of what approach to take depends on the local market's culture, media sophistication, and economic and political situation. However, one need not separate national from international news. With fewer companies taking a domestic approach, many issues now have relevance to people around the world. Moreover, editors often want to hear from public relations professionals back at the corporate headquarters. They are also eager for contact with top executives, since most reporters often have contact only with corporations' overseas representatives.

Local considerations still come into play, however. People and companies with high profiles in one country may not be as well known in other parts of the world. Relevance, timing, and wording are key requirements when operating across time zones into local markets. *International Public Relations in Practice* suggests that companies answer the following questions before carrying out public relations efforts in local overseas markets:[11]

- Do the local press accept news releases? Or do they expect payment?
- What types of promotions work?
- Do the local media accept tie-in promotions?
- Does the government have a strong "corrupt practices" branch? (If so, it can be very restricting.)
- What is the local attitude toward sponsorships?
- Are charity donations accepted or construed as bribes?
- Are newspaper supplements used?
- Is there a local trade or technical press? (This is a good beginning for media relations campaigns.)
- Has public relations drawn up an attitude survey, which differs from marketing research?
- How will the organization's local standing affect its credit rating and hiring ability?

BUDGETING AND MEASUREMENT CONSIDERATIONS

Cost management challenges all multinational companies. And the fact that media relations must by done on the local level creates extra program costs. Careful budgeting becomes crucial, not only as a way to decide the cost of your media campaign, but also for management evaluation. Dispelling the myth of "free" publicity enables media relations professionals to prove their worth. This requires educating management on the difference between disseminating press releases and building credibility for a company's products and services. The former, unfortunately, is the popular definition of publicity; the latter is what responsible media relations accomplishes. But neither effort is "free," or easy.

Creating skeleton budgets of all relevant expenses helps to document media relations' efforts. When allocating funds, leave enough aside for incidentals and a contingency fund. With press conferences and special events, in particular, always expect the unexpected. Budgeting is made easier by consulting such resources as *The Professional's Guide to Public Relations Services* (H&M Publishers, Rhinebeck, N.Y.). The services listed can be contacted and then compared based on current prices and written estimates.

TACTICS

EXECUTING A MEDIA RELATIONS STRATEGY

Tactics set media relations objectives in motion and thus play an important role in media relations strategy and planning. A company that is trying to build sales in a specific industry, for example, could use media relations to provide the industry with helpful information on the company's products. The tactics to achieve this strategy can include sending press kits to industry trade publications and holding receptions at industry trade shows (Exhibit 4–1).

For instance, USG Corporation, a *Fortune* 250 building materials manufacturer, has decided to increase its R&D and marketing efforts in its repair and remodel business. This

E X H I B I T   4–1

Example of Media Relations Plan for Building Materials Manufacturer

Objective:	Increase product awareness in the repair and remodel segment.
Strategy:	Supply timely, accurate product information to those publics who influence the sale of repair/remodel construction products.
Possible tactics:	Distribute timely, usable information to industry trade publications; personally call industry editors and syndicated writers to determine and bolster interest in the company's remodeling products; submit case studies on successful renovation projects to the trade press; exhibit remodeling products at industry trade shows; supply product for use on promotional remodeling projects.

segment offers companies more stability than does the highly cyclical new-construction segment. To help carry out the marketing end of this strategy, the media relations department supplies product information to those publics who influence the sale of repair/remodel construction products.

Tactical examples include distributing timely, useful information to industry trade publications; personally calling editors and syndicated writers to determine and bolster interest in the company's remodeling products; submitting case studies on successful renovation projects to the trade press; exhibiting remodeling products at industry trade shows; and supplying product for use on promotional remodel projects.

The choice of tactics depends on your media relations objectives. The following is a list of just some tactical options available:

- Audio releases (for radio).
- Backgrounders (supplement news).
- B-roll (unedited video).
- Bylined articles (authored by "experts").
- Community calendar listings (similar to public service announcements).
- Computer or CD ROM disks (can include product demonstrations and other detailed graphics but be sure your recipient has the capability to view them).
- E-mail (can transfer everything from computer files to pictures).
- Fact sheets (supplement news releases).
- Faxes (make sure they are welcomed).
- Features (publication articles or broadcast programs).
- Fillers (supply sidebars, illustrations, lists, and other "quick reads").
- Letters to the editor (one of the most under-used media relations tools).
- Mat releases (camera-ready copy and photos).
- Media advisory (for press invitations and very timely items).
- Media kits (range from simple folders filled with information to elaborate packages of giveaways and samples).
- Op/ed pieces (take a side on an issue).

- Phone calls (preferred by some editors, especially those with tight deadlines).
- Photos (avoid clichés and make them eyecatching; may help to get your story published or can be used alone as filler).
- Pitch letters (personalize them).
- Press conferences (make sure your reason is *very* newsworthy).
- Press releases (target recipients carefully to avoid wasteful mailing).
- PAs or PSAs (public service announcements).
- Talk and interview shows (more risk involved, but can be worth it).
- Trade shows (multitude of opportunities from exhibiting products to hosting elaborate press receptions).
- Video (be careful not to skimp on quality).
- Video news releases (VNR) (satellite-fed to TV stations; aim for broadcast quality and make your news integral to the story).

The main consideration when selecting appropriate tactics is to know what your target media prefers. With financial-related news, certain disclosure requirements *must* be followed. News that could have a bearing on your company's stock price should be disclosed simultaneously by the quickest means possible. This requires sending it through a fax service bureau or over a newswire. Choose these services carefully and ask lots of questions, particularly about how they handle recipients who cannot be reached.

Overseas, these tactics carry many idiosyncrasies. For instance, the press in other countries often meets with companies at the close of the business day—not at the time-honored U.S. lunch meeting. And press conferences in some countries begin promptly at the appointed hour, while others make it customary to wait 30 minutes. Also, the list of attendees to press conferences can include everyone from government officials, local bankers, and dignitaries to the company's customers and sales representatives.

The language issue can be resolved by composing press kits in English as well as the host country's official language. Company spokespersons should also be trained to avoid American slang and business jargon. And any giveaways must consider local taboos. Ways to learn about local customs and make media contacts include in-depth "briefings" from local public relations agencies; the U.S. community "over there;" local press clubs; and your own marketing people.

Here and abroad, relationships depend not only on cultural understanding, but also on professional conduct. For instance, media relations professionals must understand journalism and be knowledgeable of their subject matter. Knowing how to "sell" one's story using strong written and verbal communications skills is also crucial.

Case Example: United Airlines

During the mid-1980s, the safety of air travel was in serious question. A recent string of airline disasters had left the American public questioning the airlines' maintenance procedures, and the media were determined to find some explanations. After being turned down by every other major carrier, a "20/20" producer contacted United Airlines, asking to tour a maintenance facility. The proposed feature was portentously titled "Is This Thing Fit to Fly?" Kurt Stocker, then United's senior vice president of corporate communications, wanted to participate. But he said he would call the producer back with his response.

Stocker immediately thought of his recent visit to United's San Francisco-based maintenance center. He remembered how impressed he was with the airline's diligence—mechanics took personal responsibility for everything they worked on and were required to sign off on every part they inspected. But how could Stocker communicate his confidence in United's maintenance procedures? Until this point, speaking publicly about safety was taboo. "Do safety; don't talk about it" was the industry practice.

Stocker went to United Airlines' chairman and posed this question: What would we say if a United plane crashed tomorrow? The chairman responded that they would first say how they felt about the situation; then they would talk about the airline's dedication to safety. It became clear that United's response would be the same, accident or no accident. They then decided it was time to end the contradiction and start speaking publicly about their strong safety record.

Confident in United's story and the company's ability to tell it, Stocker invited the "20/20" producer to visit the San Francisco maintenance center. United insisted on three stipulations, however, which were intended to prevent a one-sided report:

1. The producer would film for at least three days to get a more accurate sense of United's day-to-day safety procedures.
2. Everything and everyone in the center would be accessible to the cameras.
3. United's employee publication would interview the producer immediately after he finished filming. This would help United to capture the producer's immediate impressions and freeze them prior to editing days later.

INTERNAL MEDIA RELATIONS

Before approaching the media, it is necessary to sell your story internally. By earning the trust of senior management, you can teach them the benefits of open communication and prepare your organization for possible media confrontations. Achieving this level of respect within the organization better enables you, as media relations professional, to turn potentially negative situations to your company's advantage.

Fortunately, this was the case at United Airlines when the ABC news program "20/20" came calling.

Not until the program aired did United know its strategy had paid off. Host Barbara Walters introduced the segment by admitting she spent more time in airplanes than she did at home. She closed the United piece by stating how much safer she felt after the visit to United. Walters' comment echoed the sentiments of viewers, who immediately began lighting up the lines at United's 24-hour reservation line. Passenger volume surged as many switched their flights to United, even if it meant paying more.

In order to extend the positive perceptions generated by the "20/20" segment, United took to the skies with its message of safety. The manager of external communications enlisted a United 747 pilot to act as spokesperson on a nationwide media tour. The pilot appeared on talk shows and granted interviews.

The media tour, coupled with the "20/20" broadcast, forever changed the airline industry's approach to safety. Other carriers soon joined United and began discussing their maintenance procedures in an effort to market safety.

In the end, United's candor had turned a potentially negative situation to the company's advantage.

MEASURING THE SUCCESS OF TACTICS

Demonstrable results build credibility and strengthen the media relations function. Accurate program measurement is difficult enough here at home and multiplies significantly as media relations takes on a global reach. Given the challenge of pan-European comparisons, for instance, media relations must depend on country-by-country evaluation. Media delivery measurements vary between countries, creating inconsistent data. Increasingly sophisticated databases and instant access to the information superhighway will simplify measurement, but understanding the actual *effects* of media coverage will continue to elude many.

Monitoring and distribution services currently provide audience profiles and can detect whether the message was mostly positive or negative. On the other hand, technology lacks the human ability to analyze. As a result, media relations professionals must rely on these existing technologies while combining them with their own interpretation. One suggestion: Include reply cards, 800 numbers, questionnaires, and other two-way communications as often as possible. These help to determine who is writing or calling in for information as a result of your media coverage.

The following lists some measurements currently available:

- *Clipping services.* Same-day services are an alternative to databases; pertinent clips are faxed to clients the morning of publication. Some vendors even "analyze" clips and assign ratings based on the clippings' position in the publication.

- *Transcript services.* Using a modem, clients can access transcripts from news summaries of network, cable, and local news.

- *Fax services.* Blast faxes are reformatted press releases sent to news directors and producers. Reply cards help to document usage. Fax-on-demand is another service, which enables consumers and the media to call an 800 number to request information; callers' names are captured and compiled.

- *Content analysis services.* Using sophisticated computer analysis, these services go beyond readership and audience figures. Lack of a human element creates shortcomings, however.

THE FUTURE

FUTURE TRENDS WILL CHANGE MEDIA RELATIONS

New forms of media monitoring and information dissemination will build on the progress described in the preceding section. Electronically scanned publications will someday combine the benefits of on-line databases and clipping services. New, imaginative forms of information distribution will emerge, requiring media relations professionals to keep up. It will become increasingly difficult to control the speed of two-way, interactive communication, while the visual influence of these communications will have impact on the corporate image more than ever.

THE FUTURE BELONGS TO FORWARD-THINKING MANAGERS

This new high-impact media will have a profound influence on public opinion. As a result, media relations must become more of a knowledge-based profession. The competition to reach these key constituencies will become intense.

Just as the speed and quantity of information will increase, so too must its quality. This means honing information and personalizing it for an increasingly diverse audience. Technology will continue to drive this segmentation, with vendors introducing new ways to reach tightly defined targets. More media relations professionals will use this information to distribute information to targeted local media. Already there are services that insert local information into press releases.

At the same time, messages must remain consistent if they are to unite the corporation's local and global interests. This integration requires media relations to join forces with issues management, law, finance, and marketing. Together, the various corporate functions can ensure clear and consistent emphasis on key messages. A constant state of readiness enables global companies to manage and influence events *before* they occur.

EDUCATION AND TRAINING RESPOND TO FUTURE NEEDS

Media relations must be part of this integrated marketing communications (IMC) movement if it is to provide consistent messages and achieve measurable results. The first requirement is an understanding of how the other disciplines operate, which can be achieved through training in government relations, employee communications, advertising, marketing, and other related functions.

Add to this a business and management background, and media relations gains an even broader framework on which to build itself into a knowledge-based profession. Public relations education must prepare graduates for positions that combine a strategic management focus with strong written, verbal, and interpersonal communication skills. At the same time, public relations and business must join forces. This requires business schools to overcome their traditional prejudice caused by a lack of understanding of the public relations practice. Public relations professionals also need to adapt business planning and accountability and be able to speak the language of business.

By strengthening its position *within* the organization, media relations will be better equipped to respond to external constituents. This balance between business strategy and public opinion is achieved by keeping an eye out for emerging social and political trends. It also means offering guidance on how management should respond. This is what true media relations is all about. For today's global companies, the added challenge is to stay alert for emerging trends both here and overseas. Such a broad perspective takes media relations beyond mere press coverage to influence public perception and behavior toward the organization.

E N D N O T E S

1. Finn, David, "The Media as Monitor of Corporate Behavior," *Business and the Media,* Craig E. Aronoff, ed. (Santa Monica, CA: Goodyear Publishing Company, Inc., 1979), p. 119.

2. Bovet, Susan Fry, "Trends in the 'New' Europe," *Public Relations Journal* (September 1993), p. 18.

3. Josephs, Ray, and Juanita Josephs, "Public Relations in France," *Public Relations Journal* (July 1993), p. 24.

4. Josephs, Ray, "Public Relations the U.K. Way," *Public Relations Journal* (April 1994), p. 16.

5. Bovet, Susan Fry, "Trends in the 'New' Europe," *Public Relations Journal* (September 1993), p. 18.

6. Seitel, Fraser P., *The Practice of Public Relations* (New York: MacMillan Publishing, 1989), p. 517.

7. Macdonald, Alan, "Financial Public Relations in a Global Context," *International Public Relations in Practice*, Margaret Nally, ed. (London: Kogan Page Limited, 1991), p. 58.

8. Seitel, Fraser P., *The Practice of Public Relations* (New York: MacMillan Publishing, 1989), p. 516.

9. Dilenschneider, Robert, "Use Ingenuity in Media Relations," *Public Relations Quarterly* (June 22, 1992), p. 13.

10. Adams, William C., "The Role of Media Relations in Risk Communication," *Public Relations Quarterly* (Winter 1992–1993), p. 28.

11. Linscott, Ann, "Consumer Marketing Worldwide," *International Public Relations in Practice*, Margaret Nally, ed. (London: Kogan Page Limited, 1991), p. 104.

## CHAPTER 5

Broadcast Media Relations

John A. Bace, APR
Principal
J. A. Bace Communications, Inc.

A STRATEGIC APPROACH

The chief executive of the multi-million dollar company was upset. "Why don't the stories issued by my PR department, like the product announcements, get picked up by television stations?"

When asked about the process used in working with the broadcast journalist, the reply was predictable: "We send the TV stations a (print) news release *and* a color slide the morning we issue the news release," he said.

This sort of afterthought treatment of the broadcast media is not uncommon among line management and many public relations professionals. Too many PR pros have no idea how the editorial process really works in broadcast news rooms, and because of wrong assumptions, they fail to use the medium in an effective manner. The tactic of a video news release, a possible radio interview, or a satellite media tour is often tacked on to the publicity plan at the last minute just to round out the offerings.

Practitioners who fail to look at an organization's strategic plan and match up the goals and objectives against target broadcast media and the relevant audiences are doing a disservice to themselves, their client, and the broadcast journalists.

Broadcast media relations is the process of providing broadcasters with timely, relevant, and interesting information that enables them to make their broadcast product more valuable in the marketplace.

The Times, They Are Changin'

There was a time when broadcast media relations was relatively simple to do. You had three major television broadcast networks in the United States and each had one powerful affiliate in every market that had a regular schedule of newscasts. To target radio audiences, you would look to the powerful 50,000-watt clear-channel AM stations. However, those days are gone forever.

Today, broadcast media relations covers the spectrum on radio from Paul Harvey to Howard Stern, and from Mike Wallace at "60 Minutes" to "Late Night with David Letterman" on television. Everything in between includes "Hard Copy," "Moneyline,"

"Inside Edition," "American Top 40," "All Things Considered," and The Weather Channel, just to mention a few. Soon public relations practitioners will be asked to use their tools and skills to build awareness and stimulate interest in their companies, products, and services with broadcasters such as the Home Shopping Network.

Cable permitted broadcasting to sharpen its focus into a narrowcast beam, giving viewers the opportunity to pick and choose from a much broader menu of programming. All-news and all-sports channels that were born on the cable stations are now joined by channels dedicated to everything from military history to bass fishing.

In the very near future, new technologies and changes in the way the public accesses its broadcast media will see a new phenomenon, pinpointcasting. Gone will be the current audience measurements of success that talk about cost per thousand (CPM), households using televisions (HUTS), and quarter-hour shares. A successful broadcast media relations placement of the future may have a target audience as small as one.

Where People Get Their News

For nearly half a century, the Roper Organization has studied the sources of news and information for the United States population.

In 1963, Roper found that, for the first time, most Americans (52 percent of those surveyed) cited television as their major source of news and information. Up to that point, printed sources such as newspapers and magazines were cited by the majority of the public as their primary source of information. The trend continues to grow. In 1996, Roper found that 52 percent of the U.S. population ranked television as their main source for local news and 71 percent cited television as their main source for national news.

A study by Gallup conducted for the Radio-Television News Directors Association found that 50 percent, exactly one-half of the U.S. population, received *all* of their news and information from television.

Nielsen and Arbitron continue to defend their estimate that the average American spends between 22 and 28 hours a week "watching" television. A more accurate estimate might be that the television set is turned on and tuned in for 22 to 28 hours. When asked "How many hours did you *watch* TV?" the actual answer comes out to be about 12 hours per week.

Recent nationwide polls conducted by the Los Angeles Times, Gallup, Harris, and Yankelovich all show a general decline in public confidence regarding the news media. Yet, when compared to other media, television comes out the most credible.

A study conducted by the Roper Organization for the Television Information Office investigated what would happen if conflicting or divergent reports on the same story were put out by television, newspapers, radio, and magazines. A convincing majority (55 percent) asserted they would be most inclined to believe the television reports.

As publicist Henry C. Rogers put it, "There's no doubt that television is the most effective tool the PR person has in getting the message across."

See You on the Radio

Think back to how you learned of the major breaking stories of the last decade. If you are like most Americans, chances are you first learned of the story via the radio.

A Gallup study conducted for the Associated Press Radio Network found that 83 percent of the U.S. population first hears of a major news story on the radio. The key radio listening times are when first awakening in the morning, going out to lunch at noon, and driving home in the afternoon. Additionally, the most recent U.S. Census Bureau data suggests that 98 percent of all U.S. households own at least one radio.

There has never been a greater opportunity for the public relations professional to get a message out than via spoken word format (all news, all talk, or news-talk) radio stations. According to the *M Street Journal*, a New York-based publication that monitors the broadcasting industry, the number of these stations has more than tripled since 1989, from 308 to 978 in July 1994.

This growth has been fueled by three forces: technology, economics, and programming.

First is technology. Spoken-word-format radio stations were traditionally very expensive to operate, and that is why, for many years, these stations could be found only in the largest markets. Small markets could afford neither the talent nor the line charges to bring in syndicated programming. Now, however, with satellite technology, the cost of running these stations has become dirt cheap. Small stations will use the satellite feeds of the syndicated shows for the majority of their programming, allocating their limited talent budget for local hosts in key time segments.

The second factor is economics. Radio is going through its second major metamorphosis. The first occurred in the late 1950s and early 1960s, just as television was hitting its "golden age." The growth and popularity of television did for radio what cable did for the television industry in the 1970s: it caused fragmentation, specialization, and niche programming. Now, AM stations in all markets are losing their music formats to FM stations, and they are hard at work trying to find a new profitable niche.

The third factor is the public's demand for real-world programming on both radio and television. Gene Burns, a syndicated host on WOR-AM New York and president of the National Association of Radio Talk Show Hosts, calls the phenomenon, "the most efficient reconnect mechanism between the governed and those who govern."

Some people suggest that this growth in all news, all talk, and news-talk radio is just the beginning of the new media of the 21st Century. "I foresee interactive media taking its place aside of and eventually replacing the traditional media as the main vehicle of communications in America in the next 20 years," said Michael Harrison, editor of the broadcast industry specialty magazine *Talker*.

On the television side of programming, Alan Sternfeld, ABC-TV's chief network scheduler, agrees that the same forces driving radio programming are also having an effect on television offerings. Electronic news gathering (ENG) and satellite remote broadcasts give all television stations the ability to produce programs quickly, from anywhere, at very reasonable costs. Also, news and news-type programs can be produced more quickly—and less expensively—than traditional entertainment shows.

And finally, Sternfeld notes, what the public wants is "reality" shows. "The interests of viewers have shifted away from fantasy," says Sternfeld. He says the days of "jiggle" television—"Charlie's Angels," "The Love Boat," and "Fantasy Island"—are long gone. Instead, viewers want TV (and radio) to be a "window to the world."

You Want It When?

Hal Fisher, a former CBS News bureau chief in Chicago had a wonderful answer for some public relations professionals (and correspondents, writers, and field producers) who had trouble dealing with broadcast deadlines.

B O X   5–1

A MINI CASE HISTORY

How well does proactive media relations work on radio? Just ask Michael Farris, the executive director of the Home School Legal Defense Association.

In February 1994, Harris spotted a minor provision in an education bill that appeared to threaten parents' right to educate their children at home. Without leaving their offices, Farris and a half-dozen other staff members sounded the alarm on more than 50 radio talk shows. In no time at all, Capitol Hill switchboards were flooded.

One veteran Capitol Hill staffer said he never saw any issue go from no calls one day to flooding the switchboard the next day. Less than a week later, the House voted to kill the once-obscure provision, 422–1. Farris gives talk shows much of the credit.

"If I wanted it tomorrow, I would have called you tomorrow," Fisher would say. "Yes, I want it today!"

Broadcast media relations is as different from print media relations as the space shuttle is from a commercial jet liner. While both fly and carry passengers, cargo, and crew, their schedules, flight paths, and preparations are significantly different.

The first is that broadcast time is finite. The deadlines occur in a continuum, and when the clock says 6:00:00, the Six O'Clock news must go on the air. Few public relations professionals, and even fewer organizations, are prepared to deal with "I need it now" deadlines.

Some forward-thinking companies are installing permanent satellite upfeeds or fiber-optic video loops to help in answering broadcast media inquiries. The satellite feeds and video loops permit executives and spokespeople to sit down in front of a camera in their own office buildings and answer questions from a broadcast reporter, à la "Nightline." The output of the camera is fed into a central point at the local telephone company, and then is routed to a leased line into the broadcast newsroom. This way, the station or network does not have to send a camera crew out to a location, or the executive does not have to go to a television studio that could be either down the street or across the country to do the interview.

Additionally, the actual amount of on-air time in a news broadcast is very small. Witness the fact that, in the traditional half hour nightly network newscast, only 22 minutes is dedicated to news. The competition for coverage is tremendous from both internal and external forces. The internal forces are the departments, such as the Washington bureau, the business editor, or the science reporter, fighting for spots within the show. The outside forces are thousands of public relations practitioners and other interested parties who want to get their messages on the air.

The key to good broadcast media relations is being able to provide the broadcaster with timely, relevant, and *interesting* information. How can you make the broadcaster's job easier and improve the return on investment he or she has to make in covering your company, product, or service?

A good test of interest value is based on the Nielsen and Arbitron ratings numbers. We know that the television is turned on in the home for between 22 and 28 hours a week. Yet, people only "watch" it for about 12 hours. Does the story you are about to pitch have the ability to make someone look up from playing with the dog or doing a crossword puzzle while the television set is turned on and playing in the background? If not, perhaps you should think twice before pitching the story and wasting everyone's time.

HISTORY, TECHNOLOGY, AND LEGISLATION AS PROLOGUE

To understand the emergence of broadcast publicity as a tool of public relations, it is first necessary to understand the emergence of TV news as a force in American culture.

Broadcast journalism grew out of the press–radio war that broke out in 1932 between the Associated Press (AP) and the major radio networks of the day—CBS and NBC. The newspaper members of the AP wanted the broadcasters cut off from news dispatches. When the wire service took this action, the radio networks started their own one-person news departments: Paul White at CBS and Abe Schechter at NBC.

For the rest of the 1930s, broadcast journalism grew slowly, gathering news as best it could. However, newspapers still held the edge in being able to tell the American public what was happening.

All that ended on December 8, 1941. Radio broke the story of the bombing of Pearl Harbor the day before and the newspaper from that point forward started playing the fill-in game. World War II did much to grow news gathering talents and technology, with such stars as Edward R. Murrow and Walter Cronkite rising to prominence, as the public strained to hear familiar voices telling them the news of the world.

In the 1950s, television came on the scene. At first, it was only seen as an entertainment medium. News was added as a public service and because it was cheap and easy to program. In the early days before color, broadcasts lasted 15 minutes and were largely radio newscasts with a still picture, a talking head, and the occasional crude graphic. The broadcasts started on the networks and spread to local stations as they found news could become a revenue producer.

As television moved through the 1960s, network television news broadcasts were expanding to half an hour and becoming very profitable. The Information Age was born as seminal events such as the assassination of John F. Kennedy, the Vietnam War, and resultant political upheaval caused people to seek more information quickly. As network news expanded to 30 minutes, most local stations were devoting an hour to developing events—30 minutes in the early evening and 30 minutes in the late evening. Formats, such as "Eyewitness News," were developed to compete for advertising revenue. Suddenly, the local news department was the profit center for the television station.

The Prime Time Access Rule

In 1974, the Federal Communications Commission invoked the Prime Time Access Rule (PTAR). This action forced the three major networks (ABC, CBS, and NBC) to give up control of the first half-hour of prime time to their local affiliates. At first, this found the local affiliates scrambling to fill this additional half-hour that had a large audience.

The television syndication industry was born almost overnight as game shows and off-network reruns were rushed to the local affiliates to fill this very profitable half-hour. Yet other stations found that they could fill the time with informal programming. The "infotainment" shows such as "PM Magazine," "Evening," and, eventually "Entertainment Tonight," were born. These quasi-news shows could be produced inexpensively and they were constantly fresh with no repeats.

In the top 10 major markets, the network owned-and-operated (O&O) television stations began to experiment with expanding their early news programs. An internal study by NBC News found that, with the five local O&O stations, for every 30-minute expansion of the early news, they would see an increase in audience of 40 percent. The added required talent and resources to cover the expanded early news cost only a fraction of the price of entertainment syndicated programming.

Technology in the Newsroom

By the end of the 1970s, a technological revolution had taken place in the newsroom that added to broadcasts the immediacy of time as well as that of presence.

WHY DO THEY CALL IT B-ROLL?

When an ENG (Electronic News Gathering) crew shoots raw video to be used to illustrate a story, it is said that they are "gathering B-Roll." What is the source of that term?

It comes from the days of film. In film editing with sound, the technology is such that it is difficult to insert film containing pictures that illustrated the subject matter of a story into the middle of a film story with sound.

To do that you have to edit a reel of film that contains the sound on film (A-Roll) that includes narration and interview soundbites. Another reel of film contains the illustrative pictures and natural sound (B-Roll). Then you have to either have the two reels printed together onto a new reel of film or project both reels on separate projectors and mix the pictures and sound through a switcher. In broadcast news, this was done live.

With the advent of ENG, the illustrative scenes along with sound-on-tape scenes and narration could be edited onto one single video cassette, often in less time than it took to develop the film and edit the A–B Roll package.

Videotape recorders and handheld cameras finally reached broadcast quality, enabling all stations, regardless of market size, to shoot and edit news packages up until deadline. Before, in using film, stations needed a minimum of a half-hour of processing time to develop film, and even longer to complete editing. Additionally, the ability to produce a "packaged" news story, with reporter's narration, soundbites, and illustrative footage, was very complicated.

These A–B roll packages required film splicing and editing, and at least two film projectors in the telecine chain to get the product on air. As late as 1976, a survey by United Press International discovered that only two television stations in downstate Illinois (outside of the Chicago market) were able to do A–B roll. By 1980, thanks to the use of videotape production technology, every television station could produce a "package."

The use of the broadcast-quality videotape technology had other benefits for the stations. The video signal from these electronic cameras and tape systems could be carried on microwave transmissions. This enabled stations to go live during newscasts from nearly anywhere in their markets on very short notice.

This technology gave birth to the "Live at Five" news programs as reporters were able to bring to their viewers the action (or sometimes inactivity) from the scene of a breaking news event.

Economic decline, inflation, increased unemployment, Watergate, and turbulent stories like the year-long Iranian hostage crisis, the Arab oil embargo, the war in Afghanistan, and the Olympic boycott prompted the public throughout the 1970s to look for more news and information. Stories on the economy, the consumer, and pocketbook issues became more prominent.

The Profit Factor

As the 1980s began, NBC's Tom Brokaw said in a *Washington Journalism Review* article that the broadcast newsroom was a profit center at both the local and network levels. News programming was expanding into nontraditional areas such as early morning, late evenings, and even regularly scheduled prime-time slots.

The 1980s also saw corporate raiders looking for ripe opportunities to make a quick buck and move on. The broadcast networks, their news divisions, and successful local affiliates were no exception. Within an 18-month period, the ownerships of the three major networks all changed hands.

The FCC had also relaxed the minimum amount of time required for station ownership. Previously, the owner of a station was required to have the financial resources to withstand at least three years of loss, if necessary. The Commission would permit the sale or transfer of a broadcast license only under a dire economic hardship. Towards the middle and late 1980s, venture capitalists entered onto the broadcast scene and began trading broadcast licenses and CPs (construction permits to build broadcast towers) as if they were frozen pork bellies or other commodities.

As with any mature and profitable industry, this meant also that the newsroom had become subject to cost cutting and retrenching. For while the newsroom is the major profit center, it is also the single largest expense in most broadcast operations.

Challenging the Giants

In the 1980s, the three major networks also found their domination of the broadcast news industry challenged. The number of homes served by cable continued to grow steadily through this period of time. At the same time, Atlanta entrepreneur Ted Turner established Cable News Network (CNN). CNN used the paradigm long established by all news radio of providing news in a structured, predictable format, at all times. A viewer who had cable could, at any hour of the day or night, turn on his or her television and see the latest news from around the world.

ABC News and Group W Broadcasting attempted to challenge Turner's entry in the all-news television game by launching Satellite News Channel (SNC) in 1982. However, Turner bought SNC two years later and closed the only serious competition ever mounted on CNN.

Technology continued to evolve during the 1980s with smaller, lighter, and higher-quality cameras and recorders. Satellite technology permitted inexpensive distribution of program material. Additionally, the use of satellites eventually evolved into a newsgathering tool. SNG (satellite news gathering) enabled the television journalist to originate a live report from nearly anywhere in the world. As evidenced with the Persian Gulf War and the collapse of the Soviet Union, television news has become the new form of intelligence gathering and diplomacy.

Papal and presidential assassination attempts, martial laws in Poland, the unprecedented expansion of the U.S. economy, the fall of the Berlin Wall and the Iron Curtain, the Persian Gulf War, and the crumbling of the Soviet Union continued to stimulate the public appetite for broadcast journalism.

Cable made the news coverage and information even more accessible to the public. There were two all-news cable channels in the 1980s, a third was dedicated to all financial news reporting (Financial News Network), and yet another two channels provided continuous coverage of the U.S. House of Representatives and U.S. Senate (C-SPAN). Additionally, there was a full-time sports channel (ESPN).

Technological developments in graphics and animation systems made business and economic stories easier and more interesting to tell. As CBS News correspondent Ray Brady said, "Suddenly, the story on the GNP, (gross national product) can be made into a visually interesting story for television."

During this 30 years of growth, broadcast journalism benefitted from, and stimulated, growing public acceptance and eventual dependence upon television news.

THE CHANGING TACTICS OF PUBLIC RELATIONS

During this period of time, the public relations profession noticed the changes and began to react.

Through the 1970s, the major focus of public relations was on crisis management and product promotion. The major tools of the time were the press release and a working knowledge of the reporters and editors at major newspapers, wire services, and magazines to place the news story. When it came to the broadcast media and their increasing interest in business news, corporations were reactive; they had to work with the journalist doing the story. If the story was critical, as in the case of Ralph Nader's attacks on General Motors or the bailout of Chrysler Corporation, the firms had to do their best to salvage whatever they could.

In the 1980s, there was a shift in both the medium and the message. Corporations were still interested in marketing-support publicity, but an increasingly important emphasis was being put on communicating to the public the corporation's culture and its good deeds. It was no longer enough to show a profit at the end of the year. The public demanded that the successful company of the 1980s demonstrate good corporate citizenship, having in place organizational ethics and executing managerial morals that gave something back to the community. So was born the concept of image campaigns for corporations.

At the same time, corporate communicators discovered what politicians had learned in the 1960s: The broadcast media were the most effective means of communications in reaching the largest audience. Two decades after the Roper Organization started to document the shift in where the American public obtains most of its news, corporate communicators assumed a proactive stance, starting to target these media with PR messages promoting products and images.

In a *Los Angeles Times* interview in March 1983, publicist Henry C. Rogers painted a vivid picture of the way life had changed for the corporate publicist. "The P.R. person of 20 years ago worked in a dingy cubbyhole turning out press releases. Today, he or she is one of his company's most prestigious and influential corporate officers."

In the "old days," a public relations person was hired because of his media contacts and the ability to handle bad news about the company as much as for his writing skills. Management viewed the PR profession as a doer and not a thinker. The business communicator was a technician, only worried about responding to media criticism and cranking out routine press releases. Exercising the valued ability to "work the press," the publicist would cruise through media organizations, attempting to lure reporters into doing stories about clients.

The work of the corporate publicist had grown into a management function. Business communicators were serving as counselors to the highest level of management on issues ranging from how to communicate with the many stakeholders of the organization to negotiating corporate involvement with trade organizations, governments, and all elements of society.

Those "olden-day" press releases that Rogers spoke of were most-often issued in support of new products or some other marketing campaign. The corporate publicist was there to "flack" or generate "free" media time, or to get the name of an executive or corporation in the newspaper. The press release was viewed as the currency-of-the-realm in the world of public relations because the professional background of most of the PR practitioners was print. They were familiar with newspaper and magazine writing styles and were able to craft, in most cases, a well-written story that would gain some play. Journalistic standards were such that newspapers would consider a press release as just another way to fill a news hole inexpensively.

The second reason for choosing the press release was that generating newspaper stories gave the publicist a ready-made measure of effectiveness. By counting newspaper clippings, they were able to quantify how successful they were in their publicity-generating efforts and show those results to their client or manager. Stories on television and radio were too hard to count and package.

Corporations and PR agencies still issue news releases, but they are no longer the sole, or even primary, vehicle for publicity. Today's print news releases are generally issued to meet simultaneous disclosure and financial legal requirements, or to blanket secondary and community newspapers. Most practitioners do not expect their releases to run "as issued" in most publications; they view the news release as an efficient way of organizing facts and presenting them to a journalist.

While counting clips is still a major measure of effectiveness in the public relations world, it is losing favor. The greater focus of the modern practitioner is a look at the outcome, rather than the output, of public relations programs.

The Move to Broadcast Publicity

With the greater news hole on television, public relations professionals began to develop a methodology to pitch stories for their clients.

Consumer product companies and the entertainment industry were among the first to use broadcast publicity effectively by staging events, courting the producers and reporters, and providing film clips. Film clips were very expensive to produce and somewhat difficult to use at first, but, in some cases, they were the only source for specific footage which the networks and television stations wanted.

The Department of Defense and NASA were also very successful with this approach, as were auto companies (with clips previewing upcoming models) and movies companies. Former United Press International (UPI) photographer and now New York City-based publicist Don Phelan takes credit for doing the first video news release (VNR) as a film clip for the Chrysler Corporation in 1957.

Many observers believe the video news release, as we currently know it, was born when the motion picture studios began sending clips from movies to television stations on video-cassettes and encouraging reporters to do stories and reviews. Gail Cottman, the owner and president of National Satellite Service in Los Angeles, is considered by many as the mother of the video news release methodology. Cottman started her career by sending out the movie clips for a major motion picture studio before starting her own agency.

Business-to-business and heavy industrial enterprises entered the field by developing VNRs and B-roll packages for use on specialized business shows, and publicists provided everything from VNRs and B-roll to live, two-way interactive interviews via satellite.

An area of growth in broadcast media relations is the use of the satellite media tour (SMT). Through the use of satellite news gathering techniques, publicists are now able to arrange a live interactive interview with broadcast journalists around the U.S. or the world.

Understanding the video shorthand, syntax, and grammar of ENG (electronic news gathering), former CBS News cameraman Del Hall and his wife Ginger demonstrate a close-up shot of a computer for a video news release. As a former broadcast journalist, Hall's Chicago-based company, Del Hall Video, Inc., is an excellent example of the type of talent needed to produce VNRs, B-roll packages, and satellite media tours that get picked up by television stations. Looking on are graduate students from Northwestern University's Corporate Public Relations program.

The way an SMT works is similar to what is seen every night on ABC's "Nightline" program. The subject of the interview sits before a television camera in one location. That image is beamed up to a popular satellite used by broadcast journalists. Journalists wishing to interview the subject arrange to telephone the publicist and have their questions fed into the interviewee's ear piece. The television station downlinks the interview from the satellite and, through the use of a "chroma key" screen, can then put the reporter and subject of the interview together. When recorded to tape, the process looks as if the interview had taken place one-on-one.

In an all-out broadcast media relations campaign, an organization can preproduce a video news release and B-roll and feed that ahead of the satellite interview. An excellent example of this type of integrated package was seen over a recent Labor Day weekend when Volkswagen of America produced both a video news release and an SMT for Mothers Against Drunk Driving. The story had major pick-ups in all top-10 markets in the United States.

Seaworld in San Antonio took the concept of the satellite and immediacy even a step further. The Texas-based amusement park uplinked via satellite the live birth of a killer whale. That feed lasted for many hours and was available to every commercial broadcast newsroom in North America. Seaworld also provided a free satellite uplink for visiting reporters to broadcast reports to home stations.

Disney uses similar techniques, but adds another wrinkle to VNRs. They will customize tapes and satellite feeds for individual markets unable to send a reporter to an event.

Good media training is a key element of successful broadcast media relations. Russ Tornabene, Midwest director for the Executive Television Workshop, Inc., a division of Rowan & Blewett, Inc., leads a media training workshop for young public relations professionals. Broadcast reporters spend years practicing their on-air skills. PR professionals and corporate executives should invest at least a day in media training so that they are prepared to speak effectively on the air.

Technology in Action

The use of VNRs is no longer limited to positive and proactive stories. When a bad or negative story breaks, television news is going to cover the event, and the corporation that is prepared to supply the broadcast journalist with material will have its side of the story represented.

Johnson & Johnson in 1982 used VNRs and satellite technology to explain to the public, its employees, and the investment community what was happening when tainted Tylenol killed several people in Chicago. Drexel Burnham Lambert issued its response to a federal indictment via a VNR soundbite. When Continental Airlines filed for Chapter 11 protection, it made available via satellite both soundbites and B-roll to all U.S. television newsrooms.

THE FUTURE:
SURFING THE AIRWAVES AND CYBERSPACE

If you work in public relations, you should watch lots of television and listen to lots of radio. And not just "Masterpiece Theatre" and "All Things Considered."

You should surf the channels looking at MTV, C-SPAN, Cable News Network, and the Home Shopping Network. Pay careful attention to how the newscasts are stacked and how the visuals are used to communicate. On radio, listen to all formats of music and talk

BROADCAST MEDIA RELATIONS SUGGESTIONS

The most effective way to reach broadcast journalists is to use a three-pronged approach:

1. Personal contact (known as special placement). This approach attempts to lure a journalist into doing a story. It seeks the reporter's personal involvement and, often, an interview. When done, such stories are better and longer than those triggered in other ways. Special placement is usually used to reach major markets and networks with the most important stories.

2. Distribution of fact sheets and news releases with B-roll and a soundbite package. This gives stations and networks maximum flexibility without the need for them to commit a camera crew and reporter. These materials can be produced in-house and are most effective in reaching middle markets.

3. Video news releases. VNRs are the broadcast equivalent of the press (as opposed to news) release. They mimic the style of a television news story. Sent via cassette or satellite, they are preproduced and tightly edited, with a narration track. Stations often will strip narration away and use them as B-roll and soundbites, or renarrate.

   Smaller market stations will run a story that interests them as is. The advantage of a VNR package to the publicist is that the script and background information is never lost from video since they are in sync. The disadvantage to the station is that it does not have as much flexibility in cutting and editing as it does with a B-roll package.

Just as the quality and likelihood of a press release being used profited from the experience of the writer, B-roll and VNR production benefit from experienced video camera crews, writers, and editors familiar with broadcast journalism's video shorthand. Such products are not slick or fancy; they are short, simple, and easy to edit and drop into a newscast.

stations. Listen to the callers and what they say. Pay careful attention to what topics stimulate the greatest number of calls and the strongest emotions. Leverage this knowledge to the benefit of your publicity programs.

Finally, become familiar with the on-line services such as CompuServe and America On-Line. Business alliances are already forged that will meld these two media together. NBC's partnership with Microsoft in MSNBC is a good example of where broadcast media relations is making its way to the new media of the Internet. Be prepared to use your skills as a broadcast media relations professional to put your messages effectively online.

The future is already here. The winners will be those who are able to see it and use the technology effectively.

THE VNRs THAT STOPPED A CRISIS: THE PEPSI HOAX

On Thursday, June 10, 1993, an 82-year-old man called the newsroom of a Seattle television station and reported that he had found a hypodermic syringe in a can of Diet Pepsi. The next four days would see this one claim of product tampering spread to nearly every state in the Union and launch a major attack on the 95-year-old trademark of the Pepsi-Cola company.

The quick and skillful use of broadcast media relations by Pepsi brought to an end this product-tampering hoax in near-record time. For when the public saw on the news the high-speed manufacturing process, the complex distribution patterns from nearly 400 bottling plants, and, finally, an actual case of tampering caught on videotape, the hoax died a quick death.

From the beginning, Pepsi's local bottler in Seattle treated the report as a case of product tampering. Yet, no syringes like those used for insulin injections are used in any aspect of Pepsi's manufacturing or quality control process. Within a dozen hours, there were additional reports of syringes found in cans of Diet Pepsi in three other states and Guam. Pepsi and the Food and Drug Administration (FDA) issued a series of advisories and suggested that consumers pour their Diet Pepsi into a glass before drinking.

By Monday, June 14, the Pepsi product-tampering hoax was the lead story on every network newscast in the U.S. The number of reports of contaminated Diet Pepsi cans was approaching 60, and these reports were scattered across 23 states. Remembering the 1982 incident with the tampering of Tylenol, Pepsi first conducted an exhaustive self-examination. "We had to be absolutely sure that this could not possibly have happened in our plants," said Rebecca Maderia, vice president of public affairs for Pepsi-Cola North America and head of the crisis response team.

Pepsi first had to answer three critical questions: First, was there a health risk? Late on Monday, June 14, the FDA reported that the first two syringes found carried no risk of infection. Second, Pepsi needed to make sure its manufacturing process was secure from infiltration. FDA inspectors checked the high-speed manufacturing lines at the various plants. Employee records were checked, shipping and customer inventories were reviewed. The result was that whatever was turning up in Diet Pepsi cans had been placed there after opening.

Finally, was nationwide tampering occurring? As more cases surfaced across the country, sabotage was ruled out. The cans in question were produced, in some cases, six months apart from each other, and in widely different locations. "For so many complaints to turn up in so many different circumstances was simply illogical," said Craig Weatherup, president and CEO of Pepsi-Cola North America.

Armed with this information, Pepsi launched a full-court public relations blitz on Tuesday, June 15. This included a video news release (VNR) that quoted CEO Weatherup saying, "A can is the most tamper-proof packaging in the food supply. We are 99.99 percent certain that this didn't happen in Pepsi's plant." Weatherup also did an extensive number of satellite media tours and appeared on every broadcast network that day. All told, Pepsi public relations and public affairs specialists conducted more than 2,000 interviews in two days.

The Pepsi crisis team also crafted a second video news release that had powerful, overwhelming images communicating just how safe the canning process is. The VNR was distributed on Tuesday afternoon, June 15, by Medialink. Within 48 hours, it was estimated that more than 296 million viewers had seen the Diet Pepsi cans whizzing by on the production line at 1,200 per minute.

On that same Tuesday, the FDA announced the first arrest in the product-tampering hoax. On Wednesday, June 16, the news coverage was moving to the "second day" angle to advance the story. The general news hook was how the Pepsi-Cola company was trying to protect its image. Criticism surfaced as to why Pepsi was not recalling its products. Weatherup conducted a second round of satellite media tours explaining the company's decision.

On Thursday, June 17, Pepsi issued a third VNR. This one included footage taken by a security surveillance camera in a Colorado convenience store that showed a woman open a can of Diet Pepsi, put a syringe in it, ask for a cup, and pour the soda and syringe out. The total time on the video to pull off the hoax is under a minute.

On that same day, Dr. David Kessler, head of the FDA, helped put an end to the hoax by declaring the notion of a nationwide tampering as unfounded. On the same day, a consumer survey taken by Pepsi found that 94 percent felt the company was handling the issue in a responsible manner.

While the crisis had a successful and positive resolution, it did have an economic impact on Pepsi. From a retail perspective, the product-tampering hoax broke at the worst possible time. The week of June 14 is when soft drink distributors deliver their product for the biggest sales weekend of the year, the Fourth of July. Some local bottlers reported the product being pulled off shelves. Pepsi estimates that it lost about $25 million because of the crisis. Yet, one week after the hoax was put to bed, Pepsi issued a $1-off manufacturer's coupon and reported a spike of almost 800,000 more cases of Diet Pepsi sold than normal.

## CHAPTER 6

Integrated Marketing Public Relations

Thomas L. Harris, APR
Managing Partner
Thomas L. Harris & Company

STRATEGIC CONCEPTS

The use of public relations to support marketing has grown rapidly in recent years. While the tools of marketing public relations (MPR) have become more sophisticated and its acceptance as an effective element of marketing more widespread, the practice is in itself not new.

The following is a good working definition of marketing public relations taken from my book, *Marketer's Guide to Public Relations* (New York: Wiley, 1991):

> Marketing public relations is the process of planning, executing, and evaluating programs that encourage purchase and consumer satisfaction through credible communication of information and impressions that identify companies and their products with the needs, wants, concerns, and interests of consumers.

Public relations historian Scott Cutlip, dean emeritus of journalism at the University of Georgia, points out that publicity as a part of marketing began as early as 1899 when the N.W. Ayer Advertising Agency helped the National Biscuit Company take its Uneeda Biscuits out of the cracker barrel and put them in a sanitary package with a distinctive brand name and trademark. The use of publicity to support this marketing milestone was so effective that Ayer set up its own publicity department in 1919.

Edward Bernays, the father of public relations, applied his skills to help Procter & Gamble sell Ivory soap by creating a fad for soap carving among American schoolchildren. He also created one of the greatest publicity coups of the century when he staged the "Golden Jubilee of Light" in celebration of the 50th anniversary of the electric lightbulb for his client, General Electric.

The application of public relations to marketing in the post-World War II era was so pervasive that articles on the subject began to appear in the business press in the 1950s and 1960s.

Burson-Marsteller, the world's largest public relations firm, specialized in industrial marketing public relations in its early days, while firms like Ruder & Finn and Daniel J. Edelman Associate (now Edelman Public Relations Worldwide) pioneered in marketing public relations for consumer products. Edelman originated the media tour by sending sets of Toni Twins to cities through Europe and the United States to support the now-classic "Which Twin Has the Toni?" advertising campaign, which challenged consumers to identify the twin that had a Toni home permanent. Charles Lubin, founder of the Kitchens of Sara Lee, another Edelman client dating to the 1950s, said that public relations was worth 100 times the cost of advertising in telling the company's quality baked goods story to both the consumer and the grocery trade.

Marketing Public Relations Today

The dramatic growth of marketing public relations is documented by a 1993 telephone survey conducted by *The Marketing Report*. The survey revealed that more than one-third of 243 marketing executives at consumer, industrial, and service companies were spending more than 20 percent of their entire annual marketing budgets on public relations.

Today, it has been estimated that marketing public relations may account for more than 70 percent of the billings of all public relations counseling firms. This chapter is primarily concerned with the uses of public relations in marketing consumer products. But it should be emphasized that public relations has become increasingly important in marketing business-to-business products. High technology has developed into a distinct specialty within marketing public relations. Other fast-growing areas of marketing public relations are the medical and healthcare fields.

In addition to its proactive role in marketing products, people, and institutions, public relations also plays a critical role in defending products at risk. This role has been accentuated by the contentious and litigious nature of contemporary society.

There is an inextricable link between the reputation of the company and the success of its products in the marketplace.

In an address to the American Association of Advertising Agencies (AAAA), Timm Crull, president-CEO of Nestlé USA, warned the country's advertising leaders that they must change their broadcast mindset; get closer to their clients' marketing, public relations, and overall communications goals; and be prepared to present clients with campaigns that take full advantage of the specialized marketing services available to them today.

Marketing Public Relations in Integrated Marketing Communications

The role of public relations in marketing has been intensified by the advent of integrated marketing communications (IMC). IMC has become the dominant marketing concept of the 1990s.

The Medill School of Journalism of Northwestern University, which now offers a master's degree program in integrated marketing communications, defines IMC as "the process of managing all sources of information about a product which behaviorally moves the customer toward a sale and maintains customer loyalty."

The process is based on the benefits of synergy and the assumption that the whole is greater than the sum of the parts. Thomas Duncan, director of the integrated marketing communications graduate program at the University of Colorado, says:

> When all brand and corporate messages are strategically coordinated, the effect is greater than when advertising, sales promotion, marketing PR, packaging, etc., are planned and executed independently, with each area competing for budgets and power and, in some cases, sending out conflicting messages.

The move to IMC has been accelerated by the need for companies to do a more effective, more cost-efficient job than ever before to survive in the increasingly competitive worldwide marketplace. The job of communicating more effectively to consumers and to those that influence them has become more difficult because of a number of marketplace factors: the difficulty of breaking through a climate of consumer resistance and indifference; the increase of commercial clutter; the splintering of the mass market; the proliferation of television channels; the declining efficiency of network advertising; and the impact of VCRs, video games, computers, and other lifestyle activities competing for consumer time and attention.

In 1991, the AAAA and its counterpart client organization, the Association of National Advertisers, commissioned Northwestern University to conduct a survey on the status of integrated marketing communications. Results showed the large majority (70 percent to 80 percent) of top management, marketing, advertising, and sales executives of large consumer products companies support the concept of integration and believe it would increase the effect and impact of their marketing communications programs.

The report of a task force of academics and working professionals from the fields of advertising, public relations, promotion, and direct marketing points out that mass-thinking "audiences" and "publics" no longer exist, necessitating new ways to segment and define message recipients and respondents. The increase in audience fragmentation is especially evident when looking at the global marketplace.

Many of the markets outside of the United States have been making greater use of integrated communications than have many U.S. companies. That is because clients are smaller and lack the budgets necessary to hire a variety of specialized communications agencies. In her book *Advertising Worldwide*, Marieke de Mooij, managing director of BBDO College Europe and educational secretary of the International Advertising Association, writes:

> With the use of a greater variety of communications instruments, there is a greater need to integrate the planning and executions thematically. Brand image is built up through a number of channels, and unanimity and one voice are required. It stands to reason that planning and coordinating many individual contacts with the brand increases the likelihood of creating the desired impression.

While some smaller U.S. clients want their advertising agencies to provide all promotional services, marketing executives of the larger consumer products companies participating in the Northwestern study said they believe that the job of integration is too big and important to be delegated to their ad agencies. They believe that they themselves must take responsibility for the coordination of their integrated marketing programs. Further, they reported that they don't want a single source for advertising, direct marketing, sales promotion, and public relations. While 6 of the 10 largest public relations firms in the U.S. are advertising agency-owned, they operate autonomously and primarily serve their own clients rather than advertising clients.

Marketing's New Emphasis: Relationship Building

The changing focus of marketing is expressed by Philip Kotler, S. C. Johnson Distinguished Professor of International Marketing at Northwestern University's J. L. Kellogg Graduate School of Management and author of the leading marketing textbook used throughout the world. Kotler now believes that marketing's first task is to retain satisfied customers, not just to produce new customers. He says:

Companies are shifting focus from creating a sale to creating a lifetime customer. They are beginning to view the customer as an asset; to retain this asset, companies are starting to shift their thinking from transaction-based marketing to relationship-based marketing.

In their 1992 book, *Integrated Marketing Communications* (Chicago: NTC Business Books) the first on the subject of integrated marketing communications, Northwestern University's Donald Schultz and Stanley Tannenbaum, and Robert Lauterborn of the University of North Carolina at Chapel Hill, state:

> You cannot depend on the product alone to build consumer confidence. It's the rapport, the empathy, the dialogue, the relationship, the communication you establish with the consumer that makes the difference. These separate you from the pack.

Professor Sandra Moriarty of the University of Colorado says, "The brain does not distinguish an advertising message from a PR message. Instead, it gathers information from an untold number of contact points and assimilates it into one picture." She concludes that people automatically integrate messages in their daily lives to arrive at an image or opinion.

Schultz, Tannenbaum, and Lauterborn believe integrated marketing communications makes relationship marketing possible: "In the 1990s, media systems have changed so dramatically that two-way systems are required. There is a relationship between the buyer and seller that normally results from interchanges and exchanges of information of mutual value."

At the heart of IMC programs is knowing consumers and utilizing modern technology to identify them not as "faceless, unknown groups of people," but as "human beings with names, addresses, purchase histories, likes and dislikes, shopping patterns, families and friends, and all the other things that help us to understand and, most of all, measure the impact or effect of various communications programs," Donald Schultz declares.

Turning tables on traditional marketing, Schultz says that tracking message delivery should always be done from the customer's view, "not what we think we delivered but what the customers or prospects believe they received."

Translated to the parlance of public relations, that means we must talk to people, not "publics," and must measure "outcomes," not "outputs."

What Marketing Public Relations Brings to IMC

The increasing acceptance of IMC has assured PR a place at the marketing table. Recent surveys of marketing executives have found not only the near-universal acceptance of the integrated marketing concept, but also the almost unanimous agreement that public relations plays an integral role in the process.

In his introduction to *The Marketer's Guide to Public Relations*, Philip Kotler states:

> Marketers are finding it increasingly difficult to reach the minds and hearts of target consumers. As mass marketing and even target advertising lose some of their cost-effectiveness, message senders are driven to other media. They discover or rediscover the power of news, events, community programs, and other powerful communications modalities. Marketing public relations represents an opportunity for companies to regain a share of voice in a message-satiated society. It not only delivers a strong share of voice to deliver share of mind; it delivers a better, more effective voice in many cases.

Public relations is winning a more prominent role in integrated marketing because it possesses a priceless ingredient essential to every effective marketing program—its ability to lend credibility to the product message. Years ago, Professor Theodore Levitt of Harvard pointed out the distinction between the public relations message and the advertising message. He labeled public relations "the credible source," pointing out that "when a message is delivered by an objective third party, such as a journalist or broadcaster, the message is delivered more persuasively."

This is particularly important because today's increasingly skeptical consumers are finding advertising messages less credible. According to a 1991 survey conducted by Video Storyboard Tests, "seven out of 10 respondents said they believe few, if any, of the ads they see on TV or in print."

A recent Yankelovich Clancey Shulman study reveals that today's consumer prefers more information about a product, rather than a sales pitch.

The growing number of consumers that resent or reject overt selling messages can be reached through public relations messages. This is especially true of so-called "Generation X" consumers who, research tells us, want to be told—not sold.

The importance of the credibility factor is underscored by a study conducted in 1993 by Golin/Harris Communications. Two-thirds of the marketing directors and brand managers surveyed said they believe that public relations is as important as or more important than advertising in building brand *awareness*. But four-fifths believe it is more important than advertising in building brand *credibility*.

Silicon Valley marketing guru Regis McKenna says the press plays a particularly important role in high-tech industries.

In his influential book, *Relationship Marketing* (San Francisco: Addison Wesley, 1991), he writes, "The press can help reinforce and broaden the credibility the product and company have already gained. It can educate and can ease fears by making customers feel secure about new technologies. In new and fast-growing industries, journalists can play the role of evangelists."

McKenna adds "Advertising can perform many of the same functions but information coming from the press is usually more credible. Articles in the media are perceived as being more objective than advertisements. If a company can win favorable press coverage, its message is more likely to be absorbed and believed."

The legendary adman David Ogilvy wrote in his book, *Ogilvy on Advertising* (New York: Crown, 1983):

> Roughly six times as many people read the average article as read the average advertisement. Very few ads are read by more than 1 reader in 20. I conclude that editors communicate better than admen.

TACTICS: HOW MPR ADDS VALUE TO IMC PROGRAMS

Marketers today recognize the need to speak with one voice, not only to consumers but also to all those more finely segmented "publics" that influence their purchase decisions. They are discovering a multiplicity of strategic uses of public relations in integrated programs, which include:

1. To build marketplace excitement before advertising breaks .
2. To drive the communications program when there is no advertising.
3. To make advertising news when there is no product news.
4. To bring advertising to life.
5. To extend promotion programs.

6. To build personal relationships with customers.

7. To influence the influentials.

8. To communicate new product benefits.

9. To demonstrate a company's social responsibility and build consumer trust.

10. To defend products at risk and give consumers permission to buy.

1. Building Marketplace Excitement before Advertising Breaks. Today, most marketers recognize that the announcement of a new product offers a unique opportunity for obtaining publicity and for dramatizing the product.

When introducing a new product, timing is the name of the game. Most marketers also understand that the news about the new product must precede the advertising break. Once the advertising is seen by the consumer, the product is no longer news to the media. For example, when the Food and Drug Administration approved an over-the-counter dosage of ibuprofen, Advil was ready with a publicity and marketing blitz, capturing the dominant share of the market. Nuprin, an identical product that did not use this tactic, has never caught up.

A successful PR introduction can have a dramatic impact on sales.

Cabbage Patch Kids dolls achieved sales of $600 million as the result of a sophisticated public relations effort that saw the dolls featured on every TV station and in every major magazine and newspaper in the country. It was not until sales slowed that the products were first advertised.

Hyde Athletic Industries doubled its sales, depleting inventories and causing retailing shortages, when *Consumer Reports* magazine awarded its Saucony Jazz 3000 shoes the top rating in the highly competitive running shoe market. *The New York Times* credited the company's success to "the power of the press."

Before its first ads broke, Goodyear Tire & Rubber Co. sold 150,000 new Aquatred tires as a result of an introductory PR campaign.

Savvy marketers use MPR effectively to build anticipation for the product long before it is available to the public. Hollywood is the past master of the art. In the movie business, there must be immediate demand for the product on release. If audiences don't fill theaters on that first weekend, the film dies an instant death.

> **A successful PR introduction can have a dramatic impact on sales.**

A masterful public relations campaign was created to build tremendous excitement about *Jurassic Park*. Many more than 1,000 stories about the film appeared in print and broadcast media a month before the premier, making it a must-see event and eventually the most successful movie ever produced.

The public sector adapted the tools and techniques of Hollywood when the U.S. Postal Service issued the Elvis Presley postage stamp. Americans voted for the Elvis of their choice: the youthful rebel or the Las Vegas superstar. The announcement of the contest, the announcement of the winner, and the festivities accompanying the issuance of the stamp dominated the nation's news for months.

Marketing public relations put the Ford Mustang and the man behind the car, a then-unknown automotive executive named Lee Iacocca, on the map. In his biography, the most successful business book every written, Iacocca described the key role that public relations played in launching the Mustang in 1964. It was an effort that culminated in what he describes as "an astounding publicity coup for a new commercial project"—the simultaneous appearance of the man and the car on the covers of *Time* and *Newsweek*.

208701-209   OCTOBER 3 RELEASE   134885-189   OCTOBER 3 RELEASE

1994 FORD MUSTANG GT   **1964 1/2 FORD MUSTANG**

The restyled 1994 Ford Mustang GT combines the best of the past,   The 1964 1/2 Ford Mustang, introduced April 17, 1964 at the New York
including pony badges and three-bar taillamps, with state-of-the-art   World's Fair, was equipped with a 170-cubic-inch, six-cylinder engine,
technology. The 5.0-liter V-8 GT offers improved power steering and   three-speed, floor-mounted manual transmission and seating for four.
4-wheel disc brakes for better ride and handling. It is available as a   Dealers had more than 22,000 orders on the first day. The car was priced
convertible or a coupe and with manual or automatic transmission.   at $2368.

FORD DIVISION PUBLIC AFFAIRS   FORD DIVISION PUBLIC AFFAIRS
(313) 446-7730   (313) 446-7730

Ford evoked nostalgia for the original Mustang when it introduced its restyled 1994 Mustang in celebration of
the car's 30th anniversary.

By the time Ford celebrated the 30th birthday of the Mustang in 1993, the company
had sold an amazing 6.1 million cars. The major Mustang celebrations not only paid tribute
to the past, but turned the spotlight on the redesigned state-of-the-art 1994 Mustang, which
was named *Motor Trend*'s "car of the year" before it went on sale. Hundreds of vintage
Mustangs were displayed at Knott's Berry Farm in California, the Indianapolis Motor
Speedway, and the Charlotte (N.C.) Motor Speedway. Some 3,000 Mustang owners from
20 countries made their way to Charlotte, including President Bill Clinton. President Clinton
was surprised when his 1967 blue-gray Mustang convertible was transported from an
Arkansas museum to Charlotte for a presidential spin around the track. "I never dreamed
I'd be invited here to this event and given a chance to drive my car," the president exclaimed.
"Nobody let's me drive anymore."

In 1989, Lee Iacocca, then chairman of Chrysler, introduced the Dodge Viper, a sports
car patterned after the roadsters of the 1960s as a concept car to buffs at the North American
International Car Show. Two years later, he personally unveiled the Viper for the press and
the public in a six-city road show called "Chrysler in the 1990s." The next step was to put
the media—television reporters and auto editors in key markets—in the driver's seat for a
test drive, eliciting enthusiastic endorsements.

The New York Times said, "Rarely has any car been so widely anticipated or so
widely ballyhooed." The three-year preemptive publicity blitz generated more than 3,000

calls and letters from interested consumers. Dodge sold the 3,000 Vipers built in 1993, despite the hefty $50,000 price tag and the absence of advertising.

Again, Chrysler made international news when it introduced the Dodge/Plymouth Neon at the Frankfurt International Automobile Show. The site emphasized Chrysler's determination to make a car for the global marketplace, and the event marked the first time an American carmaker had unveiled a car outside of the United States. Simultaneous media events were held in eight U.S. cities with interactive satellite feeds from Frankfurt. A delightful advertising campaign emphasized Neon's friendly, smiling face in a word "Hi!" The public relations campaign also emphasized the car's personality and associated Neon with the music, politics, clothes, and lifestyles of the target 18- to 29-year-old market. Borrowing a page from high-technology PR, Chrysler won early support of key auto trade and business media by inviting them to participate in backgrounders on the car during its preproduction stages. Two hundred international and domestic reporters were chosen to ride and drive the Neon in the Austin, Texas, area. To immerse them in the "Generation X" milieu, reporters were outfitted with Doc Martens shoes, provided with lava lamps, and even given in-line skating lessons. Neon was an immediate sales success with the target market.

No matter how good the publicity, the product must be able to live up to its press notices.

Apple Computer pulled out all the PR stops in introducing the Newton Message Pad. The product was announced in grandiose fashion at a press conference at the 1992 Consumer Electronics Show before a prototype even existed and a year before consumers could get their hands on Newton.

When Newton was ready to go to market, the Apple PR team orchestrated a dramatic demonstration on ABC's "Good Morning America." The first faxed Newton message was transmitted from the network's New York headquarters to weatherman Spencer Christian, who was covering the great flood of 1993 in Des Moines, Iowa.

No matter how good the publicity, the product must be able to live up to its press notices.

The trouble with Newton was that it had a problem recognizing an individual's handwriting, a problem widely noted in the business press. The advanced publicity for Newton was so effective that it raised expectations that the product was unable to deliver.

Another product that was a great publicity success but that also faced problems in the marketplace was McDonald's reduced-fat hamburger, McLean Deluxe. When it was introduced, the McLean story was big news on the evening and morning network news shows. *The New York Times* ran a front-page story headlined "Leaner Hamburger Undergoes Trial by Taste," including eight pictures of people enjoying the new sandwich, all of whom pronounced the McLean a winner.

The media relations blitz was so successful that McDonald's achieved four-week awareness levels in two weeks from PR alone. However, the public—which had expressed interest in a low-fat hamburger—continued to choose McDonald's original burgers, and the McLean began to disappear from the menu.

2. Driving Marketing in the Absence of Advertising. When Binney & Smith, makers of Crayola crayons, announced the addition of eight child-tested, bold, bright colors to replace some of the old colors, the company had no funds available for advertising and decided to rely on public relations. The PR program, which included an event enshrining the old colors in the Crayola Hall of Fame, attracted unanticipated negative national attention in print and broadcast media. Unexpectedly, protest groups formed to challenge the disappearance of their favorite colors. The crayon maker called in the press to announce the return of the "extinct" eight in a special Collector's Edition.

To bring attention to 16 new colors being introduced in its new 96-crayon box, the company sponsored a national contest to determine the new crayons' names. From two million names submitted, the company selected 16 colors like Tickle Me Pink, Granny Smith Apple, Purple Mountain's Majesty, Robin's Egg Blue and Macaroni and Cheese. The winners were announced at a press event at Hollywood's Universal City on the company's 90th birthday, the same day the 96-color box went on sale. The company conducted a poll to determine the top crayon colors of all time among celebrities such as "Peanuts" cartoon creator Charles Schulz, children's television program host Mister Rogers, actress Whoppi Goldberg, and comedian Mike Myers. Crayola birthday-year sales rose 12 percent and the company sold $23 million worth of the new 96-color boxes.

To mark the 50th birthday of its famous advertising character, Miss Chiquita, Chiquita Brands did not advertise. The company used public relations to celebrate the character and advertising jingle from its 1940s radio and television commercials. The search to find Miss Chiquita 1994 culminated in public auditions where hopefuls performed wearing 10-pound bowls of fruit on their heads in front of judges and television cameras from all major networks and local stations. The winner then toured major markets to meet media, make store appearances, and hand out bananas.

3. Making Advertising News. Phil Dusenberry, chairman of BBDO, says: "When you get this type of publicity, it's like somebody coming along and handing you a whole pile of money you didn't have. The advertising takes on more value because the product is being mentioned in a nonadvertising context." He advises his clients: "Anytime you release a new advertising campaign, you would be wise to bring in your PR people and ask: 'Is there anything in this that can stretch it beyond our media expenditure?'"

Advertising guru Jerry Della Femina told *USA Today* that his work "doesn't stop with an ad" and that "in many ways, the PR overshadows the ads."

Since Apple's startling commercial introducing the original Macintosh during the 1984 Super Bowl, the Super Bowl has become the venue of choice for new product introductions and new campaign launches. Advertisers, who are spending close to a million dollars per 30 seconds of airtime these days, want to ensure the impact of their Super Bowl spots through a supporting teaser publicity blitz.

Advertisers like Nike, Budweiser, and McDonald's have learned how to build anticipation for the spots by providing sneak previews for the media. Typically, the video packages include outtakes from the making of the commercials and interviews with the company spokespersons and celebrities who appear in the commercials. Budweiser even provided player profiles and scouting reports for the animated bottles that played in its "Bud Bowl" commercials.

4. Bringing Advertising to Life. Some advertisers have gone a step further, by capitalizing on the popularity of their commercials by bringing them to life. Advertising "spokescharacters" like Morris the Nine Lives Cat, the Dancing California Raisins, and Kellogg's Tony the Tiger have toured major markets, appearing at high-traffic locations and participating in newsworthy events. For instance, Tony visited every major league ballpark and even conducted his own spring training camp for major league baseball mascots.

Miller Lite used public relations to extend the visibility of its "Combinations" campaign. The theme of the campaign was that a beer that can combine "great taste" and "less filling" can combine anything. Its Sumo Divers have staged live demonstrations in hundreds of bars where Miller Lite is served. The company sponsored Weiner Dog Races to celebrate one of the most popular commercials in the campaign. The first race attracted more than 2,000 entrants and 17,000 fans, breaking a Texas track's attendance record.

Kentucky Fried Chicken supported the launch of Colonel's Rotisserie Gold, a new roasted chicken product, by unleashing hundreds of Colonels in all shapes and sizes in New York before the advertising break. Sporting the traditional white suits, string ties, and goatees, these Colonel look-alikes invaded the Big Apple on motorcycles, rollerblades, open-air buses, and trolleys to deliver the new product to media and consumers. At lunchtime, they converged on Grand Central Station to lead commuters in the World's Largest KFC Chicken Dance, and later took over the bleachers at Yankee Stadium for a ball game. KFC reports it generated more than 300 million national media impressions from newspapers and audio and television reports, causing many of its restaurants to double their business.

5. Extending Sales Promotion Programs. Integrated marketing public relations can be effectively used to extend sales promotion programs as well as advertising campaigns.

When McDonald's launched a promotion in celebration of the 25th anniversary of the Big Mac, the company effectively used public relations to generate consumer excitement about the famous sandwich. The story generated more than three hours of air time, including network interviews with the McDonald's owner-operator who invented the Big Mac.

McDonald's research shows that publicity generated increased awareness of Big Mac's anniversary prior to the promotion. That awareness translated into a 13 percent increase in Big Mac sales during the three day publicity period that preceded the advertising.

Midas Muffler's Project Safe Baby established the company as the leader in child automotive safety and increased traffic in Midas shops across the country by offering certified child safety seats at wholesale cost, plus brochures and videos providing "Tips for Safer Travel with Children." As a result of extensive public relations efforts in support of the promotion, Midas distributed 54,000 car seats to target market consumers, many of them women car owners who had never been in a Midas shop. Endorsements from governors, mayors, police and fire chiefs, safety advocates, and the National Highway Traffic Safety Administration positioned Midas franchisees as heroes in their communities.

Marketing public relations was used as a cost-effective way to generate awareness for the The Purina Big Cat Survival Fund promotion, a program designed to raise awareness of and funds for keeping tigers and lions alive. Ralston Purina gave donations to the National Zoological Association and individual zoos designated for research into big cat survival. Then, for a two-month summer promotion period, consumers were given an opportunity to help their local zoos raise funds by purchasing Purina cat food products. Using celebrity spokespersons and staging local "roar-a-thon" contests at zoos in key markets, Purina achieved a publicity bonanza and, more importantly, a 12-percent increase in cat food sales during the promotional period.

6. Building Personal Relationships with Consumers. Some companies have become household names by providing consumers with helpful ideas, information, and answers through the years. By earning a reputation as the consumer's friend, they have been able to create a climate of acceptance for their products, advertising, and promotions. This concept is particularly important in IMC and in today's marketplace since it costs far less to keep a customer than to find a new one.

Midas was widely lauded for Project Safe Baby. Booklets in both English and Spanish on tips for safe travel with children were made available to parents at Midas shops.

The Butterball Turkey Talkline, a public relations initiative created a dozen years ago, has become the brand's principal marketing tool. The Talkline is promoted primarily by publicity, including live network coverage on Thanksgiving Day. Butterball generates two billion print and broadcast media impressions, and dispenses personal advice on how to prepare a turkey to 25,000 callers during the peak holiday turkey sales season. On Thanksgiving Day alone, a corps of 48 Butterball home economists handles 8,000 calls for help.

The Pillsbury Bake-Off has proven to be a superior vehicle for maintaining and building a loyal core consumer base. The grand dame of all public relations events, it has become an American institution. Pillsbury receives tens of thousands of recipes from eager bakers aspiring to the grand prize: $50,000 in cash, plus a $10,000 Sears Kenmore Appliance Kitchen Makeover. The annual event translates into purchases of countless thousands of packages of Pillsbury products used to create the contestants' very best recipes. Media coverage of the event is so universal that the Pillsbury products used in the winning recipes register huge instant sales jumps when the publicity hits.

7. Influencing the Influentials. While consumer audiences are often the targets of our efforts, MPR programs also are frequently targeted at opinion leaders who play important roles in influencing consumer attitudes and actions.

Continental Baking Company, bakers of Wonder Bread, targeted the nation's dietitians with an information program designed to counter the notion that white bread is unhealthy. The company underwrote a study that dispelled the myth that bread is fattening and even suggested that bread improves the daily diet. Four thousand members of the American Dietetic Association who attended its annual meeting in Washington, D.C. were invited by Continental to two convention events: a business session where the results of the study were to be announced, and a fun event, a "Thumbs Up" for white bread rally, at the Washington convention center. The rally was widely covered on network TV and made newspaper headlines. The message that white bread is healthy was dramatically delivered to the ADA, as the most important single group influencing American diets. Sales experienced an 8-percent increase when the research was carried by the news media.

8. Communicating New Product Benefits. One of the most effective uses of marketing public relations is to promote new product uses and newly discovered product benefits.

Arm & Hammer has sustained interest in and expanded the market for baking soda, an aged product category, by promoting and publicizing dozens of new uses for its product over the years. Among them are its use as a refrigerator deodorizer, freezer deodorizer, dentifrice, and antiperspirant.

Aspirin industry-funded studies over the past decade have found a link between the product and prevention of heart attack, stroke, and cancer. Consumers who once took aspirin only for headaches and colds now take it daily as a disease preventive.

In 1994, Ocean Spray Cranberries announced the results of a company-funded Harvard Medical School study that proves regular use of Cranberry Juice Cocktail can help protect women against urinary tract infections. The results of the study were published in *The Journal of the American Medical Association.*

When the news was widely reported in newspapers, radio, and TV, Ocean Spray's consumer hotline calls doubled and sales of Cranberry Juice Cocktail increased as much as 35 percent.

9. Demonstrating Social Responsibility and Building Consumer Trust. Marketing public relations is uniquely qualified to meld the corporate interest with the public interest. Today, more than ever before, consumers want to do business with companies that share their social concerns. Examples abound of programs designed to win support by identifying companies and brands with causes consumers care about.

Trend-spotter Faith Popcorn says, "It used to be enough to make a fairly decent product and market it, but not anymore. In the 1990s, the consumer will want to know who you are before buying what you sell." She says corporations must form relationships with their customers based on trust, and corporations that *do* good and *are* good will inspire trust. She calls it "Marketing the Corporate Soul."

When customers make purchase decisions, they are, in a very real sense, deciding to buy two things: the product and the company. People want to do business with companies they know and trust. This trust is earned by being accessible and responsive to consumers and by sponsoring activities and identifying with causes popular with consumers.

One company with soul, Ben & Jerry's Homemade ice cream has won consumer loyalty by identifying with new "consumer values" and contributing a percentage of its profits to support social and environmental causes.

Ben & Jerry's integrates social concerns into its business mission, "Doing Well by Doing Good." The company markets an ice cream bar called Peace Pops in support of an organization whose goal is to divert 1 percent of the Pentagon budget to programs that build understanding between nations. Likewise, sales of Ben & Jerry's Rainforest Crunch ice cream benefit rain forest preservation. They are convinced that consumers are most fiercely loyal when they believe both in the product and in the company behind it.

If the marketer can tie specific benefits of the product to a meaningful cause, so much the better.

Body Shop built a $50 million natural beauty care products business in this country in three years exclusively on word-of-mouth endorsements and publicity about the social and environmental causes of its founder, Anita Roddick.

First Brands Corporation's Glad Bag-a-Thon program teams Glad Wrap and Bags with Keep America Beautiful, Inc., in the nation's largest organized cleanup and recycling effort. The program has evolved from a five-city pilot in 1986 into a full-scale educational cleanup program. More than half a million people in more than 100 cities now help clean up their communities through this program, collecting millions of pounds of litter and diverting equally large amounts of recyclables from landfills. Local media have reported the positive impact of the program in their communities, increasing public awareness of the program and of the Glad brand as a corporate leader.

If the marketer can tie specific benefits of the product to a meaningful cause, so much the better.

There has been no bigger winner in earning consumer trust than McDonald's corporation. It's no coincidence.

From the beginning, founder Ray Kroc has believed that McDonald's should be committed to giving something back to the society that generates the company's profits and, specifically, investing in the local communities where it does business. He knew instinctively that good citizenship is good public relations and that good public relations is good for business.

To this day, McDonald's believes that its distinctive difference, beyond food and service, is its image and community involvement. In the fast-food industry where the public's perception of real product and service differences is becoming blurred, McDonald's believes the way people feel about the company and the trust they place there sets McDonald's apart from and above its competition.

For instance, when McDonald's announced its decision to replace the ever-present polystyrene foam clamshell packages with paper packaging several years ago, President Ed Rensi told the media, "Our customers just don't feel good about it so we're changing."

The significance of the announcement was underscored when Rensi appeared with a spokesperson for the Environmental Defense Fund, a public-interest group that had formed a joint task force with McDonald's to study the solid waste problem. By joining forces with the critics in response to public concerns, the company was widely commended by environmental groups and the media and rewarded by consumers for its pro-environmental industry leadership. McDonald's is rated No. 1 on the public's top 10 list of companies with a good reputation on environmental issues compiled by the Roper organization.

10. Defending Products at Risk. Marketing public relations builds brands. Public affairs defends brands. In today's marketplace, consumer buying decisions are increasingly impacted by public issues and by the words and actions of a host of influential new players including state, local, and federal government officials, consumer groups, activists, health-care professionals, and academics. Most issues affecting marketing are environment-related, nutrition-related, safety-related, crisis-related, or corporate behavior related. Harlan Teller, executive vice president of Burson-Marsteller, says that, when an issue gets in the way of closing a sale, marketing public relations and public affairs must work together to give consumers "permission to buy."

A single incident, the Tylenol crisis of 1982, raised the crisis consciousness of American business. The success of Johnson and Johnson in handling the crisis has become the classic example of the interaction of responsible management action, media relations, and marketing communications. By communicating openly and frequently with consumers through the news media and advertising, Tylenol survived a life-or-death crisis with its credibility, integrity, and market share intact.

Pepsi-Cola provides another textbook example of how to successfully survive a public relations crisis. As Pepsi was gearing up for its peak 1993 summer selling season, the news flashed across the nation that an 82-year-old Tacoma, Washington, man claimed he had found a syringe in a can of Diet Pepsi. News accounts of alleged tamperings began to surface across the country. The Associated Press surveyed its newspaper clients and found 50 reports of tampering in 23 states. *The Chicago Tribune* reported that "a minor panic developed, with the media leaping to legitimize the reports and, perhaps inadvertently, lending credence to the sense that something was happening on a truly national scale."

Pepsi quickly assembled its crisis management team and designated North American Division CEO Craig Weatherup as its point person. Weatherup used broadcast media to assure Pepsi drinkers the company had determined with "99.99 percent certainty" that the incidents reported could not have occurred simultaneously in Pepsi plants in such diverse locations and on production lines that fill thousands of cans in seconds. Weatherup appeared on evening newscasts and morning shows of three major networks and on CNN's "Larry King Live," PBS' "McNeil-Lehrer News Hour," and ABC's "Nightline," and was inter-viewed by other news organizations.

Pepsi's response was extraordinarily effective. The company satellited video of its high-speed production process, showing how the empty cans are turned upside down, blasted with hot water and air, inverted, filled, and sealed, all in nine-tenths of a second. The tapes were seen by more than 185 million viewers. Production photos and pictorial flow charts provided by Pepsi ran in key print media like *The New York Times* and *USA Today*. Soon the FBI and police around the country began arresting people who had falsely claimed they found needles, nails, and other objects in their drink cans. Key media credited Pepsi's intensive public relations efforts for limiting the company's losses. The company buried the hoax with ads in 200 local newspapers thanking its millions of customers for standing by the company. The headline read: "Pepsi is pleased to announce . . . nothing."

THE FUTURE OF MARKETING PUBLIC RELATIONS

Media advertising was the dominant marketing communications method until the 1990s. Today, more than 65 percent of all marketing expenditures in the United States go to sales promotion, database marketing, trade promotions, special events, sponsorships, and public relations. The total advertising budgets of the past are giving way to more targeted, more diverse ways to sell goods and services, maintain consumer confidence, and build brand loyalty. More than ever, this will require a custom mix of advertising and sales promotion and direct marketing and marketing public relations.

Public relations consultant Mitchell Kozikowski says that, where ad agencies formerly set the strategies and the other disciplines created compatible programs to reach a target audience, under integrated marketing communications the ad budget is not a given. IMC requires collaboration by the key disciplines on strategy and use of the best combination of communications disciplines to build relationships with consumers.

Integrated marketing public relations is positioned to play an even greater role in marketing because:

It is a discipline that has expertise in audience segmentation.

It uses two-way communication that listens to and communicates with these publics to gain their understanding and support. The new IMC relies on dialogue with and feedback from consumers.

It is a cost-effective way to gain positive awareness and create a favorable climate for sales.

It has the power to enhance the sales message with the third-party endorsement of powerful influencers, including the media, who have no visible commercial ax to grind.

It is versatile and can apply a wide spectrum of awareness-generating tactics (see Figure 6–1) that reach target markets. The marketing public relations programs cited in this chapter alone employ such diverse tactics as product anniversaries, contests, community involvement, celebrity endorsements, fan clubs, festivals, funded research, hotlines, junkets, media events, media tours, polls, publicity stunts, public education programs, road shows, sampling, seminars, television demonstrations, and video news releases.

It can reach the consumer directly through a variety of nonmedia tools and tactics ranging from personal contacts such as speeches, seminars, and symposiums to various uses of technology like teleconferences, telemarketing, informational videos, computer discs, and on-line messaging.

It can lead the company to gain a competitive advantage by supporting causes.

It can help marketers identify societal issues that can impact the marketplace for their companies' products.

It can influence key marketing decisions in the public interest, such as the repackaging of McDonald's hamburgers and the decision of Star Kist tuna to market "dolphin free" tuna.

It can help marketers avoid pitfalls that might lead to consumer backlash.

And it can restore consumer confidence in product safety and efficacy.

Integration offers public relations a greater opportunity to influence not only what companies say about their products and how they say it, but what they do and how they do it.

F I G U R E 6–1

A–Z List of Marketing Public Relations

Awards	Newsletters
Books	Official endorsements
Contests, competitions, and created events	Product placement
	PSAs
Demonstrations	Questionnaires
Exhibits	Radio trade-for-mention contests
Expert columns	Road shows
Fan clubs	Sampling
Festivals	Symbols
Grand openings	Tours
Hot lines	Underwriting
Interviews	Vehicles
Junkets	VNRs
Key issues	Weeklies
Luncheons	Youth programs
Meetings	Zone programs
Museums	

Source: Thomas L. Harris, *The Marketing Guide to Public Relations* (New York: John Wiley and Sons, 1993).

## CHAPTER 7

Investor Relations for Shareholder Value

Nancy A. Hobor, Ph.D.
Vice President, Communications and Investor Relations
Morton International

A STRATEGIC APPROACH

Imagine: During 1993, investors poured an average of $500 million into stocks or equity funds in the United States *every business day*. And the pace has continued with the stock market hitting new highs in 1996. Additionally, bonds or fixed-income funds received more than $400 million daily in 1993, although bond fund investors have been more cautious since then. The total number of investment decisions—whether to buy or hold or sell, and what—is as staggering as the money invested.

To make a decision on which stock or bond to buy, investors need information. Many did some research before investing, and, as long as they are shareholders, most will require ongoing news and information.

That's where the investor relations function steps in. A working definition of the investor relations professional is one who brokers information between the investing community (audience) and publicly traded corporations.

The number of people involved in the investment process is huge. More than 47 million Americans own stocks outright, with an average portfolio worth about $6,000. Many who do not own individual stocks—and some who do—also have invested in the 17,000 money management firms which have investments totaling more than $2 trillion. And that's just the U.S. investment community.

On the other side of the communications process are some 34,000 publicly held companies headquartered in the United States.

Looking only at the United States today is myopic, however, for the investment industry knows no national boundaries. Corporations are available around the world as information and money move across borders at electronic speed. Investors are equally widespread and increasingly numerous.

The United Kingdom is the largest fund manager in Europe, with approximately $1.6 trillion of total assets under management, 20 to 30 percent invested in non-British firms. The Swiss, Germans, Scandinavians, Dutch, and French also have money management firms investing wherever the opportunity to make money exists. And the largest stock market in the world is in Japan, although most of the stocks traded on it are Japanese companies.

Sophisticated investors seek opportunities all around the globe. Some funds invest only in Asian companies, or South American and European companies—even African companies. A survey done in 1994 found most major U.S. financial institutions, including banks, insurance companies, and mutual funds, expected to increase their investments in Europe, Latin America, and Asian markets, areas where they perceived the best opportunities.

The Audiences of Investor Relations

To practice investor relations, a communicator needs thorough knowledge of the global investment community, including the important intermediaries between individual or institutional investors and companies: buy- and sell-side financial analysts, stockbrokers or registered representatives, and reporters and editors from influential financial publications.

At the same time, the communicator needs to know the messages a company must deliver to those critical audiences to inform and persuade. For the company, those messages are anchored in its strategic direction, a subject of importance to the chief executive officer and his or her key management team.

Therefore, investor relations practioners tend to become involved with discussions relating to where the company is heading and how it plans to get there. Only then can the investor relations person have the information to respond accurately to questions and, more importantly, to develop communications plans to address the reasons why investors would want to own the stock or bonds of the company.

In the United States, most publicly traded companies today have some investor relations activities that go well beyond the required filings and meetings prescribed by law. But other parts of the world are just beginning to develop investor relations functions. An example is South Africa, where an aggressive investor relations professional is trying to get investor relations courses incorporated into the curriculum of the business schools. Another professional in France teaches investor relations to finance and communications students.

Most investor relations professionals also play a key role in the integrated communications of the firm because the relevant publics or audiences aren't just investors.

Employees—even if they don't own stock in the company they work for—are aware of the financial community's opinions about their company. One important employee group, senior management, frequently has a financial interest if the compensation program includes stock options, so executives follow the price of the company's stock with intense interest.

Customers, too, are influenced by what the financial community is saying about the company from which they're buying. The products might be great, the service outstanding, the price right, but if the financial media is attacking the company—raising concerns about what the future may hold and quoting knowledgeable financial analysts or major institutional shareholders—customers may pause, want more guarantees, negotiate harder. They, too, are influenced by the company's reputation as defined by the investment community.

Similarly, *suppliers* watch and read about the companies they sell to, as do the *community* leaders in the areas where a business operates.

The financial health of companies as defined and discussed by the financial community has repercussions well beyond the shareholders themselves. Investor relations, therefore, becomes a critical communications task for all publicly traded companies, and practioners have a major impact on the future of the corporation. That wasn't always the case.

Trends in Investor Relations

Just as the field of communications or public relations is changing in other areas, investor relations also has evolved and grown, along with the size, power, and sophistication of the financial community.

Less than 45 years ago, the important buyers of most stocks and bonds in the United States were individuals who held almost 95 percent of the stock owned. By 1991, the majority of the shares of U.S. companies was no longer in the hands of individuals. Today, the movers and shakers are institutions.

On a daily basis, institutions represent more than half of the shares traded on the major stock exchanges. Institutions such as banks, insurance companies, pension funds, and mutual funds can influence dramatically the price of a stock and thereby the business decisions and direction of most firms.

Investor relations professionals make distinctions between two different kinds of institutional investors within the United States: passive and active. Passive institutional investors make buying and selling decisions based on computer models that try to replicate some index, such as the top 500 companies in the Standard and Poors' Composite. While these investors are not swayed in their buy or sell decisions by company fundamentals, they are increasingly important and often permanent shareholders. For example, many of the largest public pension funds, such as the California Public Employees Retirement Fund (CalPERs), are managed passively, but have become very active in making their views and importance known on corporate governance issues.

Active institutional investors make their buy and sell decisions based on information they receive from analysts, the sales force of brokerage houses, companies, newspapers and magazines, and, increasingly, electronic databases. Fund analysts and managers around the world sit surrounded by telephones and personal computers—often more than one—and feed the information they receive into their own computer models. That information comes instantly and constantly.

Want to find out what communications clutter is all about? Visit a busy financial analyst or fund manager whose office is strewn with papers and reports and who typically keeps an eye on one, or maybe two, computer screens. The computers are constantly monitoring the globe for information, including changes in stock prices. If a stock they are following goes up or down dramatically and without apparent explanation, the analyst or manager will pick up the telephone to try and find out why.

Legal and Practical Requirements

All of this activity takes place in a well-regulated world. In the United States, the Securities Acts of 1933 and 1934 created the framework for the interchange between companies and the investment community. The Securities and Exchange Commission (SEC) is the watchdog. All legally required documents (such as 10Ks, 10Qs, 8Ks, and proxy statements) are filed with the SEC in a prescribed manner. In addition, the courts have and are interpreting the provisions of the acts to ensure there is no selective disclosure of material information.

Not only does the SEC regulate companies, but also the various exchanges (New York, American, etc.) on which stocks are traded as well as the Financial Accounting Standards Board (FASB), which dictates the way financial information is reported. Thus, the investor relations professional must also understand such laws, regulations, and financial bulletins, relying heavily on the input of lawyers and accountants in communicating with the firm's shareholders or bondholders.

But fundamentally, the task of investor relations is to communicate. Read any issue of the *Financial Times*, *The Wall Street Journal*, or *Investors Daily*. Many stories, particularly those on controversial subjects, quote at least one sell-side analyst. If a reporter can't find out what is happening at the company or needs an additional industry source, he or she will call a financial analyst. A financial analyst might call a company's competitor. Not communicating takes the message out of the control of the company and puts it in the hands of others.

The company whose investor relations professional masters the communications challenges within the legal and accounting framework should see the benefit in its shareholder value. Investor relations consultants argue that an effective program reduces the risk of owning a stock and that is therefore reflected in the price of the stock.

Value: To Help Achieve Corporate Objectives

A well-planned and executed investor relations program facilitates the communications process. On one side is the investing community wanting accurate, timely information to make the best decision. On the other side is the company with facts and figures that must be marshalled logically and persuasively to convince investors that the company's future is sound. While any stock price appreciation does not directly affect corporate results (as indicated earlier, it may do so indirectly by influencing customers, suppliers, etc.), corporations are paying more attention to what investors expect.

In a recently completed study by the Financial Executives Research Foundation, the chief financial officers of more than 100 major U.S. firms confirmed the importance of communicating directly with shareholders—particularly large shareholders—and highlighted how important shareholders' opinions are when making major business decisions. In fact, shareholders' opinions came before those of customers, employees, the community, suppliers, and bondholders.

But how does a company find out what the shareholder wants? The investor relations function at most companies is charged with that task. The investor relations professional, on the daily firing line with investors, knows intimately the issues and concerns of the investor.

> **Fundamentally, what the investor wants is an understanding of the strategic direction of the firm and what competitive advantages will allow it to improve returns for the shareholder.**

Fundamentally, what the investor wants is an understanding of the strategic direction of the firm and what competitive advantages will allow it to improve returns for the shareholder. That information, usually reduced to some key numbers for entry into a computer spreadsheet, helps the investor evaluate the price of the stock today using discounted cash flow and other financial models.

At some companies, the firm's strategies are laid out in the annual report with milestones or goals to allow shareholders to measure results.

B O X 7–1

ANNUAL REPORT MESSAGES

One of the best examples of laying out goals and strategies can be found in Sara Lee's 1994 annual report. The firm has three key financial goals: "real (inflation-adjusted) growth in earnings per share of 8 percent per year over time; a return on equity of at least 20 percent (raised to 22 percent beginning in fiscal 1995); [and] a total-debt-to-total-capital ratio of no more than 40 percent over time."

The financial community now can make a judgement about whether to invest in a company with these strategies and goals versus another company (assuming the company's management team has the reputation for being able to accomplish what it sets out to do). The ease of making this comparison when the firm is willing to set forth its strategies and goals usually tilts the balance toward such a firm, all other factors being equal. The company should see the benefit in the price of its stock.

Investor Relations and Capital Formation

While a "fairly" valued stock price is the desire of all companies, that result may be only one of the benefits of an investor relations program to a corporation. Another one that most companies recognize initially, and then periodically throughout their history, is that investors help companies raise capital.

A small company with a big idea needs capital to grow. Investor relations usually starts when the company first goes public with an initial public offering (IPO) and continues later when there may be a need for more capital and the firm must go before the investment community again with a secondary offering. Effective communications with investors are critical to the price and number of shares the company will realize, especially with the secondary offering. Forward-looking companies know an effective investor relations program is a vital investment for them, for it is a key determinant of how much the company will have to pay for new capital.

But a company may not need to raise more money in a secondary offering and still want to use the stock price to raise capital. Companies on an aggressive acquisition program may use stock as a financial device to buy another company.

Investor Relations and Compensation Plans

It may not be only the owners of companies that enjoy an appreciation in the stock price. The top managements of most major U.S. companies also receive various stock incentive plans. Developed as a means of tying the interests of the shareholder and management team together, stock options, stock appreciation rights, and more recently stock ownership requirements for senior managers rely on stock price escalation for realizing considerable financial benefits. This makes the investor relations role a highly visible one within a corporation.

Another group is also very interested—the board of directors. Pushed by major institutional shareholders, the boards of directors of publicly traded firms are very active today in the oversight of their companies, especially, where results are poor, in regard to the hiring and firing of the CEO and the compensation of executives. In fact, at several companies the board is being compensated in shares of stock to ensure the members and the shareholders share the same interests.

Investor Relations and Global Strategic Planning

The investor relations function can help companies beyond raising money and providing additional compensation. It is also critical to the strategic planning process of the organization. Investors' requirements have become the test of whether a corporation's objectives or goals are appropriate. In other words, do they benefit shareholders by adding value to the investment? At the end of the plan period, will the shareholders see an improvement in their wealth as measured by the total return provided to them each year? Will earnings have increased significantly? Will dividends have been raised appropriately? Has the return on equity improved? All other goals—increasing sales, improving customer service, streamlining operations, finding acquisitions—are means to what should be the end: improving shareholder value.

In the globalization of the financial world, the accounting profession is helping investors make better decisions. Companies listed on multiple exchanges already allow access to global investors who want to buy into them more easily. Now, the financial and accounting information is becoming more homogenized. For example, one expert predicted that annual reports of companies in the United Kingdom would follow the U.S. model rather than the European Community's. Further, the expert concluded that European Community standards would converge with U.S. accounting practices. Increasingly, the financial portion of the annual reports of international companies will reflect this global trend.

Planning and Budgeting for Investor Relations

An investor relations function needs its own strategic plan to move ahead. And just as a corporation's strategic plan has measurable goals, so, too, should the investor relations function.

What those goals are depends upon the company. For example, some companies are heavily institutionally held, while at others individuals own the majority of shares. To shift that mix might be an appropriate investor relations goal. Similarly, an investor relations goal could involve the geographic distribution of the stock, with a desire to move more shares into European, Asian, or Canadian accounts.

To accomplish the goal will require a clear understanding of where and why the shares are currently held. To find out where, there are several services that monitor stock activity and report results on a regular basis, as discussed below. As to why a shareholder bought or sold, research firms using techniques similar to those of marketing research firms can help companies understand the motivations.

Attracting more individual shareholders may be an appropriate goal, but achieving the goal requires more resources. Reaching individual shareholders and communicating with them typically demands significant money. Consider the task of reaching the 47 million Americans who own stock. Motivating them to buy a particular stock requires the same tools and techniques used to get the

ESOPS—EMPLOYEE STOCK OWNERSHIP PLANS

The tying of management and shareholder interests together goes one step further in employee stock ownership plans, or ESOPs. Stock appreciation is a part of most employees' compensation. Under the 1994 United Airlines buyout program, for example, pilots, mechanics and nonunion employees are buying their shares in the company through reduced wages, banking on future stock price increases as a way of seeing a greater return in exchange for what they are giving up. The United Airlines ESOP has become the most visible of the great experiments in investor/employee linkups.

general public to buy a consumer product, such as ads or articles in publications read by active individual investors.

In addition, many individual investors rely on stockbrokers for advice and help in executing buy and sell orders. Some 60,000 stockbrokers are spread out across the United States. The task of motivating them to recommend a particular stock to clients is daunting. Hundreds of stockbroker clubs in major cities throughout the country host companies wanting to present their stories to the members.

Many active individual shareholders belong to investment clubs, so reaching them through the National Association of Investment Clubs (NAIC) is an avenue some companies have embraced. National or regional NAIC conventions with booths manned by investor relations professionals allow companies with active individual shareholder programs to distribute their messages to these potential shareholders.

Because of the expense of reaching individual investors, many companies—particularly those without any consumer presence to help with recognition—concentrate on institutional shareholders, who typically require less expensive communications efforts. But institutional shareholders are more expensive in executive time. Because the majority of the approximately 17,000 institutional investors in the United States are located in major money centers—New York, Boston, Chicago, Los Angeles, San Francisco, Denver, Houston, Dallas, Newark, Detroit, Philadelphia, Baltimore, Pittsburgh, and Minneapolis—efforts to reach these investors can be more targeted. However, meetings with senior portfolio managers typically require the attendance of senior executives such as the chief executive officer, chief financial officer, or chief operating officer.

Shifting the geographic distribution of shares to Europe or Asia also requires a commitment of executive time to meet with investors in the major European money centers, including London, Paris, Zurich, Geneva, Frankfurt, and Edinburgh, and in Tokyo. European investors, by virtue of their distance, often place more importance on meetings with senior management, especially the chief executive officer.

If the investor speaks a different language, translations may be necessary, and this is especially true if the company decides to list on various stock exchanges. In Tokyo, the cost of listing includes translations, making listing an ongoing, expensive process.

Whatever the investor relations goal, the tools and techniques to reach that goal will require some resources. Most publicly traded companies print an annual report. The cost of an annual report averages between $1 and $4 a book, according to a recent National Investor Relations Institute survey, with the number of reports printed, the number of photos, the use of color, and the length of the book affecting the price. Most annual reports are slightly longer than 40 pages.

Hosting analyst meetings and making visits to larger shareholders or money centers around the globe also are factors to be considered in developing a budget. In addition to travel costs, there may be the need to rent a room and equipment for presentations.

Whether emphasizing individual or institutional shareholders, companies are finding access databases such as First Call, Zacks, IBES, Bloomberg News, Reuters, Dow Jones, and the Internet helps to keep track of what is being said. When inaccurate or misleading information is public, correcting that misimpression becomes more difficult and time-consuming the longer it goes unchallenged. These databases provide a range of services, but can cost thousands of dollars.

Similarly, some way of monitoring the shareholder base is important, particularly if a goal is to switch that base. Firms now specialize in following the buying and selling of stock, so it is possible to know within a week which institutions have liquidated their positions and which are becoming major shareholders. While proxy firms such as Georgeson are among those providing such services, several small firms with computer linkage to the exchanges can provide the same information. Knowing the trends is important in targeting visits as well as in determining the success of the geographic distribution of shares.

The size of the budget for investor relations, therefore, depends on the elaborateness of the plans.

TACTICS TO EXECUTE A STRATEGY

Once the investor relations professional has developed an approved plan with specific goals, he or she will need to use multiple tactics: annual reports, quarterly reports, presentations before financial audiences, fact books or fact sheets, press releases and reprints of news articles, letters or bulletins, and a variety of telecommunication devices, from the Internet to the old-fashioned telephone.

The investor relations professional is a conduit of information about what is happening in the company. By marshalling resources, he or she can increase the probability that a buy- or sell-side analyst will follow a particular company, understand the growth and profitability dynamics of that company, and encourage the buying or holding of its stock. Each of the tactics needs to help accomplish that goal.

Annual Report

The annual report typically consumes the most resources and much of the time by virtue of its importance to a company's many stakeholders, including suppliers, customers, and employees. For example, most companies use annual reports as recruiting tools and have copies for suppliers to pick up when visiting.

Divided into two distinct sections—a front half, typically future-oriented with photographs or illustrations to support a message, and a financially oriented back half that reports on how well the company did the prior year— the annual report should establish the company's investment theme for the coming year.

Because it is reviewed by many different groups within and even outside the company (legal, financial, and auditing, at a minimum), careful attention must be paid to keeping the book coherent and clear, especially with regard to the message.

The shareholder letter, often the most-read part of the annual report, should set the overall theme and must reflect the personality of the chairman and chief execu-

BUDGETING

A typical investor relations budget might include:

Salary and fringe benefits of investor relations professionals;

Administrative support for investor relations;

Telephone, fax, computer, modem, and access to various services;

Annual report including design, printing, and photography;

Quarterly reports;

Fact books, fact sheets, and other handout materials;

Annual meeting space, refreshments, giveaways;

Slides, videos, and other audio visual materials;

Analyst meeting(s);

Teleconferences;

Letters or dividend stuffers to shareholders;

Travel; and

Consultants, including those able to help in targeting, developing lists, etc.

tive officer. Where possible, the letter should included milestones to allow investors to measure progress toward meeting the company's goals.

Under the operations report, the company can expand both upon what happened in the prior year and the outlook for the coming year. A discussion of what's going on in the industry and how the company is responding helps to position the company relative to competitors and establishes it as a knowledgeable source.

While the financial report is bound by accounting convention and SEC requirements, there are enhancements that can make the book attractive to investors. Defining accounting jargon for those investors not as familiar with the terms is one way. Calculating the major financial ratios is another. Providing charts and graphs in the financial section is a third.

In its annual review of investor relations programs, the Association for Investment Management and Research (AIMR) describes what makes an annual report—as well as other aspects of the investor relations program—helpful for analysts. The AIMR evaluation is a useful guide to review before starting an annual report, particularly if increasing analyst coverage is an important goal for the investor relations function. (The AIMR also ranks firms by industry categories, so the evaluation provides criteria specific to the industry as well to overall efforts.)

Presentations

Most companies get invitations to discuss their operations and performance before many groups, including security analyst society chapters, stockbroker clubs, investment clubs, and analyst meetings hosted by investment firms such as Merrill Lynch, First Boston, and Goldman Sachs. Many companies supplement this routine by hosting a meeting of their own, often combining it with a tour of nearby facilities. The choice of which meetings to attend should match the audience focus of the investor relations function.

Presentations involve preparing material and slides to highlight information. The project starts with the message, parlaying off of the investment theme highlighted in the annual report.

The goal of the presentation is to persuade investors to buy or hold the company's stock. All presentations should be scripted, and slides should be used only as memory enhancers, not to supplement the message or detract from the presenter. Slides that are too busy and confusing graphs or charts dilute the effort. If there are specific facts that bolster an argument, the investor relations professional uses them as handouts rather than cluttering the message with too much detail.

Fact Book/Fact Sheets

The fact book or fact sheets augment the annual report and other financial documents. The fact book contains information that the stockbroker, financial analyst, or portfolio manager typically wants. For many industries, statistical data over time is crucial; for other industries, descriptions of complex businesses help the analyst dissect and understand the company.

The information in the fact book or fact sheets can usually be found in other documents produced by the company. By gathering these facts and grouping them together in a simple format, the investor relations professional makes it easier for the financial community to follow the company. Fact sheets also can help supplement and reinforce the messages.

Press Releases

Press releases are used to disseminate material information, such as quarterly earnings and dividend declarations, widely and simultaneously. Typically, the company sends via modem or fax a copy of the press release to one of the services (PR Newswire or Business Wire), which then makes the release broadly available to newspapers and wire services such as AP, Bloomberg, Dow Jones, and Reuters. Whether any newspaper or wire service picks up the release, however, is up to the various editors.

One way to enhance the possibility of coverage is to ensure the news is easily understood. While that thought is not very profound, accomplishing it is extremely difficult. With 34,000 publicly traded companies and the number of press releases issued each day—particularly during reporting season—it's imperative that the news jumps out of the headline and first paragraph, rather than be buried in later paragraphs. However, if the news isn't positive, it is human nature to want to bury that news. Second, don't let the lawyers and accountants add jargon or obfuscate what really happened. And don't use too many numbers in the text; include the numbers in appropriate tables at the end of the text. Finally, try to add reasons why the news happened. Treat each important news release as an opportunity to explain how the information accomplishes the corporation's goals or strategies.

In addition to using press releases for material information, investor relations professionals can use them to emphasize a message. For example, new contracts, new products, or even the chief executive officer's speech to a group of analysts could be transformed into a press release. While the speech may not merit the attention of the media, it represents another opportunity to reach the financial community by reprinting and sending copies of the press release to analysts or stockbrokers. Just be careful to include information in the press release (and the speech) that has some value for the audience, such as the potential size of the market for the new product or what the contract can do for future sales. A worthless press release wastes everybody's time and will cause the recipient of future press releases to ignore them.

Letters and Other Written Materials

At times, companies should write directly to their shareholders. Events that happen between quarterly reports or receive a great deal of media attention may warrant a letter to shareholders. When Philip Morris changed strategies and CEOs, the new CEO wrote to shareholders to explain what was happening and to assure them of his attention to their concerns. The device proved so successful that, about six months later, he wrote of his decision to retire and his confidence in the management team taking over.

Similarly, information may need to go to financial analysts to put events into perspective. When continual snowstorms hit the East Coast in the winter of 1995–1996, the financial community raised the estimates of Morton International's next quarterly results. But there was a limit to how much salt could be delivered to customers, and that salt was sold at preestablished prices. A bulletin to investors helped explain the situation and cool the overheating expectations.

Telecommunications

Most investor relations professionals spend much of their time on the telephone, answering the myriad questions asked by financial analysts, stockbrokers, and individual shareholders. One way some companies have answered these questions successfully is with a teleconference call. After major news announcements such as quarterly earnings, analysts are invited to call a number and hear what happened from the company's executives. Usually, the analysts can ask questions or probe further if the information is unclear. If the calls are scheduled appropriately, investors from across the Atlantic can also call, listen, and ask questions.

Teleconference calls help the investor relations professional, since repetition of the same information to each of the analysts is frustrating and time-consuming. The message is also kept more consistent since many analysts can hear the same news simultaneously. However, teleconferences don't necessarily reduce the number of calls, and getting back quickly to the financial community remains an ongoing challenge.

The information superhighway is opening up new ways of communicating with the investment community, some of which are discussed in the final section of this chapter.

A Case Study: Maintaining Shareholder Interest

Throughout this chapter, the challenge of investor relations has been to disseminate information to interested audiences. For many companies, the bigger problem is finding interested audiences. In the case of United Airlines, long-term investor interest dried up during 1987 and 1988, a period of time when the company was selling off its hotels and car rental business and restructuring.

United Airlines ordinarily received steady investor interest. Yet for this critical period of time, the phones stopped ringing—except for calls from arbitragers interested almost exclusively in the sale of the hotels and rental car businesses and the eventual distribution of the proceeds to shareholders. Maintaining even scanty interest in airline operations was impossible.

Yet, once the proceeds had been distributed, the airline would require investor interest so the stock price wouldn't languish at unreasonably low levels. To revive interest in the company's future required using many of the tactics described earlier.

The first step was to determine what the strategies should be. The goal was obvious: develop interest in United Airlines (UAL) so an institutional shareholder base would replace the arbitragers after the proceeds were distributed. The new shareholder would have to believe that UAL could improve financially at a time when the costs for all airlines were rising and the price of airline tickets was falling.

The message UAL developed was to explain the airline's unique strengths, including a fleet of aircraft largely owned (not leased and therefore burdened with additional costs); a hub system unsurpassed by competitors; well-trained employees; and a new management team being assembled by an executive with an excellent reputation on Wall Street. The challenge was to communicate this message to an audience not currently interested in UAL and to do so very persuasively so investors would buy the stock after the arbitragers left. The strategy chosen to accomplish the goal was to find ways of helping investors understand what was happening in the industry. While the investor might not read material on United Airlines alone, he or she was inclined to read an analysis of industry changes.

The annual report was an obvious and important vehicle. (Because it takes almost six months from start to finish, other devices (discussed later) were used in the meantime.) The annual report's theme played off what the investors currently were interested in: perspective. Entitled "Addressing Airline Issues," the text identified five issues which transcended United. Each issue had two messages: how the industry was being affected, and how United was responding or positioning itself to address that issue.

For example, the issue of profitability was of intense interest to the investment community, and United addressed it head-on. The section dealing with United's response began: "United Airlines' expenditure levels for wages, training, fleet maintenance, and overhead put it among the high-cost carriers in the industry. Today, United has several programs in place to contribute to improved profitability."

Simultaneously, work began on a new fact book. Paralleling the annual report, the fact book described strategic issues facing the company, as well as the new management team and the company's strengths. Included was a description of the 327 airplanes United owned as well as the 55 it leased; the five hub cities that allowed the company to board about half the passengers locally; and a changed financial position as a result of the share repurchase.

Since both the annual report and fact book were months away from getting into the hands of investors, an aggressive program to get the new management team out in front of analysts and portfolio managers began almost immediately. Within a month of taking over as chief executive officer, Stephen Wolf stood in front of 300 or so analysts at an annual airline conference. While Wolf was short on specifics, he was long on what issues he would be confronting. As a long-time airline executive with an excellent reputation among the financial community for delivering shareholder value, he provided credibility before there was much positive operational news.

Another way of getting United's messages across and enhancing the level of interest in the airline came from knowing that many of the analysts following the industry were enamored by the glamour of flight. This was particularly true on the sell side. So the company invited about 10 of the top sell-side analysts to the airline's training center and offered them the opportunity to get into a simulator and "fly" the latest plane from the glass cockpit. Along with the fun went a discussion of the airline's latest safety training techniques (where United stood out from other airlines) and of what the airline was doing to maximize the resource of a well-trained crew to run the airline more efficiently.

How well did these tactics pay off? Ultimately, the board of directors decided to distribute the proceeds in the form of a stock buyback program. Within a month of the distribution, the price of the stock rose above the price established by the buyback, and the share base returned to the traditional investor institutions.

THE FUTURE OF INVESTOR RELATIONS

The tactics used by most investor relations professionals are based on old-fashioned media: print (for annual reports, fact books/sheets), telephone (including conference calls), and face-to-face meetings, whether individually or in groups. Future tactics are likely to involve computers and the information superhighway.

Financial analysts were among the first professionals to become computer-literate. Almost every analyst has at least a spreadsheet on which to develop financial models (hence the need to reduce information into numbers). Software programs, based upon the valuation models used, enable money managers to compare companies using ratios and other financial measures to determine which firm's stock price is likely to rise.

Investor relations professionals need to know how to tap into the computerized databases springing up to provide investors with meaningful information. On-line services, for example, provide a way to tap into investors looking for information electronically which is available 24 hours a day.

The key to success in the future will be the same one that provides success today: an understanding of how people want to get information. Facilitating that exchange remains the investor relations professional's responsibility—whether by telephone or by keyboard—remembering that the message must be clear and credible and the facts to support the message accurate and disseminated quickly and broadly.

> **The key to success in the future will be the same one that provides success today: an understanding of how people want to get information.**

Future investor relations professionals must be computer-literate and willing to keep up with the information trends of the investment community. In addition, they must understand finance and marketing (an MBA or integrated marketing communications [IMC] degree are pluses). While some investor relations professionals come from the finance or accounting side of the company, others originate in marketing or communications. Those without a strong grounding in numbers must become conversant in what they mean and help to translate the meaning to others. So, investor relations professionals must therefore have excellent written and oral communication skills, as well as a strategic planning orientation.

But most of all, they must enjoy the process of communications. While the skills just listed are beneficial and desirable, the one skill that is essential is the ability of the investor relations professional to communicate effectively.

CHAPTER 8

Labor Relations: Union–Management Relations and Negotiations

Mary C. Moster
Vice President of Corporate Communications
Comdisco, Inc.

Terence Franklin
President
Franklin Associates

A STRATEGIC APPROACH TO LABOR COMMUNICATIONS

Effective labor communications is based on solid, continuous employee communications. The basic tenets of honest, two-way communications apply, yet, because of the many complex legal and political considerations surrounding management's interaction with organized labor, the process of labor communications has taken on an aura of mystery.

This is not to suggest that the legal and political considerations are not important. However, communications professionals cannot allow legalities to impede the important process of communicating to employees. Now, more than ever, companies need informed, motivated, and empowered employees to be able to compete effectively in the global economy. Communications can be a key to building and retaining such a workforce, whether or not they are represented by a union.

The practice of labor communications has traditionally centered around high-profile, crisis situations—union organizing drives, contract negotiations, strikes, plant closings, and layoffs. These emergency situations demand the full breadth of an organization's crisis communications skills. Regardless of how skillfully an organization responds to a particular emergency, the foundation of effective employee communications must be built long before a crisis occurs. An organization's long-term practice of open communications and fair, consistent treatment of employees becomes its most effective tool during a crisis.

Target Audiences

A prolonged, high-profile contest between management and organized labor affects all of an organization's key stakeholders. All employees are critical targets for communications during contract negotiations or a strike—not just those who are represented by the union. It is essential that nonrepresented employees, and, where they exist, employees represented by other unions, also be considered in the communications process, especially when there is a highly visible labor–management conflict. Other employees need to be assured that their interests will not be compromised or forgotten as management and the union resolve their issues.

The impact of labor relations also extends beyond internal audiences. The confidence of customers can be strained during times of labor–management unrest, particularly when unions raise questions about product quality or availability as negotiating ploys. The confidence level of shareowners, lenders, and financial analysts may be eroded during crisis situations, especially if issues remain unresolved for a long time. Other key audiences may be drawn into the process, such as suppliers, dealers, regulators, and community leaders, particularly if the problem is high profile and long term.

Too often, management sends mixed messages. To the unionized labor force, the message is that costs are too high, that wages and benefits must be reduced or the company will be unable to compete in worldwide markets. To the financial community, management sends the message that the company is a market leader with effective strategies to achieve a global competitive advantage. With just cause, these conflicting messages often become powerfully persuasive tools in the hands of organized labor to undermine management's credibility. The complexity of the relationship between labor and management demands a more rigorous communication process.

Trends in Labor Relations

Over the past 50 years in the United States, following periods of tremendous growth during the first part of the century, there has been a significant decline in the strength of organized labor. By the mid-1990s, union membership was down to about 16 percent of public and private employment from a high of around 36 percent in 1945. The only glimmer of growth came from the public sector, which showed a slight increase in membership in 1993. And, although the change was small, the proportion of working women belonging to unions in the U.S. continued to rise in 1993, to 13 percent, while the proportion of working men continued to decline to about 18 percent.[1]

Levels of union membership vary greatly across national boundaries. Unionization rates in the U.S., which are near the lowest worldwide, are contrasted with rates of about 30 percent in Japan and about 75 percent for many of the Scandinavian countries. In the United Kingdom, however, the level of union membership has nearly halved over the past 15 years, due in large part to the legislative program of Margaret Thatcher when she was prime minister. In general, the trend over the decade beginning in the mid-1980s shows that unions in already weakly unionized countries weakened further, while those in strongly unionized countries showed less decline. The trend toward growth in the unionization of public-sector employees is also consistent throughout many countries worldwide.[2]

The decline in the strength of organized labor in the U.S. has many causes, but the shift in the economy from the traditional union stronghold of heavy manufacturing to the service sector, which has historically been more difficult to organize, is a major factor. Deregulation of key industries, such as airlines, communications, and trucking, have also eroded membership, as nonunion companies have emerged as major employers in those industries. Demographic shifts and changes in education have also been cited as reasons for the decline.

The threat of employers hiring replacement workers also seems to have had a chilling effect on organized labor throughout the past decade. While management has had the right to permanently replace striking workers for more than 50 years, companies have been more willing to use the strategy in recent years. According to the General Accounting Office, a re-

BOX 8–1

IS UNIONS' POLITICAL CLOUT DECLINING?

The political tide in the U.S. in the 1980s turned heavily against organized labor. President Ronald Reagan's decision in 1981 to fire more than 1,000 illegally striking air traffic controllers and replace them with new workers has come to epitomize unionism in decline. Reagan's decisive action was perceived by many in corporate America as a signal that organized labor had lost its clout in Washington, D.C. Thus began a decade of much tougher stands by corporate management in dealing with labor issues. Changes in leadership in Washington have so far had little impact in restoring labor to its prior position of power and influence.

search arm of Congress, more than 30 percent of all companies involved in strikes in the late 1980s said they would hire permanent replacements.[3] Not surprisingly, the number of major work stoppages (those involving at least 1,000 workers) declined to 46 in 1987 from a peak of 235 in 1979, according to the U.S. Department of Labor's Bureau of Labor Statistics.[4]

Does this lessening of the strength of organized labor in the U.S. suggest that the pressure is off to improve communications between management and represented employees? Absolutely not. Union actions still have the power to paralyze companies or force abrupt about-faces by management. In the U.S., the 1992 strike by flight attendants at American Airlines at the height of the Thanksgiving holiday travel rush and the intervention of President Bill Clinton is just one example of a union's ability to use consumer and political clout to force quick resolution of an issue.

Yet, while the traditional confrontational tactics are often effective, the global economy of today makes it imperative that management and labor find ways to work together more effectively. Labor–management relations around the world demonstrate that other approaches can be more effective than the adversarial model that is so prevalent in the U.S. For example, Japanese management and labor relations have evolved from a difficult, confrontational mode in the 1940s to a highly cooperative approach today. Enterprise unions, as they are called, are usually specific to a given company and include all lower-ranking white-collar and permanent blue-collar workers. Union members are the "elite" of the Japanese workforce, and the union takes on the status and prestige of the employing company. The emphasis is on cooperation between labor and management. A significant portion of the average worker's income comes from bonuses tied to overall company profits. As a result, labor actions are designed to show solidarity and determination, but not hurt the economic health of the company.[5]

Germany has strong unions that work under the principle of codetermination. In some cases, work councils composed of 50 percent employees and 50 percent management run the plants. There are also joint supervisory boards where both labor and management have equal representation and voting rights.[6]

The resolution to everyone's satisfaction of the differences in self-interest between a company and its workers is at the core of good employer–employee relationships. Today, particularly in the European Community, the scales are being tipped more and more in the employee's favor. New pension regulations, for example, allow transferability, thus removing the traditional "golden handcuffs," which tied an employee to a particular company in order to receive full pension benefits.

B O X 8–2

UNIONS APPLY PRESSURE TACTICS

Certain types of companies, such as consumer products or service-oriented companies, are particularly vulnerable to the bad publicity generated in a corporate campaign. In its strike against Nynex in 1989, the Communications Workers of America International Union (CWA) used corporate campaign tactics by focusing on the Public Service Commission in New York State, which approves utility rate increases, as a major lever to pressure the company. In an effort to generate negative publicity about the company, the union worked with a coalition of senior citizens, religious leaders, consumer activists, and community organizations to oppose proposed rate hikes. They distributed hundreds of thousands of flyers, gathered 100,000 signatures for petitions, and enlisted the support of high-profile activists such as Ralph Nader and Jesse Jackson to convince the company its reputation was at stake. The final coup was convincing 60 percent of the New York State legislature to sign ads in major newspapers opposing any rate increases during the strike. According to the union, the company ultimately realized that, if the strike continued, their political relationships would be destroyed and their rate increases would never pass. So the strike was settled.

Source: Herbert R. Northrup, "Union Corporate Campaigns and Inside Games as a Strike Form," *Employee Relations Law Journal* 9, no. 4 (1994), p. 7.

Changing Strategies of Labor Unions

Unions in the United States have also been undergoing a period of intense change in the past decade. The downward pressure on membership resulting from economic shifts has forced union leadership to better hone their skills in many arenas, notably the use of communications strategies and tactics. Unions have traditionally held the upper hand over management when it comes to projecting a simple, basic message, usually with great emotional appeal. Union spokespersons are also often more accessible and quicker to respond to breaking news than their corporate counterparts.

The unions' communications edge was further refined throughout the 1980s with the advent of the "corporate" or "coordinated" campaign, first popularized by union organizer Ray Rogers in the prolonged action against J. P. Stevens & Company, the textile manufacturer. In a corporate campaign, the union attacks not only the company it is seeking to bargain with or organize, but also other companies or individuals who are associated with the company, such as banks, directors, regulators, customers, vendors, and the like. The goal is to bring pressure on management from all sides. The corporate campaign has been refined over the past decade to include sophisticated use of negative publicity, issues advertising, confidential background briefings, white papers, presentations to financial analysts, and other techniques to attempt to undermine the company and sway influentials to the union's cause.

Another approach gaining in popularity is the "inside game," which is aimed at disrupting both production and the relationships between line management and the workers. Tactics include convincing employees to impede or slow down production by slowing the work pace, "working to rule," refusing overtime, or filing mass grievances. The integration of an inside game with a corporate campaign results in a formidable assault on an organization.[7]

In the face of the sophisticated communications strategies of organized labor, companies that choose a traditional route of little or no comment essentially cede to the union control of communications. This does not have to happen. In the United Kingdom, there are many examples where inventive management has gone over the heads of union leaders and appealed directly to the workforce. This technique has been used by many companies, including Ford, British Leyland (now Rover and part of BMW), British Rail, British Coal, and P&O Ferries.

Legal Issues

Labor communications in the U.S. have long been centered around two critical pieces of legislation: the Wagner Act, or Sec. 8 (a)(2) of the National Labor Relations Act of 1935, which prohibits employers from dominating or interfering with the formation or administration of any labor organization; and the Taft-Hartley Act of 1947, which permits an employer to express its views on any subject of labor relations as long as it contains no threat of reprisal or force or promise of benefit.

From a communications perspective, the focus has often been on what this legislation prohibits, rather than what it allows. While it is critical that all communications between management and labor be crafted with the help of expert legal counsel, legislation should not be a screen for management to hide behind in either a crisis situation or in ongoing employee communications. Management clearly has the right to take its messages directly to employees, to express its views on unions generally, to justify company practices, or to explain any issues or answer questions that arise during negotiations or organizing drives. Corporate communicators, together with legal counsel that takes an enabling approach to communications, can clearly work effectively within the constraints of the legislation to communicate the organization's message fully and directly to its employees.

Relationship to the Strategic Planning Process

Labor communications objectives must work hand-in-hand with the organization's overall strategic mission and goals. As we discussed earlier, labor communications should be integrated into a regular, ongoing program of employee communications, which in turn should be closely aligned with the organization's overall strategic objectives. The "selling" of a company to its employees is a marketing and public relations function. Workers have to buy the company, and all it offers, with their minds, rather than with their pocketbooks.

During crisis situations, such as a prolonged strike or extensive contract negotiations, labor communications professionals need to craft their strategies and messages with all of the organization's key publics in mind, from customers to suppliers to the financial community. To do so, the labor communications specialist must be a part of the strategic planning process and have access to all relevant information. As an informed spokesperson for the company, a labor communications professional can help to shape the message that will be directed to all the company's key audiences.

Measurement and Budget Considerations

The effectiveness of a labor communications program is often measured against the overall success of the organization's labor relations strategy. Did communications help to contribute to a settlement that was in the best interests of all concerned—employees, the company, and its shareholders? Was the company's side of the issue fairly represented in the media

BOX 8–3

AVOIDING THE COMMUNICATIONS VACUUM

Today's employees expect communications. But even in the most sophisticated companies, in the most advanced countries, most employees are communicated "at" rather than "with." Often, little more than lip service is paid to the concept of two-way communications. Management needs to question whether this one-way information activity is productive.

The real objective of employee communications is to create understanding and support among employees, enabling the company to operate more efficiently. The key is never to let a communications vacuum develop. Otherwise it will be filled with speculation and gossip. Employers need to recognize that employees have information rights, needs, and desires.

In the European Community (EC), for example, rights to information are laid down by law. Apart from contracts of employment that set down basic information on sickness, holidays, pensions, and safety at work, some companies have negotiated agreements covering extra information to be shared with employees. These often become established rights. There is also an increasing amount of legislation in the EC that identifies and defines the information rights of employees. This trend is likely to continue and could be expanded to companies outside the EC who make decisions affecting their employees in EC countries.

coverage surrounding the event? Did internal communications help to minimize the negative effects of a strike or to bolster morale of nonstriking workers? Did the financial community maintain its confidence in management and its ability to perform up to expectations, despite the labor crisis?

Budget expenditures vary widely depending upon the nature of the event facing an organization. A relatively routine contract negotiation may involve only a small group of specialists, relying primarily on in-house talent. A major issue, such as a prolonged and acrimonious strike, or a major restructuring of benefits or compensation practices, may call for assistance from various outside communications, legal, or human resources experts. When the issues threaten the company's financial future, or even its survival, labor communications expenditures often will dwarf an organization's other communications costs.

A TACTICAL APPROACH TO LABOR COMMUNICATIONS

As we discussed earlier, the most important element of a successful labor relations communications plan is a regular program of open, honest, two-way employee communications. Assuming such a program is in place, we will focus on recommended tactics for times of unusual activity, such as negotiations, strikes, plant closings, and the like. It is also important to note that a communications program should be carefully crafted with the advice of legal counsel.

Here are ten steps to consider:

1. Form a multifunctional task force. A labor communications plan cannot be developed in a vacuum. When a major event is anticipated, a multifunctional task force should be formed, including representatives from public relations, human resources, labor relations, legal, investor relations, and government or public affairs. Input should be sought from those who interact regularly with customers, suppliers, dealers, or distributors. The task force should include or report to senior management to ensure that its strategies and action plans are consistent with overall corporate strategy. Once the action starts, the communications professional should be in constant contact with all members of the task force, as well as senior management, to incorporate the new developments into the communications strategy.

2. Develop a comprehensive communications strategy. A communications strategy and a plan for implementing it are critical. Whenever possible, the strategy should be prepared well in advance of an event that could trigger a crisis. When developing a strategy, the key factor is to think through actions to their possible conclusions. Go through "what if" scenarios to anticipate the consequences of various actions and reactions. Because anticipating bad outcomes is sometimes seen as disloyal or defeatist, a common mistake is the failure to push far enough in planning. The communications professional has the responsibility to explore and plan for all possible contingencies.

3. Simplify the messages. It is essential to distill the information into a set of core messages. Once the action starts, there will be a barrage of often-confusing and contradictory information. In this atmosphere, an organization's messages need to be concise and easy to articulate. They also need to be consistent in order to be credible. Finally, it is important to demonstrate concern for your key audiences. Negotiations or strikes involve issues that evoke highly emotional responses, such as the loss of jobs, threats to retirement security, or cutbacks in health care benefits. It is essential to acknowledge the impact the organization's actions will have in human terms and to explain why they are necessary and what alternatives were considered.

4. Prepare materials in advance that are tailored to the use and the audience. Labor relations issues are invariably complex. Materials for both internal and external audiences, such as backgrounders or white papers on key issues, can be anticipated and prepared in advance. Whenever possible, use charts and graphs to illustrate information—a practice which aids comprehension and adds impact to the message. Graphics are also becoming increasingly popular with the media and may heighten the possibility that a story or statistic is picked up. Use fact sheets to cover commonly asked questions, such as basic data on the company, its unions, its labor–management history, and key financial facts. Tackle tough issues in a question-and-answer format, which can be used by the organization's external spokespersons and line management in responding to queries.

5. Background the media on the issues before the crisis occurs. Many labor relations events can be anticipated, such as the opening of contract negotiations or the announcement of a plant closing. This gives communications professionals a chance to brief the media weeks, or sometimes even months, in advance. Reporters, editorial board members, and key columnists from newspapers, television, and radio stations in both corporate headquarters and plant locations can be briefed on the upcoming issues. The briefings should result in more knowledgeable reporting, especially with fast-breaking news once the action begins. It also provides an opportunity to use the media as a sounding board to test the organization's message.

6. Be on the offensive in getting the message out. Often in the past, management has taken the position that negotiations are best left to the negotiating table, rather than debated in the press. As a result, management was usually on the defensive or simply silent. Labor, on the other hand, has traditionally taken the offensive in communicating with the media and with union membership before, during, and after the negotiations. While the balance has changed appreciably in recent years, there is still a tendency on management's side to be

BOX 8-4

CONFRONTING A CORPORATE CAMPAIGN

For several years, the United Food and Commercial Workers International Union had been attempting without success to organize the 60,000 workers of Food Lion, a subsidiary of a Belgian company and the fastest-growing grocery chain in the Southern U.S. When broadcast journalists did an exposé on Food Lion cleanliness in the meat department, the union then shifted its tactics to a corporate campaign by helping employees appear on prime-time television with the charge that Food Lion was selling tainted meat. Earnings for the year for Food Lion fell by 13 percent, due in part to the negative publicity and the cost of advertising to counteract it. The company fought back, charging that the publicity was slanted, and sued over the television coverage. But the corporate campaign tactics of the union had hit their mark.

Source: Richard Greer, "Unions Go for the Gut with Corporate Campaigns," *The Atlantic Journal and Constitution* (February 8, 1993), sec. G, p. 8.

overly conservative in both internal and external communications. There may be times when it is strategically essential to refrain from commenting on certain issues. But as a general rule, management has a responsibility to its stakeholders—employees, shareholders, customers, suppliers—to be proactive in explaining its positions on the issues and responding, fully and quickly, to allegations by labor.

7. Enlist third parties to support the organization's position. Third-party experts add a dimension of credibility to the organization's message. Before a crisis occurs, identify academics, industry experts, commentators, or religious and community leaders who can be enlisted to support or expound on the company's position. Clearly, these should be experts in their own right, because their value is in their objectivity. Provide the names of these third-party experts to reporters and financial analysts to provide background or quotes. Use their comments in employee publications to demonstrate that others support the company's position.

8. Take the message directly to employees. In the supercharged atmosphere of a labor–management action, unionized employees are often under intense pressure to show solidarity with their fellow members. That makes the job of communicating with them particularly difficult, as listening to management in a face-to-face meeting, for example, could be construed as a sign of disloyalty. It would be a mistake, however, to assume that represented employees do not want to hear management's message. The key is the delivery process. Copies of the company's newsletters, updates on company activities, letters, or even videotapes can be sent directly to the home to be read in private and discussed with family members. For example, one company explored the idea of local access cable television to allow the chairman to communicate directly to employees. Advertising in local newspapers, letters to the editor, or commentary columns all provide a means of directly accessing employees.

9. Choose the right spokesperson. The spokesperson for the company should be someone who is credible to the media, authorized to speak for the organization, and accessible, especially after hours and at other inconvenient times. While the spokesperson will need ready access to inside experts, such as lawyers, labor negotiators, and senior management, specialists from these disciplines are rarely good candidates for the spokesperson role. In recent years, some companies have been very successful in humanizing the

B O X 8–5

TAKING THE MESSAGE DIRECTLY TO EMPLOYEES

Caterpillar used advertising to appeal directly to its target audience before the long and bitter strike with the United Automobile, Aerospace, and Agricultural Implement Workers (UAW) that began at the company's Peoria, Illinois, plant in November of 1991. For more than six months preceding the strike, Caterpillar ran a series of advertisements in newspapers in the small Midwestern communities where most of its UAW employees live. The message was straightforward. The company must be able to compete in the global marketplace. Its health care costs were too high. It was not an auto manufacturer and should no longer be tied to the "pattern" agreements that linked its fate to that of the Big Three U.S. automakers. The same message appeared in executive speeches, press releases, and company publications. Caterpillar established its position early on and consistently reinforced it through various media as the strike stretched into the weeks and months ahead. While the UAW later fought back with similar tactics, its campaign never achieved the clarity of the company's message.

Source: Stephen Franklin, "Specter of a Strike Darkening Cloud over Caterpillar Country," *Chicago Tribune* (August 21, 1994), sec. 3, p. 1.

voice of the corporation in troubled situations by choosing a spokesperson who projects those qualities.

10. Don't stop communicating once the crisis has passed. Communications shouldn't stop once the contract has been signed or the workers come back after a strike. In fact, the conclusion of a labor–management action should trigger more, not less, communication from management. The focus needs to be on moving forward, trying to heal whatever rifts developed. Also keep in mind that the best time for real progress in labor–management relations is *between* contract negotiations, when the spotlight is off and fewer lines of demarcation are drawn. Communications can also help in that process.

An example we'll explore indepth (beginning on p. 128) demonstrates how Navistar's management worked cooperatively with its major union to solve a critical problem threatening the company's survival.

THE FUTURE OF LABOR COMMUNICATIONS

In the United States, union membership in the private sector has been dropping steadily and there is little to suggest that the trend will be reversed in the near future. Many point to organized labor itself as the major culprit. Even those sympathetic to labor say that the movement is in need of a facelift. Victor S. Kamber of the Kamber Group, a Washington D.C.-based consulting and public relations firm that counts many unions among its clients, said:

> Unions haven't sold their message of why in the 1990s joining a union is important . . . Even the worst critic of labor will say that, back in the 1930s and the 1940s, unions were really important—even in the 1950s—but that today they have outlived their usefulness. Labor has an obligation to keep reminding its own base, as well as those they want to influence on the outside of that base, why they are important if they want to still be players, and labor has failed to do that.[8]

BOX 8-6

NAVISTAR'S LANDMARK HEALTH CARE RESTRUCTURING
A Case of Management–Union Cooperation

After surviving more than a decade of labor strife, high-profile plant closings, divestitures, and radical downsizing, by 1992 Navistar (formerly International Harvester Company) had restructured to two core businesses—truck and engine manufacturing. The once highly diversified company with worldwide operations now had just a handful of plants in the Midwestern U.S. and a workforce of 13,000, trimmed from a peak of more than 100,000 employees a little over a decade before. It also was the market leader in both of its lines of business, with a strong dealer network and a loyal, blue-chip customer base.

While many problems had been resolved, Navistar still faced one more major hurdle— staggering health care costs. Because of its earlier downsizing, the company was providing benefits to 96,000 active and retired employees and their dependents, creating an untenable competitive cost disadvantage. Confidential studies by investment bankers projected that the company would face a severe cash drain, and even potential bankruptcy, if costs were not reduced.

Changing the plans would not be easy. Navistar retirees were covered by literally hundreds of different plans, but almost all were very generous by national standards and were provided virtually free of charge to retirees of the company's major union, the United Auto Workers (UAW). Previous court rulings on similar cases were inconsistent on whether plans could be changed. Plus, the UAW had taken a high-profile stance that health care benefits were nonnegotiable and would likely resist any attempt to set a precedent on the issue. Yet, the company determined that restructuring the plans through a class action lawsuit against retirees was the only viable solution.

STRATEGY AND ACTION PLAN

A communications strategy was developed to address the many challenges Navistar faced: (1) present a convincing message that the company's very survival was at stake, while still retaining the confidence of a fragile coalition of suppliers, dealers, customers, and the financial community despite a barrage of negative news; (2) avoid polarizing the issue, because management believed the best hope for a quick resolution to the issue was a negotiated settlement with the UAW acting as representative for all retirees; (3) avoid attacking the opposition, because sympathy was more naturally with the retirees than with management; and (4) bolster the morale of active employees to keep them motivated through yet another high-profile negative issue.

Yet, some suggest there are new stirrings of life in the labor movement that may have implications for communications professionals in the future. As noted earlier, unions in the U.S. are having some success in organizing public-sector workers. The wrenching downsizings of once-stable and secure giants such as Sears and IBM have sent shock waves through the American public, leaving many workers feeling insecure and disenfranchised. Some believe that anger could be a fertile ground for organized labor. Unions are discovering that they can organize workers they formerly ignored or gave up on, such as service sector or part-time workers. The unions themselves may also be changing, attempting to be more responsive to changes in the workplace. A recent AFL-CIO report emphasizes the need for more worker–management collaboration in order to create more productive, humane, and democratic work organizations.[9]

B O X   8–6 Continued

The initial announcement of the restructuring, which was made virtually simultaneously to employees, customers, suppliers, financial analysts, bankers, and the media, was followed by widespread media coverage. While many of the stories were negative in that they focused on Navistar's precarious financial condition and included the strident comments of local union representatives, the company met its goal of reinforcing the message that its survival was at stake. As the months progressed, the union countersued the company and various motions were filed in court, all keeping the story on the front of the business pages.

Throughout the barrage of media coverage, Navistar strove to keep a delicate balance between its firm commitment to winning the litigation and signaling that it was ready and willing to discuss a settlement. Maintaining that balance meant taking some hard hits from the local union leadership, who constantly whipped up antimanagement sentiment in the local media. It also meant turning down opportunities, such as appearances on network television, that in other circumstances would be a publicist's dream. But the company was determined not to jeopardize its chances of a settlement with the union by polarizing the issues through the media.

At the same time, the company decided to take its message directly to retirees through personalized letters, monthly newsletters, and more than 100 face-to-face meetings staged across the country to explain the proposed new plan and why it was necessary. The company also provided a toll-free number, which remained open for nearly a year, so that retirees could discuss how the changes would affect their individual health care plans. Employees were informed regularly through management update meetings, stories in the company newsletter, and videotaped messages from the chairman. Navistar also communicated regularly with its dealers, financial analysts, suppliers, and customers to update them on the litigation and its impact on the company.

RESULTS

Three months after the first suit was filed, the company and the union agreed to begin settlement talks. After a further three months of intense examination and unusually candid discussions about the company's financial situation, Navistar and the UAW announced a plan for restructuring retiree health care benefits (see the Readings at the end of the chapter). This innovative, complex, and far-reaching agreement called for compromise and a share in the sacrifice and the gain for all those with a stake in the company—retirees, employees, and shareholders. It was possible because neither management nor the union leadership allowed external pressures—from the media, the local union representatives, or shareowners—to interfere with the overall goal of finding a fair settlement.

What are the implications of these trends for communications professionals?

These trends indicate that it will become increasingly important, and, concurrently, increasingly challenging, to communicate effectively within organizations. Communications professionals will need to expand their thinking and skills to be up to the task. In addition to education and training in traditional public relations and related communications disciplines, effective internal communicators in the future will need to develop a wide range of new skills.

Communicators involved in labor relations will need exposure to many disciplines that are traditional strengths of the human resources department, such as organizational development practices and effective negotiating techniques. Shifting demographics in the workplace will place new and different demands on communicators as they attempt to find the message

B O X 8–7

COMMUNICATIONS: A MANAGEMENT TOOL

In a well-run organization, the communications responsibilities of each manager are fully understood and implemented. In fact, communications responsibilities are included in each manager's job description. Communicating effectively then becomes the responsibility of all managers, not just the communications professionals or top management.

Some people believe that information is power and are very careful about how they give it away. This covetous attitude towards information can create extremely weak links in the communications network. Any information bottlenecks must be identified and cleared.

Training will improve communications weaknesses, but the most critical point is for each manager to realize that the organization requires him or her to be an effective communicator. This cannot be a voluntary option.

and the method to build loyalty and motivation in an increasingly diverse workforce. The widespread and growing availability of communications technologies that span the globe not only provides a powerful tool for communicators, but also a challenge to keep the company as a viable and relied-upon source of information for its employees. And, more than ever, communicators will need to understand their organizations' business strategies and be able explain why employees need to share in and support the company's goals.

In the United States, and throughout the world, it seems clear that the traditional role of organized labor will change, perhaps dramatically, in the future. However the new tenor and shape of labor–management relations develop over the next decade, it is clear that there will continue to be enormous opportunities for communications professionals.

E N D N O T E S

1. Bureau of National Affairs, "Number of Union Members Rose in 1993 as Public Sector Membership Grew," *Government Employee Relations Report* 32, no. 1552 (February 14, 1994), p. 226.

2. "OECD Employment Outlook: Highlights," *OECD Observer* 172 (October, 1991), p. 51.

3. Uchitelle, Louis, "Labor Has a Big Job for Its New Friend Clinton," *The New York Times,* (June 27, 1994), sec. 4, p. 5.

4. Victor, Kirk, "Striking in the 1980s," *The National Journal* 21, no.1 (January 1989), p. 18.

5. Sypher, Beverly Davenport, ed., *Case Studies in Organizational Communications* (New York: The Guildford Press, 1990), p. 249.

6. Fox, Kelly, "Caterpillar Impasse Highlights Unresolved Labor Issues," *Corporate Legal Times* (December 1992), p. 15.

7. Northrup, Herbert R., "Union Corporate Campaigns and Inside Games as a Strike Form," *Employee Relations Law Journal* 9, no. 4 (1994), p. 7.

8. Victor, Kirk, "The Labor Movement: This Old House," *The National Journal* 26, no. 25 (June 18, 1994), p. 1446.

9. Judis, John B. "Can Labor Come Back? Why the Answer May Be Yes," *The New Republic* 210, no. 21 (May 23, 1994), p. 25.

R E A D I N G 8–1

NAVISTAR PRESS RELEASE

This press release by Navistar International Corporation announced a tentative agreement with the United Automobile Workers (UAW) union on its retiree health care benefits restructuring. The press release provides details of the innovative, yet highly complex, structure of the agreement.

NEWS

**For additional information: Mary Moster
Navistar International Corporation**

Navistar and the UAW Reach Tentative Agreement on Retiree Health Care Restructuring; Main Labor Negotiations to Resume in Early January; Dividend Suspended on Series G Preferred

CHICAGO, December 17, 1992—Navistar International Corporation (NYSE:NAV) announced today that it has reached a tentative agreement on a settlement with the United Automobile, Aerospace and Agricultural Implement Workers of America (UAW) for restructuring its retiree health care costs. The innovative agreement enables Navistar to achieve a competitive cost structure, helps ensure its long-term ability to provide jobs and benefits to employees, and provides retirees with a modified medical plan for life. The agreement also provides for retirees and employees to share in the benefits of the Company's return to profitability and long-term financial health.

The UAW has been leading negotiations with Navistar since mid-October under an order agreed to by all parties involved in a class action suit in the U.S. District Court for the Southern District of Ohio in Dayton.

The Company also announced that negotiations with the UAW on a new collective bargaining agreement for active employees will resume on January 8, 1993, in Louisville, Kentucky. Approximately 7,500 of Navistar's 12,500 employees in the United States are represented by the UAW. The Company also will be negotiating concurrently with its other unions to achieve changes in post-retirement health care benefits for current active employees.

The agreement reduces Navistar's liability for retiree health care and insurance benefits under accounting rules (FAS 106) from $2.6 billion to $1.0 billion and achieves the Company's goal to begin implementing $200 million in cost savings. In return, 255 million new shares of Navistar common stock will be issued to a trust fund for current and futures retirees. A new profit-sharing program will make payments into the same trust fund.

The Company's board of directors also announced today that the dividend for Navistar's $6 cumulative convertible preferred stock, Series G, will be suspended until the legal process is completed and the new health care program can be implemented.

The settlement is subject to court approval in the Ohio litigation, shareowner approval for the issuance of new shares of common stock and amendments to the corporate charter, various regulatory approvals, and the successful negotiation of the new collective bargaining agreements. The Company also said that, because the agreement is complex and many parties are involved, timing will be difficult to predict and there may be delays in implementation.

– more –

Specific details of the medical benefits and life insurance programs are still being finalized and will be announced soon. Retirees will be required to share in the cost of their medical benefits through premiums, deductibles, and co-payments.

Navistar plans to implement the new program for all retirees as expeditiously as possible after the U.S. District Court in Ohio approves the settlement.

"With the savings achieved from this settlement, combined with anticipated savings from our upcoming main labor contract negotiations with the UAW and a number of other aggressive initiatives already underway to improve operating efficiencies, we are confident Navistar will achieve its goal of $200 million in savings annually and become a strong, profitable company," said James C. Cotting, chairman and chief executive officer.

The Company previously had disclosed that it has a $200 million cost disadvantage when compared to other industrial companies in generally the same line of business, with $150 million resulting from health care costs and $50 million from operating costs. Because of downsizing, Navistar currently has more than three retirees for each active employee, while its major competitors have retiree to active ratios of less than one-to-one. During fiscal 1992, Navistar's medical and life insurance benefits for retirees totalled $146 million.

"We are very pleased that the Company and the UAW have been able to reach this agreement, which is a major step forward in making Navistar more cost competitive," said Cotting. "We have substantially reduced our liability for retiree health care and resolved key issues that caused uncertainty about Navistar's long-term solvency."

According to the agreement, Navistar will establish a trust qualified as a VEBA for the purpose of paying its share of the retiree health care benefits. (A voluntary employee benefits association, or VEBA, is a mechanism approved by the IRS and ERISA to allow employers to provide employee benefits other than pensions in ways that are tax-advantaged.) The trust will have two subtrusts—a "base plan" subtrust and an "upside benefit" subtrust—each of which will operate on a wholly independent basis.

Base Plan Subtrust

The "base plan" subtrust will be established to pay retiree medical costs and provide a vehicle for future Company funding. While retiree health care costs initially will be paid on a pay-as-you-go basis, it is the Company's intention to prefund up to $500 million of the $1.0 billion liability over time from the proceeds of the sale of new shares of Navistar common stock. In addition, the Company will pay into the trust the current service costs of the new plan.

"Funding the base plan subtrust will provide additional security to retirees for the future of their benefits," Cotting said, "as well as cost savings and increased financial flexibility for Navistar by lowering our unfunded liability."

An independent financial institution will serve as trustee of the base plan subtrust and the company will administer it and make investment decisions. A seven-member committee composed of Company and retiree representatives will be established. The committee will resolve claim and benefit disputes and review premium calculations, but will have no authority to modify benefits or change Company contribution obligations.

– more –

Navistar–UAW Agreement / Page 3

Upside Benefit Subtrust

The "upside benefit" subtrust will be established for the benefit of current and future retirees to be used to reduce retiree costs and/or provide additional benefits. It will be funded with an initial contribution of new shares of common stock equal to the total amount of the Company's outstanding shares at the time of implementation of the settlement, or about 255 million shares. In addition, the Company will make an annual profit-sharing contribution to the subtrust based on a formula that determines income eligible for this profit sharing and has a minimum amount based on total hours worked that progresses in steps from one percent to a maximum of 16 percent. For example, based on hours worked in 1992, had eligible profits exceeded $250 million, the maximum contribution would have been approximately $9 million, plus 16 percent of eligible profits in excess of $200 million.

The upside benefit subtrust will be governed by a five-member committee composed of two UAW appointees, two other appointees, and a chair approved by the U.S. District Court. The committee will be restricted from selling the Navistar shares for up to a five-year period following the date of implementation of the settlement to allow Navistar full market access to sell shares to fund the base plan subtrust. During such period, the committee will vote its shares in favor of the recommendations of the board of directors on matters submitted to the vote by the shareowners.

Corporate Governance

Navistar also agreed that, as long as the upside benefit subtrust holds at least 20 percent of the Company's outstanding common stock, it will be entitled to select two members of Navistar's board of directors. When the subtrust holdings drop below 20 percent but still exceed 10 percent, it will be entitled to select one director. In addition, until the base plan subtrust is fully funded, the UAW will have a right to select an individual to serve on the Navistar board of directors. All three directorships are newly created positions and will bring Navistar's total board membership to 15.

The agreement also provides for an amendment to the Company's charter so that any merger or sale of all or substantially all of the assets of Navistar will require the vote of 85 percent of the common shareowners.

"The Company and the UAW have a mutual goal for Navistar to be a strong, profitable company," said Cotting. "Navistar is a fundamentally strong operating company. It is in the best interests of our shareowners, our customers and suppliers, our retirees and employees, as well as the unions that represent them, for Navistar to return to financial health and grow profitably. This agreement makes these goals achievable."

# # #

UAW PRESS RELEASE

This press release by the UAW on the tentative agreement with Navistar was released simultaneously with the company's announcement—another sign of the cooperation between the two organizations.

NEWS FROM THE UAW

For Release: Immediate—Thursday, December 17, 1992

UAW and Navistar Reach New Understanding

The UAW and the Navistar International Corporation have reached an understanding designed to help keep Navistar viable while at the same time protecting and maintaining the core benefits of active and retired UAW-Navistar members.

The understanding creates a new framework for the payment of retiree health and insurance benefits, provides greater input for Navistar retirees and the UAW, and creates a mechanism to allow retirees to benefit from the company's profits and future growth.

"It has taken sustained hard work, aggressive legal representation, and solidarity in the Navistar ranks to achieve this understanding," said UAW Secretary-Treasurer Bill Casstevens who directs the union's Navistar Department.

"After performing a detailed analysis of the company's financial situation," Casstevens said, "we reluctantly concluded that unless current retiree health care benefits levels were modified, Navistar would be forced to liquidate the company through bankruptcy. That would leave Navistar unable to provide any retiree health or life insurance benefits and would cause the permanent loss of Navistar jobs."

"Given the very poor business conditions resulting from 12 years of deeply flawed Reagan/Bush economic and trade policies, Navistar's high ratio of retired workers, our nation's inefficient and costly health care delivery system, and new accounting procedures requiring companies to account now for benefits to be paid in the future, we have crafted the best possible solution to the difficulties facing our members at Navistar and the company," Casstevens stated.

While specific details about the revised medical and life insurance benefits are still being finalized, Casstevens today advised UAW members via letter of the following broad provisions of the understanding:

- The company's liability for retiree health care and retiree life insurance will be reduced from $2.6 billion to $1 billion by a combination of retiree co-payments; deductibles; premium sharing; the elimination of some benefits including dental care, vision care, and Medicare Part B payments; and by limiting the amount of company-paid life insurance.

- The company has agreed that the new retiree health and life insurance program will be provided on a lifetime basis, thus forfeiting any claim that it can unilaterally modify or terminate benefits for retirees.

- The $1 billion necessary to assure company payment of retiree health care and life insurance benefits will come from pay-as-you-go payments from the company, together with

– more –

up to $500 million from the proceeds of new stock offerings deposited in a fund devoted solely to that purpose.

- A new "upside benefit" fund will be established for the purpose of reducing retiree costs and/or improving benefits. It will be funded with an initial contribution of new shares of common stock equal to 50 percent of the total amount of the company's outstanding shares at the time of implementation of the settlement, or about 255 million shares. In addition, the company will make profit-sharing contributions to the fund under a new profit-sharing plan providing for payments up to a maximum of 16 percent of eligible profits.

- The upside benefit fund will be governed by a five-member committee composed of two UAW appointees, two other appointees, and a chair approved by the U.S. district court. Navistar and the UAW have also agreed that, as long as the upside benefit fund holds at least 20 percent of the company's outstanding common stock, the UAW will be entitled to select two members of Navistar's board of directors. When the fund holdings drop below 20 percent but still exceed 10 percent, it will be entitled to select one director. In addition, until the base plan fund is fully funded, the UAW will have a right to select one member of the Navistar board of directors.

- The current UAW-Navistar collective bargaining agreement will be extended and modified in three specific areas: suspension of the penalty on excessive overtime; temporary elimination of the 1-for-2 attrition recall retirement; and implementation of a managed health care program. Other provisions of the current collective bargaining agreement will remain in place. In coming weeks, the UAW bargaining committee will meet with management to work out details of the changes to be made in the current agreement. The new collective bargaining agreement will then be presented to the membership for ratification.

Implementation of the modifications in the retiree benefits are subject to review by the representatives of the other retiree groups, the U.S. District Court in Dayton, Ohio, and appropriate regulatory agencies.

"While this new understanding means some changes and sacrifices for UAW-Navistar members, the alternatives were clearly worse. The prospect of no retiree health care or life insurance and the loss of thousands of good-paying jobs was clearly unacceptable," Casstevens stated.

"At the same time," Casstevens added, "The situation which we face at Navistar is compelling evidence that meaningful national health care reform must be achieved if we are to maintain a healthy industrial base and preserve a middle-class standard of living for America's workers."

# # #

R E A D I N G   8–3

NAVISTAR NEWSLETTER

A special edition of Navistar's internal newsletter, *Inside Navistar*, was published whenever there were significant developments in the health care restructuring case. It was distributed immediately throughout all company locations, often following a face-to-face meeting with management. The special edition was produced internally on desktop publishing to provide the greatest flexibility and speed in getting the message out.

January 23, 1993
Special Report
INSIDE NAVISTAR

NEW NAVISTAR/UAW LABOR AGREEMENT RATIFIED BY EMPLOYEES

Over the weekend, Navistar employees who are represented by the UAW ratified a new labor agreement, which became effective immediately upon ratification this weekend and will extend through October 1, 1995.

Approximately 7,600 production, maintenance and clerical employees at Navistar facilities in Georgia, Illinois, Indiana, Maryland, Ohio and Texas are covered by this new labor agreement.

The previous UAW/Navistar agreement, which had been in effect since November 1990, was scheduled to expire on October 1, 1993, but was opened by mutual agreement as the next step in addressing Navistar's $200 million competitive cost disadvantage.

Says Chairman and Chief Executive Officer Jim Cotting, "We have said all along that the mutual goal of Navistar and the UAW is for Navistar to be a strong, profitable company.

"This new labor agreement is based on a thorough analysis and understanding of Navistar's competitive cost position. Through the tremendous effort of the UAW and Navistar negotiating teams, we were able to reach agreement quickly. This joint effort proves that by working together, we can make real progress toward the goal of returning Navistar to a strong, profitable company," he says.

Highlights of the Agreement

Briefly, the new labor agreement includes the following:

- UAW-represented employees will receive two 3 percent lump sum payments (one on October 1, 1993, and the second on October 1, 1994).

- The pension benefit levels that were negotiated for the previous agreement will remain in effect for this new agreement. Two lump sum payments of $400 each will be paid to retirees in March 1994 and March 1995 in addition to a previously scheduled $200 payment in June 1993.

- A joint Navistar-UAW Committee will mutually select health care providers to form a coordinated "managed care" network with the goal of improving quality and reducing costs. Current health care plans for UAW-represented employees will remain in effect until these health care networks are established by the joint committee. Once the coordinated health care networks are established, employees residing within designated network areas who choose to use network providers will receive coverage for physician office visits with a $20 per visit co-payment. Currently, they receive no coverage for physician office visits.

– more –

New Navistar/UAW Labor Agreement Ratified by Employees / Page 2

Employees residing within a designated network area who do not choose to use network providers will be required to pay 25 percent of the usual and customary charges. The maximum out-of-pocket expenses for employees who do not use health care providers within a designated network will be $1,000 per individual and $2,000 per family. Employees who reside outside a designated network will continue with their current benefit program without penalty, and will be allowed access to the coordinated network program.

- The two-for-one attrition provisions of the Navistar Employment Target Program have been suspended. These suspended provisions previously required that for every two UAW-represented employees who retire, one laid-off worker would be called back to work from the Master Recall list.

- The Excess Overtime Account was suspended. Under the previous contract, Navistar had been paying penalties for all overtime worked in excess of an amount agreed upon by Navistar and the UAW.

- The company and the UAW agreed that there should be equality of sacrifice between represented employees and nonrepresented employees, and no annual incentives or bonuses will be paid unless there also is a profit sharing payout.

- The procedures for being placed on the Master Recall list have been changed to provide for a 30-day notification period and a one-time, final opportunity for laid-off employees to be included on the list. Under the previous contract, laid-off employees were allowed to go on and off the Master Recall list at any time.

Details of Tentative Retiree Health Care Agreement Released

The new labor agreement was the second step in addressing the company's competitive cost position. The first step was previously announced in December when Navistar and the UAW reached a tentative settlement for restructuring retiree health care costs.

The tentative retiree health care settlement reduces Navistar's liability for retiree health care and life insurance benefits under accounting rules (SFAS 106) from $2.6 billion to $1.0 billion and provides retirees with a modified medical plan for life. The new plan has a present value of $1.39 billion, of which $1.0 billion is Navistar's obligation and the other $390 million will come from retiree contributions in the form of premiums. (See attached fact sheet for more details of Navistar's Retiree Medical Plan.)

The retiree health care settlement is subject to court approval in the Ohio litigation, shareowner approval for the issuance of new shares of common stock and amendments to the corporate charter and various regulatory approvals. Navistar plans to seek these approvals expeditiously so that the new health care program can be implemented for all retirees as soon as possible.

A special edition of Inside Navistar, published for the employees of Navistar International Transportation Corp.

455 North Cityfront Plaza Drive
Chicago, Illinois 60611
Editor: Sherry Scott
312-836-2103

– more –

New Navistar/UAW Labor Agreement Ratified by Employees / Page 3

Supplement to *Inside Navistar* Special Report

NAVISTAR RETIREE MEDICAL PLAN

The retiree health care agreement that has been negotiated reduces Navistar's liability for retiree health care and insurance benefits under accounting rules (SFAS 106) from $2.6 billion to $1.0 billion and provides retirees with a modified medical plan for life. The plan has a present value of $1.39 billion, of which $1.0 billion is Navistar's obligation and the other $390 million will come from retiree contributions in the form of premiums. Those retirees over age 65 who are covered by Medicare will have the same range of benefits which Medicare covers, with the negotiated health care plan covering the Medicare deductibles and co-payments in excess of $200 per person. Dental, hearing, and vision coverage has been eliminated. Other changes to retiree medical and life insurance coverage are summarized below.

	Under Age 65	Over Age 65 (and/or Medicare Eligible)
Contributions (premiums) per person	$70/month	$34/month
Deductibles per person	$200/year	$200/year
Co-payments	20% of expenses after deductible has been met	None
Out-of-pocket maximum per person (includes deductibles)	$500/year	$200/year
Office visits covered	No	Yes
Part B Medicare premiums	None	Paid by retiree
Prescriptions drug co-payments	$8/generic drug $18/brand name drug $7/mail order (30-day supply)	$8/generic drug $18/brand name drug $7/mail order (30-day supply)
Life insurance	$5,000 maximum (limited additional coverage can be purchased at group rates)	$5,000 maximum (limited additional coverage can be purchased at group rates)

# # #

Connecting with Consumers

Lisa Fortini-Campbell, Ph.D.
Associate Professor, Medill School of Journalism,
Northwestern University,
and President, Fortini-Campbell Co.

A STRATEGIC APPROACH TO CONSUMER-BASED PUBLIC RELATIONS

Of the many stakeholders responsible for making our corporations and organizations successful, it would be easy to argue that consumers are the most important. An organization may have a product or service, a method of distribution, and an internal support structure, but if it does not have a consumer, it cannot exist or sustain itself. In the corporate world, consumers buy products or services, generating the cash flow that allows a company to grow and expand, to invest in improving itself, and to make a profit. In the not-for-profit world, consumers are the end-users of an organization's services, creating for that organization a sense of purpose and focus. The opportunity that consumers represent is the reason we organize in the first place. Consumers are an organization's greatest assets, and ones to be carefully managed.

The consumer audience also commands our attention because of its size. In any particular industry, there may be several government regulators, a hundred industry analysts, a thousand reporters, tens of thousands of employees, and a hundred thousand investors. But, there may be tens of millions of consumers, buying and using the industry's products and services every day. Each one of these consumers is a stakeholder in that organization's current success, and each represents an opportunity for the organization to build a relationship which will sustain its success in the future.

The diversity of the consumer audience is also a unique characteristic of this stakeholder group. We group consumers together into one audience simply because they share a common behavior, that is, they have purchased or used a product or service. However, the needs which prompted their desire for that product or service may differ widely, as may the benefits they derive from it. There may be widely different attitudinal and behavioral segments within any group of consumers, there may be different cultures within any one country's consumer base, and certainly there is a great diversity of cultures across an international consumer franchise. Both the size and diversity of our consumer audiences present exciting challenges to public relations and communications professionals.

Influencing, persuading, and motivating this critical stakeholder group is a fundamental activity of any organization. Marketers and communications professionals are particularly dedicated to this task, and always have been. Public relations professionals, as one type of communications expert, are also highly involved in this influence function, but their role has evolved over time. Public relations, like other communications functions, has evolved a far more central role in an organization's planning process than it once had. Its particular tools are less likely than they once were to be used only in narrow, tactical ways to achieve certain marketing objectives or to solve particular short-term problems. Today, public relations and other communications programs actively contribute to an organization's broad, strategic goal of reaching out to its consumers. An organization's outreach efforts increase its understanding of this critical stakeholder group, as well as potentially increase the consumer's commitment to, preference for, or loyalty to the organization. Communications professionals and the tools at their disposal are critical to the effective functioning of today's private and public organizations.

Perspective

Because consumer audiences are so large and diverse, it would be inappropriate to attempt to draw general conclusions about how communications and public relations should be used to affect them. However, an important issue shared by all communications practitioners is the need to understand consumer motivations fully and richly enough to be able to design programs which persuasively and effectively "connect" with those consumers. As any communications professional knows, the programs he or she creates are far more likely to be effective at influencing, persuading, and motivating a consumer audience if they are constructed from the beginning with the wants, needs, and motivations of that audience in mind. To that end, this chapter will focus on ways in which communications professionals and their organizations can learn more about consumers as a foundation for effectively influencing and persuading them.

Definitions

Before beginning the next section, it is necessary to define a few terms. "Consumer" is a word used quite broadly, but it generally refers to the "end-user" of a company's product or service, that is, the person who pays for and "consumes" that product or service. In a not-for-profit context, a consumer may be a "client" of a public organization, benefiting from the services that organization has been created and funded to offer. In a political context, a consumer may be a "voter." Inasmuch as the corporation or organization provides a product, service, issue, or candidate to someone to be used or affiliated with, the corporation or organization has a consumer. Equally, a consumer can be defined as the person on whom the organization depends for the money, effort, time, or votes which sustain it. The relationship between an organization and its consumers is indeed an interdependent one, and one which should work to the benefit of both parties.

For purposes of this chapter, we broaden the definition of "consumer" to include a type of person often called a "customer." Customers are, in fact, consumers, but in a business-to-business context. For example, a food manufacturer's first "consumer" is the grocery store buyer. A clothing manufacturer's first "consumer" is a department store buyer. A mutual fund company's first "consumer" may be the stockbroker whose own consumer is the investor. Because these people are essential elements of the distribution system of most corporations, they should be considered part of the broad consumer audience.

Indeed, it would be reasonable to consider a consumer to be anyone from whom the organization wants something. And, using that logic, we could extend the definition of a consumer to include any of an organization's many publics, stakeholders, or audiences. However, extending the definition of a consumer to include everyone an organization hopes to influence is over-broad for the purpose of this chapter. And while many of the techniques described below can be applied to the understanding of audiences other than consumers, we will restrict our definition to those end-users and intermediate users commonly known as consumers and customers.

Strategic Approach

For at least the last 40 years, consumer and customer marketing have been increasingly important functions in any sophisticated organization. They are functions perhaps most fully developed in for-profit commercial enterprises, but they are gaining in sophistication in not-for-profit and political enterprises as well. And, as more companies become multinational, the techniques used to market to consumers and customers are widely shared all over the globe.

However, it is important to reiterate that, regardless of how widespread or how sophisticated they have become, marketing and marketing communications are essentially tools for organizing and formalizing the process of consumer and customer persuasion. In fact, with all of the tools of the marketing mix—product, pricing, distribution, packaging, communications, and customer service—we hope to persuade consumers that our organization is more capable of satisfying and delighting them than any other.

As with any persuasive activity, a marketer or communicator's programs are only as effective as the insights into consumers and customers which inform them. Indeed, we will always find that an organization that is effective with its consumer audience is one that is highly skilled at gathering and interpreting useful information about those consumers. It is an organization dedicated to distilling key insights into its most important stakeholder and aligning its programs with those insights. Therefore, perhaps the most critical foundation stones for organizational success are the development of a base of knowledge about the consumer, the ability to carefully listen to and interpret that knowledge, and the ability to disseminate consumer and customer insights throughout the organization.

Of course, in many organizations consumer and market research have long been important tools in planning marketing and communications strategies and tactics. The techniques for conducting such research vary widely, but they are well-established, and range from small-scale qualitative research (often called "soft soundings" in a public relations context) to large-scale and projectable quantitative research, including surveys. It is difficult to say which of the many available techniques is most appropriate in a particular circumstance, but many excellent marketing research firms exist in virtually every country which can help formulate a program of marketing research relevant to a particular consumer target.

As you formulate a program of marketing research or consider the base of information your organization has already collected, it is important to remember that there are many ways of knowing and understanding consumers and customers. While there are a great number of techniques available to help us learn about consumers "in general" or "on the average," and they are critical to intelligent decision making, other techniques help us to get closer to the consumer, closing the inevitable distance between ourselves as marketers, communicators, and public relations professionals and the consumer.

It is an unfortunate fact of organizational life that, as an individual rises in authority and decision-making power, the more detached he or she often becomes from the consumer. In today's organizations, with so much to do and so few people to do it, the chief executive, division president, marketing vice president, and communications director spend most of their time ensconced in headquarters offices, making decisions that are well-informed but based on little first-hand information about the wants and needs of the object of their actions: the consumer.

Many facets of organizational life conspire to keep an organization's members at all levels away from direct contact with their consumers, but it is a tendency which must be fought. The more often organizational managers, and particularly communications professionals, decide how to best influence consumers based on executive summaries of distantly collected data, the greater the likelihood that those decision makers will miss important nuances and details of the consumer's experience. And it is often the nuances of the consumer's experience that lead to greater and deeper insights into their motivations, and better ideas about how to use communications tools to persuade them.

Interacting directly with consumers need not be an overly time-consuming or onerous task, but it should be one which is routinely incorporated into the activities of anyone who is responsible for work designed to influence, persuade, or motivate the consumer. Perhaps one useful way of thinking about our responsibilities to interact with consumers is to imagine them as "constituents," and ourselves as their "representatives." Inasmuch as we have organizational goals to which we are accountable, nonetheless we will always find ourselves more successful at achieving them if we embrace the consumer as part of that process. Therefore, as you plan, execute, and evaluate public relations and other communications programs, it is very important to include tools that allow you to reach out to consumers, making yourselves a part of their lives, and tools that allow consumers to reach in and become a part of the way the organizations operates.

TACTICAL APPROACHES

Reaching Out

There are a variety of ways of reaching out to the consumer, all within the capabilities of every public relations practitioner, marketer, and communicator. The simplest is to spend time with consumers, observing the way they shop for, purchase, and use our products or services. Marketers at Wal-Mart, a large discount retail chain, for example, spend several days each week in their own stores (and those of the competition) watching consumers shop, questioning them about their purchases, and asking them for feedback. At the end of each week, they return to their headquarters office and, in conjunction with their colleagues who have also spent time in stores in other locales, they discuss what's on the consumer's mind, what trends they need to watch, and what problems they need to correct. Armed with that information, they can tailor all manner of programs to the immediate needs of customers in a very specific local area.

At Anheuser-Busch, the largest American brewery, people from all of the functional departments get to know consumers in an interesting way. When they are considering a new product, for example, they often have it bottled and labeled as if it were already on the market, and take it to a tavern or bar in a nearby town. After making arrangements with the tavern owner, they offer it for sale to the consumers who happen to be in the tavern. As the consumers try the new product, representatives from Anheuser-Busch from marketing, sales, research and development, promotions, advertising, and public relations wander around the tavern, watching who orders the product, how much they order, and talking to them about how they like it. A technique like this certainly lessens the distance between the people who work at Anheuser-Busch and the consumers they are trying to delight.

In fact, visits with consumers and customers should be a part of the routine activities of people in all functional areas of an organization. If an individual's work touches the consumer in any way, there is always the opportunity to improve that work based on a greater insight into the consumer.

Indeed, customer outreach visits have long been the hallmark of some of the best-managed companies in the world. In fact, two years ago, when Louis Gerstner took over management of the giant IBM corporation, he spent much of the first year on the job traveling the world and meeting personally with customers in every product and market segment. He learned there is no better way of understanding the wants and needs, satisfactions and dissatisfactions, and hopes and aspirations of customers than to visit with them himself. His visits with customers influenced decisions in product design and development, pricing and distribution, and, importantly, how to organize and brand the wide variety of IBM products and services all around the world. In fact, many chief executives and divisional managers subscribe to the same philosophy and routinely include customer visits in their work schedules.

Consumer outreach need not be limited to the highest levels of an organization, however. The entire organization has the opportunity to benefit when the widest variety of employees possible have the opportunity to interact directly with consumers. At Mercedes-Benz in Germany, for example, a customer can take possession of his or her automobile at the factory, and have a chance to meet with and talk to the people who designed and built it. At John Deere & Co., a manufacturer of agricultural and construction equipment, factory workers are sent to customer sites to learn more about their needs directly. The information they bring back not only benefits the design and manufacturing processes, but also the marketing and communications processes. The customer knowledge they gather becomes a part of what the entire organization knows about its customers, making it better able to serve their needs with every product, marketing, and communications tool at its disposal.

Of course, these outreach interactions can be useful for gaining insight into other audiences as well. In particular, our marketing efforts and communications programs can often be vastly improved when we use these techniques to help us understand the employees who directly serve consumers. Certainly frontline employees are important "communications tools" themselves, leaving indelible impressions on the consumer about how much the organization cares about them and is interested in delighting them. It clearly behooves us to keep our fingers directly on the pulse of employee sentiment as much as it does on that of the consumer.

At many companies, in fact, management encourages headquarters employees throughout the organization to work as frontline employees themselves at least once a year to better understand the wants and needs of consumers. At Hyatt International and McDonald's, managers work at registration desks, as bellhops, serve in the restaurants, cook hamburgers, and ring up purchases so that they have actual experience interacting with consumers. With that experience, their decisions back at headquarters are informed with a reality about both the consumer and the employees who serve them that would be difficult for them to get otherwise.

Working in the company's own customer service department is often a much-overlooked way of getting to know the customer first hand. Unfortunately, in many organizations, the customer service department is located far away from the rest of the organization, and its members are often excluded from discussions about the wants and needs of consumers. Perhaps that is a result of the fact that many of these departments were formed with the goal of handling customer complaints, and so those customers who do phone or write are seen as dissatisfied, hard-to-handle complainers who do not represent the majority of the organization's consumer franchise. However, with the increasing use of toll-free numbers in virtually every category of consumer good, customer service departments can provide an important way for companies to gather direct information from their consumers. In fact, it might be argued that customer service representatives are some of the most powerful tools of a company's public relations programs, capable of answering questions, solving problems, and otherwise creating the goodwill that any organization wants to have with its consumer stakeholders.

Naturally with any of these techniques there is always the fear that, with the limited time available to any member of an organization, particularly a key decision maker, the interactions he or she can have with consumers is likely to be very idiosyncratic and unrepresentative, and therefore the conclusions this decision maker might draw could be suspect. This, of course, is possible. But if we agree that the most fundamental purpose of our organizations is to gather and share information, and that all employees should be committed to this purpose, then there is little to fear. All of the information, gathered in any way by any person, becomes a part of the organization's collective knowledge base, and the effect of any single piece of information is tempered by the rest of what the organization knows.

Reaching In

Inasmuch as the organization can reach out to its customers and consumers, there are ways in which organizations can provide more formal opportunities for consumers and customers to enter into its decision-making processes. Today, many companies have created consumer advisory panels or boards which can be consulted at a variety of points in the processes of devising business, marketing, and communications strategies and tactics. In some cases, the consumer may be aware that he or she is part of such a panel; in other cases not. But in either case, the company has ready access to people who can serve as representatives of the larger consumer audience and as a reality check for decisions and programs under consideration.

The most-detached form of consumer advisory board is a traditional form of market research known as a panel study. In this case, a sample of consumers is selected to represent the large population of consumers in a particular industry or category. These consumers generally do not know they are members of a panel for a particular company, which tends to encourage their objectivity. The size of the panel can vary from several hundred to several thousand and is usually selected and maintained by an outside market research firm. These kinds of panels are used to gather information about general consumer wants and needs, as well as emerging trends in behavior and attitudes. They form a reliable base of data on which behaviors and attitudes can be quantified, and therefore they are a source of information on which many marketing decisions can confidently be based. The major disadvantage of such a panel is its high cost and the lack of direct interaction between the organization's personnel and its consumer constituents.

Beyond the traditional market research panel, organizations often form panels of consumer experts and opinion leaders to help them stay on top of trends that can affect their marketing and communications programs. This kind of advisory panel is particularly useful in a fast-moving industry such as the computer industry, or in industries subject to quickly shifting trends such as the toy and fashion industries. Here, an organization might identify early adopters of new technologies or innovations, or people who have amassed an influential expertise in a particular area. An organization can monitor the information-gathering, shopping, and purchase behavior of these consumers in a detached and unidentified way, or it can directly interact with them and question them in a roundtable discussion format. Of course, there is always the fear that such direct interaction will taint the validity of the information and insights these consumers have to offer. On the other hand, if the members of the organization learn to interact with these consumers in a way that emphasizes their ability to listen and observe, then this risk can be minimized and these consumers can serve as extremely valuable advisers to the organization.

The longitudinal study of consumers is unfortunately a greatly overlooked way of bringing the consumer closer to the organization. Traditional market research tools tend to take a "snapshot" of the consumer at a single point in time. For example, we might conduct a focus group on a topic of interest with a group of consumers in one month, and then conduct a survey among a different randomly selected sample of consumers during another month. The concept of selecting independent samples of consumers for different research projects is the norm in the market research community. In fact, there is a definite bias against "reusing" consumers in research projects for fear that they will become consumer "experts," so self-conscious of the role they play in an organization's information-gathering process that they will no longer represent the average consumer.

The view that only the most objective and clinically gathered information should be used by organizations in their marketing and communications planning processes may be mistaken. Certainly market research which conforms to the strict standards demanded by the social sciences should be the foundation of our base of knowledge about the consumer. But preventing casual and ongoing interaction between the organization and its consumers in the name of pure research works to the disadvantage of the entire organization by making statistically defined consumers unknowable to the average employee.

It can be very valuable for an organization to establish a long-term, ongoing relationship with a set of everyday consumers who can be consulted for their opinions on both broad and specific questions. It may be that consumers are selected as consultants or advisers for only a year's time, but during that year they can be available to the organization for visits in person or talks on the phone. Having these kinds of consumers readily available encourages organization members to contact them spontaneously, as well as encourages the consumer to contact the organization with thoughts or ideas. And having contact with the same consumers over an extended period of time helps to make the consumer's point of view better understood by the whole organization. It is easy to see how this kind of contact can help draw the consumer and the organization closer together by making the consumer a real person, rather than a set of summary statistics.

Small panels of everyday consumers are also valuable resources to organizations as ways of testing early drafts of new product ideas, packaging, marketing programs, or communications tactics. In this particular case, consumers who represent the general consumer base, but who may be more self-aware, articulate, and creative in their expression than average, can be identified and selected to be part of an ongoing panel. Such panels have been put together by companies like Intuit (a maker of financial software packages) to work closely with software designers who strive to create software that is easy to install and use. Automobile companies such as Oldsmobile also bring consumers to their design factories to help them get an early reading on automobile prototypes. At Kraft Foods, members of the Creative Kitchens staff may go to consumers' homes to watch them prepare dishes with new products or with new recipes.

The same kinds of consumer panels can also be used to give an organization early reactions to public relations and communications programs. If, for example, a company is working through a crisis, like Johnson & Johnson during the Tylenol tampering case or Exxon during the Exxon Valdez crisis, a consumer panel can be of great use. First, these consumers can help the company understand the kinds of questions that segments of consumers are likely to have, or understand the nature of the fear or anger they may be harboring. They can also react to and provide feedback on alternatives the company is considering for handling such a crisis, helping the organization refine its programs so that they are maximally effective.

Companies whose products are purchased by specific age groups, such as alcoholic beverages, may also find longitudinal consumer panels of particular use. It is often the case that consumers gravitate to a particular brand of alcoholic beverage during their young adult years but then, as time passes, find themselves experimenting with other brands and eventually becoming loyal to some other brand than the one with which they started. This pattern of trial and experimentation is a difficult one to manage, and we often find that certain brands of alcoholic beverages enjoy a short cycle of popularity, after which they decline and are virtually impossible to resurrect.

Nevertheless, close contact with a set of early triers of one brand would help the company anticipate when and why a consumer eventually moves on to another brand. Armed with that information, particular communications programs can often be designed and employed which help to keep the brand fresh and relevant to current drinkers over time and to generations of new consumers as they emerge. Anheuser-Busch, for example, designs communications programs relevant to each year's new crop of young adults. That kind of close contact, and the willingness to modify programs each year, has helped to sustain Budweiser's popularity among young adults for 20 years.

It is often valuable for a company to maintain particularly close ongoing ties with its outside distribution system. Whenever an organization relies on dealers, distributors, trade partners, or another form of nonproprietary sales force to interact with the ultimate consumer, the organization must stay on top of their attitudes and ideas which certainly affect the consumer. John Nuveen & Company, a well-known sponsor of tax-free mutual fund products, maintains a panel of stockbrokers, bankers, financial planners, and insurance agents who sell Nuveen's products directly to the investor. These financial advisors are directly consulted by Nuveen's marketing and communications professionals and offer them a unique and helpful way of understanding the financial adviser's relationship with the investor. The financial advisers also benefit because they are often informed of new products or programs first, and enjoy an opportunity to offer input into the design of products to benefit their investors.

This idea can be easily extended to include panels of industry experts, media representatives, and employees. Any "constituency" can be drawn closer to the organization by making a sample of its members easily accessible to members of the organization.

THE FUTURE

Too often today, we think of consumers as the quasi-military objective of our marketing and communications efforts. We speak of "capturing" the consumer, "locking up" their purchase patterns, employing "guerrilla" tactics or "flanking" maneuvers to "destroy" the competition and establish a "beachhead" with a consumer market. This way of conceptualizing our efforts and of describing them to one another is antithetical to the view described above and the feeling we must have towards consumers to ensure our organization's future survival.

As markets in more industries and in more countries mature, and as supply exceeds demand in many of those markets, it will become increasingly clear to organizations that maintaining a long-term relationship with consumers should be the organization's most important goal. Organizations that embrace consumers as true stakeholders in their success will benefit from the long-term asset value those consumers represent. Organizations which find unique and effective ways to reach out to the consumer and to allow the consumer to reach into the organization will be ones with the greatest chance of building those relationships. The form that these "outreach" and "inreach" activities take may vary organization by organization and corporation by corporation. Nevertheless, establishing these activities and making them a continuing part of the marketing and communications planning processes will reap great benefits. If organizations are to survive and thrive in the market conditions under which they must operate, the consumer and his or her wants and needs must become central to the way the organization perceives itself.

Rather than a military metaphor, we might be better served with an agricultural one, conceiving of our consumers the way a farmer might of his land. Our consumers are people we cultivate and care for; if they are stewarded carefully, they ensure our survival. Like the farmer, we can never afford to forget the consumer. All of the resources of our organizations must be expended in ensuring the complete satisfaction, if not delight, of that person. If we achieve that goal, consumers will reward us with their continuing goodwill and loyalty, and will work with us through any crisis or difficulty that we may encounter.

The most important activity a forward-thinking manager can do to help encourage this way of thinking is to set a good example. If the highest levels of an organization dedicate themselves to some form of regular and direct contact with consumers, other levels of the organization will follow. Indeed, if the management of an organization goes further to reward the contributions of all employees or members who get closer to the customer, the organization will much more easily orient itself in that direction. A manager can never allow disassociation from the consumer or customer to become a corollary of increasing authority in the organization.

And while it is critical for the organization to maintain access to high-quality market research information, it can never afford to rely on it exclusively as the organization's only way of knowing about the consumer. Market research and the researchers who assure its quality and help to interpret its meaning are essential to the objective knowledge base from which any organization must operate. To operate without it, the organization risks making serious and costly mistakes. On the other hand, to cut the rest of the organization off from direct contact with consumers is to run the risk that consumers become dry, stereotyped representations, worthy of neither true respect nor cultivation. In fact, the two ways of knowing can work happily together to create a "stereo vision" for the organization, so to speak, providing greater clarity and more depth than either could alone.

If a formal market research department has already been established at an organization, relatively little expensive training or education is necessary to help the rest of the organization become "consumer advocates." A formal market research department can act as a useful quality-control mechanism to ensure that the information on which the organization will make major business or strategic decisions meets the necessary standard of quality. But such a department can also help to raise the skills of everyone else in the organization, helping them to become better consumer observers and listeners, and more astute interpreters of what they see and hear.

In fact, some organizations, such as Hewlett-Packard, have reoriented the charters of their traditional market research departments from "information gathering" to "consumer advocacy," and have encouraged their "research analysts" to become "consumer evangelists." What is important about this reorientation is the change in focus from the information itself and how it is collected to what it means and how it is incorporated into the planning and decision-making processes of the organization. These consumer advocates have become responsible for sharing information and insights, gathered in a wide variety of ways throughout the organization, with whomever can use them. They have also become instrumental in encouraging employees from all over the organization to become "customerized" and to have direct experiences with consumers that they can share with everyone else. The experiences of companies such as Hewlett-Packard have shown that it is essential to close the inevitable distance between the organization and its consumers with constant reminders of what these consumers want and need and how they think. And they have shown us that it is possible.

Fortunately for all of us, embracing the consumer as the most essential stakeholder in our success is more a matter of commitment than financial expenditure. It does not need to be expensive to get closer to the customer. But employees of our corporations and members of our organizations will not make the personal commitment to participate unless they are encouraged and rewarded for doing so. They must understand that success depends in part on bringing back to the rest of the organization the insights and the sense of reality that come from ongoing contact with consumers. As a manager of a consumer-oriented organization, your commitment to that goal will breed theirs, and together you will draw the consumer closer.

The Strategic Uses of Corporate Philanthropy

John A. Koten
President
The Wordsworth Group

A STRATEGIC APPROACH

Introduction

Public relations is popularly described as doing good things and getting credit for it. The strategic use of philanthropy not only can make this possible, but can go beyond to help ensure the very survival of the corporation. That's because corporate contributions are one place where a company's interest and the public interest can intersect. When properly used, both parties benefit.

The Business Roundtable of leading corporate executives in 1981 proclaimed, "All business entities should recognize philanthropy as good business and an obligation if they are to be considered responsible corporate citizens of the national and local communities in which they operate."

Today, corporate contributions are viewed not only as beneficial to communities and as helping companies fulfill the role of good corporate citizen, but increasingly they are being used to help improve profitability. For many companies, the nature of their reputation is a major factor in their ability to gain a competitive edge.

An essential role of public relations is to maintain or enhance a company's reputation so it can serve its customers profitably.

One of the tools available to the public relations executive to help fashion a favorable public identity is the company's contributions program. Ideally, this function falls within the corporate communications department. If not, it is desirable to have a member of the department (preferably the senior person) sit on the company contributions committee. In either case, the public relations executive should ensure that contributions are being made that are consistent with the company's overall interests and objectives. Every effort should be made to minimize the possibility that a contribution might in some way embarrass a company or be unintentionally controversial.

Developing an effective contributions strategy can assist the corporation in establishing a positive identity with each of its key stakeholder groups, most important of which are investors, public officials, and employees. Many companies, large and small, have used contributions to successfully build their images with the public. Among them are AT&T, Mobil, Texaco, Philip Morris, Nike, and Ben and Jerry's.

Unfortunately, grant making in many corporations is reactive rather than proactive. Companies with well-defined grant criteria, which are used to attract or select grant requests, generally have the most-effective programs. Company programs that involve the company in public/private partnerships, encourage employee giving and volunteering, and, in one way or another, effect change are the most satisfying.

It should be pointed out that not everyone agrees that corporations should be permitted to make contributions. The noted economist John Kenneth Galbraith believes that corporations should *not* be allowed to make contributions. He says it gives them a chance to use undue influence in social and economic matters.

In contrast, David Finn, former CEO of Ruder and Finn, laments, "companies and their leaders don't get enough credit for what they do for society and, out of fear of criticism, they don't make the effort to tell what they and their companies are doing for their communities and the nation.

"The public," he says, "may approve or condemn a specific corporate action, but if it knows what kind of person is responsible for the company's policies and what values he or she believes in, it is possible to be responsive to that leadership. Instead of being anonymous instruments of impersonal corporate interests, top executives can be understood as conscientious individuals doing their best to fulfill the responsibilities to society which they believe to be of great importance." [1]

Today's CEO takes this a step further and seeks to find out how the company contributions program also can be used to meet the company's self-interest as well. Weyerhaeuser, for example, conducted a study to determine where their contributions actually were going and what was resulting from them. The study was prompted by a concern of top management that the company was donating money to activities that didn't coincide with the company's basic objectives. They wanted to give money that tied in with the company's identifiable interests and strengths. The result was a decision to make most of their contributions to the preservation of forests.

In determining how the company can make the best use of its philanthropic dollars, the advice of the corporate communications professional is critical. As the link between the company and its various publics, this executive is in the best position to see that the needs of all constituencies are being met. This includes those whose objectives are internal, and those whose objectives are external. If analyzed correctly, all parties will benefit—and the possibility of making a wrong move will be minimized.

Contributions, Sponsorships, and Event Marketing

Philanthropy must be distinguished from sales promotion, advertising, sponsorships, and the newer field of event marketing. In one sense, they all relate. All are intended to better "position" the company in the minds of its stakeholders. In another important way, however, they are separate.

The essential *internal* difference in each of these activities is the source of funds. Contributions are made from a company's profits. Funds for sales promotion, advertising, sponsorships, and event marketing are taken as part of operating expenses. In recent years, because of the rapid growth of sponsorships and event marketing, the source of funds for these activities has blurred somewhat. The Internal Revenue Service, companies, and charities are working together to assure these expenditures are properly allocated.

Contributions must be made with no expected direct monetary return to the company. To do otherwise would be to engage in "self-dealing," which is illegal. Neither can contributions be made to candidates for office or to political parties or organizations.

Nevertheless, a company is not required to give money to simply any organization, and it can be selective about whom it chooses to receive its contributions. The strategic company makes selected gifts to further its broad goals and to identify with causes in which it has a particular interest.

As a matter of fact, several watchdog groups regularly berate companies for giving money to organizations that are described as "antibusiness" or "antidemocratic." Though a company is free to give to whomever it chooses, sometimes, because of the great number of requests received for contributions, not enough research is done into what an organization actually does or advocates. This can result in a contribution being made to a cause a company might not normally favor. Tactical errors such as these are all the more reason for putting a public relations lens on all contributions to assure they enhance the corporation's goals rather than detract from them.

The Internal Revenue Service permits a company to give up to 10 percent of its profits to charitable (nonprofit) organizations. They are, for the most part, known as 501-(C)(3) organizations (the reference is to the section of the IRS code). Few actually give this much. The majority of companies give approximately one to two percent of their pretax net income (PTNI).

The example most frequently cited of enlightened giving is the Minneapolis-St. Paul area, where companies such as the retailer Dayton-Hudson giving up to five percent of their PTNI are not unusual. Other communities have two-percent clubs which challenge local businesses to give more to charity. All these local "clubs" are designed to encourage businesses to use their expertise as well as their money to take a more active role in helping their communities.

In recent years, many corporations have set up foundations to ensure consistency and stability in their giving programs. In good earnings years, they contribute more money to their foundations in order to cover years when their earnings may not be as good. Many foundations build up a large capital base, the earnings from which are used to provide a financial base for their annual giving programs. In almost every case, a company foundation has key members of the senior management group on its board of directors. They attempt to keep their programs on a parallel track with the corporation's strategic goals. To assure a degree of objectivity in making grants, enlightened foundations have "outside" directors on their board. Some foundations, though they may share the name (i.e., Ford), have no direct connection with the company.

Many companies have "pass-through" foundations in which the company gives to its foundation annually and the foundation then distributes the money it receives directly to designated organizations. This method provides some insulation for the company since it does not directly make the contribution. This has positive and negative aspects. The Exxon Education Foundation was regarded as a model of this form of corporate giving. The Foundation, acting independently of the corporation though receiving money from it regularly, gave to causes it believed best—thereby insulating the corporation from any direct criticism (or praise). Unfortunately, the Foundation, which gave heavily to educational institutions, did not support environmental groups. So when the corporation was confronted in 1989 with the Exxon Valdez disaster, it had no environmental allies it could turn to immediately for help or support. It's a good example of what can happen when a giving program doesn't match the parent's strategic needs.

Companies with steady earnings do not need to set up a foundation since they are capable of maintaining their giving programs at stable levels. The importance of steady earnings for a contributions program is to have the ability to make and keep multiyear commitments. The source of contributions, whether made through a foundation or directly, is corporate profits.

A number of critics have wondered aloud whether some companies' giving activities are being turned into subliminal marketing ploys. They say that mixing marketing and philanthropy has the potential of pandering to the sentimentality of a naive public—or the elitism of the rich. This is a legitimate complaint as, increasingly, there appears to be a convergence of image making with do-gooding. As one critic commented, it's a "triumph of sleaze over virtue."[2]

Since funding for sponsorships and event marketing comes from operating funds, this money is spent with an expected return in sales. However, in their zeal to promote or sell products, some marketing people choose activities that are not consistent with corporate objectives. This is a significant reason for having a public relations professional involved in the decision-making process to provide oversight, since it is that executive's job to be concerned about the company's overall reputation.

Philanthropy has been part of the American tradition since the founding of this country. Initially it was fostered by the religious community; later, wealthy families and individuals accepted responsibility for helping others by making financial contributions. Names like Carnegie, Rockefeller, and Mellon are frequently cited as some of the earliest philanthropists. Some of these names now have far more favorable reputations in the public's mind as civic-minded philanthropists than they do as the hard-driving, monopolistic businessmen they were.

History of Corporate Contributions

The first companies known to use contributions as part of their business strategy were the railroads in the early 1890s. Recognizing that many of their passengers and employees needed clean, comfortable, inexpensive places to stay overnight as they made cross-country journeys requiring connections, the railroads made contributions to support local YMCAs located in various key crossroad communities. Generally, the railroads provided 60 percent of the Y's operating budgets and expected rentals from passengers and employees to cover the remaining 40 percent. These contributions for "supervised economical accommodations" at the turn of the century not only furthered the railroads' goal of helping passengers travel safely, but they did much to stimulate the growth of YMCAs. These Ys also served as homes for train crew members who, having finished a "run," needed a place to stay before they returned to their place of origin the following day. This early use of company contributions served two important stakeholder groups—customers and employees. As railroads prospered during those days of extensive train travel, a third group, investors, also benefited as the contributions made longer, more expensive (and more profitable) journeys possible.

Over the years, corporate contributions philosophy has broadened considerably. Prior to World War II, most company giving programs (of those few that existed) were the private purview of the CEO and/or a handful of senior executives. Sometimes the CEO's wife was influential in determining where corporate contributions were directed. In the 1950s, contributions programs began to take on an entire new look.

In 1955, the Ford Motor Car company, which initially funded the Ford Foundation in 1936 with a grant of $25,000, announced that it would spin off $641 million of its stock to the Foundation when it changed from a private to a publicly held company. Concurrently, the Foundation announced that it would make grants in 1956 totaling $260 million to more than 600 private four-year colleges and universities to help increase faculty salaries. Ford's action provided an enormous stimulus to corporate giving.

Also in 1955, General Electric started the landmark matching gift program which enabled employees to have a say about where corporate money was donated. Originally viewed as a fringe benefit to attract and retain employees, the program grew into an effective device for directing corporate contributions.

It wasn't long before matching gifts were extended to a wide variety of cultural, social, and health-related organizations. Andrew Heiskill, former CEO of Time, Inc., said, "Matching gifts are one of the best ways of boosting employee morale and building a good feeling about working for an organization that supports the causes chosen by its employees." Heiskill went on to say that "50 percent of a company's giving should be 'employee driven.'"[3]

From modestly matching approximately $200,000 in employee contributions to colleges the first year, by 1980 more than 900 companies were participating in the educational "match," providing about $40 million for higher education. In 1993, the total match by companies to education, culture, and health-related and other nonprofits amounted to well over $100 million annually.

In the late 1950s, Sanford Cousins, a vice president of AT&T, proposed in an article in the company magazine that the company and its employees "begin helping the *communities* we serve." In that way, he argued, the company would benefit because, as the communities grew and prospered, so would the company. Employees would benefit since they would be helping neighbors in *their* communities with the company's support. Shortly thereafter, the Bell company in Illinois made "help the communities we serve" its fourth "guiding principle" following (1) serve the public, (2) benefit investors, and (3) deal squarely with employees. So began an era of targeting corporate contributions to a broad range of local or regional social programs and economic development efforts.

Other companies followed suit, and there was a considerable increase in support for social service agencies and community groups through the 1960s and 1970s. As conditions in many communities deteriorated, it was apparent that, if a company was to maintain a viable pool of labor in its area, it needed to help stabilize such social problems as housing, crime, transportation, education, health care, and racial friction.

Specific targeting of contributions to aid a particular aspect of a corporation's interests came next. In the mid-1970s, General Motors, seeking to improve its management recruiting efforts on college campuses, decided to concentrate its educational giving on the 13 business schools and 14 engineering schools it deemed crucial to its own future.

In 1980, Kenneth L. Albrecht, a vice president of Equitable Life Assurance Company, said, "There is really no point in any corporation wasting its time on matters in which it has no interest and with which it is not equipped to deal. For example, Equitable, a life, health, and pension company, will almost always have a segment of its program devoted to health. If we made musical instruments, our interest in the performing arts would likely be great."[4]

Through the 1980s, as it became clear the federal government was shifting the burden of support for many social activities back to the local community, enlightened companies, recognizing that individuals couldn't take on the increased burden completely by themselves, stepped in to help out. Those that did won the plaudits of the public and, importantly, government officials. The impetus for these activities usually came from public relations personnel—those either engaged in the contributions area or those involved with community relations activities.

The public relations person, as the external "eyes and ears" of the company, is in the best position to assess shifts in societal trends and economic conditions. Support for economic development activities arose when it became clear that jobs were shifting from region to region within the country and overseas. By supporting groups or activities that helped keep jobs within a community, corporations helped protect their customer base and their community's tax base—both of which had considerable economic implications for companies.

In 1984, the Amoco Foundation, headquartered in Chicago, decided to target its giving to improving the quality of housing in the inner city. It began by giving $150,000 to Bethel New Life, a neighborhood group on the city's Near West Side. By stabilizing housing in the city, it reasoned, it could help protect its investment in an area where it had many gasoline service stations. The initial effort was so positive that, by 1990, it had given $990,000 to 60 community development and neighborhood rehabilitation organizations in the Chicago area.

In the 1990s, most companies have become more "customer focused." This has meant a greater emphasis on marketing activities and developing ways of building the customer base, either by increasing market share, increasing unit volume, or bringing out new products. This sometimes has been accomplished through internal growth, but also, increasingly, through mergers and acquisitions. As this occurred, companies increasingly tried to better "position" their images and products. The vehicle for doing this was called "targeted" marketing. After identifying the "target," the companies then sought to relate themselves to something positive to earn customer goodwill.

McDonald's, for example, established Ronald McDonald Houses, comfortable guest houses located near major children's hospitals, so that family members of critically ill children would have an affordable place to stay during a child's hospitalization. Ronald McDonald became an icon for children everywhere as a symbol of care and concern.

McDonald's was so successful in establishing the concept through its Ronald McDonald House charities, that it was able to get other companies (including many suppliers in addition to its franchisees) to contribute to its not-for-profit corporation. According to Phil Webster, former vice president of corporate communications at Scott Paper, "Our involvement with the Ronald McDonald Houses was the most successful in Scott's history. Not only did it significantly increase profits and enhance Scott's national image while raising some $4.5 million for the houses, but importantly it helped us build a business relationship with McDonald's whose 15 million customers go through a lot of paper napkins, bathroom tissue, and tray linen that Scott manufactures."[5]

Officials at McDonald's say that its entire product line benefits from its association with the more than 175 Ronald McDonald Houses in 14 countries.

IBM, the largest corporate donor, links its giving to the interests of its employees. Recognizing the benefits of giving on employee morale, it seeks to encourage volunteerism and gives to nonprofits where employees volunteer. This strategy was regarded as helpful when the company had to significantly reduce its workforce in the early 1990s. Employees believed that the company really cared about people and wasn't just being arbitrary in making its decisions about layoffs. A different attitude could have had long-term negative effects.

As companies have become more global, so has their underwriting of activities overseas. This has been a little more difficult since most countries outside the United States do not have a history of corporate giving, and many of the nonprofits located overseas, accustomed to government support, are uncertain about corporate support. As the amount has increased, however, these concerns have gradually diminished, and more overseas charitable groups have sought to get their fair share.

Companies establishing giving plans in areas where they do business are likely to see dividends from their efforts in the years ahead as they develop a cadre of supporters appreciative of their actions. As in domestic situations, giving should be looked upon as a long-term investment, one which serves the interests of both the community and the company. Selecting the appropriate areas to support is the job of the corporate communications executive.

James Burke, former chairman of Johnson & Johnson, noted, "I have long harbored the belief that the most successful corporations in this country—the ones that have delivered outstanding results over long periods of time—were driven by a simple moral imperative—serving the public in the broadest possible sense—better than their competition. We as businessmen and women have extraordinary leverage on our most important asset . . . goodwill. The goodwill of the public . . . If we make sure our enterprises are managed in terms of their obligations to society . . . that is also the best way to defend this democratic, capitalistic system that means so much to all of us."[6]

Corporate Philanthropy Today

Corporate philanthropy is the fastest-growing part of philanthropy in the United States. About $7.4 billion is given annually by U.S. corporations, which is just about even with the amount given by all private foundations. When noncash items are counted, corporate philanthropy is by far the largest source of income for nonprofits. Noncash contributions include the use of loaned executives, time off given to volunteers, and the donation of goods and services. The latter might include overstocks of food given to local food depositories or it might include outdated computers given by companies such as IBM or Apple to schools. Of course, the donation of items such as computers is not completely eleemosynary since the donors hope that, by learning on their instruments, the users will ultimately become customers. AT&T's manufacturing division took an opposite approach, saying that giving computers to universities does nothing to advance its relationship with these potential customers.

In terms of total dollars, corporate giving has leveled off. However, when measured against the increase in corporate profits (percent of pretax net income), giving has been falling. This measurement may indicate that businesses are losing some of their social consciousness. Fewer and fewer CEOs are championing corporate giving, suggesting that corporate communications chief executives have their work cut out for them.

"Giving money away intelligently," said John E. Corbally, former president of the $3-billion MacArthur Foundation, "is the hardest job there is."

Budgeting for philanthropy is ticklish. Most companies tend to divide their contributions budgets according to the five traditional categories established by the Council of Foundations:

- United Way.
- Health and human services.

156   PART 2 Organizational Chart of Public Relations

- Civic and community.
- Education.
- Arts and culture.

To these, many corporations have added the categories of (1) Economic Developoment and (2) Environment.

In most cases, United Way and Education get the majority of the grants, though there is no set pattern. A pharmaceutical company, for instance, might give the largest share of its budget to health and human services. The scope of a company's giving program most likely will be tied to the nature of the company's operations. National companies tend to give to national organizations, regional companies to regional groups, etc.

Geography always has played a major role in contributions decisions, with the bulk of the money going to agencies in the headquarters or plant or office locations. This is because most companies—regardless of size—believe in helping their local communities. With their gifts, they attempt to improve the areas where they live, work, and do business. This serves both to help stabilize their workforce and to make their location attractive when recruiting new employees. In all cases, local presence of a company is a major factor in giving decisions.

With the increase in targeted giving aimed at assisting the sales or marketing effort, there has been a gradual shift in the designees for contributions. Instead of giving money to organizations for general operating funds, companies now seek specific projects that relate to some aspect of their business. Also, they look for activities that provide opportunities to host their customers. For example, a company might contribute to an exhibit at an art museum with the expectation that they could host an opening night reception for their major customers. In this way, both the museum and the company benefit. The museum receives underwriting for its activities, and the company gets an opportunity to have "quality" time with its customers.

The amount of money spent on such activities might be as little as $5,000 or as much as $2,500,000, depending on the nature of the event and the company's resources. In any case, a company should figure that, in addition to the amount of money contributed to the organization, it should set up a budget to properly promote its involvement and to cover the costs of whatever tie-in activities it holds in conjunction with the event.

Measuring the value of contributions is difficult. Seldom do they directly move a product off the shelf or out of a showroom. Yet their long-term benefits in building goodwill and establishing positive relationships with targeted audiences cannot be denied. Like any other corporate activity today, *contributions should be measurable*. Whereas in earlier times results might have been measured by the success of the organization receiving the money, today it is more likely to be measured in terms of what it does for the giver. This puts a premium on being able to trace results from the donation to the bottom line. Or perhaps, just as importantly to the company, the value is placed on being able to see that attitudes toward the company have improved, thereby creating a better climate for the company to present its message—either sales or perhaps political.

A company might choose to endow a chair at a university. In such a case, the chair invariably, though not necessarily, would relate to a field of special interest to the company. The going rate for chairs at major universities ranges from $1 to $2.5 million. By making such a commitment, the company obviously isn't expecting an immediate return, nor does the university promise one. But both hope that, out of such a collaboration, something useful will occur that will be mutually beneficial in the long run. This is particularly true in a case in which contributions are made to support research or educational achievement.

When contributions are made with an eye on sales, generally the expectation is that the amount of the contribution will be recovered over time through the reinforcement or changing of attitudes about the company. It is important to point out, so donors understand, that the IRS will disallow any contribution that is made to *directly* further sales.

In every case, the person responsible for making the contribution should have some measure in mind which will enable him to judge whether the contribution was successful or not. Without such a measure, making a contribution is likely to be pointless. When that measure is used to compare philanthropy to other ways of maintaining or improving a company's reputation, philanthropy is by far the most cost effective.

A TACTICAL APPROACH

Developing Effective Contributions Programs

To develop an effective contributions program for a company, it is necessary to:

- Determine objectives.
- Establish measurable results.
- Assure the budget is sufficient to achieve and quantify objectives.

Strategic objectives of the company's contributions program may be achieved or supported by using a variety of tactics, such as:

- To establish a favorable reputation, associate with a "quality" or "innovative" activity.
- To position senior executives, create visibility for them.
- To establish a political presence, host opinion makers.
- To motivate employees or thank them for a job well done, invite them to an open house at a museum or to a special concert.
- To improve the quality of education of future employees, adopt a school or class.
- To improve the quality of life in a community in order to attract and keep employees, support activities involving job creation, improved education, better housing, or cultural activities such as theaters, orchestras, museums, and so on.
- To build relationships with political leaders and develop "quality" time with them, invite them to special events.
- To improve health care delivery for employees and the community, support hospitals, clinics, etc.
- To promote an image of quality and innovation, support or assist in research in areas of special interest.
- To attract customers, generate hosting opportunities at sporting or cultural events for sales people.

The list of tactical tie-in possibilities is endless. The list of tactics is increased by the great number of ideas for mutually beneficial collaboration being sent to companies by nonprofit organizations. A plaque to hang on the wall or having one's name engraved on a building isn't enough these days to attract corporate underwriters who are looking for measurable returns for their investment. More and more nonprofits are discovering that their constituents—upscale or otherwise—make a good "target" audience for corporate goals. Matching audiences provides another means for nonprofit organizations to raise money.

Like a customer orientation in marketing, looking at corporate philanthropy from the recipient's viewpoint can help build a better relationship between the company and the nonprofit agency. A stronger relationship can lead to further ventures if the activities are beneficial to both. In earlier times, corporate modesty frequently caused a company to take a low profile. Managers worried about being criticized for taking shareowner money and using it for contributions. This reluctance was coupled with an uncertainty about whether it was the right thing to do in the first place. Increasingly, in today's more competitive environment, many companies are seeking a higher profile and casting aside old concerns in their desire to become more visible and known for doing good works.

However, there are negatives from the nonprofits' standpoint as well, and they should be considered by the company. First, the greatest fear on the part of many nonprofits is the "over-commercialization" of their activities. Selling its name or facility to a company for what can be viewed as commercial purposes can work to a nonprofit's disadvantage in the eyes of *its* constituency. If that is a possibility, then the company should avoid the activity so it doesn't generate negative publicity for itself or create an environment in which its intended audience may feel uncomfortable. Second, becoming involved in a joint venture often creates additional expenses for the nonprofit. In order to participate in a joint venture, it incurs costs in personnel and promotion that aren't covered by the original grant. Instead of benefiting from the venture, the nonprofit loses money, and therefore the relationship sours. Third, most nonprofits need *operating* money. Accepting a targeted grant from a donor for a specific activity frequently doesn't help a nonprofit balance its budget. So from a fund-raising standpoint, the association with a company may not be profitable. It also puts pressure on them to respond to their regular donors who ask, "what are you doing for *me* to give recognition for *my* gifts?"

Over the years, corporate philanthropy has become much more acceptable as the benefits to the public and shareowners have become more apparent. The sheer volume of corporate philanthropy also has made it so common that the public rarely separates it in their minds from advertising. This, of course, has its benefits and drawbacks. The benefit is that it is less likely to draw public ire; the drawback is that the public may not give as much credit to the company for going "good things" as it did formerly.

Examples of Successful Ventures

The decline in literacy in the United States has been a concern to many—especially to businesses which are dependent on the product of the educational system for its workers. With increasingly sophisticated technology rapidly moving into the marketplace, workers who can read and write are essential. This is particularly true for businesses such as newspapers, magazines, book publishers, booksellers, etc.

Harold McGraw of McGraw-Hill became so concerned about the decline in literacy that he set up the Business Council for Effective Literacy and put $1 million of his own money into it.

B. Dalton, the 700-store national booksellers chain, has an obvious interest in literacy. The company makes no bones about who qualifies for *its* contributions. It proclaims, "Dalton's Bookseller is firmly committed to increasing functional literacy within the United

States. As a national full-selection, full-service bookseller, we recognize our responsibility to help solve the illiteracy problem, which affects not only our business, but the quality of life in the communities we serve."[7]

CEO Sherman Swenson took the company's policy a dramatic step further. In the early 1980s, he started an in-house push for volunteers among employees to teach reading to school-age children and adults. The goal was to get 10 percent of his employees involved with local literacy programs over a three-year period. He backed this up by saying the company would donate $3 million over three years to the organizations with which employees became involved. Not surprisingly, with such an incentive, backed up with a good in-house explanation of why improving literacy was important to the company, the goal was exceeded.

Because of the good citizen reputation the company had built up over the years by supporting community activities, Illinois Bell (now part of Ameritech) executives were welcome members of civic groups and other community organizations. When important issues such as zoning or taxes came up, the company's viewpoints were accepted because of the halo effect created by its community involvement. When the company sought to increase rates for service, it was able to find supporters among the groups it had aided. Similarly if the company was going to be hurt in some way by the passage of legislation or local ordinances, it could count on groups of citizens to join its protests about specific distasteful provisions.

Occasionally, ratepayers would protest Illinois Bell's contributions, saying they didn't want any of *their* money going to charity. The chorus against such protests was deafening as charity after charity would point out the benefit of the company's contributions to the community and how those gifts helped stimulate other giving by individuals, corporations, and foundations.

Perhaps one of the most successful of all marriages between corporate philanthropy and strategic goals has been accomplished by Philip Morris. Few industries have been under more constant attack than the tobacco industry. Concern about smoking and children, smoking and pregnant women, aggressive marketing to minorities, dependency on the leadership of controversial North Carolina Senator Jesse Helms, and a host of other tobacco-related issues made the company an easy target for consumer groups and the press.

Fearing the impact of a hostile public environment on its business, the company set out to dramatically change its image from being "just a tobacco company" to one of being a diverse public-minded conglomerate. To be sure, some of this was accomplished through strategic mergers and acquisitions, most notably the acquisitions of General Foods and Kraft Food. But parallel to the merger strategy was the remaking of the Philip Morris image.

Armed with an annual budget of $60 million in cash and some $20 million in food services, philanthropy played a key role. The easiest route might have been to choose to support local United Ways, with minimum demands for visibility. But Philip Morris, under the guidance of Senior Vice President Stephanie French and Corporate Contributions Manager Anne Dowling, decided on a more aggressive approach.

Interested in education and in trying to improve the learning capabilities of elementary and secondary schoolchildren, they decided to earmark 40 percent of their budget for education. Initially as part of the school reform movement, they intended to focus on helping children directly, especially in the inner city, with classroom programs. However, when a Washington, D.C., school board member accused the company of using a $1 million grant to the schools there to recruit minority children to cigarette smoking, they backed off quickly.

To avoid the charge and to keep it from reoccurring, they decided to help *teachers* rather than *children* directly. Consequently, they became involved in programs nationwide that were designed to change the ways teachers are taught and the way they teach.

Selecting AIDS as a high-visibility social and medical problem, Philip Morris became the largest supporter of the National Community AIDS Partnership. The company clearly became catalytic in getting other companies involved in helping to fund treatment for this growing problem. However, their involvement was not without controversy. They found themselves caught in the battle between the gay community and Senator Helms, a well-known gay basher. The company, for political reasons, had been a supporter of the Jesse Helms Institute, to which they had given $200,000. In retaliation, the gay community called for a boycott of Miller Beer and Marlboro cigarettes. The boycott was called off only after the company agreed to double its funding of the AIDS organization. This underscores the importance of building partnerships with leading nonprofits when a company either wants to advance a particular issue or to minimize controversy about an issue.

In a separate effort to remake its image, Philip Morris took a leadership role in the campaign to reduce hunger in the United States. About 20 percent of the contributions budget and all of the food services in-kind donations are directed to this cause. Working to reduce hunger is a natural for Philip Morris since its Kraft Foods and General Foods divisions now account for about 66 percent of the company's assets. "Anti-hunger projects are a way of building consciousness that Philip Morris is in the food business," says Dowling.

On another front, Kraft's Yuban Coffee division provided $100,000 to the Nature Conservancy for a program known as Kraft's "Adopt an Acre," which is designed to help save the rain forest in South America. As a tie-in, working with *Scholastic Magazine*, it developed a curriculum for use in schools about the rain forest and its importance to the environment.

Still another way Philip Morris has worked to change its image is through its support of the arts. The company has been a major underwriter of exhibits appearing nationwide in America's most prestigious museums. In fact, the company has become known as the arts "corporate angel." It has supported arts-related events with advertising in major national and local magazines calling attention to exhibits, promoting attendance while identifying itself with quality of the highest nature. Frequently after making a contribution to an organization, the company uses marketing dollars for receptions, special events, press materials, and brochures. It also assists the organization with design elements and promotional materials, and with public relations help on how to market the event. For example, in connection with an exhibit of Frida Kahlo's work in Houston, Philip Morris asked a public relations firm that specializes in reaching Hispanic audiences to help get word out about the exhibit to Houston's Hispanic community. The result was a diversified audience, many of whom had never been invited to an art exhibit. As another example, to help support the Next Wave Festival at the Brooklyn Academy of Music, Philip Morris tapped one of its ad agencies to develop a film that not only informed, but helped market the festival.

To assure maximum effectiveness, Philip Morris operates its contributions program through three levels within the company: corporate headquarters, major operating units, and local plants (which between them have 76 local contributions committees). Oversight for the entire program is provided by headquarters, though each of the entities has considerable autonomy. Asked about the future, Dowling said, "We determined we would keep arts support because we have so much invested in it; and that we would have hunger and nutrition to reflect that fact that we were the nation's largest food company, and the world's second largest." Finally, "we want to focus on education reform because that is a workplace issue for us."[8]

Over the years, the company has garnered favor nationwide from opinion leaders and the public at large for its support of these programs.

An example of a partnership with some unusual tie-ins was the Times-Mirror's partnership with the Smithsonian Institution's Museum of Natural History's exhibit entitled "Ocean Planet." Times-Mirror contributed $750,000 to the museum and recruited partners for a $2.5-million advertising campaign to promote the exhibit. They offered advertising pages in their magazines *Field & Stream, Yachting, Golf*, etc., and radio and TV spots on stations they owned. They also developed licensed products, editorial inserts, books, CD-ROMs, on-line service, and merchandising. Times-Mirror customized each program to meet its partners' needs. Participating underwriters were asked to provide each other with advertising opportunities and promotional recognition. This collaborative effort is a good example of how one company can leverage its gift by getting others involved. Frequently a project may be too big for one underwriter, but, by getting other noncompeting companies to help with various pieces of the project or providing "in-kind" services, they all may benefit.

The Advent of Cause-Related Marketing

A recent companion of philanthropy is "cause-related" marketing. Also labeled "event" marketing, "image" marketing, and more recently, "lifestyle" marketing, it is the newest phenomenon in public relations and marketing.

Often described as "linking a worthwhile charitable cause in a market to the growth of [a] business through the fusion of marketing, public relations, promotion, and special events," this newcomer has swept business in recent years. It is differentiated from philanthropy for two main reasons. First, the source of its funds usually comes from the advertising or sales promotion budget. This means the money for these activities does not come out of the contributions budget or the profits of the company, thereby allaying any shareowner concerns about spending "their" money. Since the advertising budgets in most companies dwarf the contributions budget, it also means a significantly larger pool of money is available for event marketing. Second, it is directly associated with sales. This puts a premium on achieving measurable near-term results—whether they are improving revenue, number of units sold, market share, or, simply, volume.

Corporate communications, since it is at the intersection of all communications to the public and employees about the company, plays an important coordinating and oversight role in event marketing.

Event marketing became significant when the "sin" industries—liquor and tobacco—were not permitted to advertise on television any longer. (Though this is still being tested in the courts.) Their huge advertising budgets needed to find a new place to work, and sports were soon discovered.

About the same time, other advertisers were finding mass media to be increasingly expensive and cluttered. It was difficult to get a message through to a specific audience and, with cable television growing in popularity, there was increasing uncertainty about who was watching what. This resulted in a significant change in mass marketing and the use of mass media. Companies seeking more efficiency from their advertising expenditures started to narrow-cast their messages to targeted audiences. Expenditures for mass media flattened out, while expenditures for product promotions rose steadily.

Advertising agencies, quick to spot the trend, broadened the extent of their activities to include public relations, sales promotion, direct marketing, and event marketing among their offerings. They even went so far as to acquire public relations firms or build their own. This new resource enabled the advertising agencies to be more responsive to their clients, while profoundly impacting the field of public relations and marketing.

It is estimated that currently about 40 percent of a consumer product company's advertising budget goes for sales promotion. This is all the more remarkable since, only a decade or two ago, sales promotion was the illicit child of corporate marketing.

Meanwhile, in-house corporate public relations organizations, under pressure to justify *their* expenditures, started looking vigorously at how they could assist their company's sales efforts. The answer from all quarters seemed to be: find an event or cause with which to become identified.

In its earliest days, event marketing was not big in the image-sensitive industries like insurance, banking, petroleum, utilities, etc. But as competition began to increase in these industries, individual companies saw the need to differentiate themselves from one another because the public saw them all as essentially offering the same product or service. So now we have the Mobil Cotton Bowl, The John Hancock Bowl, The Kroger Senior Classic, Paine Webber Invitational, The Ameritech Senior Open, etc.

The events themselves range from Red Lobster restaurants paying for a traveling exhibit on sharks, Nutrasweet Kelco and Breath Mints sponsoring a garlic festival, Pepto Bismol sponsoring a chili cook off, and Domino's Pizza sponsoring a competition for good drivers. All relate one way or another to meeting a company's specific interest.

Sales can be measured, too. General Foods provided Mothers Against Drunk Driving with $100,000 to help with their "March Across America," which they said helped boost the sale of their Tang drink mix by 13 percent.

An estimated 3,000 companies now are involved with event marketing, and expenditures for "events" have reached a booming and growing $1.75 billion annually. Interestingly, the focus, which was initially on sporting events, is increasingly shifting toward more community-based events. This allows companies to get closer to their markets and develop stronger local ties, supporting the notion that "all business is local."

Jerry Welsh, when he was executive vice president of worldwide marketing and communications for American Express, is credited with inventing the term "cause-related marketing." At the time, he made it clear that the term is meant to imply "marketing—not charity."

The first use of cause-related marketing was in connection with the funding of the Statue of Liberty restoration. In 1982, President Reagan asked Lee Iacocca, dynamic head of the Chrysler Corporation, to head a private-sector effort to restore the Statue of Liberty by 1986, which would be the statue's 100th birthday. In 1983, American Express entered into a mutually beneficial arrangement with the Statue of Liberty Foundation to promote the restoration. As a result of its promotion efforts, other companies joined in, and a national fund-raising campaign was held among private citizens and particularly among schoolchildren.

In the early 1990s, underwriting of events grew at three times the rate of advertising spending. Business sectors creating the most activity were: banks, cruise lines, makers of candy, coffee, photo supplies, paints, and security systems. The top corporate underwriter was Philip Morris, which spent about $95 million, followed by Anheuser-Busch at $90 million and RJR Nabisco at $40 million.

Time magazine sponsored a "Forum for Freedom" program which involved advertising agencies. AT&T underwrote a large exhibit in the Ellis Island Immigration Museum which displayed artifacts of immigrants to this country. As a tie-in, AT&T developed a marketing program which urged Americans to call internationally as part of the Ellis Island opening. American Express said that, during the period of their promotion, credit card usage jumped 28 percent and card applications jumped 45 percent—a resounding success by any measure.

Fred Wilkinson, senior vice president of corporate initiatives at American Express, observed, "In all our programs, cause-related marketing was at least as successful as other ad campaigns. In many cases, it blew the roof off the business."[9]

When combining corporate philanthropy with event marketing, keeping a low profile frequently works best for all concerned.

Reebok International, the $1.5-billion shoemaker, decided it wanted to support Amnesty International, the Nobel-prize winning human rights organization. First, it created a $100,000 Human Rights Award to be given to the person or organization doing the most to champion human rights in the world. To provide funding for the award, it agreed to put up $10 million to promote a 19-city "Human Rights Now!" music tour that had top rockers, including Bruce Springsteen and Sting, taking the Amnesty International message directly to the people. The Reebok Foundation, which normally received $500,000 annually from the company, was given $2.5 million to help support the tour. The remainder of the money came from in-house marketing sources. Wherever the tour's title was displayed, discretely below it in small type was "made possible by the Reebok Foundation."

Reebok's CEO Joseph LaBonto said, "If we were to do a lot of advertising with our name all over it, it would undo the purity of the event."[10] Reebok didn't ask the performers to wear their apparel. The low-key approach had an important benefit, as far as the tour was concerned. The "Boss," Bruce Springsteen, who heretofore had refused to have his name linked with any company, agreed to participate.

Though Reebok was more than satisfied with its involvement, it did have two disappointments. First, there were a few countries where the concerts didn't attract as large an audience as had been anticipated. This was because Amnesty International previously had singled out the regimes in those countries as being uncooperative, which created ill will toward the organization. Second, Reebok had hoped more corporations would join it in various countries as sponsors. The failure to achieve as much money as anticipated from this source was attributed to the concern many companies had about the controversial nature of Amnesty International. (It's true companies tend to shy away from political causes because they are often seen as using their financial muscle in an unfair or biased manner—winning favor with some while alienating others.)

All in all, studies showed Reebok reaped good publicity and a favorable image among the young people who buy their shoes—which was exactly what the company had hoped to do while promoting a cause its employees favored.

The major reasons for becoming involved with event marketing are to:

- Increase awareness of a product or name.

- Identify a company with a certain lifestyle (family-oriented, fitness, etc.).

- Differentiate a product from competitors'.

- Create new opportunities to sell merchandise.

- Help a company call attention to its product's benefits.

Sometimes an organization can get into trouble for an activity to which it *doesn't* donate money. Heublein's brand of Canadian whiskey sponsored a national search to find a model for its advertising campaign. Originally, it intended to donate money in connection with the contest to the March of Dimes. But when it realized that the March of Dimes often works with babies suffering from fetal alcohol syndrome, it changed its mind because it (and the charity) feared they might be criticized for trying to buy goodwill. Instead, Heublein donated the money to the National Multiple Sclerosis Society.

Evaluating cause-related marketing events begins with asking the question: Was it worth it? What were the cost/benefits? Did it increase volume, market share, or both? Other measures might be: Did it meet our trade or industry objectives? Were our salespeople, retailers, and others in our industry happy with the activity? And, importantly for the long run: How did it affect the reputation of our company?

For the public relations counselor, the phenomenon of cause-related marketing is of special importance since the activities that companies engage in frequently are designed to shape public opinion or to promote a product or business unit of the company. In their enthusiasm to generate sales, marketing people are not always sensitive to the public relations implications of their activities. This is not because they aren't well intentioned, but more generally because they are working on a short time horizon, interested in generating current sales so they can meet a specific sales objective.

Sponsorships

Texaco has been known for its sponsorship of the Metropolitan Opera Saturday afternoon radio broadcasts for over 40 years. It is hard to think of radio and the Metropolitan Opera without thinking of Texaco.

When Mercedes Benz wanted to identify its product with quality and to bring it to the attention of an upscale audience, it underwrote the opening night of the Chicago Symphony Orchestra's season. One of the features it insisted upon was the opportunity to display one of its cars in the lobby of Orchestra Hall. Although there were some objections about this "commercialism" at first, the benefits soon were apparent to all as both Mercedes and the CSO profited.

Interestingly, about 75 percent of event sponsorships have been related to sports (see Chapter 28). Recently, the emphasis has been gradually shifting toward cultural activities. This trend, from a marketing standpoint, is obviously a good one, since women make an increasingly large percentage of the buying decisions.

According to the International Events Group, sponsorships in the United States in 1993 grew 17 percent to $3.7 billion. This topped the previous year's growth of 13 percent. Cause-related marketing receives about $314 million, far ahead of the arts, which receive about $245 million in sponsorships.

Originally, companies sought just name recognition. Oscar Mayer, for example, provided $500 cash for each blocked punt by a member of the Los Angeles (now St. Louis) Rams special teams. Budweiser sponsored the National Hockey League's Man of the Year Award, donating $1,000 to the special charity of each team's nominee and $70,000 to the charity selected by the winner. Thriftway gave $1.6 million in profits from a golf tournament it produced to a children's hospital.

More sophisticated uses of sponsorships also are possible. An example of trying to adjust perceptions can be found in the case of the "Illinois Young Performers Competition."

Illinois Bell, 30-year sponsor of the annual state high school basketball championship tournament on television, during which time the event and the company almost became synonymous, decided to withdraw its sponsorship. The withdrawal occurred because of changes in the format of the tournament and in what were deemed exorbitant fees charged by the state high school athletic association for the television rights.

Working with television officials and educators who had become concerned that athletes and rock stars were becoming the sole role models for young people, the company decided to show a different kind of competition on television. Thus was born the Illinois Young Performers Competition in which young people in two age groups (8–12 and 13–18) participate in a series of eliminations leading to an opportunity to compete for scholarships while playing "live" on television with the Chicago Symphony Orchestra. The annual state-wide telecast rapidly became one of the most popular on public broadcasting, winning a coveted Emmy Award, the applause of educators throughout the state, and the praise of opinion leaders and the press. In this case, all parties (except the high school athletic association) benefited from the change in direction by the company.

With the aid of their public relations associates, corporate marketers have discovered that, with $1 million spent on a museum exhibit or festival, they can reach a target market segment more cost-effectively than with paid mass-media advertising. Once they associate themselves with a charity their market cares about, by tieing sales promotion activities into the event, they create a mutually beneficial collaboration.

Stealing a page from the Cadillac ads of the 1950s, which featured the famous Cadillac "V" juxtapositioned next to a necklace of diamonds, emeralds, and rubies to connote quality and value, many companies today are associating their names or products with quality in the art or cultural world.

Developers of events should recognize that people prefer quality and they want authenticity. They want to be moved by what they see. They want the best for their families. They continually look for ways to enhance the quality of life for their families.

This partially explains such major sponsorship successes as Tutankhamen (Exxon), *This Old House* (Sears), *Nicholas Nickleby*, *Masterpiece Theater* (Mobil), *Hallmark's Hall of Fame*, and Ken Burn's "The Civil War" and "Baseball" (General Motors).

The biggest mistake a sponsor can make is to attach its name to a program or event and then not augment it with advertising and marketing dollars. These are usually drawn from the corporate advertising budget. Most frequently used are "tune-in" ads or "place and date" advertising. By leveraging the activity, sponsorship is greatly enhanced.

Coordinating Activities at One Company

Though it is a relatively young company, a good mix of corporate philanthropy, sponsorships, and event marketing has been achieved at Ameritech, the regional communications company headquartered in Chicago. This was possible because oversight was provided by the corporate communications department, which not only managed the activities but also was responsible for a major portion of the budgets used.

Corporate contributions, for the most part, were made through the Ameritech Foundation, and sponsorships and event marketing activities were funded through the corporate advertising budget. In cases of event marketing, additional funds were supplied by the company's various sales units.

The Foundation's stated objectives were to:

■ Support national and regional organizations.

■ Encourage the local operating units to support local organizations consistent with company policy.

These guidelines were intended to provide direction to minimize any questions about "turf" battles. In a number of cases, it was deemed advisable for both the national and local units to provide support when the magnitude of the undertaking seemed to warrant it.

The Foundation's special areas of interest were described as:

■ Supporting activities that enable communications to add value to society.

■ Addressing public policy communications issues.

■ Stimulating the Great Lakes economy.

■ Improving the quality of life in the region, including providing assistance to major educational and cultural institutions.

To further research ways that communication could add value to society, grants were made through one of the Foundation's programs, called the Ameritech Fellowship Program, to the University of Michigan and the University of Chicago. Public policy issues were addressed in research grants provided to Ohio State University and Northwestern University. In addition, national organizations like the Brookings Institution and Citizens for a Sound Economy were given funds to do additional research in the area of telecommunications policy.

Support for stimulating the Great Lakes economy was provided to the Council of Great Lakes Governors, Jobs for Metropolitan Chicago, Case Western Reserve University, and Indiana University. Each of these groups worked on activities to stimulate job creation in the five-state region served by Ameritech.

One of the Foundation's most innovative undertakings was the creation of the Ameritech Partnership for Independent Colleges. This five-state venture was designed to support the area's independent colleges in an effort to maintain the nation's pluralistic system of higher education, which is regarded as the world's best. By calling attention to the distinct contribution of the independent colleges, it was hoped to maintain some balance between their need for funds and the needs of state-supported institutions.

These contributions were all made with the intention of furthering specific corporate objectives. To build the company's reputation for quality and excellence, associations were developed with the prestigious Chicago Symphony Orchestra, Lyric Opera, and the Art Institute of Chicago. Special concerts of the Symphony were underwritten, and telecasts of them on PBS were arranged in order to reach that medium's high-profile, upscale, opinion-making audience. The production of Lyric's *I Capuleti e i Montecchi*, starring Cecilia Gasdia, and *Turandot*, featuring Éva Marton, also were underwritten by the Foundation and supported with receptions and dinners for key opinion leaders.

To reinforce the company's association with quality on a year-round basis, opening night opera performances were sponsored on radio, and broadcasts of the Symphony were sponsored each Sunday afternoon. The broadcasts provided a continuous link with the special performances underwritten by the Foundation.

An audience of significance for the new company was the federal government in Washington, D.C. Prior to its separation from AT&T, all negotiations on behalf of the company at the federal level were handled by the parent company. Once on its own,

Ameritech was forced to represent itself before federal regulatory agencies, the courts, and with Congress. This meant establishing a presence in Washington and building a favorable reputation.

One of the company's first undertakings (in addition to opening a Washington office) was to help Congress celebrate its bicentennial. This was done in collaboration with the congressional bicentennial committee cochaired by Senator Robert Byrd and Representative Lindy Boggs. The centerpiece of the company's efforts was underwriting a 90-minute documentary on the history of Congress. The film was made by award-winning director-producer Ken Burns (later of "Civil War" and "Baseball" Program fame). The film, made for showing on national PBS television, was premiered at the National Theater in Washington, followed by a black tie dinner at the nearby Hyatt Hotel. Congratulatory speeches were made by the leaders of both houses of Congress, as well as the bicentennial chairpersons, at both the premiere and dinner. With over 400 members of Congress and their guests present, experienced Washington observers said it was the largest attendance by members of Congress and their guests at a social function in the history of Congress.

The film was shown on national PBS several times, but, most importantly, a teachers guide and handbook were prepared and distributed to every school in the United States. These pieces carried appropriate credits to Ameritech in addition to the authors and producers. A videotape of the program was provided, at cost, to every school which requested one—resulting in the ultimate distribution of some 7,000 videotapes.

Two other activities helped cement Ameritech's presence in Washington. One was the enormously successful exhibit, "Circa 1492," at the National Gallery of Art. The blockbuster exhibit, which was held in connection with the 500th anniversary of Columbus' discovery of America, was the largest ever undertaken by the National Gallery. It was underwritten in part by the Ameritech Foundation. "Circa 1492" turned out to be popular with the public, resulting in record-breaking attendance, a best-selling catalogue, and a gala black tie opening night dinner which attracted the political and cultural elite of Washington. Coupled with appropriate advertising promoting the exhibit in "think" magazines, the result was "positioning" the new Ameritech corporation at the most sophisticated level of American institutions and culture.

Another activity resulting in superior positioning of Ameritech was the reestablishment, during President Ronald Reagan's term in office, of Sunday afternoon concerts in the East Room of the White House. The concerts, taped by WETA for public television rebroadcast, gave Americans throughout the country an opportunity to witness first hand a legendary White House social event. Hosted by the President and featuring a variety of entertainment, the concerts were called "In Performance at the White House" and were underwritten by Ameritech. The select audience, chosen by the president and first lady, was invited to a reception in the state dining room following the concerts. As sponsor, Ameritech invited a limited number of guests, subject to presidential approval, to each of the concerts as well. Presidents Bush and Clinton continued the tradition.

Recognizing that Asian and European business and political leaders have more of an inbred interest in cultural activities than their American counterparts, the company used that means to build a bridge between it and its overseas customers. When the company sought to expand to overseas markets, it underwrote a tour of the Chicago Symphony Orchestra to Japan. The tour coincided with the launch of an English-language yellow pages directory produced by the company for Tokyo. Business leaders and prospective customers were invited to the concerts, along with the governor of Illinois, as guests of the company.

Ameritech also underwrote tours of the Cleveland Orchestra and Indianapolis Symphony to Europe, with similar objectives in mind.

To assure Europeans that the Midwest (or the "rust belt," as it was sometimes called in the business press), was also a center of creativity and American culture, the company sponsored an exhibit at the Pompidou Center in Paris, in conjunction with the Art Institute of Chicago, of internationally acclaimed Chicago artist Ed Paschke's work. Key European business leaders were invited to the opening night black tie dinner, which was held at the Center overlooking the enchanting city. (The event was so successful that European businessmen in attendance asked how they could sponsor similar exhibits in America. Officials of the Pompidou Center acknowledged this was the first time they had ever held an exhibit which was underwritten by an American company.)

In a unique collaboration between philanthropy and event marketing, the company, recognizing the benefits of using computers with local area telephone networks, organized a demonstration of the technology called "Super School." The demonstration, complete with model classrooms and home learning centers, was set up at Chicago's McCormick Place Convention Complex. It was designed to show educators how electronics could provide "distance learning" at economical prices. The marketing people assembled the equipment used in the demonstration of the networks, while contributions by the Ameritech Foundation were made to develop the seminars which showed how the systems could help improve education achievement while lowering overall instruction costs for the schools.

After the initial demonstration was held in Chicago, "Super School" eventually was rotated to major midwestern cities and, ultimately, to Washington, D.C., where members of Congress expressed an interest in it as part of creating the "Information Highway." This activity was a significant marriage designed to further the corporation's interest in expanding its networks while providing tangible benefits to society.

Recognizing that it was moving into a more competitive communications environment, the company knew that it needed to do more in the way of developing "quality" time with its major customers. Aware that golf was the most popular businessman's sport, the company agreed to sponsor an event on the Professional Golf Association's Senior Tour. Thus was born the Ameritech Senior Open. The Senior Tour (as distinct from the "regular" tour) was selected because the primary audience for its matches was composed of senior executives who were the ones most likely to be responsible for major purchases in their companies and who would readily recognize the names of the senior players. These decision makers also were candidates to be invited by the company to the "pro-am" tournament (in which professional players are teamed with amateurs) which would be held in conjunction with the regular tournament.

The first Ameritech Senior Open was held at the Canterbury Country Club in Cleveland, Ohio, in 1989. The final two days were telecast nationally on CBS, which delivered a target audience of prospective purchasers of Ameritech's communications equipment and services. The company not only received recognition as sponsor of the event, but it also ran sales commercials of its own during the telecast to cement the tie-in. The first event was so successful in meeting revenue objectives

When it was in the midst of a competition in Germany to obtain a license to sell cellular phone service, Ameritech used an appearance of the Chicago Symphony Orchestra to invite business and government leaders to Munich and Frankfurt. It followed up these appearances with advertising in selected local media which reinforced the association of the company with the Symphony and nonpromotionally linked the company with quality.

and delivering brand name recognition for Ameritech that it has been sponsored by the company ever since.

Throughout the 1990s, the Ameritech Senior Open has been held in the Chicago area, which is the company's headquarters, largest market, and media center. The event sparked the greatest media interest in 1993, when basketball superstar Michael Jordan and legendary golfer Arnold Palmer were paired in the pro-am tournament. The excitement generated by these two sports icons playing together not only garnered considerable national publicity, but it impressed customers. Perhaps even more importantly in the long run was that it created considerable enthusiasm among employees and prospective employees who believed that, if these two megastars would play together at a company event, it must be a pretty good place to work.

Though much of the cost of the event is covered by the marketing department's budget, the proceeds from the sale of programs, souvenirs, food, exhibits, parking, etc., are contributed through the Foundation to local charities. Thus the tournament not only serves to meet customer sales objectives, it also meets some of the company charitable objectives as well.

As a positioning event for Ameritech, it has been extremely successful, not only from the vast amount of publicity the week-long event generates, but from the collateral advertising created to promote the tournament.

The overall cost of the event, including the tournament purse, TV rights, and hosting expenses, are more than recovered through sales attributed to the tournament. The marketing and sales organizations, consequently, are enthusiastic supporters. Other companies vie for space at the tournament to invite their customers and special guests. The players, a key constituency since it's important to keep the "names" coming back each year, consistently have ranked the Ameritech Senior Open since its inception as one of the two or three best tournaments on the senior circuit each year.

LOOK TO THE FUTURE

With most major companies having restructured or in the process of restructuring, it is no surprise that corporate philanthropy also is undergoing change. As companies seek to shift their giving programs to match their own interests, so too are they adjusting the amount of money they are putting into various giving categories. Although corporate giving has not grown significantly in recent years, neither has it, in the aggregate, been cut significantly.

With the current corporate emphasis on creating shareowner value, companies are retaining most of their profits in the business for future growth or using them to pay dividends leaving less for charitable purposes. Many nonprofits see this trend in a discouraging light. But the good news is that, as competition intensifies, companies will seek ways to differentiate themselves from their competition. So, increasingly, companies will look for ways to improve the perception of their business, service, or products. Corporate philanthropy, along with its cousins—sponsorships and event marketing—clearly can help in this process. Winners in the competitive arena in the long run will wind up with more money for philanthropic purposes, while the losers will have less.

Companies have tended to model their contributions functions after charitable private foundations. They tend to do the same things the foundations do, the same way. In so doing, they lose the opportunity to capitalize on their uniqueness as companies. In the future, companies will continue to reevaluate their giving programs to assure they are doing what is right for their long-term best interests.

Effective corporate philanthropy is dependent upon persons who have broad interests and open minds. They also need to be able to "broker" the interests of society with the interests of their corporation.

Though frequently the people in charge of contributions are seasoned people with a company, more and more CEOs are looking for persons with good judgment, capable of seeking good opportunities with which to identify the company. In this way, they are increasingly likely to have a marketing sense as well as the ability to spot future trends that the company can use to help build its reputation.

The administrator also must be able to use "head" more than "heart"; he or she will be confronted with thousands of choices, many of which will seem worthwhile, but the decision maker will want to get the biggest bang for the buck, and this will depend on the strategy for philanthropy that is adopted. It may be that the choice is to concentrate on one or two areas. It may be to give the bulk of available money to one or two organizations. Or the decision may be to spread the money to as many organizations as possible in an effort to assist (or please) many groups, rather than having to say "no" to so many.

Some of this will depend upon whether a "reactive" or "proactive" strategy is adopted. Reactive is likely to spread money; proactive is more likely to concentrate on a few special projects.

In any case, the executive must be able to analyze proposals. First, he or she must determine whether the proposal is consistent with the company's objectives. Then the likelihood of whether the proposers can meet their stated objectives must be determined. When a proactive strategy is used, the company seeks partners to help accomplish its objectives. Frequently it issues a "request for proposals" (RFP) inviting organizations to send proposals that meet specific criteria.

Considering the volume of work entailed in either process, particularly in evaluating proposals, invariably it seems that company contributions departments are understaffed. Since they are not profit centers, per se, frequently the work is delegated down in the organization, and the opportunities to fully benefit from the reputation-enhancing activity that philanthropy provides aren't fully realized. The correct way to measure the amount of staff required is difficult. One study showed that corporations had one person for every $2.3 million in grants, while foundations averaged one person for every $1.2 million. The total dollar amount isn't as critical a measure as the number of requests received, actual grants made, and whether the company is proactive or reactive. An accurate assessment of the amount of staffing needed should relate to the volume of work undertaken.

As more and more organizations seek corporate help, the number of proposals a company receives will increase dramatically. They will come from a variety of sources— nonprofits, television writers and producers, auto and balloon racers, parade organizers, educational institutions, think tanks—the list is endless. These proposals will come to a wide variety of people in the company. Most will sound very interesting at first blush—especially to the inexperienced. Having a well-coordinated, centralized place to sort out the proposals and deal with all of them will take on increased importance. Even the way "no" is said has public relations implications. This is a key role for the corporate communications executive who is responsible for guarding the company's reputation.

This "new" synergy makes it all the more critical that corporate philanthropy be integrated into corporate communications, if it's not already there.

The corporate communications counselor has an important role in assuring that the way the company chooses to identify itself will truly help to perpetuate it, and not diminish it by reflecting negatively. It's too easy for the sales-minded person to misuse philanthropy so that it becomes a negative rather than a positive for the company. Also, with many business units competing with one another for sales, it is possible that events sponsored by the corporation might work in opposition to one another.

Traditionally, United Ways have been major recipients of corporate largess through the support of both the company and its employees. This is likely to change somewhat in the future as more and more groups seek and receive access to employee contributions through payroll deductions. Among them will be groups representing education, arts, environment, and certain minorities.

Corporations will continue to support education, but there will be increasing emphasis on achieving measurable results. This will be true at both the higher education and K–12 levels. At the collegiate level, there will be interest in promoting improved technology as well as in developing people with broad, diverse backgrounds. At the K–12 level, there will be emphasis on improving skills: literacy, math, spelling, science, or geography. On all fronts, there will be interest in exploring new ways of doing things because of the widespread belief that the old ways of doing things aren't working.

With the possibility of increased government spending at the federal and state levels in the health field, it is likely that, unless a company has a specific interest in this field, it will divert its resources to other areas where it believes it can get a bigger return for its investment.

If the corporation does not believe it is making investments that will ultimately pay off for them, they will cease to make them. This necessitates taking a long-term view, because helping education, health, etc., frequently does not have an immediate payoff.

There is no question that a company's philanthropic strategy should be aligned with its communication's agenda and overall corporate strategy.

As companies become more global, they are expanding their philanthropic efforts internationally. If they are to be world-class competitors, then they must behave that way in the marketplace. For example, if they want skilled workers in the areas in which they want to do business, then developing relationships with universities or other educational institutions in those areas makes a great deal of sense. With the improvements in communications technology, it is increasingly possible to bring the benefits of such associations back home, and vice versa, as cross-border exchanges of students, cultures, and business practices enable both ideas and trade to move globally more easily.

By the same token, globalness means more requests for support from agencies and organizations worldwide, cutting down on the amount of money available domestically. The speed with which information flows these days exacerbates the problem.

Interestingly, foreign companies are taking a cue from their American counterparts and are aggressively introducing philanthropy into their marketing mix. Companies like Siemens, Hitachi, and Sony have found that a sure way to win acceptance in the American marketplace is to become identified as sharing some of their profits with American nonprofit organizations. At present, more

Motorola has donated communications equipment in Vietnam to link health clinics in rural areas with hospitals in urban centers. IBM instituted a model hiring program for the handicapped in Japan. As a result of this and other employee-driven activities, it has won favor with government, business, and its customers. In fact, a recent survey in Japan ranked IBM second only to Sony in social responsibility. Surveys in cities elsewhere in the world show that people's expectations for corporate social responsibility are just as high there as they are in the United States.

than 200 Japanese companies have established formal giving programs in the United States. Companies like Toyota and Matsushita have set up elaborate giving structures in the United States. So, while some American companies have been putting contributions on "hold," their competitors are seizing the opportunity to fill the gap.

Consequently, the chief contributions officer in the future is likely to devise a new set of guidelines for his business. These are likely to include:

- Discouraging unsolicited proposals. More and more companies will send out requests for proposals outlining activities they are willing to support. They will decline all others.

- Multi-year grants, which will be reconsidered because of new Financial Accounting Standards Board rules.

- Greater use of gift matching programs in an effort to stimulate more giving by individuals for particular activities which may be of interest but which lie outside a company's main field of interest.

- Outsourcing of routine tasks, such as the matching gift program or sending of acknowledgments of gifts to meet the tax code requirements.

- An increase in cause-related marketing initiatives. This will work two ways: (1) to improve the company's reputation, and (2) to help improve the nonprofit's reputation. These longer-term relationships will work toward both partners' best interests.

By developing strategic plans for philanthropy which parallel the corporation's objectives, the competent contributions manager can turn the world that *is* into the world that *ought to be*.

ENDNOTES

1. David Finn, "Public Invisibility of Corporate Leaders," *Harvard Business Review,* November/December 1980, p. 102.

2. Craig Smith, "Triumph of Sleaze Over Virtue," *Corporate Philanthropy Report,* Vol. 7, no. 3, November 1991, p. 1.

3. Brian O'Connell, "Unique Dimensions in Philanthropy," *Philanthropy in Action,* The Foundation Center, p. 220.

4. Mary Tuthill, "The Growing Impact of Corporate Giving," *Nation's Business,* October 1980, p. 68.

5. Philip J. Webster, "Our Involvement with Ronald McDonald Houses: Strategic Corporate Public Relations: What's the Bottom Line?," *Public Relations Journal,* February 1990.

6. Andrew W. Singer, "Ethical Conduct Pays Off for Corporations—Probably," *Christian Science Monitor,* November 10, 1991.

7. Corporate Philanthropy Report, Vol. 2, no. 4, November 1986, p. 4.

8. Craig Smith, "Focus on Education Reform," *Corporate Philanthropy Report,* Vol. 8, no. 8, May 1993, p. 8.

9. *Corporate Philanthropy Report,* July 1990.

10. Craig Smith, "Undo the Purity of the Event," *Corporate Philanthropy Report,* Vol. 4, no. 2, October 1988, p. 3.

CHAPTER 11

Issues Management: Managing Trends through the Issues Life Cycle

Raymond P. Ewing, APR
Professor of Corporate Public Relations (Retired)
Medill School of Journalism
Northwestern University

A STRATEGIC APPROACH TO ISSUES MANAGEMENT

Beginnings and Definitions

From the very beginning, those who pioneered the development and definition of issues management considered it to be a management process concerned with *public policy* foresight and planning for an organization in the *private* sector. It is not the management of issues through the public policy process in our democracy or the management of the public policy process itself. Not even the most powerful person in the world, the president of the United States, can do that.

Instead, it is the management of an institution's resources and efforts to participate in the successful resolution of issues in the public policy process that will affect the future viability and well-being of the organization and its stakeholders.

In 1992, at the Public Relations Colloquium sponsored by the public relations firm of Nuffer, Smith, Tucker, Inc., San Diego State University, and Northwestern University's Medill School of Journalism, a group of practitioners developed a goal-oriented definition: "Issues management is the management process whose goal is to help preserve markets, reduce risk, create opportunities, and manage image as an organizational asset for the benefit of both the organization and its primary stakeholders"—customers, employees, the public, and shareholders.

The term "issues management," was formally and publicly coined by W. Howard Chase on April 15, 1976. That is the date of Volume 1, Number 1, of his newsletter, *Corporate Public Issues and Their Management.*

The newsletter, now usually called *CPI*, stated that its objectives were: "To introduce and validate a break-through in corporate management design and practice in order to manage corporate public issues at least as well or better than the traditional management of profit-center operations."

Chase went on to say: "The thesis and impact of CPI inevitably lead to fundamental revisions of costly and divisive practices of traditional line-staff management. There can be today only one management with one objective: survival and return on capital sufficient to maintain productivity, whatever the economic and political climate."

Chase was 66 years old when this newsletter came out in 1976, having retired the previous year as public affairs vice president of American Can Company. In 1977, he and his associates, Barry Jones and Teresa Yancey Crane (now the publisher of CPI), created the first issues management process model, which involves five steps:

1. Issue identification;
2. Issue analysis;
3. Issue change strategy options;
4. Issue action programming; and
5. Evaluation of results.

All issues management models published by others since 1977 are variations of this model.

Early full-time practitioners of issues management have always called Chase the "father" of issues management. He has more than earned that title for coining the term, publishing the first newsletter on the subject, creating the first issues management process model, and devoting his life, from age 66 to the present, to advancing the theory and practice of issues management.

At this point, three things should be noted:

■ Issues management as a new process management concept evolved from the public relations and public affairs (PR/PA) professions after Chase coined the phrase in 1976.

■ Chase did not "invent" issues management (although he created the name) because, from Ivy Lee's time to 1976, counselors of senior management had been "doing" issues management—but on an ad hoc, hit-or-miss basis under various names. Chase moved the field to a foresight and planning basis from the ad hoc practice.

■ Chase's basic concept of issues management (for senior management's use in integrating the management of public policy and profit matters) moved public relations/public affairs professionals who could practice issues management to the center of corporate or organizational management.

So long as PR was confined to media relations, practitioners were operating at the outer edge of the organization. In the 1960s, when PR and government relations were combined to create a public affairs function, they moved closer to the center of operations because senior management became more involved in decision making. With the evolution of issues management (public policy planning) as a companion to strategic planning (profit planning), again they moved to the heart of the company where senior management focuses (see Figure 11–1).

Chase ensured that the 1976 newsletter and concept were publicized throughout the public relations, public affairs, and management media. There was much debate, discussion, and experimentation with techniques during that year.

Signs of Growth and Maturity

In 1977, according to Chase's records, the first two companies to adopt "formalized directorates of issues management" were Allstate Insurance Company and Stauffer Chemical Company. That year, Allstate appointed me Issues Management Director and secretary to Allstate's Issues Management Committee, a senior officer policy-making group.

F I G U R E   11–1

Time Line of the Evolution of Issues Management

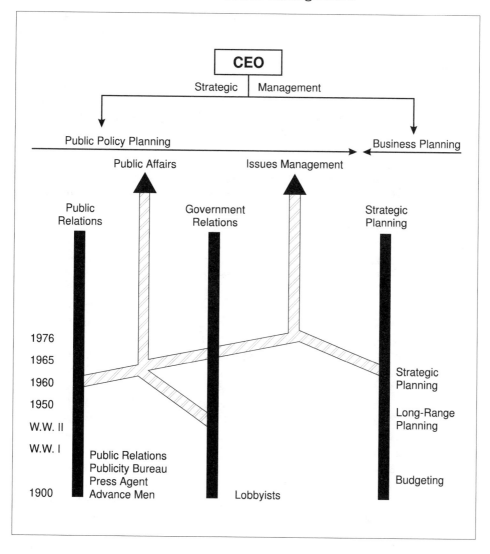

Also in 1977, the Public Affairs Council, under Ray Hoewing's direction, held the first Issues Management Conference for corporate PA officers, and they have done so every year since. Howard Chase was the main speaker at that first conference. In a sense, if you think of Chase as the *creator* of the issues management concept, you can think of the Public Affairs Council as the *innovator*—the agency that spread the concept through corporate PA offices around the country.

In 1977, Howard Chase and Barry Jones published the first issues management process model, which helped various PR/PA professionals relate their techniques to the overall tasks. In the same year, PRSA members at both the national and local levels began to explore the new field and share techniques.

In 1979, The Conference Board published its study, "The Business of Issues: Coping with the Company's Environments." This study was undertaken at the request of the Board's Public Affairs Research Council. Over 100 corporate managers participated. Publication of the study had the effect of further validating the importance, at least in the corporate world, of an issues management system. The 74-page publication was the first large collection of issues management techniques and systems, and it established by consensus various definitions and procedures based upon practice.

By 1979, there were at least three issues management network centers in informal operation. First was Chase and his newsletter, second was Ray Hoewing at the Public Affairs Council, and third was a small group of corporate practitioners (including myself as the first practitioner identified by the title) who were active in PRSA. For the next few years, this group helped organize programs for trade and professional organizations, circulated papers, and spoke at as many conferences as possible. By the early 1980s, at least 60 major corporations had issues management/policy operations, according to CPI.

By early 1981, there were so many phone calls and written requests for information that the group met to discuss how to help those people who were already involved in issues management jobs and those who were interested in careers in the field. Efforts to get the Public Relations Society of America (PRSA) and other organizations to create special sections went without success. Because only about half of the people interested in issues management were PR/PA professionals, it seemed obvious that a separate organization should be created.

On August 25, 1981, *The Wall Street Journal* mentioned on the front page (in the labor column) our intention of creating an issues management association. For the next two weeks, we received hundreds of phone calls and letters. In December 1981, Howard Chase and I invited 10 practitioners to the Harvard Club in New York City to form the Issues Management Association. At that meeting, Howard was elected chairman and I was elected president and COO.

The first meeting of IMA was held in March of 1982 at the Library of Congress in Washington, D.C. One hundred individual letters of invitation were sent; 104 attended the meeting and joined the association. The membership grew to over 400 later that year and stabilized at that level.

Also in 1982, I was asked by PRSA to help form a new national Public Affairs Section, which would also focus on the practice of issues management. Edie Fraser was the first chair.

Although dozens of articles on issues management were published from 1976 onward and dozens of chapters in books have appeared, books devoted completely to issues management were late in appearing. The first, Howard Chase's book, *Issue Management: Origins of the Future*, was published in 1984. (*The Public Affairs Handbook*, published in 1982, was only partially devoted to issues management.)

Guy Stanley's book, *Managing External Issues*, was published in 1985. Joeseph Coates' book, *Issues Management: How You Can Plan, Organize, and Manage for the Future*, was published in 1986, as was Robert Heath and Richard Nelson's book, *Issues Management: Corporate Public Policymaking in an Information Society*.

My book, *Managing the New Bottom Line: Issues Management for Senior Executives*, was published in 1987. *Strategic Issues Management* by Robert Heath and Associates was published in 1988. *Issues Management in Strategic Planning* by William L. Renfro was published in 1993.

There are other books, but these are cited to show how issues management as a modern management technique has evolved over time, despite an initial disbelief among some practitioners who held that it had nothing new to teach us.

According to the Institute for the Study of Issues Management at the University of Houston, over 240 scholarly and professional articles, scholarly books, and PR textbooks dealing with issues management have been published. This is proof to Professor Robert Heath, director of the Institute, that issues management is a new discipline which has emerged, not to replace public relations, but to strengthen it. Most professional practitioners agree, and formal courses in issues management have appeared at universities teaching public relations as well as at some business schools.

A Boston University study of 400 PR/PA professionals (1982) found that 75 percent of them were involved in their companies' issues management activities, and 61 percent reviewed their companies' strategic plans to make sure they were sufficiently sensitive to sociopolitical trends that might affect the future of their organizations.

However, another study of eight companies conducted in 1986 with the support of the Public Affairs Council and the IMA found that, where issues management was conducted as a separate staff function, the staff had the greatest input and impact on senior management decision making. In companies in which issues management was integrated in the public relations department, the study found that issues management had a lower profile and was more task oriented.

My experience at Allstate and in counseling professionals in other companies is that the CEO determines the role of issues management in the company's policy-making decision stream. If the CEO views issues management as an important technique in support of his duties, as did CEOs at Allstate, it doesn't matter whether the issues management staff is located in the PR department or as a unit in the corporate planning department.

Many CEOs have seen the advantage of an issues management system since Chase first gave it a name. By one count, over 200 issues-related titles could be identified in as many companies, and more than 60 public relations and management consulting firms were offering issues management services.

The earliest companies adopting the technique were mainly the regulated industries: chemicals, petroleum, banking, insurance, etc. That is, the earliest practitioners were found in companies like Allstate, Bank of America, Chase, Dow Chemical, PPG, AT&T, Rexnord, Sears, Monsanto, Union Carbide, and various electrical utility companies. However, over time, this management system spread to companies in all sectors.

It is important for PR professionals to understand that this management technique emerged from our profession, and it should be led by practitioners from our field.

Although Howard Chase argues that issues management is a new profession that transcends the PR/PA profession, I consider issues management to be one of the major functions that the PR professional can perform today. It is of equal or more importance than our other major functions: media relations, marketing public relations, investor relations, public affairs, employee communications, community relations, and corporate philanthropy. The addition of strategic planning and issues management to our duties in the past two decades completed our maturing into a modern profession.

In fact, the theory behind establishing the Graduate Program in Corporate Public Relations at Northwestern University's Medill School of Journalism was that public relations is now a modern management profession based on both the communications and management disciplines. It is now clear that, when PR professionals properly execute their issues management duties, they are functioning well beyond the communications field and deeply into the management problem-solving field, which is where we belong.

The Relationship of Issues Management to Strategic Planning

Issues management and strategic planning together form the planning platform on which CEOs and their senior management team can stand to strategically manage their organizations.

While issues management focusses on *public policy* research, foresight, and planning for the organization, strategic planning is concerned with *business* research, foresight, and planning for the organization. The first is concerned with policy planning; the second is concerned with profit planning. This chart illustrates what each system is concerned with or can affect.

Issues Management	Strategic Planning
Outside-in planning	Inside-out planning
Issues 1–5 years in future	Issues 1–5+ years in future
Operational (annual) plans	Organizational plans
Defense/opportunity	Opportunity/defense
Best of a contentious bargain	Best of self-created bargain

Under this construct, issues management is concerned with plans that groups outside the corporation are making in the sociopolitical and economic environment (the public policy process) that would impact the corporation's future and viability. It is also concerned with the outside plans it must make to counteract or support the plans of others as the corporation seeks to participate in the public policy process where the issues will be resolved.

Strategic planning is primarily concerned with the corporation's internal planning for its own business future, as it seeks to meet and beat its competitors in the economic arena.

On the time frame, issues management is primarily concerned with issues that will be resolved 12 months to 5 years in the future. (Of course, it monitors issues that won't be resolved for many years into the future—and brings those into the system as they move toward the five-year time frame.)

Because of the shorter time frame and the need to react quickly to public issues, issues management is more concerned with adjusting current operations and operational plans to best benefit its stakeholders.

Strategic planning can and does operate in a longer time frame, five or more years out, which gives ample time to plan organizational changes to exploit current and expanding markets or move into new businesses or industries. In the extractive industries, planning may work in a time frame of 20 to 50 years or more. However, most strategic plans are five-year rolling plans.

Issues management's first responsibility is to make sure the corporation is well defended against whatever tactic or move the many organized actors in the public policy process chose to execute. This is designed to meet the first planning/management goal of every CEO: "No surprises!"

Issues management's next goal is to search out inherent opportunities in issues others generate or the company decides to generate in the public policy forums.

The primary duty of strategic planning, on the other hand, is to seek economic opportunities and to find ways to exploit them with internally created business plans. Strategic planning has a secondary responsibility of "contingency planning" in which plans are made to protect against competitive reversals, economic uncertainties, and other upheavals.

Thus, issues management is concerned with achieving the best resolution for its company's stakeholders in a contentious arena where bargains are struck. Strategic planning is concerned with harvesting the benefits of marketing that its plans have created.

One of the first senior executives to see the potential of these two processes working together was Archie R. Boe, CEO of Allstate Insurance Companies. In 1979, he wrote: "Issues management and strategic planning are both born of the dynamic tradition in American business management that rejects the passive approach of hoping to know the future and merely adjusting to it, for an affirmative posture of *creating* the future and *fitting* the corporate enterprise into it."[1]

Both issues management and strategic planning are guided by the corporation's mission statement, which attempts to tell who the corporation is and what it hopes to become, and makes commitments to its primary stakeholders—customers, employees, the general public, and shareholders. For issues managers, the company's mission statement frames the issues they must seek.

Issues managers scan for, monitor, and seek resolution only of those issues that might have significant impacts on their company's stakeholders, and hence the company's future.

Both issues management and strategic planning use similar techniques, share research, and reinforce each other in support of the organization's bottom line.

A TACTICAL APPROACH TO ISSUES MANAGEMENT

The public policy process in a free society is the meeting ground of the public sector (federal, state, and local governmental units) and the private sector (citizens, corporations, organizations, etc.). It is the process, facilitated by the media, where the public's aspirations and dissatisfactions work their way up through public issues debates into law and regulation, if they are not voluntarily resolved in the private sector.

The social control of business is effected through this mechanism. It has only been in the past three decades that business has come to realize that it is not only controlled by the economic environment, but is in fact effectively controlled through the broader social and political environments. This realization forced the development of issues management to give corporations a rational way to manage their participation in the process.

The public policy process can best be understood through a simplified graphic model (see Figure 11–2), which I developed from an earlier Yankelovich, Skelly, and White description of the process.

The base of the pyramid is where public dissatisfactions with the present emerge, prompted by perceived injustices and exclusions, new aspirations, new concerns about the environment, new ideas relating to "rights" and "entitlements," or other issues. But at this

F I G U R E   11–2

Public Policy Process Model (social control of business)

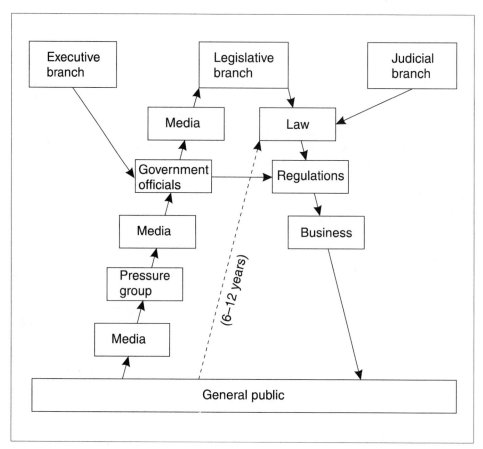

level, nothing happens until it gets a name and visibility, when the media can take it up and talk about it, broadcasting the issue of concern beyond those affected.

The media don't create issues unless there is an underling reality, but they are essential in issue development and its life cycle. However, nothing really happens to the issue until an organized group takes it up and adds it to its action agenda.

Once an organized group decides to add it to its agenda, the pressure group—a public interest group, Chamber of Commerce, trade association, religious institution, political party, or other group—seeks to mobilize social and political forces beyond its own membership. Because the media become critical at this point, the pressure group holds demonstrations and public meetings, making headline-grabbing charges. When this happens, the pressure group becomes the issue champion and, in effect, co-opts the issue, defining it as it wishes.

Frequently, the pressure group approaches a leading company as representative of a targeted industry, or some service organization, demanding a meeting to negotiate the issue, complete with notices to the media. If the company or other organization in the private sector does not respond, the pressure group moves on to the appropriate regulatory agency, demanding public hearings. Again, this is accompanied by notices to the media.

The regulatory agency, because of the publicity and accompanying demands of the pressure group, will take notice of the issue and consider holding public hearings to investigate the charges. These actions generate more media attention. If the agency decides that new laws and regulations are needed, it moves the issue to the elected legislative bodies—the U.S. Congress or state legislatures.

Finally, the Congress or the state legislature, standing at the top of the public policy process, considers the conflicting demands and the interests of key publics. The legislative body will pass a new law if it thinks a law will resolve the problem the issue represents, and if it thinks there is sufficient public consensus for a legislative solution. If the legislators do not think the issue can be resolved or that there is not sufficient public consensus for any one solution, they will not act. In effect, they kick the issue back down into the public arena, hoping the issue will be privately resolved through voluntary actions in the private sector.

If the Congress or state legislature decides a law is needed, it passes one. This law and any accompanying regulations come down like a straitjacket on the business community.

As many commentators have pointed out, the business community gets involved in the life cycle of an issue far too late—at the regulatory or legislative phase when business is considered the problem, not the solution. That is why business is famous for killing legislation, not advancing broad solutions. This was true before the issues management system was developed.

Researchers have found that, at the federal level, it takes from 6 to 12 years for an issue to emerge at the general public level before legislation is passed. (At the state level, legislation can be passed in 1 to 2 years under certain conditions.)

Issues management is designed to take advantage of the time lag so that senior management can develop policy positions and supporting action programs. It sets up systems to monitor all stages of the public policy process stream to identify emerging and developing issues.

Figure 11–3 gives a picture of how issues management arms corporate management with the tools to intervene early in the resolution of an issue while the most options are open to it.

The Seven-Step Process

Issues management can be thought of as a seven-step model.

The first step involves issue identification. This is done through scanning of the sociopolitical environment, seeking emerging issues. Scanning is likened to a constant 360-degree radar sweep, looking for blips.

Once a relevant issue is identified, it is monitored and its development is followed from then on.

After groups of issues that might be relevant to the future viability of the corporation are identified, those issues which appear to be most important are selected for further analysis.

Issue analysis is the second step in the model. Greater rigor is used to define the issue in a manner relevant to the corporation. Then impact analyses are run to consider how different resolutions of the issue would affect the future of the corporation. These analyses

F I G U R E   11–3

Public Policy Process Model

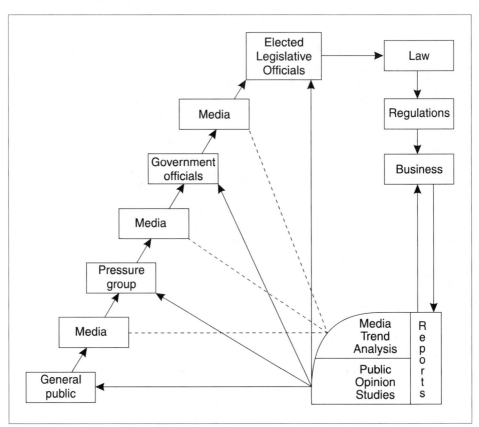

are frequently written in scenario form. The final phase of the issue analysis step is to isolate the issues with the highest priorities for further work.

The first two steps are generally done by issues management staff members. Committees or issue task groups are required for the third and fourth steps. These groups are composed of corporate employees with the most expertise in the issue field under consideration.

As shown in Figure 11–4, steps three through five, which mark the peak of activity in the issues management curve, occur well before the proposal of new legislation—the traditional point at which corporations respond to an issue.

The third step involves the development of a corporate policy position on the issue, in accordance with the organization's strategic plans and goals, to be recommended to senior management for approval.

The fourth step requires the development of specific action plans (tactics) to carry out the strategy inherent in the approved corporate policy position. This step involves setting the time frame when the company will intervene in the issue resolution process, identifying the company's actors, and setting necessary budget parameters.

F I G U R E 11–4

Life Cycle of a Strategic Issue

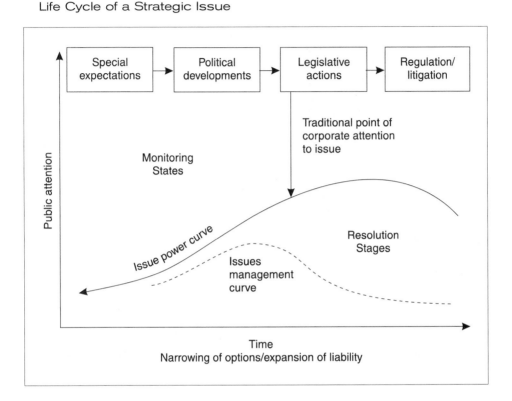

The fifth step involves implementation of the action plans and communication of the company's positions on the issues involved.

The sixth step—review of reaction, adjustments responding to legitimate objections, negotiation, and repetition of the company's positions and their supporting arguments—cannot be omitted, no matter how successful the fifth step appears to be. Those who raised the issue may well pause, regroup, and amend their stance, changing the surface issues but not the underlying goals.

The seventh step involves keeping management's and staff's attention focussed on the issue until it is resolved in a manner the company can live with during the current phase of the issue's life.

Examples of Issues Management in Action

There are many examples of companies which have used the issues management analysis and resolution process. One example of interest is the global issue of Nestlé's infant formula. Infant formula, which is vital for the survival of many infants, was a successful product in the developed world. But when it was marketed by various companies into Third World countries, the lack of safe water and ignorance of how to follow sanitary procedures resulted in many cases of infant deaths and illnesses.

Activists in the United States and Europe took up the issue and picked Nestlé as the company most representative of the industry, even though Nestlé neither manufactured nor sold infant formula in the United States at the time. Boycotts, U.N. petitions, and media campaigns resulted in placing Nestlé under siege. Matters grew worse so long as Nestlé tried to use rational, scientific, manufacturing, and marketing arguments to explain its position in the market.

Nestlé's senior management found the issue was absorbing all of their time, and stockholders were concerned for the effect the issue was having on the company's ability to market its many other products. At this point, Ray Pagan, an issues management professional, was hired. Using the issues management process to analyze the problem, he divided its opponents into two groups: "critics of conscience" (World Federation of Churches, Teachers Associations, etc.) and "critics with other agendas" (groups using nutritional issues as a cover to achieve other goals, some political).

Pagan worked with the critics of conscience to develop and support the World Health Organization's Code of Marketing Infant Formula. He then created a respected third-party organization, with representation of some of the critics, to monitor Nestlé's compliance. This resolved the issue, but monitoring is still going on and the issue could reemerge in another form if good marketing procedures are not maintained.

National Can Company provides an example of how a company used the process to take a unilateral step to remove itself from the negative force of an issue—and gave itself a competitive advantage. During most of the decades of this century, all metal food cans were soldered, allowing small traces of lead to filter into the food inside. Even though these traces were less than the lead in the air one normally breathed in the home, National Can's issue analyst concluded that the public, over time, would come to demand that any trace of lead in the food chain be removed. Hence, the federal government's strict regulations on the manufacture of food cans would become so strict that solder could not be used in the manufacture of cans.

National Can made a policy decision: It spent $80 million to convert its manufacturing process to produce cans with no lead in them, before government regulations demanded such actions. Thus, it was in an advantageous marketing position, compared with its competitors, as the tougher federal regulations rolled into place.

Other industries, after careful issue analyses, have made similar anticipatory moves. International animal rights groups mounted strong campaigns to stop major fisheries from using nets in tuna fishing that entangled and drowned dolphins. Major tuna canneries, including Chicken of the Sea, moved to stop buying tuna from fisheries that used the tuna harvesting method that killed dolphins.

Likewise, evidence was produced in the early 1990s that ozone depletion in the global atmosphere was caused by CFCs (chlorofluorocarbons) used in refrigerants, aerosol cans, and the manufacture of foam products. As the scientific evidence became clear, DuPont and Dow Chemical, which were early users of issues management systems, announced that they were converting to foam manufacturing systems that would eliminate the use of CFCs as blowing agents in the creation of their foam products.

Perhaps the most interesting international case involving the use of the issues management process has taken place in Venezuela, where the government-owned international energy corporation, Petroleos De Venezuela, SA, adopted the process in 1991.

PDVSA ranks in the middle of the Fortune 100 list of the world's largest industrial companies. It operates in Europe and the United States, where it is the sole owner of CITGO.

In recent years, PDVSA has accounted for 13 percent of Venezuela's gross domestic product (GDP), 51 percent of government revenues, and 81 percent of the country's exports.

PDVSA's approach was outlined by its public affairs manager, Janet Cesar de Polarnik, at a 1994 Issue Management Council conference in Washington, D.C. Cesar pointed out that, although the company is wholly owned by the national government, it is managed as a private corporation. Being government owned, the organization believed or acted as if it were insulated from external forces and crises.

However, changing world trends such as economic globalization, slumping oil prices, growing competition, and environmentalism, as well as national trends involving the eroding quality of life in the country causing social instability, prompted PDVSA to take a fresh look at its planning and management style. In addition, there had been an increase in public awareness of institutions in this democratic country as political power shifted from the central government to state and local authorities, who were now elected for the first time. This resulted in the formation of local organizations capable of bringing community pressure on the government and its institutions, including PDVSA. The privately owned media were also a factor in generating public action.

To close the gaps between corporate performance and public expectations and between the public opinion environment and its reactive managerial style, PDVSA decided to adopt the issues management approach in 1991. In describing this shift, Cesar introduced us to a delightful new word. She said the organization wanted to move from management style of reactivity to "proactivity." [2]

At PDVSA, the Public Affairs unit developed a multimedia issues management training program in the various languages of the organization's international subsidiaries. The training program can be used by large groups or by individuals who want to use a laptop computer.

Four issues monitoring centers were established in the operational centers. From these centers' reports, PDVSA prepares a single report which also includes international and national information and analysis. This report is sent to the various boards of the company and its subsidiaries, senior managements for each of the companies, and to the governmental ministry responsible of PDVSA oversight.

Cesar reported on the achievements of the program: a reduction of the national exporting tax from 80 percent to 60 percent; strategic associations with foreign corporations to explore and produce natural gas; and a greater responsiveness from PDVSA's boards and operating affiliates.

THE FUTURE OF ISSUES MANAGEMENT

It has been 20 years since W. Howard Chase had the brilliant insight which resulted in the naming and formulation of the issues management process. In the intervening years, thousands of men and women have applied this management technique for as many organizations.

However, the warning given in a white paper in 1981 still applies:

> To date, issues management is being staffed not only by PR practitioners, but also by long-range planners, lobbyists, lawyers, public affairs specialists, and public policy analysts. If we in the public relations profession don't make a major effort to study this new management development and shape our skills and techniques to serve it, we will be squeezed out by economists, public affairs specialists, and, especially, the public policy analysts from the nation's think tanks.

> In its present form, issues management is a new management science for which the rules are being written now. Let's make sure our profession matures and helps write our share of the rules, instead of finding ourselves in the back of the bus again, restricted to once more running glorified news bureaus.[3]

Currently, several organizations affiliated with our profession run conferences and workshops on issues management. PRSA runs several workshops each year on the subject for its 17,000 members. The Public Affairs Council offers an annual Issues Management Workshop to the PA management staffs of its 525 corporate members. And the Issues Management Council, under the direction of Teresa Yancey Crane, runs several workshops and conferences every year for its 150 professional issues management practitioners from leading corporations.

A number of other trade associations also offer conferences and training on the subject. However, as predicted, many of the attendees do not come from the PR field, but from other specialties (human resources, corporate law, engineering, marketing, etc.). Many of these people wish to control the issues management system in their organizations and restrict it to their specialties, especially corporate lawyers responsible for legislative and regulatory relations. In companies where corporate lawyers control the issues management process and wish to restrict it to current legislative/regulatory affairs, all too often qualified PR professionals are squeezed out of the loop. So it has been in the past; so struggle will continue in the future.

But a strong trend in college and university PR degree programs has emerged over the last several years and promises to gain strength for the profession in the future. More and more schools are offering issues management courses in their graduate and undergraduate curricula. For example, Northwestern University has offered an issues management course in the graduate corporate public relations sequence at the Medill School of Journalism since 1987.

Thus, an ever-growing cadre of PR graduates trained in issues management will continue to emerge over the next decades. With every major PR agency offering an issues management capability to clients, the practice will continue to grow in the consulting field. But more importantly, with the increasing numbers of CEOs discovering that crisis management doesn't cut it, but that issues management offers a better way to steer through the shoals of potential crises, the future of issues management as a rewarding career path is assured. Our task is to convince senior management that our training, experience, and knowledge of the public environments our organizations live in make us, as PR professionals, uniquely qualified to staff and lead an internal issues management system.

This some of us have done in the past; many more will do so well into the next century.

E N D N O T E S

1. Archie R. Bol, "Fitting the Corporation to the Future," *Public Relations Quarterly* (Winter 1979), p. 5.
2. I have always detested that limp rag of a word "proactive," which some PR people stole from educational psychology. Proactivity, however, has muscle and direction. It reminds me of Mark Twain's observation: "The difference between the right word and the almost-right word is the difference between lightning and the lightning bug."
3. Raymond P. Ewing, "Issues Management: Public Relations Comes of Age" (paper prepared for the Counselors Academy, Public Relations Society of America, Chicago, IL, 1981).

B I B L I O G R A P H Y

Books

Ashley, William C., and James L. Morrison, *Anticipatory Management* (Leesburg, VA: Issue Action Publications, 1995).

Brown, J. K., *This Business of Issues: Coping with the Company's Environment* (New York: The Conference Board, 1979).

Chase, W. Howard, *Issues Management: Origins of the Future* (Stamford, CT: Issue Action Publications, 1984).

Coates, Joseph F., *Issues Management: How You Can Plan, Organize, and Manage for the Future* (Mounty Airy, MD: Lomand Publications, 1986).

Ewing, Raymond P., *Managing the New Bottom Line: Issues Management for Senior Executives* (Burr Ridge, IL: Dow Jones-Irwin, 1987).

Heath, Robert L., and Richard Alan Nelson, *Issues Management: Corporate Public Policymaking in an Information Society* (Beverly Hills, CA: Sage Publications, 1986).

Heath, Robert L., and Associates, *Strategic Issues Management* (San Francisco, CA: Jossey-Bass Publishers, 1988).

Nowlan, S. E., and D. R. Shayon, *Leveraging the Impact of Public Affairs* (Philadelphia, PA: Human Resources Network, 1984).

Renfro, William L., *Issues Management in Strategic Planning* (Westport, CT: Quorum Books, 1993).

Stanley, Guy, *Managing External Issues* (Greenwich, CT: JAI Press, 1985).

Chapters in Books

Chase, W. Howard. "Issues Management." In *The Public Affairs Handbook* (Chicago, IL: American Management Association, 1982).

Ewing, Raymond P. "Sociopolitical Forecasting: Managing the Black Hole of the Future." In *Through the 80s: Thinking Globally, Acting Locally* (Washington, DC: World Future Society, 1980).

Ewing, Raymond P. "The Uses of Futurist Techniques in Issues Management." In *A Managerial Odyssey: Problems in Business and It's Environment* (Reading, MA: Addison-Wesley Publishing, 1981).

_____. "Modeling the Process." In *The Public Affairs Handbook* (Chicago, IL: American Management Association, 1982).

Newsletter

Corporate Public Issues and Their Management. Issue Action Publications, Inc. (Leesburg, VA).

Journal Articles

Chase, W. Howard. "Public Issue Management—The New Science." *Public Relations Journal,* (October 1977).

Crane, Teresa Yancey. "Issue Management: Service Growth Area for Associations." *Association Trends,* (January 20, 1995).

Ewing, Raymond P. "The Uses of Futurist Techniques in Issues Management." *Public Relations Quarterly,* (Winter 1979).

_____. "Evaluating Issues Management." *Public Relations Journal,* (June 1980).

_____. "Advocacy Advertising: The Voice of Business in Public Policy Debate." *Public Affairs Review,* III, (1982).

_____. "Moving from Micro to Macro Issues Management." *Public Relations Review,* (Spring 1990).

_____. "The Role of Issues Management in Managing the New Bottom Line." *Journal of Corporate Public Relations,* (Winter 1990).

Heath, Robert L., and Kenneth R. Cousino. "Issues Management: End of the First Decade—Progress Report." *Public Relations Review,* (Spring 1990).

Long, Richard K. "Getting the Jump on Public Issues." *Vital Speeches*, (February 15, 1986).

Pedersen, Wes. "Challenges and Concerns of Issues Management." *Public Relations Journal*, (February 1984).

Unpublished Material

Ewing, Raymond P. "Issues Management: Public Relations Comes of Age." (Paper prepared for the Counselors Academy, Public Relations Society of America, Chicago, IL, 1981.)

A Strategic Approach to Crisis Management

Kurt P. Stocker
Associate Professor, Integrated Marketing Communications
Northwestern University,
and Principal, Stocker & Associates

A STRATEGIC APPROACH

Definitions

Crisis management, by definition, is the preparation and application of strategies and tactics that can prevent or modify the impact of major events on the company or organization. At best, crisis management is a way of thinking and acting when everything "hits the fan." At it's worst, crisis management can be the life-or-death difference for a product, career, or company. A crisis will demand the use of all our skills. Gaining credibility with all our audiences, under extreme stress and with severe time constraints, is a true test and too often we come up short.

Crisis management is often confused with a "business interruption plan" which helps an organization when faced with facilities issues such as loss of power, fire, or computer breakdown. While operational emergencies should be addressed in a crisis plan, the majority of business interruptions are easily dealt with through redundancies or purchased backups. For example, computer and financial systems are often supported in this way. On the other hand, crisis management incorporates all the decisions, communications, and personnel necessary to either prevent or deal with a crisis.

Crisis management begins with the answers to two very important questions: What is a crisis, and when did the crisis start? Finding answers isn't as easy as it sounds. Sure, when a fire starts or a product malfunctions, it's easy to understand, but when a company goes "into play," or when questions are raised about the actions of a CEO, or when one of your restaurants turns away someone of color, it's a little more difficult to predict the enormity of the consequences.

In the book *Overdrive*, Michael Silva and Terry McGann offer a fairly simple "Five-Minute Audit" to determine if an event is a crisis. They define a crisis as a violation of your vision, and then ask four questions:

1. To what degree will this event affect your ability to meet your mission?

2. What is the intensity and the urgency of the crisis? How big can it get?

3. Which of your values are affected and what is the long-term potential for damage?

4. What relationships are threatened?

Crisis management crosses all organizational boundaries to have an impact on every stakeholder, either as a direct result of the problem or as a potential supporter of the solution. Just think about strikes or plant closings, which affect everyone from the institutional investor to the local car dealer. Consider the impact of a product defect on your stock price and your brand equity. Above all, it is important to remember that a crisis affects people first, then organizations. Employees, customers, and shareholders are the early losers in a crisis, especially one that is out of control.

Crisis management is "you bet your company," and at warp speed. It is this level of pressure and stress that makes a crisis either a real high for all those involved or a nightmare. Nothing else in the practice of public relations is so all-consuming and tests us in such an unforgiving climate.

Trends

As with other functional areas in the public relations profession, organizations in the United States have shaped the approach to crisis planning, response, and management. With each crisis situation, organizations develop better tools to prevent, prepare for, and handle the inevitable. Unfortunately, too often, it is too late. In fact, if we look back at the evolution of crisis management, it parallels the rise in the practice of public relations. The trends in crisis handling are based in the changing face of the standards of our society and the resultant attention of the media. Organizations increasingly put greater emphasis on quality, ethics, and respect for employees. Communities look beyond economics at the environment, crime, and child care. Health risks and environmental concerns dominate our thinking. With the new global village, differences in culture and ethics cause the return of issues of child labor and bribery. Corporate restructuring has undermined traditional employee loyalty. Similarly, customers and investors are better informed, and are instantly notified of anything that affects their perceptions and actions.

Prior to the late 1960s, crisis handling was deliberate and legally dominated. Without the pressures of instant communications and immediate public reaction, a crisis could be dealt with by thoughtful and determined people, normally lawyers who were concerned exclusively with lawsuits and communications strategies designed to conceal rather than reveal. Not that everyone has seen the light and every lawyer has been checkmated, but we have come a long way in understanding what a crisis is, how to handle it, and what the ultimate penalty is—that is, the damage to the brand or the company which far outweighs the cost and fear of the courts.

The bottom line is clear. The combination of increased standards and improved communications have made corporations into glass houses. The reduced loyalties of all audiences, driven by restructuring and outsourcing of employees; the dramatic move of corporate ownership from individual to institutional investors; and an increasingly better-informed customer, have created an environment that will spawn and nurture crisis. Along with this change in climate, the approach to crisis management has evolved beyond the dusty and out-of-date three-ring binders that still populate many shelves.

Today, companies see a crisis for what it is: a potential marketing issue, with lasting effects beyond just an isolated event. Consequently, how a company handles a crisis creates a lasting impression that ultimately changes or supports the company's reputation.

Along with changes in corporate and community climates and the corresponding evolution of the approach to handling a crisis, several other current trends continue to impact crisis management.

1. *Trial by media.* Today, more news outlets exist than ever before and the demand for sensationalism is at an all-time high. More media attention combined with the lack of restrictions on lawyers fosters the current strategy for lawyers on both sides to "prepare the jury" through the mass media. Lawyers do not have to prove allegations outside the courtroom; instead, they use the press to tell the story and nurture public opinion. We've seen this tactic in the tobacco industry's allegations about nicotine addiction and passive smoke, and in the recently settled Dow Corning breast implant case. In both cases the company and the accusers used both paid and free media to tell their story in order to influence the outcome of the case.

2. *Sue the media.* Two clear examples with two different outcomes illustrate the trend. Both General Motors and Food Lion sued the television "news magazine" that accused them of terrible deeds—GM of an unsafe pickup truck gas tank and Food Lion of selling old meat and produce. GM won the day using a television press conference and evidence of fraudulent test manipulation. GM eventually received an apology from the network. On the other hand, Food Lion failed to make the case that the union, in an effort to pressure the company, faked the hidden camera tape. Food Lion is still suffering the consequences. More recently, the tobacco industry threatened suit to block an interview on "60 Minutes," and then followed by publishing an in-depth investigation of the executive in an attempt to destroy his credibility.

3. *Give something back.* This concept is taken from the complaint-handling formula. People who are disadvantaged want an apology, assurance that—whatever it is—it will not be repeated, and then, something extra. Give something. Companies now try to compensate key stakeholders, at least in a small way, for the disturbance a crisis causes. Food companies often use coupons after product recalls to get customers back. As an apology after the failure of its system, AT&T offered a day of free calls.

The change in the attitude and specialization of media has led to crises becoming national events, and the speed of coverage has shifted a company's successful handling of a crisis from reaction to preparation.

Relationship of Public Relations and Communications to Missions and Goals

Crisis management has three sequential objectives. The first, ideally, is to prevent a crisis when possible. The second, if a crisis should occur, is to modify the negative effect on the company or its products. The third, through its behavior, is to provide a platform for the company's future. Arthur W. Page of the old Bell System (AT&T), reputed to be the first corporate public affairs officer, said that you must "conduct public relations as if the whole company depends on it." The outcome of a crisis has to do with how well the organization was prepared and how faithful its conduct was to its mission and values.

All responsible corporate relations strategies boil down to two objectives: (1) to produce new revenues, or (2) to protect current revenues. Crisis planning may be at the top of the protect list, along with various competitive issues, market share concerns, and ownership questions.

Consequently, the strategic implications are broad and integration into the organization's planning, missions, and goals is imperative. In contradiction to current thinking, most companies are not prepared for a crisis. They either have failed to prepare or the plan sitting on their shelf is outdated and incomplete.

Crisis planning is insurance, just as important as, and arguably more important than, a fire policy or a system to back up tapes and records. The potential cost of a poorly handled crisis will exceed any damage done to plant or records. The accountants call it "goodwill," and the marketers call it "brand loyalty," and Wall Street puts a price on it.

The key to crisis management is planning—knowing what can happen to you or your industry, and what you can do about it. Most crises can be anticipated and preparations can be made, even though the timing and magnitude remain in doubt. The stated objective must be to prevent the crisis, although, in most cases, what happens is out of the company's hands. But, all crises can be at least partially anticipated.

Consider the examples:

- Should Intel have suspected that its chips had a flaw?
- Should NASA have been prepared for a failure in one of its missions?
- Why would one of the largest restaurant chains, Denny's, ignore the possibility of charges of discrimination?
- Was it a surprise that Exxon had an oil spill, or that Jack-in-the-Box had cases of food poisoning, or that Union Carbide had an explosion?

When you look at the majority of crises in the last 10 years, what happened should have been on or near the top of the list of possible events. Why wasn't anyone prepared? The first reason for this is a feeling that it is impossible to plan for everything; therefore, plan for nothing. The second reason is an inherent arrogance, an assumption that we can handle anything that happens.

The first step in crisis management involves analysis—knowing what can happen to you or your industry and what you can do about it, if anything. Getting information about a potential crisis can be as sophisticated as a formal issues management program or as simple as interviewing your own employees about what could go wrong, or what may be going wrong. Keep in mind that top management, by definition, is the least-informed group in the company when it comes to bad news. Nothing moves more slowly than bad news running up a hill, a very steep hill. In most internally generated crises, the knowledge and potential for a problem was known well in advance of the onset of the public crisis, and top management found out about it as it was going public.

The four most important questions in formulating a crisis plan are:

1. What are the potential threats to your company?
2. Can you plan for every eventuality?
3. What is your plan trying to protect?
4. Do you need a plan, or just good preparation?

The four most important questions in formulating a crisis plan are:

1. **What are the potential threats to your company?**
   - Product-related incidents or defects.
   - Natural disasters, fires, explosions.
   - Employee or industrial relations events.
   - Corporate or personal behavior issues.
   - Accidents and terrorism.

2. **Can you plan for every eventuality?**
   - You can plan behavior, not specific tactics.
   - You can assign responsibility based on threat potential.
   - You can communicate "upstream" to provide early warnings.
   - You can centralize control and handling of top-tier crisis situations.

3. **What is your plan trying to protect?**
   - The reputation of the company.
   - The immediate bottom line.
   - The house brands or vendor products.
   - The current management.

4. **Do you need a plan, or just good preparation?**
   - There is no need for elaborate manuals.
   - You can make directional decisions now.
   - You can anticipate the tough questions and prepare the best answers.
   - You can create a proprietary distribution network.

Determining if you are at risk of a crisis is easy, but some organizations are more at risk than others. The source of crisis has traditionally been attributed to what happened, rather than the more important cause of what happened. First let's look at the risk of something happening to your organization.

The Risks of Crisis

Is your organization in a high-risk category? Consider yourself at high risk if you are in manufacturing (especially if there are environmental or medical products) transportation, food products, even lodging or construction. These deal primarily with products and services which imperil someone's life if something goes wrong.

The second category is medium risk. There is no low risk.

Is the risk preventable? Certainly many are. Preventable risks generally fall into the category of manufacturing rather than service industries. This group of crises is normally handled in the safety programs, audits, and quality programs commonly found in manufacturing companies. The only question is how well they are followed and in many cases, ignored.

All incidents are different. They have different characteristics, but many are similar in some ways. Some of the more notorious can be grouped as follows:

1. Product-related cases:
   - Gerber baby food was alleged to contain glass shards.

- Pepsi had to deal with a syringe allegedly found in a can.
- Dow Corning continues to deal with the issue of silicon breast implants.
- Audi faced concerns about runaway acceleration.

2. Terrorism and random violence:
   - Post Office shootings damaged the Postal Service's image.
   - Shooting in McDonald's California drive-in affected business.
   - Miami shootings had major effects on international tourism.

3. Financial, takeover, and ethical issues:
   - Continental Bank's failure led to bail out by the FDIC.
   - United Airlines' strike led to an attempted takeover and employee purchase.
   - Kidder Peabody and Drexel both faced the implications of management improprieties.

4. Rumors and allegations:
   - Procter & Gamble faced recurring rumors that their logo was somehow connected to the devil.
   - Chicago's Cardinal Bernadin was falsely accused of sexual abuse.

The Real Source of Crisis

A study was done at Northwestern as part of the Crisis Management Practica, on what is the real source of a crisis. The study was based on the premise that a crisis is not what happens to you but its outcome—how you handle it. The results change the conversation and give foundation to crisis management principles. The study titled "The Seven Deadly Sins," analyzed contemporary cases for common mistakes that led to bigger and more costly events. These "sins" are, in every case, sins of commission.

1. *Erroneous ethics*. This describes situations where, it is alleged, management's ethics were responsible for the crisis. Denny's Restaurants founder was accused of poisoning the corporate culture of the company, which led to a highly publicized discrimination case. More recently, Archer-Daniel-Midland was accused by a government "mole" of price-fixing and questionable securities dealings.

2. *Incentive crisis*. One of the most-overlooked root causes of a crisis is misguided incentive programs. In an effort to improve productivity, the company provides incentives and pressure for results. When workers overachieve, they cause huge problems. Consider Sears Automotive Center's problems which originated with an incentive to sell additional parts to customers beyond those they needed. Food Lion Inc. is another example, which we will cover in detail later in this chapter.

3. *Mixed values*. When your organization's values clash with those of your public, it can cause big problems. Time Warner, a family media company, marketed Gangsta Rap (spoken verse that encourages or praises illegal or disrespectful activities, set to a musical beat) in the face of a rising tide of "family values." Issues now boil up around the tobacco industry, questioning how much the companies knew about nicotine and its drug-like effects.

4. *Stonewalling stakeholders.* This is the worst and most invoked of all the sins. The issue here is trust—telling what you know when you know it. When a company or individual refuses to admit a problem, even for a short period, they lose credibility. In the case of Intel's Pentium chip, the defect was first broadcast on the Internet. Competitors waded in to take advantage, and Intel tried to downplay the defect. It turned into an expensive mistake. Consider the Dow Corning breast implant controversy. Would the outcome have changed if they had spoken earlier about the leaks and the science surrounding the problem? Through early denial, they destroyed all their credibility; which has plagued them for years.

5. *The Peter Syndrome.* Almost all crisis handling can benefit from truth telling. When a company refuses to accept blame or even express regret, the public turns on it. The organization looks guilty, even if it isn't. When Jack-in-the-Box was accused of food poisoning, their first response was to blame the vendor and the inspectors. It may have been true, but the public voted with its feet and sales tumbled.

6. *Walking the high wire without a net.* It is the slow-burning crisis that should have been anticipated. When France decided to conduct eight nuclear tests in the South Pacific, they should have been prepared for the reaction, but they were not ready. When people started dying as a result of a heat wave in Chicago, someone should have had a plan of action, not words. Communication is not a substitute for action.

7. *Addiction to repetition.* Never become an expert in the same mistake. One event is a situation, and two is a crisis. It may not be within your control to prevent the repetition, but it is in your control to anticipate it and plan for the result. When the computers at an airport crash for the third time, or another shooting occurs in the Post Office, or another train leaves the track, it should not be a surprise to you or the public.

The Porter-Novelli Survey

In 1993, Porter-Novelli, a well-known public relations agency, conducted a survey to track the impact of crises and the public dynamics of anger. The results of the survey were not surprising in their content, but for the first time quantified the damage. The survey supports and documents the real damage to reputations and gives real substance to the dynamic of crisis handling.

1. The larger the crisis, the longer the public remembers. (At the time of the survey, Exxon, Sears Automotive, GM's fuel tanks, Dow Corning, Food Lion, and IBM's business problems dominated the list.)

2. How the company behaved influenced the public reaction. When a company refused responsibility, or put out inaccurate information, the public was angry. When the company seemed to put profits above public interest, or was not quick to rectify a problem, the public got angry.

3. Eyewitnesses and third parties are believed. Company spokespersons, no surprises, are not credible. We are seen as what we are, especially when we

defend rather than admit. Most people believe that companies do not tell the truth.

4. A damaged reputation affects the customer's decision to purchase. This is the real cost.

Preparing for a crisis means developing the internal mindset necessary to survive a turbulent period. When a company is prepared for a crisis, it is reflected in the corporate attitude during tough times. At Johnson & Johnson, the corporate mission of "people first" provided the foundation for managing the Tylenol crisis. When syringes were found in Pepsi cans in Seattle, the company quickly responded to public concern in a different, but appropriate, manner. Similarly, a very public emphasis on safety allowed United Airlines to maintain the perception of safety in the face of a series of accidents.

A crisis tests a company's mission, values, and strength. During a crisis, the company operates under a microscope. The way the company behaves day to day and how it stratifies its priorities will carry over into a crisis, for better or worse. The public will give the "good corporate citizen" a break, but will punish the organization that does not seem to care about its employees, community, or environment.

The globalization of the business community also has important implications for crisis planning and handling. In each country, a company's acts are held up against local laws, customs, and public perception. This complicates risk analysis. For instance, does a global company comply with each local environmental law, even if it is far short of those of its home country or the country with the highest standards? Many companies are currently making these decisions. With the advent of economic zones like NAFTA, the issues are real and the penalties severe. The media acts like a global whistleblower. Child or prison labor, toxic dumping, government bribes, and employee abuses no longer go unnoticed or unpunished by the consumer. Boycotts and public criticism demonstrate how crises impact marketing.

Budgeting and Measurement Considerations

Justifying the budget for crisis planning involves elementary cost-benefit analysis. First, the initial cost of creating a plan is relatively small, and second, the potential cost of not planning can be astronomical. The initial financial impact of losing a product, of a strike, or of a damaged reputation can be easily calculated and result in a big number—frankly, a much bigger number that is readily attributed to a crisis.

Recent studies done at Northwestern University's Integrated Marketing Communications program found that the majority of costs associated with a crisis are not legal costs or judgments. The potential for legal costs tends to determine how companies respond to a crisis and, in almost every case, ends up being a minor segment of the ultimate costs. The largest single segment of costs is market costs—the cost of lost sales, either through damaged products or damaged reputation. The ultimate effect is on market share, ability to grow, and margins.

The second major cost is the company's market value or equity. Stock price is generally hammered when a crisis occurs. The stock market instantly understands the effect on sales and growth. Shareholders, employee-owners, and management options are immediately discounted, and rarely rebound over time.

Consider this example. Sears' reputation with customers was severely damaged in 1992 when its automotive centers were accused of selling unnecessary repairs. Auto center revenue declined by $80 million and generated a third-quarter loss. Legal fees were about $11 million. Reimbursing California for its investigation and providing mandated employee training added another $5 million. By far the biggest losses were to the shareholders and employees. The stock immediately lost 1.5 points, or about $565 million. Finally, 1993 revenues declined by $1.5 billion. How much of that was a result of Sears' weakened reputation with its customers?

Conduct a simple experiment. Consider the most likely crisis that could happen to your company, even one that is out of your control. Apply the "one percent rule," that is, if it affected the price of your stock by one percent, how much would that cost the company's pubic owners, or your chairman personally? Now consider that most companies that undergo a major crisis take a 5 to 50 percent hit on their stock price.

The new model of crisis planning (which follows) no longer takes large expenditures. It is the agreement and understanding of top management on how they will behave, and the preparation of public relations practitioners on how they will manage the event, that carries the day.

A TACTICAL APPROACH

The Crisis Plan

Planning in advance of a crisis may be the prime determiner as to the depth and cost to a company's reputation and bottom line. Once an event occurs, there is no time for a considered, thoughtful approach.

1. Start with an Approach

The crisis plan begins with a corporate statement outlining the company's crisis management approach, providing a decision base and behavior path for all actions. The statement will summarize the company's philosophies and ethics, and delineate what the company plans to "protect." This is the corporate conscience section.

While it is possible to list the most probable events that can befall an organization, the details, twists, and turns have the ability to handcuff. With an approach that has the agreement of top management, all decisions become faster, safer, and sounder. If the organization needs to have a meeting to make a directional decision, it is already behind and may never catch up.

> Conduct a simple experiment. Consider the most likely crisis that could happen to your company, even one that is out of your control. Apply the "one percent rule," that is, if it affected the price of your stock by one percent, how much would that cost the company's public owners, or your chairman personally? Now consider that most companies that undergo a major crisis take a 5 to 50 percent hit on their stock price.

2. Build a Strong Reputation

Banking some goodwill in advance is the best and cheapest of crisis tactics. An organization with a solid reputation will survive a crisis better than one without. It is nearly impossible to build a relationship and credibility with stakeholders in the middle of a crisis. It has to be done when the wind is down and the seas calm. Each player's initial approach to the crisis will be strongly influenced by its perception of your historical behavior. This is as true for regulators and reporters as it is for customers and communities. Putting something in the bank is just good sense and becomes very powerful when the subject is your greatest vulnerability. Each audience will look at your record, and most of it can and will be retrieved in seconds from existing databases.

3. Create a Crisis Team

Someone has to be in charge of a crisis, and in most cases it will consume all of their time. The person should be a member of top management who can step away from the day-to-day duties and assume control of the crisis team. The selection of the team will be critical to the process. Representatives from most key policy and operational areas are needed to bring appropriate thinking and management to the event. Then choose the team. Candidates for the team include:

> Corporate communications
>
> Legal
>
> Human resources
>
> Medical
>
> Research
>
> Operations
>
> Safety
>
> Security
>
> Transportation
>
> Government affairs.

4. Establish a Crisis Center

There is a need for a Crisis Center. This can be an established conference room, preferably one that is already wired and equipped for these communications technologies:

> Preinstalled jacks for phone lines.
>
> Computers with modems to access databases.
>
> Faxes, video conferencing, and VCRs.
>
> Satellite television, radio, and wire services.

In addition, the room should contain:

> Communications lists for key groups:
>
> - Top management and board of directors
> - Company directories
> - Investors and analysts
> - Customers and distributors
> - Regulators and government officials
> - Media
> - Vendors

Stationary and overnight envelopes

Grab bag—duffel or box that is already stocked and ready to be taken to the site of the crisis. It should also contain lists, stationery, cellular phones, lap top computer with modem, and, additionally, some cash, credit cards, tape recorder, camera, film, batteries, and beeper.

5. The Network Alert System

The bigger you are the harder it is to know what is going on in your company: lots of suits, product issues, advocate groups, investigations, and safety issues. Knowing which ones have the potential to create a crisis can give you a real edge. Forge a link with the legal department. Help them to understand what kinds of suits you want to be informed about, even if they don't have large price tags. Discuss with the human resource group the unintended consequences of incentive programs. The dark side of sales incentives can damage a corporation's reputation. Look at the results of Sears rewarding automotive service personnel for extra sales, or Prudential Insurance's bonus program for their insurance salesmen. In both cases, they were good incentives—maybe too good.

Eliminate all surprises. There are no good surprises.

6. Prepare Materials in Advance

Every organization is different, and every crisis is different, but every response is not different. We can prepare a great deal in advance. The thought process is straightforward. If something bad happened today, what would I need to respond immediately? The list will differ with each situation, but some suggestions to get the thinking started include:

- A press response stating that you have incomplete knowledge of the crisis details, describing your conceptual approach, and giving your promise to inform.

- Your best answer and information if the product fails, or the plane crashes, or the tank leaks, or the broker cheats, or personnel discriminate, or the union strikes.

- Some generic but positive information about the company that has some bearing on the crisis. For example, if you are an aircraft engine manufacturer and a plane crashes, put out diagrams of how engines work and how they are tested, and reliability charts, all without speculating on the cause of the accident.

- In the "normal" crisis there is an early vacuum of information. Fill it with information that will form a background and control media speculation. Don't be reluctant to say good things about your company, your products or services, your safety record, audits, and management. If you don't, nobody will.

Managing the Crisis

The first response to a crisis can be very important. Even though it is on a much larger scale, the rules of complaint handling and the "4 Rs" still apply:

1. *Regret.* They want you to say that you are sorry it happened. Not that you're guilty, or even responsible, just that you regret the event. This is very hard for some overprotective lawyers, who will caution that "these very words will come back to bite us in court." First, the real costs are not in the courtroom, and

second, crisis research is clear; if you do not express regret, nobody will listen to anything else you say. You cannot skip the first R and jump to the second.

2. *Resolution.* State, if appropriate, what you will do to resolve the issue. Put safety caps on the medicine, buy double-hull ships, test the chips before you ship, or, if it is not your fault . . . nothing.

3. *Reform.* The third step is to assure, if we can, it will not happen again. And then, in some cases . . .

4. *Restitution.* Everybody wants something. This doesn't refer to legal judgments, but product coupons when the product returns to shelves, or free phone calls in return for outages. The formula works.

To assure an accurate and fair reporting and understanding of your position, your facts, and your attitude in a crisis, you cannot allow the media to control the entire dialogue. Think of the media as the only distribution system, and one that has its own agenda, unless you establish your own proprietary systems.

- Develop direct, unedited information systems to reach your important audiences.
- Utilize all forms of media. Overnight delivery and faxes can be used for small, important groups like your board, legislators, or institutional investors.
- Consider direct mail, group faxes, 800 numbers, Internet pages, regional meetings, or advertisements for larger, more diverse groups like customers, employees, or the community.
- Hold the media to the truth. Form a "Truth Squad" to monitor and correct any and all media errors or omissions. Understand that each instance will not or should not result in a correction. The objective is to make sure the database is reasonably accurate, as each new reporter on the scene will use it as a basis of their coverage.
- Test messages for understanding and impact. A quick focus group or telephone research is helpful in sensing the mood of the public and testing your response for sincerity and credibility.
- Supplement everything you do with third-party support. Everyone will have "experts" to support or explain the terrain.
- Keep a log of all press releases and key accurate stories as the crisis develops, and use it to "upload" new members of the press as they enter the story. This will improve the accuracy of the coverage.
- Provide a location for the press to meet, communicate, and get briefings from your organization. If you want to get your messages across, you need to be a source of information.

Real Cases, Real Costs: Food Lion

There are more examples of organizations that have done it wrong than those that did it right. Some just aren't ready; the crisis gets ahead of them and they can't catch up. Some think they can tough it out, stonewall, and it will pass. Some just blame it on someone or something else, and a lot just don't get it.

The two most celebrated cases of crisis handling have been the Johnson & Johnson's Tylenol tampering case and the Pepsi syringe tampering case. In both cases, the companies handled the crisis perfectly. They had good reputations going into the crisis. They were not at fault, but they didn't play the victim. They communicated broadly, openly, and often. Understandably, it's a bit easier when you are not at fault, and a bit harder when you have actually done something wrong and must confess. But the rules of engagement are the same. Let's take an in-depth look at such a case and see how it was handled.

Food Lion Inc. was the darling of Wall Street in the early 1990s. It was a $7 billion retail food chain, with 1,000 stores in 14 states and big growth plans. Their net profits were in the $200 million range and they had margins three times the industry average. The fastest-growing chain in the decade, it doubled its size in four years.

This was a nonunion company located primarily in the southeast. The United Food and Commercial Workers were engaged in an organization drive, and had filed complaints of child labor violations and "off the clock" workers.

Late in 1992, Food Lion was contacted by "Dateline" with requests for interviews and information on worker abuses and policies surrounding the sale of outdated foods. Food Lion refused, denied all allegations, and blamed it on union campaign tactics.

"Dateline" pursued the story with a hidden camera and ABC employees. On November 5, 1992, "Dateline" aired a 25-minute segment that allegedly "showed" old meat being re-dated and sold, unclean conditions, and even food being taken back out of dumpsters and placed on the store shelves.

The company's first reaction was to blame the union and accused ABC of falsifying the tape and their employees of creating the situations. Food Lion stock dropped about five dollars, about half its value. The cost to officers and directors alone was over $958 million, and lost revenues were over a million a week.

What should the company have done? Why did all this happen? Was this really a bad company? The answer is, clearly, no. The problem might have been created by the unantici-pated consequences of what seemed to be a good business decision. Food Lion had installed benchmarked task times for all operations. Employees were measured on adherence to the policy, but some couldn't keep up with the regulations. The result might have been overtime without compensation and cutting corners. That wasn't the entire reason, but it could have contributed to the issue and the resultant publicity.

What would you do? You might have made a statement that sounded a little like this. "Food Lion is embarrassed and angry at what the "Dateline" show uncovered. It has always been our policy to run our stores the way our customers run their kitchens. Keep everything clean and healthy. Unfortunately, it appears that an aggressive cost-cutting program got out of hand, and we owe an apology to our faithful customers. As of this moment, we are closing all 1,000 stores and will go through them with outside inspectors to ensure they meet our high standards. When we open again, Food Lion will again be the store you can count on for fresh foods and good prices."

What did Food Lion do? They continued to claim foul, blame the union, and sue the network. All during 1993, the stock continued to drop. The ambitious growth plans into Texas and other states were canceled. A new group, The Consumers United with Employees (CUE), claimed the stores were selling outdated baby formula. The Department of Labor settlement cost $16 million, and profits for the year were $3.9 million, down from $178 million the prior year.

This is the crisis that never ends. It continues today, with Food Lion's suit against ABC Television, claiming that ABC employees lied about who they were when they applied for jobs at Food Lion. A North Carolina court, without examining the truth or falsity of the broadcast, charged the network with a meager $5.5 million in a punitive damage settlement for their deceptive methods of gaining access to the stores.

The enormous costs to Food Lion could have been avoided. Since we were not in the room, we can only speculate who and why these decisions were made. Our best guess is that legal concerns drove the strategy, claiming all sorts of dire consequences for any admission of error, and huge rewards from suits against everyone from the network to the union.

The bottom line, a damaged reputation, lost revenues, portfolio losses for shareholders, and a slap on the hand for the network that started the whole mess.

You can't always control what might happen to you, but you can control how you deal with it . . . and, in the end, that's what matters.

THE FUTURE OF CRISIS MANAGEMENT

A company's probability of and vulnerability to crisis is increasing. The front page of *The Wall Street Journal* and most issues of *Forbes* often features stories about crisis. People simply love to read about other people's problems. Should disaster strike your company, it is important to be prepared.

What top management is doing today is to make a small investment in staff time now, and prepare the organization for any tough days ahead. Crisis planning provides clear, measurable benefits. It is risk management in the best sense of the term. Very simply, it is possible to reduce the risks associated with unexpected events by planning an approach to handling a crisis—not by planning for a specific crisis. On a much larger scale, it is similar to hedging currency or interest, insuring a plant or process, or getting performance guarantees on contracts.

As companies restructure, as CEOs are fired by boards, as new shareholder challenges face corporations, as the media becomes faster and investigations deeper, as whistleblowing increases and employee loyalty is tested, companies are turning to crisis planning in order to sleep at night. Competitors are sifting your garbage, invading your computers, and listening to your cell phones. There are no secrets left; if it happened, someone knows and may tell. This is a new age of mandated openness. There are no constraints. All audiences feel a need to know everything and to tell everything they know.

You can reduce the risks associated with unplanned or unexpected events. More companies and more not-for-profits are beginning to plan. Issues management, which made a brief appearance a couple of decades ago, is coming back. It is a stronger, smarter, and leaner approach. It is one way to limit surprises and to know at least as much as the public.

Smaller companies, which are more vulnerable, are planning, and more private companies are creating plans. That a crisis is instantly a costly event is now understood. That there is a residual cost to the reputation of the company, the nonprofit, or the product is just now surfacing through studies.

Crisis management will change little from its current state of planning and execution without external pressures that broaden the definition of a crisis. The potential for crisis events increases as government continues to insert itself into the business arena, as regulations grow, and as agencies seek more oversight.

The media, which now is virtually instantaneous, continues toward the ultimate in narrowcasting—programming customized for the individual. As narrower categories of people can be discretely reached and communicated with on personal subjects, the level of interest in smaller events will increase. But, as it increases, communicators will have the ability to get the right message to the right person, cheaply and with some impact.

As more companies become more global, the potential for crisis increases. The ability to handle crises well decreases with distance and lack of homogeneity.

Preparation and training will separate the winners from the losers, and that training can't wait for the promotion to CEO. Graduate schools understand that crisis handling is management at its zenith. It is "bet your company or your job" time, and the schools spend more time with future CEOs and chief communicators to give them the training and understanding of the process and the tactics. It's a little like learning to become a pilot in a flight simulator. You confront every nasty thing that can happen at you and you learn to fly through it. Crisis training is exactly that; experience in the hanger, not in the sky.

BIBLIOGRAPHY

Augustine, Norman. "Managing the Crisis You Tried to Prevent." *Harvard Business Review* (November–December 1995).

Barton, Laurence. *Crisis in Organizations* (Cincinnati: South-Western Publishing Co., 1993).

Caywood, Clarke L., and Raymond P. Ewing. *The Handbook of Communication in Corporate Restructuring and Takeovers* (Englewood Cliffs, NJ: Arthur W. Page Society and Prentice Hall, 1992).

Richards, Lisa. "The Seven Deadly Sins" (paper presented at the Northwestern University/IMC Crisis Communications Conference, Evanston, IL, 1995).

Silva, Michael, and Terry McGann. *Overdrive* (New York: John Wiley & Sons, 1995).

Soro, Michael, "The Cost of Crisis" (paper presented at the Northwestern University/IMC Crisis Communications Conference, Evanston, IL, 1995).

Stocker, Kurt, and Clarke L. Caywood. "The Ultimate Crisis Plan." In *Crisis Response*, Jack Gottschalk, ed. (Visable Ink Press, 1993).

## PART THREE

Current Issues and Topics in Public Relations and Communications

## CHAPTER 13

Environmental Issues in Public Relations: A Matter of Credibility

Susan Croce Kelly, APR
Executive Vice President
The Cresta Group

THE DEVELOPMENT OF ENVIRONMENTAL PUBLIC RELATIONS

Probably nothing has changed business so much in the past generation as the growing recognition that the earth is a finite resource and that waste can be hazardous not only to the earth, but to its population as well.

Environmental issues can have an impact on corporations far beyond the normal scope of a company's day-to-day business. Discovery of an old hazardous waste dump, for example, suddenly pits a company against homeowners in a community where it may not have done business for a generation. That, in turn, may lead to legislative response affecting company products or to shareholder retribution. Environmental problems, real or perceived, can be costly.

As companies have come to recognize the importance of managing their environmental profiles and relationships, environmental public relations has become a significant part of the practice of corporate communications.

Thought of primarily in defensive terms, environmental public relations is a management function that was born out of the need to minimize the cost of environmental issues and potential problems. In recent years, the practice also has taken on a positive aspect as the public and government have begun to appreciate positive environmental efforts and environmentally sound products.

Once considered a fringe issue, environmentalism went mainstream in the 1980s. Today, approximately 80 percent of all Americans consider themselves to be environmentalists. There are 150 major nationwide environmental organizations and more than 12,000 grassroots groups in the United States. About 14 million Americans were members of one or more of these groups in 1993.[1] Corporate America is learning to take them seriously.

Most public relations specialties are born because someone, somewhere, has a problem. Environmental public relations, a growth profession for the 1990s, is no different. Corporations, which had driven the United States to world economic dominance after World War II, lagged in recognizing a major change in national sensibility that arose as a result of the general affluence in the nation in the 1950s and 1960s.

People with enough to eat, a comfortable place to live, employment, and reasonable amounts of material possessions have time to turn their attention to the world around them. Probably the first modern nationwide environmental initiative occurred in the 1950s with the movement to clean up the nation's highways. People who are in positions of power today participated as children in "Don't Be a Litterbug" campaigns led by schools and children's television shows.

In the 1960s, the environmental movement firmly took hold in the United States. The trigger event is generally agreed to have been the 1962 publication of a book by naturalist Rachel Carson. The book *Silent Spring* warned of the misuse of chemical pesticides, specifically DDT, and the danger of a corresponding buildup in the environment. (DDT was essentially banned in the United States in 1972.) *Silent Spring* was the call to action for environmental activists. The movement gained momentum as increases in scientific and technical understanding (and the elapse of time) began to reveal the downside of the amazing technology that had nurtured the nation's economy after World War II.

The relationship between human health and environmental concerns reached the front page in the early 1960s when Dr. Irving Selikof, a research physician at Mt. Sinai Hospital in New York City, published data on the health problems of people who installed asbestos insulation. On the heels of the asbestos crisis came information about the adverse health effects of vinyl chloride on workers. Both the Johns-Manville Corporation, the leading American producer of asbestos, and the corporations that manufactured vinyl chloride recognized the importance of public relations in telling their stories as they dealt with the issues.[2] Other companies were not so farsighted, and adversarial relationships sprang up among much of industry, the government, the media, and the public.

By 1970, environmentalism in the United States was becoming institutionalized—as was the need for environmental public relations. In 1970, when the first Earth Day was celebrated, Congress also authorized the nation's two top environmental offices: the Occupational Safety and Health Administration (OSHA), to deal with worker health and the workplace environment, and the federal Environmental Protection Agency (EPA). Although laws already existed to protect workers and the environment, they did not have the clout of the new laws of the 1970s: Clean Air Act; Clean Water Act; the Resource Conservation and Recovery Act, to deal with solid waste; the Toxic Substances Control Act; and, in 1980, the Comprehensive Environmental Response and Liability Act, also known as Superfund, to deal with cleanup of contaminated dumpsites.

The early 1970s was also an era of large-scale environmental "accidents" and events that, more than activists ever could, focused public attention on the need for a national policy. The nightly news had plenty to report when it came to industry and the environment: Love Canal; the kepone poisoning of the James River by Allied Chemical Company; the contamination of animal feed in Michigan with polybrominated biphenol (PBB); the contamination, in Japan, of cooking oil with polychlorinated byphenol (PCB); publication of studies that showed an accumulation of various chemicals in the fatty tissue of fish and other animals; an explosion of a pesticide plant in Seveso, Italy, that put tons of dioxin into the atmosphere; and mercury poisoning of fish. And if not the most abominable, certainly one of the most photogenic incidents occurred when the Cuyahoga River in Cleveland, Ohio, reacted to a high level of pollution by spontaneously bursting into flames.

During the 1970s, environmental issues were festering across the United States. As various widely televised accidents and incidents reinforced their message to the public, environmental organizations gained members and operating budgets grew.

Industry was slower to react.

A few thoughtful companies paved the way for environmental public relations by appointing individuals to help staffs deal with the multiplicity of new laws and to respond to environmental issues. Some companies went even further and became proactive in responding to growing concern about the environment in Washington. Cummins Engine, a Columbus, Indiana-based manufacturer of diesel engines, recognized that the best way to deal with the Clean Air Act was not to fight it, but to spend time in Washington working cooperatively with the EPA to draft regulations. Cummins received a lot of positive publicity for this effort. The CEO further enhanced the company's image by seeking out opportunities to speak about corporate responsibility and industry/government cooperation.

A STRATEGIC APPROACH TO ENVIRONMENTAL PUBLIC RELATIONS

As far as the environment is concerned, I am convinced that the only companies which are going to survive into the 21st century will be those with the vision and resources to manage their environmental impact. That's going to happen sooner in some parts of the world than others. Ultimately, it will affect everyone everywhere. So there is a very strong business case for getting on top of those issues right now, before you're forced to.[3]

Vincent A. Sarni
Chairman and CEO of PPG Industries

Today, good environmental practices and a prudent environmental policy translate to the bottom line.

Because of widespread and growing public attitudes toward environmental preservation, business strategy today is almost required to include environmental policy among the most basic tenets of the company's operating philosophy. In 1990, Deloitte Touche and the Stanford Graduate School of Business conducted a survey of industrial businesses. Among those surveyed, 45 percent of the executives believed that environmental issues are critical to a company's well-being. A larger group—68 percent—said they felt that environmental issues will increase in importance.[4] And well they should: In 1993, industry and government were spending more than $100 billion per year on pollution control; the federal EPA has estimated that amount will reach more than $150 billion by the year 2000.

Those American CEOs who prefer to see environmentalism as a passing fad only need look to the European community, where the Green Movement has become a strong political force. Especially in the Scandinavian nations and Germany, "Greens" have significant representation in the federal legislative bodies and have had an impact on important legislation. For example, because of public concern heightened by Green activism, biotechnology is almost impossible to employ as an industrial tool in Germany, and voters in Switzerland only recently defeated a referendum that would have prevented genetic engineering research in that country.

Currently, a Greenpeace initiative to eliminate the use of chlorine, a basic industrial chemical that has been vital in maintaining the quality of drinking water, is in the process of moving from Europe to the United States. In past years, such a notion would have been dismissed as ridiculous by the American business community; today, companies recognize that a Greenpeace initiative needs to be faced squarely and addressed. Even ridiculous ideas can take on a life of their own if nobody is there to explain.

The immediate significance of many environmental issues—Greenpeace initiatives, new manufacturing plant emission requirements, groundwater pollution, or waste site cleanup—is the potential negative effect on company finances. While environmental stewardship often does not add to the bottom line, environmental problems (real or perceived by the public) can quickly diminish not only profits, but stock prices as well. Within the past decade, socially responsible investing on the part of public pension funds and other investment organizations has broadened from considerations about South Africa to include a company's environmental activities.

Moreover, in 1993, the federal Securities and Exchange Commission issued new guidelines requiring companies to disclose environmental issues that might depress their shares' value. This means companies must disclose any environmental trends or uncertainties expected to have a material impact, such as being named a responsible party in a Superfund site. They also must inform the public about the material impact on any investment of complying with environmental regulations, and of any "material" environmental proceedings involving the company.[5]

When business strategy addresses the environment, nearly all parts of the company are involved and the strategy should always be accompanied by a communications component.

A TACTICAL APPROACH TO ENVIRONMENTAL PUBLIC RELATIONS

The secret of success in business is honesty and sincerity, and if you can fake those, you've got it made.

Groucho Marx

Like all other public relations specialties, the environmental specialty is about relationships. It begins with the company's relationship with its customers, its employees, and its neighbors. From there, it extends to encompass representative group such as the local, state, and federal government, environmental organizations, and the media. Up to now, much that has gone under the rubric of environmental public relations has really been crisis management, as companies sought to put a good face on environmental situations gone awry. That is unfortunate because most environmental crises could be predicted, and many, with the right approach, could have been avoided altogether. Today, with the institutionalization of the environmental movement into America's mainstream, business is waking up to the potential value of effective, proactive environmental public relations, not only to the company image but also to the bottom line.

When dealing with environmental issues, traditional public relations approaches don't always work. Issues affecting the environment involve a variety of audiences, often with different agendas, and have an overlay of human fear and emotion. Because of this, corporate policies and strategic decisions need to be taken with their communication ramifications in mind, in addition to the traditional business considerations. This makes it more than a little important that the company's top communicator be part of the up-front policy setting and decision making.

Successful environmental public relations depends on the involvement and support of the company's chief environmental officer: the CEO. In today's world, a company's activities are everybody's business: the public, the government, customers, employees, and especially environmental groups. As a result, how a company operates in relation to the environment, and how it is *perceived* to be operating, can have a direct impact on financial results. Truth, of course, is the foundation for all business communication. In the case of environmental public relations, honesty is vital, and (as Groucho Marx put it) so is the appearance of honesty. Often the public is as concerned about how the company acts about what it actually does. Certainly that was true in 1989 when firemen fighting a chemical fire at the Swiss chemical and pharmaceutical giant Sandoz Ltd. inadvertently washed a large amount of agricultural chemicals into the Rhine River. The resulting fish and eel kill affected the river through several European countries. Sandoz, a company that had traditionally focused its communication on financial and marketing areas, was neither prepared for nor able to respond to the onslaught of media and government inquiries and concerns. While the company's image was suffering in the press, Sandoz poured many millions of Swiss francs into cleaning the river, and supported numerous academic studies of the river itself, nearby wetlands, and the river's wildlife population. Ironically, the Rhine, long polluted by hundreds of industrial companies along its banks, has not only recovered from the Sandoz disaster but also is now far cleaner than before. Nevertheless, because of the company's initial inability to express concern and explain its willingness to make amends, Sandoz is still working hard to regain public trust.

A company that is serious about its environmental image must remain in tune with the issues by which it could be affected.

This requires a strategic approach to environmental communications, beginning with an assessment of important outside issues and applying to them the traditional analysis that guides any other strategic plan.

The job of the environmental public relations officer is to alert management to issues that may be of concern in the future; to develop and execute plans to manage stakeholder relationships concerning existing issues; and, when possible, to provide a communication perspective to environmental policy settings.

Given the environmental climate among members of the public, the widespread growth of environmental activist groups, and the strength of environmental concerns in Washington and among state legislators, any kind of environmental public relations program should include the following:

- Issue scanning and analysis.
- A strategic environmental communication planning based on SWOT (strengths, weaknesses, opportunities, and threats) analysis.
- Plan execution with ongoing media/community relations/government affairs programs.
- Measurement, analysis, and refocus of the program.

Issue Scanning and Analysis

Any company may be the subject of environmental controversy.

Most environmental media crises are predictable and can be planned for (and therefore probably avoided—or at least minimized).

To assure that the company/organization is as up-to-date and aware of potential environmental issues as possible, a company must have, or have access to, an issue-scanning program to stay abreast of environmental initiatives, new legislation, and public concerns

F I G U R E 13–1

The SWOT Analysis

STRENGTHS	WEAKNESSES
■ Safe products ■ Safe plant	■ Plastic jugs
OPPORTUNITIES	**THREATS**
■ New packaging plan	■ Pending legislation to limit bulk transport of raw materials ■ Public concern about pesticides on fresh fruit

(see Chapter 11, Issues Management). This information is vital to accurately assess the company's strengths, weaknesses, opportunities, and threats (SWOT) in the environmental arena (see Figure 13–1). Whether the actual issue scanning is done inside or outside the company, an inside assessment group must review, consider, and decide whether the company should act on, or prepare to act on, the issues that surface. A number of survey organizations that can track environmental issues exist today, and many public relations firms also have issues-scanning and analysis groups. Problems also can be identified through regular review of publications that have a reputation for publishing topical articles before they reach the mainstream media. Another way to get early warning of important issues is to survey employee, customer, and supplier groups.

Wherever the issues come from, they should be brought up before a management group that includes legal, environmental, manufacturing, and marketing people in addition to communicators. This cross-section mix is crucial in gaining consensus and buy-in for the group's conclusions. It is up to this group to discuss and prioritize issues. Even under the best circumstances, however, management may decide to delay thinking about an issue even though it will obviously affect the company in the future. It is easy to find people who predicted a decade ago that water quality issues would be of paramount importance, even though few corporations heeded that warning, and now many are scrambling to deal with multiple clean-up laws under consideration in many state legislatures.

Even if the company chooses not to address an issue from a business perspective, the corporate communications department should keep an active list of current and potential issues, their relationship to the company, and strategies for addressing them. Today, as we watch chlorine move to center stage in the U.S. environmental debate, there are few companies unaware of the Greenpeace campaign underway in Europe for years. Any company that makes or employs chlorine in its industrial processes or sells products that use chlorine as a raw material (such as some children's toys) should understand their role in the debate.

While external issues analysis is taking place, it is also important to determine exactly what the company wants to accomplish in the environmental arena. This may come from the corporate strategic plan, annual business plans, individuals' personal objectives, or a conversation with the CEO: Do you want to modify or circumvent a potentially disastrous law now wending its way through city council/state legislature/Congress? Do you want to be seen as the most environmentally conscious company in the industry . . . Gain permission for a facilities expansion through a local zoning board next year . . . Minimize costs of environmental compliance and pollution control . . . Have a "heads up" on which raw materials may have to be phased out . . . Hire top-quality, skilled workers in a tight labor market? Or do you simply want to help assure your long-term right to stay in business?

Because of the nature of environmental issues and of environmentalism in the United States, the best way to address any specific goal is with a long-term, strategic answer. A pundit wrote that a long-term plan outlines what you plan to do in the future, but a strategic plan tells you what you're going to do today to make sure that you're still around in the future. Both are important. In other words, good intentions must be supported by ongoing hard work.

Creating the Plan

To create an effective environmental public relations plan, a successful public relations practitioner needs to know about the history of U.S. environmentalism, key legislation, and regulations; as well as to understand the ins and outs of technical processes, distribution, and product use. Company stewardship—and public expectation—increasingly requires cradle-to-grave product responsibility. Finally, the environmental public relations practitioner also must understand risk communication and know how to address people's fears as well as the science or economics and the issue at hand.

An environmental public relations plan should be prepared with consideration for the pertinent outside issues raised in the issue scanning and analysis process and for how those issues relate to current and future company operations. The SWOT analysis should be incorporated into the formation of the public relations plan to address particular environmental concerns. A SWOT analysis considers inside actions and plans, along with outside influences, and rates them according to how they could affect the company.

To assure its comprehensiveness and acceptance, a SWOT analysis for communications purposes (like the issue analysis) should be handled by a group of people in operations, legal, human resources, and manufacturing jobs, as well as the public relations officer. This group's purpose is to provide a document that can be used to assess issues and determine priorities for environmental communication.

If, for example, an agricultural chemical company decided to undertake a SWOT analysis, it might consider the following:

The company may market only pesticide products with extremely good environmental profiles. That would be a strength in these environmentally sensitive times, not only because there is little risk from the products, but also because environmentally sound pesticides are a marketing plus.

The company also may have a state-of-the-art manufacturing plant and an occupational safety and health program that shows a history of healthy workers and a healthy workplace. Again, that is a strength both in terms of not having to face any major cleanup costs, but also a potentially valuable bit of marketing information.

However, a weakness may exist in that the company's products are sold only in throw-away plastic jugs, which are a disposal problem nationwide. Another weakness may lie in the existence of an old hazardous waste site on land once used for chemical loading operations. However, if the cleanup is dealt with effectively, then it also may be a potential opportunity to talk with the media and position the company as a leader in taking responsibility for the environment.

The company may have an opportunity to develop some kind of new packaging, thus giving it an advantage over competitors. Another opportunity could exist in an exciting new research project.

There also may be a threat from state legislatures and the EPA in pending legislation and regulations that limit bulk transportation of certain kinds of chemicals. Such actions might pose major threats to the company's manufacturing operation. There also may exist a threat from the general public's growing concern about chemical pesticide residues in food.

This kind of internal and external analysis provides the basis for a long-term environmental communications plan and also should be an integral part of the company's marketing and strategic business plans.

Ongoing Community/Employee/Government/Media Relations Plans

Once issues are identified and a SWOT analysis has been completed, public relations should draft a plan that identifies important audiences, addresses the priority needs of the corporation, and considers unforeseen crises. If the company is ahead of the curve, a carefully prepared and executed communications plan should preclude the need for a crisis plan. If, however, potential environmental issues are ignored, a crisis situation will occur without the benefit of a prepared plan with clear objectives, messages, and tactics. Crisis planning is an integral component of environmental PR (see Chapter 12, A Strategic Approach to Crisis Management).

For an environmental issue, who are the key publics?

■ **Customers**, obviously. Statistics show that, increasingly, buying decisions are made on the basis of whether the products are sound and the manufacturers are environmentally credible.

■ **Employees**. In some cases, as with waste or hazardous exposure situations at manufacturing facilities, employees must by law be informed about exposure. In all cases, however, a company can benefit from an informed employee population that understands the issue and the company's response.

In 1989, when the Natural Resources Defense Council (NRDC) and Mothers and Others for Pesticide Limits (MOPL) stirred up national hysteria against Alar, a growth regulator used on apples, people employed throughout the food chain should have been the first source of information for much of the general public. The better they could answer questions for their families, friends, and neighbors, the more quickly the situation could have been controlled. Unfortunately, they couldn't.

Years of public questions about pesticides—often not adequately answered and never well addressed by the agriculture industry—had set the stage for the unnecessary concerns that developed as a result of the environmental groups' (and their public relations agency's) fear-mongering. Not even the NRDC, which had led the publicity event, intended to upset people to the extent that they dumped apple juice and school districts banned apples. But public concern about chemicals and pesticides was at such a high level that a well-orchestrated publicity campaign, and a disorganized and defensive federal EPA and pesticide industry, allowed things to get completely out of control.[6]

Besides maintaining the company's credibility with employees, careful communication of potentially "hot" issues with the people closest to them can assure a well-informed and loyal group of ambassadors to the world at large. (This assumes, of course, the issues are in fact being properly handled.)

■ **Neighbors**. Whether the situation involves a manufacturing plant or a company's product, the people who live in the vicinity of the company need to be reassured with the facts and explanations of the risks, or lack thereof. Because so much of what we describe as environmental issues involves fear of the unknown, people closest to the company must be reassured and must understand what is manufactured, what types of raw materials are used, and what steps are taken (if necessary) to protect workers, the environment, and the community. Inadequate environmental communication on a local level leads to undesirable potential consequences such as pickets, local laws and regulations, and "No" votes by zoning boards that are barriers to future expansion.

In the chemical industry, members of the Chemical Manufacturers Association have signed on to an initiative called Responsible Care. This involves not only upgrading industrial processes and emissions standards, but also requires a high level of interactivity and communication with employees and local communities.

One example of proactive community relations took place during the summer of 1994 when a number of chemical plants in the Kanahawa River valley of West Virginia joined forces to tell the community about potential "worst case" scenarios that could befall their facilities. These scenarios, described in a series of public meetings, provided a basis for further communication and opportunities for the plants to revisit some of their operating procedures as well.

Unfortunately, multiple surveys indicate that the general public simply doesn't trust corporations. This fact has to be one of the basic assumptions for any communication plan involving the environment.

■ **Shareholders**. Increasingly, shareholders are taking an active interest in the company's environmental profile. The concern is not entirely idealistic: the amount of money spent to comply with environmental regulations in America today is astronomical, the cost of environmentally related lawsuits is considerable, and other goodwill-related costs can affect a company's performance for years. In 1991, more than 50 environmental resolutions were proposed at board meetings of large U.S. corporations; of those, 31 actually were put to a shareholder vote.[7]

Today, more than 150 multinationals and some smaller companies prepare environmental reports for their stakeholders and shareholders. Some of the best, according to a report by London's *Financial Times*, are by companies headquartered in the U.S. including Dow, DuPont, and IBM, although the newspaper singled out British Petroleum as having the best such report.[8] Annual reports, on the other hand, have been much slower to turn green. A 1993 survey of about 100 large companies revealed that nearly two-thirds either did not intend to mention environmental compliance at all or only did so in a small way.[9] This will change as the SEC takes note of the cost to corporations of maintaining/improving their relationship with the environment.

A number of corporations have also invited environmentalists to join their boards of directors. After the Exxon Valdez disaster, John Steele, a senior scientist at Woods Hole Oceanographic Institution, was named to Exxon's board. John E. Bryson, the founder of and a former litigator for the Natural Resources Defense Council, is on the board of the Times Mirror Company and two other organizations. William Ruckleshaus, the first head of the EPA has been a member of the Monsanto Company's board. Moreover, Monsanto and other major chemical companies also appointed their senior environmental officers to their boards.

■ **The General Public**. Because environmental issues by definition extend broadly into the world and because the American population is increasingly concerned about its world, it is important to make information available about situations of potential concern. It also is important to make opinion leaders knowledgeable about the issues and the company's response and stance. Depending on the issue, there are various ways to address these groups including national advertising in the media, public speaking campaigns, and special events that offer opportunities for dialogue and feedback. The goal in dealing with the public is to establish a conversation that involves as much listening as telling, and to work toward consensus for what the company is going to do.

■ **Government**. The government is concerned because elected officials are convinced that their constituents are concerned. Environmental groups have been instrumental in sounding the alarm about situations that needed to be addressed, but also have been known to stir up the public unnecessarily. In addition, these groups are extraordinarily successful in keeping elected officials in Washington and several of the state capitals aware of issues and their positions. As former EPA administrator, Lee Thomas noted, "Congress frequently mirrors the mood of the American people. When citizens are frightened by hazardous wastes, air toxics, and other threats to their health, they look to government to solve the problems." [10]

In environmental communications, knowing your audiences, keeping in touch with them, and listening are essential actions. Once the audiences have been identified, they should be surveyed periodically to determine perceptions, attitudes, and opinions. Knowing the audiences, and what is important to them can be of untold value should an environmental issue turn into an environmental crisis.

Successful tactics to address these publics and nearly any environmental issue begin with open, honest, and frequent communication through the media and directly with the audiences involved.

Tactic 1: Educate the Media, but Look for Other Communication Routes

Unfortunately, business believes, and members of the media agree, that news gatherers generally pay more attention to statements of environmental activists than business people. [11] Part of the reason for this bias is that activists are traditionally more accessible and willing to talk to the press. Business people, who often feel that, when they do talk to the media, they are not only misquoted but also misrepresented, are not eager for more encounters. This, of course, only exacerbates the situation.

As was shown so graphically during the 1992 presidential campaign, direct communication that bypasses media interpretation often can be more successful than traditional communications. This is especially true when the media has predetermined stances on the issue. On the other hand, since few environmental issues are actually surprises, there is no excuse for not building a line of communication with the people and members of the media who will most likely be out in front should an environmental disaster occur or if a back-burner environmental issue comes to the forefront. Media lunches, executive briefings, mini-seminars on environmental issues, editorial board meetings, and tours of research, manufacturing, or waste disposal facilities all help educate the media and public, as well as build relationships that are so important when something goes awry.

Tactic 2: Build a Relationship with Pertinent Environmental Groups

By doing your homework and picking groups (or members of groups) who are open to communication, potential exists to educate people about the company's goals and even find areas of common interest. True partnerships are not possible with all environmental groups—Greenpeace will not even accept donations from corporations—but, more and more, both business and environmental groups are realizing that if their goal is really to clean up the environment, they will be successful if they work together, rather than in opposition. The Environmental Defense Fund, for example, teamed up with McDonald's Corporation in the 1980s to phase out polystyrene burger containers. The Chemical Manufacturers Association, which represents most of the country's largest chemical companies, and the World Wildlife Fund made history in 1984 when they joined forces to form Clean Sites Inc., a nongovernmental organization dedicated to cleaning up orphan hazardous waste sites.

A somewhat different example is General Motors' Chevrolet Motor Division agreement with Tree People, a Los Angeles-based tree planting group, to use the Tree People logo in advertising and sales promotion materials for the Geo car, which had been commended by EPA for its fuel efficiency. In return, General Motors became a corporate sponsor for the organization and provided financial support for citizen forestry workshops and tree plantings.[12]

Other kinds of partnerships between business and environmental groups include unrestricted grants, cooperation on technical projects, political coalitions, and workplace fundraising. If handled correctly, these partnerships can result in positive publicity, access by the corporation to group members, credibility for the corporation, and even access to the group's political clout. Nine of the 10 largest environmental groups have been involved in cooperative programs with industry (Greenpeace is the exception).

Tactic 3: Plan for a Crisis

Even with a long-term strategic environmental plan in place, it is a good idea to also have a crisis plan should an environmental issue erupt in an unforeseen way. The crisis plan will vary somewhat depending on the industry and the potential for disaster, but all should share the same core segments and all should be updated on a regular basis. Confrontational media training for company executives and a blueprint for contacting key publics at a moment's notice, plus an internal emergency network that is tested periodically, are always a good idea, as is a list of well-informed outside experts who can speak on behalf of the company, or at least offer an informed perspective on what happened. Besides, an active crisis plan keeps executives attuned to the need to stay on top of potential crisis issues—and that in itself is worth the time and effort because creating and maintaining top-of-mind awareness among company management can go a long way toward preventing a crisis.

Tactic 4: Sensitize Marketing People

Inside the company, make a practice of finding a way to sensitize marketing people and others who are paid to focus on brand competition and not the corporate reputation. Their practices need to square with the corporate environmental policy. They should be aware that a misstep in the area of the environment can cause serious problems for the company. Regular briefings on the corporate environmental communications strategy are one way to inform marketers and others who do not deal daily with these issues. Another means is to bring in outside pollsters who can talk about environmental issues on the public radar screen. Such presentations are a good way to initiate dialogue on these matters.

A company's positive environmental image also can be a marketing plus. As public buying habits have begun to shift toward pro-environmental products and services, we are beginning to see the integration of the corporate environmental message into the marketing message. After all, it enhances the sales message if the seller of a "green" product is an environmentally friendly company at the outset.

Tactic 5: Increase Visibility in Washington and Key State Capitals

Congressional staff members who handle environmental issues are quick to point out that environmentalists are on the Hill year-around talking about their issues, but that industry people rarely show up until drafted legislation becomes a concern. In dealing with Washington, as with dealing with any other relationship, an ongoing association is bound to be more successful than an intermittent, adversarial approach. Likewise, when business can offer positive alternatives to troublesome legislation, more opportunity exists for a happy solution. One well-known lobbying firm in Washington always registers "FOR—with amendments" regarding bills they are working on because they believe that anything can be modified effectively, and a positive approach is always in their, and their client's, best interest.

Although things are changing, business has done a less-than-outstanding job of getting a true and honest message to lawmakers and regulators, not only about problems with potential legislation but also about the positive things that business has accomplished. Developing a simple grassroots system for asking employees to write to their elected member of Congress on key issues that affect the company can have monumental returns for a business dealing with pending legislation.

It is also important to tailor governmental communication to those who may question, as well as those who support, your issue. Stuart Price, a public relations practitioner for Westinghouse Electric Corporation's Waste Isolation Pilot Plant project for the Department of Energy, wrote in the April 1994 *PR Journal* about his belief that a faulty communications strategy led to the 1991 cancellation of a $1.5 billion nuclear waste disposal evaluation project for his company. The project, begun in the 1970s, involved plans for underground contaminant testing in New Mexico. Over the years, Westinghouse had initiated little or no communication with members of the public and environmentalists. On the other hand, the Natural Resources Defense Council, Environmental Defense Fund, and other groups that opposed the underground experiment had lobbied members of Congress, testified at hearings, and met with the media and public. This became very important in 1991 when the Clinton administration took office.

When Westinghouse failed to readjust its communication strategy from the Bush to the much more environmentally conscious Clinton administration, serious problems arose and funding for the project was canceled.[13]

Tactic 6: Make Sure You Do the Little Things Right

If you are trying to present an environmental image, make sure that not only your employee newsletter or magazine, but also your annual report is printed, at least in part, on recycled paper. Involve employees in a recycling program. Encourage other kinds of conservation, such as taking public transportation, if possible, and be prepared to deal with questions about waste if your company has a corporate jet. Although such gestures may not make a difference individually, taken together they send a message to employees and other stakeholders about your commitment to the bigger issues.

Tactic 7: Learn About and Practice Risk Communication

Since so many environmental issues turn on questions of public risk, a communication strategy that does not consider the emotional side of the issue probably will not succeed. Companies that once said, "Trust us, we know there is no danger present in our product (or process, or raw material, or plant emissions)" have learned that what the public wants to hear first is an acknowledgement of and a respect for their concern. People often are actually less concerned about the risk to themselves than they are outraged over their lack of control and the sense of fairness of a situation. That is why smoking and driving, both high-risk but voluntary activities, are accepted in a much different way than airline accidents or the threat of pesticide residues in food, which are low risk but not controllable by the individual.

Environmental communicators must understand there are several components of risk communication, including acknowledging that people have a right to be concerned and that technology is often scary. A key to successful risk communication is ultimately based on honest, open, two-way communications which offer the audience opportunities to express fears and concerns and allow companies to address those particular fears. Understanding the trigger points on both sides of an issue can greatly increase the opportunity for real dialogue to take place. Otherwise, if the public is concerned about one thing and the company is busy telling them about something else (as is often the case), nothing is resolved and the problem is magnified.

Measurement

Successful environmental communication is like a successful company safety program: Often the best results are that nothing happens. That having been said, however, it is always useful to measure what has taken place and look at the results against original goals. If results are not exactly as desired, then the communications plan must be reassessed and revised if necessary. Just because no environmental crisis has occurred, you must be confident that the company is in the best position possible to make sure one is not lurking over the horizon. Measurement is crucial.

As mentioned earlier, a number of public relations firms and polling organizations conduct annual surveys of public attitudes toward environmental issues. These reports can be useful in assessing the value of your program. Is your industry rated higher or lower than a year ago in terms of public credibility? Are your particular environmental issues higher or lower on the list of public concerns? Such national (and, increasingly, international) data are also useful in convincing management of the necessity of an environmental communications effort.

TACTICS FOR ENVIRONMENTAL PUBLIC RELATIONS

1. Educate the media, but look for other communication routes.
2. Build a relationship with pertinent environmental groups.
3. Plan for a crisis.
4. Sensitize marketing people.
5. Increase your visibility in Washington, and key state capitals.
6. Do the little things right.
7. Learn about and practice risk communication.

Another excellent determination of success is a periodic survey of key audiences. Sandoz Agro Inc., a manufacturer of chemical and biological pest control products, hired The Gallup Organization to conduct surveys of key customer groups on their attitudes toward the use of chemical pesticides in general (not product-specific). From these surveys, the company has been able to determine customer attitudes toward use of pesticides (they're wary), toward federal and state regulations with which they must comply (they expect more), toward much-publicized public concern (it's overblown, but they have some concerns of their own), and toward what they expect from companies in the way of products and support in the future (safer products). Not only did Sandoz publicize the survey results to all of the various customer groups through trade publications, but the company also used the results to look at corporate environmental strategy, products in development, and specific marketing plans to see whether or not they were aligned with customers' expectations and visions of the future. Happily, they were.

Other less quantifiable forms of assessment also must be taken into consideration. Does the company have a good relationship with the necessary government organizations such as the city council, the state legislature, the EPA, OSHA, etc.? What about fines from various inspections? Do neighbors or customers write or call regularly to complain? Does employee turnover have anything to do with environmental issues? (Most companies conduct exit interviews, and employees on their way elsewhere can be surprisingly candid. Don't overlook this source of information.)

THE FUTURE OF ENVIRONMENTAL PUBLIC RELATIONS

Corporate public relations is often a mystery to the vast majority of line managers in the company, and sometimes even to the CEO. They understand finding out about issues. They understand about developing relationships with legislators to beat bad legislation. They understand about responding when the media calls, giving speeches when they are asked, and sponsoring a company picnic and newsletter. But much of the time, a corporate public relations practitioner is so busy carrying out the program that he or she fails to point out how all of these actions—the newsletter, public speech, lunch with the mayor, membership on a community board, or upgrades in the plant emission system—contribute to the image the company presents to its various audiences and should be structured accordingly.

For too long, corporate dealings with the environment were considered part of day-to-day business and of no one's particular concern nor of any interest to anyone outside the company. Today, because of widespread environmental awareness, a plethora of environmental laws and regulations, and advancements in science that allow for greater understanding of health issues and the human relationship with the environment, companies know that they no longer operate in a vacuum. They also understand that practices that are acceptable today may not match up tomorrow—a cause for concern, given the tremendous cost of environmental compliance, but also a challenge to go to the next step in developing new products and processes.

In recent years, the environment has become a subject for corporate policy. Because of the tremendous costs of present environmental compliance and the potential risks involved, corporations are recognizing that environmental communication is not something to be dusted off in the case of a crisis, but something that must be tended to on an ongoing basis—and an issue tied directly to the strategic future of the company.

Also in recent years, there has been growing understanding that public relations practitioners need to know a great deal more than simply how to write a press release and interact with the media. Corporate finance, law, business operations, and technology, in addition to the traditional communication tools, are all required knowledge for a successful professional in environmental public relations. Quick thinking, initiative, an ability to interact with all kinds of people and understand why things happen (or don't happen), and a desire ultimately to make the world a better place are also parts of the job.

It is probably the fervent desire of every corporate CEO, as it is also the desire of every leader of an environmental organization and each elected official, that the need for environmental public relations will simply go away. But, so long as there are industrial accidents, so long as the advance of science changes the way we interact with the environment, so long as groups exist with an avowed goal of banning the use of certain chemicals, there will be a need for environmental PR. Not only will there be a need, but it will be a major growth profession.

E N D N O T E S

1. Harris, James T., "Working with Environmental Groups," *PR Journal* (May 1992), p. 24.

2. For a detailed report on the development of the asbestos story from a public relations perspective, see Matthew M. Swetonic, "Death of the Asbestos Industry," in Jack A. Gottschalk, ed., *Inside Stories on Managing Image Under Siege* (Detroit: Gale Research, Inc., 1993).

3. Black, Jane A., "Red Tape Blocks Off Green Attitudes," *Business Dateline Executive Report* (July 1992), p. 37.

4. Harris, James T., "Working."

5. Murphy, Margaret, "Warning: Disclose Environmental Costs," *The Wall Street Journal* (September 4, 1994).

6. Fenton, David, "How a PR Firm Executed the Alar Scare," *The Wall Street Journal* (October 29, 1989).

7. Thomas, Lee M., "The Business Community and the Environment: An Important Partnership," *Business Horizons* 35, no. 2 (March 1992), p. 21.

8. Knight, Peter, "Business and the Environment: The Advantage of Coming Clean," *Financial Times* (January 24, 1994), p. 22.

9. Murphy, Margaret, "Warning."

10. Thomas, Lee M., quoted in "One Year after Bhopal: A Briefing Package," unpublished report by Chemical Manufacturers Association, Washington, D.C.

11. Knapp, Inc., "Journalists Admit Environmentalists Get More Attention than Business," *PR Newswire* (January 13, 1992). This is a report on a survey of 100 media and 100 business people in 43 states.

12. Harris, James T., "Working."

13. Price, Stuart, "Communication Fallout Derails Waste Project," *PR Journal* (April 1994), p. 30.

C H A P T E R   14

Media Transformation and the Practice of Public Relations

Kevin A. Clark
Director, Communications, Networked Applications Services Division
International Business Machines Corporation

A STRATEGIC APPROACH TO NEW MEDIA

New forms of media change the scope of communications practice, but not the fundamental nature of the profession. Even as media's boundaries shift, their fundamental role as extensions of human perception remain unchanged.[1] Media collapse time, overcome distances, and extend the range of the eye, ear, and mind.

The primary cause of recent media transformation is the widespread deployment of digital technology. Digital media move with ease from one form to another—from voice to print to disk—by wire, wireless, or satellite.

In a briefing at the Naval War College in Newport, Rhode Island,[2] now-retired instructor Capt Frank Snyder, USN (Ret.), said during a discussion about communications, "We're all 45,000 miles away from each other these days." What he meant was that, in an age where the geosynchronous orbit of a communications satellite is 22,300 miles above the earth, data and voice go up and down all day and night to make connections in this interconnected world of ours. The necklace of satellites around the earth doesn't care if the information is coming up to be sent back down to the other side of the world or to your neighbor next door.

Snyder's comment is a leading indicator of what practicing public relations will be like in the future. Digital forms of media will make the distance between sender and receiver irrelevant. What will constitute a "public" will change because publics will be able to group electronically and behave differently.

New media are being generated at an astounding rate. They have created the opportunity for the nature of work and play to blur. As the distinction between going to work and being at home diffuse, the challenge for the public relations professional will be choosing media to bring in information that will help organizations adapt, and delivering messages through selected media to appropriate publics.

New media also diffuse what constitutes a public and where it exists. The concept of virtual communities has gained currency—a community based on common interest and linked electronically. Concepts such as virtual communities make global citizenship and international issue management increasingly important to public relations practitioners.

Geographic boundaries will become irrelevant as new virtual communities of interest spring up. Where digital media are widely in use, people will derive their identities from self-selected communities of interest rather than just national, professional, or company affiliations.

This imposes a new demand for client counsel based on improved access to relevant information from around the world. This counsel must be coupled with completed staff work—recommendations for action that reach newly segmented and ever-shifting publics.

Practitioners have many of the tools needed to reach these publics, but they will have to apply them in new ways to mediate the new future rushing toward clients.

One implication of digital communication and media convergence is a global population that is becoming increasingly iconic, gaining less information and fewer cues from the written word and more from pictures. This trend has profound implications for education, commerce, and governance and clearly needs to be studied in the practice of public relations.

Public relations has its roots in the written word. Today's practitioners have keen ears for the language; equally keen eyes will have to be developed for an iconic world.

For instance, print has taken on the imagery of electronic games and television. Just as *USA Today* is television in print, new print publications are springing up to parallel the spread of digital media. After surfing the Internet, you can curl up with a copy of *Internet World.* Once you've stopped working on your new interactive television plan, you can kick back with your favorite interactive publication.

A decade ago, the "P" section of *Bacon's* magazine directory was fairly empty. Then the advent of personal computers filled the section up with "PC this" and "PC that." The "I" section is exploding now with "Information Highway" titles—Internet or Interactive week, world, age, etc.

Employee communications is also rapidly emerging as a distinct challenge. When employees no longer report to work, communicating with them becomes a problem only new forms of media can overcome. Pagers, cellular phones, and notebook computers have replaced the tools of the office—indeed, the office itself—creating an office anywhere the worker is in the world at any time.

The cork bulletin board has all but disappeared in many companies, replaced by electronic notices on computer networks. On-line electronic services provide forums that open new sources of external information for employees; when these networks connect with other networks publicly, the result is the Internet. Global communication becomes possible between employees, suppliers, contractors, and customers. In the face of these changing relationships, even the notion of "employee communications" as a discrete audience begins to break down.

Electronic messaging and the Internet change the nature of disclosure for investor relations as well. Who knows what is radically different. What will constitute simultaneous disclosure on market-making news will push the professional communicator to scrupulously orchestrate the release of information.

Speed is the key advantage of public relations. PR professionals are well-equipped to deal with breaking events and crises. With greater percentages of knowledge and information moving at the speed of light thanks to digital technology, public relations should benefit from the quick response capability it brings to the table.

Our industry has traditionally been a highly reactive profession and this can be a great strength in organizations in which time and speed are valuable commodities that bestow great competitive advantages. In fact, as information moves faster and faster, more and more of the problems organizations face will be defined as public relations problems. They will be problems rooted in an imbalance of information—either incorrect, misinterpreted, incomplete, or disinformation.

The role of the public relations practitioner could become so pervasive that it is no longer a specialty staff function. Many skills will be transferred to the management team itself, since public relations is simply part of the fabric of many organizations.

Practitioners must redefine themselves to be highly relevant within these trends and become the coaches, teachers, and inventive consultants who create and deploy new ways of practicing public relations, not just perform the tactics themselves.

The greatest advantage beyond speed, then, may be in the practitioner's ability to define new ways of using the new media being developed. The practitioner must fully understand all forms of media and the roles they play between organizations and individuals.

In this role, the public relations professional must continue to find ways to understand and create credibility. This is the role of advocacy communication. As new media emerge, the credibility of the source will become a much larger issue than it is even today.

For instance, what is source credibility in the age of the Internet? Is information received online sitting at a work station hooked up to a network the same as getting information from CNN? For some, the distinction will be lost that CNN is a news-gathering organization that puts information into some kind of edited order and context for viewers, while the Internet, at the time of this writing, is a form of organized chaos. The underlying value system of the Internet is freedom of expression and expanding frontiers—popular themes for democracy.

That's why new forms of digital media are making it possible for democracy to flourish. Digital information is democratic information—it likes to spread and does not respect the boundaries of authoritarian ownership, or of objectivity, or even accuracy.

The implication for public relations is that source credibility will blur at the first stages of the digital communications revolution, and people will get burned.

Just as in a new democracy, having information freedom doesn't mean having access to useful information, such as information that will sustain a strong economy. It doesn't guarantee jobs. Freedom doesn't mean that if the right information is available it can be found or put to any useful purpose.

That's why source credibility will invoke itself. Information franchises such as Associated Press, CNN, Dow Jones, Nikkei, Reuters, and others will find renewed following around the world as people seek accuracy, order, and priorities out of information chaos.

The desire for random access freedom brought on by emerging interactive media such as the Internet, interactive television, and wireless personal data assistants will not be replaced. Cellular phones and personal computers (PCs) celebrated their 10-year anniversaries during the early 1990s. Along with fax machines, PC printers, and modems, they swept over the planet and rewired our global and political priorities.

In each case, the introduction of new media has reflected the needs of the culture using them. In the case of North America, the first use of digital media was to send money electronically. This export caught on rapidly around the world, and the digital dollar is now the common denominator for the world economy. Since accounting is a command-and-control language that expresses value by what gets funded and what doesn't, the first phase of the digital media deployment taught the world to trust numbers more than words. A decided preference exists now for automated teller machines (ATMs)—the first public-access terminals. It's now considered a hassle to stand in line and wait for a person.

In Brazil, a leading department store lets consumers shop for merchandise in "virtual stores" with video kiosks—the shopping extension of the ATM. Products ordered are delivered to customers' homes or offices the next day.

In recent years, cyberspace has tackled many messy instances of human interaction and expression, and has expanded and increased the value of information and entertainment franchises.

North America has traditionally been a net exporter of culture, information, and education around the world. Existing media fuel the dissemination of popular culture in the form of film, video, recordings, and software to even the most remote locations. New forms of media will speed this trend with the addition of instantaneous networked delivery of content worldwide. The Internet is a relatively low-capacity testament to the success of this networking phenomenon. When global broadband interactive media, such as interactive television and wireless communications, move vast quantities of information to people around the world, we will search the globe for ideas to create local solutions.

The new global media hold the potential to similarly extend world-class higher education to classrooms everywhere. News franchises that have been extended from their North American base, fueled by the success of CNN, Dow Jones, and the Associated Press, reflect the values of the culture that created them.

The European continent will continue to find pressure to unite, trading sovereignty for economic power. Media patterns will follow this trend. The practice of public relations will become less of a local phenomenon and more of a continental one. Finding and creating durable relationships across borders will become a staple of the public relations business during this consolidation period.

For instance: "From the network of *trains a grande vitesse* to the construction of a new national library, France has a penchant for *grands projects*," said John Ridding in Paris for the *Financial Times*.[3] "Today, the government will consider a project which could rank with the grandest—the creation of a national *autoroute d'information*, a Gallic information superhighway."

Consider Minitel, the French teletext system created by Gerard Thery. Thery was a former managing director at France Telecom, that currently has more than 23,000 services: "Like Minitel at its launch in 1979, Mr. Thery's new project is ambitious. His report proposes the establishment of a network of fibre-optic cables linking every household by 2015. The aim is to build a national infrastructure allowing the French public and businesses to connect to a network of interactive television, telephone, entertainment, and data services. The cost of the infrastructure alone would be between Fr50 and Fr200 billion (£18 to £24 billion)." (U.S. $27 to $36 billion.)

In the Far East, Japan and the Seven Tigers will likely be net global importers of information as well. Information acquisition, which will then be adapted to their needs, will have a strong role in these societies. As a result, the Far East likely will be among the greatest information aggregators in the world. These cultures may more rapidly develop the ability to synthesize new knowledge from that which exists. In this environment, public relations will provide a strong role to help organizations adapt to a rapidly changing world. Many leading-edge counseling practice methodologies will be developed for Far East clients and then be disseminated as new public relations methodologies.

In the same way that a garage became the birthplace of the personal computer over a decade ago—and small workshops gave us the telegraph, telephone, and the technology of flight—so will some remote parts of the world find their way racing into the age of knowledge.

What seem to be insurmountable barriers to the deployment and use of new communications and information technologies are melting in the face of equally new communications practices and techniques.

The least-wired half of the world, the Southern hemisphere, will quickly find it has the leverage to compete in the communications revolution as satellites and wireless communication make the need for wires and extruded glass unnecessary over broad expanses of unwired oceans and continents.

The Wall Street Journal reported in 1994 that "The rebellion that erupted in Mexico January 1 began on the edge of a rain forest in the poorest part of the country. Yet within days, the insurgents or their supporters had signed on to the Internet and used its collection of electronic bulletin boards to broadcast the rebel manifesto around the world."[4] Saul Alinsky would have been proud and might have added a chapter about the Internet, if it had been around at the time, to his 1971 book *Rules for Radicals*.[5] Essentially, this was proactive public relations in the cause of reform.

NEW MEDIA TACTICS

Consider five new major media tactics at the time of publication. Expect more tributaries from each of these basic ideas to emerge over the next decade.

1. Internet Home Pages. If you have access to a server that's connected to the Internet, you can put up a "Home Page." A Home Page is simply a convenient way to retrieve information on a particular organization—usually with nifty graphics and links to other servers with related ideas and information. Many computer companies and consumer products companies have started Home Pages to offer product and technical information only available in print or by phone or fax in the past. At the time of this writing, "Home Page Editors" or "Webmasters" was one of the fastest-growing job categories in the public relations profession—recruiters can't find enough of them for the tens of thousands of Home Pages already in existence on the estimated seven million servers connected to the Internet in 1996.[6]

Hyperlinks to other Internet Home Pages are essentially brand extensions and cross-brand promotions—ripe territory for public relations to make significant contributions to marketing communications activities and existing customer relationship marketing.

2. Interactive Print. Here's a huge reversal on digital communications: an explosion of print media extensions covering the information revolution. As mentioned earlier, there already are several "Interactive" publications. People want to read about the interesting things they'll be able to do in the future—the same motivation that leads readers to science fiction literature or investors to the pages of *Barron's*. What the future holds is a legitimate market for new subscribers and a place practitioners can mine for new placements—especially in the realm of new marketing technologies.

3. Wireless Communications. The Information Highway has already presented itself as a powerful force in the marketplace. The cellular telephone marketplace is growing at a rate of 30 percent a year, and wireless services seem to benefit from unlimited demand. Public relations professionals will be able to use these wireless technologies to make their services more readily accessible to clients around the world. Wireless communications also present the practitioner with expanded placement opportunities as on-line computer services become on-the-air services. The segmentation of the users of wireless services will help practitioners more readily identify targets that need access to up-to-date, in-depth information. Information targets will become self-selecting based on new agent technologies that allow individuals to scan the electronic environment for relevant information and have it presented when, where, and how they want it. Wireless distribution represents the greatest degree of flexibility and access once the information has been found. Practitioners armed with knowledge about wireless services have a competitive advantage in the marketplace of ideas.

4. Collaborative Communications Interviews and Press Tours. Let's face it, it's hard to get enough executive time to make the external appearances needed to form lasting impressions in the marketplace of ideas. With the advent of collaborative communications services, people will be able to connect, do interviews, and participate in conferences remotely. "Virtual appearances" by executives at conferences will become commonplace. Press interviews, already done in many cases by phone, will increasingly be conducted through videoconference on collaborative computer systems as the prices of these systems plummet with the cost of personal computers. Network time charges also will fall as bandwidths increase through the competition of phone, satellite, and cable companies.

5. Management Consulting from Afar. Underneath the technologies that instantly connect people anytime, anywhere, is the need to have something relevant to say. The public relations practitioner as global management consultant becomes possible only if the practice methodologies are well thought out and valid across cultures and time. What is discovered in one situation needs to be documented and applied in the future. The savvy public relations practitioner can ill afford to create "new" practices over and over again for clients. To create once and apply many times around the world will become a unifying theme for many agency and corporate practices and will result in tremendous competitive advantages.

Successful Application of Tactics

1. Global Press Conferences. IBM, Siemans, and Toshiba held a joint press conference in 1992 to announce a technology alliance to develop the next generation of large-scale semiconductors. Held in New York City, the announcement was carried live in Germany and Japan. Reporters, consultants, and analysts around the world were able to ask questions and participate via a live private television satellite conference. The impact was significant and underscored the global nature of the alliance.

The cost of this kind of satellite conference is dropping, and commercial services such as IIN from Redgate Communications increasingly make this a global commodity service.

2. Internet Crisis Communications. For a leading consumer products company, the world of public relations was turned upside down during 1993. Over the course of three days the president and chairman of the company received hundreds of faxed letters from all over the world condemning them for acts of violence against their workers. What was most unusual was that the faxes were all the same—not just the same words, but even the same typeface! The VP of corporate communications wondered how someone could have orchestrated such an elaborate worldwide communications strategy using the exact document. Certainly, the larger issue was who was doing this, why, and what response would appropriately control it.

Discussions with their public relations agency revealed that many faxes had similar writing at the top of the page. The writing related to different on-line computer services the sender was using to either send or receive the materials. The agency accessed the Internet to track down the antagonists who had started this campaign.

The public relations agency immediately started hunting more than 5,000 "conversations" taking place on the news groups section of the Internet. Under the category "activism," they found the copy of the fax along with instructions for fax delivery to the company. Now the question was how to respond, or whether to respond at all since this could incite the originator of the campaign (who still was not identified).

What made this situation so unusual is that the Internet has no publisher or policing organization an accused or maligned organization can approach to properly address the facts of a situation. Users are free to say just about anything they want. This vast network of networks is accessible throughout the world to anyone with a computer and a modem, and provides a unique and potentially potent communications vehicle to people who have similar interests. In this case, it was working.

The company decided to respond with the real facts of the situation, just as they would with any normal public relations crisis experience. In the meantime, more faxes kept pouring into the chairman's office, but from many more places. The public relations agency continued to ferret out the on-line services responsible and found that the Peace Network and CompuServe also were serving as outlets for the campaign. In each case, the same response was posted.

After about a week the faxes slowed down. Nobody responded to the company's statement. There was no real conversation—the fax campaign was over.

3. Politics on the Information Highway. The U.S. president's home, the White House, has an Internet address, recognition that the information highway should move information both ways in a democratic society. Electronic messaging is forging new links between elected officials and their constituencies. Like any medium, time and space are compressed to bring the elected and the electors closer together. Peter Lewis in a 1994 *New York Times* article, reported:

> The Internet and other spurs of the information superhighway have emerged as powerful new links between politicians and voters in this election year, adding forums for debate by the candidates, nearly instant voting results, and vast pools of background information for local, state, and national races. The idea of electronic democracy has spread to nearly every state along with the rapid expansion of on-line bulletin boards, which are used by more than five million Americans.[7]

Even in nondemocratic societies, digital media are exerting their influence. If China thought the facsimile machine was a problem during the Tiananmen Square turmoil, they won't believe the boundary-spanning capabilities of electronic messaging.

Measuring Success

How is success measured in the use of new media for clients? In an interview with an advertising publication, the question boiled down to this: If you had to allocate scarce media dollars to a new medium, how would you put it into your media mix and how would you evaluate its success?

To answer this in a public relations context requires that the practitioner forget about the newness of the medium and ask, "What can it do for me better than any other media form?" For instance, on-line media and the Internet foster the creation of communities of interest—a reversal of the mass audience created by consumer advertising. Therefore, using on-line media for mass media objectives is inefficient.

On the other hand, once you have identified yourself as being part of a community of interest, the ability to listen to these focused—and many times influential—parts of society can reveal broader societal trends. Such communities also make creating close cyber-relationships possible. Any purchase—of a computer, car, or mutual fund—identifies the customer as a member of a community of interest. Opportunities exist to join groups such as the on-line IBM Think Pad Forum on CompuServe, Jaguar owners bulletin board, and Fidelity Investors chat session. Regardless, these smaller, self-selected publics are key opportunities for practitioners to contribute to broad organizational goals such as information gathering, existing customer marketing, reducing post-purchase cognitive dissonance, and focused issues management.

FUTURE TRENDS

Public relations is, by nature, an acquisitive profession. Since it serves every conceivable type of organization and profession, public relations also has the opportunity to learn from them.

PR must discipline itself, record what it knows, and rapidly adapt to the changing needs of clients and to the demands of the environments in which these organizations exist over time.

Professionals need to share what they know with each other. The new forms of media being created today will not only allow them to deliver ideas and information to finely segmented publics, but will allow them to interact with other practitioners more readily. A true dialogue between professionals should parallel the high-stakes poker games being played around the world. Networks of media should foster networking among practitioners. Public relations needs to be its own best client during this time of media transformation.

The future of public relations practice hinges on how well the profession adapts to the new media environment, and how it translates this understanding into useful counsel for clients. Everyone should be considered a client, whether the counsel is provided by internal or external practitioners.

Public relations will need to draw from a broader cross-section of professions over time. Knowledge of computer and digital communications technologies, or alliances with professionals in these disciplines, are required for future success. Being able to render ideas iconically will be as important in the future as writing them down. Public relations will diffuse into the broad fabric of organizations, making everyone responsible for company image and adaptation.

To truly benefit from the deployment of digital media and the spread of networks, practitioners must become "knowledge networkers"—people who are comfortable fusing what public relations knows how to do today with "cybermedia."

Public relations professionals should become among the most adept people in society at using computer and network technologies. "What you know" and "who you know" will increasingly be exercises in distance relationships—relationships developed by phone, fax, on-line services, and videoconference.

In education, this points to the need for communications curricula to find alliances with the information processing community. The same holds true for commerce. In a conversation with John Soysen, the director of university relations at the University of Portland in the Pacific Northwest, the question arose as to who should "own" the university's Internet Home Page, the college computer community or university relations? The answer is both, since skills from both communities are needed to make the new medium work. He agreed; only a blend of technical and editorial competencies would make the new Home Page work for the university.

Just as the maxim "publish or perish" is a compelling notion in the academic community, "connect or collapse" might be a fitting warning for the savvy public relations counselor in the age of media transformation. Connect with new media and digital networks, or suffer professional collapse as others take on these roles and create the "cyber-relationships" needed to compete in an emerging digital world.

ENDNOTES

1. McLuhan, Marshall, *Understanding Media, The Extension of Man* (New York: McGraw-Hill, 1964).

2. The United States Naval War College Current Strategy Forum, June 14–16, 1994.

3. Ridding, John, "France Ponders Superhighway Gamble," *Financial Times* (October 27, 1994), p. 2.

4. Carroll, Paul, "Foreign Competition Spurs Mexico to Move into High-Tech World," *The Wall Street, Journal* (July 5, 1994), p. 1.

5. Alinsky, Saul, *Rules for Radicals* (New York: Random House, 1971).

6. *The Internet Society.*

7. Lewis, Peter, "Voters and Candidates Meet on Information Superhighway," *New York Times* (November 6, 1994).

## CHAPTER 15

Managing a Diverse Workforce in a Changing Corporate Environment

Marilyn Laurie
Executive Vice President, Public Relations
AT&T

The AT&T Corporation (formerly the American Telephone and Telegraph Company) literally began with the invention of the telephone and a vertical integration strategy that became the heart of our very culture. Once strictly a provider of telephone service, AT&T provided all sorts of communications services and products, as well as network equipment and computer systems, to businesses, consumers, telecommunications services providers, and government agencies.

In 1995, AT&T announced the largest voluntary breakup in business history. By the end of September 1996, we had already spun off our $20 billion equipment company and were planning to spin off our $8 billion computer company by the end of the year. That would leave the new AT&T as a $51 billion communications and information services company. A key component of AT&T's strategy which spans both the old and new AT&T involves managing and valuing diversity, a strategy that impacts our employees, our customers, and the communities in which we conduct business.

Diversity Defined

What is diversity? At AT&T, it is "the quality of being different or unique at an individual or group level." That definition recognizes that every member of the company and every group in which employees choose to acknowledge their membership can bring value to the workplace. And the company seeks to recognize, and respond positively to, the variety of differences among customers and in the wider community.

We define managing diversity as "creating and sustaining an environment in which everyone can achieve his or her full potential" for contributing to the success of the business. And *valuing diversity*—perhaps the hardest part—we believe means "recognizing and respecting the value of human differences" in moving the business ahead.

These definitions differentiate diversity from equal employment opportunity and affirmative action. Unlike EEO and AA, which remain the laws of the land, diversity initiatives are not driven by the need for compliance. Nor are they grounded in religion or morality, although many will acknowledge that valuing and managing diversity have the feel of being "the right things to do." Rather, diversity initiatives are a response to three

B O X   15–1

Within the increasingly competitive markets [we seek to serve], on both the domestic and international fronts, it is critical that the AT&T family reflect the diversity of our customers, communities, governments, and all the groups with whom we are in contact. In addition, it is our belief that in creating a richly diverse family of AT&T employees whose talents and potential are fully utilized, we will gain strategic competitive advantage. How we respond in spawning a culture designed to fully engage our people will determine AT&T's future viability in the marketplace.

As leaders, we must accept the challenge to create a work environment that sets the world-class standard where individual differences not only are recognized and valued, but indeed embraced because of the richness they bring to thinking, creating, problem solving, and understanding our customers and communities.

Our management challenge is to be proactive and forward looking in establishing effective support systems and processes that remove existing barriers to full productivity, development, and advancement. In so doing, individuals can feel fully empowered and encouraged to achieve their potential.

business needs: the need to attract, hire, and promote the best people we can find—wherever in the world we can find them; the need to stimulate all employees to contribute their best ideas to the work they do; and the need to better understand and serve different markets and market segments.

When we say that the challenge for AT&T people is to "value and manage diversity in all its dimensions," we mean, of course, recognizing and respecting such traditional dimensions as age, color, physical ability, gender, national origin, physical characteristics and level of ability, race, and sexual orientation. But our definition of diversity goes beyond that to include such dimensions as educational background, ethnicity, family responsibilities, geographic background, language, level in the organization, lifestyle, marital status, military experience, political beliefs, religion, skills, socioeconomic status, thinking patterns, and work background. By valuing all these dimensions of diversity, we increase the pool of creativity on which our future as a business depends. In this way, we increase our responsiveness to the customers we serve and the communities we inhabit.

AT&T's concern for diversity was sharpened and enhanced in 1993 and 1994 as the result of an incident described in the case study near the end of this chapter. But this concern goes back at least to the 1960s and 1970s, when a variety of programs were established, above and beyond those required by law, to bring equality of opportunity into the workplace and to bring women and minorities into professions such as engineering, then dominated by white males.

By the early 1990s, these efforts had broadened to include a corporate-level Diversity Process Management Team composed of business leaders and Employee Resource Group leaders (with public relations serving as counsel). The term Employee Resource Group at AT&T refers to a voluntary association of employees who share an element of diversity in common, or who support that element. Currently, there are Employee Resource Groups for African Americans; Hispanics/Latinos; Asians and Asian Americans; people with disabilities; Native Americans; gays, lesbians, and bisexuals; and women. The Diversity Process Management Team was formed to help accelerate the awareness and understanding of diversity issues throughout the company.

In 1992, AT&T executives also issued a public statement (see Box 15–1) that put them on record with regard to diversity.

In addition, diversity managers in most units of the company were developing ways to improve awareness and understanding of diversity-related issues—again, because doing so was perceived by line management to be "good business." And a portion of all executives' compensation was linked to their organizations' score on a "diversity index" derived from questions in AT&T's annual employee-opinion survey.

AT&T was not alone among American companies in its incorporation of diversity into its business concerns. A survey of 406 U.S. companies, conducted in 1991 by Louis Harris and Associates for The Conference Board, found 79 percent of them either offering or intending to offer diversity training for managers; 66 percent either possessing or intending to develop a statement on diversity from senior management; 55 percent either offering or planning to offer mentoring programs for women and minorities; and 53 percent either sponsoring or planning to sponsor a diversity task force.

The Broader Pressures for Action

Clearly then, especially over the past five years, pressure has been mounting to stimulate American business to focus on diversity. What are the sources of this pressure?

Most importantly, perhaps, as noted in the Hudson Institute's landmark study, *Workforce 2000*, profound changes are occurring in the U.S. labor force. A team of strategists in AT&T's Human Resources Division summarized these changes as follows:

> The stereotypical U.S. worker—white, male, head of household—is no longer the norm. With fewer workers entering the workforce, employers will have a more diverse employee base that comes from a predominantly female and minority labor pool . . . .

> Women are entering the workforce in greater numbers worldwide, and their participation will result in substantial changes in working conditions and patterns . . . .

> By the year 2000, more than one-half of all new workers hired will be minorities, nearly three times the number in the 1980s . . . .

> Another factor that impacts the size and diversity of the U.S. workforce is the role of immigration. Immigrants currently account for 30 to 35 percent of the annual growth of the U.S. workforce. . . .

> Employers competing in a shrinking pool of new workers will have to respond to the needs and demands of working parents for more workplace support for family obligations. The focus will be not only on day care, but also on a broader concern for better integration of home and work life . . . .

> Successful companies will have to treat all employees as strategic resources by providing an environment in which all employees can learn new ways to contribute to the company's success . . . .

Other pressures also are helping to drive the current corporate concerns about diversity. For example:

Knowledge work is growing in importance. In a world in which sustained competitive advantage will come to those companies whose products cannot be duplicated easily by low-cost competitors, success will depend increasingly upon the knowledge and insights of employees—all of them, not just some of them.

The global economy continues to expand. As it does, the growth opportunities for many U.S. companies will be increasingly in non-U.S. markets. Those companies will prosper that best satisfy the needs of non-U.S. customers—a process that usually works best when it includes the contributions of workers closest to the customers, that is, non-U.S. workers.

Information technology continues to evolve rapidly. The increasing, inexpensive availability of this technology is driving other changes as well: in the nature of work, the places and times when work gets done, the increasing availability of information, the democratization of the workforce. All of this is making it possible to put real decision-making power into the hands of more and more employees.

The hierarchical organization continues to flatten out. The capability of new technology to disseminate information across the firm is a necessary, but not sufficient, condition for fast new-product introduction. New products will actually emerge only if the traditional bureaucracy gets out of the way and allows networking, self-managed teams and informed front-line employees to drive the work of the organization.

The boundaries of the corporation continue to expand. Mergers, acquisitions, and alliances of all kinds are blurring the once-distinct borders of the firm. Total quality management blurs the distinctions even further, with customers and distributors and suppliers—and sometimes even competitors—being considered "inside the tent." How we define who is "us" and who is "them" will require new levels of understanding of diversity.

The democratization of the workforce continues. The collapsing hierarchy, the knowledge worker's value to the firm, self-managed teams, the increasing availability of information, lifelong learning, the increasing interest in social contracts as a means to build a workplace community—all combine to place more power in the hands of all the people of the firm.

IMPLICATIONS FOR THE STRATEGIC PRACTICE OF PUBLIC RELATIONS

These are just some of the workforce, workplace, and marketplace pressures driving American companies to develop and deploy corporate diversity strategies and the initiatives to support those strategies. As we have learned in our journey of managing and valuing diversity at AT&T, a constellation of public relations issues surrounds this business concern, especially at the strategic level.

Key Issues

Partnership between the diversity and public relations organizations: In AT&T, the diversity effort is managed from within the company's human resources organization, while corporate public relations and employee communications are managed in a separate staff organization. Execution of the diversity strategy demands close, daily cooperation (really a strategic partnership) between PR and HR—for example, as elements of the strategy are crafted and communicated to a variety of audiences; as progress is made toward strategic goals; as organizational and individual role models are identified; and as setbacks or problems arise that must be addressed and communicated. At AT&T, this partnership has been forged over time as PR managers and HR managers participate together on the teams in which overall diversity strategy and tactics are developed and deployed.

Diversity and corporate reputation: For public relations people involved in enhancing corporate reputation (sometimes called "brand management"), a diversity initiative can have a major payoff. Here's why: Surveys have shown that external stakeholders gauge corporate reputation in part according to how they feel the company treats its employees. AT&T's stakeholders, for example, say that the attributes they most value in a company are innovativeness, helpful service, and trustworthiness. We believe all three attributes are strengthened by our diversity initiatives: innovativeness as diversity increases the pool of good employee ideas; helpful service as diversity helps to build employee empowerment and understanding of customer needs; and trustworthiness as diversity creates a work environment in which all employees are valued and spurs more inclusive community involvement.

Diversity and employee communications: For public relations people involved in employee communications, a company's diversity initiatives can have a profound impact on the ways in which information is shared within the company. Here's why: Since one of the goals of a corporate diversity initiative is to open the business environment to new ideas, employee communicators will have to reflect the new openness by opening internal communications channels as well. This means including new voices and new ideas in traditional communications media, and it may mean the creation of new media as well—new ways for employees to communicate directly with the leaders of the business and new ways for them to communicate with one another.

In all of this, of course, a high level of candor—on all subjects, but particularly on the subject of diversity itself is critical. Employee communicators play a key role in telling the success stories (and analyzing problem areas) related to the company's diversity initiatives. If such stories smack more of hype than substance, or if they get only occasional, back-page coverage, the diversity initiative will not be advanced.

Diversity and marketing support: For public relations people involved in sales and marketing support, including advertising, a company's diversity initiatives may create opportunities to identify new market segments and to communicate with those markets in new ways. Clearly the demographic changes occurring in the U.S. labor force are similarly occurring in the nation's consumer marketplace. Collaboration with diverse employee groups in accurately and swiftly targeting diverse market segments can bring real competitive advantage to the firm. Communicators can facilitate this collaboration by seeking out (or assembling) diverse employee groups to serve as informal advisers, sounding boards, or colleagues in the creation and delivery of marketing support materials. This wider source of input also can help the firm enhance its traditional sales and marketing efforts. For example, the focus on diversity helps to assure that marketing plans and targets include and reflect the increasing diversity of the general population.

Diversity and community relations: For public relations people involved in community relations, a company's diversity initiatives may stimulate the development of much deeper relationships with a wider variety of community (local, state, and national) organizations. Such organizations will be increasingly critical to the firm's success because their constituencies will represent a growing proportion of the labor force and the consumer population. Public relations people will be called on to develop new ways to facilitate communication between the firm and such groups. The roles of executive participation, employee volunteerism, corporate donations, supplier relationships, and joint business-community ventures will be broadened. In all elements of this relationship-building, of course, openness and candor of communications are critical.

Diversity and the media: For public relations professionals involved in media relations, a company's diversity initiatives can offer opportunities to develop deeper relationships with new media (those serving ethnic communities, for example) and to promote positive coverage, in all media, of diversity initiatives within the company. Such coverage might focus, for example, on the changing composition of the workforce, the increasing flexibility of the workplace, the growing bonds between the corporation and the community, the increasing use of minority- and women-owned businesses as suppliers, and the contributions to the company's success by employees who represent diverse groups. Here again, as in the arena of marketing support, the engagement of diverse employee groups as advisers and participants in the communications process can facilitate the effort.

Diversity and recruitment/hiring: For public relations people involved in the support of corporate recruitment, a company's diversity initiatives can offer a number of new opportunities—for example, the opportunity to align community relations activities more closely with recruiting; to engage representatives of diverse employee populations in the recruiting process; to strengthen relationships with diverse groups on traditional college and university campuses and to build new relationships with non-traditional colleges; and to build new partnerships with the labor unions associated with the company. The public relations department should also serve as a role model by assuring that the composition of its own employee population reflects the employees, communities, and customers it serves.

Diversity, quality, and labor relations: For public relations people supporting labor relations or quality organizations, the company's diversity initiatives can directly enhance any activities designed to engage and empower employees to serve customers better. This is because all three efforts—diversity, labor relations, and quality—are aimed at transforming the workplace into a place where employees' hearts and minds as well as hands are engaged. Work done by public relations people to align all these efforts (and perhaps additional ones as well) into a single, well-orchestrated initiative can bring efficiency and effectiveness to the culture-change process, while reducing the number of different employee programs initiated by the firm.

Diversity and executive support: The company's diversity initiatives will offer new opportunities in executive support for leadership positioning, participation, and endorsement. PR people can help leaders be role models for the diversity strategy or policy by ensuring that they have the continuing opportunity to hear, and respond to, the variety of voices present in the firm; to take visible stands, inside and outside the company, on appropriate diversity-related issues; to hold up for recognition those people and organizations in the company who are driving the diversity initiatives; to challenge those organizations that are not doing their part; and to participate in community activities that challenge and expand their comfort levels. Also, as PR people help executives align culture-change initiatives, they will help to create an effective and efficient leadership approach to workplace transformation.

Downside Risks

So far, we've been talking about opportunity—the opportunity offered by diversity initiatives to drive the business in new directions to the betterment of both the workplace and the bottom line. Let's take a moment now to look at some of the potential downside risks associated with a corporate diversity initiative. These include, most prominently, heightened expectations, fragmentation of the workplace community, customer and employee reaction to inclusiveness, downsizing issues, and the globalization of diversity.

Heightened expectations: A corporate diversity initiative tends to put the firm's intentions on record with regard to issues that can be very accurately observed and measured—for example, increases in the diversity of the executive ranks; improvements in workforce satisfaction as measured in the employee attitude survey; increases in community participation; or increases in purchases from businesses that are minority- or woman-owned. To put the issue simply, good intentions are not enough. If employees and other stakeholders do not see results, the damage to the corporation's reputation—to its "good word"—can be significant. Public relations people can play an active role first in helping to frame the promises, then in reminding the corporation of its promises and helping it to deliver on them in ways that stakeholders perceive to be valuable.

"Fragmentation" of the workplace community: A corporate commitment to diversity may lead to the formation of various active and vocal employee organizations. These organizations often work to assure that the interests of their constituents are heard at the highest levels of the firm. To some, the presence of these new voices may be taken as a sign that a once-harmonious workforce has been broken into splinter groups. Public relations people can help to explain that the earlier sense of harmony may have been more illusory than real and that the formation of employee affinity groups may be a necessary step to a more concrete and lasting harmony.

Negative reactions to "inclusiveness": These can arise both inside and outside the company—inside, in response to the company's promise of nondiscrimination against certain groups or individuals whose beliefs or lifestyles may offend other employees; outside, in response to the company's efforts to market its products to certain individuals or groups.

Internally, for example, the problem may arise in response to company policies against discrimination on the basis of sexual orientation; externally, the problem may be caused by marketing strategies aimed at gays and lesbians. In both cases, members of certain religious groups may object loudly to the company's actions—and may register their objections, both through the media and in the marketplace, by boycotting the company's products or services. On the other hand, approval of the company's actions by the gay and lesbian community may create positive publicity and generate additional sales. The role of public relations people here is to make certain that, before the company decides the issue, it has as many facts at hand as possible—with regard to stakeholder opinions and also to economic, legal, and ethical issues (especially the linkage to the company's values statement).

Downsizing: This unhappy fact of current business life can adversely impact the company's diversity initiatives in two ways. First, if seniority rules alone govern downsizing, the last to come in the door—who often comprise the firm's most diverse cohort—may be the first out. And second, even for employees not directly affected, lowered morale may seriously compromise the firm's efforts to engage and empower all employees. The role of public relations people here is twofold: first, to help assure that the diversity of the employee population is maintained (and enhanced if possible) during downsizings; and second, to counsel leadership on ways to maintain employee morale during and after downsizing episodes.

"The globalization of diversity": A global company can be tempted to want to deploy the diversity strategy and initiatives on a global basis; after all, differences on a global scale are significant, and the firm must understand and value these differences if it is to succeed in global markets. On the other hand, it's important to recognize that some aspects of diversity reflect American values that are not shared by other cultures. As just

one example, in the United States we hire and promote almost exclusively on the basis of individual merit; in other countries, family, citizenship, and age may be equally important qualifiers for hiring or promotion. PR people who help deploy diversity initiatives in other countries should be aware of these differences and work to adopt the basic principles of diversity—fairness, inclusiveness, engagement, and empowerment—in ways that are aligned with local cultural values.

"RULES OF THE ROAD": SOME TACTICAL GUIDELINES

Beyond the specific strategic support and counsel that PR people can provide on diversity initiatives, there are more general behaviors that all public relations and other employees can practice to help manage and value diversity in the firm. The following points are taken from an all-employee publication called "Diversity Matters," prepared by AT&T's PR and Diversity organizations.

- Remember that competence is shown by what people accomplish, not what they are or, usually, how they do the job. Clearly define the work to be done, and allow people to do the job in the way that suits them best.

- Learn about others. Take someone different from you, someone you don't know, to lunch. Read about diversity and study cultural groups other than your own. Study another language. Join one of the AT&T employee resource groups—they're open to all employees. Take one of AT&T's many courses in diversity awareness or team dynamics.

- Honor individual differences by treating people equitably. That doesn't mean you treat everyone exactly the same. Remember that the "right" way to deal with others is determined not by you, but by those you work with.

- Understand how your standards affect others, and apply those standards consistently with everyone. At AT&T, standards should be consistent with the values in "Our Common Bond" [the company's values statement, given in Box 15–2, page 243].

- Adjust your outlook. Don't focus only on how others are different, but remember the many things we all have in common.

- Broaden your problem solving. Go out of your way to find someone with a different life or business experience, and ask how that person views the problem.

- Don't pretend everything's fine if it isn't. If you encounter discrimination or lack of awareness, speak up. Kindly but firmly point out the behavior that makes you uncomfortable.

- Accept the feelings of others as valid, even if you don't share those feelings.

- Don't let assumptions about people interfere with your professional work relationships. If you are simply unable to avoid thinking of some people in terms of stereotypes, examine your behavior at work to make sure your biases do not get in the way of your performance.

- Watch your language. Learn the appropriate words to describe groups. Sometimes it's a matter of accuracy, sometimes choice—the choice of the person or group you're talking about.

Here are a few additional points, particularly for PR people:

- Understand that diversity initiatives constitute a continuing *process* and not a program of some finite duration.

- Don't get smug and assume that you've "got it." There are dimensions of diversity we haven't even begun to think about yet—like the individual assumptions about work that every one of us brings *to* work each day.

- Don't run away from, or bury, contention. Contention is an inevitable part of the openness that diversity initiatives seek to nurture. Instead, use contention as a vehicle to achieve new levels of understanding and cooperation.

- In communicating the diversity journey, don't assume that "one size fits all." There's a world of wisdom in the simple phrase "Different strokes for different folks."

- Think about the idea of 360-degree communications channels—downward, upward, lateral. Diversity initiatives stimulate, and thrive on, complex communications networks.

- Be aware that some employees see diversity as a zero-sum game—that gains for some groups and individuals are necessarily won at the expense of other groups. Work to position the diversity initiative as a process that stimulates greater engagement and empowerment of *all* employees.

- Learn to listen. And listen to learn. Valuing and managing diversity involves the continuing acknowledgment that the traditional leadership does not have all the answers.

- Understand that if diversity means anything, it means respecting different approaches to public relations—everything from opening up the pages of the employee magazine to different voices, to segmenting employee and media audiences in new ways, to counseling leaders on the extent and direction of their external involvement.

- Be prepared for criticism. The products of public relations—advertising, employee communications, marketing literature, etc.—are sometimes more visible to stakeholders than the products of the firm. Understand that if diversity values and encourages differences of opinion, there will be differences of opinion about PR's product line. Accept and learn from such criticism, and use it as a basis for future cooperation.

- Understand that as the firm learns to get closer to diverse segments of the external customer base, the voices of those segments will be heard more loudly inside the corporation. People inside the firm should be prepared to receive criticism as well as compliments from such voices—and to treat such criticism as an opportunity for improvement, not as evidence of ingratitude.

Tactics at AT&T

A number of initiatives are under way to support the execution of AT&T's strategy. All are being developed and deployed by teams that include officers of the company, representatives of the employee resource groups, representatives of a new high-level Diversity Quality

Council, managers in the Corporate Diversity Office, and representatives from public relations. Here are some of those initiatives:

- Establishment of diversity training objectives for all employees, beginning with top officers.

- Appointment of a vice president for corporate relations to strengthen ties between the corporation and the communities—*all* the communities—drawn upon for support.

- Creation of a methodology to help each unit of AT&T improve its ability to attract, develop, and retain a diverse employee population.

- Creation of a Business Development Diversity Action Council to deepen relationships with minority- and women-owned businesses.

- Creation of a chairman's diversity excellence award to recognize AT&T organizations making significant progress in managing and valuing diversity.

- Creation of an "executive partnering process" to develop mentoring relationships between diverse officers and employees.

- Development of a strategy for extending the company's concern for diversity to its locations and people outside the United States.

- Establishment of a "diversity progress report" to help leadership mark the progress of the diversity journey.

- Strengthening of the tie between leaders' compensation and their performance in managing and valuing diversity in their organizations.

- Formal inclusion of diversity planning in the business planning process to ensure that diversity initiatives are under way in every organization.

- Increasing levels of collaboration between sales, marketing, and employment organizations on the one hand, and representatives of diverse employee groups on the other, to improve the company's sales and recruiting performance in diverse external communities.

- Development and deployment of a large number of informational and educational materials for AT&T employees at both corporate and unit levels.

Case Study: The *FOCUS* Issue

A large number of AT&T's current diversity initiatives are the result of an incident that we call, inside the company, "the *FOCUS* incident."

The *FOCUS* incident occurred in September 1993. At that time, *FOCUS* was AT&T's all-employee publication—a colorful monthly magazine of company news and features, edited by a staff of corporate public relations professionals, that had won national attention for the appeal of its graphics and the candor of its contents. During the *FOCUS* incident, for example, AT&T Chairman Bob Allen received a letter from President Bill Clinton praising an earlier issue of the magazine for its forthright treatment of AIDS in the workplace. On the cover of that issue, an AT&T employee displayed a piece of an AIDS quilt commemorating the deaths of several AT&T colleagues.

The *FOCUS* staff prided itself on the magazine's sensitivity to, and continuing editorial coverage of, issues related to diversity in the AT&T workplace. The September 1993 cover, for example, portrayed a diverse group of employees involved in ethnic marketing; inside, another piece highlighted the diversity of an award-winning factory. And a special issue on diversity was in the works.

Unfortunately . . . and unfortunately is too mild a word . . . a short article on page 50 of the September 1993 issue—an article on patterns of international telephone usage—was accompanied by a drawing: a map of the globe on which small cartoon figures were making telephone calls. All of the cartoon figures were humans except for one. On the continent of Africa, the caller was portrayed as a monkey.

The appearance of that cartoon was an unintentional, but extremely offensive, slur on Africans and African Americans. The appearance was the result of a breakdown in the quality process—specifically, a breakdown in communications between the magazine staff and the external contractor who provided all the magazine's graphics, often with the use of third-party freelancers. In the heat of putting the publication to bed, and working from faxed and refaxed copies of page layouts, the magazine staffers simply missed the cartoon's offensive detail.

Hours after the magazine had been mailed to some 300,000 employees, a *FOCUS* editor, leafing through an advance copy, spotted the cartoon for the first time. Without waiting for reader feedback, the *FOCUS* staff apologized to all the people of AT&T through the company's daily electronic newsletter. On the following day, I added my apologies to theirs through the same medium. And before the week was out, Chairman Bob Allen had written to all employees, at their homes, conveying his own sense of acute embarrassment and apology.

Whether these letters of apology raised or lowered the outpouring of employee emotion that followed the cartoon's publication is debatable in retrospect, but that sort of calculation did not figure into the decisions at the time. Throughout public relations, and at the top levels of the company, we were mortified. And we said so.

A great number of AT&T people were outraged. An 800 call-in number, set up to allow employees to voice their thoughts and feelings, drew thousands of calls. This firestorm of emotion caused us quickly to understand that the offending cartoon had uncovered a much larger corporate problem: Just below the surface of a workplace environment that was consistently winning awards for its support of diverse groups, many of the people of AT&T felt like second-class citizens. Not just African Americans, but Asian Americans. Hispanics/Latinos. People with disabilities. Women. Union members. Supervisors. White males. Native Americans. Gays and lesbians. Citizens of other countries. What these AT&T people were telling us, in no uncertain terms, was that the company did not value them as individuals; did not capitalize on the variety of different points of view available to it; and did not make the connection between valuing diversity inside the firm and winning in diverse market segments outside the company. Passionate, inflamed emotions on this issue—so frequently sparked in the larger society—were suddenly everywhere inside AT&T.

The workplace wasn't the only place where we felt the heat. Our customers, federal and local government officials, the media, and community organizations all registered their own feelings—usually outrage and betrayal—in a variety of ways that added to our pain.

It was not a happy time to be in public relations at AT&T. But the events of 1993 triggered by "the *FOCUS* incident" taught us that diversity is indeed a central and critical business issue that profoundly touches the daily lives of many of the firm's stakeholders: employees, customers, and communities. These lessons we vowed to translate into changed corporate behavior just as soon as we thoughtfully could.

Chairman Bob Allen engaged the senior executives, the employee resource groups, diversity managers, public relations counselors, and a wide variety of other members of the AT&T community. Allen challenged these people to develop, by the end of 1993, a major, company-wide strategy for addressing the issues of diversity that our people had told us needed to be addressed . . . *if* we wanted honestly to claim that we valued diversity in all its dimensions; and if we wanted to hold our head high in the diverse markets we served and in the communities we belonged to.

Some of the people on the diversity strategy team did not sleep much during the fall of 1993. But their work, when completed, gave AT&T an extraordinarily comprehensive and detailed plan for stepping up to this business issue that led to many of the initiatives described earlier.

The strategy team's mission statement set the tone and direction:

> AT&T will create a work environment that sets the world-class standard for valuing diversity— where individual differences are not only recognized and valued, but are embraced because of the richness they bring to thinking, creativity, and problem solving, as well as enhancing our understanding of employees, customers, and the communities where we live and work.

The team also took pains to align its diversity strategy with the company's values statement, which we call "Our Common Bond" (see Box 15–2). The team stated:

> Fundamental to AT&T's long-term business success is its ability to embrace and live Our Common Bond values. Our values start with respect for individuals, which embraces the fundamental tenet of valuing diversity. Respect for individuals and valuing diversity serve as the cornerstone for our other four values:
>
> - If we do not respect one another and value each other's diversity, we cannot respect and therefore help our customers.
> - If we do not respect all people, we cannot demonstrate integrity.
> - If we are not open to alternative views, we will not hear and act upon the innovative ideas that we can offer each other.
> - And lastly, if we do not value diversity in the workplace, we cannot hope to work together as a team.

The implementation plan developed by the diversity strategy team focused on ways to improve internal awareness and understanding; to increase the diversity of the AT&T workforce; to expand relationships with supplier companies owned by minorities and women; and to enhance AT&T's involvement in the communities where we live and work. Behind all of these initiatives was another goal critical to our business: to improve our ability to satisfy—indeed, to delight—an increasingly diverse set of customers around the world.

The diversity strategy is not windowdressing. It is a plan that the leaders of AT&T are determined to execute—that the leaders of the business are enthusiastic about executing— because it's going to add to the bottom line. Bob Allen framed the issue succinctly when he spoke to AT&T's association of African American employees just two months after the *FOCUS* incident:

> One of the mistakes we have made, I believe, is that we have managed diversity at the edges and not in the mainstream of our operations. That is a mistake because the diversity of our customers, both domestic and global, and the growing diversity of the workforce demand that diversity be at the center of things—not on the side.

B O X   15–2

OUR COMMON BOND

We commit to these values to guide our decisions and behavior:

Respect for Individuals: We treat each other with respect and dignity, valuing individual and cultural differences. We communicate frequently and with candor, listening to each other regardless of level or position. Recognizing that exceptional quality begins with people, we give individuals the authority to use their capabilities to the fullest to satisfy their customers. Our environment supports personal growth and continuous learning for all AT&T people.

Dedication to helping customers: We truly care for each customer. We build enduring relationships by understanding and anticipating our customers' needs and by serving them better each time than the time before. AT&T customers can count on us to consistently deliver superior products and services that help them achieve their personal or business goals.

Highest standards of integrity: We are honest and ethical in all of our business dealings, starting with how we treat each other. We keep our promises and admit our mistakes. Our personal conduct ensures that AT&T's name is always worthy of trust.

Innovation: We believe innovation is the engine that will keep us vital and growing. Our culture embraces creativity, seeks different perspectives, and risks pursuing new opportunities. We create and rapidly convert technology into products and services, constantly searching for new ways to make technology more useful to customers.

Teamwork: We encourage and reward both individual and team achievements. We freely join with colleagues across organizational boundaries to advance the interests of customers and shareowners. Our team spirit extends to being responsible and caring partners in the communities where we live and work.

By living these values, AT&T continuously aspires to set a standard of excellence worldwide that will reward our shareowners, our customers, and all AT&T people.

LOOKING AHEAD

Today, in response to a number of factors, corporate America has embarked on a journey of massive workplace and workforce transformation. Some of the dimensions of coming change we can calculate with considerable precision: For example, the demographic composition of the workforce in the year 2005 is fairly certain, for those workers have already been born. Other dimensions of change we can only guess at, such as the impact of advancing technology.

The task for all of us in business today is to develop tools and methods to manage the required transformation in ways that create sustainable competitive advantage. Diversity initiatives offer a powerful tool for the engagement and empowerment of the men and women who will populate the workplace of the future. Whether we have the courage and foresight, today, to forthrightly address and value individual and group differences in the workforce may determine whether the firms we work for are the winners or losers of tomorrow.

## CHAPTER 16

Maintaining Effective Client-Agency Partnerships

David R. Drobis, APR
Chairman and Chief Executive Officer
Ketchum Public Relations Worldwide

John W. Tysse
Vice President of Public Affairs
DOW North America

"**S**urprise me once in awhile. In fact, seduce me occasionally—even if we've been together for a long time."

That's what many a client has in mind in a healthy relationship with a public relations firm.

Provocative? You bet. But upon reflection, maybe not so surprising. As with any long-term relationship—the best kind in public relations but, regrettably, now becoming the exception rather than the rule—familiarity can breed not contempt but boredom. And boredom is one of the things you just can't afford in the client-agency relationship.

Besides, there's no reason for it. With the many exciting developments in our field—new kinds of assignments and new strategies, tactics, tools, and players—there's plenty to keep the music playing.

Clients often look to their agencies to deliver that excitement—the rush that comes with discovery, but more important, the fulfillment that comes with having applied the right strategies and tactics, whether traditional or leading edge—to public relations challenges.

But we're getting ahead of ourselves. Let's go back to basics and start with the right way to establish the client-agency relationship.

THE FIRM FOUNDATION

There are, of course, many reasons for hiring a public relations firm.

The search and the ultimate relationship will be shaped by these objectives: Is the need broad-based or quite specific? Are we talking audit, research, development of strategy, implementation—or all of the above or more? Is the relationship likely to be short term (a project) or long term (a relationship)? Will it be local, regional, national, or international?

Whatever the prospective assignment, there's no substitute for candor from the outset. These days, no one has time to waste on lack of clarity or, worse, hidden agendas.

The client wants to know the agency's credentials and, quite possibly, its preliminary approach to the assignment.

The agency needs to know the *precise* nature and status of the public relations challenge, not just seat-of-the-pants guesswork; what's been done about it so far; and what kinds of resources will be applied and for how long.

Obviously, proprietary information must be protected. In such cases, the prospective firms will be more than willing to sign confidentiality agreements. Too, the firms should be willing to assert that they serve no organizations or products with directly competitive objectives.

In short, the client and agency must clear the air on expectations from the start.

Going in, the client should expect informed objectivity, creativity, follow-through, and a business-like approach—in short, professionalism. The agency quid-pro-quos include client consistency, realism, and respect.

The modus operandi, including progress reports, budgets, billing, and other administrative procedures—all essential to a smooth-working relationship—have to be agreed upon up front. Many a productive relationship has foundered on these "mighty minutiae."

Perhaps the most important early agreement is on what constitutes success. Will we know it when we meet it? Increasingly, the client's internal constituents are looking for *evidence of the value* of the public relations effort.

That's not as hard as it used to be. With rapid advances in research techniques, such as the Ketchum Effectiveness Yardstick (KEY), it's increasingly possible to document changes in audience awareness, attitude, and even behavior—and to demonstrate public relations "fingerprints" on those changes.

In all of these establishing-the-relationship activities, one very simple maxim pervades: "When in doubt, spell it out."

STRATEGIES FOR NURTURING THE RELATIONSHIP

A 1993 Ketchum national survey of desirable agency attributes as seen by clients is revealing. Clients and potential clients listed these priorities:

- An internal strategic thinking process (75 percent).
- Long-standing client relationships (66 percent).
- Specialized expertise in the client's field (65 percent).
- Expertise in coping with the client CEO's most-pressing business challenges (59 percent).
- A commitment to total quality management (58 percent).

Less-impressive agency attributes included: A sustained "leader" in the public relations field (meaning a "top-five" size), 22 percent; commitment and expertise outside the U.S., 11 percent (this is obviously changing rapidly); and industry recognition (awards), 11 percent.

The attribute, "long-standing client relationships" deserves a bit of scrutiny. The survey support data lead to the conclusion that the respondents feel, understandably, that a long relationship means long-term client satisfaction.

But the question of long-term "relationship" accounts versus "project" accounts is also roiling waters in the public relations field.

In an August 1994 edition, *Public Relations News* reported that "a dramatic discrepancy exists in the amount of public relations counselling (that) corporations say is done on a project basis . . . versus retainer (long-term commitment) work the firms says they are conducting . . . Surprisingly, 48 percent of public relations firms reported their billing is set by retainer and not by project . . . . These figures contrasted sharply with the response from corporate executives surveyed."

Nevertheless, the *PR News* survey indicated that project work is becoming more prevalent: "A whopping 58 percent (of counsellors) said more clients are becoming project-based." In other words, the "typical" client now uses more than one agency at a time, choosing the best available for a given assignment. The idea of "agency of record" seems to be changing. There's much to be said for *both* "relationship accounts" and "project" assignments.

The long-term relationship is obviously beneficial to the agency as a *business*. The agency can better project income, staffing, and resource requirements. But ultimately, if it's not in the client's interest, neither is it in the agency's interest.

A case can be made that it often *is* in the client's interest. Public relations is by nature a long-term activity. Awareness, attitudes, and behaviors are rarely changed quickly. It often takes many incremental gains to reach critical mass. An agency that has built an institutional memory on the client's public relations—and overall business—challenges and achievements "comes out of the gate running" on subsequent challenges.

Equally important, in this situation the agency can function as a truly effective external monitor, or environmental scanner, for the client. It's not just more eyes and ears, it's more brains as well.

Any number of initiatives can result. Perhaps the most delicious sentence in client relations begins with the account executive calling first thing in the morning and saying, "You know, just before I dozed off last night, something occurred to me that might just help you start . . . "

Of course, budgets and other exigencies sometimes make the relationship account an unrealized ideal. In these and other cases, the project assignment is quite necessary and appropriate.

For project assignments, a specific agency expertise is paramount. And the agency either has it or doesn't—no faking it. Candor is critical because the client is obviously looking for the most experienced, most creative talent available in a very discreet area.

Track record is important. But so is creativity, an *informed* approach (especially in this age of rapidly-evolving communications technology), and—as in all client-agency relationships—personal chemistry ("What will it be like working with these folks? Will it be fun, or at least not tedious?").

Once established, the healthy client-agency connection evolves toward symbiosis—the intimate living together of two kinds of organisms, especially where such association is of mutual advantage. Some readers, especially in client organizations, may feel squeamish about the term symbiosis. For them, we offer the overworked but equally appropriate term "partners." Either way, we're talking about a very close professional relationship, in many ways rivaling that of the client's legal or financial counsel. The matters to be addressed are that important. They're often at, or near, the heart of the future of the organization. They are vital.

This is no mere buyer-vendor relationship. This is a swim-or-sink-together, if-you-don't-look-good-I-don't-look-good kinship. It requires mutual trust and respect and, above all, the kind of candor that such trust and respect generates.

In preparing this chapter, we talked to several Dow and Ketchum communications professionals who have long been involved in the 20-year relationship between the companies. A few seminal comments from Dow managers:

"I want—and feel I have—an agency that can tell me flat out that I am wrong."

"I want a minimum of protocol and a maximum of hands-on by the worker bees."

"I want respect for budgets, certainly. But keep in mind that people remember the quality of the work product longer than the cost of it."

Among the agency's account service team, we heard:

"Dow has come a long way in the evolution of its corporate reputation because it's willing to listen to objective, hopefully informed, outsiders—us."

"How do we show that the Dow account is important to us? By pouring on the effort whenever it's needed—not by a lot of schmoozing and entertainment."

"We really enjoy being on the lookout for things we can take to Dow to advance their cause."

Nurturing the relationship also has a hazards-to-be-avoided side.

Potential agency pitfalls include lack of cooperation with the client's other agencies; over-promising (if you say you have a capability, you'd better have it); and the crucial mistake of going over the head of the client representative who has responsibility for the account.

On the client side, it's a mistake to be overly protective. If the account executive isn't cutting it, even after a fair trial period, it's in everyone's interest—client, agency, and the account executive—that a change be made. It's by no means the end of a career. Many agency people prosper on other accounts after being removed from a client relationship that just didn't click.

The most toxic element in the client-agency relationship is, of course, repeated—or worse, continuous—disagreement on communications philosophy, strategy, or tactics. And when such disagreements are about ethics, they are usually deadly.

Ultimately, the agency is the hired consultant, and the client has the right to accept or reject the counsel for which it is paying. But if it happens frequently and without constructive resolution, the marriage is in trouble. There *are* instances when account relationships are severed because of "creative differences" (although not nearly as many as announced).

Still, disagreements can be healthy. If handled with intellectual honesty, they can actually reinforce trust and respect. The right attitude should be, "I'm going to listen carefully; after all, neither I, nor anyone else, has a monopoly on wisdom and truth."

Respecting Respective Strengths

With the increasing flow of client professionals into public relations agency jobs—a very healthy recent development—there is sometimes a blurring of the strengths that each player brings to the client-agency relationship. It's worthwhile, therefore, to recall some of the realities about these respective strengths.

Most importantly, agency people must remember that, in most cases, the client representative is a *colleague, an experienced communications professional* (or has one or several such professionals on staff). That means that the client is usually quite familiar with the many tried-and-true public relations strategies and tactics. Too, and quite significant, the client knows the culture, the business strategic plan, the personalities of key players—*the pace*—of his or her organization. And institutional memory here is invaluable. The agency should be thought of as the qualitative and quantitative extension of the client's public relations capability, or, put another way, the complementary and supplementary support.

Most well-developed agencies can provide today's public relations core services: media relations; investor, employee, and community relations; public affairs; consumer and business-to-business marketing communications; healthcare communications; special events of many kinds for many purposes; and graphics and video design and production.

But the truly valuable agency is aggressively monitoring the communications-services landscape—and beyond—for the emerging tools that will help get the job done. That's the true added value of an agency. It's not just the fire brigade for crisis situations or the validating auditor, although in themselves these are not inconsequential roles. It's the ability to identify, adapt, and apply *whatever works* to the client's public relations problem that distinguish the truly valuable agency.

Before getting more specific about this, it may be useful to offer a description of public relations that serves as the context for the Dow-Ketchum relationship (and, hopefully, many other client-agency relationships): *Public relations is the management function that, through communications, helps an organization build or maintain quality relationships with those groups of people— "publics"—who can influence its future.*

Public relations is the management function that, through communications, helps an organization build or maintain quality relationships with those groups of people– "publics"– who can influence its future.

Within that broad but serviceable description, we have found creative outlet by exploring and introducing several relatively "exotic" activities including:

- *Outreach to critics*. At Dow, we have learned— along with companies such as McDonald's and General Motors—that it can be much more efficient and productive to examine a public relations problem cooperatively, rather than combatively, with those with whom we disagree. So we've proactively established dialogue with environmental groups, and have established local and national citizen advisory groups.

- *Alternative dispute resolution*. A conceptual extension of "outreach," ADR is a cluster of negotiating, mediating, or arbitrating activities that can reduce or eliminate the need for costly litigation and public confrontation.

- *Leadership on public policy*. Reflexive reaction just doesn't cut it anymore. And we feel that business, which must implement most government-mandated public policies, can and should play a proactive, positive, and central role in the formation of many of those policies. So Dow has offered top executives for such assignments. Example: Senior Vice President David Buzzelli accepted the co-chairmanship of President Clinton's Council on Sustainable Development, a seminal activity which will likely impact U.S. and international environmental policy for the rest of the century.

Happily, sometimes the client and agency commit to exploration of a public relations frontier on separate, but simultaneous, tracks. This is more than coincidence. It's an example of the old bromide about "great minds . . . "

That's been happening at Dow and Ketchum in the application of new electronic communications and information processing technology. Of course, virtually everyone in public relations is trying to sort out how best to capitalize on the vast potential of this technology. When client and agency alike have parallel "laboratories" pursuing such a holy grail, some good things are bound to happen.

For example, Dow is confident that database marketing can help greatly in meeting customer expectations around the world. Dow is, after all, a global enterprise, manufacturing in 33 countries with about 50,000 employees generating about $20 billion in revenues annually. Those revenues result from sales to an ever-changing mix of customers who buy more than 2,000 or our "product families."

Dow marketing communications professionals are hard at work evolving an information management system that will manifest a commitment to value-based management. Basically, it will demonstrate great value to top management by delivering marketing intelligence on what customers really value in their relationship with the company. This will involve some mighty sophisticated gathering, processing, and interpreting of data elicited by Dow customer information managers. The net result will be marketing strategies that are truly customer based.

Not coincidentally, Ketchum, like many agencies, is also deeply involved in applying the new communications technology to help solve clients' challenges. As a unit of a major worldwide communications services company, Omnicom Group, Ketchum Public Relations Worldwide is a beneficiary of the parent company's high-priority group of companies which are advancing the sophisticated application of interactive television, CD-ROM, on-line kiosks, the Internet, virtual reality, and other communications vehicles of the future.

These twin efforts, at client and agency, are already crossing as Dow and Ketchum share their incremental insights on the evolving communications technology.

Appreciation by Top Management

There is a self-defeating myth among too may public relations professionals that top management in client organizations doesn't appreciate the value of public relations. While there are undoubtedly good examples to support this opinion, the weight of accumulating evidence demolishes it. The distinction is vital at the outset: Given Dow-Kethcum's description of public relations—"building or maintaining quality relationships with the groups of people who can influence the organization's future"—can anyone seriously doubt that top management has any reservation in its support for this management function?

Function. There's the key—as contrasted with, unfortunately, the popular perception of public relations practitioners as only publicists. Is it any wonder that the function is often managed under a myriad of other titles?

On the contrary, the true top corporate public relations professional—bearing whatever title—is sometimes so tied to the CEO's agenda, style, and accomplishments that their terms of office coincide.

A related example shows the high value top management often places on the function. In recent years, several high-level corporate public relations professionals (again, bearing other titles) have taken relative early retirement as millionaires because of the stock options they originally received to become key players in corporate turnarounds.

As yet another indicator of top management's support for public relations, for many years, *Public Relations News* has annually honored dozens of public relations professionals who attained officer status in corporations, trade associations, nonprofit organizations, and other institutions.

No, it is not that top management doesn't value public relations intrinsically. It's that today—and, most assuredly, tomorrow—the kind of *value-based* management practiced at Dow is becoming the rule. Whatever its philosophy—"re-engineering," "right-sizing," "lean-and-mean"—top management, increasingly pressured by more active boards of directors and newly energized institutional investors, is insisting on clearly demonstratable value for each surviving corporate function.

In many organizations, the old "doughnut-factory" philosophy of business has taken hold: "There's the guy who makes the doughnuts and the guy who sells the doughnut. Everything else is overhead." Never mind that in the sophisticated world of contemporary business-in-society, this doughnut business philosophy is hopelessly simplistic. The public relations professional has three choices: Debunk the philosophy by dissecting and re-interpreting overhead (are the people who help you build the corporate brand overhead?); or become invaluable to the maker and seller of doughnuts; or do both.

The way to become invaluable to operating people is to relate centrally to their business plans. That's what the Dow Database Marketing mission is about. Better yet, *help develop* those business plans by delivering valuable early input on social, economic and political changes that can impact the business. The corollary is to develop public relations objectives directly supportive of the business plan and to accept—even welcome—measurement against those objectives.

Will all such public relations objectives and accomplishments be strictly tangible, without interpretative aspects, or achieved unilaterally? Of course not.

Take the financial value of a brand, and public relations' contribution to that value. In recent years, one of the most important elements in the acquisition prices of consumer products companies has been the accounting principle of "goodwill," which means, mainly, the value of the company's brands and reputation. Building and sustaining the brands (never mind the corporate reputation) is largely the task of media relations, promotions, and other efforts within, or contiguous to, the public relations department.

Public relations professionals are becoming better armed for measurement, or value analysis, with the more-empirically-minded top management. Outputs, outcomes, and outgrowths of our work are increasingly documentable—if such documentation is planned for at the outset.

A final note of management appreciation: Don't the recent staff cuts in client's public relations departments argue against such appreciation? Not necessarily. In an effort to boost productivity, managements are cutting jobs in virtually all departments. Manufacturing and marketing—vital functions—are not escaping, so how can public relations be immune?

Growing Together Internationally

We have purposely delayed our observations on the international aspect of the client-agency in order to offer a more focused discussion.

Much has been written about global marketing and worldwide public relations. Understandably, a lot of it is strictly conjecture. But there is now a growing body of experience that will truly inform such thinking and writing.

First, to be perfectly candid, many public relations firms have not as yet prospered financially from their overseas operations.

In the 1980s, establishing overseas offices was a combination of being visionary and wanting the caché of offices in Europe, in the Pacific Rim, or around the world. Finding and solidifying relationships with compatible agencies abroad was no easy task. And the market for such services among American clients was not brisk. With a few notable exceptions, these international offices were unprofitable and were mainly investments in a market that was to come.

But come it did! With the advent of the 1990s, many more clients, especially multinationals, wanted their agencies to have capabilities in international markets.

The Dow-Ketchum experience may be instructive in terms of how important such additional resources have become because, in a sense, that experience violates a principle advanced earlier in this chapter—that clients engage agencies largely on the basis of *existing* capabilities.

When Dow became seriously interested in European public relations, it asked Ketchum to develop such a capability. The meld of interests was achieved when Ketchum assigned the longtime leader of its Dow account team to run its modest but burgeoning European affiliate network and service the Dow Europe account. This just illustrates the value of a long-term relationship of mutual trust.

Most of the attention given to international public relations—or, for that matter, international advertising—has been related to international marketing. Justifiably so, because this usually addresses the delicate balance of delivering a core, universal message in a variety of cultures. This is no easy task.

What is too often overlooked, however, is the rapid proliferation of international public policy issues and the special capabilities that this requires of both client and agency. A key consideration is the rapid—sometimes instantaneous—movement of information internationally. An announcement in New York can be "news" simultaneously in London, Paris, Moscow, Beijing, and Tokyo.

And public activist groups such as Greenpeace International have become quite adept at using the latest communications technology to move information internationally and to coordinate strategies in various parts of the world. Corporations, trade associations and other institutions, some of whom are faced with survival issues in these debates, can do no less. In these situations, client-agency coordination in various parts of the world is crucial.

One of the more important international resources being applied in these disputes— and another outreach for today's public relations agencies—is the international scientific community.

In 1992, a handful of leading scientists, some of them Nobel Laureates, created a short but telling document called the Heidelberg Appeal. While supporting progress in global environmental improvement, the scientists cautioned political leaders against chasing chimeras, thereby wasting valuable resources needed for more genuine health threats. The Appeal, with more than 3,000 signatories, is now a valued source of expert scientists around the world who are willing to play a public policy role on their own terms.

But let's not overlook the needs of another kind of international client—the overseas client entering or expanding in the American market or marketplace of ideas. One of the faster-growing segments of international public relations is composed of companies and, indeed, governments who have a need to favorably impress American consumers and voters and the American government. The challenge for the agency here is twofold: To educate the foreign client on the American system and culture, and to formulate client messages that have a good chance of acceptance here.

Yet another international client-agency relationship has sprung up with the "global triumph of democracy and free enterprise." Working with overseas governments, often in cooperation with U.S. State Department agencies, American public relations agencies are increasingly being called upon to aid in the transition from state-controlled to "democratic capitalism" politico-economic systems. This is happening not only in Eastern Europe, where the vestiges of Communism are eroding, but also in South American, African, and Asian countries.

This is high-purpose public relations. But it is also high-frustration public relations, not only because of international culture clash but also because many of the clients are governmental or quasi-governmental agencies with traditions of very deliberate progress.

TACTICS: "TREMENDOUS TRIFLES"

In the spirit of the inverted pyramid, we've left until last a brief discussion of what some may feel to be more marginal aspects of the subject—some of the day-to-day, in-the-trenches aspects of good client-agency relations. Nevertheless, even though some are less dramatic than the foregoing, woe be it to those who ignore them!

In this respect, the agency account team owes the client:

- *An understanding of the client's business.* What are the success factors? What are the business challenges?
- *Constant monitoring* of developments in the client's industry and in related industries as well as any general events that could impact the business.
- *Polished communications skills.* All documents must be presented in ready-to-publish quality.
- *True professionalism.* Absolute confidentiality. Near-instant accessibility. Punctuality.

The client owes the agency:

- *Objectivity, honesty, and accuracy.* Ultimately, *two* reputations are at stake.
- *Consistency in direction.* Flexibility is a virtue, but arbitrary veering is sinful—the sin of waste.
- *Trust and access.* Once trust is earned, the account team needs to have access to company experts (while at all times keeping the client informed of such contacts).
- *Considered use of professionals' time.* The days of personal favors are long gone. Voluntary socializing is, of course, still "in"; we still need to know, like, and respect each other.
- *Timely payments and/or rapid resolution of billing issues.* It's still a business, and cash flow is not inconsequential. Besides, old bills fester and sour otherwise-sound relationships.

In the final analysis, "partnership" *is* the right word for the ideal client-agency relationship because it connotes a common interest, mutual support, and, most important of all, a sharing of risk and profit.

CLIENT MANDATES, AGENCY EVOLUTION

Ketchum Public Relations has been blessed with many long-term clients. The blessing had to be earned.

Over the decades since the agency was founded in Pittsburgh in 1923, the firm has learned that the best way to serve—and keep—clients is to indulge regularly in creative listening. And decades is the operative term for the core client list. Ketchum has worked for more than 10 years not only for The Dow Chemical Company but also for such leading organizations as The California Strawberry Board, The Potato Board (San Francisco office), Miller Brewing Company (Chicago), H.J. Heinz, Inc. (Pittsburgh), and Hoffmann-La Roche (New York). The grandaddy of them all is Mine Safety Appliance (MSA), which has been a Pittsburgh client for almost 50 years!

In its most recent exercise in creative listening, Ketchum asked four leading clients for analysis of their priority needs in the decade ahead. Heinz, Merck AgVet, Clorox, and FedEx said that agencies must now be prepared to meet five compelling client expectations.

1. Agencies must be "insiders" who know the client's business and contribute significantly to the solution of its business problems.

This, of course, might suggest an eventual increase in agency-of-record business. (If you are part of the client's institutional memory, you save a lot of time and effort not reinventing the wheel or suggesting strategies that are just a bit off center.) In the meantime—while project relationships are virtually the rule—agencies will have to scurry to become ad-hoc insiders as rapidly as possible.

Too, the need for insiders is making it more attractive for agencies to hire a certain kind of client public relations professional. This person must combine the understanding of business (and, frankly, "turf" considerations) with the ability to work for clients with many diverse missions.

To be insiders, successful agency people will have to be able to dig deep, identify what keeps the CEO up at night, and offer the communications component to solutions for these problems. Communications, however, is taking on a very broad definition. In many cases, it includes advance advice on how proposed policies will fly with key publics.

2. Clients will need agencies that can fully exploit the emerging media.

Technology is giving birth to what we call "affinity media." Small or large groups of people with relatively narrow interests can now be reached with little or no waste circulation. And these groups of people, these publics, can be given as much information as they want on a subject, virtually whenever they want it. That can be a boon to clients and agencies who know how to use the technology that gets this done.

The Internet is perhaps the paradigm for such tailored communication technology. You can reach many niched audiences via Internet, but remember that antagonists can also use the technology to advance antibusiness agendas.

And what of the rapidly evolving "cyberspace democracy"? How many Americans will avail themselves of the on-line ability to read all Congressional bills and decisions? What will they do after reading them?

"Brave New World" takes on new meaning when you consider the smarts—and courage—clients and agencies alike will have to demonstrate in mastering the coming communications technology.

3. Agencies will have to produce measurable results.

These days, *everyone* is accountable. So agencies will have to mirror their clients' internal accountability. The really valuable public relations program of the future will: bring input to the business planning process; set component public relations goals within the business-plan goals; and submit to ongoing measurement of accomplishments against those goals.

Ketchum has urged clients to think about three categories of public relations measureables—outputs, outcomes, and outgrowths.

The mistake is to think that *all* such measurements must appear in numbers. There are some, especially in the outgrowths category, that may be less empirical but still very valuable to the business plan. For example, when General Motors achieved "partnership" with the Environmental Defense Fund, thereby relieving the company of much time- and resource-consuming environmental confrontation and potential public embarrassment, was this (outcome? outgrowth?) not an important "measurable"?

Agency creativity and commitment will have to extend to this vital area if clients' interests are to be truly served.

4. As the many client projects surface, agencies must bring to them a "best teams" approach regardless of geography.

Although there is much to be said for the agency-of-record relationship, the reality is that a great deal of agency work for clients today is done on a project basis (although repeated projects lead to an ongoing relationship). Many of these projects are extremely important to the client. They often generate plenty of facetime with the client's top management. This is true not only in product launches, analyst meetings, and government relations, but particularly so in crisis management.

Nothing but the best team will do under these circumstances. And it doesn't matter to the client how far some of the team members have to travel, or from which agency profit centers they come. The client has a serious problem or an outstanding opportunity that requires outside counsel and implementation manpower. It needs quality help and it needs it *now*.

Ketchum has handled this in two ways. One is to assemble specialists in the major professional practice areas. Second is an internal accounting system that encourages total cooperation among profit centers, i.e., offices, around the world.

5. Your clients are going global. So should you.

In the agency business, as in all business, it's axiomatic that you go where the business is. In recent years, that has meant Europe, the Pacific Rim, and, now becoming increasingly important, Latin America. In all of these places, there has been a rapidly growing demand by local clients for "American-style public relations" (adapted, of course, to local culture, politics, and media).

But there is another important factor: Some large American clients and potential clients say that the definition of a full-service agency is changing, that full service now means the ability to handle their current and future needs around the world. As a result, leading agencies now monitor developments such as GATT, NAFTA, and the European Community almost as closely as domestic megatrends because this is where the rapid changing business world, taking advantage of the new communications technology, is leading.

"Creative listening" can serve an agency well. Customers (clients) can tell you a great deal about where your business is heading—or *should be* heading. Armed with that, all you need is the courage and flexibility to get there ahead of your competitors.

Ethical Implications of Corporate Communications

Cornelius B. Pratt, Ph.D., APR
Professor, College of Communication Arts and Sciences
Michigan State University

Kihyun Shin
Manager of Programming Team
Arirang, Korea World Network
The Korea International Broadcasting Foundation

This chapter examines two major corporate crises and draws lessons from managements' attempts—or lack thereof—to resolve them through ethics-based risk communications. However, it does not accomplish that purpose by a philosophical discussion on ethics. Models by which businesses can avoid unethical conduct have been presented elsewhere.[1,2] Neither does it do so by a step-by-step and an ethical approach to corporate dilemmas; much work has been done on management approaches toward ethical conduct.[3,4]

Rather, the purpose of this chapter is to use two Asian case studies to illustrate two outcomes: (1) management's strategic approach to demonstrating ethical conduct, as exemplified by Samyang Foods Co. Ltd., headquartered in Seoul; and (2) management's failure, in large measure, to demonstrate such conduct, as exemplified by Showa Denko K.K., based in Tokyo. The importance of the case-study method in accomplishing these outcomes is emphasized by Frey, Botan, Friedman, and Kreps: "Case studies examine a single, salient social situation to interpret the role played by communication. . . . The goal is to identify appropriate strategies that were used . . . to solve problems experienced in that particular situation."[5]

Stakeholders and Cases

The selection of the companies for this chapter was guided by several factors. First, their headquarters are in countries that are major U.S. trading partners, South Korea and Japan.

Second, while there are management differences between Japan and Korea,[6] both are profoundly influenced by Chinese culture, by the Confucian work ethic, and by worker harmony and solidarity.[7] Beyond these, Japanese management style was practiced widely in Korea until the end of World War II, during which Korea fell into Japanese control.[8]

Third, both South Korea and Japan did not have product liability laws at the time events associated with the case studies were unraveling. (Japan's first product liability law went into effect July 1995, following two decades of debates among government officials and industry and consumer groups on whether the country needed such regulations.)

Fourth, the companies' handling of their respective crises has implications for managements in other countries, particularly as businesses worldwide influence each other's behaviors and marketing environments and adapt to the increasing realities of global marketplace competition. For example, shortly after World War II, the Japanese improved the cutting-edge practices of U.S. manufacturing management, marketing, and research and development to the extent that they began to play leadership roles in those areas.[9,10] Such Asian successes are so phenomenal that U.S. companies are now studying and improving Japanese manufacturing practices.[11] Similarly, the practices of U.S. companies regarding corporate citizenship are actively considered by Japanese managers in setting courses of action.[12]

Finally, the two firms confronted comparable corporate dilemmas. A case study of similar issues is a relevant data-collection strategy that enhances issue comparability and facilitates the study of the relationships between the firm's public affairs function and its social-political environment.[13] A firm's actions do compromise or enhance its image as a good corporate citizen. Even though some argue that ethics are not related to corporate profits,[14] the reverse relationship has been documented.[15–19]

Past and Current Trends

Prior to the turn of the twentieth century, analyses of corporate ethics, let alone the ethics of company communications, were uncommon. This was so primarily because the 1800s were an era during which businesses disregarded, for the most part, consumer interest. The robber baron was king. However, the advent of a new form of thinking sparked an interest in how businesses could adapt their practices in ways that signified responsibility to the public interest.

The Friedman view,[20] which represents the classical, "free market" philosophy of big business, holds that the "business of business is business." While this view connotes that property rights and interests of shareholders are supreme,[21] it became laced, beginning particularly in the early 1970s, with an even more practical aphorism: The business of business is the public interest.

Thus, the "public-be-damned" image of the global corporation generated consumer ire worldwide. Corporate communications have been used to respond to such consumer concerns. Governmental agencies and corporations thrust into heated debates on their financial interests have found it imperative to be a part of the ongoing discourse on public policies.

One major struggle of companies worldwide is the establishment of a reputation consistent with the interests and expectations of their stakeholders. At the minimum, the demise of the Cold War has led to three global developments: the trend toward the adoption of open-market economies in the former Eastern bloc countries and the strengthening of economic ties among members of the European Union; the intensity of the competition in the global marketplace; and the emergence of stiffer competition from the newly industrialized Pacific Rim nations, particularly from the Four Tigers (South Korea, Hong Kong, Taiwan, and Singapore).

Relationships to Corporate Goals

Reputation management—or credibility enhancement—is a key element in the looming competitive mix. It is the key to generating public support, which is, among other things, a step toward attaining an organization's healthy financial status. Organizations also typically use a number of public affairs and credibility-restoration strategies to turn around their sullied reputations.

A reality for both global corporations and economic alliances, purposeful risk communications are pivotal to success, particularly during crises. The U.S. National Research Council defined risk communications as:

> an interactive process of exchange of information and opinion among individuals, groups, and institutions. [They involve] multiple messages about the nature of risk and other messages, not strictly about risk, that express concerns, opinions, or reactions to risk messages or to legal and institutional arrangements for risk management.[22]

Crises call into question corporate reputations. Examples include A. H. Robins and its recall of the Dalkon Shield in the early 1970s; the Upjohn Company and the Halcion controversies of the 1980s; the Union Carbide explosion in Bhopal, India, in December 1984; the Chernobyl nuclear station disaster in April 1986; NASA and the *Challenger* accident in 1986; the *Exxon Valdez* environmental pollution in March 1989; Dow Corning and its continuing problems with silicone breast implants; the Alar agricultural chemical scare of 1989; and Sears, Roebuck and Co.'s commission-and-quota system in its automobile repair centers.

If a crisis is left unchallenged, it can escalate, fall under news media or government scrutiny, interfere with the normal operations of business, jeopardize the company's image, and damage the company's goals and objectives.[23] Communication strategies are a major option companies can use to avoid false first steps in responding to crises.[24]

CASE STUDY NO. 1: SAMYANG FOODS CO., LTD.

Samyang Foods Company was established in 1961 by its current president, Choong-yoon Chun. The company introduced instant noodles in Korea in 1963. Ramen, a popular Samyang brand of instant noodles, soon became a common food because of its reasonable price, its convenience in preparation, and its taste.

With the sharp increase in sales, Samyang, by the 1970s, became a profitable Big Ten company in Korea. Encouraged by the success of this product, the company invested in developing additional food products, establishing more than 10 affiliated companies and creating a big ranch in a mountainous area. Chun constructed a "kombinat" system, which enabled each affiliated company to provide raw materials to others involved in the production process. The resulting Samyang group comprises companies involved in breeding stock, processing agricultural and marine raw materials, producing livestock feed and soybean oil, importing oil and fat, manufacturing containerboard for boxes, and distributing a variety of products.

In addition to Ramen, Samyang Foods Co., Ltd., the parent company of the Samyang group, produces more than 100 varieties of foods, including snacks, vegetable oil and fat products, dairy products, and several sauces. Although Chun had been advised to invest in different businesses, he focused on food-related industries based on his belief that people's balanced nutrition was the business of food companies. That philosophy is reflected in the mission statement of Samyang, whose characteristics are more consistent with those of a public enterprise than of a private business.

The number of Samyang employees in 1988, before its crisis, was more than 4,000. Ramen sales amounted to $160 million, while Samyang's total sales were $333 million.

T A B L E 17-1

Samyang's Product Sales and Percentage of Total Sales, 1988–1994

Product Category	1988 Sales*	1988 Percent	1989 Sales	1989 Percent	1990 Sales	1990 Percent	1991 Sales	1991 Percent	1992 Sales	1992 Percent	1993 Sales	1993 Percent	1994 Sales	1994 Percent
Ramen	$159.5	48%	$136.5	46%	$ 94.6	33%	$112.4	37%	$103.2	35%	$111.3	37%	$150.0	41%
Snacks	16.7	5	16.0	5	15.5	5	21.1	7	20.3	7	20.1	7	18.0	5
Oils	26.3	8	19.2	6	22.2	8	23.0	8	21.7	8	25.0	8	28.0	8
Sauces	11.0	3	10.1	3	8.8	3	7.5	2	8.9	3	7.6	2	7.6	2
Dairy	62.4	19	58.5	20	55.5	19	56.8	19	53.4	18	56.5	19	61.6	17
Others	57.1	17	59.2	20	91.1	32	80.4	27	86.0	29	81.1	27	99.4	27
Total	$333.0	100%	$299.5	100%	$287.7	100%	$301.2	100%	$293.5	100%	$301.6	100%	$364.6	100%

*Dollars in millions.

258

After the crisis hit, the number of employees dropped to about 2,500. By 1992, sales of Ramen had dropped to $104 million, with total company sales of $294 million. Total sales then inched up to $302 million in 1993, and in 1994 they increased to $365 million. (Samyang's seven-year sales trends in each product category are shown in Table 17–1.) Even though there are no data that explain the increase in sales volume, a plausible reason is that the company's ethical handling of the "fight of its life" may have restored consumer confidence in its products.

The Crisis

Korean prosecutors announced on November 3, 1989, that Samyang and four other food companies—Samlip Oil and Fat Co. Ltd., Seoul Heinz Co. Ltd., Ottogi Foods Co. Ltd., and Pusan Oil and Fat—had violated regulations on food manufacturing by using "inedible" beef tallow to manufacture instant noodles, margarine, and shortening. In reality, Samyang had used a mixture of beef tallow and palm oil for frying Ramen. The problem, according to prosecutors, was in the use of beef tallow. Samyang's processing of instant noodles, according to prosecutors, violated government regulations in one key area: the company's use of raw materials was inconsistent with consumers' traditional dietary habits or with consumers' expectations that the content of foods prove safe for consumption. Prosecutors said that the "top white tallow" (second grade) and "extra-fancy tallow" (third grade) used by Samyang violated the government's requirements because the tallow was classified as "inedible" in the United States, where Samyang bought it. Table 17–2 shows various specifications for the different grades of tallow, as determined by the American Fats and Oils Association.

The government charged Samyang with violating additional regulations which required that (1) fat tissue of cattle be of good quality; (2) raw materials be free of impurities such as soil, sand, and straw; and (3) raw materials be properly kept and cared for in ways that prevent deterioration in quality.

To substantiate their charges, prosecutors said the raw tallow refined by Samyang had an acid value of 0.4, while 0.3 was the highest permissible value specified y the government. They also said the high acid value may have resulted from the use of low-quality beef tallow by Samyang.

To further substantiate their charges, prosecutors asked two public agencies—Seoul Metropolitan Government Institute of Health and Environment (SMGIHE) and the National Institute of Health (NIH)—to test tallow samples from Samyang. On October 12, 1989, two such samples were taken, and SMGIHE tests indicated an acid value of 0.4, which exceeded the allowed maximum value of 0.3. Tests by NIH showed a value of 0.06.

The test results generated further controversy. Samples taken by SMGIHE were tested on October 16, which was four days after they were collected. Reliable results required testing within four hours.

Consequently, on October 18, SMGIHE re-collected and reanalyzed samples. Test results showed that the acid value was within the limits required by the government.

Samyang and other food companies, in arguing their case, cited four flaws in the prosecutors' charges. The first was that there was no such thing as "inedible tallow." During hearings, Professor Chae-Sun Cho of the Department of Food Processing at Kyung-hee University, Seoul, testified there was no scientific justification for classifying top white tallow and extra-fancy tallow as either edible or inedible.

T A B L E 17–2

Standard Grade: Specification and Quality Tolerances for Tallow and Greases as Established by the American Fats and Oils Association*

Grade	Titration[1] Minimum (milliliter)	FFA[2] Maximum (percent)	FAC[3] Maximum	R and B[4] Maximum	MIU[5] Maximum (percent)
Edible tallow	41.0	0.75	3	none	6
Top white tallow	41.0	2	5	0.5	1
Extra-fancy tallow	42.0	2	5	none	1
All-beef packer tallow	42.0	2	none	0.5	1
Industrial extra-fancy tallow	41.0	3	5	none	1
Fancy tallow	40.5	4	7	none	1
Bleachable fancy tallow	40.5	4	none	1.5	1
Prime tallow	40.5	6	13-11B	none	1
Special tallow	40.5	10	19-11C	none	1
No. 1 tallow	40.5	15	33	none	2
No. 2 tallow	40.5	35	none	none	2
Intermediate special tallow	39.0	10	21	none	1
"A" tallow	39.0	15	39	none	2
Choice white grease	36.0	4	13-11B	none	1
Yellow grease	36.0	15	37	none	2
Feed grade fats[7]					

*Effective January 1, 1983.

1. Titration: Quantity of menstruum (or solvent) required to neutralize acid or alkaline.
2. FFA: Free fatty acid.
3. FAC: Fatty acid color.
4. R and B: Refining and bleaching.
5. MIU: Moisture and insoluble impurities.
6. Maximum moisture is 0.20 percent; maximum insoluble impurities is 0.05 percent.
7. Must be within the limits for pesticides and industrial chemicals.

Source: Korean Society of Food Science & Technology, "The Opinion of Korean Society of Food Science & Technology on the Trouble of Imported Beef Tallow," *Journal of Food Science & Industry* 22, no. 4 (April 1989), pp. 78–81.

The second flaw was that charges were based on a simplistic invocation of U.S. standards, which, prima facie, need not be applied to products manufactured in other countries.

Third was that refined tallow and its products had met the standards for acid value set by the government.

Finally, until the occurrence of the crisis, no problems had been identified during random inspections regularly done by government officials.

All five companies believed they had been using the proper tallow, which exceeded government standards. Nevertheless, the issue was fair game in the nation's media, which described Samyang's tallow as "industrial oil" rather than, at worst, "inedible oil." Korean consumers generally interpreted the term "industrial oil" used by the press as "motor oil."[25] They believed, for 26 years, they had eaten noodles fried with an "inedible tallow."

B O X   17–1

WHAT IS "INEDIBLE OIL"?

By U.S. standards, raw beef tallow has 16 grades. U.S. consumers are provided only with the first grade of tallow, not because the lower grades are inedible, but because consumers customarily consume only the first. The first grade, a form of pure tallow, makes refining unnecessary. So, by U.S. standards, the first grade is conveniently labeled "Edible Tallow" because it can be eaten in its raw state, without any refinement. Other grades are considered "inedible" before refinement, based on the notion that it is inadvisable to consume them in their raw states. The reason for refining is simple: It removes substances that would otherwise make tallow impure.

Interestingly, the United States does not label other grades "inedible." A November 7, 1989, letter from the National Renderers Association, Inc., in Washington, D.C., to Samyang stated that, with proper refining, processing, and handling, the second and third grades can meet or exceed edible tallow standards. Worldwide, food experts say that it is unnecessary to differentiate edible from inedible tallow because beef tallow of any grade can be used in food and for industrial purposes. Samyang used the second and third grades, after having them refined, for frying instant noodles; no company uses raw tallow in foods without refining it.

The prosecutors' contention was based on a convenient interpretation of U.S. standards. That contention was not backed by scientific evidence that the second and third grades were considered "inedible." Additionally, the prosecutors did not demonstrate knowledge that other countries used standards different from those of the United States. The Netherlands, Belgium, Spain, and Mexico permit the use of 14th-grade tallow in foods. Australia and New Zealand refine all beef tallow, without classification.

In summary, U.S. food habits require the use of the first grade in foods and of grades 2 through 16, in spite of their edibility, for manufacturing "industrial products" such as soaps, cosmetics, and candles. Because of such industrial use in and the classification standards of the United States, Korean prosecutors concluded that the five food companies had, indeed, violated government regulations on the use of raw material in foods.

Samyang was *the* media target because it was the first and largest producer of instant noodles in Korea. Even though prosecutors said that it was not definite that the tallow was hazardous, rumors were rife that industrial oil was injurious to public health.

On November 16, 1989, 13 days after Samyang's problems became public, Chong-In Kim, the Minister of Health and Social Affairs, said in a news conference that raw tallow was "inedible," but that the manufactured product—instant noodles—was definitely safe. This conclusion was a sequel to the findings of the Committee on the Inspection of Food Sanitation, which was established by the government after the charges were announced. Minister Kim said, however, that because the five food companies had violated government regulations, such tallow could no longer be used in food production. Immediately after the news conference, Minister Kim demonstrated its safety by eating a bowl of Samyang's Ramen for lunch.

Twelve days later, a high court released on bail representatives and chief directors of the food companies. At issue was whether the use of second- and third-grade tallow was a crime. The defendants were found guilty on January 27, 1994. On appeal, a higher court ruled on July 14, 1995, that the defendants were *not* guilty. The prosecutors are appealing the court's decision to the Supreme Court, which is yet to set a date for the case.

BOX 17-2

SAMYANG AND CODEFENDANTS' ADVERTISEMENT RESPONDING TO GOVERNMENT CHARGES*

AN EXPLANATION

We are sorry for creating a situation that has created public concerns.

1. The refined beef tallow we have used meets the standard for raw material for food set by the Ministry of Health and Social Affairs.

    According to U.S. standards, beef tallow has 16 grades. However, even first-grade "Edible Tallow," when imported, should be refined for use in foods. Similarly, "Top White," the second grade, which we imported, was refined and exceeded standards set by the Ministry of Health and Social Affairs. Therefore, the products that we have sold for several decades are not only edible, but pose no risk to the consumer.

2. Every edible oil is inedible in its raw state; however, refining makes it edible.

    The water in reservoirs is not appropriate for drinking; however, it becomes drinkable by a cleaning process. Similarly, palm oil, coconut oil, rapeseed oil, rice bran oil, as well as beef tallow, are inedible in raw states. They also become edible when they are refined and meet or exceed the standards of the Ministry of Health and Social Affairs.

3. We regret that the prosecutors' announcement resulted from the difference between the government's simplistic interpretation of the term "inedible tallow" and the views held by the food science community.

    Our country is up-to-date on developments in food science.

4. It is untrue that the food companies made excessive profits from industrial tallow.

    This is based on the fact that the import price of beef tallow is about $100 higher per ton than that of palm oil.
    The food industry is doing its best to develop a more advanced food culture for the 21st century and to make healthful foods.

    We solicit your continuing patronage.

November 5, 1989
Korea Foods Industrial Association
Samyang Foods Co., Ltd.
Samlip Oil and Fat Co., Ltd.
Seoul Heinz Co., Ltd.
Ottogi Foods Co., Ltd.

---

*English-language translation.

Ethical Implications of the Crisis and Responses

The crisis spawned reactions from four major groups: Samyang's consumers and dealers, the government, Samyang, and the news media.

Telephone calls from angry consumers encouraged the company not to do business as usual. Consumers, retailers, and wholesalers returned the product in hand and asked the company for a recall. The military suspended its use of the product, and foreign dealerships canceled their orders. The coalescence of these actions cost Samyang $13 million in unsold Ramen.

The prosecutors' charges were applauded by consumers because businesses were perceived as largely interested in meeting their narrow financial goals. Additionally, a number of the company's competitors capitalized on Samyang's crisis.

Prior to the prosecutors' charges, the company's public information department had obtained some information about the investigation, and the company's vice president and a managing director were summoned for preliminary investigation by prosecutors. However, top management did not consider the investigations worrisome because they believed the company operated within the law, and, more important, within high ethical standards.

When the crisis broke, political considerations discouraged Samyang from making a prompt public response to the charges. The company's manufacturing process soon became a communication crisis. Its initial response came on November 5, 1989, two days after the prosecutors' charges were announced. Samyang and three other companies ran advertisements (see Box 17–2) in which they explained that their refined tallow met government standards and that the prosecutors' association of "inedible tallow" with the companies' products resulted from their misunderstanding of beef tallow and its classification. The advertisement also outlined the company's refining process, thereby potentially debunking any fears associated with consuming Ramen.

Responding to the advertisement, the prosecutors reaffirmed their justification for prosecuting the five companies. Their contention was also based on the opinions of two professors from Yonsei University and Hanyang University, both in Seoul. They held that such tallow posed health risks and that its quality did not improve with refinement. They further argued that public safety could not be guaranteed with the consumption of such "inedible raw tallow."

Samyang struggled to overcome its crisis through other tactics such as using door-to-door persuasion and distributing fliers on the street. Chun, argued that Samyang would eventually be cleared because its slogan, "honesty and credibility," always had driven its operations. One line of response adopted by Chun was that the beef tallow that his company used was more expensive than the palm oil used by his competitors. At the time the crisis reached its peak, imported second- and third-grade tallow cost $100 per ton more than palm oil. Chun explained that Samyang used the more-expensive beef tallow because the average consumer needed some animal fat for balanced nutrition.

Samyang and the other three companies apologized in advertisements in which they re-emphasized the safety of their products (see Box 17–3). In keeping with top corporate managers' belief that the use of multiple media to communicate with employees and with the external world is important for implementation strategy and for improved relations with strategic publics,[26,27] the ads were run in 14 national newspapers.

News media responses to the crisis were initially inimical to Samyang's interests and created distortions without presenting facts. "Industrial tallow" was essentially the media's own label, and they charged food companies with making exorbitant profits by using such cheap products. Some broadcast journalists who visited Samyang's headquarters rejected scientific evidence.

Although Minister Kim had announced Ramen's safety, Samyang ran advertisements the following week in 17 major newspapers. In the ads, the company apologized again and stated it would make every effort to provide "better products" (see Box 17– 4).

On March 19, 1990, to demonstrate its commitment to manufacturing "better products" and to respond to negative public reactions to the word "industrial," the company changed its name from Samyang Foods Industrial Co. Ltd., which it had used for 29 years, to Samyang Foods Co., Ltd.

B O X 1 7–3

SAMYANG AND CODEFENDANTS' ADVERTISEMENT APOLOGIZING TO CUSTOMERS*

AN APOLOGY TO OUR CUSTOMERS

Our managements believe that it is meaningful to contribute to the improvement of people's health and diet.

We apologize for public concerns created by importing, refining, and using second-grade beef tallow when manufacturing some of our products.

Food experts say that beef tallow, when refined, is safe for manufacturing foods.

However, in spite of the testimonies of food experts, we deeply apologize for creating public uneasiness and confusion.

In the meantime, we promise to redouble our efforts to ensure people's health and improve their dietary habits by using raw materials whose quality is in compliance with government regulations.

November 11, 1989

Samyang Foods Industrial Co., Ltd.
Samlip Oil and Fat Co., Ltd.
Seoul Heinz Co., Ltd.
Ottogi Foods Co., Ltd.

---

*English-language translation.

On the heels of the crisis, Samyang accounted for less than 20 percent of the instant noodles market. Concerned about the future of the company more than 1,000 employees resigned, a move that cost Samyang $6.7 million in retirement benefits.

Samyang's Risk Communications Strategy

Samyang's success in surviving the crisis hinged on scientific evidence and on its communications strategies. Were there political communications options that the company could have adopted to halt any further erosion of its public reputation?

In our view, an overall strategy based less on an understanding of the substantive issues facing Samyang than on an understanding of the process by which the company could influence public policy vis-à-vis the food manufacturing regulations would have been beneficial. That strategy, based on studies of persuasive political communication, identifies three agendas of interest to the business communicator: the media agenda, the public agenda, and the public policy agenda.

The media agenda comprises issues disseminated by the media. The public agenda includes those issues the public knows, thinks, and talks about, while the public policy agenda refers to topics and issues on which policies may be formulated.

The company's communications strategy called for influencing all three: the media agenda through a systematic use of corporate communications, such as video, electronic

B O X   17–4

SAMYANG AND CODEFENDANTS' ADVERTISEMENT APOLOGIZING TO THE PUBLIC*

WE APOLOGIZE TO THE PEOPLE

We are sorry for creating public concerns and will work hard, through research and the development of better-quality products, to live up to your expectations.

It has been proven that Samyang's Ramen is safe.

Our Ramen has been subjected to rigorous analysis by the Committee on Food Sanitation, which was established on November 9. Our product has been shown to be safe.

We have, for the past 30 years, focused on food.

Since its founding, Samyang Foods Co. has made every effort to improve people's health and diet. The damage done to our image by the beef-tallow controversy will be reversed by your warm heart and sound judgment. You will be able to ascertain the credibility of Samyang.

We appreciate your views.

Because we value your opinions and concerns, we, Samyang Foods, will take the initiative in providing more healthful foods, using only vegetable oils in their manufacture.

You will have better products.

We, the 5,000 workers of Samyang, promise to be at the cutting edge of developing and producing excellent foods. You can count on Samyang.

We hope you will continue to patronize us.

> All the staff,
>
> Samyang Foods Industrial Co., Ltd.

---

*English-language translation.

---

news releases, and position statements; the public agenda through proactive social responsibility programs; and the public policy agenda through lobbying, indirect lobbying, and interest groups.

While the company had attempted to influence all three, current evidence suggests that corporate efforts on the policy agenda, which should have been the ultimate target, had been minuscule.

On February 17, 1993, *Mun-Wha I!bo,* a Korean newspaper, carried an article about the case, saying that it raised troubling questions for the judiciary, the prosecutors, and the company.

Twenty-two hearings were held in 50 months. As indicated in a preceding section of this chapter, on January 27, 1994, 10 company representatives and the four other food companies were found guilty. The judge ruled that all five companies used raw materials inconsistent with consumers' traditional dietary habits and with their expectations of food content. The prosecutor had demanded penalties totaling $580 million, but the judge lowered the fine to $279 million. However, the judge commuted the monetary penalties because he thought they might drive the companies into bankruptcy. The defendants and prosecutors appealed the judge's rulings; the defendants were dissatisfied with the judge's finding of guilt and the amount of the fines, whereas the prosecutors thought that the penalties were too low.

Tactics to Be Learned

This case presents corporate risk communicators with several lessons. First, it is important for a maligned company to encourage consumers to understand its crisis. In Samyang's case, its success in doing just that, as evidenced by its sales recovery, hinged on both scientific evidence and communication strategies. The company used the pages of the print media, which were initially hostile, and encouraged the public to call its headquarters to have questions answered or concerns addressed. Such communication options helped Samyang draw in the reins on its plummeting public reputation. Even the government could not challenge the company's rebuttal.

Second, it is important that manufacturing methods adopted by companies exceed those stipulated by law or approved by government regulators. For communications practitioners, such a step gives them elbow room to demonstrate nonpecuniary interests toward their strategic publics.

To what extent should U.S. standards influence Korean manufacturing standards? For the global practitioner, the issue of local versus headquarters' standards does not have a direct answer. As a rule of thumb, however, companies that do business globally should adopt standards higher than those available locally. The labeling standards for beef tallow, for example, are obviously more explicit and rigorous in the United States than those adopted by Samyang. If the company had adopted such standards and had not been satisfied with those of its home country, the government would have been hard-pressed to charge it with improper manufacturing processes. The reader will recall that, following a December 1984 chemical leak that killed more than 2,500 people and injured more than 200,000, Union Carbide confronted charges of shoddy construction of its plant in Bhopal, India. A similar accident at the company's Institute, West Virginia, plant injured about 100 people but did not cause any fatalities perhaps because of its more stringent safety rules and because that plant was constructed according to U.S. codes, which were more exacting than those required by the Indian government for the Bhopal plant.

This issue of manufacturing standards raises two companion questions: Did Samyang's responsibility go beyond economic and legal concerns? Where does the social responsibility of the company lie? There is no evidence that the company violated any national regulations. However, the nonviolation of a regulation is not tantamount to behaving aboveboard; neither is it equal to a full-blown demonstration of adherence to its discretionary responsibility. One scholar defines discretionary responsibilities as "those about which society has no clear-cut message for business."[28]

Third, the Samyang experience provides the practitioner some guidelines for fomenting public discussion about a crisis. Free and fair discussion of the issue must be encouraged by the company. The coalescence and the clash of a number of views could benefit the company in the long run. Understandably, the news media in South Korea, officially free, are susceptible to government pressures, which suggest that they will support the official mind-set. For South Koreans, such an expectation, albeit subtle, compromises the extent to which the media can play a viable role in setting the agenda. Communications practitioners in the West have few media restrictions in comparison with their Asian counterparts. They are, therefore, better positioned to set and influence the media agenda, and, thereby, the public responses to the company.

Fourth, Samyang's lack of preparedness demonstrates that companies must establish crisis management teams (CMTs). "What fundamentally distinguishes crisis-prepared from crisis-prone organizations," write two top researchers, "is their overall and integrated view of CM [crisis management] . . . One of the first tasks of the crisis-prepared organization is the formation of a crisis management team (CMT)."[29] Even though such teams have the potential to manage crises, companies tend not to use them. Among more than 200 companies the researchers studied, no more than 15 percent had developed systematic strategies or CMTs for dealing with crises

Admittedly, because CMTs use game plans and forecasting techniques to address crises, such plans and techniques tend to have an obvious weakness: they cannot predict, with a high level of certainty, the nuances of possible outcomes. Such weakness can be tempered by using scientific and philosophical theories in strategic planning, an approach that makes management more proactive and less reactive in crisis situations.

Finally, public perceptions of business ethics may rub off on perceptions of businesses in general, that is, that the latter, at best, have mixed motives that indicate a much higher level of loyalty to their stakeholders and dominant coalitions than to their other publics. The public is less apt to be forgiving and less likely to be understanding if corporate handling of a major crisis does not meet even its modest expectations. Past corporate responses provide benchmarks for evaluating similar futures occurrences.

Samyang's ethical lesson for other organizations that are pitted against government regulatory agencies is to adopt communications strategies that are ethically sensitive to three agendas: the media, the public, and the public policy. Those agendas call for the use of persuasive tools such as lobbying, speeches, interviews, and debates. However, given the relationships between two of the three agendas and the Korean national government, the task ahead for Samyang gets even more challenging by the day.

TACTICS CASE STUDY No. 2:
SHOWA DENKO K.K., JAPAN

Showa Denko K.K. was formed June 1, 1939, through the merger of Nippon Denki Kogyo Company, which had been established in 1926 as Nippon Iodine Co., and Showa Fertilizer Company, founded in 1928. Both Nippon Denki and Showa Fertilizer had been founded by Nobuteru Mori as units of the Mori group of companies.

Showa is the seventh-largest chemical company and among the 100 largest companies in Japan. It is a major manufacturer of an essential dietary supplement, the aromatic amino acid L-tryptophan, which it began producing at the end of 1982. A major crisis hit Showa in the summer of 1989, when some people who had consumed health foods containing the amino acid developed cramping muscle pains and skin rashes. The symptoms were known as eosino-philia-myalgia syndrome (EMS) and were believed to have been caused by the supplement.

In that same year, Showa halted production and marketing of the amino acid and requested its affiliated companies in the United States and Europe to recall products in which it had been used. On April 27, 1990, Japan's Ministry of Health and Welfare requested that the company recall any L-tryptophan still on the market.

By September 10, 1990, the company faced claims totaling $1.18 billion from 122 cases; by November 30, 1990, 28 deaths had been attributed to EMS.[30] Another writer estimated that 10,000 people may have developed EMS and that 31 had died.[31]

Showa was ordered by an arbitration panel to pay damages to victims of EMS. In November 1989, the U.S. Food and Drug Administration (FDA), and in November 1990,

Ross Laboratories in Columbus, Ohio, recalled all preparations to which the amino acid had been added. In February 1991, the FDA expanded its recall to include all medical foods, infant formulas, and other food supplements that contained the supplement.

Showa's Ethical Nightmare

The absence of product liability laws in Japan absolved the company from making any restitution to victims. Individuals had to prove civil negligence on the part of Showa, which only offered to reimburse dissatisfied Japanese customers their purchase price. The claim–settlement system is a blend of strict product safety regulations, customer protection requirements, and informal methods for settling disputes. Because even Showa itself has not ascertained what went wrong, and Japan is still debating changes in product liability laws, it is unclear what future recourse consumers may have. Nonetheless, the company's handling of the issue raises major ethical questions.

In Japan, the legal impact of this case was minuscule. Showa walked away from the problem with its head held legally high. However, it can hardly be said that the company took the high road to ethical judgment. It seemed interested in paying some restitution only to those victims who had the time and resources to take the corporate giant to court.

A 50-year-old Tokyo housewife said she was barely able to walk and sleep because of muscular pains she thought resulted from her use of L-tryptophan. Showa refused to accept her claim, stating that she would have to prove that the company was negligent in manufacturing and marketing a defective product and that she suffered as a result of her use of that product.

Studies cast doubt on a causal link between L-tryptophan and EMS;[32,33] others show some evidence of such a relationship.[34,35,36] And still others report cases of EMS not associated with the use of tryptophan and suggest that other nutritional supplements be considered as possible etiologic agents in EMS.[37,38] It appears, then, that the causative agent of EMS remains unclear.

In the United States, sufferers of EMS allegedly induced by Showa's product were treated much differently, possibly because of the legal climate under which product liability cases are adjudicated. Stricter product liability laws, for example, led to a more than 300-percent increase in product liability suits filed in federal courts from 1975 to 1983.[39,40] Consequently, sufferers of a mysterious blood disorder linked to the intake of L-tryptophan were able to extract some concessions from the company.

Showa has since awarded grants totaling more than $3 million to research groups at universities and institutes in the United States, and has supported similar research in Japan. In fact, Showa has been cooperative in supplying data on its production processes and samples of the material. However, the company's aggressive legal strategies—requiring U.S. government researchers to provide their data to Showa before they are published, for example—have been a cause of public concern.

Showa's 1989 health fiasco had a 24-year precedent. In 1965, there were allegations that the company's Kanose plant had dumped methyl mercury into the Agano River, contaminated fish in Minamata Bay, and engaged in practices that precipitated an outbreak of Minamata disease, which caused at least six fatalities. Victims and relatives of the deceased filed suit in district court. The company insisted that plaintiffs should prove that methyl mercury was responsible for their ailments, but the court maintained that it was the defendant's responsibility to prove that such a link did not exist. Showa was found negligent and fined ¥270 million.

This case, among many others, has forced some changes in the attitudes of Japanese businesses toward the public and in the cozy relationships between big business and government.[41] However, Showa's current legal maneuvers are reflective of the Japanese concept of corporate social responsibility and business ethics.

While corporate social responsibility is a widely accepted feature of U.S. businesses,[42] a number of Asian countries[43-47] are still grappling with their own strategies for a synergy between corporate and public interests.

The ethical ramifications of Showa's environmental and health risks are similar to those of two U.S. companies: Johns Manville's problems with asbestos in the late 1960s and early 1970s, and A. H. Robins's handling of the Dalkon Shield fiasco in the mid-1970s. For one thing, all three companies demonstrated a diminished sensitivity to consumer interests. In addition, stakeholder allegiance seemed more consistent with company interests than with those of larger constituencies. A pivotal question was how quickly corporate action should be taken to avert any likelihood of product risk to the consumer. Also, how promptly responsive were those companies to the concerns of their consumers?

Granted, the value system that signifies Japanese business ethics is more central to that country's belief system than it is to Western values.[48-50] Japanese ethics are predicated on two normative environments, the transcendental and the group.[51] The perspective of the transcendental normative environment is that all individuals and things are linked to an ultimate reality—a higher force.

The group normative environment stems from the transcendental environment. Japanese employees, for example, exemplify *kaizen* (or the gradual progress), which develops a relatively high degree of cooperation between leaders and workers—a cooperation believed to contribute to everyone's well-being in the long run.[52] Similarly, *kaizen*-oriented corporations foster cooperative relations within and among companies, which, in turn, build trust. They also adhere to *wa*, harmony and unity, which is significantly different from those in the West. But these group attributes have created ethical problems in a workplace where women tend to be excluded and unconventional ideas tend to be suppressed.[53]

Ethical and Questionable Tactics

Showa's handling of the fallout from EMS was ethically sound in three areas. First, without government prodding or intervention, the company halted the manufacturing and marketing of its amino acid. Second, it cooperated with government and independent agencies to identify the cause of the health problems. Third, it awarded research grants to agencies and research centers in their attempts to establish or refute any links between use of the food supplement and alleged health problems.

Beyond these measures, however, Showa kept a close tab on its pecuniary interests. While its response made economic sense, there were instances of foot-dragging and of employing legal maneuvers in the United States to interfere with studies being undertaken to test for causation between L-tryptophan and a myriad of health problems.

Showa employed a double standard in its response to the food-supplement crisis. It settled lawsuits in the United States but discouraged similar suits in Japan. In Japan, because the burden of proof lies with the alleged victim, bringing a chemical giant to justice was a far-fetched reality. Yet, it was in the best interest of the company to demonstrate, without government prodding, an ethically rigorous interest in the welfare of a number of claimants who had complained about side effects from their use of the acid. Risk communications, as used by Samyang, were not considered by Showa—at least not for the U.S. consumer public—because the company feared

increased vulnerability to lawsuits. But corporate social responsibility is about the fundamental relationships between a business and its consumers. And, as Clarkson concluded, "To
be socially responsible is to be ethically responsible and profitable."[54]

CASE QUESTIONS AND FUTURE ISSUES

The two case studies presented here leave us with the following questions:

1. Regardless of legal proddings, is there a universal sense of normative,
   ethics-based corporate behavior that pervades the boardrooms of major
   businesses?
2. Is there a universal agreement on what constitute normative benchmarks?
3. To what extent are companies cognizant of the importance of operating
   consistently in the public interest?
4. Do domestic companies, let alone the multinational types, work consistently in
   the public interest?
5. What are the universals of the public interest?
6. How could organizations, particularly their communications staff, demonstrate
   such universals?

Moral behaviors are a function of societal values. Thus, the responses of both Samyang
and Showa to the crises that confronted them indicate that, for the most part, answers to the
first four questions are in the negative. If they are, then it is understandable how corporate
risk communications are as much a Rosetta stone in an ethical minefield as they are a
corporate Achilles' heel.

This chapter used two Asian case studies to present strategic lessons for managers who
are potentially or regularly confronted by crises. The two studies are based on countries that have
common business philosophies. Beyond that, Japan is the largest and the wealthiest of the Asian
economies; Korea is the third-largest. The Samyang Foods Company case focuses on the virtues
of prompt, forthright response to a corporate dilemma; that of Showa Denko K.K., which has as
much export business as it has domestic business, exemplifies the dilemma of a company caught
between two competing legal and social environments. Showa settled lawsuits differently abroad
and within its own country, in effect ignoring the health needs of local consumers. Unlike
Samyang, Showa did not tell its story through a proactive risk communications program, which,
as Arnstein notes,[55] has the potential to rebuild public trust in a company.

Even though social responsibility in Asia is still in its infancy and consumer protection
laws in Korea and Japan are not as protective of consumers as U.S. laws, Samyang
accommodated the immediate and long-range interests of its consumers. In spite of the
absence of product liability laws, South Korea's largest manufacturer of Ramen saw the
necessity of thinking *both* long range and ethically; a good step now begets better consumer-
company relationships in the future. Shortly after Samyang was absolved, on appeal, of any
wrongdoing, its president said: "I do not plan to sue for damages. It is my hope and belief
that, through this ruling of not guilty, our reparation would come from consumers' regained
trust toward Samyang."

On the other hand, the absence of strict product liability protections in Japan meant
that Showa did not have legal liability to individual consumers. In effect, consumers were
exploited in an ethical sense for the pecuniary advantage of Showa.

All organizations of the next millennium, however, will place more emphasis on their quest for continual product improvement, rapid research and development, and reduced time-to-market turnover. An increasingly dynamic marketing environment that requires corporate strategic responses to crises will be even more of a litmus test of the corporate social credibility and culture of the next century than it is today.

E N D N O T E S

1. Bivins, T. H., "A Systems Model for Ethical Decision Making in Public Relations," *Public Relations Review* 18 (1992), pp 365–383.

2. McElreath, M. P., *Managing Systematic and Ethical Public Relations* (Dubuque, IA: Wm. C. Brown, 1993).

3. Evans, J. R., and B. Berman, *Marketing,* 3rd ed. (New York: Macmillan, 1987).

4. Bivins, T. H., "A Theory-Based Approach to Public Relations Ethics," *Journalism Educator* 17 (1991), pp. 39–41.

5. Frey, L. R., C. H. Botan, P. G. Friedman, and G. L. Kreps, *Investigating Communication: An Introduction to Research Methods* (Englewood Cliffs, NJ: Prentice Hall, 1991), pp. 209–210.

6. Kelley, L., A. Whatley, R. Worthley, and H. Lie, "The Role of the Ideal Organization in Comparative Management: A Cross-Cultural Perspective of Japan & Korea." In *Management Behind Industrialization: Readings in Korean Business,* D-K. Kim and L. Kim, eds. (Seoul: Korea University Press, 1989), pp. 253–271.

7. Chang, C-S., "Comparative Analysis of Management Systems: Korea, Japan, and the United States." In *Management Behind Industrialization: Readings in Korean Business,* D-K. Kim and L. Kim, eds. (Seoul: Korea University Press, 1989), pp. 231–252.

8. Ibid.

9. Pascale, R.T., and A. G. Athos, *The Art of Japanese Management: Applications for American Executives* (New York: Simon and Schuster, 1981).

10. Pegels, C. C., *Japan vs. The West* (Boston: Kluwer, 1984).

11. Lewin, A. Y., T. Sakano, C. U. Stephens, and B. Victor, "Corporate Citizenship in Japan: Survey Results from Japanese Firms," *Journal of Business Ethics* 14 (1995), pp. 83–101.

12. Ibid.

13. Pasquero, J., "Comparative Research: The Case for Middle-Range Methodologies." In *Research in Corporate Social Performance: A Research Annual,* L. E. Preston, ed. (Greenwich, CT: Jai Press, 1988), pp. 181–209.

14. Aupperle, K. E., A. B. Carroll, and J. D. Hatfield, "An Empirical Examination of the Relationship between Corporate Social Responsibility and Profitability," *Academy of Management Journal* 28 (1985), pp. 446–463.

15. Abratt, R., and D. Sacks, "The Marketing Challenge: Towards Being Profitable and Socially Responsible," *Journal of Business Ethics* 7 (1988), pp. 497–508.

16. Boroughs, D. L., "The Bottom Line on Ethics," *U.S. News & World Report* (March 20, 1995), pp. 61–66.

17. Clarkson, M. B. E., "Corporate Social Performance in Canada, 1976–86." In *Research in Corporate Social Performance: A Research Annual,* L. E. Preston, ed. (Greenwich, CT: Jai Press, 1988), pp. 241–265.

18. Davis, J. J., "Good Ethics Is Good for Business: Ethical Attributions and Response to Environmental Advertising," *Journal of Business Ethics* 13 (1994), pp. 873–885.

19. Lydenberg, S. D., A. T. Marlin, and S. O. Strub, *Rating America's Corporate Conscience* (Reading, MA: Addison-Wesley, 1986).

20. Friedman, M., "The Social Responsibility of Business Is to Increase Its Profits," *The New York Times Magazine* (September 13, 1970).

21. Carson, T., "Friedman's Theory of Corporate Social Responsibility, *Business & Professional Ethics Journal* 12 (1993), pp. 3–32.

22. National Research Council, *Improving Risk Communication* (Washington, DC: National Research Council, 1989), p. 21.

23. Fink, S., *Crisis Management: Planning for the Inevitable* (New York: AMACOM, 1986).

24. Carney, A., and A. Jorden, "Prepare for Business-Related Crises," *Public Relations Journal* 49, no. 8 (August 1993), pp. 34–35.

25. Yang, S-H., "Overexcitement of Nonexperts Like Prosecutors Cause Consumers to Be Confused," *Weekly Chosun* (December 3, 1989), pp. 48–51.

26. Daft, R. L., K. R. Bettenhausen, and B. B. Tyler, "Implications of Top Managers' Communication Choices for Strategic Decisions." In *Organizational Change and Redesign: Ideas and Insights for Improving Performance,* G. P. Huber and W. H. Glick, eds. (New York: Oxford University Press, 1993), pp. 112–146.

27. Higgins, R. B., and J. Diffenbach, "Communicating Corporate Strategy—The Payoffs and the Risks," *Long Range Planning* 22 (1989) pp. 133–139.

28. Carroll, A. B., "A Three-Dimensional Conceptual Model of Corporate Performance," *The Academy of Management Review* 4 (1979), p. 500.

29. Mitroff, I. I., and C. M. Pearson, *Crisis Management: A Diagnostic Guide for Improving Your Organization's Crisis-Preparedness* (San Francisco: Jossey-Bass, 1993), pp. 115, 117.

30. Suguro, T., "Showa Denko Suffers from Health Damage Suits," *Tokyo Business Today* (March 1991), p. 6.

31. Abelson, R., "Killer Acids," *Forbes* (September 2, 1991), pp. 144–145.

32. Shapiro, S., "L-Tryptophan and Eosinophilia-Myalgia Syndrome," *The Lancet* 343 (1994), pp. 1035–1036.

33. Shapiro, S., "L-Tryptophan and Eosinophilia-Myalgia Syndrome," *The Lancet* 344 (1994), pp. 871–818.

34. Slutsker, L., F. C. Hoesly, L. Miller, L. P. Williams, J. C. Watson, and D. W. Fleming, "Eosinophilia-Myalgia Syndrome Associated with Exposure to Tryptophan from a Single Manufacturer," *The Journal of the American Medical Association,* 264 (1990), pp. 213–217.

35. Eidson, M., R. M. Philen, C. M. Sewell, R. E. Voorhees, and E. M. Kilbourne, "L-Tryptophan and Eosinophilia-Myalgia Syndrome: Authors' Reply," *The Lancet,* 343 (1994), pp. 1036–1037.

36. Kamb, M. L., J. J. Murphy, J. L. Jones, J. C. Caston, K. Nederlof, L. F. Horney, L. A. Swygert, H. Falk, and E. M. Kilbourne, "Eosinophilia-Myalgia Syndrome in L-Tryptophan-Exposed Patients," *The Journal of the American Medical Association,* 267 (1992), pp. 77–82.

37. Clauw, D. J., D. A. Flockhart, W. Mullins, P. Katz, and T. A. Medsger, "Eosinophilia-Myalgia Syndrome not Associated with the Ingestion of Nutritional Supplements," *The Journal of Rheumatology,* 21 (1994), pp. 2385–2387.

38. Patmas, M. A., "Eosinophilia-Myalgia Syndrome not Associated with L-Tryptophan," *New Jersey Medicine,* 89 (1992), pp. 285-286.

39. Mergenhagen, P., "Product Liability: Who Sues?" *American Demographics* 17 (1995), pp. 48–54.

40. Settle, S. M., and Spigelmyer, *Product Liability: A Multibillion-Dollar Dilemma* (New York: American Management Association, 1984).

41. Sethi, S. P., *Japanese Business and Social Conflict: A Comparative Analysis of Response Patterns with American Business* (Cambridge, MA: Ballinger, 1975).

42. Lewin, A. Y., et al., "Corporate Citizenship in Japan."

43. Ibid.

44. Mafune, Y., "Corporate Social Performance and Policy in Japan." In *Research in Corporate Social Performance: A Research Annual*, L. E. Preston, ed. (Greenwich, CT: Jai Press, 1988), pp. 291–303.

45. Paul, K., "The Impact of U.S. Sanctions on Japanese Business in South Africa: Further Developments in the Internationalization of Social Activism," *Business and Society* 31 (1992), pp. 51–57.

46. Taka, I., "Business Ethics: A Japanese View." In *Business Ethics: Japan and the Global Economy,* T. W. Dunfee and Y. Nagayasu, eds. (Dordrecht, The Netherlands: Kluwer, 1993), pp. 23–59.

47. Watanabe, K., "Not Just Profits," *Look Japan* (February 1992), pp. 14–15.

48. Taka, I., "Business Ethics."

49. "Will Tokyo's Ethics Invade Wall Street?" *Business and Society Review* (Winter 1992), pp. 10–18.

50. Taka, I., and W. D. Foglia, "Ethical Aspects of Japanese Leadership Style," *Journal of Business Ethics* 13 (1994), 135–148.

51. Ibid.

52. Ibid.

53. Taka, I., and W. D. Foglia, "Ethical Aspects."

54. Clarkson, M. B. E., "Corporate Social Performance," p. 263.

55. Arnstein, C., "How Companies Can Rebuild Credibility and Public Trust," *Public Relations Journal* 50 (1994), pp. 28–29.

CHAPTER 18

Making the CEO the Chief Communications Officer: Counseling Senior Management

John D. Graham
Chairman and Chief Executive Officer
Fleishman-Hillard, Inc.

Public relations has reached a significant turning point in its evolution as a profession. In today's highly competitive business environment, with more public attention focused on business actions and their consequences, public relations has the opportunity to become one of the key management disciplines of the future. The ability of the PR profession to meet this management challenge will depend heavily on the success with which public relations counselors can perform a crucial function: *advising senior executives in protecting, managing, and marketing an organization's single most important asset, its reputation.*

Data show that business leaders recognize the importance of closely guarding corporate reputation. A 1994 Opinion Research Corporation survey showed that 90 percent of the business executives polled (two-fifths of whom were senior executives) agreed strongly that a company's reputation is a vital corporate asset that must be maintained as carefully as any other asset. This sentiment has remained virtually unchanged since the time of a similar survey taken a decade before. The poll also indicated that most executives believe a good corporate image has a direct impact on a company's profitability by influencing the buying decisions of consumers.[1]

As more and more corporations around the world come to rely on public relations professionals to guide them through the complex communications issues they face in an increasingly global marketplace, those professionals must have expertise in strategic and analytical skills as well as tactical tools. For example, they must be "futurists" in their thinking—able to anticipate with reasonable accuracy the potential impact of trends and issues on corporate growth and profitability. They must also have a broad perspective on their entire industry (and related industries), rather than a narrow focus on a few companies. They must be mindful of the consumer's growing influence over corporate behavior, and be able to interpret how that influence will affect specific products and services. They must align communications plans with the organization's present and future objectives, and be willing and able to change accordingly. At the same time, public relations executives must have the ability to respond rapidly in handling an unforeseen crisis or in supporting a marketing effort.

To provide the strategic counsel senior management requires, these skills—as well as good judgment—are fundamental attributes. PR executives will be positioned to engender conditions for success if they possess these characteristics:

- Public relations professionals will have access to the highest levels of management, thereby enhancing their effectiveness in managing the organization's reputation.

- Senior executives will recognize public relations as a key management discipline—one that is distinguished by the need to cut across all management functions to address a range of issues affecting the corporation's reputation.

- The PR function, in a broad sense, will be credible and will command the respect of other management functions within a corporation.

Increasingly, public relations will be called upon to interpret external developments and formulate plans to address a broad range of issues. As a result, public relations executives must understand the major issues and trends confronting business and society, and be able to effectively communicate their long-term implications to management.

The key issues of concern today will remain key issues throughout the decade: global competition, technological innovation, the environment, and regulatory developments at the local, national, and international levels. These issues and others (see Figure 18–1) will persist and will command higher visibility and greater priority in communications plans.

A STRATEGIC APPROACH TO COUNSELING SENIOR MANAGEMENT

The challenge confronting the public relations profession is partly a function of technology and changing times. Media coverage of business has increased exponentially to the extent that business now operates under a level of scrutiny that would have been unthinkable a decade ago. As recently as the late 1970s, for example, business news primarily focused on relatively mundane, traditional areas such as the occasional labor dispute, the rise and fall of stock prices, new products and services, and largely uneventful stockholder meetings. Overall, much of the attention devoted to business was neither significant nor sophisticated, and few people objected to this relatively uncomplicated state of affairs.

Today, the situation is far different. Scores of publications are devoted exclusively to business news. Corporate actions that once were small items on the business pages now appear on the front pages of newspapers. Those actions, and the attention focused on them, can have profound effects on a company's reputation. Some chief executive officers—for example, Chrysler's Lee Iacocca during the 1980s, and, later, Michael Eisner of Walt Disney and William Gates of Microsoft—have attained a degree of celebrity status rivaling that of movie stars. Other business figures, such as Michael Milken or Ivan Boesky, achieved notoriety of a different kind.

Television viewers frequently find that news coverage of business begins early in the day, filling a combined total of two hours or more of programming time on network, cable, and local channels. More important, reporters for both print and electronic media approach business in a more informed way than ever before, asking more pertinent questions on a broader range of business issues than would have been imagined a generation ago.

F I G U R E 18–1

Key Issues Affecting Public Relations

- Corporate governance, composition of corporate boards, shareholder activism
- Global competition, international and offshore operations
- Environmental protection
- Product liability
- Social responsibility—domestically and internationally
- Reengineering the corporation
- Technology
- Information management
- Workforce education and training, professional development
- Workforce satisfaction
- Labor-management relations
- Women and minorities in management
- Hiring and promotion, equal opportunity, managing diversity
- Mergers and acquisitions
- CEO compensation
- Ethics
- Regulatory issues
- Healthcare management and costs
- Retirement benefit costs
- Total quality management (TQM)

At the same time, consumer activist movements have grown considerably in the United States, while in Europe, groups such as environmentalists have attained a notable degree of political power. Overall, business activists have successfully brought pressure to bear on a wide variety of companies and industries in areas such as product liability, environmental responsibility, labor relations, nutrition and health. Though this development has been viewed as both a blessing and a bane, it has nonetheless given rise to an entirely new set of concerns in corporations worldwide. Activist pressures have afforded public relations professionals an uncommon opportunity to develop ways to more closely and responsibly align the goals of society and the goals of business.

Today, the public is better informed about business organizations, business issues, and how corporations are managed. Interest in the business world has been driven by the public's expanded participation in shareholder ownership and by employees' heightened concern about issues ranging from job security to changing benefits. This level of sophistication in the general population has greatly altered the ways in which businesses seek to achieve their fundamental objectives. Surveys of public opinion lend credence to the fact that public approval increasingly is necessary if sales are to be maintained, plants are to be sited for construction or relocated, legislation is to be passed or defeated, or shareholders are to feel comfortable holding a company's stock.

An Organizational Structure for Reputation Management

As a result of these public pressures, executives have become increasingly aware of the importance of corporate reputation as a bottom-line asset—an asset that must be managed carefully and given as much professional attention as other corporate assets. Corporations that acknowledge this fact must be willing to let their corporate structures evolve in ways that depart from traditional models in order to accommodate the task of managing reputation.

The most useful organizational model suggests a chief executive officer at the top of the organization, and an Office of the Chief Executive consisting of several individuals who work collaboratively with the CEO. These executives should include the chief financial officer, the chief legal officer, the chief operations officer, and the chief communications officer (CCO). The first three individuals are, for the most part, already in today's corporate boardrooms helping to make decisions. But the fourth person is not, in many cases, and that situation must change if a company is serious about the importance of its reputation.

Every time a significant corporate decision must be made, these four people should sit down with the CEO and review its ramifications. These are decisions that involve more than just marketing issues or obvious external forces; they involve actions such as changing the capital structure, opening or closing a plant, laying off employees, choosing new outside directors, introducing new products, or changing a major supplier. The legal officer discusses the legal implications of the action, the operations officer details the operational implications, the financial officer deals with the financial implications, and the chief communications officer discusses the implications for the company's reputation among a wide range of audiences. This suggests a primary responsibility to *protect* the company's reputation. More important, the CCO has the unique ability to serve as a catalyst for positive change as a result of the additional responsibility to *enhance* a company's reputation among a wide range of audiences.

The purpose of this structure is not merely to confer status on the position of the chief communications officer. On the contrary, its purpose is to assure that major corporate actions, including potential crises, are communicated properly. Unless management gives corporate reputation the type of consideration given many issues of equal importance, damaging news will be standard fare in newspaper headlines—disasters such as the Exxon Valdez oil spill, for example, or the Bophal catastrophe, or product recalls, ethical violations, forced resignations, and other negative issues and events. Moreover, unless companies recognize the value of the corporate communications function, consumers and the general public will become increasingly skeptical of business and its ability to act responsibly.

This structure is only one organizational possibility. Many companies continue to debate who should fill the role of the chief communications officer. Some believe that the CEO should fill that role. This would be a difficult task, however, given the fact that the CEO also has to take some responsibility for financial, legal, and operational decisions. It would be difficult for the CEO to be guided by the requirements of those perspectives *and*, at the same time, take into consideration the wide range of perspectives that enter from the public relations point of view.

In a general sense, however, the CEO must be considered the de facto chief communications officer of a corporation. The CEO is viewed not only as the individual who makes the final decisions regarding a company's operations—everything from what and where it manufactures, to the services it provides, to marketing, advertising, acquisitions, divestitures, etc.—but also as the individual who sets the tone for the corporation. A CEO cannot avoid this role. As a result, the job of a public relations executive is influenced by at least two factors: (1) the unique communications needs of the individual organization, and (2) the degree to which a CEO wishes to emphasize his or her role as the CCO.

The Role of the Chief Communications Officer

Given the inherent importance of the CEO as the chief communicator of a corporation, the appropriate role for the CCO is twofold. First, he or she is the person who brings news to top management or to the boardroom of what interested third parties are saying about the company. In this sense, the CCO provides intelligence and counseling based on the perceptions of others that will help the CEO make the right decisions. Second, the CCO's role is to communicate to internal audiences a central message: that everyone in the organization—from the top down, throughout the company—has a responsibility for assuring that the company's reputation is maintained and enhanced, just as they have a responsibility for helping the company meet its operational and financial goals. This is the direction in which public relations is headed—and must continue to move.

In this regard, it is useful to contrast the public relations functions with the marketing function. Clearly, marketing is much narrower in scope than public relations, except when it is in the form of an integrated marketing communications program designed to reach multifaceted, multitiered audiences. Marketing typically focuses on one audience, the consumer, and on only one transaction or a single stage of the commercial process in which goods change hands from the company to the consumer. Public relations, however, involves many diverse audiences: employees, stockholders, local communities, governments, consumers, and the general public (whether or not they buy the company's products or services). Public relations has the flexibility to focus on those audiences that are appropriate to a company's priorities and objectives.

Marketing professionals often argue that the consumer must always be the most important audience, because if consumers do not buy the company's products or services, then the company will cease to exist. This is a superficially attractive argument, but it focuses on only one corner of the picture. For example, if employees are on strike, then the company's ability to serve customers will be at risk. If your products are being boycotted, then the existence of your company is in jeopardy. If shareholders and lenders lose confidence in the company, its ability to raise debt and equity may be significantly impaired. If federal, state, or local governments restrain you from operating a plant or selling your products or services, then you essentially do not have a company.

Businesses must transcend the exclusively consumer-oriented focus of marketing. The marketing perspective is too narrow to serve the scope of the company's key interests. Corporations must realize that the job of reputation management involves a wide range of significant perspectives, and the concerns of marketing are only one slice—though an important slice—of the issues public relations professionals must deal with.

This viewpoint is supported by the previously mentioned Opinion Research 1994 survey measuring the importance of having a favorable corporate image in the eyes of various publics. Executives stated that shareholders are the most important group that must have a favorable image of a company (79 percent), followed by management-level employees (73 percent), and securities analysts (66 percent). Overall, emphasis was placed on the business and financial community whereas a decade earlier, management-level employees (77 percent), the general public (67 percent), and corporate shareholders (66 percent) headed the list of most-important publics.[2]

F I G U R E   18–2

The CEO as Visible Symbol

Strategy: Spotlight the CEO as an exemplar, leader, visionary, and embodiment of the organization.

Tactics: Focus all communications to all audiences on the CEO as the spokesperson or as the symbol for the organization.

Advantages:

- The CEO provides ease of control in communications.
- The media love personalities.
- Investor audiences like to see and get a sense of the CEO.
- A strong individual personality most easily creates a strong personality for the organization.
- Employee audiences react strongly and positively to an individual they want to follow.
- Personalities are unique and provide an inherent differentiation from other organizations.

Disadvantages:

- This structure most often used as a strategy when little else is possible and/or when a commodity product or institution is involved; the structure itself may convey that impression.
- Media can turn on a person quickly and, thus, on an institution.
- Investor audiences want a sense of depth beyond the single individual.
- If anything happens to the CEO, transitions are difficult (internally and externally).

TACTICAL MODELS OF REPUTATION MANAGEMENT

The preceding discussion advocated the importance of the CEO as the chief communicator of a corporation. That model structure is described in Figure 18–2.

In this prototype, the communications strategy of a company involves spotlighting the chief executive officer as the visionary leader who serves as the embodiment of the organization. All communications to all audiences are focused on the CEO as the spokesperson or symbol of the entire organization.

This approach has several clear advantages, not the least of which is simplicity: it involves a single individual and one, straightforward approach. It also appeals to the media's tendency to focus on personalities, as well as the general preference of investor audiences to see and hear a company's chief executive officer. An additional strength of this approach is the fact that a strong individual personality helps to create a distinctive personality for the entire organization, with the further benefit that employees will react strongly and positively to a charismatic leader whom they want to follow. The personality approach also lends uniqueness to a company, providing differentiation from other companies.

Disadvantages of this model are its frequent use as a strategy when little else sets the company apart, and when a company's products are fundamentally not unique. Over the years, this has been the case, at least in part, in the American automobile industry. Further drawbacks of this approach are the fact that the media can quickly grow disenchanted with a personality—and consequently an organization—and cautious investor audiences usually want to see depth beyond the leader of a corporation. Moreover, if anything happens to the CEO, it is difficult to provide a transition for internal or external audiences.

F I G U R E   18–3

The Executive Team Model

Strategy: Spotlight the senior executive team for its unified vision and its depth and breadth of expertise and experience.

Tactics: For major media and internal audiences, focus on the whole team; use individual members to deal with appropriate individual audiences (the CFO with the financial community, the chief scientific officer with technical audiences, etc.).

Advantages:

- Time and energy commitment are spread over a group of people.
- The team approach makes use of both individual and collective strengths.
- The team still involves the CEO as a leader and visionary.
- The team provides an external image of institutionalized excellence.

Disadvantages:

- A team can be faceless at a time when faces are needed most.
- Getting time and energy commitment from a group of people can be difficult.
- Team-developed strategy can be conducive to internal political jockeying and/or Kremlin-like internal speculation.
- The company may be difficult to differentiate from other organizations within an industry if it includes many similar organizations with similar management teams.
- A team approach requires open discussion of business strategy (which may not be welcomed) and proof of problem-solving successes (which may not be available).
- The team model works best when there is external endorsement from the financial community of management's capabilities.

A number of other models are worth examining for their differing methods of positioning a company's top management and promoting corporate reputation. These approaches may not necessarily be employed in a pure form, but may be mixed and blended to one extent or another.

The Executive Team model (Figure 18–3) spotlights the executive team as a whole both for its unified vision for a company and for its depth and breadth of experience and management expertise. Tactically, this approach focuses on all top executives as a team, and uses individual members to deal with appropriate individual audiences. Advantages of this model are that it is time efficient as a result of spreading commitments over a number of people, it makes use of individual and collective strengths, it still involves the CEO as a leader and visionary, and it provides an external image of institutionalized excellence.

Disadvantages of the Executive Team model are that it is faceless (especially at times when faces are needed most), it can prove difficult in getting time and energy commitments from a group of people, it can be conducive to internal political jockeying and Kremlin-like speculation, and it may not be sufficiently differentiated from other companies with similar management teams. Perhaps more important, the approach can involve discussion of business strategy that some companies may not want to engage in, and proof of problem-solving successes that may or may not be available. The Executive Team model generally

The Products and Services Model

Strategy: Emphasize what the organization is doing, rather than who is doing it.

Tactics: Focus on customer successes with existing products and services and on new products and services.

Advantages:

- Products and services are tangible and, potentially, dramatic.
- Focus on products and services provides a clear sense of the present and an expectation of the future.
- The model allows for third-party verification of credibility through case studies and endorsements.

Disadvantages:

- Investor audiences need individuals as well as products and accomplishments.
- The media prefer faces to embody accomplishments.
- R&D people are often poor at public relations.
- Heavy reliance on customers for credibility can be risky and is often cumbersome.
- A product emphasis requires publicizing innovations at the time of a patent filing or at commercialization, when they have less news value than at other times.

works best when there is external endorsement of management's capabilities from the financial community.

An approach that avoids the issues of personality altogether is the Products and Services model (Figure 18–4), which emphasizes what a company does rather than who is doing it. The approach focuses on customer successes with existing products and services, as well as on new products and services.

The positive aspects of this model are that products and services are tangible in the sense that they are used by or affect customers, and those products and services potentially can be used to tell dramatic stories. It also provides a clear sense of the present and future via the company's goods and services, and allows for third-party credibility through case studies, endorsements, and similar testimonials. The drawbacks are that the approach could become faceless among general or investor audiences, that research and development people who may be called on to discuss products often are not good at PR, and that a heavy reliance on customers for credibility can be risky and cumbersome. The approach can also be time sensitive, since it may require publicizing innovations at the time of patent filing or commercialization, which may afford less news value than could be attained at other times.

The History as a Guide to the Future model (Figure 18–5) makes use of the successful history of a company as an implicit predictor of future performance. The approach focuses on past successes and the individuals still with the corporation who are creating future successes. The advantages of this method are that past successes tend to provide a sense of third-party credibility, that it sustains or builds a strong internal sense of self for the organization. The approach also can be orchestrated to indicate future direction for the company, implicitly or explicitly. On the other hand, heavy reliance on this historical

F I G U R E 18–5

The History as a Guide to the Future Model

Strategy: Use the (successful) history of an organization as an implicit predictor of its future.

Tactics: Focus on past successes and on the responsible individuals who are still with the organization and who are creating the success of the future.

Advantages:

- Past successes provide third-party credibility.
- Success sustains, or builds, a strong internal sense of self.
- History can be orchestrated to indicate future directions, implicitly or explicitly.

Disadvantages:

- Heavy reliance on "Trust us, we've done it before" is risky in anything but the short term.
- The strategy essentially looks backwards.
- The company needs an established, celebrated past with few, if any, difficulties.
- The approach requires that an organization have a view of the future that it wants to talk about, in order to provide context for expectations of future achievements.
- The model may not allow adequate differentiation from other successful peer organizations in an industry characterized by rapid, serial innovation.

approach is risky in anything but the short term, since trust based on past performance has inherent limits. It is also a strategy that essentially looks backwards, and requires an established, celebrated past with few, if any, difficulties. At least implicitly, this method requires that an organization have a view of the future that it wants to talk about, so as to provide a context for expectations of future achievements. It also may not afford a company adequate differentiation from successful peer companies in an industry characterized by rapid, serial innovation.

Another approach that avoids any focus on personalities and individuals is the Financial Performance model (Figure 18–6), which includes financial messages in all communications, even those which are not obviously about financial performance issues. This method, which is essentially quantitative—a statistical variant of the History as a Guide model—is best suited to organizations that must concentrate on investor audiences which are likely to prefer this approach. It is worth noting that external validation and positive comparisons with peer companies are easier to obtain with this approach than with qualitative approaches. However, a drawback is that a company must have smooth, predictable financial trend lines to make this approach successful, or retribution by critics will be swift. This method also has little attraction as an internal communications device, and can, in fact, be counterproductive among employees. Moreover, it ignores what a company does—a questionable approach, given the fact that financial performance is essentially a result of what the company does and how it is managed.

A final method takes a broad, panoramic approach to managing a company's reputation by spotlighting the business strategy and vision of the company as a proxy for the industry as a whole. The Defining/Redefining an Industry model (Figure 18–7) focuses on the larger environmental context for strategic decisions, and operates within it to offer

F I G U R E   18–6

The Financial Performance Model

Strategy: Concentrate on financial performance of the organization and of its financial supporters.

Tactics: Include financial messages in all communications, even those which are not obviously about financial performance matters.

Advantages:

- Investor audiences may say they prefer this approach.
- Unlike other approaches, this one is essentially quantitative.
- External validation and positive comparisons with peer organizations are easier than with qualitative approaches.

Disadvantages:

- The company must have smooth, predictable financial trend lines, or retribution will be swift.
- This is a statistical variant of the History as a Guide model.
- This approach does not work as an internal communications device, and can be counterproductive.
- It ignores what a company does—after all, financial performance is not what a company does, but a result of what it does.

predictions for future directions of aspects of the business. The approach has the advantage of conveying vision and leadership, appeals to the media's tendency to look ahead, and is safe insofar as predictions about the company and the industry can be wrong as long as they are thoughtful (and well thought out). This method also allows a company to speak beyond itself—a useful device when news is either neutral or bad—and gives employees a sense of pride in being part of a company that sets the pace for an entire industry.

Cautions involved in this approach include the fact that it requires legitimate content for it to work, complete confidence in the company's strategy and its vision for the future, and underpinnings of actual business success to be credible. It also can be relatively short-lived in its effectiveness, since a company that sets itself up as a proxy for an industry can be an easy target for criticism in an environment of continuous change or negative results.

In the real world, any company consciously—or, more usually, unconsciously—uses a mix of strategies to communicate about itself, with one model being dominant and another, or others, being subordinate themes. For example, one of the best examples of the CEO model— Chrysler's positioning of Lee Iacocca—used the CEO very strongly as the spokesperson and exemplar, but did so with a heavy dose of new products to back up what the CEO was saying.

For many companies, the most effective strategy would seem to be a slight modification of the Defining/Redefining an Industry model. It allows—actually, demands—the use of the whole executive team, with the CEO as an important voice and the key player. However, it also allows each member of that team to be visible for his or her important audiences. In addition, this approach allows each individual to stress what is important in his or her own area—financial performance, new research breakthroughs, new customer products and services, and so forth.

F I G U R E   18–7

The Defining/Redefining an Industry Model

Strategy: Spotlight the business strategy and vision of the organization as a proxy for the industry as a whole.

Tactics: Focus on the larger environmental context for strategic decisions; offer predictions for future directions of aspects of the business.

Advantages:

- The approach conveys vision and leadership.
- Media love to look ahead.
- Safe. Predictions can be wrong, as long as they're thoughtful.
- It allows a company to speak beyond itself—a useful device when news is neutral or bad.
- It gives employees a sense of pride in being part of a company that sets the pace for an entire industry category.

Disadvantages:

- The method needs legitimate content to work.
- It requires confidence in the strategy and a vision of the future.
- It requires underpinnings of actual company business success to be credible.
- The effect can be short-lived, and can make a company an easy target in an environment of continuous change (e.g., "So what will they do for an encore?").

What must be made clear in this approach, particularly internally, is that the group is, in fact, a team, not a huddle of people jockeying for power. Another implicit factor is the role of the CEO as team captain, team manager, and overall strategic visionary.

The key to making this modified approach work is the corporate communications function. With the concurrence and active support of the CEO, corporate communications collects information internally about the substance of what can and should be communicated, and collects information externally about where and to whom that information should be communicated. Then, the corporate communications function determines (or, at least, strongly recommends) who should take what opportunity. Only through this kind of coordinating role can a company avoid a confusion of voices and messages.

THE FUTURE: CEOs WILL HELP SET COMMUNICATIONS AGENDAS

A company's reputation—and sometimes its very survival—depends on how well it communicates with key audiences, including stockholders, the financial community, governments, business groups and partners, suppliers, the media, consumers, the general public, and others. This is especially true at a time when corporations are under increased public scrutiny. Strange as it may sound, it is no longer good enough for a company to be ethical and forthright in its dealings; it must be perceived as such. As a result, many companies are investing in communications efforts which ensure that their good deeds are communicated to the right audiences.

In the future, corporations will face increased challenges in maintaining a positive corporate image, but the benefits of having such an image will also increase. Those companies with a strongly favorable image are likely to have an advantage over those that do not. Communicating quickly and efficiently with a diverse range of audiences will be more important—and more difficult to manage—than ever before. Modern technology assures that news on one side of the globe is news virtually everywhere in the world within seconds. And in an increasingly sophisticated business arena, there is more interaction among audiences than has historically been the case.

Corporate management increasingly realizes that important audiences can no longer be treated merely as communications targets; they must be treated as partners in the communications process. This positive change in objectives has significant consequences for the public relations executive who must analyze, understand, and approach key audiences with arguments that are meaningful and clearly understood.

CEOs in the future are likely to play a more active role in setting communications goals for their firms, as well as insisting on measurable programs to achieve those goals. Attaining the best reputation for the organization will be an asset prized by management, and more chief executives, assuming the responsibility of communicating clear visions and strong values, will set aggressive benchmarks on which to build their corporate reputation goals.

ENDNOTES

1. Opinion Research Corporation, Corporate Reputation Center, *Management Profile: The Corporate Reputation* II (June 1994).

2. Ibid.

CHAPTER 19

Excellence in Public Relations

Larissa A. Grunig, Ph.D.
Associate Professor
University of Maryland College of Journalism

THE EXCELLENCE STUDY

Excellence may well be the byword of the next generation of entry-level practitioners and students of public relations. In the 1980s, Peters and Waterman analyzed 43 top-performing organizations, looking for common management principles or practices that made these companies truly outstanding. Their book, *In Search of Excellence*[1] spawned any number of lines of inquiry seeking quality in specific realms of the organization, including public relations.

Our pursuit of excellence in public relations began a decade ago, in 1984. The Research Foundation of the International Association of Business Communicators (IABC) wanted the answers to two main questions:

1. How does public relations contribute to organizational effectiveness?
2. What is that contribution worth?

The professional society committed more than $400,000 to answering these bottom-line questions. There was one important caveat: the answers had to extend beyond the United States and be truly international.

A six-person team, of which I was a part, was selected to seek answers. The team started in a somewhat audacious way, by rephrasing or adding to the research questions posed by the IABC Foundation.

We reasoned that only *excellent* public relations programs would contribute at all to organizational effectiveness. And we knew that not all communication programs have the characteristics that Peters and Waterman (or anyone else) probably would consider high quality. Some public relations efforts—undoubtedly too many—are mediocre at best. They contribute little, if at all, to the success of the organization; they merely contribute to the income of the practitioners involved.

To complete the focus of the research, we proposed a third question: What are the characteristics of an excellent communication department? And we imposed a title on our research project that echoed the Peters and Waterman tome (and, we hoped, capitalized on the popularity of their writings!). We called it *Excellence in Public Relations and Communication Management.*[2]

The Excellence Project, as it came to be known, was led by James E. Grunig of the University of Maryland. In addition to myself, also of the University of Maryland, the team included David M. Dozier of San Diego State University; William P. Ehling, now retired from Syracuse University; Jon White of the City University in London (formerly of Mount St. Vincent's University in Halifax, Nova Scotia, Canada, and the Cranfield School of Management in the United Kingdom); and Fred C. Repper, consultant and retired vice president of public relations for Gulf States Utilities in Texas. Over the years, we were assisted by a succession of able, highly motivated graduate assistants and former students whose perspectives and hard work have been invaluable.

The research described in this chapter was not developed from any single perspective—not the academic perspective nor the industry perspective, and not the American or even North American perspective. Although we were constrained by our lack of fluency in other languages, we did include in our research design a sample of organizations in the English-speaking United States, Canada, and the United Kingdom. The project was developed and conducted not only by established scholars in the field of public relations but by a seasoned practitioner as well. This concern for cultural pluralism and for both the applied and basic nature of the research should make the findings compelling. Perhaps most important, readers should discover important implications for communication policy and practice.

The research speaks most directly to the strategic management of the communication function. Through an exhaustive review of relevant literature and subsequent field work, the researchers became convinced that certain generic principles of public relations management supersede geographical or cultural barriers. Each country or culture may require specific applications of those general tenets.[3] However, the general theory of public relations that resulted from this ten-year, three-country study should apply throughout the globe. The theory helps explain the current practice of public relations and—significantly—it points toward a development of the field that should enhance its integrity, its professionalism, and its effectiveness.

If the project were developed today, it might have been labeled "quality." When the project was defined, the buzz word was "excellence." By whatever label, though, the research evaluates the best possible practices.

What, exactly, are the qualities that distinguish the best public relations programs, the best practitioners, and the best organizational cultures in which to practice public relations? The review of relevant literature took us into the journals of fields as disparate as marketing, anthropology, psychology, sociology, business management, women's studies, communication, and philosophy. That conceptualization, which we initially envisioned as a modest few pages, resulted in a book of almost 700 pages.[4]

Definitions

An overview of some of the key terms would be helpful at this point. In this study, we do not distinguish among "public relations," "communication management," and "organizational communication." These terms encompass programs traditionally and more narrowly defined as media relations, government relations or public affairs, employee communication, financial relations, product publicity, community relations, and so forth. The key element of our definition of public relations, in addition to the breadth of its scope, is the notion of *managed* communication. To the Excellence team, then, all of these concepts refer to the *management of communication between an organization and its publics*.[5]

We go on to say that, because of this managerial emphasis, the head of public relations must function with the organization's group of senior managers. Sociologists call this power elite the *dominant coalition*. They reason that today's organization typically is too large and complex to be run by a single (even charismatic) leader. Thus it is the group, or coalition, that makes policy decisions. Sociologists astutely have avoided calling the group simply "the big bosses" because "boss" suggests position power, or influence simply by virtue of someone's official role in the organization. We know, of course, that the typical organization is directed by both the obvious holders of power (people with job titles such as president, senior vice president, chief financial officer, and so forth) and those whose influence is less apparent but equally formidable.

We define *effectiveness* by combining several major schools of thought taken from business management and organizational sociology. We conclude that the effective organization is one that balances its own goals with the expectations of its strategic constituencies. Public relations contributes by helping reconcile those often-conflicting expectations. It does so through the development and maintenance of high-quality, long-term relationships with the publics most in a position to support or to interfere with the organization. Public relations is likely to make this contribution only when the manager of the department is a member of the dominant coalition and thus in a position to help determine appropriate goals for the organization and appropriate publics that are most strategic at the time.

The first part of the book, then, develops a basic theory of excellence in public relations along these lines. The second part describes the effective planning of communication programs, and the third part describes the characteristics of excellent public relations departments. The fourth part of the book analyzes the organizational characteristics that make excellence in public relations likely—or at least possible. The final part projects what public relations contributes to the bottom line. Throughout, we develop a model for the effective management of communication and an understanding of communication's contribution to overall organizational goals. The essence of our theory is that effective communication helps manage an organization's interdependencies with its strategic constituencies.

Each chapter within each of these parts includes propositions of the theory that grew out of our synthesis of the literature. Much to our gratification (if not surprise), each of the propositions was supported by the data we subsequently collected and analyzed. These data have been published in book form, so readers of this chapter truly are on the cutting edge of our understanding of excellence in public relations.[6]

This chapter will define each of the characteristics that we know contributes to an excellent department of public relations. It will talk about how the outstanding programs we studied got to be that way, how top management views those programs and the professionals who manage them, and what the participants in our research told us about the value of public relations to their organizations. It concludes with a discussion of the effects that excellent public relations has at both the organizational and societal levels.

Methodology

First, you need to know how we conducted the study. Only by understanding our methodological approach will you be in a position to judge the credibility of our claims.

We began our pursuit of excellence in public relations with a survey of almost 300 organizations. The sample included small-, medium-, and large-sized operations chosen purposively to represent a mix of corporations, associations, governmental agencies, and not-for-profit organizations. Some had been identified as "excellent" organizations; others were listed in such publications as the "Mis-Fortune 500." (Interestingly, some organizations appeared on both kinds of lists simultaneously.) Thus we were intent on exploring the characteristics identified in the relevant literature as likely to affect the effectiveness of public relations, rather than adopting the Peters and Waterman approach[7] of first seeking excellent companies and then trying to deduce what made them that way. We reasoned, first, that excellence was in the eye of the beholder, as evidenced by several organizations appearing on both "best" and "worst" lists. Second, a number of the companies touted in *In Search of Excellence* had gone out of business by the time we began our study. To us, this signalled the potential inappropriateness of the Peters and Waterman design for our own research. And, because each aspect of our theory has been strikingly confirmed by the data, we are convinced that our approach was well suited.

We surveyed some 5,000 people in all—chief executive officers (CEOs), communication managers, and about a dozen other employees (outside of the public relations department) in each organization. One factor that sets our study apart from most others in public relations is that we included CEOs (or some other member of the dominant coalition, if the chief executive was unable or unwilling to participate). We deemed top managers' participation imperative because of their role as cultural leaders within their organizations, and also because the power-control perspective in organizational theory suggests that members of the dominant coalition tend to determine the approach to public relations practice.

Our set of three questionnaires—one for top management, one for heads of public relations, and one for other employees—included a total of about 1,700 variables that tapped into the key attributes of communication excellence. Central to the reduction of this massive amount of survey data was factor analysis. This statistical procedure reduced those 1,700 discrete measures to a parsimonious set of about a dozen characteristics of effective public relations. These results suggested a scale of excellence measuring the kinds of programs that contribute meaningfully to organizational goals. Scores from each organization, then, were juxtaposed against this scale of excellence.

While we were analyzing these data, several graduate students from the University of Maryland, working under the direction of members of the IABC research team, were applying our survey instrument in their own countries. They explored public relations excellence in southern India,[8] Taiwan,[9] and Greece.[10] Their studies, in particular, led us to agree that the cross-cultural nature of our research would be diminished if we were to rely solely on quantitative methods. These scholars all had used a face-to-face, qualitative approach. They modified the questionnaires as necessary to convey the *sense* of the questions to practitioners whose customs, values, beliefs, norms, and language all differed from ours.

Thus the second stage of the Excellence Project was qualitative. We went back into the field to probe in greater depth a few of the 283 organizations surveyed in the initial stage. We relied primarily on long interviews, augmented by reviewing the survey data about each organization and media coverage and internal documents such as annual reports relevant to it. In some cases, we were participant observers as well.

Through this triangulation of methods, we helped determine the economic value of excellent communication departments to their organizations. We studied a smaller number of less-than-excellent organizations as well, in an attempt to gauge the cost of *not* having effective communication programs. In this second phase, we also investigated the roles and status of practitioners of different races and ethnicities, the seeming inconsistency between what CEOs reported as the value of public relations and the support they offer it, and the historical factors that led, at least in part, to programs we deemed excellent through our survey research. The two dozen organizations chosen for this kind of up-close scrutiny were as different as a cosmetics company and a state lottery, a hotel chain and a public utility, an aerospace corporation and an arts organization, the chemical industry and a real estate developer.

Our multiple-case design offered the advantage of more compelling evidence than either the single-case study or the survey.[11] Despite its strength, however, this kind of comprehensive study is rarely feasible. Only with an ample team of researchers—ours had grown to 16 members by this point—and sufficient funding can such robust research be undertaken.

Thus we were able to combine a quantitative, statistical analysis of a large number of different types and sizes of organizations with a qualitative study of a handful of both outstanding and more average organizations in three countries. Data came from top management as well as from high-ranking public relations practitioners and rank-and-file employees. The study is, in a word, comparative.

CHARACTERISTICS OF EXCELLENCE

Peters and Waterman (1982) had their eight basic principles for staying on top of the heap.[12] We developed about twice that many variables that explain effective public relations. More important, we explored the relationships among all of these characteristics. By so doing, we have created a comprehensive theory that not only describes excellence in communication management but explains how and why things work as they do. With a deep understanding of such concepts as power in public relations, the value of two-way, balanced communication, and corporate culture, we have the advantage of preparing ourselves for future challenges in the field, wherever they may be. As a "Gem of the Day" item in Ann Landers' column put it: "The person who knows how will always have a job. The person who knows *why* will always be his boss."[13]

More specifically, our initial data analysis yielded 14 main hallmarks of communication excellence.[14] We also determined the main effects that such public relations programs are likely to have. A brief discussion of each characteristic or way in which public relations should be organized, managed, and conceptualized follows. The effects of these variables will be explained along the way.

Strategic Management

Excellent public relations programs are managed strategically. Strategic departments develop programs to communicate with the publics that provide the greatest threats and opportunities to the organization. Ironically, dealing effectively with these strategic publics, also called stakeholders, ends up maximizing the organization's autonomy. Public relations contributes very concretely by helping forestall costly litigation, regulation, legislation, strikes, or pressure campaigns by activist publics that may try to interfere with the organization's goals.

Managing conflict with strategic publics, then, reduces the potential costs associated with their dissatisfaction. Participation in strategic management also elevates public relations from its traditional reactive style of responding to communication crises to a proactive, responsive style of anticipating and then helping reduce emergent conflicts.

By contrast, the operation of average departments can be explained as more historicist—or doing what they do because they always have done so. For example, the mediocre department may focus on employee relations because at some point in its history employees were the most strategic public. Managers of this kind of static program fail to conduct the kind of research or engage in the environmental scanning necessary to identify emerging publics that may prove vital to the organization's long-term viability. They may manage their own programs adequately; however, they do not tie in their departmental objectives with the larger goals of the organization. As a result, their contribution to overall organizational effectiveness is minimal.

Separation from Marketing

Public relations and marketing are both essential to organizations. In certain efforts, such as product promotion, these functions may be complementary. However, when one is sublimated to the other, the organization loses much of the value of that function. The organization may indeed end up "speaking with one voice" (often a rationale for integrating marketing, advertising, and public relations), but it is able to listen with only one ear. That is, public relations and marketing bring distinct perspectives to the organization. As a vice president of strategic planning in a chemical company described it, public relations adds unique value because it involves "the sharing of thoughts from all directions."

Marketing represents primarily the viewpoint of customers or clients. We consider public relations a broader discipline, responsible for developing relationships with consumers but also with governmental agencies, the mass media and trade press, financial publics, the community, the employees and their unions, suppliers and competitors, and—perhaps most important—special interest or activist groups. The Excellence team concluded that coordination of the two complementary functions of public relations and marketing, rather than integration, seems to provide the best working relationship between them.

Direct Reporting Relationship to Senior Management

The strategic management of public relations must be integral to the management of the overall organization. For the perspectives of the organization's diverse strategic publics to be factored into the decisions made at that top level, the head of public relations must be a part of the dominant coalition, or at least have ready (if informal) access to those powerful decision makers.

Membership in the dominant coalition, then, is an important characteristic, *but not a mandatory requirement,* of excellence in communication. This finding is a fortunate one, since we learned that few organizations—excellent or average—include their top communicators in the power elite. And only slowly, over time, does even the most expert communicator become a true part of this influential group. But gaining access to the group of players who make policy hinges on several factors, only one of which is longevity. Other key determinants include past successes in public relations (especially during crises), knowledge of the business or industry, and respect on the part of top management.

Single, Integrated Department

Public relations in the less-than-excellent organization often is splintered into discrete functions that support other departments (primarily marketing, finance, or personnel) or respond to different publics. Indeed, we found ourselves surveying several "heads of public relations"—people who managed such programs as human resources, member relations, media relations, industrial relations, public affairs or lobbying, investor relations, and community relations. These departments typically develop from an historicist, rather than strategic, direction. As a result of their fragmented structure, they cannot respond and change as the strategic nature of their publics fluctuates.

By contrast, the excellent department is an integrated one. It encompasses all communication functions and thus has the flexibility to shift its resources to respond to the inherent dynamism of today's environment. Consider the example of a metal manufacturing organization that initially scored in the bottom 12 percent of the companies we surveyed in terms of communication excellence. A new CEO with a sophisticated understanding of public relations brought all communication activities under the umbrella of a vice president of public affairs, who is a member of the dominant coalition. The new vice president is expected to play the communication manager role and does so, thus increasing significantly this organization's potential for excellence.

Two-Way Symmetrical Model

Previous research identified four typical ways in which public relations is practiced.[15] The most common model is called press agentry or publicity. It is a one-way approach that relies primarily on getting favorable publicity in the mass media. The public information model values relatively objective information disseminated from the organization to the so-called general public through mass media and other controlled media such as newsletters, brochures, and direct mail. Like press agentry, however, this approach to public relations is not based on research or strategic planning. Both of these traditional one-way models characterize the average (or worse) departments we studied.

Excellent communication programs stress two-way interaction with strategic publics. Communicators practicing these models serve as the eyes and ears of the organization. They use research and dialogue with stakeholders to "find out what's going on out there." As a result, they serve as a kind of early warning system, able to alert the organization to potential conflicts with strategic publics. (And, in the process, they establish a base for themselves in strategic planning and management decision making.)

Two-way programs may be asymmetrical, trying to convince the publics to change, or symmetrical, assuming that both the organization and its stakeholders may have to compromise and collaborate with each other. Asymmetrical public relations relies on research to develop the messages most likely to persuade the publics. Symmetrical communication, the more effective approach, uses research to manage conflict, to negotiate with publics, and to improve understanding all the way around. One immediate payoff for balanced, interactive internal communication is increased job satisfaction among employees.

Our data show that organizations ranked at or near the top of the Excellence scale typically combine elements of the two-way asymmetrical and symmetrical models. Their professionals in public relations operate from what game theorists call mixed motives—the assumption that they are advocates both for the organization that employs them and for the publics it affects. However, they tend to emphasize the more balanced, symmetrical model over the asymmetrical advocacy.

CEOs participating in our survey rated the two "non-excellent," one-way models of public relations low and the two "excellent," two-way models high. They responded most affirmatively to the statement that "the purpose of public relations is to develop mutual understanding between the management of the organization and publics the organization affects." They also told us that they believe research should be an integral part of the communication process. Heads of public relations tended to underestimate the extent to which their CEOs or the dominant coalition value this kind of excellence.

Senior Practitioner's Managerial Role

Research has established that public relations practitioners play one of two major roles in organizations. They may be *managers*, who plan and supervise communication programs, or *technicians*, who write, edit, design publications, conduct special events, and so forth.[16] Two more minor roles are the communication liaison, who facilitates communication and gives advice on communication without having real power to manage the function, and the media relations expert, who maintains close relationships with the press and prepares news releases to distribute to them.

We had proposed that excellent departments would be headed by senior managers and staffed by technicians skilled in the craft of the field. Although this proposition was supported by the data, we also discovered that there are at least two types of managers. Some merely supervise their departments. Others, a more executive type, serve at the highest level of the organization. They are senior advisers. As such, they become members of the dominant coalition or have such immediate and frequent access to this power elite that they are in a position to affect policy for the overall company.

Finally, we found that CEOs prefer their top public relations person to be a manager or communication liaison rather than a technician. A close third, however, was preference for the media relations role. We think this reflects top management's continuing preoccupation with the media, despite much evidence suggesting that the media play a marginal rather than central part in the effectiveness of most organizations.

Potential for Public Relations

Excellent public relations programs require expert practitioners. Not every communicator knows how to manage the department strategically and symmetrically. We learned that practitioners may acquire mastery of the rapidly expanding theoretical body of knowledge in this field from several sources. Many of the professionals we interviewed gained their understanding from college coursework in public relations; we predict that their numbers will increase exponentially. We are especially encouraged by the development of university programs that go beyond technical training to emphasize the managerial role and two-way models of public relations. Other participants in our research, however, relied on experience, self-study, and professional development courses.

Such workshops and programs often are sponsored by groups such as the IABC or the Public Relations Society of America (PRSA). In fact, professionalism is another aspect of what we have termed "potential" for public relations. The practitioner with a professional orientation—one who is active in professional associations, reads the literature of the field, and subscribes to its ethical norms—contributes significantly to excellence. Potential, then, hinges both on professionalism and on knowledge.

Our findings show that the typical department has less potential for excellence than for mediocrity. *Having the expertise required of a strategic manager is the single greatest determinant of communication excellence.* That expertise allows the top communicator to operate almost independently, as professionals typically do. Some management structures, as we will soon see, also lead to this kind of free rein. For example, the matrix design we observed in both an industry association and a development company requires each director to manage his or her department autonomously on communication-related issues, yet integrate the operation with the organization's overall mission through cooperation with peers in other functional areas.

Schema for Public Relations

Psychologists tell us that people use schemas to make sense of their world. A schema is roughly equivalent to the anthropologists' notion of world view. Whatever we call it, public relations practitioners and their top managements both think of or have a schema for one model of public relations. Those with an asymmetrical world view use knowledge about stakeholders to try to gain their compliance, manipulating and dominating both internal and external publics to further the goals of the dominant coalition. Those with a symmetrical world view exchange information with stakeholders in an effort to devise win-win solutions to their common problems or issues. One director of communication services for a midwestern utility described her CEO's "revolutionary" philosophy of communication—which we consider symmetrical—as "more open, up front, and honest than the company has known before." In this case, the transformation from a closed to an open schema resulted from a combination of factors: support from the top, several serious and embarrassingly visible crises, operational expertise (primarily in electrical engineering), and expert public relations counsel.

Asymmetrical world views limit the effectiveness of public relations. If, on the other hand, senior managers value symmetrical communication, the department is more likely to be excellent. Similarly, if the world view for public relations is as a technical function, then it is unlikely to be headed by a strategic manager.

Equal Opportunities

One of the most dramatic shifts we observed during our decade with the Excellence Project has been the rapid feminization of the field. Although public relations cannot be considered female dominated, it clearly is female intensive. That is, women are not represented in managerial positions to the extent that their numbers would suggest. On the other hand, women constitute about 60 percent of the practice and about 80 percent of the student population.

Because of the large and growing number of women practicing public relations, the department that discriminates against women will fail to capitalize on its human resources. (Women often are the best educated in public relations.) By contrast, excellent public relations departments develop mechanisms to help women gain the power they need to advance from the technician's role to the managerial role and to implement their knowledge of the two-way symmetrical model of public relations.

The growing multiculturalism of both the workforce and the environment means that the successful public relations department of the future will be equally heterogeneous. Without what social psychologist Karl Weick[17] called this "requisite variety," the organization will fail to consider adequately the concerns of all of its diverse stakeholders. As a senior vice president in a chemical company explained it in plain language, "If I have a communication department that is made up of all white, male, Pulitzer Prize-winning people off the *New York Times*, I might have some great writers but I'll probably have a tough time making sure all points of view are reflected."

Activism

Counterintuitive though it may be, we found that activism pushes organizations toward excellence. In fact, activism emerged as the second-greatest determinant of the value top management holds for public relations (first was providing a broad perspective both inside and outside of the organization). Coping with turbulent, complex environments requires sophisticated, strategic, two-way public relations. Activist groups put pressure on organizations; excellent public relations programs are most successful in contending with that pressure.

Consider the example of strategic, symmetrical communication resulting from a crisis in a public utility in the midwestern United States. Problems with the construction of a nuclear power plant in the 1970s led to a rude and expensive awakening for the company. Before, it had focused on the technology and engineering aspects of the business. Public protests forced the company to be sure it was "attending to perceptions of people," in the words of its top communicator. A counterpart in an insurance company held out the hope that even the *threat* of increased government regulation may spur her employer toward a stronger public relations program if it does not respond appropriately to, in particular, the issue of redlining.

Threats to organizational autonomy can come from small groups as well as from powerful government agencies. One veteran CEO who had come to appreciate the legitimacy of even the smallest groups explained: "You can be closed down or closed out by a handful of people with some placards who go down on the steps of your company and the camera comes in and they zoom that thing down as tight as they can and there are only 14 but it looks like 1,400." Listening to such groups and attending to their concerns acknowledges that all business operates under a public franchise. It also may result in a shared intelligence that, in turn, helps the organization make better decisions. The same CEO emphasized this value of involving community groups in his association: "We've learned a lot from them and we're making a lot of improvements because of public involvement." Communicating openly with activists and demonstrating a willingness to change, rather than simply trying to dominate them, also may result in an all-important credibility for the organization.

Top Management Support

CEOs who most value public relations spend more time in external communication themselves than do CEOs who value it less. Their world view for excellent public relations is exactly what our theory suggests: two-way and symmetrical. They are determined that the senior person in public relations be a strategic manager. All of this sounds very promising, until one remembers that the potential we found for public relations is, on average, low to moderate. Thus what the CEO wants and what he or she is able to hire may be vastly different.

This led us to ask what we called the "chicken or the egg" question. Which comes first—good communication, or value and support for communication that leads, in turn, to the hiring of an expert? Typically, we heard that having a skillful practitioner on board begets increasing value and support for the function. Additional factors leading to support in the somewhat mixed picture that developed include facing a crisis, having the company's performance improve, and initiatives within a company's industry association.

On balance, excellent departments are valued by the dominant coalition, and mediocre departments are not. Members of the power elite are more likely to include the senior public relations person in organizations with excellent communication initiatives than in more average programs. The most effective programs we studied were characterized by a state of equilibrium between top management's expectations for public relations and the potential of that department. Further, if the head of public relations does not understand the demands or perceptions of the dominant coalition, frustration and miscommunication are likely; excellent communication is unlikely.

The state government-run lottery we explored provides a perfect example. This organization initially ranked higher than 98 percent of the organizations we surveyed on our Excellence scale. Then, a new CEO overhauled the public relations program. He equated public relations strictly with marketing communication. As a result, he demoted the top communicator, moved her into a subordinate role in marketing, and removed her from the dominant coalition. By the time we conducted our depth interviews, the communication department had become a technical support unit for marketing and other organizational functions. Now, communication makes little or no contribution to strategic planning. The staff consists largely of "journalists in residence," capable only of practicing the public information model. Contrast this scenario with the continuing support—in fact demand—for excellent public relations from the CEO of an industry association. He said, "If you can't deal with a bilateral communication relationship, or what you call 'symmetrical,' then find another job."

Multinational companies tend to place a similarly high value on two-way communication, especially for coordinating their operations. A public relations manager for an oil company affiliate, which does business in a country apart from the parent company, described the decentralized structure that allowed for each affiliate's autonomy. Each company had a distinctly local system of internal communication, yet all needed to be linked strategically to headquarters.

Supportive Organizational Context

We conceptualized the organizational environment for public relations in four main ways: structure, culture, internal communication, and the status and treatment of women. Analysis of several questions in the survey of employees resulted in reliable indices of each of these concepts. The interrelationships among them provide strong support for the general theory articulated earlier in this chapter.

Excellent organizations have symmetrical internal systems of communication and decentralized, organic management structures that offer autonomy to their employees. The top communicator in a real estate company explained it this way: "Very open. It's a very supportive environment which will allow people to take on jobs which aren't in their job descriptions." As with most participative cultures, people in her organization are allowed to make mistakes—"even big ones once in a while"—and still feel supported. As a result, job satisfaction (both with one's own job and with the organization itself) is high. Less-excellent operations communicate more asymmetrically with employees and are both mechanical and centralized; they control decision-making at the top and fail to empower employees. Understandably, job satisfaction is low.

The culture of the excellent organization, then, is participative; the culture of the less excellent is authoritarian. The key is that excellent organizations distribute power throughout. The significance for public relations, in particular, is that it is vested with enough power to implement effective two-way programs.

Although we encountered more authoritarian than participatory cultures in our study (and we also learned that no organization is purely one type or another), we also found that organizational culture is not such a strong determinant of excellence as the literature had suggested. Thus effective communication is possible even in an environment that values such attributes as individual over collective responsibility, short- versus long-term employment, decisionmaking by authority rather than consensual process, tradition over innovation, and so forth.

In our in-depth interviews with the most- and least-excellent organizations we sampled, we were impressed with a structure that seems to lead to the most open communication of all—the matrix structure. Levels do exist within the matrix, but it is less hierarchical than most organizational configurations. As the CEO of a chemical industry association explained it: "You don't have lines and boxes, turf. What you have is grazing rights. So you have the opportunity to go over into the other guy's pasture, and that person has the opportunity to come over into yours. We share our problems and we share our conclusions."

Recall that, in theorizing about the treatment of and opportunities for women in public relations, we maintained that excellence also requires diversity in both race and gender for the organization to understand adequately the diversity in its environment. As the deputy director of an engineering research agency told us: "We don't worry as much about the numbers we have of women, Blacks, and Hispanics. The main thing is, in the process of making decisions, that we get the opinion of people and staff with different backgrounds. That way we come up with better solutions."

Thus the effective organization provides an hospitable environment for its increasingly multicultural and female workforce in all departments. The CEOs and employees we surveyed seemed to agree on all 22 aspects we measured on how women are treated in their organizations. Although top management's perceptions were at least somewhat more optimistic, we were encouraged by the general correspondence.

Both groups of respondents clearly differentiated between areas in which women are most and least supported. Taken together, the survey data suggest that equitable treatment of women (as evidenced primarily by economic equity) and programs to foster their careers (such as policies against sexual harassment and efforts to encourage women's leadership abilities) are an integral component of excellent organizations.

During lengthy conversations with interview participants, we heard how the organization intent on diversifying its workforce does so. Some relied on TQM programs, primarily to change from a masculine to a more diverse culture. Others advocated promoting from within, being aware of the special problems people of color and women may face simply because of their race or gender, developing diversity-training programs, mentoring, and making an issue out of women's concerns as a way of sensitizing top management.

Unlike treatment of women and minorities, societal culture was at best a weak discriminator between excellent and average operations. We found far more similarity than difference among the organizations in the United States, the United Kingdom, and Canada. Thus we concluded that characteristics of excellent public relations transcend national boundaries, at least in these three Anglo cultures. Our graduate students' results from Greece, Taiwan, and India, and subsequent studies by practitioners in France[18] and Slovenia,[19] all confirm these generic principles.

Summary of the Characteristics of Excellent Public Relations

To summarize, excellence in public relations can be conceptualized in three broad arenas: expertise, mutual expectations between the dominant coalition and the public relations department, and a participative organizational culture. Participatory culture provides a conducive environment for excellent communication programs—but only when given the necessary expertise in the public relations department and a set of shared expectations about communication with the dominant coalition.

Sadly, most organizations we studied did not have the potential for this kind of excellence. Their cultures were typically authoritarian. However, even a nurturing, empowering internal environment fails to guarantee excellence. Why? More organizations conceptualize and practice public relations as press agentry or public information than as a two-way, interactive process that legitimizes the concern of the publics. Few heads of public relations are strategic managers, and fewer still are included within the dominant coalition. In particular, these top communicators lack the knowledge of evaluation research, environmental scanning, and segmentation techniques that would allow them to determine, characterize, understand, and ultimately communicate with all of their stakeholders.

Encouragingly, many CEOs demand just that kind of sophisticated, credible public relations of their communication managers. Along with the emergence of more and more educational programs in public relations—whether on college campuses or provided through professional associations—should come more practitioners qualified and eager to negotiate with strategic publics, to support the organization's marketing initiatives, to sit at the decision table with the dominant coalition, and—especially—to provide it with the broad perspective of all stakeholders that distinguishes this organizational function from any other.

The growing importance of the international arena suggests a corresponding escalation in the expertise of communication managers. Decentralization of operations within the multinationals we studied and contention with competitors and suppliers from other countries both presage a need for two-way public relations. The globalization of business and an increasingly multicultural workforce are just two of the factors we found to be complicating the lives of top managers. The much-touted new, wireless interactive technology is a necessary but insufficient condition for effective global public relations.

THE VALUE OF EXCELLENT COMMUNICATION

Communication is a highly valued function in the typical organization. Both CEOs and their heads of public relations rated the contribution of communication about equally in our survey research. That is, both groups of participants told us that public relations tends to return more than it costs to implement—on average, about 185 percent return on investment (ROI). Survey respondents with the most-effective public relations programs cited an even higher ROI—about 300 percent. Whereas only 5 percent of our sample of CEOs said public relations returns less than what it costs, a full 40 percent credited communication with returning twice the cost or more. CEOs and managers of public relations alike tended to value public relations more highly than the typical department in their organization.

The questions for our follow-up series of in-depth case studies were to determine why public relations is valued so highly and what, exactly, is its worth.

The answer begins with activism. Most organizations are pressured by activist groups, and most included in our survey considered themselves more beset than the "typical organization." Public relations was credited with helping the organization deal with major social issues—but only if the head of public relations was in a strategic management role. In such cases, we found, the benefits of avoiding costly crises can be expressed in financial terms.

However, even organizations with excellent public relations have a hard time attaching a monetary value to their communication programs. Our interviewees talked about the intangible benefits of such concepts as goodwill, credibility, reputation, and image enhancement. Fortunately, others were more concrete. One common explanation for the difficulty (or undesirability) of attributing money made or saved to public relations efforts was perhaps best articulated by the top communicator in a real estate company. Much of her work involves forestalling crises. This kind of help, she reminded us, is rarely acknowledged or appreciated because it is largely invisible. Another communicator told us that she was unwilling to attach a financial value to her work because the number would be so "staggering," it probably would not be believed. Others—public relations professionals and their CEOs alike—talked about the "infinite value" of public relations, especially during times of crisis or activist pressure.

Through the process of "compensating variation," the team of Excellence researchers actually helped our participants assign monetary values to communication benefits.[20] The process begins by isolating communication as the primary cause or at least an important contributor to a beneficial outcome. Typical outcomes included rooting out waste in work through employee communication programs, turning around declining stock prices through financial relations, raising the national ranking of the operation through media relations, unblocking overseas markets formerly frozen because of insensitive intercultural communication, averting lawsuits and restrictive legislation through relationships with activists and regulators, gaining acceptance for rate hikes through customer relations, and simply surviving tough economic conditions that doomed competitors with less-effective communication programs.

These kinds of benefits turned out to be very tangible indeed. The second step in compensating variation, then, is to assess the monetary value of such outcomes. For example, an equipment manufacturer based in America placed the value of two successful containment strategies for crises in its European and Asian subsidiaries at more than $100 million. A U.S. oil company estimated that it saved a minimum of $890 million by successfully influencing legislation affecting its corporate taxes and environmental activities. A blood bank credited its bone-marrow donation campaign with saving approximately 30 lives. The cost of a bone marrow transplant is $100,000, so the benefits to the 30 leukemia victims total $3 million.

Despite these often-staggering figures, the real reason top communicators and their CEOs value public relations is because they understand that communication works with other managerial functions to build quality, long-term relationships with all strategic publics. To do so, public relations professionals must go beyond their traditional communication role to function as counselors, negotiators, and strategic planners. They must be involved in every dimension of the organization, and especially with the dominant coalition. Thus we consider the bottom-line contributions of public relations to combine conventional financial return and social responsibility.

E N D N O T E S

1. Peters, T. J., and R. H. Waterman, Jr., *In Search of Excellence: Lessons from America's Best-Run Companies* (New York: Warner Books, 1982).

2. Grunig, J. E., ed., *Excellence in Public Relations and Communication Management* (Hillsdale, NJ: Lawrence Erlbaum Associates, 1992).

3. Vercic, D., L. A. Grunig, and J. E. Grunig, "Global Principles of Public Relations: Evidence from Slovenia" (paper presented to the International Conference on "The State of 'Education and Development': New Directions," Association for the Advancement of Policy, Research, and Development in the Third World, Cairo, November 1993).

4. Grunig, J. E., ed., *Excellence in Public Relations.*

5. Grunig, J. E., and T. Hunt, *Managing Public Relations* (New York: Holt, Rinehart and Winston, 1984), p. 6.

6. Dozier, D. M., L. A. Grunig, and J. E. Grunig, *Manager's Guide to Excellence in Public Relations and Communication Management* (Mahwah, NJ: Lawrence Erlbaum Associates, 1995).

7. Peters, T. J., and R. H. Waterman, Jr., *In Search of Excellence.*

8. Sriramesh, K., "The Impact of Societal Culture on Public Relations: An Ethnographic Study of South Indian Organizations (Ph.D. diss., University of Maryland, College Park, 1991).

9. Huang, Y., "Risk Communication, Models of Public Relations and Anti-Nuclear Activism: A Case Study of a Nuclear Power Plant in Taiwan" (master's thesis, University of Maryland, College Park, 1990).

10. Lyra, A. "Public Relations in Greece: Models, Roles and Gender" (master's thesis, University of Maryland, College Park, 1991).

11. Yin, R. K., *Case Study Research: Design and Methods*, rev. ed. (Newbury Park, CA: Sage, 1989).

12. Peters, T. J., and R. H. Waterman, Jr., *In Search of Excellence.*

13. Landers, Ann, "Dear Ann Landers," *The Washington Post* (August 4, 1994), p. C8.

14. International Association of Business Communicators Research Foundation, *Initial Data Report and Practical Guide* (San Francisco: Author, 1991).

15. Grunig, J. E., and L. A. Grunig, "Toward a Theory of the Public Relations Behavior of Organizations: Review of a Program of Research," *Public Relations Research Annual* 1 (1989), pp. 27–63.

16. Broom, G. M., and D. M. Dozier, "Determinants and Consequences of Public Relations Roles" (paper presented at the meeting of the Public Relations Division, Association for Education in Journalism and Mass Communication, Memphis, TN, August 1985).

17. Weick, K. E. *The Social Psychology of Organizing*, 2nd ed. (Reading, MA: Addison-Wesley, 1979).

18. Laufenburger, A., *Excellence in Public Relations in France* (Paris), in press.

19. Gruban, B., D. Vercic, and F. Zavrl, "Public Relations in Slovenia," *pristop,* Special issue (January 1994).

20. Ehling, W. P. "Estimating the Value of Public Relations and Communication to an Organization." In J. E. Grunig, ed., *Excellence in Public Relations and Communication Management* (Hillsdale, NJ: Lawrence Erlbaum Associates, 1992), pp. 617–638.

The Role of Public Relations in Mergers and Acquisitions

Stan Sauerhaft, Fellow, PRSA
Vice Chairman, Burson-Marsteller
Managing Director, Global Mergers
and Acquisitioins Practice

CORPORATE ACQUISITION HISTORY

The rapidly changing world economic scene is often reflected in the fast-paced arena of mergers and acquisitions. As a result, the complexion of the takeover business can change radically from decade to decade. It is currently in the throes of another "sea change," and corporate communications people should note from past patterns what may repeat.

Modern corporate acquisition history probably traces back to the early 1970s, when International Nickel (INCO) made a sudden move to take over ESB Batteries. The financial community was shocked that an "establishment" company would engage in such naked aggression.

Previously, corporate takeovers were considered to be mostly the domain of raiders or financial gunslingers. Soon after World War II there was a movement toward conglomeratization, which was mainly a piling together of companies to achieve size for size's sake. Sometimes the conglomerators, when faced with a reluctant marriage partner, would use hostile tactics to encourage a more compliant atmosphere.

Those aggressive financiers were viewed as a new strain of robber baron, harking back to the kind of characters that muckrakers like Ida Tarbell and Lincoln Steffens wrote about in best-selling books. They were never admitted to the "quality" business world and were considered outsiders whose money was tainted.

But then came INCO and its hostile takeover campaign orchestrated by a pillar of the investment banking community, Morgan Stanley. Soon such establishment companies as Mobil Oil, Philip Morris, and General Electric began acquiring other organizations with the use of pressure. Most of the top investment banks saw the benefits of this type of action (at least to their bottom lines), and some of the leading law firms in the United States built the most lucrative segments of their practices on the tactical takeover advice they gave and the strategies they devised for dealing with government regulatory agencies. A few public relations firms with special expertise in business press relations and investor communications frequently were retained to capture favorable attention for the corporate combatants. This was especially true in hostile takeovers.

The Rise and Fall of Creative Financing

Then along came some new and even more creative financial tactics. The leveraged buyout, often used to help corporate insiders mount a defense against hostile attackers when the "poison pills" were not daunting enough, became very popular. LBO's in the 1980s were generally made possible by high-yield bonds, looked upon by some as "junk."

The proliferation of junk bond financing enabled smaller companies to take over much larger ones. For example, small-time financial lawyer Reginald Lewis, with the aid of Michael Milken and Drexel Burnham's financial machine, was able to buy all of Beatrice International's overseas food operations, with approximately $1 billion in sales, for a personal investment of little more than $1 million. Lewis later sold off some pieces of Beatrice International to reduce much of his TLC Company's huge debt and debt service costs, thereby keeping the company afloat.

The 1980s saw an increasing number of junk-bond-financed takeovers, powered by Drexel, Merrill Lynch, Morgan Stanley, and even conservative Bankers Trust. The movement reached a crescendo with the awesome display of greed and hubris in the battle to take control of RJR Nabisco. That war, launched avariciously by Ross Johnson, the CEO of the company, was eventually won at an exorbitant cost by Henry Kravis and his partners at Kohlberg Kravis Roberts (KKR). The months of detailed reporting on the financial maneuvers of the deal uncovered the extremes of this business practice. The popular book, *Barbarians at the Gate,* dramatized the story.

After that, hostile takeovers declined sharply. Big leveraged buyouts disappeared, while many of the highly publicized takeovers that had utilized junk bond financing began to run into trouble. Federated Stores and its dashing Canadian partner Campeau crashed into bankruptcy. WPP, the multi-advertising agency company that had been put together largely through the "successful" hostile takeovers of J. Walter Thompson and Ogilvy & Mather, teetered on the brink of bankruptcy for years. The company's monstrous annual debt payments dwarfed the profits of its wholly owned ad agencies and forced CEO Martin Sorrell to restructure his debt and give away much of his ownership to banks to stay afloat.

Even the biggest of them all, RJR Holdings, the winner in the RJR Nabisco drama, is having a hard time making ends meet and has greatly dimmed the luster of the former glamour kings of the leveraged buyout, KKR.

Return of the Takeover

In the early 1990s, the acquisition business was to become a more moderate affair. The reaction against the excesses of the 1980s encouraged small, strategic, friendly mergers with only minimal use of debt. Many banks, burned by the results of the late 1980s, had tight zippers on their wallets. Big Debt, which was equated with Big Action in the 1980s, began to be regarded as Big Trouble in the early 1990s.

The early phases of what seems to be a strong comeback of the takeover business are emerging. We have recently witnessed perhaps the first successful hostile takeover of a foreign company by an American company—the winning of Arnott's Biscuit Co. of Australia by Campbell Soup of the United States. Arnott's is the biggest biscuit and cookie manufacturer in Australia, if not all of Asia. Campbell's, already big in cookies in the United States with Pepperidge Farm and in Europe with Delacre, saw the big Far Eastern markets as a major opportunity to gain new customers. The company needed closer production facilities and a regionally recognized brand name, neither of which Pepperidge or Delacre had in Asia. When Arnott's declined a merger offer, Campbell insisted. After a hard fought contest, it succeeded in gaining a majority ownership.

The complex, multibillion-dollar battle for control of Paramount Communications between Viacom (backed by Blockbuster Video and a host of others) and QVC Shopping Network (led by Barry Diller and backed by an equally impressive coterie of companies) became the biggest takeover war since RJR Nabisco. The resulting monumental legal battle was carried to the highest court. At one point, it looked almost certain that QVC would win the overpriced Paramount's hand because it had prevailed in court and dismantled the Viacom lock-up. But cooler numbers prevailed and Viacom eventually won the deal. So impressed was Wall Street that the victor's stock (Viacom) dropped sharply upon victory, while the loser's stock (QVC) went up.

We have also seen in the last few months the first big bidding battle of the 1990s that was entirely bank financed. The multibillion-dollar tugging match between Martin Marietta and Northup for control of defense contractor Grumman was almost a fight for survival by the winner Northup as Defense Department budgets were tightening.

The hostile proxy battles of the 1980s may also be coming back in force. GE Capital's campaign to gain several board seats and ultimate control of Kemper was rebuffed long enough for a higher bidder to eventually steal the prize.

The giant $5 billion chicken processor Tyson Foods launched a sudden hostile campaign to take over WLR Foods, a $700 million turkey and chicken processor in the Shenandoah Valley of Virginia. It seems that Don Tyson desperately wanted to get into the turkey business, and, by his own admission, nobody in the business wanted to sell to him. So he decided to try to forcibly gobble up the biggest publicly owned turkey processor, WLR. But Tyson encountered great antipathy on the part of the grower-stockholders of WLR, and was also faced with perhaps the toughest state antitakeover laws in the country. Virginia requires the acquirer of more than 5 percent of a target's stock to win a majority vote of disinterested shareholders in order to be allowed to vote its acquired shares. Tyson announced that, if he lost the vote, he would withdraw.

Tyson lost the proxy vote, but proceeded to challenge the voting procedure in court. He lost there, too. Now he would have to challenge the whole Virginia law in a higher court. Possible, but expensive. And even a victory there wouldn't ensure a takeover win, because the Shenandoah Valley grower-owners were by now almost all aligned against him. Tyson decided to fold his cards.

These and several other developing transactions announced in the mid-1990s indicate that the acquisition business is beginning to build again. The leveraged buyouts and heavy-debt-financed takeovers, which became notorious more for their ability to enrich a few rather than create value for many, are not returning in their old form. But takeovers and mergers are definitely on the rise again, and hostile takeovers also are coming on strong.

There are several reasons why more and more top managers are becoming emboldened to return to the battlefields.

First, relatively cheap equity is available to many. After recent market corrections, some companies have fared better than others. Some have rebounded well, while others have languished. This makes acquirers' treasury stock proportionately more valuable than their targets' stock, giving them a stronger hand to play.

Low long-term interest rates have enabled many companies to cut their interest bills by refinancing debt taken on in the 1980s. This, too, boosts each company's cash flow.

The banks are also getting interested again. Financing takeovers is one of the more profitable ways for cash-rich banks to employ some of the capital they have sitting around.

STRATEGIC FORCES DRIVING TAKEOVERS

What are some of the new forces beginning to drive the takeover business? First, there is the need to cut costs. With prices under pressure in many industries, growth can be accomplished by greater efficiency and broader market coverage. Strategic acquisitions are called for. That is what Don Tyson saw attractive for his company in WLR Foods. WLR, on the other hand, felt it was accomplishing those things on its own, and therefore found the avaricious Tyson unattractive—particularly after WLR had invested almost $200 million in plant and equipment modernization. They didn't want to let Tyson reap the fruits of their hard work, and they told that to their shareholders.

One service sector with a big cost problem is the banking industry. Thus we have seen a wave of takeovers and mergers there—big ones marrying other big ones, like Chemical Bank and Manufacturers Hanover; big ones taking over smaller ones that are strong in a particular region; and two smaller ones getting together to put up a stronger front against a big competitor.

Something similar is happening in the healthcare industry as pressure is applied by the government and insurance companies to restrain prices to cut excess profits.

A second factor driving takeovers is technological advance. The much-ballyhooed information highway is putting pressure on the cable television, telecommunications, network broadcasting, and entertainment industries to form new alliances to compete for the consumer's dollar or drop out of the race.

Even the staid electric utility industry is beginning to be concerned about competition. These companies, which are multigovernment-agency regulated, are seeing developments that may force them to choose between production of power and distribution of power if they are to survive. There are new companies that can manufacture power inexpensively and have the ability to supply whole regions of the country.

A third factor, the changing regulatory and legal environment, is pushing many companies to acquire or sell out. In the electric utility business, the wheeling regulation, which loosens the exclusive control of a company's own transmission lines in its service territory and allows outside companies access to its customers through those lines, forces a change of strategy with regard to production of electricity. The regional Bell telephone companies are moving into cable television and mobile telephones as their own local service territory monopolies are threatened by upcoming legislation.

International Takeovers

Just as some American companies are getting more active in foreign takeovers, we are seeing some foreign companies taking major acquisition steps in the United States to broaden their product lines, as Roche Holdings did recently with Syntex. Some are moving into allied fields, as Sandoz has done by acquiring Gerber baby foods. The Gerber acquiescence to a rich takeover price also enabled that company to sidestep any forcible takeovers that were rumored on the horizon. A weaker dollar, of course, was making it cheaper for these overseas companies to acquire U.S. firms.

PUBLIC RELATIONS TACTICS IN THE TAKEOVER ENVIRONMENT

What should be the role of public relations in this shifting mergers and acquisition world?

Defensive Postures Before an Attack

Let's start with takeover defense. Assuming you are dealing with a vulnerable publicly owned company, the best defense should begin well before a takeover attempt is encountered.

Dissuading the potential takeover attacker is the key, because once your company must begin a defensive campaign, whether it be successful or not, the costs to the company are immense and the upset to hundreds of people's lives can be devastating.

Moving a languishing stock price up is one way to discourage a takeover attack. Likewise, showing that management of the company is likely to be strong and stubborn, and showing that management has good support down the line in the company and from the company's board are also helpful.

Getting the company's stock to sell at its proper multiple may involve sophisticated investment community research to learn what misinformation and misunderstandings exist about the company among financial advisors and portfolio managers, and even the company's own stockholders. Then an effective communications program must be implemented.

But let's assume this has not been done, or has been done half-heartedly, and your company is now the target of a takeover attack. What are some principles to observe to give your company that best chance to survive, or at least last long enough to make a favorable deal with a friendly merger partner or "white knight"?

Tactics for Takeover Targets

As the takeover attack unfolds, rapid and forthright disclosure is essential to maintain the loyalty of the company's various stakeholder groups.

The financial audience is, of course, the primary focus—stockholders and bondholders, security analysts, and portfolio managers. Investment decisions made by the core financial audience determine whether the takeover will be successful or not.

In defending your company in a proxy contest, you can point out the character deficiencies and questionable legal and business records of the leaders of the opposition. Stockholders should know who they are being asked to vote for and who might become the future managers of their company.

On the other hand, in defending against a hostile tender offer, you have to be careful not to frighten stockholders unduly or they may sell out their stock to avoid being associated with the unpleasant marauders. This plays right into the hands of the attackers.

Because communications must be prompt and effective, the public relations people cannot afford to waste much time in framing the company's responses. It is a good idea to form a core crisis committee, composed of a small group of executives empowered to act quickly. This committee should include the company's general counsel, the chief public relations officer, and senior members of the company's investment firm, law firm, outside public relations firm, and proxy soliciting firm.

Some means of feedback should also be built in to enable you to learn how the recipients of the communications that are, coming both from the opponent and from your own company, are reacting to what they are reading and hearing. Daily logs should be kept of telephone and letter inquiries, and there should be a monitoring of street rumors. Subsequent communications directly to stockholders and indirectly through the financial media should take into account what points were being missed and correct those factors that were being distorted.

Almost as important are the constituents who are responsible for maintaining the viability of your business. Chief among these groups are the company's employees—the office and factory workers, middle management executives, and salespeople. Keeping up the morale of these people, who will feel they are literally under attack, is critical. If these people begin to feel they are likely to end up on the losing side, some may begin to look for other jobs, or succumb to the blandishments of headhunters. Unfortunately, the better and more skilled employees are the ones who may find it most easy to locate other jobs. Substantial key personnel losses can severely damage your business even if you win the proxy fight or fend off the tender raider.

Frequent in-house video reports by the CEO, cafeteria rump sessions run by corporate officers, and a lot of one-on-one meetings with the known employee opinion leaders can help keep the rumors from going wild and undermining morale all over the company.

Certain external stakeholders must also be assured of the company's stability during the fight process, or here too there can be irreparable harm. Major customers may become concerned that product lines important to them could be terminated or altered if your company is taken over and new management comes on the scene. These customers may seek alternative sources of supply to protect themselves from any possible interdiction. Once they have lined up other suppliers, your company may lose business it may never regain. Thus it is very important that executives of your company personally reassure those big customers as soon as possible that they have nothing to fear.

Other external publics who should be promptly informed of the hostile action are your legislators, both federal and state. Your company brings jobs and tax income to the communities in which you operate, and your employees vote for the government representatives. Losing even part of the company in their districts can be quite serious to those politicians, who have to do something to earn the respect of their constituents.

Sometimes the last line of defense is an appeal for government agency or legislative intervention. The public relations managers must work closely with the legal affairs consultants to prepare the best case for your company and get it widely accepted. This not only brings pressure on legislators to do the right thing, but it can cause concern to such Wall Street forces as arbitrageurs who make decisions to buy or sell the company's stock based on perceived value, the likelihood of the takeover happening, and the length of time it will take.

Possible federal or state government interference creates great uncertainty as to whether the deal will be allowed to go through. Even a long delay will be costly to traders who buy stock with borrowed money, hoping to sell that stock fairly quickly when the final takeover offer comes in several dollars higher.

The likely increase in proxy contests as the preferred medium for taking over a company puts a special premium on telling the company's positive story while disparaging that of the aggressor.

Vendors and suppliers are often-neglected external publics who are frequently left to follow the developments of a merger/takeover action, and its aftermath, through public, unofficial sources. If they become uncertain of the continued viability of the company to be acquired, they may interrupt the flow of supplies or services, making it temporarily difficult for the target to maintain normal operations. Certainly they will become more wary of extending credit. All of this increases pressure on the target company.

Still another significant group of external stakeholders of a merger are the community leaders and local businessmen in the locales where the target company conducts its business. These groups can affect community opinion about a proposed merger. Where an attempted acquisition is judged to be hostile, these people can be rallied in support of the target company and bring pressure on congressional representatives, the governor's office, and other potential disrupters of the deal. This tactic can be especially effective in fending off a foreign raider who may be sensitive to xenophobic charges of invasion, and who may further be scared off by the prospect of acquiring a hostile workforce supported by hostile government officials.

But even if the proposed merger is friendly, it is very important for the acquiring company and its target to establish a decent relationship with community leaders and businessmen. These people will know that changes in management can result in consolidations, leading to fewer local jobs and reduced reliance on local suppliers and retailers. You will have to sell them on the plus side of the company's entrance into the community, perhaps by showing them that the entire plant might have had to be shut down if it were not for the merger.

The Role of PR for the Aggressor

But what if you are on the side of a distinctly *un*friendly takeover? What if your company is the clear-cut aggressor?

Suppose you are the communications strategist and your company has just made a sudden hostile offer to buy all the stock of another company in a related field. The offer is so much above the market price that there is little chance for a white knight to gallantly ride onto the scene and help out your target by bidding higher.

Because the share price offer you made is so high, there is speculation in the press that most of the differential will be made up after the takeover by closing plants and terminating thousands of employees of the target company. As it is, your company was never too popular with the press anyway. Now you have very little in the way of goodwill chips to call in. How do you make your company's actions palatable so that there will be a minimum of negative feeling after the transaction is completed?

When American Home Products moved quickly with an all-shares takeover offer for American Cyanamid's stock that was 60 percent higher than the market, it won with hardly a fight.

AHP then set about explaining to the general public that the combining of those two pharmaceutical behemoths would create a new and much better company that would benefit everybody. More than $1 billion in research and development would be spent annually to develop new medicines and new therapies to help more people stay well and live better lives. Corporate advertising as well as carefully placed articles were developed to carry the message that everybody would gain by this new $12 billion AHP.

Post-Merger PR

This brings us to the final phase of the takeover: post-merger communications.

More than half of the "successful" transactions fail in the end because key employees depart, important customers are lost, communities turn hostile, and costs of doing ordinary business rise and cut profit margins.

This is where the work of the public relations people is often most valuable, after the deal-making lawyers and investment bankers have moved on to their next transactions.

Post-merger communications campaigns should be well planned to go into action as soon as the deal is done. Not only announcement ads but multilevel conversations with top management participation must be inaugurated. The morale of the target company employees must be a first priority. Vital technicians and managers should be identified and given special attention, showing them how their opportunities will now be greater than ever.

The acquiring company must be depicted as an important new asset to the communities, and as a company where it will be a fine place to work. The press will play a major role in shaping the relationships that the newly merged company will have with all its varied stakeholders. And, of course, the press will be skeptical or even downright cynical. They must be won over.

Introducing important corporate executives to stakeholder groups, either in person or on specially made videos, will help humanize the new company and ease some of the fear and concern.

Securing media visibility for the new company to show the importance to society of its products or services can begin to instill some pride in the "taken over" employees, and reassure local opinion leaders and customers that they can trust this new company.

Finally, it should be emphasized that any promises made, during the transaction days and thereafter, must be kept religiously. The new company is being watched warily in the few days and weeks following the merger. Integrity is the critical characteristic that must be proven. Any wavering will be magnified in the eyes of the various stakeholders. Unraveling is the certain payment for duplicity. In the end, then, everybody loses.

## PART FOUR

Advanced Public Relations Practice in Key Industries

## CHAPTER 21

Public Relations in the Food and Beverage Industry

Richard L. Nelson
Vice President, Public Affairs
The NutraSweet Kelco Company

A STRATEGIC APPROACH TO PUBLIC RELATIONS

When you think about it, few things are more personal—more *intimate*—than food. To begin with, it goes into our mouths and inside our bodies. It satisfies our first appetite and provides us with the longest-lasting source of human pleasure. The enjoyment associated with eating extends far beyond the food itself. Consider the friendships and family ties forged and renewed over meals, or the cultural signposts they provide for immigrant ethnic groups, or the ways in which certain aromas can trigger the sights and sounds that accompanied them in the past . . . the whiff of a fresh apple pie conjuring memories of Grandma's house, for instance.

On a less-romantic level, food and beverages long have dictated the most personal concerns of the human species: health. Ever since the Old Testament's King Og discovered that eating certain plants could cause harm—or, conversely, that swallowing an oyster whole would *not* kill him—mankind has realized the inseparable relationship between the things we eat and the way our bodies react. Today, as we stagger under the onslaught of nutritional studies, vitamin debates, or issues such as the irradiation of food to remove microbial contamination, the selection and preparation of food plays an increasingly large role in everyday life and health.

As Michelle Stacey writes in her book *Consumed,* "Food is no longer simply food but preventive medicine, a scientific abstraction, a moral test, and, sometimes, a mortal enemy. This love/hate relationship invests food with more freight than it can carry . . ." It also opens the door to unusual abuses, such as the tendency to exaggerate a product's extra-nutritional values which has led to government regulation of health claims for food and beverages.

Stacey writes specifically about Americans, but in cultures the world over, food represents the most personal of choices. These choices are made from a huge variety of options, multiple times each day. This fact alone distinguishes the food industry from all others and plays a paramount role in shaping and coloring the whole mix of marketing strategies.

Within that mix, public relations plays an especially important part. Advertising almost always creates a slight suspicion among consumers because they know the advertiser paid large sums to paint the best picture of the product. The third-party endorsements that public relations professionals seek from the press, universities, government, and other stakeholders can ease this suspicion in many industries, such endorsements take on a particularly important and credible role in the case of products as personal and essential as food and beverages.

How, then, should we promote food? The strategies and tactics employed can take as many forms as there are creative public relations specialists. In every case, however, the strategies must reach at least one, and preferably several, of the many relevent publics.

The Influence of Stakeholders

Chief among these, of course, is consumers. Public relations reaches them in both direct and indirect ways. The direct approach includes influencing consumers through general-market press releases and news conferences, pitching individual stories to general-interest newspapers and magazines, and placing qualified spokespeople on a seemingly ever-expanding array of radio and television talk shows. A more indirect approach includes "influencing the influencers": developing programs to reach health professionals, retailers, trade media, and other interested parties, each of whom plays a part in helping the consumer choose which food or beverage product to buy.

Other influencers include the scientific community, including academic scientists, whose critiques and validations play an essential role in the efforts just described, and trade associations, which can act as third-party spokespeople on behalf of a product. Not to be left out of the dialogue are the manufacturers themselves (as well as their shareholders, who expect to see profits and dividends from these companies); advocacy groups such as the Center for Science in the Public Interest; agricultural firms and organizations, whose interests and agendas may or may not dovetail with those of the groups already mentioned; and the elected officials and government regulators charged with safeguarding the consumer from both unhealthy food and unwarranted nutritional claims. Finally, there are the employees of food and beverage companies, one of the most important audiences of all. Without their ownership and support, an external marketing communications program becomes immeasurably harder to execute.

Industry Changes

To understand the public relations opportunities and challenges that are particular to this industry, it is important to understand the three distinct waves of influence that have affected it during this century.

First, as in most industries, food and beverage companies have seen their industry completely transformed by technological advances, which have led to geometric growth, an endless array of potential new products and markets, and rapid changes in the manufacture and transportation of food. These technological developments in turn have spurred an equally profound series of sociological changes, from the days in which families prepared all their meals at home (and often from food grown on their own land) to today, when many people eat out more often than in (and frequently simply heat or reheat preprepared meals when at home). Meanwhile, the food and beverage industry in the United States, Canada, and Europe, and to varying degrees throughout the world, has had to accommodate itself to a growing network of regulatory rules and restrictions.

The technological revolution in the food industry began with the development of more efficient farming and production techniques. These include the use of agricultural chemicals to reduce losses due to insects and other pests, and other chemicals to quicken the maturation of crops and livestock. The improved yields that resulted from these advances helped reduce prices for food. Related economies of scale have favored large and even "factory" farms, leading to the decline and near demise of family farming. In 1900, nearly 42 percent of the American public made a living from farming. In 1990, that figure stood at less than 2 percent.

Other technological leaps have had similar impacts on the industry, while at the same time spurring analogous sociological developments. Most important among these was the packaging revolution, which began with the invention of large-scale food canning in the 19th century. The canning industry made great strides during the Civil War—canned and tinned goods were used to feed both armies and at the same time became popular with civilians— and World War II provided a similar impetus to the development of the ready-to-eat foods that later caught on with the general public. Around 1920, Clarence Birdseye, an explorer and inventor, became fascinated with the way Canadian Eskimos stored their food. Birdseye developed a process for the successful quick-freezing of fresh produce, and the frozen-food industry was born.

These developments—along with advances in transportation, such as refrigerated trucks, trains, and air transport that permit the nationwide distribution of perishable goods— have revolutionized the ways in which Americans purchase and consume foods. A hundred years ago, Mom walked down to the corner food store and asked that nice Mr. Jones behind the counter for a pound of flour from the barrel in the back. Today we shop in supermarkets that have grown into virtual town squares of aisles, departments, and subsections, carrying every variety of American, ethnic, and imported foods, many of which are designed for once-undreamed-of convenience.

At the same time, this craving for convenience has fostered the exponential growth of the quick-service restaurant and has exported the fast-food phenomenon throughout the world. This, too, is part of the revolution in how we eat—a revolution of sociological impact and technological achievement. Not long ago, families gathered around the dinner table in an exercise in communication and connection necessitated by the labor-intensive home-cooked meal. Today, that "quality time" is spent in the car en route to McDonald's, where we eat and then often disband to separate work, school, and leisure activities.

The success of quick-service restaurants would not have been possible without the availability of national advertising vehicles—magazines, national newspapers such as *USA Today*, and network broadcasts on radio and television. These national media were important for another reason as well: earlier, they had played a major role in the development and marketing of the national-brand products that replaced the regional specialties defining America's food production. This was perhaps best seen with the rise of national brands of beer—most notably Budweiser—to replace the local beers once produced by community breweries.

But technology not only drives sociological change, it also must respond. In recent years, the food industry's vaunted technological skills have dovetailed with retailing innovations to meet changing, and even contradictory, consumer needs. Thus, in the midst of the proliferation of quick-service restaurants—which have come under heavy criticism for offering foods high in fat and low in nutrition in a dull, "plastic" environment—modern America also finds itself obsessed with healthful foods and gourmet treats. From salads, yogurt, free-range turkeys, and sugar-free sundaes to natural peanut butter, fat-free cookies, gourmet coffee, and bottled water—all of these serve as examples of the backlash against fast-food restaurants and generic uniformity.

These changes play out against the background of government regulatory control, which has attained an increasingly higher profile as the public's concerns over health issues grow. These concerns date back a century and reached their first great peak in 1906, when publication of *The Jungle*, Upton Sinclair's muckraking exposé of unhygienic practices in the meat industry, led to the passage of the Pure Food and Drug Act. Today, the federal government spends more resources than ever on issues that range from the original concerns of food safety—including the growing and manufacturing processes—to claims made in advertising, public relations materials, and packaging. The reason? The proliferation of new concepts, new products, and line extensions; to wit, a shelf in the supermarket soft drink aisle might hold regular, sugar-free, low-sugar, caffeine-free, diet caffeine-free, flavored, and even "clear" versions of the same label. The dairy case across the way displays regular, cholesterol-reduced, low-fat, and no-fat versions of the same brand of cheese, and a visit to the produce section reveals a tomato that's been genetically altered to ripen more slowly.

Uses of Public Relations

In this dizzying vortex of new products, multiple brands, and competing health claims, a savvy and well-executed public relations campaign can have an enormous impact. By giving the consumer some specific, unadvertised reason to think well of a product, the public relations manager can create respect and sometimes even demand that will separate the product from the large and confusing pack.

One such example is the Butterball Turkey Hotline that Swift & Company cooked up in 1981. Shortly before and through Thanksgiving Day, the hot line is open to the public. Free calls to the 1-800 phone line are fielded by more than 40 home economists who answer questions about correct preparation and salvage last-minute disasters for up to 6,000 callers a day. The publicity that surrounds this service—which seems to yield a feature story in food sections of every newspaper annually—garners tremendous attention for the company. The coverage does something else: It positions the Butterball brand's makers as experts, the people who know everything there is to know about turkeys. In consumer's minds, this equates to Butterball turkeys being better than other brands.

Public relations positioning is part of an overall integrated marketing communication program and an integral component of the mix that allows the company to meet its corporate goals and project a calculated image. Public relations professionals always have been known as creators of the image; they also must help preserve the image. Part of that responsibility lies in the counseling function.

PR's role as counselor comes into play most urgently during times of crisis. In recent years, crisis communication has become its own subspecialty, due in part to the proliferation of tampering incidents and in part to increasingly sophisticated methods of packaging. The more elements and stages involved in the process, the greater the chance of something going wrong. However, sometimes a crisis occurs when, literally, nothing happens.

On Valentine's Day 1986, a New York woman complained of finding glass in a jar of Gerber baby food. Even as the company was investigating the claim, local television stations and wire services picked up the story, resulting in copycat complaints cropping up from as far away as Florida even as the New York health authorities were giving Gerber a clean bill of health and the Food and Drug Administration was declaring that it was unable to substantiate any claims. Ultimately, complaints occurred in 40 states and in countries as distant as Australia.

This case study is of particular importance because of the strong, uncompromising stand Gerber took against something the media urged them to do—recall the product. Still smarting from a 1984 incident in which Gerber recalled baby juice said to contain pieces of glass—even though no regulatory agency found any reason to do so—Gerber remained firm in its decision not to recall the baby food. However, much like their counterparts at Pepsi-Cola during the 1993 Diet Pepsi tampering incidents in which syringes were "found" in various cans of Diet Pepsi, Gerber executives did not let matters stand with a mere announcement of their intent. Rather, they embarked on an aggressive communications campaign with one clear objective: demonstrating Gerber's safe procedures to the media, the trade, federal, state, and local authorities, healthcare providers, and even their own employees. Interviews, direct mail, and other communication vehicles were employed. The results were significant: Less than a year later, Gerber had maintained and even slightly increased its market share. In both the Gerber and Diet Pepsi crises, the companies successfully portrayed themselves as victims and thereby won the sympathy of the public.

Not so lucky or skillful were apple growers and processors attacked by an environmental group in 1989 for using the chemical Alar to protect and cosmeticize their apples. Caught unprepared in the glare of *60 Minutes'* spotlight and by the effective rhetoric of actress Meryl Streep, the growers appeared unsympathetic to consumer concerns. They also failed to garner support from third-party groups that could speak credibly to the scientific issues raised by the environmentalists. Many of the growers were forced out of business as a result.

Clearly, the benefits of building and nurturing alliances can prove most critical in times of crisis. One example involved the StarKist Company, the target of negative publicity for tuna fishing practices that resulted in dolphin deaths. As the 20th anniversary of Earth Day approached, awareness reached a critical mass; boycotts were initiated against both StarKist and its parent, H.J. Heinz, and Congress pushed for regulation.

The company decided to take the lead in adopting a worldwide "dolphin safe" policy that would set a standard for the industry. Critical to their strategy and success was coalition-building; positive response from environmentalists and congressional leaders was needed to change consumer distrust to support. Public relations counsel worked with environmental leaders to involve StarKist in Earth Day, to be held one week after the company's announcement of its change in practices. Influential environmental leaders and members of Congress praised the company and issued statements of support. The boycott was lifted on StarKist, and the boycott leader, Earth Island Institute, took out an ad in the *New York Times* specifically thanking the company. The change in policy gave the company a positive message; getting that message out successfully involved the thoughtful building of strategic alliances to provide influential third-party endorsements.

International Issues

Coalition building has been a tactic employed by sophisticated public relations practitioners since the pioneering days of Edward Bernays and John Hill. But since public relations and marketing sophistication can be an elusive quality, outside of North America and much of Europe, marketers need to be especially sensitive to cultural differences when pursuing initiatives outside their traditional geographic spheres of business.

Consider the case of a U.S.-based food manufacturer seeking to market its cake mixes in Japan. The company knew that few Japanese kitchens, because of their tiny size, had an oven; they also knew that almost every Japanese household had a rice cooker. So they developed and marketed a cake mix that could be baked in a rice cooker, hoping to make great inroads into the market . . . without fully appreciating that, to the Japanese, rice is sacred. They eat it white and unsullied. And they certainly don't want to make it in a cooker that has leftover smells or flavors of vanilla or chocolate that remained no matter how hard they scrubbed.

Other problems can occur because of the different forms of communication and tools available (or not) to public relations professionals. In Latin America, Eastern Europe, most of Africa, and much of Asia, newspaper stories are frequently bought and, just as frequently, editorial mentions will be directly linked to advertising expenditures. In the late 1970s, a major U.S. food company embarked on a program to promote breakfast nutrition throughout the world by placing health-oriented articles in the foreign press. The company found not just its greatest success but its only success in publications in which it advertised.

Still, advanced communications technology has brought about Marshall McLuhan's predicted "global shrinking," resulting in an increasingly sophisticated concept of marketing throughout the world. Such powerhouse global marketers as Nestlé, Pepsi, and others have sought local marketing partners in other nations to help spread the word about their products, and this has accelerated the acceptance and comprehension of modern marketing tools. In addition, the marketing conglomerates themselves—the WPP Group, Saatchi & Saatchi, Euro RSCG, Young & Rubicam, and others—have effectively created worldwide networks of advertising and public relations agencies to support both multinational and local clients.

This gives the food and beverage industry several options when it comes to public relations suppliers in foreign markets. Manufacturers can connect with one of the global firms such as Hill & Knowlton, Burson-Marsteller, Fleishmann-Hillard, or Edelman Public Relations worldwide to enjoy the much-touted advantage of a network of offices wired into a central headquarters. They can work with networked independent agencies or they can construct their own networks of independent agencies, choosing from the best vendors in each individual locale whether or not these vendors are owned by or affiliated with a large multinational. Not surprisingly, each has its advantages and disadvantages.

The large-firm approach affords the client a coherent, centralized public relations strategy across all markets. It also locks in (theoretically, at least) all of the services and capabilities offered by the agency throughout its network. The client can often save time and money by dealing directly with headquarters, rather than with a series of office managers. But despite their best efforts, each large agency network has strengths and weaknesses spread throughout its system. Its Frankfurt office might be the standout player in all of Germany, but the Hong Kong office may lack anyone with food or beverage expertise. Some offices may be affiliates, as opposed to agency-owned, diluting the already tenuous influence of headquarters. And finally, the local office in, for example, Buenos Aires may choose to take on a competing client and resign the multinational client; if the agency's control is weak enough, even the corporate office won't be able to prevent this from happening.

On the other hand, setting up a network can prove daunting. Without a lot of time or a large enough staff, the public relations practitioner will be hard pressed to keep each individual regional agency briefed and up to speed on the company's products and programs. The network approach also makes it tougher to establish a coherent campaign, since each agency will want to add its own entrepreneurial touches to the well-crafted strategy—often whether or not they're on target. The practitioner may spend more money, since the minimal fees for acceptable service from all these individual offices may eclipse the package deal that could be made with a multinational. The superb service received in all markets may well offset such drawbacks, but then again, the Hong Kong market just might not be that important.

As global marketers continue to expand their reach, the vendors of global communications services seem likely to do the same. By early next century, a few dominant food and beverage brands from North American and European manufacturers may well be supported by a few dominant advertising and public relations service organizations. This is already a trend in such products as alcoholic beverages and carbonated soft drinks, convenience and snack foods, and chocolate candies, and in the quick-service restaurant industry.

Regional products will continue to have their place, of course. Few in the United States, for example, have heard of a "squash," but in Britain that word denotes a popular form of fruit-based soft drink. Local traditions dictate that Norwegians like their cheese one way, Italians another, and Chinese not at all, with Americans among the few cultures that embalm cheese in plastic wrap and then place it in cold storage until it's consumed. Pasta, rice, tea, coffee, sauces, and soups are the stuff of local preference, and they will likely resist the trend toward globalization. In addition, some products are destined to remain regional commodities due to problems with distribution or large-scale manufacturing: frozen foods, most dairy products and baked goods, and fresh meats, fish, fruits, and vegetables.

Whether utilizing public relations to benefit a product here or abroad, however, one thing remains clear: Public relations no longer works in a vacuum. It's no more logical to think in terms of stand-alone public relations programs than it is to think of stand-alone advertising programs. The dividing lines among elements of the marketing communications mix are blurring; the public relations function is as apt to implement a direct mail program as the advertising group is to propose a contest.

As marketing budgets shrink and audiences for traditional forms of advertising become more fragmented, public relations plays an increasingly important role in the marketing mix. While public relations programs cannot generate brand awareness as effectively as mass-market advertising, public relations is often more effective than its marketing cousins in motivating consumer behavior, shaping consumer attitudes, deflecting criticism of a product or brand, and refining the contours of brand imagery. By its very nature, public relations is a more targeted discipline, and marketers—who are finding it less attractive to spend large sums on television advertising that reaches fewer people in desirable demographic groups—are turning to public relations as a more efficient, more focused vehicle of persuasion.

Food and beverage marketers, along with most consumer product marketers, generally allocate between 10 and 20 percent of total marketing funds for public relations programming. This rule of thumb applies most often when the total marketing budget includes a substantial sum for advertising. When marketing budgets do not allow for enough advertising to achieve a threshold of effectiveness—in today's dollars, a media spend of $8 million to $10 million is considered a minimum requirement for a national campaign—publicity budgets are likely to constitute an even larger percentage of the total marketing budget.

Some companies still maintain large staffs of public relations specialists who plan and execute public relations programs that support marketing objectives. Increasingly, however, corporations are reengineering their communications functions and eliminating many public relations specialists from the payroll. Integrated marketing communications departments are taking the place of many traditional—and traditionally separate—marketing and public relations functions. The thinking is that advertising, promotion, public relations, direct mail, and so on are simply tools that should be employed as needed in support of the strategy. In a fully developed integrated marketing communications function, there are very few specialists of any kind. Rather, marketing and communications strategists serve a dual role—as strategists and as astute purchasers of outside services from vendors such as advertising and public relations agencies, promotion agencies, and media buying services.

The field of food and beverage public relations abounds with subspecialties. Media-trained registered dietitians are available as temporary product spokespersons for national media tours or defensive work in a crisis. Home economists and food technicians develop recipes for public relations programs, and food stylists are available to ensure that specialist food photographers find the most attractive ways to portray the client's product for the daily newspapers' food sections. Health communications agencies, which also work for pharmaceutical clients, develop strategies for gaining third-party endorsements from healthcare professional groups for foods and food ingredients. Many generalist public relations agencies will not employ these specialists themselves, but hire them on a project basis and sometimes mark up their costs. Some corporations explore whether a network of individual specialists or small agencies is cost-effective for work on a project basis.

Food and beverage companies also are more heavily reliant on production and distribution services for the creation and dissemination of mat releases, R.O.P.s (run-of-press), recipe books, custom-designed press kits, and video and radio news releases (tactics that will be addressed later in this chapter). Once again, careful consideration should be given to the advantages of working directly with these services versus the probable added cost of working through an agency. Clients with limited internal public relations staff support will probably opt to let the agency handle it, as the additional cost will be worth the reduced aggravation of having to deal with multiple vendors on a single product or campaign.

A TACTICAL APPROACH TO THE INDUSTRY

As pointed out earlier, the strategies and tactics employed on behalf of a product can take as many forms as there are public relations professionals. But certain tried-and-true formats are worth noting in some detail (see Figure 21–1).

1. Few consumers can resist, and few critics can attack, an activity of true good will. One sterling example in the food industry comes from McDonald's Corporation. Its creation of the Ronald McDonald Children's Charities begat the Ronald McDonald Houses, which provide housing and support for the families of critically ill children. McDonald's also has funded such national programs as an all-star marching band for high-school musicians, and, as part of marketing efforts, the company places particular emphasis on giving back to communities through sponsorships and donations. Together, these activities become a strategy for painting a glowing picture of the entire McDonald's concept.

Such actions help build consumer trust and community loyalty. While it takes time to establish such faith in an institution, the rewards are great because the consumer's positive viewpoint adheres beyond specific products to the company behind them—and, by extension, to new products the company subsequently develops. This in turn creates a

F I G U R E   21–1

PUBLIC RELATIONS TACTIC FOR THE FOOD AND
BEVERAGE INDUSTRY

1. Engage in activities that generate true goodwill.

2. Use nostalgia to evoke warm memories and positive associations.

3. Heighten product interest in an indirect way, such as preformatted recipes for newspapers.

4. Use consumer surveys to uncover newsworthy messages for the media.

5. Complement and extend a newsworthy advertising campaign.

6. Match a product's profile to shifting public wants or concerns.

7. Deflect interest-group or consumer concerns and complaints with third-party information.

8. Use selected traditional tactics, such as recipes, demonstrations, and media tours, to
     introduce new products.

"trust bank," a concept pioneered by McDonald's public relations counselor Al Golin, in which gifts to the community serve as "deposits" upon which the company can draw when needed.

2. When a food or beverage product reaches a milestone anniversary, one effective tactic is the use of nostalgia to evoke warm memories and positive associations. This tactic, as old as advertising itself, is especially well-suited to the subtleties of public relations and is particularly useful when attempting to revive an older product or brand. Examples from recent history demonstrate the potential effectiveness of such campaigns.

In 1988, Kraft General Foods used the 60th anniversary of Velveeta to revive interest in the cheese, whose popularity had eroded. The company initiated a media blitz that emphasized two main points: Velveeta, a product so identified with the technologically obsessed 1950s, had in fact appeared three decades earlier in a "simpler, purer" world; and, rather than a nutritionless food product, Velveeta was actually a blend of all-natural ingredients (colby, Swiss, and cheddar cheeses). Different tactics, including a strong media relations program and the development and publicizing of recipe booklets, were employed, all in honor of the food that "brought back childhood memories."

In 1993, McDonald's chose to recognize the anniversary of one of its cornerstone products, the Big Mac, created by a McDonald's franchisee back in 1968. In addition to a nationwide publicity campaign, the company focused on one particular city, Pittsburgh, where the Big Mac had been created. The mayor renamed the city "Big Mac City, U.S.A." at an anniversary party featuring a marching band, the worlds biggest Big Mac cake, and local citizens singing the famous "Two All-Beef Patties" jingle.

3. The food sections of daily newspapers provide a ready-made outlet for several tactics that can heighten product interest in an indirect way. One of the most effective of these is the "run-of-press," or R.O.P. This preformatted page of recipes and food suggestions, suitable for either black-and-white or four-color reproduction, features recipes that call for use of the provider's product. The R.O.P. is a version of the mat release, also a staple of food and beverage publicity programs.

4. Often consumer surveys can provide interesting, relevant, or otherwise newsworthy messages with which to approach the media. An ice cream manufacturer, for instance, might conclude a scientific consumer survey with the somewhat unscientific question, "When are you most in the mood for an ice cream treat?" When the public relations department later releases the news that 67 percent of respondents crave ice cream immediately following an evening of passion, it is sure to garner a few headlines and broadcast news bits.

5. A marketer can complement and extend an advertising campaign by piggybacking its public relations efforts. "Integrated marketing communications" has become the rallying cry of the 1990s, frequently yielding the types of results neither public relations nor advertising can yield alone. Sometimes this integrated approach means taking two different aspects of a product and communicating one through advertising and another through public relations. Other times a particularly inventive advertising campaign can be a vehicle for publicity in and of itself.

In 1994, Hormel Corporation came up with an historically themed way of redefining its canned pork and ham mix, Spam, for a new generation. Spam was patented back in 1937 but gained recognition when it became a wartime staple in Britain in 1939. Enter the 50th anniversary of D-Day, which provided an irresistible public relations platform and gave the company an opportunity to go to the press with an "update" message on Spam's new uses, redesigned logo, and line extensions.

In 1984, for instance, Wendy's International caused a remarkable stir with its "Where's the Beef?" ad campaign, designed to tout the size advantage of Wendy's burgers over the competition. Starring an unlikely spokesperson, a septuagenarian actress named Clara Peller, these offbeat commercials established "Where's the Beef?" as a national catchphrase, punch line, and subject for parody, each usage serving as a subtle reminder of Wendy's. Usage was so widespread that, in the 1984 presidential campaign, Democratic challenger Walter Mondale adopted "Where's the Beef?" as a challenge to the policies and accomplishments of the incumbent administration. Wendy's took full advantage of the situation by immediately capitalizing on the enormous popularity of Clara Peller through media tours, press conferences, and one-on-one interviews. Subsequent commercials featuring Clara and "Where's the Beef?" were debuted at press conferences and highlighted on *Entertainment Tonight*. Outtakes of commercials were publicized on various national and local television shows.

With public relations, it's also possible to generate excitement in advance of the advertising campaign and thus help to improve viewership in an age of commercial "zapping" via remote control. The best example of this is the way in which companies known for their imaginative commercials—Coca-Cola, Nike, Pepsi-Cola, and Miller Brewing, to name a few—target and preannounce the Super Bowl broadcast as the nationwide debut of a new ad campaign. This influences viewers to stay tuned for that "hot new ad" with rapt anticipation—more anticipation, in the case of most Super Bowl contests, than is generated by the game itself. Another successful publicity program in this vein comes from Taster's Choice, whose eagerly anticipated ads featuring an intriguing liaison between "that British woman and that American man" are the subject of articles in periodicals ranging from *TV Guide* to *Newsweek*.

6. As discussed above, the examples of both Velveeta and Spam succeeded in matching a product's profile to shifting public wants or concerns. In the food industry, this has attained a pronounced importance and most often takes the form of highlighting the nutritional benefits of a product or exploiting the latest scientific research in related fields. This tactic goes back to the last century, when a young vegetarian doctor and health-spa operator named John Harvey Kellogg designed a diet and regimen that minimized fats, proteins, and caffeine. To promote his theories, Kellogg created a mixed-grain breakfast food called Granola, which became the cornerstone of the Kellogg Company's breakfast cereals.

Recent years have seen a burgeoning of foods designed to capture a health-conscious public's attention, and public relations efforts have proved an invaluable part of the subsequent campaigns. To name just two—The NutraSweet Company's introduction of its all-natural fat substitute Simplesse, and The Quaker Oats Company's exploitation of the phenomenon that surrounded early anti-cholesterol claims for oat bran products—both of which depended heavily on unbiased media support and health-professional outreach. These are precisely the sorts of arenas in which public relations opens far more doors than do traditional advertising efforts.

7. From a defensive standpoint, a savvy communications blitz can help deflect interest-group or consumer concerns and complaints. In fact, this strategy seems tailor-made for public relations sweeps: Countering such charges with a major advertising campaign would foster a Goliath versus David scenario in relation to the common-man imagery of those making the charges. Consider the example of the food and beverage industry's successful crusade to reverse the FDA's ban on the sugar substitute saccharin from U.S. products. In 1977, when the ban was announced, protest was coordinated through the Calorie Control Council. This group, an international consortium of food and beverage manufacturers, focused on such issues as overly cautious test analyses, and called attention to the benefits of saccharin to diabetics and the morbidly obese—two groups that were greatly affected and able to generate sympathy on the part of the public.

A related tactic allows the preemption of consumer backlash against a product by taking responsible action that not only mitigates the problem, but also accrues "deposits" in the "trust bank". Consider the "Know When to Say When" campaign launched by the country's largest brewer, Anheuser-Busch, to promote responsible drinking—a campaign that can be seen as advocating a *reduction* in consumption of the advertiser's own products.

8. Finally, many companies employ a selection of reliable tactics when introducing a new product. The development and effective distribution of recipe books or cards help promote product usage; cooking demonstrations, spokesperson media tours, satellite media tours, video news releases, and audio news releases are all tactics that have proven effective for the food and beverage industry. Many companies have had success by establishing a presence in national or regional conferences or cooking schools, such as the respected Southern-market cooking school developed by *Southern Living* magazine.

Whatever tactics a public relations practitioner chooses, the plain fact is that garnering publicity for a new food or beverage product (or a revitalized old product) is predicated on one thing: *Is it newsworthy?* The media will generally be open to your product if the information breathes life into one of the following categories: safety; taste; functionality; cultural relevance; familiarity; convenience; seasonality; health or nutritional value; presentation (or packaging); or contemporaniety. If you have to stretch too hard to make it newsworthy, you may best be advised to save money until a more newsworthy product comes along.

Case Study: Mr. Magoo's Satellite Media Tour

The demonstrated success of (and clear demand for) NutraSweet® brand sweetener never has been taken for granted by its manufacturer; in fact, the company has conducted an ongoing integrated marketing campaign since the product was introduced. But while the now-famous red-and-white "swirl" logo has remained intact, the company has changed gears on a regular basis to keep the campaign rolling.

Perhaps the most innovative tactic came in June 1994, when NutraSweet presented to the public a new spokesperson, the well-known, highly myopic cartoon character Mr. Magoo. But the mere selection of Magoo to represent NutraSweet® brand sweetener would not, in itself, qualify as a uniquely innovative stroke: Magoo has haunted the airwaves and commercial byways for some time and, in fact, has even represented other companies and products (most notably General Electric in the 1970s).

What garnered attention for The NutraSweet Company's selection of Magoo was the nature of the press activities used to unveil his selection. The announcement provided an opportunity for television reporters around the country to speak directly with Magoo; not an actor in costume nor a preproduced video clip, but the cartoon character himself, able to interact with each reporter in the course of a spontaneous interview. Using breakthrough computer technology in tandem with state-of-the-art electronic puppeting controls and standard modern communications devices, Mr. Magoo on became the first cartoon to conduct a satellite media tour for interested reporters across the country.

There was, of course, an actor—a gifted mimic able to duplicate the tone and vocal mannerisms created for Mr. Magoo by the late Jim Backus—and this event depended heavily on his quick-witted responsiveness and his familiarity with NutraSweet® brand sweetener. But rather than fit his voice to a predrawn animated sequence, the director—in this case, the puppeteer controlling the computer—was able to match Magoo's on-screen actions to the things he said.

The effect proved even more remarkable than the company had hoped. Some of the reporters, purposely suspending their disbelief, literally could not let go of this new toy. They continued to talk with Magoo, discussing this and that as if he were an old friend, for several minutes after the interview had officially ended. About half of the interested stations aired their Magoo interview live, with the other half taping the event for later use. The total number of impressions generated from television coverage came to more than two million and included 20 television interviews, plus an article in *TV Guide* with a circulation of 14 million.

Almost as important was the print coverage of the satellite media tour. No less than eight of the targeted publications, including the *New York Times*, *Adweek*, and *Brand Week*, ran stories detailing the innovative techniques used for this event. The entire effort generated a total of 43 million impressions announcing to the American public Mr. Magoo's association with NutraSweet® brand sweetener.

The Magoo event more than satisfied the three major tactical objectives for this project. First, it allowed the company to leverage heavily the Mr. Magoo advertising campaign (see Figure 21–2) with separately generated media coverage. Second, it filled the media pipeline with images of Magoo and with concomitant positive messages about NutraSweet® brand sweetener—specifically, the myopic Magoo's pointed reminder to "LOOK for the logo." Third, the widespread publicity helped create awareness of the Magoo campaign among The NutraSweet Company's manufacturing customers (the thou-

F I G U R E 21–2

TRADE AD FOR THE MR. MAGOO CAMPAIGN*

*Retained Rights —Notwithstanding anything to the contrary, the Nutrasweet Company ("NSC") retains the nonexclusive rights to repro-
duce all copyrighted material covered by this Transfer and to include said material in publications distributed by or on behalf of NSC. In
addition, NSC retains the nonexclusive rights to prepare derivative works based upon said material, to reproduce such derivative works,
and to authorize the publication of such derivative works with acknowledgement of your organization's copyright. NSC may extend such
retained rights to its affiliated company, Monsanto Company, a corporation of Delaware, and to each company that said Monsanto Company now or hereafter owns or controls, directly or indirectly, fifty percent (50 percent) or more of the stock having the right to vote for or
appoint directors thereof.

sands of manufacturers who use NutraSweet® brand sweetener as a branded ingredient in their own products) and, in the process, demonstrated again the added value of manufacturing with NutraSweet® brand sweetener.

THE FUTURE

The future practice of public relations will be shaped by several factors: the continual shrinking of the globe by new communications media; the globalization of brands; the "tabloidization" or lowering standards of media; the public's growing distrust of all institutions; and the trend toward integration of marketing disciplines organized around a central strategic need.

It has been several decades since news and information—good or bad, accurate or inaccurate—could be practically confined within local or regional boundaries. The interlinking of national and international wire services and the proliferation of satellite-delivered television and radio news services dictates that a food scare such as the 1996 outbreak of "mad cow disease" in the United Kingdom can instantaneously raise concerns about the safety of the meat supply in Germany. Just as certainly, debates in the United States about the safety of genetically modified foods can and do generate parallel fears in Europe and elsewhere in the world. And the ready access to computer databases on virtually any topic means that public relations practitioners must be on constant guard to ensure that these unfiltered sources of sometimes erroneous or misleading information do not form the basis for news coverage about a marketer's company or product.

Debunking the media-hyped myths about the safety of the food supply may be the public relations challenge of the 1990s.

As brands migrate across borders, continents, and hemispheres, marketing communications practices are exported with them. This should be good news for the public relations profession since the brands that globalize generally originate in those parts of the world where public relations is practiced by competent professionals in an ethical manner.

At times, tabloid television and talk radio in the United States stretch the boundaries of truth while preying on the credulousness of viewers and listeners. "Experts" with a shingle and little else to recommend them are indiscriminately booked on talk programs to peddle their wares, and their claims often go unrebutted by program hosts and producers ill-equipped to sort fact from fiction. While independent groups such as the American Council on Science and Health and the food industry-supported International Food Information Council attempt to counter this trend, they are frankly underfunded and outgunned. Debunking the media-hyped myths about the safety of the food supply may be the public relations challenge of the 1990s.

This challenge becomes tougher in light of the citizenry's pronounced cynicism about all institutions. It is simply not enough to say that the United States Food and Drug Administration or the U.S. Agriculture Department has determined that a food is safe—the public no longer believes that the government can be trusted. And who can blame them? Those same agencies have, with justification, complained for years of underfunding, which they admit affects their ability to police the food supply as well as their capacity to approve beneficial new foods, food ingredients, and food technologies. Meanwhile, self-styled consumer groups position themselves as the only real protectors of the public's health, often raising spurious claims about food safety to enhance their fundraising efforts. As government agencies and advocacy groups battle it out, food and beverage companies take advantage of common fears about health and nutrition to sell so-called designer foods. The public ends up confused about the issues and believing no one.

Page, the public relations pioneer of the original AT&T, put it this way: "All business in a democratic country begins with public permission and exists by public approval."

Neither public relations as a single discipline nor integrated marketing communications as a strategic communications approach can eradicate cynicism. In fact, traditionalists in our profession may assert that the practice of public relations and the marketing of products using public relations techniques are inimical, because marketing itself is in large measure responsible for this lack of collective faith. But there is no reason that, as public relations, advertising, promotion, and other tools in the strategic communications arsenal merge under the umbrella of integrated marketing communications, the principles of Arthur W. Page cannot govern even more broadly. Page, the public relations pioneer of the original AT&T, put it this way: "All business in a democratic country begins with public permission and exists by public approval."

We're all selling something. Whatever tactics we use, let us make honesty and fairness the cornerstones of our strategy.

## CHAPTER 22

Image Management through Public Relations in the Insurance Industry

Robert E. Gorman
President
Communication for Change

James M. Dudas
Director of Corporate Relations
Allstate Insurance Company

A STRATEGIC APPROACH TO PUBLIC RELATIONS

Public relations practitioners in the insurance business today face significant challenges as they work to improve the industry's image with the public, as well as with customers, employees, regulators and shareholders.

Negative perceptions among the public are well-documented. In a 1994 survey by the American Council of Life Insurance, only 28 percent of American adults said they view the insurance industry in a favorable light. A higher share, 36 percent, had a negative view. In fact, insurance garnered more negative opinions than any other rated industry.

In addition, public attitudes about the industry have been trending downward for some time. In 1967, for example, 79 percent of the public said the life insurance industry was "humane and understanding" in dealing with the public. By 1975, that share had dropped to 57 percent. In 1994, it was only 45 percent. (See Figure 22–1.) While life insurance is only a part of the larger industry that includes property and casualty lines (auto, home, and business), the attitudinal trends still are cause for concern.

Claims and Other Causes

What's to blame for the industry's image problems? People's perceptions are based on personal experiences, as well as what they hear from friends, family, and others, and what they see and hear in the media. This is no different for insurance companies than for any other industry.

What is unique to insurance companies is that people are paying substantial sums for something they hope they never have to use.

In auto and home insurance, claims are generally considered the single most important "moment of truth" in the relationship between insurance customers and companies. But since only a small percentage of customers experience a claim in any given year, insurance companies start out on negative footing. If a customer has an accident, the company works to make the best of a bad situation. Those customers who do not have a claim are likely to think they have paid something for nothing.

F I G U R E 22-1

Insurance Industry Loses Share of Heart
Percent Who Agree That the Life Insurance Industry Is "Humane and Understanding"

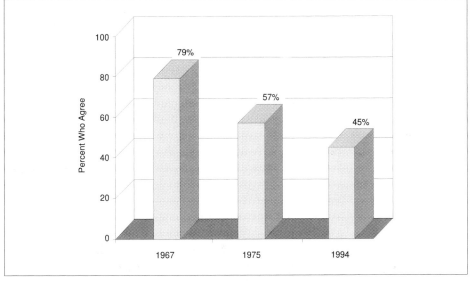

Original graph by author.

Part of the cost/value assessment consumers make about insurance companies is influenced by perceptions that the insurance business is highly profitable, that service is unresponsive, and that insurance policies are hard to understand. As the image experts say, perception is reality. Insurance companies need to begin changing consumer perceptions or risk negative consequences from customers, employees, and other stakeholders.

One clear opportunity area is in customer communication. Insurance policy language, loaded as it often is with legalese and complex contractual jargon, does meet the requirements of regulators. But the resulting policies and sales literature can unintentionally distance companies from their customers. Once a sale is made, things can begin on an adversarial rather than empathetic note at least partially because customers aren't always clear about what they have purchased. When accidents do occur, customer expectations may or may not be consistent with policy language and actual coverages.

Partially counterbalancing this negative image has been the industry's claim performance during record levels of natural disasters in the early 1990s. Earthquakes and fires in California, tornadoes and flooding in the Midwest, hurricanes in Florida, Hawaii, and the Carolinas, along with other catastrophes ranging from mudslides to ice storms to droughts, have reminded policyholders and the public why they need insurance in the first place. Accounts in the media and word of mouth growing out of the industry's catastrophe claim handling generally have been positive.

However, catastrophe losses in the billions and resulting solvency concerns have forced some companies to stop writing or renewing some coverages. Insurance is one of the few businesses in which companies actually turn away potential customers, essentially because the rate being charged (which often must be approved by insurance commissioners in each state) is not adequate for the risk or exposure the company is being asked to cover.

When financial concerns lead insurance companies to cancel some existing policies, it doesn't play well with the public in general or with policyholders in particular. Cancellations reinforce an image of insensitivity and profit at the expense of customers, and they fuel negative word-of-mouth comments that have plagued the industry for many years.

Of course, insurers are not the only companies suffering from image problems. In fact, almost all industries have shown declines in public confidence and support during the past 25 years. But the issue is especially important in the insurance business, for several reasons.

The Trust Factor

A negative public image is especially troubling for insurers because this business is built entirely on trust.

Although some insurance coverages are mandated by certain states and by lenders, customers still want to trust that companies will make good on the promises made by agents, in sales literature and advertising, and in insurance policies themselves. People want to have peace of mind about their families, their homes, their cars, and other belongings and responsibilities.

For example, Allstate, which has one of the most recognized names in the industry, has built its entire consumer franchise around the promise that "You're in Good Hands with Allstate." Anything that undermines that customer promise can undermine the company itself.

Anything that undermines that customer promise can undermine the company itself.

Trust also is extremely important to life insurers such as Prudential and Metropolitan and to multi-line insurers such as CNA, Aetna, and Travelers. Selling "a Piece of the Rock" is more difficult when prospects read about fines levied by state insurance commissioners for not complying with regulations on sales practices, for example.

Unfortunately, the insurance industry and certain companies in particular have had their share of negative headlines in the past few years. Over time, this bad news can chip away at the trust people have for a company and even an industry. And trust is at the heart of the strong relationships with customers, prospects, employees, shareholders, regulators, and others whom companies rely on to be successful. For example, building positive relationships with state insurance commissioners is critical to building the favorable business environment insurance companies need to operate successfully.

Trust also is a major issue in dealing with shareholders. Investors have a right to expect that insurance companies will protect themselves adequately against catastrophes, invest wisely, operate as efficiently as possible, and provide a competitive return.

For insurers, however, the trust factor is perhaps most critical when it comes to their own employees. Many employees deal directly with customers, or they support agents and claim and service professionals who are the heart of the company relationship with customers.

If employees don't trust their employer, it can influence how willing they are to deliver customer satisfaction. Ultimately, this can gravely damage a company's financial performance.

Today, public trust and consumer confidence in the industry are unacceptably low. This, then, is the strategic and communications challenge facing virtually every insurance company in the 1990s.

The key to restoring that trust and generating positive word-of-mouth comments is serving and satisfying customers in ways that exceed their expectations. And that, in turn, means maximizing the potential and the contributions of individual employees.

A Case in Point

The challenges of building a good image and positive relationships with stakeholders were brought into sharp focus for Allstate and other insurers when Hurricane Andrew slammed into south Florida in August 1992.

When Andrew hit, Allstate was a wholly owned subsidiary of Sears. It also was the country's second-largest property and casualty company and owned the second largest share of the Florida property insurance market.

The huge losses resulting from Andrew caused Allstate and other insurers to reduce their exposure to future severe hurricanes in Florida so they could stay fiscally strong for the benefit of all their customers. While the industry got great press for its catastrophe claim service in the aftermath of Hurricane Andrew, Allstate's image became tarnished once it started canceling customers and limiting the writing of new business in those areas of Florida most prone to these disasters.

To understand the situation facing Allstate post-Andrew, it is first necessary to understand how the business of insurance works.

For much of the 1960s and 1970s, property and casualty insurance companies expanded rapidly. This focus on top-line growth meant taking on some high-risk customers at rates contained by stiff competition, and counting on income from investment of the premiums to earn a profit. Many insurers now pay out more each year in claims than they receive in premiums, but still make a profit because of investment income on prior accumulations.

As investment profits began to decline during the 1980s, however, companies needed to return to the fundamentals of the business: making money from underwriting insurance, not just from investment income. Consequently, companies began placing more emphasis on finding and keeping the most profitable customers—those who offer the maximum opportunity to establish a mutually beneficial, long-term relationship. One such market segment was the growing group of upper-middle-class retirees who began moving into upscale developments in Florida. Florida became one of the hottest real estate and insurance markets in the country during the 1980s.

Meanwhile, many insurance companies, including Allstate, were in growth modes for property insurance—especially homeowners' and condominium owners' policies. They grew as fast as Florida was growing. Insurers were making a fair profit. They were contributing to the state's economy. Homeowner rates were among the lowest and most competitive in the nation. There were few regulatory problems. Even the climate cooperated. The number of hurricanes between 1961 and 1991 was the lowest in any 30-year period since 1871.

In 1987, however, Hurricane Hugo in South Carolina made insurers sit up and take notice. It not only caused $4.2 billion in damages, but also showed clearly that major hurricanes were still a serious threat.

By 1991, more-sophisticated hurricane modeling techniques allowed insurers to improve the accuracy of their risk assessments. But the assessments didn't result in good news. The models showed that many companies in Florida were overexposed to hurricanes. Indeed, they suggested that a serious storm could put some insurers out of business. In response to this new information, some companies—including Allstate—developed plans to reduce their risks. Unfortunately, however, plans take time to implement. And on August 24, 1992, time ran out.

The Worst Ever

Hurricane Andrew roared over 1,100 square miles of south Florida with wind gusts that may have reached 200 mph. Actual wind speeds remain unknown because National Weather Service measuring devices were destroyed by the storm.

Andrew spawned and nurtured more than 200 tornadoes that ripped a 20-mile-wide path through south Dade County and 50 miles into the Florida peninsula. The storm damaged 107,000 homes and 82,000 businesses. At least 28,000 homes were completely destroyed and as many as 45,000 became uninhabitable. Some 180,000 South Floridians were suddenly homeless. At $20 billion, it was the costliest natural disaster in history.

The devastation was so great it would be months before the true enormity of the storm was known. Help, however, began arriving immediately. Like other insurers, Allstate has formed catastrophe, or CAT, teams comprised of experienced and specially trained employees—some called out of retirement—to handle the aftermath of natural disasters.

In the case of Hurricane Andrew, Allstate couldn't predict how serious the devastation would be, but at least company leaders knew the storm was coming as it was tracked on radar. So, the day before Andrew hit, catastrophe plans were already in full swing.

Staffing at Allstate's National Claim Service Center in St. Petersburg, Florida, was boosted, and the company began broadcasting an 800 number to customers who were in the hurricane's potential path. Allstate contacted 29 regional offices throughout the country; by the next morning, 100 claims people were on stand-by for deployment. Arrangements were also made with a local claims adjustment contractor to provide about 200 people to handle the losses.

When Andrew blew ashore in Homestead, 30 claim offices around the country were wired into the 800 number, ready to take loss reports. Another 20 offices were standing by. Allstate's claim staff set up a catastrophe center in the Marriott Biscayne Hotel. In fact, they took over the hotel, installing computers, distributing hundreds of cellular phones and two-way radios and coordinating customer-service efforts.

As soon as the National Guard allowed entry into the affected areas, Allstate staff fanned out across the shattered neighborhoods. Though many of the 500 sales agents in the area experienced total or partial losses of their own homes and offices, they were nevertheless on the scene immediately, often writing checks for customers on the hoods of their cars or on sidewalks.

They encountered a catastrophe unlike any in their experience. Many street names and house addresses had been blown away, so even locating customers' homes was a daunting challenge. Finding the home owners, some whom were forced to vacate uninhabitable dwellings, was even more challenging. With virtually no mail or phone service in the area, victims were helpless. They gravitated to a huge tent city set up by the Federal Emergency Management Agency, where they lived on donated food and water. Some storm victims were living in their cars, driving from handout to handout while getting their lives in order. Some rented apartments and homes.

Meanwhile, their homes sat idle—in some cases looted, in others damaged even further by steady rains that fell for weeks after the storm. Reputable repair contractors, booked months in advance, turned away far more business than they accepted. Others, some of whom were clearly carpet-baggers, feasted on the tragedy, making promises, taking payment and then flight, leaving their hapless victims in worse straits than before.

In the midst of all this, as the enormity of the damage became clear, some insurance companies were running out of money. Even the giants were not spared. Prudential of Florida was forced to take a huge capital infusion from its parent company. State Farm's Fire and Casualty unit in Florida literally went bankrupt, although policyholders were protected by the parent company. Some smaller companies fared worse. With no parent to bail them out, they became insolvent. At least 12 companies were unable to pay their policyholders' claims.

Still, by February 1993, six months after the storm, 95 percent of claims had been settled and more than $13 billion had been distributed to policyholders. Most companies were overly generous in their efforts, providing services and cash that sometimes went well beyond the contract. The Florida Department of Insurance described customer satisfaction as "relatively high," citing complaints on only 2.7 percent of storm-related claims. According to a *Miami Herald* survey, 88 percent of policyholders felt their settlements were "generous" or "fair."

Good News and Bad News

So, amid all the destruction, the months immediately following the storm included some positive developments. Andrew was, in one sense, a public relations dream opportunity—a chance for companies like Allstate to show their customers that the premium dollars they had paid over the years would pay them back—and then some. The company, especially its Florida employees, took great pride in helping customers put their lives back together.

On the financial side, however, the post-Andrew perspective was not nearly so positive. To quote a Chrysler television commercial from the recent past, "*This* changes everything." The losses from Andrew were bad enough by themselves. In Florida alone, the equivalent of 53 years of Allstate profits in the state—about $1.9 billion—blew away in just four hours (see Figure 22–2). But Allstate's total countrywide 1992 catastrophe losses (which also included the Oakland Fire, the Loma Prieta earthquake, and Hurricane Iniki) were nearly equal to the 17 prior years of catastrophe losses combined.

Rating agencies such as Standard & Poor's and A.M. Best expressed concern about Andrew's impact on Allstate, as well as on other companies with large shares of the Florida market. Rating agencies scrutinize insurance industry financial stability and assess their ability to meet obligations. A reduction in financial rating can have major implications for a company because insurers sell a promise that they will "be there" for customers when they are needed. Downratings can threaten the trust that customers and others place in a company.

Financial ratings are especially important to a company—like Allstate—that was about to go public. Just 36 days after Hurricane Andrew hit, Allstate's parent company, Sears, Roebuck & Co., announced it would be offering Allstate shares to the public for the first time in history. It would become the largest initial public offering (IPO) of common stock in the 200-year history of the New York Stock Exchange. On June 3, 1993, Sears sold 20 percent of Allstate, or 89.5 million shares, at $27 each and generated $2.4 billion in gross proceeds. The IPO also had an impact because it magnified pressure from potential investors, who wanted to see whether the company would act quickly and decisively to lower its exposure to future catastrophes in Florida.

F I G U R E 22–2

Comparison of Allstate's Florida Operating Profits, 1939–1992,*
to Allstate's 1992 Florida Operating Loss from Hurricane Andrew

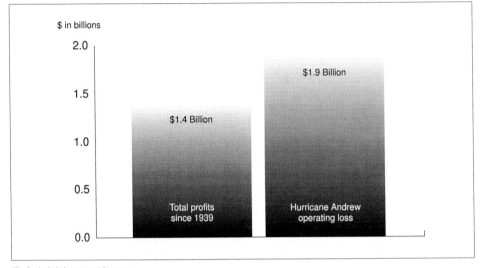

*Profits include investment income.

The heavy losses from Hurricane Andrew, combined with projections about the possibly devastating impact of future storms, basically left the company with three options. First, Allstate could buy reinsurance spreading the Florida risk with other insurance companies. Given the past several years of huge catastrophe losses, however, the reinsurance market did not offer coverage in the amounts Allstate needed. And what was available was prohibitively priced.

A second option involved working with the Florida State Legislature to pass a bill that would create a public-private partnership to share the risk. Allstate and the industry worked very hard to get this accomplished, but they could not complete this work before the legislative session concluded.

The final option was the most difficult because it meant reviewing the company-customer contract. Allstate insured 2.8 million personal property customers in Florida. Unfortunately, about 300,000 of them lived in areas highly vulnerable to hurricanes. Management was faced with, on the one hand, potentially jeopardizing the insurance protection for Allstate's 25 million other customers across the country, or, on the other hand, not renewing the existing property coverage of some of its customers in Dade, Broward, and Palm Beach Counties, the areas most prone to hurricanes.

Given Allstate's exposure in some of the areas most prone to hurricanes, there was no option other than to protect the financial viability of the company. The company established a goal to ultimately limit its hurricane exposure to $1 billion per catastrophe event. On April 23, 1993, Allstate announced its decision to not offer renewal coverage to about 300,000 homeowners. The action was to be phased in over a two-year period. A rate increase averaging 30 percent also was announced to more accurately reflect the hurricane risk Allstate faced.

After receiving Allstate's plan, the State Department of Insurance issued two mandates. First, *all* customers had to be notified, thus generating unnecessary concern, anger, and complaints among those who would not ultimately be affected.

Second, the company had to participate in public hearings to which it must invite all of its customers. The hearings posed some public relations risks, to be sure, but company leaders had no choice but to comply with the insurance commissioner's order. The hearings were held May 17 and 18, 1993. Allstate officials testified concerning the reasons for the company's nonrenewal decision. They told attendees that the customers ultimately affected would still have property insurance. Allstate agents would handle the transition from Allstate to a state-run Joint Underwriting Association.

The hearings were held in hotel ballrooms with standing-room-only and sometimes very angry crowds. The second hearing had an atmosphere one Allstate participant later called "circus-like." People came with prepared remarks and hand-lettered signs. Many were senior citizens on fixed incomes. Others included heads of consumer groups, retired employees, and a representative from an environmental watchdog group.

To the extent that time permitted, everyone had an opportunity to speak. Company representatives listened patiently to comments such as: "If I'd known what I know today, I wouldn't have bought a policy from Allstate." And: "They just want to insure people who will never have a claim so they can make money."

Allstate spokespeople also had their say: ". . . an Andrew-like storm—or worse— can, and indeed will, strike again. The risk, together with a realistic appraisal of our own resources, demands that we act and act now." And: "These changes are dictated by the necessity to remain financially strong in order to honor the commitment we have made not only to the citizens of Florida but to more than 25 million policyholders across America."

Media Tables Turn

Press reports on both days of the hearings accurately reflected the anger of many attendees. The situation quickly escalated into a public relations nightmare. Company hero had turned almost overnight into company goat—at least for the time being.

All the positive press and word-of-mouth comments growing out of Allstate's Andrew claim performance disappeared. It was an unpleasant reminder of how long it takes to earn a good reputation and how quickly it can disappear. Allstate became the butt of political cartoonists and Jay Leno's jokes on *The Tonight Show*. The "You're in Good Hands with Allstate" promise was held up to question and ridicule.

It was a painful time for employees—especially Florida employees. They could put themselves in the place of customers, some of whom would now have to turn elsewhere for their property insurance. But they could also see the company's side of the situation. They just had a hard time with all the negative press and comments from friends, family, and associates. Florida employees—and their managers—repeatedly asked the company to do something to make the atmosphere change, to restore Allstate's good name.

By focusing on a workable solution to the problem of severe hurricanes, the company's leaders felt Allstate could move beyond the immediate situation, act in the best long-term interests of its customers, and begin to improve its image. This became the direction of the company's strategy: Allstate began working on a legislative solution to the state's insurance crisis.

F I G U R E 22–3

F I G U R E 22–3

Allstate's Strategy to Restore a Good Image

1. Communicate clearly with employees so they understand and support the company.
2. Work with others in the industry and related fields to restore stability to the market.
3. Implement solutions that are in the best long-term interest of customers.

From a company standpoint, three things quickly became clear, as shown in Figure 22– 3. First, Allstate employees needed to understand and support the company's difficult decision. Second, Allstate needed to work with others in the state to bring stability to the Florida insurance market. The best way to do that was to support legislation that would share the risk of severe catastrophes between insurance companies and the state. And third, Allstate's reputation, although tarnished, could be repaired by standing for solutions that were in the best long-term interests of its customers. Allstate leadership believed that an industry-sponsored catastrophe bill would do just that.

Allstate's and the industry's key message was that ongoing losses the size of Andrew's were simply beyond the financial scope of private insurers. Only a public-private partnership, they argued, could fund a long-term solution that would bring stability to the insurance marketplace. And that stability, in turn, was critical to the long-term growth of Florida's economy.

Allstate needed a plan to mobilize action internally and externally. But first, the company needed to know how key stakeholders were reacting to the decision, so it surveyed employees, customers, and the public in Florida and across the country. The surveys showed that employees everywhere were aware of the company's nonrenewal decision. And while most understood the reasons and thought it was the right thing to do from a business standpoint, some felt less favorable about Allstate as a place to work after the announcement. Only about 30 percent of the public and customers outside of Florida were aware of the decision, according to the surveys. But customers who were aware of the decision were less likely to recommend Allstate to friends and family. Agreement that "Allstate has a good reputation" was significantly lower among those customers across the country who were aware of the nonrenewal plan.

THE TACTICS OF RESTORING AN IMAGE

Rebuilding from the Inside Out

The research findings obviously were cause for concern on employee and customer fronts. Among employees, it was clear that communication had been successful in "capturing" their heads. They understood why the risk reduction strategy was necessary. But the company also needed their hearts. It needed their help in building grassroots support for the catastrophe bill that was being drafted.

With customers, Allstate worried that the decision could devalue a company core strength: the Allstate brand name. Would purchase and renewal decisions be negatively influenced? The company needed to act quickly and decisively to redress any possible loss in trust and confidence.

The strategy was an effort to work from the inside out—starting with employees and agents, and, through them, communicating with customers, legislators, and related businesses that would benefit from a stable insurance market.

The plan had four components: employee communication, political action, media contacts, and coalition building.

Employee Communications

Of these, employees were the most important audience. The message to them—and subsequently, to others—was that this issue affected much more than insurance companies. A stable insurance marketplace affects every Florida resident and is critical to the state's economic well-being. Communications positioned the industry-sponsored bill as the best short-term solution. For the longer term, employee communications attempted to build support for the Federal Natural Disaster Protection Act in Congress. The bill proposed a nationwide public-private plan covering losses from hurricanes, tornadoes, and earthquakes.

Allstate sent a communication package to all employees on June 1, 1993, which included highlights of the Florida research so they could understand how the decision was being received by customers and the public. It also included "talking points" that employees could use to inform themselves and to answer questions from customers, family, fellow employees and others. Also included in the package were a series of questions and answers, a chronology of key events, and a sample customer letter that addressed questions and concerns.

On June 2, a taped interview with the president of Allstate's Property and Casualty division, was broadcast by satellite to the company's regional offices across the country. The interview provided a historical context and a rationale for the decision. The president added his perspective that it was very difficult to read the bad press and see the company you love being "dragged through the mud," but that the company was doing the right thing for its 25 million customers long-term.

The interview with the president was brief but candid. Employee feedback was favorable. After the broadcast, video and audio tapes of the interview also were distributed to ensure that every employee had the opportunity to review the message.

Another employee communication package was distributed a month later. This offered a more detailed historical summary leading up to the legislative solution and discussed how employees could help support it. While Florida employees were encouraged to participate in grassroots efforts, employees in other states were briefed about the federal bill in development.

Political Action

At the same time, political action efforts capitalized on an active group of Florida employees who were members of a Political Action Team. Their strategy was to sponsor roundtable discussions and educational forums that would mix employees with invited legislators. These meetings focused attention on the advantages of an industry-sponsored catastrophe fund that, by this time, was being reviewed by a special session of the state legislature.

Political Action Team members—about 100 statewide—held open houses in several company offices. They contacted their representatives about the bill, and they encouraged fellow employees to do the same.

Media Contacts

The media strategy involved partnering with other insurance companies, industry groups, and other businesses with a stake in the catastrophe fund bill. The group made editorial board visits with national and state newspapers and magazines, as well as with television and radio stations.

Coalition Building

Allstate and other companies worked closely with the Florida Insurance News Service, an industry information and advocacy group, as well as the Hurricane Insurance Information Center sponsored by the Insurance Information Institute, a national trade organization.

The Florida Hurricane Catastrophe Fund passed on November 9, 1993. Passage of the bill was very important for Allstate because the risk-sharing mechanism established by the bill meant the company could reduce the original number of customers affected by nonrenewals from the originally announced number of 300,000 to about 30,000. While the fund was an important first step, Allstate and the industry continue to advocate the need for a federal bill that will establish a public and private sharing of large-scale risks such as severe earthquakes and hurricanes.

Lessons Learned

Growing out of some painful lessons in Florida, Allstate has recently taken several major steps to improve its image.

These steps are based on a better understanding of the severe catastrophe risk the company faces and the things it can do to mitigate that risk. They also are based on a new understanding of reputational risk—the threat to the trust upon which a business is built—and what the company can do to protect that trust.

In addition to the company's ongoing efforts to decrease exposure to natural disasters in states such as Florida, Texas, California, and New York, senior managers meet regularly to discuss pending business decisions and consider how they will affect Allstate's image.

The company also formed a senior-level Image Team to identify how they would like Allstate to be perceived by the public and suggest ways to perform up to those perceptions. The work also includes estimating the dollar value of the Allstate brand and considering how the value of this asset could go up or down depending on marketplace performance, actions and decisions, and communications.

Another related effort is to articulate an Allstate aspiration; a nonfinancial statement that describes what the company intends to become. This aspiration will guide decision making and actions at all levels and help employees connect their jobs to the larger company purpose.

Tough decisions certainly lay ahead. Allstate will need to balance the interests of shareholders with those of customers and employees. But the lessons of Florida have given the company a useful perspective for balancing those interests.

The aftermath of Hurricane Andrew and its related consequences clarified that a good image is critical to Allstate's ability to grow and prosper. People's perceptions influence their choice of whether or not to do business with a company. So image is not something soft or separate *from* the business—it *is* the business.

This heightened sensitivity to the importance of image will be especially valuable as company leaders make decisions and as Allstate—now a 100 percent independent company and the largest publicly owned personal lines insurer—matures as a public company. It also will help employees deliver on the promise the company makes every day to 25 million customers around the country— "You're in Good Hands with Allstate."

> **Image is not something soft or separate *from* the business– it *is* the business.**

TRENDS FOR TOMORROW

What about the future? Several trends already underway will significantly affect insurers and their communications programs. Consolidation and globalization will decrease the number of competitors while increasing the level of competition. Nontraditional marketing programs in areas such as direct response will expand. Technology advances such as interactive television may redefine distribution systems and customer relationships.

No matter what other changes occur, however, the importance of quality and customer focus will intensify. Satisfying customers will be key, not only to improving profits, but to improving the industry's image. And the key to satisfying customers will be harnessing the efforts of employees throughout the organization.

Technology can help. But in the end, it will take comprehensive communications efforts, driven by overall business strategies, to cement and strengthen the critical bond between company and customer.

To quote Daniel Yankelovich:

> Every one of us knows from daily experience how frustrating it is when the companies we personally depend on—banks, phone companies, airlines, car rental companies, insurance companies, etc.—substitute a computer-driven system for employees who don't give a damn and don't know what they are doing. What the logic of the 1990s recognizes is that, in a world awash with bigness and technology, the competitive edge will go to those businesses whose employees care about the customer rather than just go through the motions. In the future, the edge will belong to those who know how to mobilize their employees' discretionary effort.[1]

And communications will be critical to achieving that goal.

E N D N O T E

1. Yankelovich. *Corporate Logic in the 1990s,* 1994 Arthur W. Page Society Spring Seminar.

Public Relations and the Pharmaceutical Industry

Elliot S. Schreiber, Ph.D.
Senior Vice President, Communications
Northern Telecom (Nortel) Ltd.*

A STRATEGIC APPROACH TO PHARMACEUTICAL PUBLIC RELATIONS

Until the early 1990s, pharmaceutical public relations primarily supported marketing communications and direct promotion of products to doctors. Today, the specialty is far more complex and heavily issued-oriented. It must now be more strategically integrated into decision-making processes, more aligned with long-term business objectives, and able to meet the new challenges of a highly regulated and increasingly competitive health care marketplace.

The New Constituency Relations Focus

With the rise of managed care and demands for health care reform, new challenges include designing meaningful responses to marketplace and government developments.

But, first, a company must identify the nontraditional audiences which are driving these developments and affecting business through legislation, public policy, and public opinion. A company must then gain an appreciation of the needs and motivations of these audiences to ensure that messages speak directly to the values of each targeted group. This need to address new audiences has moved pharmaceutical public relations away from its marketing communications or financial relations orientation toward a more strategic constituency relations focus.

An important step in understanding pharmaceutical PR's sharpened focus on constituency relations is to recognize that manufacturers have been thrust from a traditional business and market environment into a highly charged political environment. As the industry's environment changes, so too do the number of its constituents and the complexities of its relationships among them. As a result, many pharmaceutical companies are struggling to realign and refocus their public relations activities, focusing increasingly on public policy and public affairs.

In this new world, companies must quickly elevate the role of public relations and recognize that powerful forces—policymakers, patient and public interest advocates, man-

---

*At the time of this writing, the author was Senior Vice President, Corporate Communications, Miles Inc. (now Bayer Corporation).

aged care groups, activists, and the media—are taking control and exerting greater influence on the business of selling pharmaceuticals. These groups, among others, accuse the industry of indifference toward patients, price gouging, and deprivation of patients who are poor or lack insurance of the medicines their physicians prescribe.

Such scrutiny requires a sensitivity toward and a complete understanding of constituency relations. Where PR professionals once used communications to help brand management increase market share, they now, like politicians, must use more-targeted, interactive communications to address their constituents' needs. While they sought message control in the past, they must now exchange information and ideas and establish, build, and nurture relationships. Market share alone will no longer be the tool to measure leadership. Constituents will reward companies that create dialogue and consensus with the respect and trust which is essential for conducting business today. With this trust, publics will, to a certain degree, give corporations the benefit of the doubt regarding product value, marketing practices, prices, and profits. Constituents will give manufacturers permission to continue in the business of selling drugs.

Putting Things in Perspective

Until recently, the pharmaceutical industry's overall charter was to develop and market products to support its primary customer, the prescribing physician. Issues of payment were of little concern: patients and insurance companies dealt with payment, with very little involvement by doctors.

It was the industry's role to develop and manufacture drugs and educate physicians. It was the doctor's role to prescribe and counsel patients on how to use the medicine. This relationship between company and doctor continued well into the 1980s, when increasingly high profit margins brought pharmaceutical companies into the public spotlight.

In the new marketing environment, pharmaceutical companies must fundamentally change the way they communicate and do business. Companies are being forced to manage operations within a highly charged political environment that holds them accountable for the cost of care. Companies must learn how to effectively respond to widespread criticism and public policy and public opinion pressures, and learn how to leverage their responses for business advantage.

Simply put, cost sensitivity is redefining the role of pharmaceutical public relations. The cost-effectiveness of therapeutics, for example, in addition to safety and efficacy, has become key to all communications and marketing. The value of each product must now be demonstrated to a diverse group of audiences (or new customer bases) such as providers, patients, and payers. Moreover, since prevention and wellness measures, as opposed to therapeutic treatment of illness, are encouraged to reduce the financial strains on the health care system, and more patients are being forced to take responsibility for their health, PR can no longer exclusively focus on product attributes. The human factor or human value of health care must become part of the message and communications process.

With patients, and all constituents, pharmaceutical communications must have four strategic dimensions. PR today must: (1) involve and form relationships with audiences to demonstrate commitment; (2) redefine questions and concerns in the context of cost-effectiveness and social value; (3) share emotion and the human value of the industry; and (4) demonstrate integrity to assure all publics that the industry acts to serve the social needs of the country.

The Industry Restructures

In 1993, the pharmaceutical industry began a fundamental restructuring which had already occurred in many other industries. In the year 1993 alone, the U.S.-based industry lost approximately $100 billion in market value and cut nearly 35,000 jobs. Many have blamed this on President Clinton's health care reforms; however, this restructuring mirrored developments in both the public and private sectors. The factor that initiated most of the restructuring was not health care reform—an industry does not downsize on the threat of change—but rather the growing forces of cost sensitivity on the part of the payers in the system. The patient, or the public, was not a major component of this bottom-line-driven mission and method of business.

Government Control of Health Care Spending

The relatively recent pressures on pharmaceuticals are a continuation of a trend begun in the 1970s, when the U.S. Congress began to consider legislation to control rising hospital spending (then, as now, the largest segment of health care expenditures). This led to the American Hospital Association's "Voluntary Effort to Contain Hospital Costs" (VE), which worked until Congressional pressure subsided. The Congress then passed the Tax Equity and Fiscal Responsibility Act of 1982 (TEFRA), which introduced the Prospective Payment System (PPS) into health care.

The Prospective Payment System created the DRG method of payment. DRGs are a patient classification system that is used not only for reimbursement but also for quality control, budgeting, and planning. Under current legislation, patients are placed in a DRG based on their primary and secondary diagnoses as determined at discharge from the hospital, and other factors including age, discharge status, and surgical procedures required. Payment rates for each diagnosis are set in advance, and the hospital is paid only that amount regardless of services rendered. All costs in excess of the DRG are absorbed by the hospital. Conversely, the institution retains the full payment if costs are lower than the DRG rate.

The objective was to drive down costs sustained by the federal government, namely those covered by Medicare, but it also was intended to be a model for the private sector to follow.

Private Sector Initiatives

The changes that have occurred in the medical delivery system and which are likely to continue have been brought about more by private industry than by government. Uwe Reinhart, James Madison Professor of Economics at Princeton University, has suggested that the pharmaceutical industry might be better off in the long run with a heavy government hand than with mega-purchasers in the private sector, simply because the government has an interest in the industry's viability as a research enterprise. As he put it: "I'd rather deal with [the government's Office of Management and Budget Director] Alice Rivlin than [now retired Chrysler CEO] Lee Iaccoca."

This, of course, was not always so. Less than a decade ago, drug companies ran a fairly simple business. They discovered and marketed drugs which they priced at a premium and watched profits roll in. However, with the rise of managed health care in the United States, drug companies have come under increasing pressure to bring their prices down. These developments began in the early 1980s with the growth of health maintenance organizations (HMOs) and other managed care practices. Companies, sensitive to the effect of the escalating cost of medical benefits on the bottom line, began to change their employee benefits policies. Companies that could—that is, those without labor unions—initiated changes which forced employees to increase their amount of co-payment with the company.

At the same time, companies in many areas began to form alliances to pressure local hospitals and doctors to control their prices. Companies began providing to their employees a list of "qualified" doctors in the local area who would perform tests, surgery, or other procedures within prescribed pricing parameters. Doctors whose fees were outside of these boundaries were blacklisted.

Companies got serious about bringing down the costs of health care when the cost of medical benefits became the third-largest employee cost for many companies, trailing only salaries and vacations. The involvement by companies, in turn, began to effect changes in the system. As hospital costs were squeezed, the marketing environment changed. The purchasing agent within the hospital became the most important decision maker. Radiologists had less involvement in the decision as to which x-ray film and equipment to buy; pathologists had less input into the decision as to which medical diagnostic system to buy. As a result, companies which had focused efforts on improving the quality of their x-ray film had to focus increasingly on cost; diagnostic companies which had fallen over one another to add more tests to their instruments to make them competitively more attractive had to think of the bottom line. Company benefits managers also began insisting that employees seek generic alternatives to ethical drugs and that second opinions be sought on elective surgeries. The focus on generics, in particular, had a dramatic impact on the industry.

The pharmaceutical and diagnostic companies were slow to change their marketing and communications activities despite these changes in the industry. Pharmaceutical salesmen, or so-called "detail men," continued to call on physicians to tout their new drugs; diagnostic companies manufactured instruments with reagents that were exclusive to their systems and could not be interchanged with another. The industry continued until recently to see its role as developing and selling drugs. Public relations professionals within pharmaceutical companies were marketing-focused, finding new ways to attract attention to their products. All along, however, there was little attention paid to cost since, by and large, this continued to be passed on to the customer who could, in turn, pass the costs along to someone else.

The Industry Defends Itself

While all of these market changes occurred long before Bill Clinton's election to the presidency, he was the first president to question the primary motivation of the pharmaceutical industry. Was the industry motivated by an interest in the health of its patients or by profits? Would they sacrifice the former for the latter? By raising these questions, one could argue that administration officials were providing their own answers. The president made it okay to question whether it was appropriate for the pharmaceutical industry to make money on its drugs. Some of these arguments were potentially dangerous. For example, one member of the health care advisory team put together by First Lady Hillary Rodham Clinton and Judith Feder of Georgetown University suggested that the pharmaceutical industry should be regulated like a public utility.

B O X 23–1

GLOBAL STRATEGY

By mid-1994, managed care represented 50 percent of all U.S. pharmaceutical sales, more than double what it had been just a few years earlier. Jan Leschly, CEO of SmithKline Beecham, suggests that by 1977 this percentage could be about 80 percent. As a consequence, the industry downsized its existing operations while, at the same time, going on a buying spree for multisource (that is, generic) pharmaceutical companies. One of the largest buys was Merck's $6 billion acquisition of Medco Containment. SmithKline bought Diversified Pharmaceutical Services for $2.3 billion. Bayer Corporation chose not to purchase outright but to invest about $310 million to buy a 28 percent stake in Schein Pharmaceutical, one of the largest generic operations, with the option to purchase the company in total after seven years.

European companies also were acquired. Bristol-Myers Squibb went into generics in Europe by buying 25 percent of Germany's Azupharma.

In response to the Clinton Administration's focus on industry profits, the pharmaceutical industry argued that, while the public focused on the cost of drugs, pharmaceuticals actually save money since they frequently treat people outside of the hospital and are, in fact, often the reason the patient did not have to be hospitalized.

Moreover, the industry pointed out that it costs, on average, $250 million to bring an ethical drug to market, and even more for a genetically engineered pharmaceutical. While drugs might be costly, the reimbursement was argued to be fair given the enormous investment and time, as much as 12 years, until a drug cleared FDA approval. Also, while a successful drug might bring large profits, few people recognized how much money and time the industry had lost with research efforts that did not bear fruit.

Companies engaged in research also pointed out that the companies that made generics did not have to bear these costs. Often, the greatest investment by generic companies was in patent attorneys who challenged the patents of existing drugs prior to patent expiration, sometimes successfully. These companies had little or no research investment. They only formulated and sold products at a lower price. What escaped scrutiny, however, was that these generic companies' margins often were equal to those of the research-based pharmaceutical companies.

What the entire industry failed to understand was that they were arguing facts against mounting perceptions to the contrary. As any student of marketing knows, fact and perception are one and the same in the marketplace.

Response to the New Focus on Cost

It is interesting to note that the 1990s arguments of the pharmaceutical industry were the same ones used in the early 1970s. Usually, if someone uses an argument for more than 20 years and discovers that it still has not convinced the audience, one changes the message. That, regrettably, was not what the industry did. For most of those 20-plus years, the arguments were being made to members of Congress who could not muster enough public support to force changes in the health care system—we do, in fact, have in the U.S. the world's finest system, for those who can afford it. However, the industry did not recognize that the audience had changed. The audience now was comprised of corporate benefits managers, hospital purchasing agents, and others of similar background. The message of recovering research costs was no longer appropriate.

By 1994, the unique selling proposition had become cost. As a result, the industry began to go through a restructuring and downsizing as margins were squeezed.

Acquiring generic companies was the strategic direction chosen by some research-oriented companies. In times of uncertainty and change, there are a variety of market movements and mergers. Merck set the direction for most companies through its acquisition of a generics and distribution company, Medco, while the giant Swiss pharmaceutical company, Roche Holdings, decided to integrate horizontally by acquiring an ethical pharmaceutical company, Syntex, for $5.3 billion. Time will tell which was the right strategy.

"What is interesting here," notes financial analyst Sam Isaly of Mehta and Isaly, "is that you have the world's largest pharmaceutical company in terms of market cap betting one way, and the world's second-largest, Merck, betting the opposite view." [1]

This merger fever has involved both U.S. and foreign companies. Everyone, it seems, is responding to what financial analyst Arvind Desai of Mehta and Isaly calls a "global trend toward frugal health care."

SLOW CHANGES IN PUBLIC RELATIONS TACTICS

The shifts in the competitive environment, coupled with health care reform proposals, wreaked havoc on the industry. Public relations messages and marketing techniques have not kept pace. It is easy to understand why it took a while for the industry to combat its critics effectively. Unlike the chemical and oil industries which have had to deal with decades of criticism, public scrutiny, and regulation, the pharmaceutical industry found it difficult to cope with the public's skepticism and distrust. Yes, some critics argued the industry needed money for research, but why so much? Why, people argued, does the industry need to grow 25 percent per year "on the backs of sick people"?

The Clinton Administration's attacks on the health care system found the industry unprepared and disjointed in its response, unlike the chemical industry. Years of Superfund and chemical phobia had helped shape the Chemical Manufacturers Association (CMA) into an organization with strong involvement by the industry's CEOs, who spent considerable time formulating common industry positions. The CMA slowly transformed itself from a group of independent-thinking companies with only a few outward-thinking leaders like Du Pont, Dow, and Monsanto, into an organization with significant resources spent on communications and public education. In contrast, the Pharmaceutical Research and Manufacturers Association (PhRMA), formerly the Pharmaceutical Manufacturers Association, remained a group of free and separately thinking executives. Little effort was given to public education; the organization was more reactionary.

GO GLOBAL

What the United States is planning to do to its health care system already has been done in much of the world, often to a greater degree than we in this country plan or should contemplate. When profitability is impacted, companies often go global to find a market. The pharmaceutical industry is no exception; the industry has become much more global in recent years. Unlike the chemical industry, there cannot be the same degree of importing and exporting of products due to regulatory requirements. However, drug companies are playing on a world field like never before.

While national meetings of the CMA concerned themselves with issues updates and trends, PhRMA's agenda was social.

The New Role of Public Relations

Today, the public relations function within the pharmaceutical industry is very different from what it was just three to five years ago. Then, the job was very heavily centered on marketing communications, promoting products to doctors. Today, the position is far more complex and heavily issued-oriented. Public relations in the pharmaceutical industry today needs to be far more integrated into strategic decision making by the company and more focused on how to help the company meet its long-term business objectives.

Several examples of recent communications by the pharmaceutical industry show signs of change and some signs of the past.

- Early in the Clinton Administration, the president suggested that all children should be vaccinated. Because millions of people are uninsured, the president suggested that the states should become the agents through which vaccines are provided free to all children. The immediate industry response was to argue that this would cut into monies needed for future research and would undermine the industry. Only later—after the initial news cycle and after a well-prepared President Clinton issued a scathing rejoinder—did the manufacturers of vaccines tell the public that they provided vaccines free to indigent patients.

  This example shows the inability of marketing-communications-oriented public relations to identify the key issue in this situation. This was an early administration challenge to determine if the industry was focused on patients or profits. What better example to choose that to question the availability of products for children.

- At the same time, the administration suggested that there might be a need for mandated price controls. The industry's trade groups argued that price controls did not work and that they would erode important monies needed for research. The industry argued that pharmaceuticals comprised only 7 percent of all health care costs and that price controls would have no impact on the nation's health care costs.

  Once again, the argument of the composition of pharmaceuticals within the total health care price tag missed the point. Certainly, the administration recognized that it could not control health care costs by simply controlling pharmaceuticals. The issue was another test of the principal of profits versus health. The pharmaceutical industry was becoming a convenient target for the administration.

  Instead of recognizing the issues and the options available to manage them, the industry's early reaction was to behave as it had in the past—to confront and argue with old messages.

  With Merck's leadership, some things began to change. Merck was the first company to announce that it would voluntarily control prices of its drugs to the rate of inflation. Miles (now Bayer) and a few other companies quickly followed. Within weeks, 17 pharmaceutical companies had made the same pledge. With that offer of voluntary price controls, the threat of mandated controls was removed from the administration-proposed legislation. Still, 18 drug companies, among which were some of the largest and best known, refused to make such a pledge. Instead, these companies stuck to their original arguments about needed research dollars and the limited impact such controls would have on the nation's health care costs.

Changing the Messages to Reach the Audiences

A pattern emerges in both of these scenarios. That is, an industry that has continued to argue the need for profits for research has a hard time changing its message, even when this message no longer works. Pharmaceutical salesmen in the early 1970s were trained to argue against generics on the basis of needed research and development costs. In 1994, the same arguments were still being used. If after so many years one learns that the message has not been heard, one has two choices. One can yell the same message louder and with more vigor. Or one can try to understand why the audience is not accepting the message and attempt to change the message to address the needs of the audience. Much of the industry remains focused on the first alternative.

At the same time, the industry continues to go through fundamental structural change. Public relations activities at pharmaceutical companies are beginning to catch up to these changes as top management recognizes that it needs public relations counsel as a prelude to public relations tactics.

The key public relations activity in the pharmaceutical industry has shifted from being marketing communications or financial relations oriented, toward counseling with a view toward constituency relations. As the industry has changed, the number of constituents and the complexities of the relationship among these constituents has changed. As a result, many pharmaceutical companies are struggling with a catch-up process, trying to realign and refocus their public relations activities and focusing increasingly on public policy and public affairs.

To some practitioners in other industries, these changes may seem, in the words of Yogi Berra, like "déjà vu all over again." The practice of public relations as constituencies relations emerged as a standard in the chemical, oil, and other industries that came under public scrutiny and criticism years ago.

The international arena is another place in which public relations is changing. For years, pharmaceuticals were managed on a country-by-country basis. Compounds developed in one country and approved by its regulatory agencies are not easily exported. While the European Community has recognized and accepted the regulatory practices of EC countries, the United States continues to require that all drugs go through a lengthy clinical trail period prior to Food and Drug Administration (FDA) approval. These regulations are in place regardless of whether the drug has already been approved in another country.

However, the issues of health care reform and cost containment are international in nature. Government and third-party pressures on medical costs are growing not only in the United States, but also in Germany, Italy, France, and Japan.

In the 1950s, social psychologists Muzafer and Carolyn Sherif found that influence and attitude change were usually determined by a "significant other" or reference group. In the medical community, influence typically resides in the medical school from which the doctor graduated and in leading research physicians at leading teaching hospitals who help establish consensus on treatments for various disorders. The public relations practitioner often is involved in medical symposia and other meetings at which medical consensus is established. Similarly, press conferences for new product announcements usually feature leading researchers who provide the important "endorsement" of the pharmaceutical as an efficacious therapy for a particular disorder. Budgets for public relations often must reflect the need to provide counseling or spokesman fees to doctors and researchers who endorse a company's products at symposia and through presentations.

E N D N O T E

1. "The Road Not Taken: How Fritz Gerber of Roche Holdings Became the Maverick of the Drug Industry," *Financial World* (July 19, 1994), pp. 38–41.

## CHAPTER 24

The Personal Care Products Industry and Public Relations

Leah Landolfi
Vice President (Formerly)
Ogilvy Adams & Rhinehart

A STRATEGIC APPROACH TO PERSONAL CARE PRODUCT PUBLIC RELATIONS

Risk and reward are major drivers in the purchase and use of personal care products. Consumers ask: What is the risk to me if this product fails? What is my reward if it delivers on its promise?

The risks and rewards for personal care products vary as dramatically as the products that make up the category which includes—but is not limited to—hair care and color, skin care, cosmetics, fragrance, antiperspirants and deodorants, nail care, shaving products, foot care, oral care, tanning products, soaps, adult incontinence products, feminine care, baby care, and bath and shower products. The risk of trying a new shampoo, for example, is very low. At worst, a consumer experiences a "bad hair day." At best, the person may experience the fulfilled promise of healthy, stylish hair. More risky is a failed deodorant—its failure can be offensive to others. Riskier still are products for incontinence. If a consumer has found one that works, the risk of switching to a competitive brand may outweigh the potential rewards.

Because risk and reward are so important in choosing personal care products—and can vary so much depending on the category—they dramatically affect the way products are marketed and the strategic role public relations can play. In a product category in which potential rewards outweigh risks, the marketing challenge may be to increase loyalty among fickle consumers who are ready to try the next new "hope in a bottle" (to use Revlon founder Charles Revson's famous definition of beauty products). In categories in which risks may outweigh rewards, marketers must convince consumers that their product will be able to deliver the desired benefits better than what's tried and true. Public relations can help consumers understand why product X performs better, what new technology makes product Y superior, and why product Z absolutely, positively won't embarrass the user.

Consumer interest and involvement also influence how and when public relations is used in the area of personal care. Risks and rewards aside, consumers are engaged much more in fashion and beauty personal care products such as hair care, make-up, and fragrance than they are in hygiene products such as deodorant, toothpaste, and foot odor spray. In developing public relations strategies for personal care, practitioners must understand the risk and reward each product offers, as well as the level of consumer interest and involvement in the product category.

For example, planning a media relations strategy for a new product requires a good understanding of media opportunities. Realizing there is far more editorial space devoted to hair and skin in women's service (*Redbook, McCall's, Woman's Day*, etc.) and beauty (*Cosmopolitan, Glamour, Elle*, etc.) magazines than to deodorants and toothpaste, will influence the strategy for launching new products. Pitching a new line of shampoos and conditioners to these magazines probably will be more successful than pitching an improved deodorant or toothpaste. The latter will require strategies for reaching consumers in different ways.

When consumer interest in a product category is low, public relations often must borrow interest from other places, be it a celebrity, a cause, an event, or a contest. Consumer interest in these things will contribute to increasing interest and involvement in the product if the tie-in is properly executed. A major trend that has defined the personal care products industry in the last decade is the proliferation of products, which has led to fierce competition and lack of differentiation. Companies are compelled to spend millions in brand marketing for differentiation among consumers. Public relations, as part of the marketing mix, can help brands stand out in the crowd and give consumers reasons and incentives for becoming involved with the merchandise.

As products have multiplied, so have environmental considerations. Consumers claim that environmentally friendly attributes (which can embrace ingredients, packaging, or biodegradability) contribute to their decision to purchase a product. Research has not always confirmed that consumers do, in fact, buy "green," but manufacturers have wisely responded to what consumers say they want. This has affected personal care products in addition to many other consumer goods. The Body Shop, for example, has made its name in part by selling products with natural, environmentally correct ingredients and packaging.

Another trend in the area of personal care is cosmetics merchandising, namely, the growth of mall boutiques like The Body Shop, H_2O Plus, Bath and Body Works, and Goodebodies. These shops have taken share from both mass merchandise brands—found in grocery, drug, and discount stores—and upscale department store products. With price points somewhere in between, these boutiques have found a niche with consumers who can't (or won't) buy the high-priced department store brands, but will indulge in a more affordable luxury. They also have succeeded because they create a shopping experience that indulges the senses in ways that mass merchandise—and even department—stores cannot.

Possibly more than any other category of packaged goods, personal care products convey something about the people who use them. Whether it is to communicate something to others, affirm a belief about oneself or aspire to an ideal, consumers buy more than just a product—they buy an image along with the cream or paste, shampoo or spray. Because of this dynamic, marketers concentrate their efforts on consumers who must be persuaded that their brand will best satisfy their needs and desires. Of course, other audiences are affected by the brand's performance and image: the financial community (shareholders and analysts), retail customers, and employees.

The relationship of public relations to corporate and organizational goals must be recognized. Marketing public relations can raise the profile of a product with key constituents, thereby increasing the profile and enhancing the image of the entire company. For example, when introducing a new product, corporate and marketing public relations practitioners need to coordinate their efforts so various audiences are reached with timely and consistent messages. Communicators also can deal with socio/political issues such as animal testing by explaining policies and addressing special interest groups. Public relations can help companies create a positive environment in which to conduct business.

Most larger personal care products companies have internal public relations staffs who handle corporate concerns, issues management, and employee relations, or these functions may be handled by an outside firm. The PR budget for personal care products depends on the size of the product's market, the competitive environment, and the rest of the marketing plan. A new product introduction budget could be as little as $30,000 for a very modest media relations plan, or as much as $500,000 or more for an elaborate, multi-faceted campaign. It is crucial to determine how much the intended results of a public relations campaign are worth to the brand. If, for example, a successful new product launch is critical to the overall reputation and image of the corporation, it may be determined that an important function of public relations will be to build brand awareness with stakeholders such as analysts, shareholders, and business media, as well as consumers and retail trade.

Tactical Approaches to Personal Care Product Public Relations

Although most of the tactics for personal care products are similar to those for any packaged good or food product, there are some distinguishing attributes and special applications.

Cause-Related Marketing Marketers are increasingly using consumer interest in a cause to draw them to a product. The company may make a donation with every purchase of the product; ingredients or packaging may support a cause; or the company may foster a long- or short-term affiliation with a project or group. Important to this tactic is an in-depth understanding of what causes are relevant to the target audience—and the realization that regardless of the cause, consumers won't buy the product unless it offers other tangible benefits.

Cause-related marketing can be supported very successfully with public relations. Because it is less commercial than straight product publicity, this tactic increases the potential for media coverage. Likewise, it can be a way to attract celebrities or other VIPs to your efforts, again increasing exposure and interest.

Celebrity Endorsements Endorsements are very common for personal care products, since celebrities—chosen for their appeal to the target audience—provide living proof of a product's effectiveness, such as Cybill Shepard for L'Oreal's Ultress hair coloring or supermodel Niki Taylor for Pantene Pro V hair care products. Trusted celebrities also can be used to help market products that may carry some social stigma or embarrassment, such as film star June Allyson for Depends incontinence products.

Due to the high cost of retaining a celebrity, many PR programs use them for limited engagements, such as judges for contests, emcees for events, and hosts for satellite media tours.

Expert Advice Less expensive than celebrities—and almost certainly more credible—is the use of experts to recommend and endorse a product. A hair care brand may hire a well-known salon stylist to speak to beauty media, a toothpaste brand might retain an advisory board of dentists and hygienists, or a baby care brand may use a child psychologist as a spokesperson.

Experts can help elevate media and consumer interest by providing useful education in addition to promoting the brand's attributes. They also can help explain more credibly than advertising why a product's ingredients deliver certain benefits. Finally, experts carry with them the credibility of a third-party endorsement.

Sports Marketing   Sports marketing—commonly associated with sports drinks and sporting equipment—also can be successfully used to market some types of personal care products. For example, a company marketing an antiperspirant for young adults may find that sponsoring a beach volleyball tournament raises awareness among its target audience and demonstrates the product's benefit of keeping consumers dry. Many products aimed at the health club crowd, such as 2-in-1 shampoos, antiperspirants, and deodorant soaps, can be given as samples in health clubs or listed as a sponsor for club tournaments. Sports marketing can be especially helpful in increasing interest in a product category in which consumer interest is generally low.

Contests   A contest or sweepstakes is commonly used to generate interest and awareness, communicate the image and attributes of the brand and reward consumers for using the product. A national contest usually includes advertising and packaging in addition to public relations. A local or regional contest may be driven exclusively by public relations and can provide a good benchmark for the effectiveness of PR.

Contests can increase involvement by inviting consumers to use the product and describe or demonstrate how the product performed. For example, a hair care brand could hold a contest for teen girls in a mall by asking them to style their hair using the product. This would provide rewards for the participants, create a good visual for the media, and build awareness with other mall shoppers.

Surveys and Research   Surveys can help sell to the media a product that might otherwise have little newsworthiness. Carefully crafted and executed surveys can create news and interest that provide a context for a product's mention. Usually, these surveys are about consumer habits or opinions relevant to the product category. Sometimes, existing consumer research conducted for other purposes can provide fodder for a good release. For example, a deodorant manufacturer may know the top 10 situations that make consumers sweat—a first date, a job interview, a final exam, a visit from the Internal Revenue Service—and can turn this into a release targeted to lifestyle writers about what makes people anxious. Then, this survey could be repeated in subsequent years to learn how consumers' fears change—or don't—change over time.

The aging baby boomer population, the older of whom are experiencing their first age lines and white hair, is a prime target for personal care marketers. For example, there's been a surge in the hair color market, both in salons and with at-home applications, that roughly corresponds with the aging of this population bulge. The products designed to cover gray (including Loving Care and Miss Clairol) have benefited from the graying of America. Likewise, facial care products have experienced a face-lift of their own with the proliferation of consumers looking for a more youthful appearance. With so many beauty products available that promise "miracles," word-of-mouth and third-party endorsements play a huge role in convincing women to try something new. Public relations can be instrumental in promoting this behavior.

New Product Introduction

Advance-formula products are driving growth in the $313-million food and drug facial category. The new alphahydroxy acid-based (AHA) skin care products account for much of this growth. According to dermatologists, AHAs improve the appearance of the skin—even aging and sun-damaged skin—by helping to slough off dead surface skin. And because AHA-based products are made from natural, nontoxic substances found in foods and plants, they are less likely to irritate skin.

Denver-based Neoteric Cosmetics (a division of Scott's Liquid Gold) launched its Alpha Hydrox Skin Treatment System in 1992, making it the first AHA product available to consumers in mass merchandise. Neoteric Cosmetics and its public relations agency, The Wharton Group of Denver, were faced with the challenge of actually creating the AHA category. Consumers and the media needed to be educated about alphahydroxy acids, to understand why they were different and better, and to be motivated to try the product.

The Wharton Group prepared a mass mailing to beauty and women's magazines. Press materials were supported with science articles explaining the properties of AHAs and why they are dramatically different than other skin care ingredients. A dermatologist who participated in the clinical studies of AHAs also was made available for interview. The magazine mailing was followed up with mailings to television, newspapers, and trade media. The Wharton Group realized it had something big on its hands when TV stations started calling for more information, and this prompted the agency to recommend creating a video news release (VNR). The VNR was produced and distributed over satellite nationwide and eventually aired on more than 70 television stations. In many markets where it aired, stores sold out of Alpha Hydrox the next day. Today, Alpha Hydrox is the number one product by unit sales in the mass market AHA category, with 12 products for all skin types.

Updating an Image

The proliferation and growth of sophisticated facial care products obviously affected older, more-traditional facial care brands. Chesebrough-Ponds, for instance, had a long-established image in the beauty market as a maker of cold cream. The company developed many new products in the early 1990s, among them cleansers, moisturizers, and skin-smoothing capsules. While the products themselves were right for the market, the company's image needed updating. To achieve this, Chesebrough-Ponds created the Ponds Institute to gather and distribute facial care information to the media and to individuals. Pond's public relations agency, Cairns & Associates of New York, worked with the company to publicize the Institute and help position the new product lines.

For national media, Cairns created the Pond's Institute Beauty Advisory, a group of experts on women's health and beauty. The insights of these experts were periodically released to the media under the auspices of the Pond's Institute. Cairns also launched a shopping mall tour which took the Pond's Institute on the road. The display, which suggested an upscale health spa, provided a venue for cosmetologists and skin-care experts to discuss facial care with consumers and allowed consumers to sample products—something usually associated with higher-priced department store brands.

Entering New Markets

The diaper, or nappy, battles began in earnest in the United Kingdom with the introduction of Kimberly-Clark's Huggies brand nappies in early 1994. As the number one seller in the United States, Huggies was in the position of trying to quickly gain awareness and trial in the £500 million U.K. nappies market.

Ogilvy Adams & Rinehart/London was responsible for launching the product and gaining exposure in media outlets. OA&R took on the U.K.'s number one brand of nappies, Procter & Gamble's Pampers, by engineering the "nappy wars" in national and regional newspapers, television, and radio. This communicated Huggies head-to-head competition with Pampers and the challenge the new product would present to the current market leader. Capitalizing on the news that British parents now had a choice in quality nappies—and confident in the product's ability to compare favorably with the market leader—OA&R arranged several tried and tested editorial consumer comparisons. These were carried out independently by the country's consumer newspapers, breakfast television shows, and parenting magazines. In most cases, Huggies proved to be competitive with the market leader, quickly positioning the brand as Britain's "number two" nappy.

To sustain editorial coverage and consumer interest in the brand beyond the initial launch, OA&R arranged a series of editorial promotions and product giveaways in key specialist and consumer media. In addition to increasing awareness, these contributed to the Kimberly-Clark direct mail database at minimal cost. To build on the growing consumer awareness of the Huggies brand and to develop an identity as the nappy for happy babies, OA&R commissioned a leading child psychologist to undertake a survey into the psychology of hugging. The survey results achieved widespread news coverage, particularly in regional newspapers and radio, reaching the brand's target audience of young mothers at home.

Ensuring Brand Loyalty

Salon Selectives, a leading hair care brand from Helene Curtis, is targeted to women aged 13 to 34. A very important segment of this target is teen girls who love the choice and combination of products that Salon Selectives provides. However, Salon Selectives does not have special advertising for its teen users. The brand managers understand that the product and its image are highly aspirational; it is something the teen girls can aspire to, making it far more attractive than products created for teens. However, teens also are very fickle consumers, ready to try anything new in the category, so programs designed to generate loyalty and use among current and lapsed users are very important.

The brand, working with *TEEN* magazine, developed the Salon Selectives Super Hair Search. This contest, exclusively for readers of *TEEN*, was designed to generate interest in Salon Selectives and reinforce the promise of "Salon-Beautiful Hair." Salon Selectives' public relations firm, Ogilvy Adams & Rinehart/Chicago, was asked to extend the contest's reach beyond the pages of the magazine.

The first task was to generate coverage and increase awareness of the contest. Since competing magazines were out of the question, Ogilvy targeted newspapers for coverage.

B O X   24–1

THE BODY SHOP

Sometimes, personal care products thrive without any advertising. The Body Shop is a case in point. Now a $500 million company operating in 44 countries, this English skin- and hair-care company, founded in 1976 by Anita Rodick, became a success without any ad spending. Instead, it produced products with natural ingredients in environmentally responsible packaging that caught the attention of a new kind of consumer. Then the company aligned itself with a number of socially responsible issues such as the environment, animal rights, and trading with indigenous cultures all communicated in its stores and through the media.

To visit a Body Shop is to be bombarded with messages: product labels implore against animal testing; signs promote recycling and conservation; and bags ask shoppers to join Amnesty International. The Body Shop has turned cause-related public relations into a way of doing business.

The Body Shop's commitment to its causes seems indisputable. But what's also indisputable is that these causes, thoughtfully communicated to consumers, have created a powerful positioning for the Body Shop. And whether it calls this PR or not, the Body Shop has used public relations to market itself to consumers around the world.

As semifinalists were identified, releases and photos were sent to hometown papers, and interviews for local media with "Super Hair" teens were arranged. After eight months of soliciting entries and choosing semifinalists, four finalists were selected to spend a weekend in New York, with mothers in tow, and attend a gala luncheon where the Super Hair Search winner would be announced. The event, which took place in a penthouse ballroom overlooking Central Park, also served to reinforce Salon Selectives' image as savvy, stylish, and salon-like. Beauty editors from noncompeting magazines were invited to attend, as were retail and health and beauty aid trade editors and representatives from modeling agencies. The brand's spokespersons, Manhattan salon owners Damien Miano and Louis Viél, presented a hair style forecast and described how each teen finalist achieved her "Super Hair" look.

Following the New York event, *TEEN* ran photos of the winner and finalists, and media coverage was obtained in local and trade publications. Pre- and post-contest consumer research indicated that the Super Hair Search was successful in raising Salon Selectives' profile with teens and reinforcing its image as the brand for "Salon-Beautiful Hair."

Educating Consumers

When Bausch & Lomb introduced Clear Choice alcohol-free mouthwash in 1992, there were more than 15 mouthwash brands on the U.S. market. Bausch & Lomb introduced Clear Choice at the peak of consumer interest in clear products; however, after six months on the market, the product was floundering. Coinciding with this was the problem of childhood poisoning from the alcohol in many mouthwash brands, moving the attorneys general of 27 states to file a petition with the U.S. Consumer Products Safety Commission (CPSC) calling for child-resistant packaging for all mouthwashes containing more than 5 percent alcohol. This presented Bausch & Lomb and its public relations agency, Edelman Public Relations, with an opportunity to raise awareness of this public health problem. By educating parents about preventing childhood poisoning the company could simultaneously raise awareness of Clear Choice.

Research uncovered that poisonings are one of the five leading causes of childhood death, and that more than 17,000 poisonings related to ingestion of mouthwashes with alcohol were reported in a five-year period. The American Association of Poison Control Centers (AAPCC) reported that only one ounce of high-alcohol-containing mouthwash can cause effects such as seizures, brain damage, coma, and death. Many parents were totally unaware that mouthwashes contain alcohol and never thought to store mouthwash out of children's reach.

Based on this research, Bausch & Lomb and Edelman Medical Communications developed a program to observe Poison Prevention Week, held annually in March, with a national media relations program. The company sought to benefit the health and welfare of children by raising awareness of the safety issues associated with alcohol in mouthwash. Another objective was to build awareness of and demand for an alcohol-free alternative: Clear Choice.

Edelman launched a national media campaign during Poison Prevention Week, building on the news of the child resistant packaging petition filed in February with the CPSC. A satellite media tour featured the president of the American Academy of Pediatric Dentistry, a director of pediatric emergency services at Cornell Medical Center in New York, and the parents of a child who almost died as a result of poisoning from mouthwash with alcohol. Media materials included a video news release, radio news release, press releases, and fact sheet describing how mouthwash works and why alcohol is an unnecessary ingredient, and a chart comparing the alcohol content of several mouthwash brands, in addition to the alcohol content of beer and wine.

The "Dangers of Mouthwash with Alcohol" campaign resulted in more than 137 million impressions, with 564 television stations airing the VNR and 760 broadcasts of the radio news release. Public relations played a major role in raising awareness of Clear Choice and, after 10 months, it had become the alcohol-free mouthwash category leader with a 70+ percent share.

Another example of the use of public relations for product-supporting consumer education took place in 1984, when Unilever was preparing to launch a new toothpaste, Mentadent P., in Colombia, South America. Designed to fight bacterial plaque, the toothpaste was entering a consumer market largely unaware of the existence and dangers of bacterial plaque, the principal cause of periodontal disease.

Centrum, Ogilvy & Mather Relaciones Públicas of Bogatá, Colombia, was retained by Unilever to make Colombians aware of the dangers of bacterial plaque and its role in dental disease, and to raise awareness of Mentadent P. among dental care providers. The agency's strategy was to launch a campaign to educate dental health professionals, hygienists, and dental students about the importance of dental health and the role that Mentadent P. could play in improving dental hygiene. Centrum, Ogilvy & Mather designed a mailing to dental health professionals with information on periodontal disease, posters to be displayed in dentists' offices, samples of Mentadent P. for patients and brochures about dental seminars. Dental health conventions and seminars were organized, and two Mentadent Scholarships were established to reach dentistry students. These efforts culminated with the launch of a nationwide oral health campaign—Colombia's first Dental Health Month. The campaign was designed to promote the concept of preventive dentistry by offering the public and dentists a complete prevention plan. The program reached Colombians through posters, videos, televisions spots, and media relations.

As a result, more than 150,000 people received dental health checkups and prevention plan materials; employee dental prevention campaigns were formed at companies; awareness of bacterial plaque as a cause of gum diseases and tooth decay increased to 70.5 percent; Unilever's oral health division data bank increased its list of names by almost 9,000; and Mentadent P.'s market share increased following the dental health awareness campaign.

Changing Consumer Behavior

Sometimes a product comes along that not only has new features and benefits, but also seeks to change consumer behavior. The Gillette Sensor shaving system, introduced to consumers in 1990, was one such product.

The result of more than 10 years of testing and $200 million in research and development, Sensor was designed to revitalize the refillable shaving category by slowing the trend away from quality shaving that had begun in 1975 with the introduction of low-priced, disposable razors. Trading up customers to the better-performing Sensor system would require a renewed appreciation for quality. Once sold, Gillette Sensor would increase growth in the blade market and enhance Gillette's already strong position in shaving technology and male grooming.

Achieving these business goals required a public relations campaign targeted at the trade and consumers in the 19 North American and Western European countries covered by Gillette's North Atlantic Group. Porter/Novelli of New York City created and executed the public relations component of an integrated marketing plan that also included advertising, direct mail, point-of-sale, and sales force support. London's Countrywide Communications assisted Porter/Novelli with communications efforts in Europe. The public relations objectives were to generate media coverage to maximize awareness of Sensor and its unique benefits; to encourage men to try the product and convert to it; to generate support in the male grooming products trade; and to lend credence to Gillette's claim as the company that understands men and lives up to its advertising tagline: Gillette. The Best A Man Can Get.®"

Because the introduction was taking place simultaneously throughout North America and Western Europe, Porter/Novelli needed to ensure uniformity of messages. This was achieved with a "North Atlantic Guidelines Manual" that emphasized the similarities rather than the differences among men in the North Atlantic market. Included were press kits with suggested story angles, a video on Sensor technology adaptable to all television formats, mechanicals for graphics, and consumer test results.

The Sensor system was first introduced to the financial community and trade media at a press conference on October 3, 1989, and similar conferences or editorial briefings were held in Europe. This resulted in advance coverage of the product in business publications—including being named a "1989 Product of the Year" in *Fortune*—before the product was even available at retail. In fact, the extensive news coverage of Sensor prior to its availability in retail outlets created an unusually high degree of interest in the product before it was advertised.

The second publicity thrust accompanied the retail launch of Sensor three months later on the Monday following Super Bowl XXIV (1990). In addition to multicountry distribution of the releases and videotape, media activities included contact with editors to arrange interviews with Gillette spokespersons; development and placement of story angles for trade, consumer, and business publications; and distribution of Sensor gift packs to 4,000 male influentials. (The list, headed by President George Bush, included prominent politicians, corporate leaders, sports celebrities, and movie stars.) Finally, disc jockeys in 30 key U.S. markets were sent special kits containing a Sensor razor, Foamy shaving cream, a terry cloth robe, and facts about Sensor for use in their morning drive-time programs.

Publicity achieved by the summer of 1990 included 840 placements, resulting in more than 403 million impressions. Among the highlights were feature coverage in *Fortune*, *Business Week*, *Newsweek International*, *U.S. News and World Report*, *Time*, *Forbes*, *Elle*, and *Mirabella*. AP, UPI, and Reuters carried stories, and feature articles ran in leading metropolitan newspapers. Segments aired on ABC's *Good Morning America*, the *CBS Evening News*, and NBC's *Tonight Show*. Dozens of radio DJs commented favorably on Sensor during their drive-time shows. In Europe, the story was carried by prestigious media including *Financial Times* (UK), *Frankfurter Allgemeine Zeitung* (Germany), *Vogue Hommes* (France), *Milan Finanza* (Italy), and *International Herald Tribune* (Europe-wide).

By the end of 1990, 26 million Sensor razors and 424 million replacement cartridges had been shipped, and demand was running nearly 30 percent ahead of the company's projections. The new razor gained a 7.8 percent market share and became the top-selling wet shaving device in every country in which it was offered.

A short time later, in 1992, Gillette was ready to introduce a female shaving product different from anything else on the market: the female version of its breakthrough shaving system, Gillette Sensor for Women. Gillette again turned to Porter/Novelli to create a national launch campaign to introduce Sensor for Women.

The team identified three primary public relations objectives for the introduction of Sensor for Women: develop and expand Gillette's female shaving franchise; energize the female refillable shaving segment; and generate immediate trial and usage of Sensor for Women.

The primary public relations strategy was to leverage the credibility of third-party editorial coverage to educate women about the differences among shaving products and the superiority of Sensor for Women in meeting women's shaving needs.

The secondary public relations strategy was to leverage Gillette's heritage and Sensor's innovative technology to communicate to the business, financial, and trade communities that Sensor for Women would be a success.

Porter/Novelli decided to announce Sensor for Women in a two-day media event: a special long-lead editor event, immediately followed by a general news announcement for all media. This would result in two peaks of publicity—the first round of coverage (from the second day) appearing in general news, business, and trade publications and broadcast outlets in February and March 1992, and the second round in influential women's magazines, newspaper consumer/lifestyle sections, and broadcast outlets in the summer of 1992, when the product became available.

For the magazine editors, Porter/Novelli created an environment to induce them to think about the summer shaving season on a dreary February day in New York. With more than 250 feet of tenting, hundreds of azaleas, tulips, daffodils, ficus trees, and even a custom-made waterfall, the rooftop of New York's Peninsula Spa was transformed into a summer garden. Fifty-seven editors received an in-depth product briefing and were offered an opportunity to sample the product at the spa. The press materials, including an 18-month editorial calendar and extensive background information categorized for development of feature stories, were contained in one media resource guide. The following day, business, financial, and general news media witnessed a dramatic photo "reveal" of Sensor for Women onto a seven-story wall of water. Concurrently, specially packaged product samples were distributed to 1,600 female opinion leaders nationwide. Following the event, B-roll footage was distributed to select broadcast media nationwide.

The results of this campaign far exceeded the expectations of Gillette and Porter/Novelli. Said John Darman, vice president, blades and razors, Gillette North Atlantic Group, "Targeting the beauty and lifestyle editors was a central element of our strategy. We understood the key role they could play in involving their readers in the shaving category and in educating them about the differences between products and the real advantages of Sensor for Women." With the introduction of Sensor for Women, Porter/Novelli helped educate women about the shaving process and drove preadvertising sales to more than 50 percent beyond Gillette's own forecast. Added Darman, "Sensor for Women achieved more than a 30 percent share of the razor market in the United States before the start of advertising, and public relations played the central role in achieving these results."

According to The Gillette Company, the public relations strategic plan and creative execution were the driving forces behind preadvertising sales that were more than 50 percent ahead of Gillette's ambitious forecast. Against its original cartridge objective of 2.2 million razors in 1992, Gillette sold 7.2 million. Against a refill cartridge objective of 8.2 million, Gillette sold 28.2 million.

Prior to any consumer advertising, more than 600 separate stories appeared in high-profile media, communicating to women across America the breakthrough technology and design of Gillette Sensor for Women. Coverage ranged from virtually every woman's magazine to the *New York Times*, *Wall Street Journal*, Associated Press, Reuters, *Business Week*, and local market dailies and television. Three separate stories ran in *USA Today*, one of which named Sensor for Women "one of the hottest products of the year."

Measurement and Evaluation

Public relations campaigns can be measured in several ways, with varying degrees of validity and expense. Regardless of the measurement selected, it is very important that the brand and its agency are in agreement about what success will look like. After the fact, it's difficult to decide what has worked and what hasn't without a benchmark in place.

Among the most traditional and objective measures is that of impressions. These are the number of consumers reached be it through editorial placements, participation in an event, or number of contest entries. Success should be determined using a number of different criteria, if possible. For example, media placements should not only count total number of impressions, but also total number of media outlets reached, message delivery, percent using photographs, and so on.

While there is no formula for calculating how many impressions spell success, a target number of impressions can be determined by evaluating the resources committed to public relations along with the kind of tactics employed. For example, a mall event to introduce a new product in 20 markets probably will reach fewer consumers at greater cost than one article in a national beauty magazine. However, the impact on the consumers who participate in the mall event will be far greater than on those who read the article. So numbers alone don't determine success, but rather an understanding of what you are trying to achieve and what is possible given the tactics used and the budget.

Another way to judge the success of a media relations campaign, especially for established products, is to evaluate a product's coverage against that of its competitors. While it may be difficult to say whether four national magazine placements each month is good or bad, it is possible to compare results against the competition's. This is called share of voice (SOV), and it can be very helpful in evaluating results that might otherwise be very subjective. Measurement of share of voice is achieved most easily by hiring a national clipping service to search not only for coverage of your brand, but for coverage of four or five of your brand's biggest competitors. This can then be evaluated on a monthly basis to determine your results versus those of competitive brands.

Pre- and post-consumer research also can be conducted to determine how great an effect public relations had on building awareness or changing attitudes. This measurement tool is expensive and is usually employed when a great deal of money has been spent on public relations or when public relations is the only marketing tool employed. When public relations is used in conjunction with advertising, point-of-purchase, or direct mail, it can be difficult, if not impossible, to determine if and how each discipline contributed to the end result.

Another way to evaluate the effectiveness of public relations is to implement campaigns in isolated markets. This may mean using advertising alone in five markets, and advertising and public relations together in five different "like" markets—markets similar in size and demographics. In this way, companies can see how the inclusion of public relations affects awareness, attitudes, and sales.

THE FUTURE OF PERSONAL CARE PRODUCT PR

The personal care industry already is experiencing a consolidation of companies, and this consolidation is expected to continue. What this means is that fewer companies will own and control more of the brands. This is significant because more and more brands will be sold against sister brands. The goal for companies will be to build a strong portfolio of brands that don't succeed at the expense of each other and the challenge will be to do this in markets that are (in the United States, at least) flat.

Public relations can play an important role in meeting this challenge by addressing the needs of smaller audience segments. While advertising is very efficient at reaching a mass market, public relations can slice and dice that mass to target smaller groups with messages that are meaningful and persuasive. Using communication in this way can secure and build consumer loyalty with audience segments. For example, a body-building shampoo might be marketed to a mass audience as a product for people with thin or normal hair who want hair with more body. Public relations might be used to target a subset—women who are experiencing hair loss and want a shampoo to add volume and mass. By using health care professional marketing, newsletters, and other media, PR can reach this target with messages appropriate to their special needs.

Another trend is that personal care products—especially beauty products—will be sold more on science than hope. As consumers become more skeptical and sophisticated, they will require more information, so communications that inform and educate will become increasingly important, as will third-party endorsements and word of mouth. Public relations, with its use of experts, editorial placements, and endorsements, is a natural fit with this trend.

Going forward, the practice of public relations in personal care—and in every industry—will require more reliable and meaningful measurements. This is a responsibility for public relations agencies and for the companies that use them. It will require committing resources to public relations programs that are big enough to make a difference as well as to measurement of those campaigns. Too often, too little is spent on public relations to make a real impact. Instead of abandoning PR, brands should test what levels of spending do produce a favorable result. Increasingly, as mass media become more fragmented, public relations should become more important for its ability to cost-effectively reach consumer segments.

Today, many companies are realizing the value and power of integrated marketing. As companies obtain more experience with integrated programs, public relations will become more important to the mix. Today, many brands see public relations as primarily a publicity tool. In the future, public relations will be able to demonstrate all the things it can achieve.

## CHAPTER 25

Marketing and Communications in the Management Consulting Industry

James E. Murphy
Managing Director of Worldwide Marketing
and Communications
Andersen Consulting
and President, Murphy & Company

AN INTEGRATED APPROACH TO MARKETING AND COMMUNICATIONS

The management consulting industry has grown at an explosive rate in recent years, with many consultants becoming powerful partners and visionary allies with their clients. Along with this exciting growth has come the strategic shaping of the marketing and communications role, creating unique challenges for marketing and communications professionals. In recent years, those challenges have been amplified by rapid change and increased competition in the industry.

All management consulting firms face a similar fundamental challenge: the marketing of intangible services. This is characterized by an exchange of knowledge and expertise, rather than a physical product. Even more challenging, to be truly successful and valuable to clients, consulting firms need to provide not only deep expertise and skills in areas clients need today, but to also develop holistic approaches the client needs to determine what business to be in, anticipate where the market is going, and survive and stay competitive. Ultimately, the successful consulting firm plays an integral role in helping clients develop and execute strategic goals, maximize the performance of their workforces, build process excellence, and enable strategy through technology. Consulting firms often offer abilities that clients do not have in-house—the ability, for example, to reengineer business processes or to rapidly formulate and execute new strategy to meet changing market conditions. Consulting firms increasingly play a critical role in counseling clients about economic trends, the marketplace, and innovative ways to achieve value and make leaps in market position.

To succeed, the management consulting firm must make these intangible services relevant and differentiated in the eyes of the client. It must convince the marketplace that it has the vision, expertise, and skills—often complex and specialized capabilities—and the ability to deliver and do this better than all the other competitors. Ultimately, it must persuade potential clients that it is the best choice to help with issues that are vital to the competitiveness and the very survival of their organization.

Historically, marketing and communications efforts in the consulting industry have been relatively minimal, mirroring other professional services, such as law, accounting, and medicine. But like many other industries, management consulting has undergone dramatic changes in recent years reflecting major shifts in the business world such as globalization, alliances, mergers and acquisitions, downsizing, outsourcing, and general acceptance of bringing in outside thinking from other industries. These changes have brought a greater need for marketing and communications, and call for an increasingly visible and strategic role in the industry to build a firm's image, understand the marketplace better, and foster the development of business relationships.

Industry Trends

The consulting industry encompasses a range of *management services,* including strategy formulation, organizational design, process reengineering, process excellence, and change management; *information technology services,* such as systems design and implementation; and *strategic outsourcing,* in which a company uses an external business partner to manage and continuously improve an entire business function enabling a company to focus on its core competencies.

Consulting firms help clients identify and maximize opportunities, increase productivity and competitiveness, create new markets, and stay ahead of changing business environments. As a result, trends in the industry are closely linked to the larger business trends that shape the needs of consultants' clients.

In recent years, most business organizations have been facing a rapidly changing competitive landscape. Competition has become global. Product life cycles have grown shorter. Customers have become more sophisticated. The need for speed is relentless; in most markets, windows of opportunity are brief, and the time between strategy formulation and execution is diminishing. Information technology has become increasingly complex and increasingly critical to success. In fact, in many cases, new technologies—such as electronic commerce on the Internet—drive change.

In this environment, the ability to find innovative, breakthrough approaches is critical to success. This has prompted more companies to look beyond their own boundaries for expertise, driving rapid growth in the management consulting industry. Since the early 1990s, the industry has grown by approximately 18 percent annually, and growth rates are expected to remain in the double digits for the rest of the decade. Based on a number of analysts' estimates, the global management consulting market today is $147 billion; by the year 2000, it is expected to reach $261 billion. This growth naturally has brought more consulting firms to the field—and with them, dramatically higher levels of competition.

Joining management consulting firms in that competition are software and hardware vendors, contract programming companies, outsourcing vendors, communications companies, and value-added resellers. The result is that buyers have more choices and are more price sensitive, and the vendors find it difficult to differentiate themselves.

Andersen Consulting has emerged as the leading global management and technology consulting firm by differentiating itself through its business integration client service model. IBM is a prime example of a hardware vendor that has expanded into professional services, as growth in its traditional product lines has slowed. It is now a highly-competitive, full-service vendor. EDS and CSC, whose core businesses historically have been data processing services, now offer a full range of services, including management consulting, business process reengineering, systems integration, and information technology outsourcing. Also, management consultants such as Booz-Allen have developed capabilities in systems integration.

As the consulting industry has grown, it has undergone other fundamental changes. Historically, business expertise has been marketed as relatively distinct sets of service. A client would look to one firm or group within a firm for information technology services; another for help developing a strategy; and yet another for assistance in reengineering business processes. To a large extent, each specialty operated in its own separate universe.

With the steady increase of global competition, a fragmented approach to using consulting firms no longer suffices. Success today requires companies to change themselves with increasing speed and frequency, and on a large scale. Change must occur simultaneously on many fronts, and the complex interplay of organizational elements must be carefully managed. Computer systems, for example, affect the nature of business processes, and vice versa. In turn, those processes and technologies must fit with the behaviors and skills of the people who use them. All those elements must align with an organization's strategy. So, if a company is to succeed, it must address change across the organization holistically and simultaneously.

In short, as a dynamic business environment demands more of organizations, those organizations demand more of their consultants. Today, a top tier management consulting firm must be able to offer an integrated array of services to the client—and it must be able to provide those services globally. Where consulting was traditionally focused on executing specific tasks and providing certain deliverables, success today is increasingly measured by the value that is delivered—overall business results, reduced operating costs, or increases in share price or market share.

Finally, the industry is experiencing a trend toward broader, longer relationships between clients and consultants. The two parties often work as partners, rather than as traditional vendor and customer. This shift is especially evident in the outsourcing arena. For the most part, outsourcing arrangements traditionally were aimed at controlling costs and eliminating the need to manage mundane operations in-house. Increasingly, these arrangements are more strategic, with the client organization looking for a strategic partner to manage an entire business process, to help in designing and planning the process, and at times, even share in the risks and rewards of the operation.

MISSIONS AND GOALS FOR MARKETING AND COMMUNICATIONS

If the marketing and communications functions of management consulting firms are to be effective, they must naturally support and reflect the overall mission and goals. Marketing and communications must create a high-profile image in a competitive marketplace. They must advance the firm's leading ideas and innovations. They must communicate with customers and other stakeholders in such a way as to foster and reinforce positive attitudes. They must maintain customer mind-share by conveying the value of the firm's intangible services. Further, they must help the marketplace understand how the firm itself is changing to help clients cope with a changing world.

In today's environment, these goals can be met only through a strategic, integrated approach to marketing and communications—which represents something of a change for the industry. Traditionally, marketing efforts have been more or less the responsibility of the individual partner or consultant who built and maintained the relationship with a client relying largely on "local," disparate marketing and communications resources. Often, this led to varied and conflicting messages and an inconsistent "look and feel" to communications across the organization.

With the trend toward broader and longer-term consulting relationships, this approach has become ineffective. In selling an intangible, yet highly critical service, the consulting firm is in a very real sense selling trust and confidence in itself. A key component of trust is consistency in behavior and messages. This consistency must be present not only in direct communications vehicles, but in all points of contact with the client, from the advertising shown on television to the attitude of the engagement partner to the way phones are answered. If the client is in Prague or Cleveland or Madrid or Johannesburg, the experience should be consistent, allowing naturally for cultural customization. Otherwise, clients infer conflicting messages from different contacts with the firm, which erodes trust. Thus, consistency, which always is an important consideration in marketing and communications, is of paramount importance in the management consulting industry.

Consistency is best achieved through integrated marketing. Integration must take place globally, and:

- *Across functions,* such as marketing communications, public relations, advertising, and special events. In the management consulting industry, integrated marketing must encompass the entire range of activities through which the firm reaches the client, including everything from external publications to market segmentation to ongoing client contacts and opportunity management.

- *Throughout the organization,* because virtually everyone in a consulting firm has some impact on the firm's image. As a result, "marketing is everyone's job," rather than a separate function. In particular, marketing and communications should be closely integrated with the activities of partners and other front-line employees who have contact with clients, to ensure consistency of behaviors, messages and, ultimately, firmwide image.

By integrating these activities, the consulting firm can focus efforts where they will be most effective. It can identify its best clients, develop an understanding of those clients' values, provide appropriate offerings and services, and target its marketing and communications resources to convey its fit with those values in a compelling and consistent manner.

An integrated approach to marketing also makes it possible to formulate consistent, global *branding* and *positioning* strategies, which are at the heart of marketing and communications in any industry. Too often, however, management consulting firms overlook the need to establish a firm's branding and positioning strategy. Defining this strategy is a critical, preliminary step.

Branding

When people think of branding, typically they think of a distinct set of physical marks that identify a company's products. At the mention of Coca Cola®, for instance, people around the world may think of the red can with the white script. But branding is more than physical elements. The mention of Coke may spark recollection of the taste of the carbonated cola beverage or even more intangible thoughts and emotions.

A management consulting organization, of course, has no such physical product. As a result, it needs to build a brand that identifies the organization itself and stirs positive feelings about the organization. In the professional services realm, this "corporate branding" is critical, because customers base their select-or-reject decisions on how they feel about the organization itself, as well as what it provides. Effective branding and image development will:

- Communicate a consistent, differentiated positioning globally (see following section).
- Lower evaluation costs and reduce the risk of the unknown for the buyer.
- Serve as a proxy for key buying criteria that cannot be evaluated easily.
- Serve as a barrier to entry for potential competitors.
- Reinforce long-term relationships and help build customer loyalty.
- Serve as a real promise of quality.

Virtually all of an organization's actions and communications add or detract from the marketplace's perceptions of that organization. A brand communicates "what you think, what you say, how you look, and how you behave." Thus, the across-the-board consistency that stems from integrated marketing plays a vital role in effective branding.

Positioning

Every brand—whether a corporate name or a product—holds a position in the minds of its key publics. This position is the distinctive net impression that people have about the organization—its purpose, its benefits and its value to clients. Ideally, the perception a client holds about a firm happens purposefully, rather than by accident or default.

The foundation of a strong brand is a well thought-out and executed positioning. Positioning is the act of defining succinctly and incisively an organization's purpose: it is the claim of what a firm does, who it does it for, and the benefit and value that it delivers. Positioning provides the basis on which the corporate brand is built.

A powerful positioning should differentiate the organization in the marketplace. It must have content—that is, it must make a compelling and clear claim about what the organization is, what it does, how it does things, or who it serves. Developing a positioning strategy can be difficult, because a good position defines not only what an organization is, but what it isn't, as well—and many firms are uncomfortable with the idea of limiting their options.

Increasingly, management consulting organizations are placing greater emphasis on the importance of the brand in their attempt to stand out in a crowded market and create support and allegiance among target audiences. To be effective, a brand positioning strategy must be buyer-oriented and reflect the wants and needs of clients. Ideally, the position should reflect not only what the organization is today, but also where it will be tomorrow—what it wants to become. This is especially important in consulting, where clients in a changing world want to know that their consulting partner will be able to meet their future, as well as current, needs.

Marketing and communications professionals play a pivotal role in managing the brand. They need to ensure the brand is projected consistently and convincingly across the entire spectrum of communications, including image advertising, capabilities brochures, recruiting videos, new business presentations, and special events. In addition, the power of the brand should be felt in the way it is "lived" by employees. The understanding of the brand should be so widespread and so deep among everyone in the organization that what people do, how they act, and what they say reinforces the desired brand image.

Budgeting and Expenditures

Given the diversity and dynamic nature of the management consulting industry, it is difficult to provide a generic rule of thumb for marketing and communications expenditures. What is most important is that the expenditures are focused on high-impact initiatives that support the top priorities of the organization and effectively reach target clients.

This means starting with the strategic priorities of the organization, before building a marketing program. With that foundation, the next step is to identify the specific targets for the marketing program before determining which tactic to use or the level of expenditure needed. This is not always as easy as it sounds: a great deal of research and planning must be conducted prior to launching a marketing and communications initiative.

One of the most effective means of determining how to best reach target clients is the "equity circle," a marketing tool that is widely used in planning activities. (The equity circle is discussed in more detail on the following pages.)

The Importance of Marketing Research

In the management consulting industry, market research is critical to targeted, integrated marketing and communications programs. Research plays two key roles:

- *Informational*—Helping organizations learn about their marketplace and their buyers.
- *Diagnostic*—Measuring the effectiveness of specific marketing strategies and tactics.

Market research provides an objective look at how clients are served and how they can be better served. In management consulting, it is becoming increasingly important to perform research that is not only accurate, but also consistent across borders and geographical units, so that markets, initiatives, and results can be compared and managed globally.

In collecting data, there are two key types of research that are undertaken: qualitative and quantitative.

Qualitative Research

Qualitative research is used to gain insight into buyer values and behavior and is often a first step or a complementary step to traditional survey research. Some uses for qualitative research are:

- Generating issues and hypotheses.
- Screening new concepts and revisions to existing services and products.
- Providing insights into brand and company images.
- Developing or testing advertising concepts.
- Developing positioning strategies.

When conducting qualitative research, management consulting firms typically use two techniques: (1) *focus groups*, which consist of personal interviews conducted within a group discussion and, (2) *personal interviews*, which are direct, face-to-face conversations between researcher and respondent.

Quantitative Research

Quantitative research focuses on statistical measures. It is conducted by selecting a representative sample from the total population being examined, interviewing the people in that sample, and projecting their responses to the total population.

Quantitative research provides an understanding of a population's attitudes toward and beliefs about an organization, product, service, or industry. Some of the uses of quantitative research are:

- Measuring the importance of existing attitudes and opinions.
- Measuring buyer preferences.
- Assessing brand, company, or advertising awareness levels.
- Determining initial and repeat purchase intent.
- Measuring product/service acceptance levels.
- Measuring client satisfaction.

The most commonly used qualitative research techniques are telephone interviews between researcher and respondent, and mail surveys consisting of questionnaires sent to designated respondents.

Market data can also be obtained from companies that publish reports on market size and forecast data, trends, and competitors. A number of such organizations cover the professional services market, including Dataquest, Gartner Group, G2 Research, INPUT, International Data Corporation, META Group, Alpha, Data Monitor, Kennedy Publications, and the Yankee Group. In addition to producing published reports, these and other analysts are available for custom consultation and research on market segments not covered by their basic services.

Employing the Equity Circle to Enable Integrated Marketing

The equity circle provides marketing and communications professionals with a framework for thinking about a client's attitudes toward and relationship with a management consulting firm. By understanding where a target—whether individual, group or entire industry—is on the circle, the firm can better understand how to shape marketing efforts.

Tactical Approaches to Marketing and Communications

Beginning with "awareness," the stages listed clockwise around the circle represent the client's current perspective on an organization. The objective is to move a prospective client from the point of "awareness" (and, actually, prior to that) through all the other stages, with the ultimate goal being a long-term partnership. Each contact with a potential client must be considered a crucial contact.

An explanation of the stages follows:

- Awareness—At this stage, the target knows the organization exists and has basic knowledge of its services and its competition.

- Perception—The initial ideas or impressions have been formed in the minds of the buyers, usually based on perceptual personality traits.

- Knowledge—Buyers go beyond the general perception phase and begin to have specific impressions of the organization's work and may even be familiar with some competitor's service or product offerings.

- Interest—Buyers become interested enough to proactively seek information.

- Consideration—Buyer moves from the "interest" stage to wanting more fact-based information and may put the organization on the short list.

- Commitment—Buyer makes actual selection of the organization or its competitor.

- Delivery, value, and success—All three are measurements of a working relationship with clients.

- Partnering—Buyer and organization develop long-term relationship.

As the relationship progresses on the equity circle, the required marketing tactics vary according to the target-focused objective(s) to be accomplished. To develop a winning marketing and sales program, it is essential to choose the right mix of marketing tactics given the marketing objective. A simple example: advertising may be the best tactic for generating awareness, but not for securing commitment. On a global basis, it is especially important to make sure that varying cultural issues are taken into account to make investments in the "right" tactics.

Regarding specific tactics and related expenditures, it may be beneficial to create a matrix of effectiveness. This is done by listing the possible tactics for a situation, such as news releases, advertising, face-to-face capabilities presentations, telemarketing, and so on. Then, with the audience in mind, as well as the organization's positioning and intended outcomes, assign an "effectiveness" level to each of the tactics. This method provides a simple way to focus on the most effective tactics. For instance, many firms may find that tactics dealing with the mass media will not be as effective as those that appeal directly to individual targets.

Message Development

Because consulting firms sell knowledge and expertise instead of traditional products, they must pay special attention to managing marketplace perceptions.

As a client moves around the equity circle, different types of messages are appropriate to fostering the relationship. Early on, messages should be targeted to groups of clients or potential clients that share specific attributes. Later, messages will need to be tailored to specific subsets of those groups, requiring a much higher degree of precision.

The most effective messages are those that help differentiate the organization in the client's eyes, and that clearly convey the organization's value to the client. The key is to develop messages that reflect an understanding of the client's point of view and that are relevant to the client. Most professions have their own jargon built around their particular expertise, which acts as a kind of shorthand for complex concepts; this is certainly true of professional services firms. While such terminology may be useful internally, it is often confusing to clients. Similarly, it is important to be aware of cultural differences, and to convey messages in ways that resonate and translate to clients globally.

To derive key messages from a host of possibilities, it is best to use an iterative development process. This process starts with a definition of clients' needs and business imperatives. These are then compared with the consulting firm's proposed solutions or strengths. The objective is to find a match between client needs/business imperatives and firm solutions/strengths.

Next, the organization should formalize message preparation. This begins by gathering existing messages, which provide a basis from which to work. From there, messages can be written in a conversational form to clearly reflect the organization's positioning and differentiate the firm in the marketplace. It is important to note that message development is not effective when done in a vacuum. To achieve the necessary buy-in and to ensure their consistent use, messages must be tested and approved by functional and subject experts.

Answering the following questions can help in the development of effective messages:

- What does the target need to believe in order to buy?
- Do messages require a large leap of faith to believe?
- Does the logic need to be improved or expanded?
- Do messages build differentiation?
- Do they address benefits to the target?
- Can these benefits be quantified? How much? By what amount? (For example, percentage ranges of savings, reductions, improvements, etc.)
- Are messages integrated horizontally?
- Are the terms being used relevant to the target? Would they use this terminology themselves?

Internal Communications

Internal communications programs are critical to an integrated marketing strategy, because they help employees understand what they need to do to support the overall brand and position of the firm. For a management consulting firm, of course, employees are the most visible and most effective contact with the client. Therefore, it is crucial that they understand the firm's direction and goals, clearly comprehend the firm's desired brand image, and, especially, personify the firm's positioning.

By nature, consulting firms tend to employ relatively well-educated and motivated "knowledge workers." Such people appreciate and respond to honest, direct information about their organization, its industry and what is expected of them. Conversely, they tend to react negatively to information they perceive as incomplete or misleading. While the role of internal communications is to foster appropriate behaviors at all levels, Generation Xers, in particular, respond best to highly innovative and personally meaningful communications. As a result, communications to a diverse internal audience should be consistent and coordinated with external communications, and convey the same fundamental messages. Internal communication vehicles should also provide opportunities for feedback and two-way interaction.

Internal communications should employ the same discipline found in external communications. For example, surveys should be used to understand the audience's needs. Or, when appropriate, individual segments of the internal audience should be targeted with precise communications.

To reach their relatively sophisticated internal audiences, many management consulting firms are enhancing print communications with electronic channels. These channels allow the firm to "push" information to employees, and allow employees to "pull" information they want on demand.

Image Advertising

Advertising is a relatively new phenomenon in the management consulting industry. Television advertising by consulting firms, for example, dates back only to the late 1980s. Indeed, it was only in 1977 that the United States Supreme Court ruled that client-serving professionals could advertise and directly solicit clients. Since then, constraints have been removed against direct-mail marketing by professionals, as well.

In this industry, advertising is best used to enhance overall brand and image, rather than tout a specific service. Image advertising, including both print and electronic media, puts the organization's name and service offering in front of prospective clients. Its goal is to make those prospects think of the organization when a need for service arises. Advertising can also help create the right mind-set so that the potential client is prepared and willing to entertain the possibility of working with the organization.

Advertising is an exciting and excellent medium for building image, but since it is expensive, it should be done strategically with a solid concept of the target in mind guiding all advertising purchase decisions. If, for example, a firm wants to reach business executives, it would probably want to buy time during prime news shows rather than during afternoon talk shows.

Finally, any advertising that is used must be integrated with and be supported by, other marketing materials. The potential buyers' overall awareness must be built through consistent messages and images.

Media Relations/External Communications

Getting a firm's name in front of targets as often as possible helps to build and enhance an organization's image. Public and media relations can be used to build reputation, educate the audience, and differentiate the organization in a crowded competitive field.

As with the other tactics cited here, successful media and public relations is based on a clear understanding of the audience. In today's fast-paced world, it would be useless to simply fill the in-boxes of reporters and industry analysts with generic releases. Editors receive from 5 to 20 calls daily from public relations practitioners. In addition, they typically are inundated with mail, faxes, and e-mail—most of which they view as irrelevant and unusable. Editors are understandably less than eager to receive unsolicited phone calls and letters.

Consulting industry media relations professionals must take the time to understand the publication it is approaching—its mission, editorial focus, readership, and deadline requirements—and even the individual editor. In other words, the fostering of relationships over the long term, as well as relevant backgrounders and press kits, is the most effective approach.

In this industry, media relations practitioners often work with national and trade publications to provide content produced by in-house experts and partners. Again, it is important to ensure that all bylined articles and thought-leadership pieces are written with a publication's specific audience in mind. Publications usually create editorial calendars far in advance, which means that organizations can develop pieces based on the publication's needs, rather than just sending items "cold." Similarly, supplements and inserts to special editions can also serve as an excellent means of reinforcing messages and promoting the organization's image.

An extremely important audience for management consulting firms is the industry analyst segment. These analysts function somewhat like the news media and somewhat like Wall Street security analysts, providing an objective view of companies in the industry. When analysts release a positive report about an organization, they provide a credible endorsement that cannot be "bought." Their views are well respected by the news media and by potential buyers of consulting services. The literature they produce is based on extensive research and experience, and can serve as excellent background kits for use with potential clients and the media. This information can also be distributed with other collateral, such as brochures, annual reports and proposals, at one-on-one client presentations, and at special events.

With external communications, again, the goal is to provide material that is directly applicable to prospective clients. Many firms produce mailers, quarterly or annual newsletters or magazines, and other publications that can be packaged and sent to specific mailing lists along with article reprints, annual reports, and more.

Special Events

Special events can take several forms. Credible forums and conferences allow firms to demonstrate their expertise and provide the latest information on critical issues. Community-oriented activities serve to ingrain the desired image in the public's mind. Client-oriented events or outings can be used to enhance and build long-term relationships and generate media coverage.

Special events tend to be more of a soft sell than other marketing activities. But the results can be far reaching for management consulting firms. Events tend to create a feeling that the client is special, and in the eyes of the organization, worth the additional time, money and attention being spent on a particular client. An invitation-only approach is an especially effective means of building a long-term relationship with an individual, because it provides "quality time," usually in a relaxed and attentive environment. It gives individual clients an opportunity to share their concerns and talk about their interests outside a business environment. On the other side of the coin, the event gives the consulting organization a chance to highlight its capabilities, thought leadership on key issues and understanding of the issues facing the client.

Another form of special event that has proven successful in the consulting industry is sponsorships, such as the hosting of a charitable fund-raiser. Event sponsorships offer an opportunity to place a firm's brand and message in front of target audiences, enhancing awareness and expanding business opportunities.

Tactics and Global Considerations

The final three tactics already described—*image advertising, public/media relations,* and *special events*—have differing levels of appeal in different areas of the world. For example, according to the Dataquest industry analyst firm, buyers of information technology services generally tend to rely most heavily on word-of-mouth, followed by the trade press, followed by past experience as their main sources of information. In the United Kingdom, however, word-of-mouth and past experience are the most-used sources. In Europe, but outside of the United Kingdom, the trade press is more highly regarded. While in the Asia/Pacific region, conferences and seminars are most prevalent. As always, global marketing and communications must take such cultural nuances into account.

Case Study: Andersen Consulting

Andersen Consulting is a global management consulting and technology firm that has brought a number of innovative marketing and communications approaches to the industry.

The organization got its start in 1913 as the consulting division of the Arthur Andersen accounting firm. Over the years, it grew in both size and scope of work, and in 1989, was established as a separate business unit. Today, Andersen Consulting is the world's largest consulting firm, with annual revenues in excess of $5 billion. The firm is established in some 50 countries worldwide, and counts three-fourths of the top 100 companies of the Global Fortune 500 among its clients.

Andersen Consulting's mission is "to help clients change to be more successful." Key to the firm's business approach is a client service model known as business integration, which takes a holistic view of achieving best business performance for a client by aligning an enterprise's people, processes, and technology with its overall strategy.

As a "new" organization at the end of the 1980s, Andersen Consulting faced two key marketing challenges. First, it had to create an identity for itself, separate from its past as part of the Arthur Andersen accounting firm and from its historical roots as a technology-oriented, systems-integration firm. Second, it had to differentiate itself in an increasingly competitive, rapidly changing industry.

Andersen Consulting has focused on developing brand and positioning strategies around an organizationwide personality that is "resourceful, committed, farsighted, and innovative." To create marketplace awareness, the firm began an image initiative in 1988, before its legal separation from Arthur Andersen. The campaign primarily used television and print advertisements and an increased emphasis on public relations and direct marketing. At the same time, the firm launched an organizationwide initiative to ensure that all graphic images portrayed the firm consistently.

In late 1992, Andersen Consulting began a program to integrate marketing and communications operations globally. This integration effort goes far beyond the traditional marketing and communications areas to encompass:

- *Image Development*—Which includes research, positioning, advertising, communications, media/industry analyst relations, events, and other activities that strengthen the firm's personality and global brand.

- *Market Development*—Which includes database marketing, special centers and forums for marketing (see Box 25–1 on page 390), research, and other activities that provide industry market focus, define best clients, and articulate what the firm can offer those clients.
- *Business Development*—Which includes market management, client management, relationship selling, and opportunity management.

This integrated approach allows the firm to focus on its highest-potential clients, shape consistent global messages to build relationships with those clients, and leverage global marketing and communications resources across the firm.

Andersen Consulting's industry-focused approach to the market is also a strength in leading the industry. For each industry that it serves, the firm develops positioning, offerings, and messages within the industry to demonstrate to clients that Andersen Consulting truly understands their business. Furthermore, within each industry, the firm identifies those companies most likely to embrace change and who desire change, and focuses on fostering relationships with those organizations.

All marketing, sales, and client efforts within Andersen Consulting are bolstered by its comprehensive Knowledge Xchange® system, an electronic knowledge management system that enables the firm to distribute core knowledge applications that store and deliver its best synthesized knowledge. This provides its professionals with ready access to and the ability to share consistent, high standards of service, experiences, and information among colleagues located throughout the world.

Several of the firm's marketing and communications efforts are described in more detail below.

Research

Market research is integral to Andersen Consulting's integrated marketing strategy. Research efforts began in the 1980s as a means of determining levels of awareness for Andersen Consulting and its competitors, creating an accurate profile of Andersen Consulting's potential clients and assessing the current and future needs of the marketplace.

Since then, the importance of market research has continually grown at the firm. Today, it examines nearly every stage on the equity circle, looking at areas such as differentiation in the marketplace, client retention, media relations research, and client satisfaction surveys. Overall, this research has provided insights into the changing nature and needs of clients that have been used to refine marketing strategies and messages.

Since 1995, the firm has paid special attention to truly globalizing its research activities, putting the same research methodologies in place on a country-by-country basis. Andersen Consulting is careful to use the same images consistently worldwide, but tests for cultural and language particularities. By testing consistently on a country basis, management now has a more precise view of Andersen Consulting's marketplace position vis-à-vis its competition.

Image Advertising

Andersen Consulting was the first major consulting firm to advertise at a significant level. Its efforts began in the United States, soon expanded to Europe and after that, ventured into Asia/Pacific. In recent years, the firm has launched a global advertising initiative, consolidating many country initiatives into one global program. The firm has been especially careful to use images and analogies that work across cultures.

B O X   25–1

ANDERSEN CONSULTING'S OTHER MARKETING FORUMS

Andersen Consulting has established various types of centers to help clients and potential clients envision new ways of working. Not only do these centers foster innovation for Andersen Consulting, they also build and solidify relationships and enhance the firm's brand and positioning in the marketplace. Examples of its centers include the following:

- **Business Integration Centers**
  Andersen Consulting's approach to helping clients is based on the concept of business integration, which aligns an organization's people, processes, and technology with its strategy for the achievement of best business performance. To make this somewhat intangible and sophisticated concept more "real" for clients, the firm has established Business Integration Centers throughout the world. Each of these centers is a working environment that enables clients to experience marketplaces of the future as well as how business integration can contribute to success in a specific industry. Examples of Business Integration Centers include the Financial Ideas Exchange^{SM}, Enterprise 2020^{SM}, and SMART STORE®.

- **Technology Centers**
  Andersen Consulting's research and development initiatives are focused on harnessing emerging technologies to the strategic advantage of clients. Centers around the world are dedicated to this purpose. The firm's Center for Strategic Technology Research in Northbrook, Illinois focuses on identifying, evaluating, and integrating technologies that are likely to drive enormous business opportunities. The Centers for Strategic Technology in Sophia Antipolis, France and Palo Alto, California help translate research into results by bringing together the latest products from technology providers, leading-edge thinking from Andersen Consulting industry experts, and the firm's business integration expertise. To explore with industry executives the strategic applications of advanced technology, Andersen Consulting sponsors the DAVINCI workshop series. Other initiatives from these centers include the development of LifestyleFinder, an experimental intelligent agent for target marketing on the Internet, and "Internet Music World," one of the first extensive Java applications.

- **Research on Market Leadership**
  Andersen Consulting has created a new business integration, pragmatic "think tank." The group's mission is to develop leading-edge ideas and insights about how organizations can achieve and sustain market leadership. Located in Palo Alto, California, the group engages in multidisciplinary research efforts focused on the issues of concern to CEOs, other top executives, and the members of corporate boards. Research topics include global enterprises, the performance impact of information and technology on organizations, and the evolving roles and competencies of executive leadership.

- **Solution Centers**
  Solution Centers are a global network of Andersen Consulting facilities where teams of professionals develop specialized, reusable, and proven solutions for clients. These centers put Andersen Consulting on the cutting edge of new ways to deliver solutions for clients. Solutions can range from better processes to improved systems. Professionals from Andersen Consulting's Technology, Process, and Change Management competencies work in these environments to explore and build innovative, creative answers to meet client needs. The centers promote continuous improvement and foster the development of deep skills while creating high-quality solutions for clients.

The ads are shown in various languages across the world, yet the images and content clearly depict Andersen Consulting. This global approach ensures that the same image, messages, and personality are delivered to every market in the same way, so that each time a client or potential client sees an advertisement, this individual will be presented with the same consistent, overall image, messages, and personality, contributing to the strength of the brand.

For example, in one television ad, Andersen Consulting communicates its creativity, innovation, and resourcefulness through a scene in an art museum where dancers and musicians from masterpieces come alive to perform together seamlessly, reflecting the firm's business integration message. It will be seen across more than 20 markets, yet communicate a single consistent message. The mission of helping clients change to be more successful is depicted in an ad using a string quartet that quickly transforms itself into a sports team; in another ad, a school of small fish takes on the shape of a shark to fend off predators. (A sample of the firm's print advertising is displayed in Figure 25–1 on page 376.)

Andersen Consulting's image advertising has helped increase awareness levels dramatically. When first researched in the United States in 1988, awareness of the organization as an information systems provider stood at 15 percent; in 1996, unaided awareness of the organization as a business reengineering services provider stood at more than 80 percent. This is especially significant in that it shows not only increasing awareness in general, but also a growing awareness of the firm's broad capabilities in the areas of people, processes, technology, and strategy.

Media Relations/External Communications

Andersen Consulting has had great success in the area of media relations. In 1995 alone, it enjoyed nearly 5,000 media articles or mentions in national and trade publications. Reporters frequently call on the organization's partners to serve as subject experts and spokespersons, and several partners contribute ongoing columns to publications. Some examples of coverage include:

- In its March 6, 1996, profile of Andersen Consulting, *The Wall Street Journal* stated, "While . . . companies . . . grab headlines by cutting their workforces, Andersen Consulting is enticing young recruits with the increasingly exotic prospect of relative job security. . . . Being that one stop for a multitude of major corporations has enabled Andersen [Consulting] to be among the most aggressive and successful recruiters on college campuses."

- In July 1996, *Consultants News* ranked Andersen Consulting No. 1 in its annual survey of the 40 largest U.S.-based management consulting firms, underscoring the company's success in expanding from its systems-integrator roots to a management and technology consulting firm.

Andersen Consulting holds an annual two-day Industry Analyst/Media Conference in which the firm shares information about its capabilities and how it helps clients change to be more successful. These meetings have been highly effective in getting the message out: Dataquest, Gartner Group, and INPUT have all produced full-length reports on the firm, and journalists from many countries have covered the event. One profile praised Andersen Consulting's ability to reinvent itself and respond to its clients' needs. Such objective third-party reports are vital in lending credibility to a consulting firm.

F I G U R E 25–1

Andersen Consulting Print Advertising Sample

Are all your talents working in concert?

An impressive range of skills can be found in almost every organization. The challenge, of course, is getting them to perform harmoniously.

Andersen Consulting works to help synchronize all of your vital components: strategy, technology, process and people.

With vast experience in each of these areas, we can help you seamlessly blend individual strengths with collective goals. Because these days, organizations don't perform. Unless they perform together.

Visit our web site at http://www.ac.com.

In terms of external publications, the firm produces an annual report, which is mailed to clients, potential clients and the media, and *Outlook* magazine, which presents views of leading luminaries and Andersen Consulting experts on current issues and trends. The organization also has produced a number of *CEO Briefs* focusing on various business trends, such as managing change and achieving process excellence. These briefs are mailed with issues of *Chief Executive* magazine, a publication with an audience that closely matches the firm's target audience. The firm has also moved onto the Internet, with a World Wide Web page that has received as many as 4.2 million hits per month.

Thought Leadership

Andersen Consulting makes a concerted effort to spotlight its thought leadership through industry conferences, executive forums, and specialized studies and publications.

Many of its industry conferences, such as the Customer Contact Forum for the communications industry and the International Utilities Executive Conference, have become the leading conferences in their industries. One-time executive forums also reinforce the firm's thought leadership. A World Forum on Change brought together a select group of top U.S. executives to discuss findings on transformational change and organizations' capacity to change. In Europe, Andersen Consulting served as the sponsor of the annual World Energy Utility Forum, a global event focusing on the energy utility market aimed at senior industry executives.

An array of publications, all with a consistent look and feel, relay insights from the firm's experts. In addition to those publications mentioned above, examples include a series of reports on Asian/Pacific business done with The Economist Intelligence Unit, Andersen Consulting's Top Executive Survey on European Economic and Monetary Union, as well as several books on important industry topics.

Special Events

Andersen Consulting sponsors a number of events that enhance its corporate image and positioning in the global marketplace, expand relationships with business partners, and extend integrated marketing opportunities worldwide. These events range from an annual CIO Workshop to golf outings to charitable sponsorships.

A key event in this lineup is the Andersen Consulting World Championship of Golf (see news release on page 394). This event has become one of the firm's most successful event-marketing programs. In 1996, the tournament received more than 300 hours of worldwide television coverage; eight of the world's Top 10 golf professionals participated in the championship and more than 250 of the firm's top clients attended events.

Andersen Consulting also sponsors a number of other sporting events around the world. In Europe, for example, the firm sponsors the Rothmans Williams Renault Formula One automobile racing team. In Australia, it sponsors the Gordon Rugby Club of Sydney and the Andersen Consulting Stakes at the Melbourne Cup, a major horse-racing event. In the United States, it sponsors the Corporate Sports battle, an Olympic-style fundraising competition among U.S. corporations. Each sponsorship is designed to meet a specific set of marketing objectives.

Internal Communications

Worldwide, Andersen Consulting employs more than 45,000 people, which means that the organization must communicate across a range of cultural and demographic audiences. A

FIGURE 25-2

Andersen Consulting News Release– January 5, 1997

ANDERSEN CONSULTING

WORLD CHAMPIONSHIP of GOLF

FOR IMMEDIATE RELEASE: January 5, 1997

NORMAN NABS MATCH PLAY TITLE AT ANDERSEN CONSULTING WORLD CHAMPIONSHIP OF GOLF

Claims Victory and $1 Million at Grayhawk Course in Arizona

(Scottsdale, Arizona, USA) – Greg Norman of Australia captured the $3.65 million Andersen Consulting World Championship of Golf, the sport's richest event, as he upended Scott Hoch of the United States, 1-up, and in so doing earned the crown of golf's international match play champion and $1 million.

N Norman, who earned the biggest individual paycheck of his highly acclaimed career, birdied the 36th hole of the championship match to claim a dramatic victory over Hoch, who also earned the biggest single paycheck of his career, $500,000.

E Norman, the number-one ranked player in the world, built a 3-up lead after birdieing the 2nd, 3rd and 4th holes on a cool (mid-50's F), cloudy day. He extended his lead to 4-up after Hoch bogeyed the 9th hole. After a see-saw battle on the back nine, Norman took a 3-up advantage at the intermission when Hoch bogied the 18th.

W After bogeying the first three holes of the afternoon 18, Norman's morning lead was gone and he and Hoch were even. A Hoch bogey on the 30th hole gave Norman a 1-up advantage which he held until he bogeyed the 33rd to deadlock the match once again. The title showdown remained all square as the duo reached the par-5 18th green where Norman drained a 15-footer for birdie and the championship after Hoch had narrowly missed his birdie attempt from 16 feet. For the 36 holes of play, Norman was 2-under par and Hoch one-under.

S Hisayuki Sasaki of Japan prevailed over Sam Torrance of Scotland, 2-and-1, to take third place in the 18-hole consolation match at the 6,973-yard, par-72 Grayhawk Golf Club/Talon Course here in the Phoenix suburb. Sasaki, who earned $350,000, birdied the 2nd, 3rd, 4th and 5th holes to build an early 3-up lead. The Scot battled back to even the match at the turn only to have Sasaki birdie the 11th, 13th and 14th to take the lead for good. Sasaki was six-under par for the 17 holes played; his opponent 3-under. Torrance collected $300,000 for his fourth place finish. Like Norman and Hoch, Sasaki and Torrance enjoyed the single biggest payday of their careers.

In yesterday's semi-final play, Norman defeated Sasaki 5-and-4 and Hoch bested Torrance 4-and-2. On a slightly warmer, yet windier day, Norman made seven birdies and no bogies in 14 holes of play as Sasaki contended with a balky putter. In an equally scintillating display, Hoch posted seven birdies and one eagle over 16 holes. Torrance's five birdies and one eagle were countered by three back-nine bogies.

The $1 million winner's prize is matched only by the first prize offered in the $2.51 million Nedbank Million Dollar Challenge.

The Andersen Consulting World Championship of Golf matches began in March with eight players representing four regions of the world (Europe, International, Japan and United States) competing in a single elimination match play format to determine golf's match play champion among the five major professional golf tours of the world (Australasian, European, Japan, Southern Africa and United States). It is the only event in golf to enjoy the sanctioning and support of the respective tour bodies of each region. Matches have been played in Georgia, Wisconsin and Arizona in the United States, and Japan, England and Spain.

The 1997 Championship kicks off in Japan on March 1-2. The 8-player Japanese field will be announced later this month. The other three region 8-player fields will be announced in early March with championships being played in April (U.S.), Europe (May) and International (July).

# # #

For further information:

Jeff Adams	Gary Beckner	Pete Arrichiello	Sam Ogawa
Andersen Consulting World	Andersen Consulting	Burson-Marsteller	Media Gain/Japan
Championship of Golf	(312) 507-2480	(212) 598-3614	81-3-3592-2454
(404) 873-5669			

1100 Spring Street
Suite 600
Atlanta, GA 30309
(404) 873-5669
(fax) (404) 873-5720

-over-

primary vehicle for addressing employees is *Dialogue*, a monthly news magazine that covers topical Andersen Consulting issues and features a question-and-answer page that lets personnel interact with management.

In 1995, the firm instituted a move toward paperless communications to maximize a number of electronic channels for internal communications. Use of electronic publications, e-mail, and databases make timely information available to a widely dispersed and highly mobile employee audience. The move reduced the use of paper and its distribution costs, and encouraged innovative developments with the Andersen Consulting Knowledge Xchange® system.

The ensuing results have greatly improved communications worldwide and provide consistent information instantaneously to all employees. Employees can now access *Headlines* for a weekly summary of news about the firm, as well as more specific Community Pages, relating to particular areas of interest within the firm, such as human resources, a competency group, or an industry. In addition, an extensive collection of databases allow employees to access information about internal policies, hold discussions, and share information about best practices worldwide.

Rather than provide traditional corporate news, Andersen Consulting's internal communications strive to foster consistent, high-quality behaviors and attitudes among employees who come in contact with clients. An Internal Communication Council has been established to help ensure that these efforts have the same look and feel across the firm, and that they embody messages that support Andersen Consulting's overall brand image and positioning.

THE FUTURE OF THE MANAGEMENT CONSULTING INDUSTRY

The pace of change that the management consulting industry has experienced over the last few years is by no means abating, nor is the rise in competition. Both trends can be expected to continue for some time.

In this environment, management consulting firms will have to not only keep up with general business trends, they will have to lead those trends. They will have to heighten their ability to bring new skills and expertise to market rapidly and effectively. They also will have to continue to seek innovative approaches to the marketplace. We have already seen fundamental changes in the arrangements between clients and consultants. Relationships are more long term, and the traditional fee-based structure is beginning to give way to value-based arrangements in which the consultant's compensation is based on the actual business results delivered, such as profits or cost reductions. Projecting these trends out, many experts see even longer and closer relationships in the future, including formal alliances and joint ventures. Consulting firms may even launch entirely new enterprises built around their key skills.

The consulting organization itself may also take on new shapes. In looking at today's networked, mobile firms, it is not hard to envision an increasingly virtual organization, with far-flung employees linked electronically, rather than gathered in a physical location. In this kind of firm, employees from anywhere around the globe could come together as a team for a specific project, collaborate electronically to complete the work, and then disband to be reconfigured into new teams. To be effective in such a firm, marketing and communications professionals will have to find ways of understanding and reaching a highly fluid workforce.

In addition, with marketing and communications human resources dispersed, they will need to develop skills that enable them to "manage what they cannot see."

Technology also is having an increasingly powerful effect on the way firms communicate with key audiences. Marketing professionals must pay close attention to the evolution of the Internet, intranets, CD-ROMs, and other interactive technologies. They must acquire an understanding of how images and messages translate to these electronic channels, and how these channels can and cannot effectively fit into the mix of marketing communications.

Professionals should be prepared to contend with new issues of control, as well. With communication resources and open channels within the hands of every individual, how does one manage the flow of information and messages in our electronic era? Perhaps the answer is not a control mind-set, but rather in the realm of encouraging appropriate communication behaviors and acceptance of candor in communication.

These emerging issues only underscore the need for a broadly integrated approach to marketing and communications. In a dynamic world of competitors, virtual workforces, and increasing speed, it is the key to consistency in messages and behaviors, and to the effective use of marketing resources across the firm.

Overall, the management consulting industry will continue to be a rapidly evolving and challenging environment. As the saying goes, however, change brings opportunities as well as problems. Those marketing and communications professionals who are willing to innovate—and willing to proactively shape the future—will find opportunity, and thrive.

The Role of Public Relations in the Hospitality Industry

John Wallis
Vice President, Marketing
Hyatt International Corporation

INTRODUCTION

Hotel, motel, inn, bed and breakfast—whatever the name, we have all stayed in one at some point in our lives. While a hotel's basic purpose of providing a safe, clean, comfortable resting place for travelers of all types has not changed much over the years, the inner workings, functions, and executive profiles of the people behind the scenes have.

As a former hotel general manager, I have spent many years working in hotels. The role of the public relations manager in the hotel has certainly come a long way from the time when I began. While I wish I could say that public relations has always been viewed in the same light, I cannot. Today, we are working in a completely different environment and the role of the public relations manager has taken on a new meaning.

In this chapter we will highlight how the hotel industry has changed its focus on public relations, some of the global differences as they relate to the role of the hotel-based Public Relations Manager, and we will explain how we can make such variances work to our advantage for a strong corporate image. By adopting an integrated form of marketing and communications, our company is beginning to change the way we communicate to our existing customers and to the press. We are beginning to understand and track the behaviors of our existing customers, particularly the loyal ones, so we can devise the proper communications vehicles needed to find more like them.

Because our hotels are spread throughout 37 countries, we have structured our company in a decentralized manner of operation. While our corporate headquarters is based in Chicago, we operate divisional offices in Hong Kong and in Lausanne, Switzerland. Under each of these offices are area offices, each with public relations managers who have responsibilities for the hotels located in their region. These offices are located in Tokyo, Singapore, Kuala Lumpur, Sydney, London, Frankfurt, Paris, Madrid, and Mexico City.

As defined in John Hill's book *The Making of a Public Relations Man* (Chicago: NTC Business Books,1993):

Public relations is a recognized and constructive force in modern society. We can see it at work in the policies and actions of almost every organization, business, and cause in the world. In its modern sense, public relations was brought into being by the ever increasing complexity of the economic, social, and political problems that have assailed the human race in the years since

World War I. Its roots are fixed in the basic fact that public opinion, confused, obscure, and unpredictable as it may seem, is the ultimate ruling force in the free world. A fundamental function of public relations is to help public opinion reach conclusions by providing it with facts and interpretation of facts.

A Historical Perspective

When examining the historical perspective of public relations in the hotel industry, we observed that the role of the hotel-based public relations executive has evolved and is continuing to evolve. Twenty-five years ago, a key role of the public relations manager in a hotel was to entertain important guests, handle customer complaints, and go shopping with the wives of important customers! The public relations manager was, in fact, a glorified VIP guest relations officer. Hotel general managers never completely understood the value of public relations or how a specialist could benefit the overall marketing and positioning of the product. Proper specialists were not hired because there was a great deal of confusion over the role and potential this person had in the makeup and ultimate success of the hotel and because the hotel never wanted to spend the amount of money necessary to hire a person with the right skills. In many cases, the hotel would do one of two things: not fill the position, or appoint a public relations manager with little or no formal training. We have also witnessed occasions when the general manager's secretary was appointed to the role.

Another reason public relations was never fully realized was because of the heavy emphasis placed on the hotel sales department. The "sales call" was believed to be the single most effective means of filling a hotel. It was easy and fast and it achieved results. Public relations, on the other hand, is often more difficult to assess because of the following questions: How do you track employee awareness? How do you determine what image a hotel has with external audiences? How do you determine the number of rooms filled as a result of an article in the local newspaper? Candidly, I do not think this even occurred to general managers in the past; but in the new age of public relations in the 1990s, we realized that we must begin building response mechanisms into our communications to allow us to better determine the results of a given promotion or campaign.

In the 1970s and 1980s, for example, the hotel's director of sales was responsible for working with the press because the public relations executive that was employed in the department had no formal training in communications. Any interaction with the press was promotional or advertising in nature and driven by the press not by the hotel. Although hotels would participate in such promotions, the newspaper or television station would derive the most direct benefit. A typical scenario: a local newspaper would call the director of sales to offer a half page of free advertising space. In exchange for the space, the hotel would give five weekend packages good for a two-night stay and a complimentary dinner that would be given away in a special promotion conducted by the newspaper. Because the director of sales was lured by the free exposure and flattered that the newspaper was calling, they often accepted the offer, no questions asked.

The secretary in the sales department would then send brochures on the hotel, as no press kit existed, and the newspaper's advertising manager would extract whatever they thought was relevant to their readers, with no direction or input from the hotel. The hotel never questioned the value and potential return on investment. Were the readers of the publication among the hotel's target customers? Would the hotel have sold the rooms if given the opportunity?

In contrast, by the 1990s, hotels had established marketing departments and professionally trained public relations specialists. At Hyatt Regency Birmingham in England, for example, the hotel launched two food and beverage promotions in its premier restaurant: one that focused on Asian cuisine and one on a California theme. When the hotel's public relations manager interviewed the executive chef and wrote the press release, she inserted information about the buffet and the chef's special skills and instantly qualified him as Birmingham's leading expert on Asian and Californian specialties. Rather than faxing the release blindly, telephone calls were placed to each local newspaper advising the features editor and forewarning them of the news that was due to arrive.

As a result of applying a strategy and process to an otherwise poorly handled practice, she was successful in getting an article and photo of the hotel's culinary team in the first section of the *Birmingham Evening Mail*, the city's largest daily newspaper read by 500,000 residents. She was also successful in pitching and placing her executive chef on a cooking demonstration that will appear for one full week on Birmingham Live Television, the largest cable station in Birmingham, with a feature placement on the promotion in *Select Magazine*, a widely read monthly magazine. By applying this process to the marketing department, the public relations manager was able to achieve two important goals: to establish a relationship with the local press and to begin to reach the hotel's target customer base in a more strategic method.

Even as the role of the hotel public relations manager began to be better understood, public relations management was still more reactive rather than proactive. The hotel public relations manager answered calls from the press, wrote and distributed press releases based on the news the hotel wanted to tell, and sat back and waited for the telephone to ring. Public relations managers at the hotel level, then and now, have two primary communications goals: internal hotel relations and external, or media, relations. If proper internal communication does not take place, an effective external campaign can never be achieved.

All internal communications efforts must exist and should flow in every direction in order to be effective. In many cases, information was only communicated to the general manager and not to the most important audience of all, the front-line staff who come into contact with the customer on a daily basis.

Think of all the people you come into contact with when staying in a hotel: bellperson, frontdesk clerk, housekeeper, waiter/waitress in the restaurant, fitness club manager; and the list goes on. Did you ever have the occasion to ask any of these people a simple question to which they did not know the answer? If the answer is yes, you are not alone. The image a guest has after staying at a hotel is often based on the collective impressions formed during a stay. We will expand on this in the section "All Marketing Is Communication—All Communication Is Marketing," but these points of contact are called *brand contacts* and are directly tied to the role of the hotel public relations manager.

Once internal communication is taking place, a targeted, well-thought-out and executed external public relations campaign can begin.

STRATEGY

A CLOSER EXAMINATION OF HOTEL PUBLIC RELATIONS IN TODAY'S MARKETPLACE

Major changes in the marketplace have impacted traditional or historical marketing and communications approaches as we knew them. These changes include technology, global economics, competition, social systems, legislation, and the political environment. Technology has had the biggest impact with regard to logistics, communications, and information technology. Because of major influences like these, Hyatt has been forced to restructure its traditional approach to marketing to meet the needs of today's traveller. Because of all the burgeoning marketing activities necessary at the hotel level, it has become crucial to establish an integrated marketing and communication (IMAC) structure in our properties. In truth, our customers integrate our marketing and communication whether we want them to or not based on how they perceive our company and our hotel products. We simply set out to better manage that perception.

The most direct impact of IMAC on hotel public relations is in the way in which we establish mutually productive relationships with the press. We are training our managers to manage their media information just as a hotel marketing staff would analyze the profile of each and every guest who walks in the door. There are a great many synergies between how to profile a model guest and the tactics a public relations executive would use to profile a model media outlet or contact to ultimately determine the vehicles needed to find more of those guests. The following chapter will place particular emphasis on the relationship between public relations managers and their most important "customer," the press. Some examples that relate to the hotel customer, or guest, will be used. By analyzing the following 11 questions, our public relations managers are beginning to model their press contacts.

1. Who is my most important (productive) press outlet/contact?
2. How do they want to be communicated with—telephone/mail/fax/electronic mail? And how often?
3. How can results generated by this outlet/journalist be tracked?
4. Do we know the productivity of each media segment, that is, travel trade, business, consumer press, and so on?
5. Do we know which media segment will reach our target customer?
6. Do we know to which media our customers are loyal?
7. Do we allocate our time wisely according to the productivity of each segment?
8. Do we protect our relationship with the press contact?
9. How do we protect the relationship once established?
10. How do we acquire new press contacts?
11. How do we determine what hotel news is newsworthy and what is not?

Our goal now is to gather media data of any type and store it in one place where it can be easily accessed. Sounds simple. In the hotel business, we are in a fortunate position because we know who our customers are, their geographic origins, and what their habits are when they are in the hotel. Few other businesses have the opportunity to gather as much data about their customers, directly from their customers, as we do in the hotel business.

The situation for hotel public relations managers is similar in that information from press contacts can be easily obtained and stored for future use. Public relations managers often spend a large percentage of their day in a reactive mode; if they do not make a conscious effort to build two-way relationships with the local press, productive results for the good of the hotel may never be fully realized.

Fortunately, the public relations departments at our hotels have been tracking and recording information about the media they work with for years in the form of monthly reports. They know such things as when their press contacts are on deadline, when material must be submitted to meet a deadline, when editorial meetings take place, who on the staff is responsible for assigning stories, and so on. We must now train our managers to turn this information into more than just information stored in their heads. In the United States, there are various computer programs available to public relations practitioners. Many such programs exist, including software that allows the public relations specialist to store and maintain records about the more than 200,000 members of the press in the United States, to log notes about various media contacts, to track hotel news or special events, to scan clippings, to create media lists for individual media segments, and to perform many other related tasks. While sophisticated systems like this don't exist in every country across the globe, the data is nevertheless important no matter what format is used for storage and retrieval.

TACTICS

The database and customer or media segmentation are the critical elements in IMAC programs. The following Nine Commandments are the basis for how Hyatt International has begun to change the way it has traditionally conducted public relations in the past. Under each example, we will explain the ways in which we are considering public relations within the IMAC environment at Hyatt.

1. Outside-in marketing, not inside-out.
2. All marketing is communication and all communication is marketing.
3. Process versus gut.
4. Not all customers (media) are equal.
5. Achieve relevance and receptivity.
6. Manage the database.
7. Set clear behavioral objectives.
8. Total customer (media) revenue.
9. Return on investment.

Outside-In Marketing, Not Inside-Out

In integrated marketing and communications, we are changing everything we do because we are beginning to use a more customized *outside-in* form of marketing rather than the more traditional and very familiar *inside-out* marketing. How many times have we all been sitting in a meeting with our colleagues trying to decide to which promotion, product, or campaign we think our customers will respond? We cannot continue to create programs just because we *think* our customers want them. We need to shift our thought process to an outside-in mode.

Each year our company attends a number of industry trade shows. Inevitably, we carry with us five-pound press kits complete with every possible story our company has to tell. We could never understand when a journalist was not eager to walk away from our booth with the information we deemed so valuable. Now we are beginning to transform this process by distributing press materials to those with a receptive ear, to those on our target database, or to journalists we have identified as being willing to accept the information and interested in doing something proactive with it.

Another example of inside-out marketing can be seen when you log on to the home pages of a majority of the companies on the Internet. We post contests, giveaways, and trips around the world because we think we know what our customers want. How many companies have taken the time to conduct focus groups with existing and potential customers to find out what they want? Although we wish we could say that we did the proper research in the beginning, we cannot. Our company is in the process of doing this necessary research now. And we are now beginning to tune in to the voice of the customer.

In recent surveys we've conducted, we have begun to ask our present and potential customers how we could best communicate with them. In many cases, their communication vehicle of preference is an electronic one. But what do we do with the mounds of information? Are we equipped and properly staffed to communicate to our customers in the ways in which they want to receive our communication? The data is important and meaningful, and the company that can best manage the data will come out ahead.

In a recent issue of *USA Today*, I was intrigued by a new product featured in a full-page advertisement by a large American photography company. The company's Internet address was printed in bold letters, so I dialed in to their site with hopes of learning more about the product and maybe even ordering it. After more than 10 minutes of browsing through their site, I was never able to even find a mention of this new product, let alone order it. How did this company expect to sell the new product if customers had no way of learning more about it? How can this company calculate a return on investment when there is no tracking method associated? An expenditure of at least $75,000 and nothing to show for it! If this company would have had an integrated program in place where it could have tied its product advertising to its Internet home page, it may have had an opportunity to sell more of its product.

All Marketing Is Communication and All Communication Is Marketing

The second step in the process is based on the premise that *all marketing is communication and all communication is marketing*. Integrated marketing and communication is not the latest "marketing gimmick" developed by the corporate office. It is a way of doing business. If one believes that a customer's perception of a brand can change with each interaction, then the bellperson is as important as the $20,000 glossy image advertisement in *Conde Nast Traveler* or *Town and Country*.

The role of public relations is to find ways to communicate this change in a manner that is simple for every employee to understand. Even the employee who is responsible for washing the pots in the kitchen must become aware that his role in supporting a restaurant is enabling the cook to prepare the food quicker and the waiter to serve a hot meal to the customer quickly and efficiently.

In addition to the five- and two-day IMAC courses we have been conducting, we have designed a series of 12 posters that are now displayed in the back of the hotel. They serve as constant reminders of the importance of the guest. A sample of these posters includes such key phrases as: "How's Our Guest Service—Ask a Guest," "It Takes Months to Find a New Guest and Only Seconds to Lose a Loyal One," "You Are the Most Important Brand Contact," "Clean Data Is as Important as a Clean Kitchen."

The prime brand contact for each of our hotels should be local, not global. Each of the overseas hotels we operate, many of which are the first to enter their respective markets, is at the center of its community. It is very different than that which we see in the United States where a hotel is seen as just another business entity. In most Asian cities, for instance, local residents and business executives will often dine or entertain in a hotel. Hoteliers in the United States only wish they could make this happen; generating business from the local community is often difficult, if not impossible.

When the Park Hyatt Tokyo debuted in June 1994, it was launched with an aggressive public relations campaign. The hotel followed all the right steps to ensure a leading position in the very competitive Tokyo marketplace: a public relations specialist from a large Tokyo-based consultancy was hired one year before the opening; with an eye toward attracting the American business traveler, the services of a Los Angeles-based public relations consultancy were retained; an aggressive promotion campaign within Japan and in the leading Asian capitals was conducted; and cross-selling among Hyatt International hotels in Asia-Pacific helped to attract loyal customers and to establish general awareness of the new property. A result of all this activity led to the hotel being named the "Best New Hotel in Japan" in 1995 by *Nikkei Business* magazine.

In the Japanese culture, being the best meant that your prices needed to reflect this position in the market. Our Japanese customers asked us to raise our prices because they were not high enough. An enviable position in which to be.

The image of the hotel can be affected either positively or negatively by every communications effort made. The role of the hotel public relations executive is often expanded to take this into consideration. Every interaction he or she makes with the guest, the staff, the local community, and the press is a direct correlation of the image of the hotel.

In a given hotel, there are more ways for a customer to be impacted by our product than could ever be counted. Every brand contact, whether it be the guest's experience with the front-desk clerk upon check-in or interaction with the housekeeping staff during the stay, can affect a person's impression of the company either positively or negatively.

Process versus Gut

The third commandment is *process versus gut*. Because public relations was a misunderstood position, proper planning rarely occurred. Hotel companies the world over were more apt to create promotions they thought would work rather than create and implement well-thought-out public relations campaigns. When our company entered a period of explosive growth in the 1980s, the work would always get done but follow-up and calculating the return on investment were unfortunately not even a consideration. I suspect this is where the flooding of the media databases around the company also broke down. When our director of public relations for the corporate office joined the company, she had an unruly media database of more than 1,000 journalists. The list clearly was not maintained and no specific value was placed on any of the media groupings. Because of her training at Hill and Knowlton where process and planning are everything, she applied a process to our public relations department, greatly aided by the use of public relations purpose-designed computer software, that had previously not been applied.

Not All Customers (Media) Are Equal

The fourth commandment is based on the premise that *not all customers (media) are equal*. In the world of travel public relations, this is especially true. If 10 babies are born every minute, then it would be safe to say that at least one travel writer is born every hour. There are probably more journalists who claim to be travel writers than any other type. Travel writing is particularly popular due to the lure of exotic travel destinations and the hope that the cost of visiting such destinations can be shared with, or subsidized entirely by, somebody else. Because of our destinations, our company has a fair share of requests for complimentary accommodations. It is a curious observation that the journalists who seem to demand the most, produce the least.

Through the use of an integrated marketing and communications effort, we can now begin to place a value on these journalists and treat them each differently. One of the premises of IMAC is to train your executives to communicate the right message at the right time to the right person. When dealing with the travel press, this is particularly true. A good database becomes especially important at this juncture. One way to determine the importance of the journalists with whom we interact, is to analyze the clippings they write, place a value on those clippings that portray our company in the best light, and keep a tally of the number of clippings that we get from a given writer and/or media outlet in a given year.

Achieve Relevance and Receptivity

Commandment number five is to *achieve relevance and receptivity.* By analyzing the behavioral patterns of the guests in our hotels, we can quickly determine many things about them, including the most effective delivery methods that we can use to reach them. For instance, we can track the demographics of where our guests are coming from based on the addresses on their folios; if they leave business addresses, we can track which industry they represent. At the Hyatt Carlton Tower in London, we know that the largest number of our guests are coming from the banking industry; because of the reputed healing effects of the Dead Sea waters, Hyatt Regency Dead Sea Resort and Spa attracts visitors who are interested in skin treatment; in Tokyo, we are attracting a large number of executives from Silicon Valley; and in Baku, Azerbaijan, many of our customers are employed in the oil industry. With data like this, we can very clearly target the magazines and newspapers that these people read with hopes of achieving two goals: reinforcing the reasons why they would want to stay at our hotels and attracting more customers from the same industries.

While a hotel is often busy with reactive work, one proactive effort that is worth its weight in gold is the telephone call made to the editors of those magazines that are read by the hotel's current customer base. The job of the public relations manager at Hyatt Regency Baku (Azerbaijan) is suddenly much more relevant to the hotel and can be viewed in a more receptive way by the magazine editors. In Baku, we know that the geographical origin of the hotel's customer base is 62 percent European, 27 percent American, 7 percent Middle Eastern, and 3 percent Asian, in addition to some other very small percentages from other regions. In America alone, we know that by targeting the business desk editors of the major daily newspapers in Houston and Dallas and the top oil trade magazines such as *Oil and Gas Journal, Oil Daily, Petroleum Engineer International,* we can reach a large percentage of existing Hyatt Regency Baku customers, and we would have a good chance of acquiring new customers from the same industry.

A common and somewhat historical mistake we don't want our public relations specialists to make is to send irrelevant press releases to journalists who don't want them. In the past, a public relations practitioner's value was determined based on the number of press releases they would send in a given week. Rather than only sending press releases when the company had real news to report, the practitioner was pressured to send press releases as often as possible, regardless of the topic or to whom it was being sent. This practice has helped to erode the integrity of the relationships that public relations professionals rely on with the members of the press who are on the receiving end of mounds of mail and endless faxes.

At a recent public relations forum, the panel of press representatives were echoing their frustrations on this point. Fax transmissions are expensive to the journalists and bear the cost of incoming communiques. Given the flood of irrelevant material, it is little wonder that the press no longer give out their fax numbers, or as one panelist threatened, consider making public relations practitioners pay a fee to send them their releases. We must train our executives to communicate the right message (in the form of a press release, advisory, or pitch letter) to the right person (a single journalist at a relevant magazine) at the right time (when that journalist either requests the information or agrees to let us send it.)

As Davis Young, president of Edward, Howard and Company said:

> In the use of the term public relations, many people believe the operative word is public. That is incorrect. The key word is relations. If listening is the cornerstone of communications, then relationships represent the foundation of public relations. If you want good public relations—if you want to build a good reputation based on sound relationships—start listening.

In countries such as Singapore and Malaysia, we have found that achieving receptivity has been the best solution for building strong relationships with the press. The media there are looking for short press releases that are relevant to the local market and they are more receptive to working with low profile public relations executives who don't try to push their way into the editorial pages.

Manage the Database

If we are to begin to achieve these goals, we must take a serious look at how we *manage the database*, commandment number six. In our industry, media groupings are broken down into categories such as architecture, arts, business, financial, food and beverage, and meetings and incentive groups, depending on the type of hotel. Determining the primary interest of each of the journalists with whom we work will help us to more effectively target the information we send them. Regularly updating the information in the database is critical. When dealing with the audience by whom we want to be portrayed favorably, directing press materials to an editor who is no longer with the publication doesn't exactly send the right message. In fact, those releases quickly end up in the circular filing cabinet on the floor.

Set Clear Behavioral Objectives

In addition to having a clean database, it is important to work with each hotel to *set clear behavioral objectives*. Behavior, in the eyes of our company, is all the ways in which a customer or guest uses or interacts with Hyatt International Hotels that demonstrate their revenue contribution, commitment, and loyalty to Hyatt. On reaching the stage where our database is in order, it is necessary to set clear behavioral objectives that we wish to achieve by a given date. For instance, a public relations goal of our company is to continue to attract the attention of media outlets such as *The New York Times* and *The Wall Street Journal*. The behavior objective of a campaign targeting media outlets such as these is for the writers from those outlets to be more proactive in calling us as often as we call them.

We have found in our hotels and marketing offices across the globe that setting clear behavioral objectives is one of the most important steps in the nine IMAC commandments because when we begin to segment the behaviors of the press, we can have a much clearer picture of the potential outcome for Hyatt.

Total Customer (Media) Revenue

Total customer (media) revenue, the eighth commandment in our process, will change the way we look at the media on our databases from a revenue-related connection to the target customer. On first glance, it may appear that a press release about a promotion at the Grand Hyatt Hong Kong would be of equal importance to both *The New York Times* and the *Chicago Tribune,* but based on the U.S. customer profile of the hotel's guests, which is heavily dependent on the East and West Coasts, it is apparent that a more targeted pitch to *The New York Times* would yield more direct benefits to the hotel than a call placed to the *Chicago Tribune.*

Every hotel has a profile of its target customer. In this step, the integration of all facets of the marketing department becomes critical. After determining who this customer is, we will be better prepared to target the media outlets that can help to attract more of this model customer. The constant communication between public relations and sales and marketing is an equation that can prove to be most profitable for the hotel if handled methodically and in relation to proven track records.

Return on Investment

As with any planning, determining your *return on investment (ROI)* is a step not to be overlooked. At Hyatt International, a proper ROI analysis is an important consideration in any program or promotion in which we participate. Return on investment is harder to determine in public relations because we are in the image-building business and can't always link our efforts to direct room revenue. However, we can apply this same principle to all of the steps I've outlined above in that we can determine an ROI for each of the target media that we determined in commandment four *not all customers are equal.* We would do this by comparing the results we received from our targeted media in a given year versus the amount of time we spent cultivating a relationship. If we find that we are not getting any closer to establishing a relationship, then perhaps there are other media outlets that we could cultivate with an eye toward increasing the amount of Hyatt coverage published.

Another example of a hotel in Hong Kong that is realizing trackable results after a recent promotion can be seen in the section below entitled Measurement/Evaluation.

In many of our hotels and marketing offices around the globe including those in such countries as Mexico, Spain, Germany, Argentina, France, Thailand, and to a large extent Indonesia, our public relations departments often receive high pressure to advertise in the local publications in exchange for editorial coverage. Fortunately, because our hotels are significant local players, they can normally resist the quid pro quo tactic just by virtue of their existing reputation and high profile position in the market.

A tribute to the reputation that our public relations professionals have managed to establish with the press can be seen through the number of industry awards we win in a given year. In 1995 alone, we received 118 awards across the globe. These awards were given by magazines that include *Asiamoney, Executive Travel Magazine, Travel Weekly,* and *USA Today* and include awards such as Best Hotel Chain Worldwide, Best Hotel Chain in . . . North America, Middle East, Asia/Pacific, Germany, and many more. Almost all of these awards were won solely on Hyatt's position in the market and on the close ties our public relations staff have been able to develop with the press in order to continually receive positive media exposure. While a limited amount of advertising space is bought by the hotels based in the United States, Canada, and the Caribbean, almost no advertising for Hyatt's hotels outside the United States is placed. A tribute to this can be seen in the fact that the company just walked away with eight awards by *Business Traveler Germany*, and virtually no advertising was placed.

THE FUTURE

THE FUTURE OF HOTEL PUBLIC RELATIONS

As part of our new IMAC way of thinking, we have created a flow chart that serves as a good basis for taking the nine IMAC commandments outlined above and placing them into a logical order to allow a more organized thought process. The steps in the flow chart are as follows:

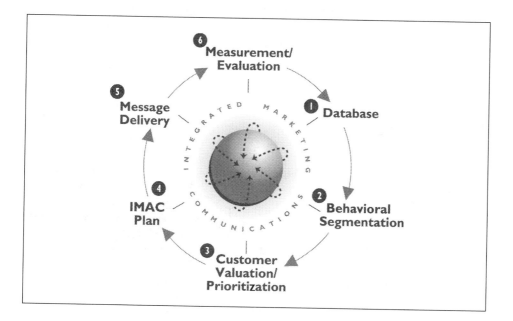

The future of hotel public relations, as we have described as a key component of integrated marketing and communications, can work if we change our way of thinking. Because the public relations departments in some hotels are more sophisticated than in others, the degrees of success will vary. But regardless of the hotel, an integrated effort will invariably achieve results. The six steps outlined above are adaptations of the nine IMAC commandments. By looking at them from the perspective of moving forward, we can begin to make advancements in the ways in which we interact with our target customers—both internal with the hotel staff and external with the press.

Database

First and foremost, a thorough analysis of the public relations database should be conducted. This is perhaps the most important step in the process because as mentioned earlier, we often have many more journalists in our database than are necessary. A telephone call from a journalist seeking information or accommodation from our company doesn't require that we add that person to our list. We will encourage our hotels to analyze the database by considering the 11 questions outlined earlier.

This process should always be cross-referenced with the media outlets that are known to be the most significant in a given market. For example, if a hotel public relations manager knows that the *South China Morning Post* is an important target but it has a relatively nonexistent relationship with the hotel, it should still be added to the target list because it is clearly an outlet that is important to the company and one that should be cultivated.

Behavioral Segmentation

As we begin to develop relationships with the press with whom we work on a regular basis, pay particular attention to behavioral characteristics. For instance, if a journalist only wants information on the food and beverage promotions that are conducted at a given hotel, that is all that should be given. Being bombarded with press releases about executive appointments, new hotels under development, or renovations underway will only upset the writer and result in a negative brand contact. We should follow the lead of hotels like Hyatt Regency Birmingham who know their food and beverage business is derived from the local market, so their primary relationships are developed with the local newspaper and television outlets.

One area where our company is already strong is in the process of segmenting the behavioral patterns of the press with whom we work. According to our public relations managers in both Japan and Santiago, many long hours are spent working with the press in social settings, getting involved in their activities, and working closely with them to maintain good relationships. In these two parts of the world, the work done outside the hotel has proven to be more effective in relationship building than that which could be done during an eight-hour work day.

In those parts of the world, and there are many, where the media outlets attempt to force our hotels to advertise in exchange for editorial coverage, we can easily segment that behavior into yet another category, a category that clearly is low on the priority list for any of our hotels.

In Spain, our public relations staff has established a number of good relationships with the press over the years by simply catering to their needs. The press want local, or country-specific angles, so our staff in Spain is quick to phone them when local developments occur or when ideas for trend pieces come to mind. Although we know the basic premise of media relations, we often fall into the *inside-out* trap of creating news angles that we think they want. As Davis Young said, if we want the press to write about our companies, we need to start listening to their wants and needs. I have never met a journalist who was not willing to spend five minutes with me to simply tell me how we could work better with his organization. In fact, an exchange of this nature can often be the first step in helping to break down any barriers between parties because it shows that you are trying to establish a mutually beneficial relationship.

Customer Valuation/Prioritization

In this step on the flow chart, we will encourage our specialists to take the information gathered in the first two steps and begin to place a value on each writer or outlet. All writers are not created equal and by virtue of the experiences we have on a daily basis when dealing with them, it is very easy to see how and why. As in any organization, the 80/20 rule quite suitably applies to the media process. Twenty percent of the press we interact with account for 80 percent of the results. So at this stage in the process, public relations specialists must begin to place a value on or assign a priority to each journalist with whom they have dealings and segment their behaviors appropriately. Our public relations team in Chicago has been doing this in such a way that the majority of their energy is now focused on the most productive press and those they want to cultivate.

Another important consideration of IMAC is the biological database. While we are beginning to track the behavioral patterns of the press with which we work, we must remember that one of the most important databases of all lies in our own heads. The amount of information a public relations manager who has been with the company for five years has stored in his or her memory bank is worth a great deal. If that person decides to leave the company tomorrow, we have lost mounds of valuable information. It should be a requirement that every public relations manager be responsible for recording this valuable information in a database for generations to come.

IMAC Plan

Embarking on an IMAC plan that is right for the hotel requires the public relations executive to apply all of the steps outlined in the nine commandments to their current process and transform their way of thinking. Partnerships between not only the marketing, sales, and public relations departments need to exist, but a more open exchange of information between all primary areas within a hotel needs to occur. For instance, our public relations manager in Guam knew that the one-year anniversary of the hotel was approaching. Rather than letting the day pass, she developed a plan that interfaced all the departments within the hotel with each other as well as with all the external audiences. In this case, she chose to have a contest in the local community whereby the hotel would select a local baby who was born in the same month and year that the hotel opened and use that child in the hotel's birthday celebration collateral and advertising materials. She liased with the food and beverage department to plan the official celebration, the fitness department to determine suitable prizes for the winners, and the rooms department to plan for the photoshoot once the child was selected, and she chose one individual from each department in the hotel to serve as a judge. Because this campaign was promotional in nature, it created excitement and awareness among the hotel staff and generated a great deal of excitement in the community resulting in an increased number of covers in the hotel's dining outlets. The media, who always identify with the smiling faces of beautiful children, loved the promotion and reported favorably on it, and the hotel's primary goal of communicating its one-year birthday was successfully achieved.

Message Delivery

This step is the most important to the public relations executive in the whole scheme of the marketing effort because it is the step that allows communication to a hotel's target customer base to begin. In the past we have always handled this phase in the process in what we believed to be a targeted, well-planned, well-executed manner. But there was one thing wrong—it was based purely on inside-out thinking. All the targeting, planning, and executing in the world won't make a difference if we are not giving our customers what they want but just what we *think* they want. What we perceive they want and what they actually want are two different matters and must be treated as such.

Message delivery can most easily be handled once we know our customers. As mentioned in commandment five, once we know our customers, we can achieve relevance and receptivity by reaching those customers through the magazines, newspapers, television stations, radio stations, and electronic forums to which they are loyal.

Measurement/Evaluation

Because public relations has traditionally been a difficult area to measure, we must do our best to build a response device into every communication that the hotel sends out. This can be done by including a toll-free telephone number inviting the customer to call for more information, an address where they can write to receive a brochure, a coupon they can send to the hotel and receive something in return. Each of these efforts must prompt a response which would result in an action both on the part of the consumer and on the part of the hotel who will then be able to add this important information to the database for future correspondence.

An example of a hotel that has conducted a promotion and has followed all steps to ensure a clear return on investment is the Grand Hyatt Hong Kong. In February 1995 the hotel decided to develop a special package called the Privilege Plan (PP) to be valid through December. The PP was implemented due to the changes in guest spending patterns. Because of the downturn in the global economy, many companies were downsizing and cutting the frills from their travel expense accounts. Per diems were imposed and many business travelers were not allowed to indulge in limousine transfers and laundry. Almost all guests who carried long-distance calling cards complained about the surcharges applied for local calls.

In response to this economic shift, the rate offered in the Privilege Plan included guaranteed room upgrade, complimentary round-trip airport transfer in a Mercedez-Benz limousine, daily complimentary breakfast, no charge for pressing one suit and for five pieces of laundry per day, free use of health club, free local calls and no surcharge for credit card calls, free London taxi service to Central and Pacific Place, and 15 percent off Business Center services. Because all services were offered in one reasonably priced package, the business traveler had a much easier time booking the rate and not having to justify all the extra expenses.

As a result of the hotel's keen sense of creating a package that was truly value-added, media clippings increased by 20 percent during the 1995 promotion period and revenue has increased by 213 percent over the same period in 1994. A campaign that clearly proved its success.

Conclusion

The organizers of a recent Pacific Asia Travel Association conference said it best when they titled their 1996 conference "Ancient Cultures: New Realities." The ancient culture of public relations through the years has formed a solid foundation for one of the most important and credible communications vehicles today. Public relations is a critical component to companies large and small and regardless of the nature of the business, the importance of the function remains intact.

While Hyatt Hotels & Resorts is only one company in the vast hotel industry, we are beginning to chart the waters in the industry like no other. If handled effectively, the new realities that we will all face as we move forward will help to continually shape the industry into the dominant force that it has become.

It is our belief that if the nine commandments that we propose in this chapter can find a place in the public relations departments of hotels throughout the world, we can truly begin to change the traditional ways public relations was conducted in the past. When application of the commandments is coupled with the flow chart, the public relations managers can begin to apply a logical process to their efforts and achieve positive, trackable results.

To summarize, Hyatt Hotels & Resorts is not a global business; we are a collection of local hotels that need intense regional data coordination. With the right marketing tools in place, we can maintain a leading position in the industry as a premier hotel management company.

Public Relations for High-Technology Industries

Michael Shore
Manager, Media Relations
IBM Corporation

A STRATEGIC APPROACH TO HIGH-TECHNOLOGY PUBLIC RELATIONS

Everyone loves high technology. It's everywhere in everything we see, hear, or buy. It appeals especially to two basic types of buyers. The first I call "early adopters" or "heat seekers" who love high technology for the sheer joy and feeling of superiority that comes with having the latest and greatest. The second and far larger group are "Joe endusers" who want and appreciate the convenience high tech brings in work or play.

Both sets of buyers have a passionate belief that high tech means progress—the latest and the best. As a purchase motivator it's hard to beat. Companies, even entire industries, have built their marketing and advertising strategies on high-tech differentiation. This is true far beyond the traditional high-tech industries such as biotechnology, aerospace, communications, home electronics, or information processing.

Often, it seems almost impossible to outdo the "techno-babble." Ski boot manufacturers, for example, publish charts showing "vibration decay rates." Clothing manufacturers publish enlarged cross diagrams of sweat pores showing "scientifically" how moisture escape rates are doubled with certain kinds of materials. Vintners public newsletters about the benefits of computerized fermentation management.

For public relations purposes, assume that high technology is any engineering-driven innovation that can help set your company's product apart by giving it unique and desirable characteristics. In other words, high technology is adaptable to virtually any product you can think of, and this brings tremendous career opportunities in high-tech public relations.

Given that high tech is a critical marketing weapon, what type of strategies should be followed in developing and implementing a good marketing communications or public relations campaign? These strategies depend on a foundation of ideas and basic skills that permit professionals to promote any company, including high-technology companies.

Some requisites for conducting a successful public relations campaign are:

- Your interest is from the client or company side, not as an employee of a public relations agency specializing in high-tech issues.

- You love or at least appreciate technology and understand how it applies to and differentiates your company's products.

- You are a skillful writer and your content, logic flow, grammar, and sentence structure make so much sense that reporters and editors actually read your press releases.

- You like talking with reporters and editors and always respect them even if they make a mistake or dare to write something you don't like.

- You are savvy, experienced, or just plain tough enough to guide or direct any marketing executive who thinks he/she knows media relations better than you do.

Ideally, to manage any corporate PR program including high technology, you already know how to compile and win approval from your company executives for:

- An intelligent and concise marketing communications plan outlining key positive news messages and hooks along with a plan to deal with the fallout when (not if) the reporter pushes you into some radioactive zones.

- A complete logistic and message delivery timetable that dovetails with any proactive or reactive engagement or event including such things as your new product announcements, trade or business shows, visit-the-editor "road shows," executive speeches, or special editions published by trade magazines.

- A fully developed, written and approved press release and contingency Q&As to lead the charge while credibly defending against the "have you stopped beating your spouse" questions.

- A target list of influential print and electronic news organizations, newsletters, and Internet files in which you want your press release to appear along with the reporters you want involved with your story.

- Investment in full print and electronic media training for your top-gun spokesperson. (Never believe your director or CEO when he/she professes to know how to "handle" reporters unless you've seen it firsthand.)

- A way of measuring and assessing results—and simple clip counting is only for starters.

Strategy #1: Know When to Keep Your Mouth Shut

Timing is everything in life and especially so with high tech because if you aren't careful you can "media relations" yourself right into a dried-up cash flow and Chapter 11. No matter how great your technology, any publicity must be timed right to make sure buyers don't suddenly stop spending on current products and instead wait for the next iteration. "Freezing the market" is a real danger with high-tech consumer products.

When to talk and when not to talk about your high-tech wonder depends on several factors. Where is your company in the current product cycle? Is the technology so new and early in the research stage that it won't impact your existing product line? Will it complement or replace all or part of your existing product line? How much should you say about something that may not actually exist? What is the competition saying and is it hurting your sales?

In some industries, notably software development, restraint of trade rules seem to be all but ignored as companies discuss upcoming follow-on high-tech products even though actual delivery may be months away. Critics call such products *vaporware* while proponents describe such "statement of direction" press releases and speeches as a way of helping buyers and consumers plan future purchases.

Beside the financial danger and the embarrassment, you risk a tremendous loss of credibility by talking too much or too soon and not delivering. Some consumers may forget what you said eight months ago about an upcoming product launch, but reporters never do.

There is no one right strategy, but I recommend looking at every high-tech press release, statement, or even demonstration at a trade show as a loaded gun that can be turned right at you. Even if you offer disclaimers, your release and statements will be looked at as an implied promise. That can both help and hurt you. The best press release describes a product that already exists, or discusses pure research without referring to a specific product or time table. The more specific the statements, the more concrete the technology and product should be.

Strategy #2: Realize the Best Technology Is No Sure Win

Having the best or most advanced technology doesn't mean you are going to win the public relations battle or gain market share and make your product a winner.

Indeed, having the best technology is just part of the total story. It's the other factors that make that technology so convenient and a "must have" from a consumer standpoint that often sway the outcome of a product marketing battle. Other factors may be related companies and their support products; existing consumer buying or usage habits; entrenchment of existing technology; and competence of competitors' marketing communication.

For example, when more movies were distributed on VHS than beta, the public swayed toward buying recorders with that technology. In the computer industry, having the best hardware doesn't mean much without an accepted operating system and a critical mass of key applications developed and sold by the software industry.

This is why industry standards are so important in helping win acceptance for a particular technology. It's hard enough to gain positive publicity and help generate market demand for a product with new technology that meets existing and accepted standards; it's 10 times harder to do that with technology that departs from the existing standard or requires consumers to abandon what they already know.

Any effort on your part to promote a particular product must show that the technology involved meets existing standards or give plenty of great reasons why consumers should spend money moving away from the standard to adopt your technology. If your product is a radical departure, you have a two-front war on your hands, (1) helping establish acceptance of a new standard and (2) helping gain acceptance of your new technology.

In showing that your technology is superior, every statement you make must show that you are not alone. You want to show your company is a leader AND that many other companies are following your lead. Even early adopter buyers don't want to buy a product with a technology heading for backwater obsolescence.

Strategy #3: A Partnership Made in Heaven or . . .

Corporate partnerships are formed for many reasons: to reduce development costs, to help exploit the new technology, or to help generate the perception that the technology you've chosen or the standard you are promulgating is the right one.

Because technology partnerships are so critical and common in high tech, the impact on your marketing communication plans and actions will be profound. If the partners see eye-to-eye, every message and every event gain added weight and substance.

But the downside is significant. Often, partners may disagree or have hidden agendas. Either way you will need a plan on how to handle your newfound communications partner(s) and what they may want to say and do. No matter how close the partnership, there will always be differences in business strategy, product goals, and this wispy thing called *company culture*.

The bottom line is that with any partnership agreement, public relations become much more complex and difficult. Your planning and approval cycles may require twice the effort, assuming you have agreement on your key messages and news content. Any message execution segment will involve executives from the other company whom you may not have even met, much less trust to say the right thing. The chances of miscommunication, misunderstanding, and discord rise exponentially.

Often, intentionally vague language within the partnership contract causes severe problems when the respective communications departments are drafting initial versions of the announcement press release. The value public relations brings to a table is to facilitate a resolution of—or at least an agreement on what to say to the media about—these vague contract points. If there's no agreement, you know better than anyone else what will happen when reporters begin their questions with the words "Let me understand exactly . . ."

Then there's the problem of leakage, especially if your counterparts want to predispose the press in a way that may not be in your company's best interest. These leaks can create internal tension within the partnership in addition to usurping the PR practioner's control of the information.

So what strategy should you follow to handle these partnership communications issues? As a professional there's no question you should do your best to work in a harmonious manner with your counterparts in the other company. If your execs want this partnership, you should do everything you can to make the joint announcement a successful one.

Realize there will always be conflicts and some of them will be significant. Never let your key messages be submerged or lost in any attempt at partnership harmony. If that happens, your partnership is costing you too much in the public opinion arena. Also remember that when you are deep in negotiations over the press plan, normal allies such as your company marketing director or legal counsel may become roadblocks. They may be so intent in having a successful joint announcement that key press issues are ignored or submerged until it's too late.

Your prepositioning strategy and your aggressiveness in conducting it will depend on several factors including the "holes" in the contract; any downside perception with the partnership itself; the potential or actual conflict over certain contract issues; and the issue of who might appear to win or lose when the announcement is made.

Sometimes disagreements or misunderstandings on relatively simple things, such as when, where, and who should make an announcement can't be ironed out. In such an instance, there may be separate press announcements and each company puts its own spin on the announcement. This should be rare if the partnership has any real hope of being successful.

How successful you are in negotiating and winning acceptance on the minor and major press issues will have a major impact on whether the partnership has a solid future.

Strategy #4: Who Cares about This Technology Stuff?

A basic rule in high-technology public relations is the same as in any other public relations effort—namely, don't forget which primary audience you want to address and don't get sidetracked from that effort. You only have so much time and so much money, and you can't waste either one. Every message and proactive event you do must be tailored to that primary audience and the reporters that write or speak to that audience.

This sounds simple, but it's easy to forget under the pressure of your engineering department's eagerness for you to spend time and effort publicizing in some relatively obscure technical journal every insignificant advancement they've made. Remember that pure technology rarely sells to the general purpose, enduser audience unless it is truly spectacular.

Be tough and confident enough to say no to requests for you to publicize any event that doesn't support your media plan. Such unimportant events might include an agreement with an original equipment manufacturer; a licensing agreement with a small company; a new title or job responsibility for a second-tier executive, and many others.

In a nutshell, stay focused on your key audience.

Strategy #5: My Plan . . . What Plan?

No matter how involved, how glittery, or how expensive, doing a kick-off announcement event is child's play compared to devising and implementing a full-scale, long-term, successful marketing communications plan. You must develop and follow a reasonable media strategy of proactive activities based on your company's marketing strategy. The aim is for you, and not reporters, to drive the news curve.

At a minimum, your marketing communications plan must take into consideration the following aspects of your technology or product:

- Are you trying to brand your technology or a product that uses your technology?
- What is the existing consumer awareness level?
- What are people's expectations?
- How big is the information gap between what your technology is and what people think of it?
- What are your technology's strongest attributes? To which target audience or consumer are they attractive? Why?
- Where do competing technologies or products stand?
- What are the pros/cons of your technology compared to the competition?
- What needs will the marketplace expect your technology to meet and what needs are left unfulfilled?

Not having good answers to these questions or a coherent marketing communications plan to answer them means you will fall into the "piece parts trap." The latter is nothing more than the willy-nilly announcing of the latest new enhancement tossed over the transom from your engineering department. You will work like a dog and be completely ineffectual. You will lose the public relations war.

You must demand and get good and right answers to those questions. Only then can you focus on the two or, at most, three key messages you want to publicize and do the proactive media activities that achieve constant repetition and reinforcement of those few major messages. This is the only way to gain not just a share of mind, but top share of mind.

Without proactive activities, reporters will do one of two things: (1) ignore or forget your product, or (2) if they do call, present a story angle that makes you cringe. With a solid communications plan you won't ever wait for reporters to call you.

Remember, all your planned activities need to be is newsworthy, and there are a lot of exciting and credible ways to generate that. If it works, your high-tech product stays in the news longer, and that recognition factor keeps inching up. From your kickoff announcement forward every event should be devoted to building and marketing momentum.

Strategy #6: Building and Keeping Momentum

No strategy is more important than getting and keeping momentum. To accomplish this, your proactive media plan should consider the following points.

First, you must always have real content—no snow, smoke, or mirrors in any event, activity, executive interview, or announcement. A majority of press releases go into the wastecan because they have no content, no story, and no hook. A steady stream of releases without content and without reinforcement of your basic messages only builds a full wastecan.

Always ask yourself what the news is. Is it some new capability or application? Does it offer some time or cost saving, reduced price, or a more efficient way of conducting business? Is the improvement immediate or in some distant time frame? Does it have some new, safer impact upon the environment?

Once you know the news, ask yourself what it means and how it fits into your key messages.

For a propeller head or "heat seeker" reading the latest engineering journal or scientific paper, the intrinsic technical facts by themselves may make up much of the news. But even with this audience, you need to show the application or the end result. This need to understand the enduser perspective and demonstrate real value is paramount when you are dealing with publications that cater to general public readers and potential product buyers.

Simple, hard technology news is not enough except for a few engineering journals. The benefit must be directly stated in any external activity or event you conduct. The benefit should be in the lead of your press release and reinforced over and over again in your executive quotes and numerous customer testimonial statements.

Even a simple release about a customer testimonial event you are sponsoring must show the benefit of your technology or product. No one cares that five different customers love your hot new technology unless they talk about how it helps them and how it will help other buyers.

Sometimes the engineering team will push hard for a press release in an attempt to either show progress or at least demonstrate they aren't falling behind the competition. Unless there's meat and it fits in with your overall key messages, don't do it. Your company's credibility is too important to waste on false news.

Building momentum also means knowing and taking advantage of every external opportunity to get your messages across. Examples include business or trade shows, technology forums, professional society meetings, government-sponsored seminars or research projects, or product comparisons, often nicknamed shootouts, sponsored by trade publications. These events offer you the chance to reinforce your messages while defending against competing claims.

One of your biggest problems will be keeping up and finding time to execute your proactive plan. You have to know when these external events are scheduled, make sure you have news to give, get the news organized into your key messages, get approvals, handle logistics and you have to have executives and customers willing to appear and speak.

Building momentum often requires outside help in the form of helpful technology consultants that follow your particular industry or product set. These consultants should understand and favor your company's business strategy, product set, or technology and be credible. There's no issue about how willing they are to talk with reporters and be quoted—they are always willing to do that. The more facts, the more straight talk and open access you give the consultant, and they in turn give to the press, the better for you. It's not that reporters don't trust your releases or your executives, but they want an outside opinion, even if it's not 100 percent impartial. Never underestimate the weight consultants carry with reporters. No press event, no release must ever happen without adequate early preparation in briefing consultants, seeking their advice, and trying to win some to your side. A full one-on-one briefing by one or more of your senior executives for the six most influential consultants is a minimum for any important announcement or ongoing campaign. You may even want to hire several of them as a sounding board for your product or business strategy. It's also common to hire one to write an "impartial" technology white paper lauding your technology and product where such a tactic is credible.

Does this destroy their credibility with the press? Surprisingly, no. Just because you have them as advisers or seek their opinions regularly doesn't mean they always agree with you and will always give glowing quotes to reporters. Never take consultants for granted even if you think they are on your side. You may not want to publish the names and phone numbers of the consultants you think are on your side in your press release, but it's a must to mention one or two of them when talking to any reporter. Often reporters will ask you for some names of consultants they can contact.

Next on the momentum-building list is to have as many security analysts as possible love you. This depends a lot on whether your company's financial outlook is strong or weak. But you need to win some to your side because reporters call security analysts as often as they call consultants. The bigger your product impact is on the company earnings, the more important analysts' opinions become.

You can brief them together the day your quarterly earnings report is made public. But it's better to hold periodic group updates independent of any blackout or earnings period. The key thing about the updates is that reporters will usually attend. These updates are a tremendous opportunity to get your key messages out to analysts and reporters together. It's also quite risky, depending on how many and how big are the holes in your product line, strategy, or execution.

Another mandatory requirement for momentum is to have at least two strong spokespersons. These speakers must be entrepreneurial enough to understand the need to meet with the press regularly and be willing to do so. In my experience, the bigger the company, the harder this requirement becomes.

Executive accessibility is one of your most powerful tools. But often this sword is made of cardboard. It's not easy to find a high-level spokesperson that knows how to listen and respond directly while emphasizing the key messages. He or she must be knowledgeable and confident, but not have a big ego. A spokesperson must always respect reporters, especially the tough ones. Saints like this aren't born, they are media-trained either by you or another expert, I don't mean training just for camera sound bites but for the entire presentation and interview process.

Perhaps the single most important factor in building momentum is customers' testimonials. The money they've spent on your high-tech products gives them instant credibility. Have them at your press event. Help them with their presentations and visuals. Pay to have them get media training—do whatever it takes to get them in front of reporters and tell their story.

At a minimum, you must have a list of satisfied customers with phone numbers as part of your press kit. Find enough happy customers that will talk about your technology, and you can triple the impact of your announcement.

Aside from a particular product announcement, you may want to consider holding a separate customer briefing dedicated to a particular aspect of your product or marketing strategy. In this instance, your top executive simply makes opening/welcome remarks and gets out of the way while a parade of customers talk about how your technology is making them more efficient and profitable. Unless your product is in deep trouble, major media won't send a reporter, but your trade publications will.

Another way of thanking these customers is by doing a press release for each and sending it to their respective trade publications in their own particular industry.

In summary, strategic considerations for good high-technology public relations include:

- Knowing when to speak up and when to stay quiet.
- Understanding the pros and cons of your technology, what it can accomplish, and where it fits in the marketplace.
- Being able to negotiate with your counterparts in any company partnership and making sure your key messages are fully publicized with the added weight of multiple companies standing behind them.
- Segmenting your audiences and making sure they get the news that will drive buying decisions.
- Developing a proactive media campaign with a limited number of factual key messages that can be reinforced and emphasized.
- Building momentum by taking advantage of every opportunity, including business shows, speaking engagements, and customer testimonials to get your news before the public.

## CHAPTER 28

A Practical Guide to Sports Marketing and Public Relations

Steven H. Lesnik, APR
Chief Executive Officer
Kemper Lesnik Communications

Howard Schacter
Vice President
Kemper Lesnik Communications

A STRATEGIC APPROACH TO SPORTS PUBLIC RELATIONS

Sports public relations is one of the youngest and fastest growing segments of the PR industry. This segment is defined by the use of a public relations tactic to:

- Achieve the communications objectives of a sports-related company or organization.
- Support and enhance a sports marketing activity executed by a company or organization.

We will begin the examination of this PR segment by exploring the importance of sports in the United States and the corresponding sports marketing explosion of the past decade.

Sports in America

The impact of sports on the American culture has been well documented. Popular language is filled with sports clichés and analogies. Sporting events annually rank among highest rated television programs. Many people can remember the starting lineup of their favorite team more easily than the names of their local government officials.

The sports phenomenon is easily understood. The same principles and values upheld on the playing field—loyalty, competition, teamwork—mirror those that drive America's competitiveness in international affairs, in business, and in our need as individuals to excel.

For example, in the United States during the past decade, America's fascination with and participation in sports across the entire sports spectrum has grown exponentially. According to a 1993 survey by the National Sporting Goods Association (NSGA), 71 percent of Americans play some kind of sport at least once a week.[1] Further, a full 80 percent of Americans have maintained or increased their participation in sports and fitness activities during the last several years.[2]

But Americans are not just playing sports more. They are also attending more sporting events. The NSGA survey says approximately one-half of all Americans have an extremely high interest in spectator sports—and that's both men and women. The average spectator pays to attend a sporting event nine times per year.[3]

Viewership of sporting events has also seen a tremendous rise with the advent of all-sports cable networks such as ESPN and SportsChannel. An analysis of TV sports programming available to Chicago residents demonstrates this point. In 1982, households with basic cable television service were provided 31 hours of sports programming during the first week of May. That number increased to 227 hours in 1992.

By all of these measurements—participation, attendance, and viewership—sports continues to grow faster than any other activity in the United States. In fact, sports appears among the top 50 industries that contribute to the Gross National Product, accounting for more than $50 billion per year.

The Emergence of Sports Marketing

The pervasive presence of sports in our culture is one of the major reasons for the emergence of sports sponsorship, now a $4.25 billion business according to the International Events Group, publisher of *IEG Sponsorship Report*.

However, other factors come into play. The amount of leisure time we have has increased over the past decade, and people are spending more of it at sporting events. Marketers recognized this trend in the 1980s and began asking how they could harness this opportunity to sell a product or enhance their company's image.

The fitness boom also has contributed to the sports marketing explosion. Americans are emotionally and physically involved in healthy living, and events such as 5K runs and aerobics competitions provide marketers new avenues through which to reach target audiences.

Sports as big business is another important influence on the emergence of sports marketing. Escalating player salaries, competition from new sports and expansion teams, and a downward economy in the mid-1980s led those who head our leagues, events, and teams to seek additional revenue generators.

The sophistication of demographic and psychographic research has also influenced sports marketing. In the past decade, companies have learned to delve deeply into the consumer's thought processes, habits, emotional outlook, and reaction to hypothetical product positioning. Companies discovered that sports provides the means to try targeted or niche marketing strategies.

Research has shown there is a distinction among baseball, football, and basketball fans. And, as a result, specific sports are being used by marketers as a reliable way to reach targeted audiences.

What Is Sports Marketing?

Marketers may be wise to take advantage of sports trends to reach key audiences, but just how do they do it? What is this ambiguous industry of sports marketing? Any program that uses sports to realize one or more corporate, sales, marketing, or communications objectives falls within the parameters of sports marketing.

It could include inviting a client to a ball game, buying an ad in a team's program book, hanging a sign with a corporate logo at a sporting event, purchasing commercials during a sports telecast, inviting an athlete to deliver a motivational speech to employees, or sponsoring a Little League team. Any of these tactics are the basis of a successful sports marketing campaign.

The best sports marketing campaigns will vertically integrate program components that together achieve many of these objectives. Public relations can support one or more of them.

By engaging in any sports marketing activity, the marketer hopes to tap the emotional investment that bonds most sports fans: loyalty—loyalty to a favorite sport or event or loyalty to a favorite team or player.

Because consumer brand loyalty is perhaps the most important attitude a marketer must influence, marketers align their companies with an entity or personality to whom their target consumer is loyal. In theory, over time the consumer will become a loyal follower of the company as well.

The following section summarizes the major areas of sports marketing. The integration of public relations with marketing and corporate goals is critical to the successful implementation of many, but not all, of these strategies.

Sponsorship

Event Sponsorship

College football's John Hancock Bowl. Professional golf's Kemper Open. NASCAR's Miller Genuine Draft 500 auto race. These are all examples of title sponsorship: purchasing the right to integrate a corporate or brand name with that of an event.

> A sports marketing program should achieve one or more of the following objectives:
>
> - Drive sales.
> - Enhance image.
> - Generate product awareness.
> - Encourage customer trial.
> - Gain access to mass media.
> - Nurture client and/or employee relationships.
> - Enhance community relations.

The benefits of title sponsorship are enormous dividends in terms of generating awareness. Any time that event is mentioned—during its television broadcast, by fans around the office water cooler, on that evening's sportscast, or in the newspaper—the sponsor receives a mention, too.

Generally, the title sponsor will negotiate additional benefits from the event's organizers. These include placement of the sponsor's logo on-site and if the event is to be broadcast, within TV camera view (often on the actual playing field). Other possibilities include one or more commercial spots during the event's telecast, the opportunity to distribute product or coupons at the event, a supply of tickets to it, and attendance at one or more VIP parties tied to the event.

The price tag for such a package can be quite steep, however. Title sponsors of nationally televised events frequently pay more than $2 million for the sponsorship.

Most event organizers will sell less expensive, associate-level sponsorships to marketers that for one reason or another do not wish to purchase the title sponsorship. Associate sponsors will receive one or more of the benefits the title sponsor receives but will not have their name tied to that of the event.

The advent of made-for-TV sporting events provided a cheaper sports marketing vehicle for companies unable to afford the title sponsorship cost of "institutional" events like the Olympics or the college bowl games.

Events like the Merrill Lynch Shootout, the Gatorade Ironman Triathalon, and the Coors Light Pro Beach Volleyball Tour could not exist without the benefit of corporate support and television.

Property Sponsorship

For marketers looking for a sports link in their advertising or perhaps in retail, property sponsorship makes sense. Sponsorship of a property means a marketer has purchased the right to use the logo, name, or likenesses of the players of a team, franchise, league, or organization in promotional efforts.

Most sports properties, such as the Olympic Games, the World Cup soccer tournament, and the National Football League, sell similar sponsorship packages to many different marketers by offering one package to just one marketer in many different business categories. For example, McDonald's (restaurant), Coca-Cola (soft drink), General Motors (automobiles), Snickers (snack food), and seven other companies constituted the group of worldwide sponsors of World Cup USA 1994.

Venue Sponsorship

Purchasing the rights to the name of a stadium or arena presents another area of sports sponsorship.

For example, United Airlines has purchased name sponsorship of a new facility in Chicago, the United Center, home to the NBA Chicago Bulls and NHL Chicago Blackhawks. In 1995, the Colorado Rockies of Major League Baseball began playing at Coors Field. And the NBA's Washington Bullets play in the USAir Arena in Landover, Maryland.

A professional sports and entertainment venue sponsorship can cost several million dollars. That investment pays big dividends, however, in terms of impressions generated each and every time members of the community and the media mention the building. And in a way, the venue sponsor is inherently linked to every event that takes place there.

Athlete Spokesperson

Professional athletes are frequently associated with excellence, commitment, and dedication—all qualities it takes to be the best. Those are the same qualities marketers want consumers to associate with their organization or product. Therefore, athletes are often hired as spokespeople to endorse the products in commercials, at special appearances, or on numerous other occasions.

For top athletes, like Michael Jordan and Joe Montana, moonlighting as a spokesperson can translate to as much as 10 times their salary. While watching TV on any given night, you might see Jordan promoting a new line of Nike basketball shoes, the great taste of Gatorade or McDonald's hamburgers, the comfort of Hanes underwear, or the ride of a Chevrolet Blazer.

The rewards of associating a product with an athlete in terms of image enhancement are great, but it is important to remember that athletes, like the rest of us, are only human. Today's superstar can be tomorrow's forgotten player.

Signage and Logo Placement

Perhaps the simplest form of using sports to generate consumer impressions is a marketer's purchase of the right to put its logo where people will see it—in the venue or on an athlete.

The next time you're at a Major League Baseball game, count how many commercial signs you can spot: On the scoreboard, by the outfield wall, behind home plate. Rotating boards that provide signage space to more than one company during a game are prevalent at courtside of NBA arenas. The goal of well-positioned signage is to generate awareness for a marketer both in the ballpark and in the thousands of homes where people are watching the sporting event on TV. The better the position of the signage, the more times it will appear during the event's broadcast.

But logos can appear on more than just signs. In many nonteam sports, the athletes themselves seem to have become walking billboards. Golfers, tennis players, and professional race car drivers, for example, are often seen with logos of sponsors on caps, helmets, breast pockets, equipment, and even socks!

Product Placement

While many marketers pay a hefty price for an athlete to wear their company's logo on apparel during competition, sporting goods companies battle and pay handsomely, to have athletes actually play with their equipment.

Nike, Reebok, Adidas, and many other athletic footwear manufacturers, for example, pay college coaches millions of dollars to ensure the coaches outfit their teams with products during the season. And Louisville Slugger provides thousands of free bats to professional baseball players every season.

Hospitality

Tickets to many professional and college sporting events are often difficult to obtain. Providing a number of seats to key clients or employees is a major source of generating goodwill among important audiences. It also enables a marketer the opportunity to get to know key influencers in a more relaxed social setting.

TACTICAL APPROACH TO SPORTS PUBLIC RELATIONS

The boom in sports marketing led to the growth of sports public relations as well.

Public relations practitioners in a corporate communications department or at an agency may one day face the challenge of supporting a company's sports marketing venture. Every sponsorship celebrity endorsement is different and the practitioner must analyze each program's individuality.

On the following pages are examples of fundamental public relations tactics that widely respected sports marketers have used to support their sponsorships and athlete endorsements. Note that companies rarely utilize their public relations budget to support signage and hospitality opportunities, and those areas of sports marketing are not covered in this section. (Readers interested in sponsorship including the arts and cause-related marketing should read Chapter 10 by John Koten.)

Supporting a Sponsorship

Event Support

As the title sponsor of an event, a company expects, above all else recognition of the sponsorship by all target audiences, including consumers, the media, employees, and other key influencers. It is the responsibility of public relations to help generate that recognition, which most often is accomplished through the activities of a corporate information bureau. The information bureau plays the lead role in undertaking all communications-related activities for the marketer, including:

- Creating, developing, and producing all media materials.
- Managing all proactive media relations efforts, including regularly distributing information on a variety of sponsorship-related stories to appropriate media outlets.
- Responding to media inquiries.
- Serving as the marketer's liaison with employees regarding sponsorship support activities undertaken by the company or organization.

Property Support

Sponsorship of a major sports property costs millions of dollars. According to the International Events Group, NFL sponsorships cost upwards of $2 million.

To support that heavy a marketing investment frequently requires an integrated PR program that includes national and grassroots elements. In addition to an Information Bureau, there are many public relations programs that could serve as an overlay to an organization's NFL sponsorship:

- Host a local youth football league sign-up party.
- Create a national education program in which youngsters are invited to enter an NFL-themed essay contest.
- Develop a free viewer's guide to the NFL offered via publicity.
- Provide tickets to NFL games to charity organizations.
- Donate equipment to high school football teams that perform a required number of hours of community service.

Venue Support

Sponsorship of a stadium or arena is big news to local media and citizens. If the site is used by a professional team, it may be of national interest as well. A carefully designed, aggressive media relations plan should take advantage of the following opportunities for publicity:

- Announcement of the sponsorship.
- Groundbreaking.
- Completion of construction.
- Walk-throughs by VIPs.
- The first event held at the venue.
- Ongoing public relations and publicity efforts throughout the year.

Athlete Spokesperson

Public relations can strengthen the relationship between a marketer and a spokesperson in a variety of ways, depending on the specifics of the endorsement contract.

The announcement of the endorsement provides a first opportunity for publicity. Consider hosting a press conference with the athlete in attendance. During the event, orchestrate a photo opportunity featuring the athlete holding or using the marketer's product or perhaps including the athlete in a posed shot with the company's senior executives.

Examples of Successful Applications of the Tactics

Maui Visitor's Bureau

A good example of a successfully implemented sports event information bureau is that which supports the Maui Visitor's Bureau's (MVB) sponsorship of the Maui Invitational NCAA college basketball tournament. One of the most prestigious events of its kind, the Maui Invitational annually invites some of the highest ranked teams in the country to compete in a preseason tournament on this beautiful Hawaiian island. Games are televised live across the United States on ESPN. The MVB sponsors the event as a means of generating awareness of the destination as a wonderful vacation spot for consumers, especially sports fans, and the information bureau is used to deliver that message.

The information bureau regularly distributes updates on the tournament to media and makes sure to include tourism information on the island in each news release. The information bureau also secures media attendance to the November event and suggests nontournament related story ideas about Maui to the media for sidebar articles to their event coverage.

The efforts of the Maui Invitational Information Bureau from 1990 through 1994 have resulted in over 1 billion consumer impressions for the island.

The following examples show how PR can take advantage of some of the annual appearances an athlete spokesperson will provide to the company:

- Secure media interviews during which the athlete can deliver predetermined messages about the marketer or wear apparel featuring the company's logo.

- Arrange for the athlete to visit with employees at the marketer's headquarters for an afternoon or perhaps deliver a speech at the company's national sales meeting.

- Schedule the athlete to appear at the company's booth at an industry trade show to help build traffic.

- Distribute information to media about a new advertising campaign or promotional effort that will feature the athlete.

McDonald's

In recent years, the television commercials airing during the Super Bowl have become as popular as the game itself. Many of the world's biggest marketers have used the event to premiere new campaigns featuring athlete and celebrity endorsers.

In 1993, McDonald's unveiled "Showdown," a shot-for-shot competition featuring basketball superstars Michael Jordan and Larry Bird, during the Super Bowl. While the spot was viewed by an estimated 133 million viewers during the game, more people actually saw previews of the commercial in the week leading up to its premiere.

B O X   28–1

CASE STUDY: EPSON

MARKETING SITUATION

Long known for its leadership in dot-matrix printers, in 1987 Epson decided to extend its business to personal computers. Despite its solid brand name, the company needed to generate awareness of its new products among its target audience, electronic data processing (EDP) decision-makers at Fortune 500 companies. Furthermore, Epson's marketing budget was dwarfed by its main competitors, IBM, Apple, and Compaq.

To compete in this environment, Epson had to find ways to gain access to its target audience and position itself as a major player in the market with top quality computer products.

OBJECTIVES

Epson developed an integrated marketing and public relations plan to:

- Reach EDP decision-makers directly with the Epson story.

- Generate brand awareness among consumers and corporate customers.

- Create an image of Epson as a "professional" competitor.

- Demonstrate product quality.

STRATEGIES

Epson selected golf as the medium to achieve its objectives. The sport made perfect sense because:

- The demographics match: golf fans are Epson customers.

- Golf provides an opportunity to meet outside the office on common ground.

- Golf events offer numerous sampling and hospitality opportunities.

TACTICS

Sponsorship of the PGA Tour

Epson's first step was a sponsorship of the PGA Tour that provided the designation "Official Computer Products of the PGA Tour." The designation appeared on PGA Tour marketing and publicity materials, generating millions of impressions and legitimizing Epson's place among industry leaders. It also provided the company business opportunities with direct sales to PGA Tour players, PGA Tour headquarters, and golf courses around the country.

The PGA Tour also granted Epson title sponsorship of its official statistics (stats). News releases distributed regularly to sports media enabled the company's name to appear in local newspapers on a weekly basis when PGA Stats were reported.

Tournament Sampling

At up to 10 PGA tournaments each year Epson executed the "Epson Fan Enhancement Program," through which the company provided a series of computers placed around the golf

Case Study: Epson (Concluded)

course so spectators could keep up with tournament scoring. At the touch of a key, spectators could find out how their favorite pros were doing at that moment, which holes they were playing, and where they stood against the field.

Computers were also placed in every tournament hospitality tent, where executives of Fortune 500 companies and their customers could experience an Epson computer in a relaxed environment. Periodically, Epson representatives would stop by each tent to discuss the computers and handle any questions. An aggressive publicity campaign, which included media demonstrations at each tournament to show how the system worked, helped provide the Epson Fan Enhancement Program story to the general public.

Athlete Endorsement

To further position Epson as a professional level competitor, the company entered into an affiliation with Greg Norman, one of golf's most dynamic and successful players. Norman appeared in Epson print advertising and in sales videos, spent time with company employees and customers at tournament hospitality sites, and appeared at charity golf tournaments on Epson's behalf.

Event Sponsorship

To generate awareness for Epson while gaining access to the mass media, the company sponsored two PGA Tour-sanctioned nationally televised events. The Epson Stats Match and the Epson Senior Stats Match also provided entertainment opportunities for Epson to build strong relationships with its corporate clients. An information bureau was established on Epson's behalf to ensure business and sports media were aware of the sponsorship and covered each event.

Traffic Building

Epson used its associate sponsorship of the Grand Slam of Golf, a Chicago-based tournament featuring the winners of the four major championships, to help local computer retailers build traffic to their stores. Through publicity, displays, and advertising, consumers were invited to visit participating retailers to "test drive" an Epson computer. At the completion of the in-store demonstration, the consumers received free tickets to the Grand Slam of Golf.

RESULTS

The golf program was the principle marketing and promotional focus of Epson during a three-year period. Over the course of the program, Epson's sales increased 500 percent, from $200 million in 1987 to more than $1 billion in 1990. In addition, the public relations components of each tactic generated tens of millions of consumer impressions each year, thereby achieving Epson's marketing and communications goals.

On the Monday prior to the big game, McDonald's distributed via satellite a video news release (VNR) on the commercial to television stations and national sports programs across the country. The VNR featured scenes from "Showdown," humorous outtakes from the making of the spot, and comments from Jordan and Bird about the ad's storyline.

Portions of the VNR aired on "Entertainment Tonight," CNN, NBC's "Today Show," and over 200 other outlets, generating 150 million impressions.

THE FUTURE OF SPORTS PUBLIC RELATIONS

In the mid-1990s sports marketing is a nearly $5 billion industry. With more marketers getting in on the action, there is no reason to believe the explosion the industry realized the past decade will slow down as we approach the next century. And the practice of sports public relations will thrive right along with it.

Sports PR will continue to grow for several reasons:

- Marketers, seeing the benefits of fully integrated programs that include strategic marketing and public relations plans, increasingly invite public relations professionals to the table when preparing strategies and plans. PR pros offer insights about the probable public response to all the elements of the marketing mix and provide ideas for connecting those elements with a thematic overlay.

- Sports speaks a universal language, as evidenced by the rise of annual NBA and NFL exhibition games overseas. As marketers learn to "think internationally," they incorporate sports marketing into their global strategies.

- Every day brings new opportunities as the demographics of the sports fan change. Women are more active as participants and followers of sports than ever before. The Generation X crowd is also more active. The result is the creation of new popular sports, like beach volleyball and mountain biking, that reach these market segments.

- Fans embrace corporate sponsorship of sporting events. According to a 1994 survey by the Sports Marketing Group, 77 percent of consumers agreed that sponsors provide "vital and necessary" funds for teams and events.

Because sports marketing is here to stay, the general public relations practitioner must add the discipline of sports PR to the knowledge bank if he or she intends to provide the

CORPORATE SPORTS SPONSORSHIP SPENDING IN 1993

$110–$115 million
- Philip Morris

$90–$95 million
- Anheuser-Busch

$70–$75 million
- Coca-Cola

$35–$40 million
- RJR Nabisco
- General Motors
- IBM
- Eastman Kodak

$30–$35 million
- PepsiCo

$25–$30 million
- McDonald's
- Quaker Oats
- Chrysler
- Du Pont

$20–$25 million
- Procter & Gamble
- Sara Lee

$15–$20 million
- Visa U.S.A.

Source: Lesa Ukman, *IEG Sponsorship Report*, IEG Sponsorship, Chicago, December 1993, p. 1

BOX 28–2

1994's "FIVE MOST WANTED" SPOKESPERSONS*

The following is *The Sports Marketing Letter's* list of the "most wanted" spokespersons in sports.

1. **Michael Jordan**

   Projected spokesperson earnings in 1994: $31 million

   Represents: Nike, Gatorade, McDonald's, Chevrolet, General Mills, Upper Deck and Upper Deck Authenticated, Electronic Arts, Ohio Art, Wilson Sporting Goods, Sara Lee, NBA Entertainment–CBS/Fox Video, Collins San Francisco

2. **Shaquille O'Neal**

   Projected spokesperson earnings in 1994: $13.5 million

   Represents: Reebok, Pepsi-Cola, Paramount Pictures, Spalding, Electronic Arts, Hyperion Publishing, Tiger Electronics, PPI Entertainment, Scoreboard, Jive Records, Kenner, Daydream Publishing

3. **Arnold Palmer**

   Projected spokesperson earnings in 1994: $12 million

   Represents: Cadillac, Textron, Pro Group, Rayovac, Pittsburgh National Bank, Penzoil, Paine Webber, GTE, Sears, Rolex, Lanier, Back Technologies

4. **Jack Nicklaus**

   Projected spokesperson earnings in 1994: $10.5 million

   Represents: Lincoln-Mercury, Hartmarx, Rockport, Warnaco, Trans Apparel Group, Nicklaus Equipment Company, ABC Sports, E-Z-GO Textron, *Golf Magazine*, Marine Midland Bank, Great Golf Resorts of the World, Yamagata, Wagonlit Travel

5. **Joe Montana**

   Projected spokesperson earnings in 1994: $10 million

   Represents: Sara Lee (Hanes), Fitness Quest, Fossil, Sports Impressions, Upper Deck and Upper Deck Authenticated, Sega, Mitsubishi, Franklin Resources, L.A. Gear, Pine Mountain Fire Logs, Salem (sportswear)

*Rankings are based on money earned and a subjective evaluation of the sports marketplace. Dollar amounts are estimates for 1994 and do not include tournament winnings or player salaries.

Source: Brian J. Murphy, "The 10 Most Wanted Speakers," *The Sports Marketing Letter,* Vol. 7, 1994.

overall expert counsel all organizations demand. It does not take a "sports junkie" to do this successfully, however. Over time, reading sports marketing trade publications like *IEG Sponsorship Report* and *Team Marketing Report* will help a professional identify emerging trends and successful programs others are executing.

The public relations students have one marked advantage over today's PR professionals: they can learn the business side of sports in the classroom. According to the International Sports Marketing Association, the number of colleges and institutions offering sports marketing programs increased from 30 to 300 the past decade.

Sports marketing and sports public relations jobs are scarce, however. It takes determination and a well-rounded background to land one. With a little luck and perseverance, in time you just may find yourself counseling a worldwide brand on the benefits of a new sponsorship opportunity.

ENDNOTES

1. National Sporting Goods Association, "Sports Participation in 1993: Series I," National Sporting Goods, Chicago.

2. Ibid.

3. Ibid.

Public Relations and Communications in the Publishing Industry

Jackie Saunders Goettsch, APR
Staff Vice President–Corporate Relations
Meredith Corporation

A STRATEGIC APPROACH TO PUBLIC RELATIONS AND COMMUNICATIONS IN THE PUBLISHING INDUSTRY

The strategic use of public relations in the publishing industry is rooted in respect—respect for the freedom of expression embodied in the First Amendment, respect for the potency of public opinion, respect for the power of the written word, and respect for those who craft, market, and read it. Two purposes drive the strategic management of public relations: (1) support for the company's mission, principles, and objectives and (2) stewardship of the company's reputation as it influences the actions of groups who are key to the organization's success.

Publics, audiences, stakeholders—the people in these groups often do not even know each other; their common interests or concerns make them part of the same public. It is those common interests or concerns that provide both the greatest opportunities for a company and, paradoxically, the greatest threats to it. In the publishing industry, relevant publics ordinarily include:

- Customers (both readers and advertisers, if the publication carries advertising).
- Employees.
- Trade and consumer news media.
- Elected and appointed government officials.
- Headquarters and branch community members.
- Boards of directors and stockowners, especially in publicly held companies.

In practice, public relations identifies all pertinent publics, both patent and latent, both existing and forming. The best practitioners quickly understand these groups, devise strategies to reach them, provide relevant advice and counsel to top management, and then plan, execute, and evaluate communications that reach targeted publics and contribute to the company's mission.

A word about mission and then a word about stewardship:

Mission: For public relations in the publishing industry to work, those who practice it must have an appreciation for the industry, a clear picture of the individual company mission (that is, what the company aspires to become), and an understanding of the operations (the magazines, the newspapers, the books, the new media) which will carry the company into the future. It is equally important for practitioners to hold a realistic view of the company's strengths and weaknesses, including the elements of company culture: history, mores, attitudes, behaviors, relationships, quirks, and practices. And most important, for public relations to work, it must weave all of the relevant functional areas—employee communication, investor communication, government relations, community relations, corporate philanthropy, media relations, board communication, special events, and customer contact—into one seamless fabric. When the functional areas of a public relations department are integrated, all of the company's communications resonate among all of its publics.

Do you want to know if a public relations department works in concert with the company's mission? Take a look at the allocation of human and financial resources within the department. The use of public relations resources and its outcomes should reflect the organization's mission, principles, and goals. The entire public relations staff should be knowledgeable about the other functions within the department and understand how their activities intersect.

Stewardship: Stewardship goes beyond conservation. Stewardship embraces the creation and maintenance of a good reputation and then builds on it. For public relations to work in the publishing world, for a good reputation to be enhanced, a company's public relations practitioners must have the ear (and the respect) of senior management. In an ideal situation, at least one public relations practitioner is a member of senior management. Public relations is properly involved not only in shaping what a company says, but also in planning and deciding what a company does.

Retired publishing executive and author James A. Autry calls management a "sacred trust." While he may have been referring especially to a manager's regard for his or her subordinates, a sacred and mutual trust of others at all levels is critical to successful public relations for any organization.

Practicing public relations in the publishing industry is not unique; it is much the same as practicing public relations in many other fields. Indeed, public relations and communications skills transfer readily, so it is not uncommon for public relations practitioners to have jumped into publishing from the outside. Nevertheless, the publishing industry claims a number of distinguishing factors.

The strongest drive

is not Love or Hate.

It is one person's need

to change another's copy.

The Currency of the Industry

The most obvious is the currency of the industry—the love of the written word itself. The old saying "everyone's an editor" rings particularly true in a publishing company. Legions of neophyte public relations practitioners have become nearly paralyzed by the awesome task of *writing* a memo, news release, speech, or simple note for a real, live editor or publishing executive. On the positive side, most public relations practitioners never have to explain production basics—from deadlines to bluelines—to their top management in the publishing business.

Media Relations

Media relations can present its own peculiar set of challenges in the publishing industry, especially when establishing a spokesperson and providing timely, accurate information to employees.

A Single-Voice Policy

Editors, publishers, and others in the company sometimes refuse coaching on how to deal with the news media or do a good broadcast interview. "After all," they reason, "we *are* the media, so we know the field." True, but as public relations professionals know, conducting an interview and being interviewed are very different things. Moreover, it is downright impossible to have a "one voice" spokesperson policy when free speech is taken literally by many in the organization. But a single voice, or at least coordinated voices, creates the strongest impression for a company and its products. A single voice yields consistent, believable content and delivery.

Employee Communication

Many publishing companies were started and grew under the leadership of a founder and his descendants. It is not uncommon for a familylike culture to exist, and with it a strong commitment to employee communication. Management and employees rightfully prize that culture and commitment. However, keeping employees informed about developments that will affect them can be particularly difficult in the publishing industry.

First, journalists are generally very curious people. Their livelihoods depend on it. Perhaps that is why the company-news grapevine flourishes in many publishing companies. In seemingly uncanny fashion, the grapevine frequently produces accurate, although premature, information. Just as often though, it is inaccurate, causing undue concern, misunderstanding, and wasted energy.

Second, many writers, editors, and others in the publishing industry are closely connected to reporters and editors at trade publications, newsweeklies, newspapers, and broadcast media. Information shared with employees in a publishing company can make its way swiftly into the hands of reporters who also are old college friends, roommates, neighbors, companions, or spouses. Even Manhattan becomes a small town when there's a rumor in the publishing business.

Third, public relations departments in publishing companies—especially those with daily newspapers—cannot afford to be the *source* of news leaks, even to their own publications.

Working with Celebrities

Unlike most other industries, publishing companies' editors, writers, columnists, and authors frequently are well known; their names are household names. Working with the stars requires not only a certain set of public relations skills but also a well-tuned set of human relations skills.

Staff Retention

Recruiting, training and, *keeping* outstanding public relations staff has a unique dimension in the publishing industry. Many good public relations people are good writers. Some are excellent thinkers. A few are even good sellers. And that is what makes them all especially attractive candidates for other jobs in a publishing company.

Public Relations for International Publishing

Publishing companies continue to expand their operations to other countries. Again, the language itself is the heart of the matter. Because people want to read in their native language, products cannot simply be exported, renamed, repackaged, or slightly reformulated. Often the product must be transformed.

Perhaps no one else understands international publishing better than The Reader's Digest Association. The company has been international since 1938. Today, it publishes nearly 50 editions of its flagship magazine in close to 20 languages and reaches a total of 100 million readers on every continent except Antarctica. Craig Lowder, *Reader's Digest* public relations director, offers these insights on international public relations:

- Remember that while English is the language of business around the world, publishing products are more successful when created and marketed in the local language. Think twice when adapting your work to their country.
- Heed the maxim "Think global. Act local." While mission and strategy can be set at home, you must respect the language, traditions, and culture of the other country.
- Do your homework, find the right local staff, and then trust their professional skills. It is the local publisher, editor, and public relations adviser who best know the local market and their audiences' attitudes and likely behaviors.
- Pay close attention to local market conditions. Understand the intensity of national and ethnic pride. Don't assume that nuances will be overlooked, even in small or neighboring countries. If you do, you risk embarrassment, failure, or worse.
- Be patient. For example, access to technology, even reliable telephone connections, is more limited and certainly not always at one's fingertips.

At *The New Yorker* magazine, Vice President of Public Relations Maurie Perl's international efforts helped increase newsstand sales, typically the heart of circulation in countries other than the United States. Because some of the international news media have reporters based in the 12 to 15 countries where *The New Yorker* is published abroad, as well as reporters based in the United States, Perl releases information to reporters in both locations.

She knows when, where, how, and to whom to provide news tips and releases. New issues of her weekly magazine become available in the United States on Monday, in other countries on Tuesday or Wednesday. Perl knows that her magazine is for readers, not browsers, and she recognizes that reporters and media decision-makers use Sundays to read and get ready for the upcoming week. Knowing the context of local, national, and world events, she collaborates with her editor to choose articles for highlighting in the Sunday distribution of each new issue. Perl adds a tailored, different-every-week list of relevant news media and opinion makers to her standing list for customized distribution of each new issue of the magazine.

She appreciates the differences and opportunities presented by international markets. For example, the August 1, 1994, issue of *The New Yorker* carried "The Unmasking of O," an article that revealed the identity of the French author of the 1954 erotic and violent novel *The Story of O*. Perl broke the story first in Europe, where the book and anything about it was not considered so pornographic or sensational. She generated interest in Europe and let it spill over to the United States. The same news release on the unmasking of the controversial book's author was part of the weekly *New Yorker* U.S. press package, but it was not the focus of domestic media pitches for that issue.

Any discussion of international publishing must include a variation on the theme of taking products abroad. Publishers based in other countries continue to buy publishing interests in the United States. Strategies differ—some want to know how to operate in the United States, so they purchase a successful concern and learn as they go; others find a profitable acquisition on U.S. shores and hit the ground running. Whatever the reason, public relations practitioners whose companies are bought by international investors frequently must adjust to a new culture and a different approach to doing business.

Origin and Growth of Public Relations for Publishing

Centuries ago, only the privileged, educated few could read and afford transcriptions of authors' manuscripts. Gutenberg's invention of movable type marked the advent of modern publishing. But it took widespread public education and post-World War I prosperity to set publishing on a real growth course. It was in wartime and the post-war milieu that the very seeds of public relations were planted.

During early 20th century America, muckraking magazine journalists took corpulent manufacturers, monopolies, and political machines to task. Avid readers were outraged by the abuses of the rich and powerful chronicled in the stories they read. The fat cats responded. One, John D. Rockefeller, retaliated with the help of Ivy Lee, whom he hired to provide advice on "public relations." Like several of his counterparts in the fledgling public relations field, Lee left behind a career as a newspaperman, shifting instead to the pursuit of influencing the editorial content of the day's magazines and newspapers. In large measure, public relations itself is a historical product of the publishing industry (see Chapter 2 by Scott Cutlip).

In Ivy's Lee's time, print ruled. Radios and telephones, and certainly, televisions and personal computers, were uncommon or unheard of in U.S. households. Likewise, business functioned without technology. The Information Superhighway wasn't even a sidewalk. Today, the publishing industry is critically aware of the dawn of new, high-tech media. Naysayers point to the demise of the printed word. But history tells us that the printed word will always be with us. So does retired communications executive Alex Kroll.

Kroll, then chairman of Young & Rubicam, New York, said in a May 1994 speech:

> If there is one thing that my three decades in the communications business have taught me, it's this: New media stimulate the use of more media.
>
> For example, the growth of network radio in the 1930s did not kill off newspapers or magazines. In fact, both newspapers and magazines had their best year ever last year. The new medium stimulates the older one. People also predicted that radio would destroy the infant record industry. (In 1993) the sale of CDs and cassettes was a $8.9 billion business!
>
> Nor did the growth of network television after World War II kill off radio. Radio also enjoyed its best year ever (in '93), with revenues of $1.7 billion! Incidentally, television gave birth to *TV Guide*—the second-largest magazine in America.
>
> And the recent growth of cable television and VCRs has not—as so many predicted—killed network television. (What's more) Americans spent more on books last year than ever before—more than $15.5 billion![1]

Approximately 500 *new* magazine titles continue to be introduced every year. Truly, the printed word is alive and well, and so is public relations for it.

Budgets and Expenditures

With regard to budgets and expenditures, most public relations budgets in the publishing industry today are lean and flat. The real value in a public relations department lies primarily in the insight, advice, and counsel of the people who staff it, rather than the programs they create and manage. Thus, it is reasonable to find the lion's share of a budget dedicated to payroll, taxes, and benefits. In publishing as in most other industries, public relations departments increasingly do more with less. Still, payroll continues to rise as experienced staff is retained, so the chief public relations officer must find creative ways to eliminate other departmental costs to keep budgets flat.

Desktop Publishing

Desktop publishing of newsletters, brochures, reports, flyers, slides, and a host of other collateral materials quickly pays for itself, reduces program costs, and improves turnaround time on production items. For instance, one public relations department's 1993 expenditure of $15,000 on a complete desktop publishing system (hardware and software) for one work station paid for itself in six months and saves about $2,500 each month in ongoing employee communication costs alone.

Agency Use

When it comes to agency use, cost-conscious senior practitioners proceed with caution. They generally believe that on-staff counsel and skill is a better buy and a better investment than an agency. Certainly, when wisdom, experience, and knowledge accrue to a staffer, the company is more likely to reap the benefits, especially over the long haul. Agencies frequently shift and juggle personnel, and it is not unusual for a company's account to be sought and signed by a senior agency executive who, in spite of promises, monitors early progress then disappears except for an annual wine-and-dine, delegating the regular contact and work to others. As technology advances, many production services that agencies provide or broker at a markup can be accomplished for much less in-house.

Agencies are best used for special needs on a project basis, not on retainer. Project examples might be a new magazine launch, a big milestone or anniversary celebration, an initial public offering, or entrance in a new market or country. It is wise to tailor the choice of an agency to the need at hand. Likewise, it is good business to agree upfront on expectations for contact, service, and billing specifics, to provide a thorough grounding and orientation to account personnel, and to treat the agency as a member of the team, not an outsider.

Many media companies own a stable of publications that are decentralized, with separate management for each profit center. While it is not uncommon for each publication's management to choose its own public relations agency if one is used, smart profit center managers enlist the expertise and opinions of their company's public relations professionals, at least during the agency selection process. Even better, on-staff public relations people help profit centers with agency orientation, ties to corporate mission and goals, and monitoring the quality of agency work and the value received for the dollars billed.

A TACTICAL APPROACH TO PUBLIC RELATIONS AND COMMUNICATIONS IN THE PUBLISHING INDUSTRY

No practitioner could disagree that modern public relations sprang primarily from publicity. Ad sellers, booksellers, circulation directors, and merchandise managers all love trade and consumer media "hits" because they pave the way, helping to create an environment in which sales can be made. In the publishing industry, good press is extremely valuable as marketing support, and a discussion of tactics often leans toward publicity through media relations.

But this point should be clearly understood: Both the company and the publication are shortchanged when public relations is approached as if it were simply publicity—the whole scoop and nothing but the scoop. Employees, investors, community groups, board members, and the company's mission itself can be easily forgotten in the quest for press. To be fair, it is particularly within reason for publishing companies to deeply respect the power of the media to shape and influence public opinion and consumer behavior. The problem occurs when public relations and media relations are regarded as synonyms and the needs of audiences other than the media are considered subordinate.

Iowa-based public relations sage Ferne G. Bonomi advises all of her protégés, "You can influence, but you cannot control, publicity." She recognizes that publicity sometimes is inescapable, whether or not you seek it. It is in the latter "bad news" situations that practitioners call on their skills to mitigate publicity, just as they call on their skills in happier circumstances to increase publicity. In any case, you cannot control publicity.

The same can be said of the news media. That is how people in a free society believe it should be. Precisely because we do not control it, relying on the news media as the exclusive means of message delivery is foolhardy. It is essential to find pathways where we can assure that our message is delivered without interpretation, embellishment, tweaking, or twisting. Regarding the media as the only piece, or even the centerpiece, of public relations practice displays disregard for the many constituencies of any organization. Media relations is simply a component of public relations.

Put another way and very, very well by James E. Lukaszewski in his book *Influencing Public Attitudes*: "Allowing the media to drive your strategy is a recipe for failure."[2] Whether you're stimulating, responding to, or deflecting the media's interest in your company or publication, media relations should be neither your sole strategy nor your most important endeavor. It is an integral part of the whole, and managed smartly, can reinforce your direct messages to your publics.

Lukaszewski says, "If you're doing the right thing, for the right reasons, and communicating about what you're doing to the people who are most concerned and affected, you are meeting your obligation to inform the 'public,' even if you don't include the news media . . ." (p. 15)

Lukaszewski votes for balance, keeping the media in its place and opting for a targeted, call-someone-who-REALLY-cares approach. As he says, "the more you engage in direct communications (with those affected), the less what the media says or does really matters." (p. 21) Lukaszewski calls his strategy a "pro-people process," (p. 32) not an anti-media one, although he heartily advocates reducing the media's power. To him, that means, among other things:

- Talking to the media primarily when it is in the interest of your strategy to do so, but never as a substitute for reaching those who are most directly affected. (p. 31)
- Structuring your communications around base audience contact . . . if you're criticized by the news media for not releasing information to the public first because you took the time to talk to your employees, the community, your neighbors or the victims, that's criticism you can live with. (pp. 31–32)

Lukaszewski's refreshing approach sharpens the axiom that calls for the right message to the right audience through the right channel at the right time.

Seeking publicity, like any other public relations tactic, must be kept in perspective. It is all too easy to concentrate on tactics and allow the means (the tactics) to become the end. Tactics carry out strategies, and strategies emanate from objectives to reach goals such as creating awareness, increasing knowledge, developing interest, or prompting or preventing action.

Nevertheless, tactics are useful. The range of tactics found in any public relations practitioner's toolbox is fairly standard. To review the most effective commonly used tactics, consider the launch of a new product—a new magazine—by audience (see Figure 29–1), recognizing that some or all of the tactics listed are appropriate for creating new product awareness depending on the magnitude and potential of the launch.

Tactics to Reach Employees

- A memo in advance of the magazine's debut from the appropriate company or magazine official outlining the new staff, its mission and editorial philosophy, target readership, advertising categories, frequency, launch size, circulation methods (subscription or newsstand), cover price, standing features, and hot topics in the premier issue.
- Complimentary copies of the first issue.
- Story in the internal newsletter.
- Face-to-face meetings or a special event for involved and interested employees.

Tactics to Reach Trade and Consumer Media

- Media packet containing a news release with the company's rationale for the launch and expectations for growth, a fact sheet with all relevant details, a list of advertisers, biographies and photographs of chief personnel, and a copy of the

Hearst Magazines/Marie Clair Album S.A. Media Packet for
1994 Launch of Marie Claire Magazine in the United States

Premier issue of magazine

Launch news release

F I G U R E   29-1

Continued

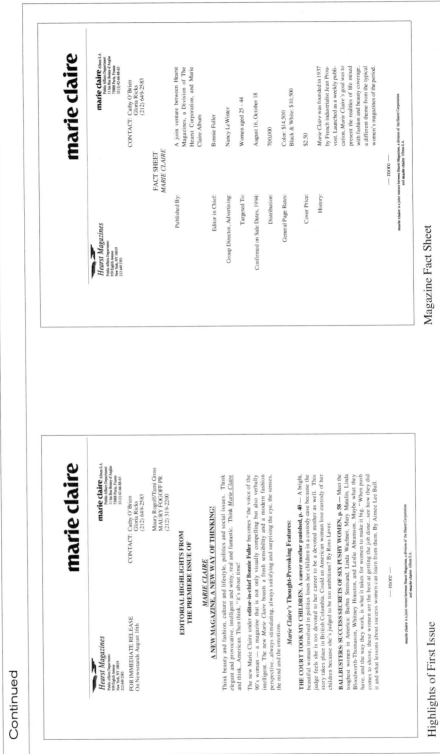

Hearst Magazines
Public Affairs Department
959 Eighth Avenue
New York, NY 10019
212.649.2383

marie claire Album S.A.
Public Affairs Department
11 bis Rue Boissy d'Anglas
75008 Paris, France
33 (1) 42-66-88-65

FOR IMMEDIATE RELEASE
On Newsstands August 16th

CONTACT: Cathy O'Brien
Gloria Ricks
(212) 649-2583

Maury Rogoff/Tami Gross
MAURY ROGOFF PR
(212) 319-2200

EDITORIAL HIGHLIGHTS FROM
THE PREMIERE ISSUE OF

MARIE CLAIRE
A NEW MAGAZINE. A NEW WAY OF THINKING!

Think beauty and fashion, culture and lifestyle, politics and social issues. Think elegant and provocative, intelligent and witty, real and fantastic. Think *Marie Claire* and think...American. Then think, "it's about time!

The new Marie Claire under **editor-in-chief Bonnie Fuller** becomes "the voice of the 90's woman — a magazine that is not only visually compelling but also verbally intelligent. The new *Marie Claire* boasts a fresh sensibility and a modern fashion perspective...always stimulating and surprising the eye, the senses, the mind and the emotions.

Marie Claire's **Thought-Provoking Features:**

THE COURT TOOK MY CHILDREN. A career mother punished, p. 40 — A bright, beautiful woman involved in politics loses her children in a custody case because the judge feels she is too devoted to her career to be a devoted mother as well. This story takes place in British Columbia. Could an American woman lose custody of her children because she's judged to be too ambitious? By Ross Laver.

BALLBUSTERS: SUCCESS SECRETS OF SIX PUSHY WOMEN, p. 58 — Meet the toughest women in America: Barbra Streisand, Linda Wachner, Mary Matalin, Linda Bloodworth-Thomason, Whitney Houston, and Leslie Abramson. Maybe what they have, and the way they work, is what it takes for women to make it big. "When push comes to shove, these women are the best at getting the job done...see how they did it and what lessons about success women can learn from them. By Aimee Lee Ball.

— more —

marie claire is a joint venture between Hearst Magazines, a division of the Hearst Corporation
and *marie claire* Album S.A.

Highlights of First Issue

Hearst Magazines
Public Affairs Department
959 Eighth Avenue
New York, NY 10019
212.649.2383

marie claire Album S.A.
Public Affairs Department
11 bis Rue Boissy d'Anglas
75008 Paris, France
33 (1) 42-66-88-65

CONTACT: Cathy O'Brien
Gloria Ricks
(212) 649-2583

FACT SHEET
MARIE CLAIRE

Published By:	A joint venture between Hearst Magazines, a Division of The Hearst Corporation, and Marie Claire Album
Editor in Chief:	Bonnie Fuller
Group Director, Advertising:	Nancy LeWinter
Targeted To:	Women aged 25 - 44
Confirmed on Sale Dates, 1994:	August 16, October 18
Distribution:	700,000
General Page Rates:	Color: $14,500 Black & White: $10,500
Cover Price:	$2.50
History:	*Marie Claire* was founded in 1937 by French industrialist Jean Prouvost. Launched as a weekly publication, *Marie Claire's* goal was to present the realities of life mixed with fashion and beauty coverage...a different theme from the typical women's magazines of the period.

— more —

marie claire is a joint venture between Hearst Magazines, a division of the Hearst Corporation
and *marie claire* Album S.A.

Magazine Fact Sheet

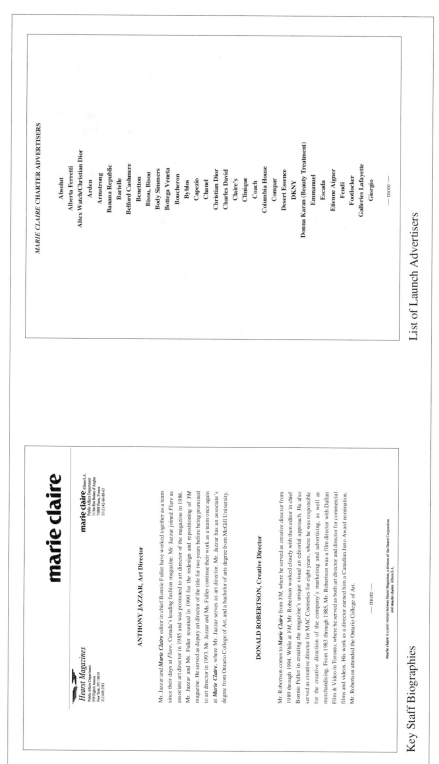

marie claire

Hearst Magazines
Public Affairs Department
959 Eighth Avenue
New York, NY 10019
212 649 2583

marie claire Albani S.A.
Public Affairs Department
11 Rue Bouley d'Anglai
75008 Paris, France
33 (1) 42-66-88-65

ANTHONY JAZZAR, Art Director

Mr. Jazzar and *Marie Claire* editor in chief Bonnie Fuller have worked together as a team since their days at *Flare*, Canada's leading fashion magazine. Mr. Jazzar joined *Flare* as associate art director in 1985 and was promoted to art director of the magazine in 1986. Mr. Jazzar and Ms. Fuller reunited in 1990 for the redesign and repositioning of *YM* magazine. He served as deputy art director of the title for two years before being promoted to art director in 1993. Mr. Jazzar and Ms. Fuller continue their work as a team once again at *Marie Claire*, where Mr. Jazzar serves as art director. Mr. Jazzar has an associate's degree from Ontario College of Art, and a bachelor of arts degree from McGill University.

DONALD ROBERTSON, Creative Director

Mr. Robertson comes to *Marie Claire* from *YM*, where he served as creative director from 1989 through 1994. While at *YM*, Mr. Robertson worked closely with then editor in chief Bonnie Fuller in creating the magazine's unique visual an editorial approach. He also served as creative director for MAC Cosmetics for eight years, where he was responsible for the creative direction of the company's marketing and advertising, as well as merchandising. From 1983 through 1985, Mr. Robertson was a film director with Dallan Film & Video in Toronto, where he served as both art director and director for commercial films and videos. His work as a director earned him a Canadian Juno Award nomination. Mr. Robertson attended the Ontario College of Art.

— more —

marie claire is a joint venture between Hearst Magazines, a division of the Hearst Corporation and marie claire Album S.A.

MARIE CLAIRE CHARTER ADVERTISERS

Absolut
Alberta Ferretti
Altex Watch/Christian Dior
Arden
Armstrong
Banana Republic
Barielle
Belford Cashmere
Benetton
Bison, Bison
Body Slimmers
Bottega Veneta
Boucheron
Byblos
Capezio
Chanel
Christian Dior
Charles David
Claire's
Clinique
Coach
Columbia House
Compar
Desert Essence
DKNY
Donna Karan (Beauty Treatment)
Emmanuel
Escada
Etienne Aigner
Fendi
Footlocker
Galleries Lafayette
Giorgio

— more —

Key Staff Biographies

List of Launch Advertisers

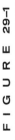

marie claire

Hearst Magazines
Public Affairs Department
959 Eighth Avenue
New York, NY 10019
212.649.2583

marie claire Album S.A.
Public Affairs Department
11 bis Rue Bisson of Anglas
75008 Paris, France
33 (1) 42-66-88-65

RELEASE AT WILL
(Biography)

CONTACT: Cathy O'Brien
Gloria Ricks
(212) 649-2583

BONNIE FULLER

EDITOR IN CHIEF

MARIE CLAIRE

Bonnie Fuller was named editor in chief of *Marie Claire* in February 1994. The American edition of the title, a joint venture between The Hearst Corporation and Marie Claire Album, debuts in August 1994.

Ms. Fuller joined Hearst Magazines from *YM* (Young & Modern) Magazine where she had been editor in chief since January 1989. Credited with one of the most successful magazine relaunches in history, Ms. Fuller's redesign and repositioning of the title boosted *YM*'s circulation, increasing the rate base from 925,000 to 1.8 million and newsstand sales from 130,000 to 437,000. The magazine also experienced solid advertising page growth. *YM*'s remarkable circulation increases prompted its selection for the *Magazine & Bookseller* Hall of Fame Award in 1992, and the title was subsequently named one of "The Hottest Magazines in Circulation" by *Capell's Circulation Report.*

Prior to *YM*, Ms. Fuller was editor of *Flare*, Canada's leading fashion magazine, for six years. Her mandate at *Flare* was to redesign and reposition the title as a major cutting-edge fashion force. She accomplished this, and newsstand sales doubled, making *Flare*

— more —

Editor in Chief Biography

Editor in Chief, *Marie Claire*

Photograph by Patrick Demarchelier

Courtesy of Hearst Magazines.

magazine itself. A short video may be appropriate. Sometimes a gift makes sense as a grabber, such as a prepared recipe from a food magazine or crayons and coloring sheets from a children's magazine.

- In-person pitch, lunch, a beer, or a telephone conversation with the right reporters at the top-tier media for the launch.

- A media tour featuring top personnel from the magazine at selected print and broadcast outlets in selected markets.

Tactics to Reach Advertisers

- Attention-getting delivery of a premium related to the magazine's editorial focus, such as a compact disc, a geranium, a holiday ornament.

- Relevant special events such as a cocktail party at a new aquarium, dinner and tours at a new museum exhibit, a Country and Western chuckwagon and dance.

- Speeches that highlight your product as an example.

Tactics to Reach Investors

- Copy of the new magazine and a fact sheet.

- Highlight of the launch and its progress in the annual or quarterly report.

Tactics to Reach Community Members

- Donation or other link with a charitable organization whose purpose is related to the editorial niche filled by the magazine.

- An open house if the size of the publication or the size of the community indicates.

- Information for government officials if the launch will create jobs or have other positive economic impact.

THE FUTURE OF PUBLIC RELATIONS AND COMMUNICATIONS IN THE PUBLISHING INDUSTRY

A campaign can, and must, be woven together into an integrated whole to reach a variety of audiences with the same message. Such integration is the most important future trend in the business. Just as the efforts of public relations, advertising, marketing and sales promotion can be multiplied by working in concert, so can the efforts of departmental functions—employee communication, investor communication, community relations, media relations—be most fruitful when linked together. Those practitioners who embrace the concept of integration and find opportunities to bring it to life will be most relevant and valuable in their organizations.

Other significant trends:

- Over the last decade, many daily newspapers have lost circulation and their staff numbers have been curtailed. Print and broadcast reporters are spread thin. At the same time, many public relations practitioners have moved toward a more comprehensive, less publicity-driven, approach to their craft. They prepare fewer, but better, news releases. The news media recognize their need for information from public relations contacts. And public relations people have become more sophisti-

B O X   29–1

CASE STUDY: MEREDITH CORPORATION

The Meredith Corporation mission statement articulated in 1990 begins "We are Meredith Corporation, a publicly held media company founded upon service to our customers. Our cornerstone is knowledge and understanding of the home and family market." The company, which publishes a large stable of magazines including *Better Homes and Gardens, Ladies' Home Journal, Country Home, Traditional Home, Country America*, and *Midwest Living,* has been focused on home and family since its founding near the turn of the century. Yet a 1992 study revealed that the Meredith name had startlingly low awareness among media buyers and advertisers.

At that time, the company set out to firmly position itself as *the* publisher with a deep and long-standing connection to the American home and family. Meredith wanted to heighten awareness that the company is the nation's authority on topics that matter to those whose focus is home and family. Realizing that many of its publications were household names, the company wanted to link the Meredith name to its titles.

To do that, Saatchi & Saatchi Pacific was called on to develop a million-dollar marketing campaign to boost name recognition for Meredith. The campaign theme, "If it has to do with home and family, it has to be in Meredith," appeared in two-page ads featuring black-and-white photographs of real people enjoying family times. A series of various Meredith magazine covers anchored the pages. The artwork popped up on roving billboards in major advertising cities. Media buyers and other decision-makers paid attention when they received periodic mailings of candy, all packaged in canisters, boxes, drinking glasses, or other containers sporting Meredith magazine titles. In addition, a comprehensive sales class and a new advertising research department sprang from the company's effort to take its rightful position in the minds of its customers.

The campaign was integrated into a variety of public relations efforts. Employees in Meredith locations nationwide received invitations to kick-off meetings via coffee mugs carrying the insignia. At the meetings, employees saw a made-for-them video which warmly outlined the home and family campaign. Employees chose magazine-title candy canisters to take back to their desks.

At the company's annual roadshow for investors, the "If it has to do with home and family . . ." insignia accented the take-home portfolios given to those who attended the meetings. Later, a photo from the ad campaign graced the cover of the company's annual report and other campaign images were featured inside. A large version of the insignia hangs on the wall in the room at company headquarters most often used to host Meredith advertisers and potential advertisers. The underlying message from the company to its advertisers: Our home-and-family readers are your customers, and we know them better than any other publisher. In addition, the campaign theme has been the linchpin for many stories pitched to the trade and business news media.

In follow-up research 18 months after the campaign launch, media buyers ranked Meredith No. 1 among its competitors in the category "Best serves home and family market." Employees now readily know the company's pride and purpose is service to the home and family. Investors recognize the company's niche. And the media often focus on the company's home and family mission in headlines, captions and articles.

cated about what they supply. The result has been a less antagonistic, less adversarial approach between the news media and PR. This trend will continue.

■ In fewer than 15 years, offices have gone from dial telephones and electric typewriters to complex phone systems, desktop computers, voice mail, e-mail, automatic fax machines, color copiers, and videoconference equipment. The speed and quality with which information can be transmitted will only increase. So will the speed with which management expects turnaround on production and creative problem solving. Research will become more important and more readily available via on-line services.

■ International publishing will grow. Publishers will make more effort to cross boundaries and waters. Familiar U.S. publications will have counterparts in other countries and vice versa. The bilingual public relations practitioner will have an advantage.

■ Excellent customer service will be a requirement for survival. Customer expectations continue to escalate, and curiously, the better the service, the greater the expectations. Customer service managers may become colleagues of public relations managers as companies recognize the convergence of skills—research, analysis, execution, evaluation, problem-solving, and relationship building.

■ Public relations will include more targeted face-to-face meetings as databases bring individual constituents into sharper focus. Also, public relations efforts will become more tailored and personalized. Results will be measured and based on actions of target groups, not by the pound of press clippings.

■ Decentralization and centralization will continue their teeter-totter exchange. The issue presents an interesting study. A centralized corporate public relations department cannot be effective if decentralized public relations operations for each publication do not respect company goals, share information, and coordinate timing. Corporate public relations directors often prefer that all publications' public relations staff be hired and report through corporate. The downside occurs when the individual magazines or newspapers regard their PR people as corporate intruders and outsiders. One solution is for the publications' public relations staff to be hired and evaluated with the corporate public relations director's input. The reporting relationship then is a dotted line to corporate and a straight line to publication management.

■ Managing public relations in the publishing industry will require people who are able to do more with less. Budgets will not increase substantially, nor will staff. Additional responsibilities such as leading customer service programs and training and staff development will find their way into high-performance public relations departments. Managers will be challenged to use technology to save time and money while workloads and productivity increase. The future and rapid change notwithstanding, great public relations departments will always set an example for the whole organization by gaining knowledge of the business, displaying a passion for it, delivering public relations counsel and programs that add value to the company, and treating their industry, company, publications, colleagues, and customers with respect.

Beyond Tactics

Tactics capture our interest; it is easy to get our arms around them, and we need to be facile with a wide variety of public relations tactics. But tactics are hollow without tenets, without touchstones. My background discussions for this chapter with other public relations professionals in the publishing industry, as well as my career contacts with many other PR pros, reminded me of these words of public relations wisdom:

- Books teach you theory and principles; on-the-job public relations practice teaches you the art and the craft.
- Those who know how will always work for those who know why.
- There's no substitute for experience. Some things you learn just by being older.
- Remember, you provide a service.
- Don't overpromise.
- Be available.
- Deliver consistent messages.
- Internal communication never stays that way.
- It's okay to say you don't know. It's better to know.
- Keep the overall goal in mind when you execute the details.
- You are an advocate for management to its audiences and an advocate for your audiences to your management.
- Approvals are a fact of life.
- Pick your spots and go to the wall for the right things.
- Handle the present for the future.
- The future depends on relationships, not on transactions.
- Make a plan.
- Adapt the damn plan.
- Timing is everything.
- Problems are our friends. When we solve them, they can make us heroes.
- Create a good team. Involve and praise your staff.
- You should always be learning; if you're not, get a new job.
- Don't be threatened by people who don't have the same background as you do.
- Maximum disclosure with minimum delay is the best way out of a bad news situation.
- People don't care how much you know until they know how much you care.
- You don't have to like the situation, but you do have to know what it is.
- In moving people to action, meet them where they are, not where you wish they were.
- Tell the truth.
- If you've never done anything wrong, you've never done anything.
- Learn from your mistakes.

ENDNOTES

1. Alex Kroll, Chairman of Young & Rubicam, New York, in a speech at the National Postal Forum in San Francisco, May 1994.

2. James E. Lukaszewski, *Influencing Public Attitudes* (Leesburg, VA: Issue Action Publications, 1992), p. 19.

SOURCES

The Academic American Encyclopedia. On-line edition. Grolier Electronic Publishing. Danbury, CT, 1993.

Autry, James A. *Love & Profit.* William Morrow & Company, Inc., NY, 1991.

Janello, Amy, and Brennon Jones. *The American Magazine.* Magazine Publishers of America, American Society of Magazine Editors. Harry N. Abrams, Inc., NY, 1991.

Kroll, Alex. Chairman of Young & Rubicam, New York. Comments from a speech presented at the National Postal Forum in San Francisco, May 1994.

Lukaszewski, James E. *Influencing Public Attitudes.* Issue Action Publications, Inc., Leesburg, VA, 1992.

Meredith Corporation. *Insider.* Kathi Woods, Editor. Des Moines, IA, 1993, 1994.

Harmonizing the Healthcare Message

Richard T. Cole, Ph.D.
Senior Vice President, Marketing and
Corporate Communications
Blue Cross and Blue Shield of Michigan

The chief executive of an American health-related business might describe the principal function of public relations as influencing government policy. Here is the logic. Government policy is made by politicians. Politicians react to public opinion. Public opinion is shaped by publicity. Publicity is the work of public relations. While politicians attempt to reshape American healthcare, public relations has shaped the debate, thereby justifying its expense.

Institutional public relations energy has been expended on derailing proposals that could have reshaped hospitals, insurance companies, and even the role of the American physician. While the effectiveness of the resistance to policy change has elevated the standing of, if not the respect for, healthcare communicators, a larger effect of healthcare communications may be lost in the shuffle. Here is an irony: many of the most effective tactics used to derail healthcare reform are tactics learned originally through communications efforts to improve America's health.

Communications campaigns have been used to influence American public health for decades. In the early 1900s, pioneer counselor Edward Bernays publicized the off-Broadway production "Damaged Goods" as a way of increasing awareness of sexually transmitted diseases. More recent campaigns have helped reduce family size, AIDS, and infant deaths. Campaigns have increased seat-belt use and reduced drunk driving. And though specific results are difficult to prove, and often less than hoped for, Americans seem more health conscious, in part, because of communication campaigns.[1]

While healthcare communicators are seen as marketing partners and image shapers within their organizations, their skill has developed through their involvement in prevention and treatment strategies aimed at individuals and groups. In healthcare, the work of communicators is often central to the success of the products and services they represent. The pharmaceuticals communicator makes sure both diabetic and doctor are aware of a new treatment. Prenatal care promotions affect the success of the pregnancy. While most public relations courses focus on commercial or political applications, the best evidence of the discipline's power to change behavior may be demonstrated by the work of the modern health communicator.

The public relations case on national healthcare reform emphasizes the role of communicators in protecting the status quo. By far, the most important work in the profession, however, results in saving or improving lives

A STRATEGIC VIEW

Communication as Behavior Change

Because of its dependence on behavior change, much of the work of healthcare communicators seems better described as marketing than public relations. Healthcare campaigns designed to produce health-related behavior change are described as social marketing, or "a framework in which marketing concepts are integrated with social-influence theories to develop programs better able to accomplish behavioral-change goals."[2]

"Integrated" communication techniques came to American healthcare long before the phrase *integrated marketing communication* was used. Two essential characteristics of integrated marketing-communications—its consumer orientation and its dependence upon relationship building—have long been mainstays of effective healthcare communication.

Silicon Valley's Regis McKenna describes the importance of relationship building in his vision of the "new marketing" for technology industries.[3] "While information is fleeting, relationships have a permanence that is very powerful in a fast-changing world. By forming the right relationship, a company can gain credibility and recognition that it would never gain through advertising."

Public relations can also be described as relationship building—adjusting organizational behavior to be consistent with the values and expectations of the audience upon which the client organization is dependent. To create an effective earth-friendly image, the chemical company must first develop an obsessive aversion to pollution. Once the behavior is consistent with the planned message, the professional communicator can use IMC to make the organization change more obvious to the target audience. This strategy strengthens a relationship between organizations in much the same way as "changing our ways" can strengthen personal relationships.

For many consumers, healthcare services are undifferentiated commodities. Healthcare is complicated, technical, and intimidating to most consumers. Organization "position" therefore may be a function of how well the organization's commitment to the customer is communicated. Position is that magical quality which, in the customer's mind, separates one supplier from the rest.

Integrated marketing communication proponents believe brand strength stems from consumer confidence. "Since your product is virtually the same as your competitor's product, you cannot depend upon the product alone to build the confidence. It's the rapport, the empathy, the dialogue, the relationship, the communication you establish with this prospect that makes the difference. These separate you from the pack."[4]

The life and death consequences of healthcare establish the special significance of consumer confidence in the marketing equation and make the communications strategy even more important. The way in which the service is described and provided speaks volumes about the commitment the doctor has to the patient relationship. An integrated communications strategy forces a company to examine what its organizational behavior communicates to the customer. Every customer transaction frames the customer relationship. A company's actions are its most powerful form of marketing communications. To some degree, therefore, all aspects of organizational performance are within the jurisdiction of the communication professional. A sharp tone of voice from a hospital security guard to a nervous visitor weakens confidence in the institution. Provider loyalty is weakened by harsh words a telephone clerk uses to defend a claim payment. Effective integrated healthcare marketing communications begins with efforts to monitor exchanges between customer and company.

Jeffrey Barach identified historical differences between social marketing programs and traditional sales-related marketing.[5] Most social marketing practitioners see themselves as "educating" the target group. Building attitude change is seen as a prerequisite for reaching a desired behavioral outcome. In sales-related marketing, on the other hand, the goal is to get the consumer to act—to make a purchase. In marketing, positive attitudes are thought to result from good experiences with the product. Marketing campaigns are aimed at trials, getting customers to use the product. Favorable experience promotes positive attitudes. And such experience capitalizes on a person's natural tendency to justify an action that has already been taken. Create behavioral change first, in the knowledge that the attitudes will eventually follow, a principle of great interest to the healthcare communicator.

Adopting the IMC Approach in Healthcare

Adopting an integrated marketing communication (IMC) approach requires first agreeing to make adjustments in one's organizational behavior in order to develop better relationships with key audiences. IMC must be designed, implemented, and evaluated from the target audience's perspective—from outside the client organization inward. The desired outcome of IMC is behavior change. Communicators must assume a broad sense of jurisdiction and responsibility given the degree to which the actions of the organization are its most powerful form of communicating.

Successful IMC is built upon clear strategy. The strategy, the clever plan that drives the messaging, should be built on long-term organizational goals, not the needs of the moment. An effective IMC strategy, or set of strategies as is most often the case in complex organizations, must incorporate the fundamental vision of the client. Equally significant is that the strategies remain flexible enough to be adjusted to the circumstances of their deployment.

Figuring out a way to clearly and consistently articulate the IMC strategy is an early step in the creation of any successful plan. I have found that strategies that can be described in terms of the desired audience behavioral change are most likely to be followed. A tenet of IMC is that each audience member forms different perceptions of an organization depending on the nature and types of messages being received. No organization can fully control all messages about itself being received by audiences. On the other hand, every organization can assess each audience to determine what messages it is likely receiving and from where and how.

The essence of IMC, therefore, is revealed through the process of discovering the messages being received by the target audience and reorganizing these messages to serve a common strategy or set of strategies. Not all messages are under the direct control of the client organization. However, such controlled communications are a major source of impression formation. These controlled communications include advertising, special events, community activities, employee communications, and marketing communications.

Successful IMC also attempts to influence messages being sent to the audience by sources beyond the client organization's direct control. From an "uncontrolled communications" perspective, the organization's image is shaped by media coverage, competitive information, and word-of-mouth.

Harmonizing Messages and Strategies

Developing an IMC strategy is like creating a score for the orchestra. Unfortunately, integrated communications has often been misinterpreted (by an advertising industry in search of regaining share of customer) as simply providing all of the musical instruments on concert night. IMC harmonizes otherwise disparate messages that audiences—customers, employees, government officials, or others—get about the organization or its products. Besides harmonizing the messages, another target of integration is the various strategies aimed at different audiences. Organizations have many audiences, and these audiences are dynamic. People are in more than one audience at the same time, and they often move from one audience to another.

The skills of the healthcare IMC team are most challenged when harmonizing various corporate communication strategies to:

1. Increase market share.
2. Develop new markets.
3. Erode competitor viability.
4. Educate audiences.
5. Enhance employee, customer, and supplier loyalty.
6. Increase product use.
7. Reduce product use, as in healthcare utilization.
8. Reduce undesirable behavior, as in wellness programs.
9. Avoid or manage crises.
10. Inoculate audiences against upcoming negative news.

An HMO may employ one strategy to increase the use of its preventive health services while employing another to reduce the use of its emergency room. Unless the strategies are harmonized, the HMO may, at once, look both stingy and generous. If wellness messages are not harmonized with messages intended to reduce the use of emergency services, money rather than care for HMO members could be seen as the motivator for the "best of health" strategy. No organization can afford to send conflicting messages. At the same time, every effective organization must have a variety of overlapping strategies in place.

Social Marketing: A Tool for Changing What People Do

Think of social marketing as a framework for integrating marketing techniques with social-influence theories to get people to change the way they behave. Social marketing borrows the planning variables from marketing: product, price, promotion, place and reinterprets them, often in a health-related context. The approach mixes these marketing-planning variables with a knowledge of modern social psychology.[6]

Cognitive dissonance theory is applied to produce anxiety in the target audience—anxiety that results when we find ourselves acting in ways that are inconsistent with what we were taught to believe. Changing our behavior reduces anxiety and alters our attitudes.

Often the goal of social marketing is to reduce the distance between the individual consumer and the desired health-related behavior. Marketing techniques are used to identify markets and individual consumers within the markets, and develop a message that they will buy. "Buying" the message is evidenced by behavioral change.

Social networks and organizational relationships can be used to accelerate the delivery of messages to the target audiences. Kellogg Company, for example, teamed up with the National Cancer Institute (NCI) to generate a public understanding of the relationship between eating habits and the likelihood of contracting cancer.[7] NCI publicized the association of increased cancer risks with certain eating habits and suggested grain cereals as an alternative food. A massive Kellogg advertising campaign reinforced this message, resulting in a higher awareness of the NCI message and an increased consumption of Kellogg high-grain cereals.

According to Wallack, "social marketing attempts to make it easy and attractive for the consumer to act in compliance with the message by creating the ideal marketing mix of right product, price, promotion and place."[8]

In some cases the product in the mix is a specific item such as a condom to prevent AIDS. In other cases, the product is behavioral change such as turning to a low-fat diet as a risk-reducing food alternative. In social-marketing theory, the price variable is often the effort required by the targeted individual or audience to make the behavioral change. Promotion translates into how the social-marketing message is delivered and what it means to the consumer. Place refers to the availability of the product.

Wallack believes the most significant contribution of social-marketing theory to healthcare communication is its refocusing of attention from the message or sender to the consumer—the target audience.

The Central Role of Formative Research

Atkin and Feimuth found that social-marketing campaigns aimed at health-behavior change have fallen short of their promise.[9] Too many organizations have begun massive behavioral change campaigns without engaging in necessary "formative research." Formative research is precampaign activity that helps develop campaign messages from the framework of "tested impact" on consumer behavior.

Formative research actually "develops" the campaigns for which it is employed.[10] It tests campaign tactics, themes, and messages to determine that they are having the desired effect on target audiences. Formative (as opposed to evaluative) research adapts public communication efforts to specific audiences. Small groups representing the target audience might be convened to solicit ideas about program strategy and test reactions to specific messages. The actual campaign messages may emerge from these sessions. At least, modifications to strategy and message can be made on the basis of focus groups.

Formative research also includes audience analysis measurement of media habits of the target population and assessment of attitudes in the target population. Simply said, formative research reduces uncertainty.

Formative research is essential to IMC because it helps retain the focus on the individual customer. The basis of social marketing is that people are willing to exchange their commitment in time, effort, attention, and sometimes money, in return for a result (product or service in marketing terms) of greater or equal value. And the value of formative research is in its power to increase the likelihood of a positive marketing outcome.

Social marketing principles have been used, with limited success, to encourage consumers to change behavior and increase the likelihood of healthier, longer (and medically cheaper) lives. These principles are also applied to a variety of other health-related integrated marketing communications efforts.

For any marketing program to be effective it must be built upon a clear strategy. For strategy to be effective, it must be consistent and harmonious with the core values of the client institution. It is for this reason that the successful integrated marketing communication program reflects and represents the qualities and intentions expressed in an organization's vision statement or similar statement of organizational purpose.

Organizing for a "Strategy of Engagement"

IMC can be organized in a variety of ways. Boiled down, however, any integrated marketing communications process includes the same basic steps which can be taken in any order and are always quite mixed in reality.

The Avenues
Schultz argues that the IMC process should begin with a determination that the organization has an opportunity to connect with the target audience. The first question that must be answered is when and how can a contact with the target audience be made. "We are simply saying that the conditions under which the communication will be delivered are as, or more, critical than determining message content of the communication."[11]

In reality, most processes that attempt to incorporate the necessary elements of IMC planning begin with identifying the opportunity as defined by the potential outcome. Nonetheless, focusing first on the media rather than the "creative" (as is the custom of advertising agencies) forces the IMC planner to address the normal interactions that occur between the organization and the target audience before beginning to plan new messages to deliver.

In a hypothetical IMC case, we need to increase use of our "birthing suite"—a hotel-style, fully equipped maternity facility—in Detroit's St. John Hospital. The problem is we currently have little or no contact with the target population. Our target population is young marrieds, especially women.

The Outcome
The second step in the process requires the IMC planner to answer the question: "Just what do I want the consumer to do?" The desired outcome of IMC must be defined in terms of desired behavior.

We want local pregnant women to insist upon having their babies in the birthing suite at St. John Hospital. We want them to select their future OB/GYN based on their preference for St. John. Advertising and public relations might support or reinforce such a decision, but it won't move prospective mothers to act. We decide we must engage them in a meaningful way with the St. John birthing suite. Once the involvement with St. John occurs, personal investment in our program is more likely. Involvement is one measurable step in the behavioral chain leading to the desired outcome. This involvement, and other involvements we can create, will become the objectives that produce the desired outcome of our "strategy of engagement." And our strategy of engagement should begin, we surmise, before the woman is pregnant. In fact, it is this logic that turns us to our special events department to create periodic "engagement parties" for local couples whose engagements have been made public.

Objectives

Step three in the process is a refinement of some of the objectives we have already touched on in our description of the desired outcome. This step in the integrated communication plan requires the planner to define how the organization will know the marketing objectives are being attained.

Our engagement strategy requires getting engaged couples who live in the general vicinity to visit our hospital before they are married. We decide to develop the "tradition" of presenting local married couples with an engraved, bronze shamrock-shaped wall-hanging which commemorates their official engagement date. A small, evening engagement party is planned for the "November announcements." During the party, an opportunity will be arranged for the guest couples who are interested to visit our birthing suite where, if the fertility gods are smiling, the couple will get a chance to meet a proud young father and mother. We'll know this tactic is working if our invited couples show up and seem to enjoy the event. It will be, at least, a few months, in most cases, before we can determine just how clever our "engagement strategy" really was.

TACTICS

Tools

The next step in our process involves deciding which communication tools and tactics best fit our engagement strategy.

We've already discussed the special events as a way to engage our couples at St. John Hospital. Our promise of a gift, a party, and a visit to the birthing suite may motivate attendance of a healthy percentage of our prospect couples. Will free media generate a news story about what we are doing? Or will such a story reveal our strategy to our competition or make us look like crass opportunists or fools if it doesn't work? Should we advertise the program to encourage involvement? Should we use direct mail to support the program or would telephone calls from our birthing suite personnel be more effective in building attendance at our parties? Would it be smart to have hospital board members from the couples' communities sign the invitations, and would this involvement in the program by our board members be a good way of encouraging deeper investment on their parts? Various tools are at our disposal. We need to make sure the tools are integrated so that the couples hear about the program in one voice. We need to make sure our strategy of engagement is integrated with any other marketing strategies aimed at this population segment. And we must remember that the families and friends of the target population will hear about this program.

This engagement strategy borrows heavily from the related discipline of fundraising, and in this case, it has been integrated into the fabric of our overall communication program.

These development principles are normally used to attract investment of a kind other than that which we are after with our betrothed couples. But our job is to get these young couples to think "St. John Hospital" and to act accordingly for their entire married lives. That's investment paying off.

Developing Behavior Change

Healthcare fundraisers also need to be mindful of the communications mix. Development officers have identified three "i"s that must occur to get a contribution or achieve *invest-ment*—the fourth "i" in the chain. The first "i" is *identification*.

The target market must be identified. In most development cases, but not all, the target market is an individual. Identifying a target market can be a complicated and daunting task. In our St. John Hospital case, it is easy. *Three local papers print engagement notices. The county records of application for marriage licenses can be cross checked occasionally. Our staff will have an easy time finding the young couples who are the targets of our strategy of engagement. Our market is discrete. We can't imagine better targets for future child-bearing than our engaged couples.*

The second "i," *involvement* should come as soon after identification as possible. And the fact that our involvement is coming before we attempt to "inform" our target audience is indicative of some new thinking, even in the development field. We advocate putting the focus of our efforts on a desired behavioral outcome. *Getting the involvement requires the target audience, our couples, to pay a small price in terms of their energy and time to come to the St. John party. We use an inducement—a small gift and the promise of a party—as the motivator to get involvement at the earliest possible moment.*

During the involvement phase, we will begin to furnish the information that provides the couple with a rationale as to why their involvement so far has been worth their time and energy. Because involvement has already occurred, the *information*, the third "i," will be much more relevant than if we provided it before some level of involvement had occurred. *The information we are providing, of course, influences our couples to understand the value that our birthing suite program can add to their lives. Beyond this initial information, and during their entire engagement, we will be providing additional information suggesting that a group of caring, high-quality people are associated with the St. John birthing suite program. We'll follow their visit with a thank you letter and a request that they help us evaluate our engagement party and tour. Besides generating further involvement, this evaluation will provide helpful information as we evolve our strategy. Another letter will offer some friendly advice on how to deal with the stress of planning for a wedding, and it may also offer discount coupons for a local wedding photographer and cake baker. A wedding card will, of course, be sent to the couple. A month or so after the wedding, the bride and groom will get a list of St. John affiliated physicians, and the name of a person at the hospital who might help them select one based upon their locale, special needs, and insurance plan.*

Our tools and tactics are designed to help young couples begin a life-long affiliation with St. John Hospital. Our hope is, of course, that our plan—our strategy of engage-ment—will touch off a series of events culminating in the delivery of a baby in the St. John birthing suite.

Our gift, party, tour, and follow-up will become subject of conversations at wedding receptions and baby showers. Hence, we have incorporated "word-of-mouth" into our integrated marketing communications plan.

Other strategies are affected by our strategy of engagement also. A separate plan to increase physician loyalty to the hospital will be advanced by a compatible effort to involve these physicians in giving tours of the birthing suites. They know, after all, that they are in a competitive environment. And they will begin to feel that whether you are a baby doctor or a brain surgeon, one value added to the affiliation with St. John is the marketing effort that keeps the birthing suites, and operating rooms, filled to capacity. This message feels good to the existing staff who are involved in it. It is also effective collateral in campaigns to recruit new physicians to St. John's staff.

Our strategy of engagement tells our nurses that we know what we have to sell and we sell it well. What we sell is caring—a holistic approach to healthcare that begins to meet family needs at the moment we identify an opportunity to do so.

Our strategy of engagement speaks volumes to our board who "get engaged" them-selves as we ask them to sign four or five invitation letters each month, letters to couples in their communities of residence, many of whose parents our board members know. Every time a board member signs a letter, he or she makes another psychological commitment to support the hospital.

Our hospital associates, doctors, nurses, staff, come to know our strategy of engage-ment not only for how it began—a plan to bring prospective parents into our birthing suite—but also for the role they play in the relationship-building that goes on as a result of the strategy. The entire staff begins to see a part of their mission as helping to find ways to "engage" the members of the community who someday will be in need of hospital services. "If the young couple is a prospect for the birthing suite," they say, "why don't we think about new grandparents who come to visit mom and baby as future customers also?" How do we "engage" the grandparents when they come to see baby in the birthing suite? And what will happen to our ability to connect with the grandparents once most of our birthing suite guests rotate out of our facility within 12 to 24 hours of the birth?

This is a simple hypothetical example of how a small hospital staff can use a clever plan, a clear strategy, to begin a process of uniting itself with its community while increasing the viability of its birthing suite and securing the future of their jobs.

The strategy we describe is integrated in the sense that a variety of "controlled" media are used to create and reinforce relationships with potential high-volume business prospects. The strategy is also integrated in the sense of its consistency with other hospital marketing strategies.

The strategy of engagement also represents actions that support and are supported by the hospital's vision statement. Hospitals provide direct service to patients. Insurance companies, which make possible the transactions between the patients and hospitals, have no less need for strategies that reflect and advance organizational mission statements.

LOOKING TO THE FUTURE—THE VISION FOR BLUE CROSS AND BLUE SHIELD OF MICHIGAN

Several years ago, Blue Cross and Blue Shield of Michigan, in Detroit, began a process of transforming its self-image. A two-year process involving a diagonal crosscut of employees from every level and area of the company produced a vision statement from which a number of important relationship-building initiatives continue to be built.

A vision statement, to be effective, first must be accepted by the workforce. All "visioning" processes are built on the same development paradigm earlier described in the

St. John Hospital hypothetical case: identification of the target audiences; involvement of the targets in the process of developing the vision; almost simultaneous informing of the targets of the significance of the process and its meaning to management; with investment in effort, energy, and attitude being the desired outcome.

Early employee involvement generates ideas that get to the root of what the company needs—where it needs to strengthen its knowledge base and performance. This may include market and competitor intelligence, cost-saving programs, product innovations, and other details. The information and the plan that evolve from it are more likely to be relevant to an audience that was involved in their development.

The vision statement of the Michigan Blues highlights the need for integrated communication in its opening line: "When people think of health benefits, they will first think of Blue Cross and Blue Shield of Michigan."

THE BCBSM VISION STATEMENT

When people think of health benefits, they will first think of Blue Cross and Blue Shield of Michigan. We will build lasting customer loyalty through exemplary service and cost-effective, innovative products. The keys to success are a skilled workforce, strong business relationships with providers, and responsive systems.

It is clear what the vision intends—top-of-mind association of our company with healthcare with all of our stakeholders. The vision statement is proactive in terms of describing exactly what we intend to do to get and keep our products as top-of-mind in the healthcare business. "We will build lasting customer loyalty through exemplary service and cost-effective, innovative products." Finally, the vision statement completes itself with a prescription for the behavior of the Blue workforce. "The keys to success are a skilled workforce, strong business relationships with providers, and responsive systems."

An appropriate integrated marketing communication strategy must relate to the organization's vision if the messages it generates are to be credible and effective. Several other criteria must also be met: (1) The IMC strategy must fit with all other communication strategies of the organization. (2) Communications of the organization must be seen as encompassing all the organization does, as well as what it says it does. (3) Strategy must be clear and unforgettable to the people charged with implementing it. (4) Strategy must be cost effective and should account for all costs including time, talent, and money in measuring its effectiveness. (5) Strategy must be selected, projected for success, and modified in the context of all available research.

The use of formative research to develop campaigns is not foreign to most large business organizations, particularly retail organizations which rely on advertising pitches to support sales. Smaller organizations, however, and especially social marketers, may believe that formative research resources are out of reach. This is simply not the case.

"Year of the Provider"– A Strategy for the Blues

In an article for the June 1989, issue of *Public Relations Journal*, the author described a relatively simple process small organizations could use to improve how they are perceived by specific audiences. The article was written in response to the frustrations of a growing number of nonprofit organizations attempting to communicate with their markets before conducting basic "formative research." (For a reprint of "Workshop: Improving your small organization's image" write the author at Blue Cross and Blue Shield of Michigan, 600 E. Lafayette Blvd., Detroit, Michigan 48226.)

A simple introspective process triggered by six or seven basic questions to a team of employees can provide the basis for an effective customer-centered communications strategy. Some of the questions cannot be answered in a meeting room and will require participants to go out and get some information for the group, but generally this process uses existing resources and information to "get a feel for" how the organization is viewed by its customers and other constituencies. The desired outcome of the process is a plan for changed organizational behavior which, if made obvious, will result in improved relationships with key constituencies. The operating premise: Effective organization managers are motivated to discuss organizational self-image and are generally capable of executing a strategy for improving it. What they may need is a basic framework. A variation of this same basic framework supported a major effort by Blue Cross and Blue Shield of Michigan in helping to improve its relationships with physicians.

The communications effort began with a one-year campaign we called "Year of the Provider." Our approach was to show Michigan physicians and their staffs that "it pays to participate with the Blues." Our formal research and our conversations with key physician "influentials" made it clear that while significant improvements were occurring in the way we transact business with and for physicians and other providers, we had yet to prove that we were a changed organization. The communication effort we designed to do this was built on the premise that the Blues were seen by many physicians and their staffs as a huge and hostile bureaucracy. And although, for business reasons, it may have been absolutely necessary for many physicians to provide services below the established market-service rates to our cardholders, they did not have to be happy about it.

The key campaign assumption was that the way to build and rebuild relationships with physicians and their staffs was for the company to continue to make adjustments in its procedures and attitudes, adjustments that better conform to the noneconomic expectations of physicians and their staffs with respect to services, consultation on matters of mutual interest, and other issues. For the adjustments to have their greatest positive impact on relations with physicians, however, the corporate communications department had to make sure the physician community recognized the many substantive changes that were being made. Our research showed that physicians and staff had to be reminded that we are motivated by a desire to improve our relationship with them. We also needed them to recognize our understanding that by becoming more provider-friendly, the company could find ways of helping physicians, especially, reduce the financial costs of doing business with us, costs that were ultimately being passed to our customers.

Corporate communicators reviewed findings from formal satisfaction research with physicians and reports from focus groups and sat in on meetings with an advisory committee of physicians working with Blues staff to resolve issues. An executive with the state medical society helped develop a list of 20 achievements we had already made, but not properly communicated, to physicians. His most revealing insight, however, was not on the list. He suggested that something the Blues could do that physicians would respond to (and to date had never received from the Blues) is "give the doctors a little social credit for some of the things they do for the public."

The process was made more complicated by this fact. Many business decision makers—the representatives of Blue Cross customers who select which healthcare plans to make available to their employees—agreed that better relations with physicians, hospitals, and other providers of care is worthwhile for several reasons. At the same time, many of these same decision makers, especially those affiliated with the larger businesses who rely on the Blues, felt that the company had a history of being "too close" to the provider community. Despite the well-publicized efforts the company was making, at that time and now, to write contracts with doctors and hospitals that contribute significantly to customer savings, a public effort to improve provider relations could fuel past doubts about whether the company defines its "customer" as the businesses it represents or the providers it relies on for direct services.

The Michigan Blues would not fit anyone's definition of a small organization. With more than four million cardholders, including a majority of America's autoworkers, 50,000 business clients, 20,000 contracted physicians, and 8,000 employees, the Blues are on the short list of America's largest payors of healthcare benefits. Nonetheless, the basic framework the communications department used to develop the "Year of the Provider" campaign is identical to the process suggested for small-organization image improvement in the earlier citation. Here are some of the questions we asked ourselves, and what our questioning produced.

How Do the Members of Our Organization Describe Our Relationship to Michigan Physicians?

Before members of an organization begin the process of determining how they are viewed by others, it's important that they describe how they see themselves and their organization— what they think they do, and how what they do fits into the overall scheme of things. One way for a smaller organization to do this is to gather communicators and others from the organization at the same table and try to settle on one word that the target audience might use to describe the company's role from the audience's perspective. To the doctor and staff, is our organization an advocate, a producer, a service provider, a defender, a collector, an arbitrator? Although these words, and others, might seem arbitrary or ambiguous, an exercise this simple may reveal many different faces of the organization in terms of how it relates to an audience on which it depends. On the one hand, diversity of opinion may be a sign of individual initiative in interpreting the organization's mission with this key audience. To the audience, such individual initiative may be seen as group drift, the absence of a clear organizational vision, or institutional schizophrenia.

One conclusion to which we were drawn was that while the success of our company depends on partnership relationships with physicians and staff, many of our processes and requirements seemed to be designed to treat these valuable partners as adversaries. The relationship begins from a rather difficult premise. The Blues negotiate agreements with physicians and hospitals under which they provide services at "below-market prices" to our customers. In return for this price concession, we provide the increased patient volume that results from having more than 50 percent of the private-pay market in the state. With such market "clout," however, comes a natural resentment compounded by complex paperwork, lengthy payment delays, surly treatment, or what physicians may perceive as insurance-company tampering in medical-treatment decisions. We concluded that while doctors and their staffs may feel forced to accept the Blues identification card as payment in full for services rendered, they didn't have to smile about it. Cardholder impressions about the value of the blue and white card, it turns out, are not impervious to suggestions of a physician's billing clerk who greets its presentation by saying: "Oh, not another one of those."

Our staff analysis began with a realization that, yes, our clients expect us to obtain necessary medical care for the lowest possible cost, and, conversely, our clients depend on our creating and keeping a large network of medical service providers. We depend on doctors and their staffs to provide care when it is needed. "We are between a rock and a hard place," we concluded. And we are here by our own choosing. So why would we act as if we are getting squeezed? We should be happy we are here. This realization brought us directly to our second question.

How Do We Currently Communicate Our Organizational Vision to This Constituency?

We found that while we did spend a great deal of time sending what from our perspective was "useful paper" to physicians and their office staffs, this paper was seen as a great burden to them. The manual that was supposed to help doctors' staffs figure out what is an eligible medical benefit was largely out of date. The manual was 1,000 pages and contained information that had been amended, deleted, or added at various times. If found, much of the information in our manuals was in conflict with information found elsewhere. We were sending out so-called administrative letters and bulletins on a variety of issues by the hundreds every year. Providers were telling us the administrative-letter process was unmanageable and unreliable. Our monthly newsletters had become complicated attempts to clarify inadequate information in the manual, and neither document was very effective except in frustrating doctors' office staff.

What Actions Do We Take as an Organization to Emphasize the Importance of Effective Communications with This Audience?

Any plan to improve relationships between an organization and its key audiences—to improve the organizational image—depends heavily on the organization's commitment to communication. Despite the company's new vision statement, with its explicit directive to improve relationships with providers, a "prevision statement" attitude prevailed. The company had been hard at work to clean up archaic systems, develop automated processes to facilitate quick payment to physicians and pay them interest for late payments, redo our manual (even involving the medical staffs as reviewers in the process), and involve physicians in a process resolving more than 40 common complaints presented by the state's largest medical association. Much was being done to prove that we wanted to treat Michigan physicians better, but we had been inhibited about promoting these actions for fear key customers somehow might think the company was softening in its resolve to contain healthcare costs. Once the communication staff pressed the issue, at the urging of and with the support of corporate leadership, we were able to proceed with the campaign to make our new attitude better known.

We had already dealt with what is normally another question that an internal group might discuss in coming to grips with its image opportunities.

Upon What Audiences Do Our Organization Depend for Survival?

We had already decided that without quality physician relationships, our organization would be deprived of strong relationships with our cardholders. What was growing was this realization that the individual cardholder is playing a much larger role in the future of our company. In the past, more emphasis had been placed on relationships with employers than on relationships with cardholders whose coverage had been purchased for them. But many of these employers are now offering "cafeteria-style" benefit plans and other arrangements that allow employees to choose from among competing plans for their healthcare coverage.

Every day, what the individual cardholder was hearing in his or her physician's office was becoming more important. A group awareness was growing that the company's image was shaped at the point of contact between the cardholder and the physician's office staff.

We also came to the realization that while the company does rely on the physician and hospital staff for the delivery of direct services, the company cannot survive without customers. Our customers, particularly the largest and most vocal of the lot, depend on us to obtain medical services at the lowest possible cost.

How Do We Learn How Our Key Audiences Really Feel about Our Organization?

Many small organizations that cannot afford formal research projects to determine how key audiences perceive them can nevertheless learn much by heightening employees' awareness of what is currently known about these groups. In our case, we had the benefit of provider-satisfaction tracking studies, formal focus groups that had been begun years earlier, and a formal structure for getting physician feedback on key issues. Smaller organizations should send team members out with lists of influentials to question about what the organization can and should be doing better. The responses can get fed back rather quickly into the structure of the overall image effort.

What Media Influence Our Audience and What Messages Are We Sending at This Point in Time?

We discussed various ways our target audience received messages about the company. Actually, we discussed this much earlier in the process than it appears here. As we stated earlier, Schulz believes that this question should be the first one asked in the development of any integrated marketing communication plan. We inventoried the controlled and uncontrolled media we use to communicate with physicians and their staff. This review revealed a wide variety of opportunities for a redirected communication program that emphasized a point our chief executive officer had first made in a New Year prediction to the state's largest business publication in December 1992.

"Closer bonds between Blues and Michigan physicians—that's my prediction for 92," Richard Whitmer told *Crain's Detroit Business*. "We have a number of efforts underway to show the doctors of Michigan that we hear, we care and we can change. 1992 will be the year of the provider around the Blues, and we're going to show one and all that it pays to participate."

This comment signaled to the corporation that permission had been granted to vigorously implement communications about the element of our corporate vision statement calling for better relationships with providers. It triggered a flurry of activity within the corporate communications division that included aggressive promotion of recent changes that had been made in provider service; dedicated regional teams to help physicians with billing and claims problems; a separate administrative unit to serve the western part of the state with employees from that area; a revised physician's manual to eliminate much archaic and useless information through a process that included text review by a team of physician assistants from across the state; and adjustments in the physician-records department to facilitate simpler and quicker transactions.

These and a variety of other significant changes were announced and reannounced to physicians and their staffs through private letters from our corporate medical director to physicians; feature articles in our physician newsletter emphasizing the importance of physician and staff involvement in the development of many of the innovations; presentations before our physician advisory board and to the leadership of the state medical societies; special advertisements and ad sections in regional medical society publications; targeted local newspaper ads that listed participating physician names and encouraged cardholders to use the services of these physicians; and the incorporation of physician messages into corporate advertising highlighting, for example, that more physicians use the blue and white card to cover themselves and their families.

Perhaps more dramatic were our efforts to highlight Michigan physicians, Blue participating physicians, in a paid advertising campaign that was arranged for at a reduced ad rate in conjunction with the state's television and radio broadcasters' association. The ad campaign featured eight physicians—one per ad—offering health tips on issues ranging from the value of reducing the rich dressings on otherwise healthful salads to the relationship between smoking and impotence. The campaign received heavy exposure and became the subject of several news columns and television and radio news features. Such visibility emphasized the nature of our unique relationships with physicians. More importantly, it gave the Blues a chance to provide Michigan physicians with a modicum of the social credit they deserve for the contributions they make to the general good.

In an additional effort, a newspaper and television campaign was developed that featured our chief executive officer reminding Michigan residents during holiday seasons that while we were enjoying our vacation meals with our families—"The doctor is in. In most lives, today is Thanksgiving Day—In some lives, however, today is just November 28. Another day of doing whatever the day demands. Making split-second decisions. Doing two things at once. Calling on every skill in the book to turn crisis into calm, despair into hope." The ad went on to ask our cardholders to express their appreciation to the doctors, nurses, and other medical personnel who are on duty while we are off. This advertising campaign was received with widespread acclaim in the medical community.

The communication effort for physicians and their staffs highlighted real changes in company policy that had been developed and implemented to strengthen relationships with the medical community. It provides a clear example of an organization adjusting to the values and expectations of an audience upon which it depends, public relations as earlier defined. Improved relations with the state's medical community were obvious. These improvements were not caused by the communications; they were the result of substantive changes in the Blues' organizational behavior. That the changes were well communicated to the medical community across the state, at the very least, accelerated their impact on this key relationship.

Results of the "Year of the Provider" effort were nearly immediate and fairly dramatic. In a report on a physician and office staff satisfaction survey conducted midpoint in the campaign, fully 47 percent of the physicians and staff surveyed reported improvement in satisfaction with the Blues during the past year, while only 3 percent reported a decline. The perception of this changed attitude at the Michigan Blues was so dramatic that a legislator who earlier had been calling for the company to be split was now telling medical reporters that he had changed his mind. And a physician who had been one of the company's most emphatic critics told these same reporters: "There is no more evil empire."

Despite the success of this effort in reestablishing our intent to reduce medical costs through efforts that reduce physician and hospital overhead and "make it easier to do business with us," feelings persist among major clients that the company is "provider driven." Rather than reflecting an unintended consequence of the previously described provider campaign, this attitude may reflect a need to redouble efforts directed at major customers to make them better aware of the tremendous cost-savings being generated by the company's unique provider contracts.

Communications as the Healthcare Marketing Position

The healthcare communicator's tool box can include advertising, public, and community relations, employee communications, media relations, customer and provider communications, special events, and where appropriate, development.

In what they describe as the new concept of marketing communications, Schultz and co-authors stress the degree to which many organizations are facing a "parity marketplace" in which production, service, logistical, and other refinements are causing more and more product and service lines to appear as commodities to the buying public. This parity condition applies to modern healthcare in America. "In a parity marketplace, the only real differentiating feature that a marketer can bring to consumers is what those consumers believe about the company, product, or service and their relationship with that brand." [12]

For healthcare companies to achieve and maintain a strategic command of the marketplace, a clear position in the minds of targeted consumers, communications activities must be fully integrated with research and marketing activities. The power of integrated marketing communications derives from its essential focus—attempting to change behavior of target audiences. To do that successfully, the healthcare communicator finds ways to engage target audience members with the organization's products and services. Through this engagement or involvement, the target audience member begins to accept the information provided by the organization.

Relations between individuals or groups improve as both sides understand that adjustments are being made to accommodate one another's values and needs. Making such adjustments more obvious to targeted audiences is often described as public relations. But disciplines other than public relations can be employed to broadcast the organization's changed behavior. The object of integrated marketing communications is to identify and employ the variety of tools through which changed organizational behavior can be highlighted. IMC demands solid research to identify audiences and modify messages, and an obsession with ensuring that the organization's marketplace is spoken to as if in one voice.

ENDNOTES

1. C. Atkin, and L. Wallack, Eds. *Mass Communication and Public Health* (Newbury Park, CA: Sage, 1990).

2. L. Wallack, "Improving health Promotion: Media Advocacy and Social Marketing Approaches," C. Atkin and L. Wallack, Eds. *Mass Communication and Public Health* (Newbury Park, CA: Sage, 1990), p. 155.

3. R. McKenna, *The Regis Touch* (Reading, MA: Addison-Wesley, 1985), p. 8.

4. D. Schultz, S. Tannenbaum, and R. Lauterborn, *Integrated Marketing Communications* (Lincolnwood, IL: NTC Publishing Group, 1993), pp. 84–85.

5. J. Barach, "Applying Marketing Principles to Social Causes," *Business Horizons*, July 1984, pp. 65–69.

6. Wallack, p. 155

7. Atkin and Wallack, p. 11.

8. Wallack, pp. 156–57.

9. C. Atkin, and V. Freimuth, "Formative Evaluation Research in Campaign Design," in R. Rice and C. Atkin, Eds., *Public Communication Campaigns* (Newbury Park, CA: Sage, 1989), pp. 131–150.

10. Wallack, p. 157.

11. Schultz, pp. 57–75.

12. Schultz, pp. 44–45.

BIBLIOGRAPHY

Fine, S. *Social Marketing*. Needham Heights, MA, Allyn and Bacon, 1990.

Johnson, H. F. *Excerpts from a Profit-Sharing Speech Made to Employees of Johnson Wax Company*, 1927.

Kotler, P. *Marketing for Nonprofit Organizations*. Englewood Cliffs, NJ, Prentice Hall, 1982.

Kotler, P. and G. Zaltman. "Social Marketing: An Approach to Planned Social Change," *Journal of Marketing*, July 1971, pp. 3–12.

Rios, B. "Healthcare Is a Boon to Lawmakers. *Detroit Free Press*, July 22, 1994.

Simmons, R. *Communications Campaign Management*. White Plains, NY, Longman, 1990.

## CHAPTER 31

Public Relations in Government

Brent Baker
Dean, College of Communication
Boston University

HISTORY

It is interesting to note that while the United States is one of the leaders in the practice of governmental public relations, it has never had a government Ministry of Information or government-run domestic national newspaper, radio, or TV station. However, U.S. government leaders, beginning with President Andrew Jackson in the 1830s, began to hire former journalists as press assistants to help get their messages out to the American people. So, the American model of government public relations practice has always involved a democratic government informing the public via a free, independent, and privately owned news media establishment.

Beginning in the 1900s, officials in the U.S. Department of Agriculture (USDA) began to institutionalize the governmental public affairs function. The USDA operated a press relations bureau in the Division of Forestry, which upset some pro-timber company congressmen. As will be discussed later, the U.S. Congress (legislative branch) has always been skeptical about the executive branch's use of public relations or publicity people to inform the public. The Congress traditionally fears that the president will use the government's public relations machine for political propaganda purposes. The major U.S. steps in the evolution of governmental public relations came during World War I and II.

On April 13, 1917 President Wilson created the Committee on Public Information (CPI) with newspaperman George Creel as head. The CPI was involved in the mobilization of public opinion before there was any commercial radio or television. The CPI produced films and had a speakers bureau of 75,000 speakers called "Minute Men." The CPI organized Victory Loan campaigns and War Expositions. Out of the CPI came the first American business and public awareness of the power of propaganda. Many who worked in the CPI, such as Edward L. Bernays and Carl Byoir left the government to apply their public relations "lessons learned" to the commercial world.

During World War II, President Roosevelt established the Office of War Information (OWI) in 1942. The OWI was under Elmer Davis, a radio broadcaster. The OWI was involved in a full range of domestic and overseas propaganda efforts building on the foundation of the CPI's techniques.

In summary, it was mainly from the wartime work of the CPI and the OWI that the U.S. government really began to institutionalize a large scale, full-time public relations function and staff. Some of those wartime government practitioners stayed after the wars to form the core group of public relations officers. Today, the U.S. federal government is one of the world's largest government employers of public information or public affairs personnel with over 10,000 practitioners.

A STRATEGIC APPROACH

There are a number of important differences between the practice of public relations in the private and public sectors.[1] The stakeholders in government public relations are a vast and diverse group of internal and external publics and audiences with different agendas. These groups include: leaders and employees in the executive, legislative, or judicial branches of government and government agencies; public interest groups, political party leaders, political action committees, state and local officials, private business people, professional interest groups, news media people, and the general public. Some of these vested interest groups closely monitor the government's public relations programs and often have either budgetary power or public opinion influence over the government's actions.

In virtually all kinds of governments the goals and functions of public relations activities are linked closely to the personal leadership styles of those in charge, as well as to unique cultural factors and the formal or informal structures of the political system. Even in democratic countries, where citizens freely elect their leaders, the nature and practice of government public relations can vary widely. For example, in the United Kingdom there is an Official Secrets Act that restricts the free flow of certain types of information to the citizens. In the United States, the Freedom of Information Act (FOIA) is designed to give citizens relatively open access to most kinds of government information and records. In contrast, in nations with difficult domestic or national security concerns, such as Egypt or Israel, the government may exercise very tight information controls in selected circumstances.

The importance of the personal communication style of senior political leaders is clearly a major factor in a government. An administration change can significantly impact how the government communicates with its publics.[2] Even within a particular administration, communication style can change very quickly, based on political events and changes in the prevailing love-hate relationship between government and the news media. For example, a pattern has developed in the United States in which new government leaders usually have a brief honeymoon with the press. During this period the news media normally provide positive coverage of the new leaders and their initiatives. But when political battles are drawn, or as other events dictate, media coverage often becomes increasingly critical.

A cultural factor among American journalists, as political scientist Thomas E. Patterson points out, is that they generally share a negative view of politics and government.[3] Furthermore, the formal structure of government in the U.S. requires that political executive leaders must share the public stage and power with legislative leaders. In contrast with European prime ministers, who often can operate with a ready-made majority, American presidents and Congress are separately elected and neither controls political power absolutely.[4] This has significant implications for public relations practices.

The American political system has additional formal features that influence the practice of government public relations. Between the president and congress, and between the major political parties, there is no clear locus of control but a so-called balance of power.

In this way, the United States is different from more centrally controlled systems. For example, in July 1994, House Majority Leader and Rep. Richard A. Gephardt (D-MO) commented on the difficulties involved in efforts such as that required to try to pass the Clinton administration's health-care bill, "I often say to people that my greatest fear as majority leader is that there is no majority, that we'll be unable to act, that there isn't enough agreement to find a majority."[5]

This division of power between branches of government causes another important difference between private business and government public relations practices. Business organizations generally have the legal right and public support to advertise or seek publicity in almost any manner they choose. In contrast, those conducting public relations in government have unique legal, political, and cultural restrictions placed on them. For example, in November 1995 U.S. Energy Secretary, Hazel O'Leary was rebuked by the White House and Congressional critics because her public affairs office had spent $46,500 to hire a commercial media tracking company to do a content analysis of media stories on the energy department's activities. The tracking company's reports ranked the news reporters in relation to whether their stories were favorable or unfavorable to the energy department. O'Leary attempted to defend her department's action saying she stood for increased government openness with the public. Nevertheless, the energy secretary came under bi-partisan Congressional political fire and news media criticism. She was ordered by the White House to repay the $46,500 to the treasury from her personal office account. *The New York Times* lashed out at the Energy Department's attempt to evaluate the content of the news media saying,

> It was a flagrant misuse of taxpayer money by a department with plenty of its own propaganda specialists. . . . The compiling of a [media ranking] list smacks of a readiness to manipulate the press by rewarding friends and punishing enemies.[6]

Actually, the government payment for measuring the media reporting was not illegal. In fact, in business public relations practice it would have been considered normal, but in government practice it was just "politically incorrect."

Congress often uses its power over the budget to restrict the size and scope of this area of the executive branch. The late U.S. Sen. J. W. Fulbright was an especially vocal critic of government public relations:

> . . . what is one to think when the apparatus is used, as we all know it sometimes is, to guide public opinion toward controversial objectives? What of the use of the government's information resources to promote intensely controversial political or foreign policy objectives?[7]

Congress has long made it difficult for government public relations to be used to achieve such goals. In 1913, Congress passed the Congressional Deficiency Appropriations Act because of concern that executive branch leaders would use public relations to influence domestic or international public opinion (and somehow change the balance between the three branches of government). This law included the stipulation that: "No money appropriated by any act shall be used for compensation of any publicity expert unless specifically appropriated for that purpose."[8] Ever since, restrictive language aimed at public relations funding has been placed in various appropriation laws by succeeding congresses. Also, Congress requires the executive branch to monitor closely and report individual department appropriations spent on public relations.

Generally, then, in carrying out their activities, government public relations specialists communicate with a vast and very diverse group of both internal and external publics. In reaching these constituents, the goals, nature, and functions of public relations, as carried out by civil government career officials or military personnel, are influenced by three major factors. These are (1) the personal communication styles of the leaders they serve, (2) shared understandings and cultural norms prevailing in their organizations and nation, and (3) both the formal and informal nature of the political process in their particular governments.

JUSTIFICATIONS FOR GOVERNMENT PUBLIC RELATIONS

In broad perspective, the practice of government public relations within a democratic society is justified by three major propositions:

1. A democratic government is best served by a free two-way flow of ideas and accurate information so citizens and their government can make informed choices.
2. A democratic government must report and be accountable to the citizens it serves.
3. Citizens, as taxpayers, have a right to government information—but with some exceptions.

Exceptions to a completely open flow of information are based on such factors as national security concerns, sensitive business proprietary issues, and, of course, citizens' rights to privacy and to a fair trial. For example, in the United States, a legal tug-of-war sometimes occurs between the Privacy Act and the Freedom of Information Act when the government's release of information is at issue. Career public relations officers frequently find themselves involved with both government and private lawyers, discussing the balance between the public's right to certain information versus the legal protection of that information due to one of the above exceptions. Often, the government leader's decision on whether to release information leads to a judgment on the balance between public interest and individual citizens' rights.

Basic Goals

While each country's government may have a different type of public relations or information context, there are four rather basic *strategic* approaches to all government public relations practice. In these four approaches, the existence of a two-way communications process is assumed, that is, a free flow of information back and forth between the government and the citizens it serves. These approaches are focused on the goals of providing political communication, information services, positive institutional images, and on generating public feedback.

Political Communication
The goal in political communication is to persuade and win domestic or international acceptance of a government's existing, new, or proposed budget, policy, law, or regulation. In pursuing this goal, political leaders usually actively sell their policies and positions to various constituencies. Simply put, this is a battle to win public opinion and gain public support.

In nations where the media are government-controlled, an effective strategy is to shape the editorial slant of all media coverage to try to control public opinion. In any democratic government, one of the key political dialogues in this strategic area occurs between the executive and legislative stakeholders. Government public relations planners will often discuss whether they should focus their communication messages directly at the legislature or aim messages "over their heads," going directly to the public. In practice, most government communicators will aim messages at both target audiences. Either way, the goal is to influence legislative votes either directly or indirectly.

In a country with free speech and a free press, the public expects elected leaders to advocate their programs. But the public also expects open and fair debate. This political communication strategy often sets the public agenda and drives the most time- and content-sensitive inquiries from citizens and the news media. Government public relations officers must deal with "political coordination and direction," sometimes at the highest levels of government. Moreover, ethical concerns often come into play when there is a conflict between political loyalty and what the public relations officer believes is the right thing to do in accordance with government laws, rules, or ethical standards of conduct.

Information Services

In information services, the goal is to inform various publics about the types of government information and services available so citizens can access them. This is the day-to-day government's customer service role—disseminating information or answering questions from citizens or the media concerning such areas as education, citizen entitlements, public health, public safety, public transportation, commerce, agriculture, government reports, and so forth. One of the best government public health communication examples was the case of the British government and the so-called "Mad Cow Disease." For over a decade (1986–1996) the British government's Agriculture and Health Ministers had publicly declared that there was no scientific evidence of any linkage between Mad Cow (brain) disease and an incurable human brain disease called "C.J.D." However, after a panel of British scientists said there "may" be such a linkage in 1996, the British people lost faith in their government's public health information and stopped eating British beef. Then, foreign governments banned the import of British beef and the British farmers faced economic ruin. The public perception was set, despite other scientific experts saying there was no such scientific linkage. In frustration, British Prime Minister, John Major declared to his European Union partners who had banned British beef, "It is a problem of confidence, not of health...."[9]

Developing and Protecting Positive Institutional Images

The goal in developing and protecting positive institutional images is to inform and influence short- or long-term public support for a government branch, department, agency, or unit. This goal often is pursued within a complex matrix of contention, criticism, and problems. Uneasy feelings and controversies can be expected when government officials try to "sell" such a positive image. Unique problems often arise when internal government critics (in Congress, Parliament, or some other agency) or external antagonists (special interests or news media) claim that type of activity is a form of self-serving propaganda and a waste of taxpayers' money. Defensively, the government unit's spokesperson usually replies that the public has a right to know what the unit is doing, and its public relations efforts are objectively and legitimately designed to inform the public about its mission, operations, and people.

Generating Public Feedback

Public relations officers seek a flow of information from the public to those who must make informed choices in the policy decision process. This is the most misunderstood strategic task of government public relations staffs. In a large government bureaucracy, leaders can become isolated from those people who may be most affected by their policy decisions. In contrast to this, government public relations officers, because of daily contact with a wide range of people (e.g., other government agency employees, news media representatives, community and civic leaders, special interest groups and the general public), hold a unique insight into how these segments of the society feel or might react to a particular government policy or decision.

In pursuing the goal of generating feedback, the personal reputation and organizational status of the public relations officer within the government bureaucracy cannot be underestimated. Bringing public feedback to the decision table isn't enough; leaders must have enough trust and confidence in the public relations adviser to ensure that such information is within the executive's policy decision process. This means providing "reality check" feedback at all stages of discussions, not just after the decisions already have been made. Veteran government public relations officers often tell their leaders, "I want to be in on the takeoff (of a policy) and not be called in only after its crash landing creates a crisis."

Feedback from the public can also take the form of scientific opinion polls. Some governments commission and use such polls, but others are more reluctant for various reasons. The U.S. Congress is very restrictive when it comes to funding domestic opinion polls due to its concern that such information would be used to pressure the Congress on pending legislation or on foreign policy. Thus, government-sponsored polls usually focus on international public opinion.

ORGANIZATIONAL FEATURES, RESPONSIBILITIES, AND FUNCTIONS

The U.S. government has one of the world's largest public relations operations. In 1993 about 10,000 civilian and military public affairs people spent close to $1 billion annually on various information programs.[10] For purposes of this discussion, let's assume that the public relations function is located in a major executive branch government department such as Energy, Veteran's Affairs, Treasury, or Transportation and that the public relations office works directly for the chief civilian department executive. This position is usually a political appointee with the title of Secretary of the department. Normally, this person will be given overall formal responsibility for several functions, including establishing public relations policy within the department as well as directing its implementation. In the United States this also includes monitoring and controlling the department's relations with Congress, higher authorities, other principal government officials, and the public.[11]

Legislative and Public Relations Functions

It is important to note that the secretary has responsibilities for both general public relations and for specific relationships with Congress. In some government offices, these two functions will be combined in one central office of Legislative and Public Relations, which makes sense with constrained administrative resources but daily presents practical problems. For example, such a single office may get the same type of inquiry from a congressional office, a news organization, and the general public. Assuming the answer to the three inquiries is the same, it seems logical for one office to coordinate the answer within the bureaucracy and respond uniformly to the customers. However, the main administrative problem is one of timing and priority. Bear in mind that thousands of information inquiries move through government offices every day. All information customers want their answers *now*! These inquiries come from all kinds of sources and there is always the question of which should get priority. Does the government employee provide answers in the order in which the inquiries were received, or in some other way?

The solution to the priority problem is shaped by the fact that in any democratic government the political priority of any agency or group is focused foremost on the annual "battle of the budget." The secretary or some "higher authority" is always trying to curry favor with Congress, and his or her success or failure is measured partly by the ability to get the department's budget or program requests approved. This simple fact of government life means that legislative inquiries usually get top priority. Indeed, most governments use special color-coded folders to distinguish top priority legislative inquiries. Within the U.S. government, different Congressional members or staff receive different priorities because some are more important in budgetary decisions than others. For example, if a request for information from the State Department is from a member or staff of the Foreign Relations Committee, which has budget authority over that agency, that request will be given top priority. As a general rule, Congressional inquiries will be answered first, followed by those from the news media, with requests from the public last in line.

Because both public relations and legislative relations are full-time jobs, most large government departments separate these functions to achieve better customer satisfaction. Within this structure, the heads of those offices carry such titles as assistant secretary, special assistant to the secretary, director of legislative affairs (or liaison), or special assistant or director of public affairs.

To illustrate the need for close coordination, politically street smart news reporters and citizens know that Congressional inquiries get top priority. The director of Congressional relations and the director of public relations will find times when either a reporter or citizen has asked a member of Congress to place an inquiry for information from an agency to get a faster response. Sometimes the same person will send the same inquiry to more than one government office. This is always discovered by some lower level bureaucrat who is the in-house expert on the particular subject of the inquiry. Obviously, a credibility problem would be created if the same question were responded to with two different answers.

To assist in legislative and public relations coordination and to give firsthand feedback to the secretary, a daily morning "lineup" meeting is usually held between the secretary, legislative adviser, public relations adviser, and the secretary's other top personal advisors. At this meeting there is normally an informal review of the events of the previous 24 hours and a forecast of expected actions in the next 24 hours, from both the legislative and public relations points of view.

Directors of public relations who also have legislative relations responsibilities normally will have two deputies: one for legislative and the other for public relations liaison. On the legislative liaison side, there will normally be different people designated to handle the upper and lower houses of the legislature. This combined office must be organized and staffed to handle about half a dozen different types of legislative actions. These include personal inquiries from legislative members, referrals from constituents of such members, requests from legislative committees (including responses to legislative investigation), general legislative inquiries regarding budgets and programs, requests for information related to internal department coordination, or development and arrangements for department witnesses to appear at legislative hearings.

Intergovernmental Affairs

In national-level government departments that interface routinely with other levels of government, there will be a separate office headed by a person with a title such as director of intergovernmental affairs which may be located either in the legislative office or within the public relations office. For example, in the U.S. government, the Department of Agriculture has a director of international affairs. The counterpart in the Department of Commerce is the assistant secretary for legislative and governmental affairs. Other major departments with similar posts are: Energy (assistant secretary, congressional, intergovernmental, and international affairs); Transportation (assistant secretary for governmental affairs); Treasury (director, office of intergovernmental affairs); and Veterans (assistant secretary for public and intergovernmental affairs). Even if there is no specific position and office with the Interdepartmental Affairs title within the major department, this function will be served by the public relations office, the legislative office, or by a specific program.

Public Relations Director or Assistant Secretary

For purposes of further discussion, it is assumed that a separate public relations office reports directly to the secretary. The head of this office is either a political appointee or a career individual to whom responsibility is delegated for daily public relations tasks.[12] In addition to advising the secretary on general areas of public concern, the normal responsibilities of such a person include:

1. Acting as the senior public relations adviser. This means the public relations adviser sees the secretary daily and attends most senior staff meetings, where policy and actions are decided upon.
2. Serving as the public spokesperson for the department. This means the daily "care and feeding" of the news media is handled by the public affairs director or staff members.
3. Coordinating public relations policy and programs within the department. This includes the planning and execution of public relations strategies and central themes.
4. Functioning as the senior public relations adviser for crisis management. This crisis role may involve public relations coordination with other government departments or agencies, as directed by the secretary or higher authority.
5. Seeking to coordinate public relations actions, as deemed appropriate, with the office of legislative relations.
6. Releasing information of special interest concerning the department in coordination with the secretary or designated higher authority. (This may or may not include coordination of requests for information under specific laws, such as the Freedom of Information Act or Privacy Act. However, all government public relations staff personnel must be familiar with the provisions of all laws pertaining to the release of information that may affect their unit.)
7. Supervising the coordination of community relations, internal information, and audio-visual programs within the department.

Functional Organization within a Government
Public Relations Office

To fulfill these public relations responsibilities, the typical public affairs office focuses its day-to-day work on the following three major areas:

Public and Media Relations   This area includes processing and coordinating department information for release to the public or the news media. The department's media relations operation and general public inquiries office conducts this activity. In most government public relations offices, the media relations function is considered the most sensitive area and requires the most higher-level coordination.

Community Relations   The organizational responsibilities of the office bring its people in direct interpersonal contact with the public. In the case of national governments, this may include intergovernmental relations with other civic and local government people. In these programs there is an attempt to gain local public support and to establish a positive image within the community through such routine activities as arranging public speaker appearances, conducting open houses and tours for local government facilities, and arranging cooperative community service projects and local people-to-people cooperative programs. An especially sensitive political aspect of community relations is that related to environmental law compliance and public safety.

Internal Relations   These are activities based on two-way communication between management and employees that normally pertain to the government's internal employees, their families, and in some cases retired employees and their families. Internal information refers not only to the communication themes and messages, but to the means by which such messages are communicated, including, for example, employee newsletters or audio-visual information covering such topics as changes in the plans of the organization, personnel policies, promotion opportunities, and training.

In conducting these activities, the public relations officer must not think in terms of internal or external media. So-called external media, that is, local television, cable, radio, and newspapers, can and should be used as internal information channels. For example, an effective approach is to think in terms of target audiences and the media they are likely to use. When wanting to reach government employees' families or retired employees, the local commercial media can be key internal relations channels.

In overview, government public relations are conducted within complex organizational structures to reach audiences both external to and within departments and other groups. Significant priorities of leaders and their missions define and limit what is communicated, in what manner, to whom, over what medium, and for what purpose.

PLANNING TACTICAL APPROACHES TO
GOVERNMENT COMMUNICATION

The first planning step in selling a government policy or program is that of central issue identification and focus. In a complex democratic governmental process, with many political players outside the government leader's control, it is difficult to tackle too many issues at

B O X   31–1

This tactic was at the heart of a White House PR interpretation of President Clinton's problems with his economic policy, which was before Congress at the time. It was offered by Michael Deaver, the public relations man turned presidential counselor who helped former President Reagan gain the reputation as "the great communicator." Deaver appeared on ABC's "Nightline" program in February 1993 along with Paul Begala, President Clinton's political consultant to discuss the selling of the president's economic policy. Deaver said if the president were to succeed, he must focus on a single issue:

> . . . the largest hurdle that President Clinton's going to have is to keep himself focused. There is so much coming in and there are so many people that want him to do things; there are so many requests to divert his attention from this (economic) goal, [that] he is going to have to be single-minded about what he does with his time and who he speaks to and where he speaks; because, otherwise, with all the information that's coming at us, this message is going to get very diluted.[13]

once. Far better is the strategy of picking an issue and concentrating all communication assets on that topic before moving to the next. Many veteran observers refer to seats of government as "one-issue towns," with the implication that people only can handle one issue at a time. Also, some media experts believe that if a government leader attempts to present more than one major topic on the evening news, the public opinion impact is lessened. This one-issue-at-a-time tactic is not an easy one in practice because there are always many issues in government, and there are other powerful political players who want to shift attention to their important concern. However, it is clear that, from a public relations viewpoint, mixed messages should be avoided.

The second planning step is formulation of a coordinated communications plan, customized to the issue. All the major government players should agree on and be familiar with the plan. The advantage of such a plan is that the entire administration can "sing from the same sheet of music." This communications plan outlines the specific themes and tactics to be followed and avoids the complaint that the administration is not speaking with one voice. Such a plan would contain a general strategic goal, major themes, and tactical steps. Usually the plan will contain "talking points" and an action listing of media and/or other public relations events used to communicate to the various target publics. For example, a member of the administration who was scheduled to appear on a television program such as NBC's "Meet the Press," or at a Congressional hearing, or in preparing a public speech would be able to review the plan's talking points to ensure agreement with the chief executive's position. It must also be stated that while a politician can get away with only a general theme such as "change" in an election campaign, when one is governing and making specific policy proposals, the themes must be backed up with more specific and detailed talking points.

The third step is to execute the communications plan. While the top leaders will be involved in the execution, many players within and outside of government (such as political party organizations) will also be involved. In the above steps we see a difference from the private practice of public relations. In the private sector, the usual sequence can be described as a four-step process including (1) research-listening, (2) planning-decision making, (3) communication-action, and (4) evaluation.

In government the research-listening and the evaluation steps are usually absent or poorly done due to the more restricted political and bureaucratic context. In addition, short-fused requests for public relations plans and budget limitations have a negative effect on practicing the four-step process. If there is a crisis in the public relations office, the first place people are pulled from to reinforce the news desk is the "plans shop." In terms of evaluation, the question of how well public relations efforts were conducted is usually answered by who won or lost the policy vote, either on the floor of the legislature or in the court of public opinion—or both.

STRATEGY AND TACTICS IN GOVERNMENT MEDIA RELATIONS

The use of the media is vital to all government public relations plans, strategies, and tactics. Each party needs the other if citizens are to be fully served by a free flow of information. Sometimes, those in high office "just don't get it" when it comes to this basic truth. For example, President Clinton was talking to a friend and he mused, "I did not realize the importance of communications and the overriding importance of what is on the evening news. If I am not on, or there with a message, someone else is, with their message."[14]

One of the most significant features of the relationship between government public relations officials and the press is the deep cynicism and negative attitude many reporters seem to have toward government. It may be some comfort to such officials that journalism schools recognize this problem. In his recent basic textbook, Melvin Mencher of Columbia University cautions journalists against such cynicism when covering government:

> Cynicism disables the reporter in his or her task of helping the public to articulate its demands on its officials. . . . The reporter must understand that for individuals to lead fruitful lives there must be systematized cooperation between the governed and those who govern and that the journalist helps to bring this about by pointing to the necessary interdependence of all the actors in the public drama.[15]

The bottom line is, like it or not, the media are the main information sources. Television, in particular, is the main source for news for the majority of Americans. If government leaders want to reach out to gain public support, they have no choice but to work with the media. If they fail to do so, they surrender valuable communication channels to their critics. It is for that reason that government officials are major players in shaping the media dialogue. One of the best documented facts about the government-media relationship is that government sources dominate media coverage of government. As writer Walter Karp reports, "The overwhelming majority of stories are based on official sources—on information provided by members of Congress, presidential aides, and politicians."[16] Therefore, the cards are not so stacked against government officials in terms of getting out their messages as some stressed-out spokesperson might think. Nevertheless, good media relationships take a lot of daily attention and can never be taken for granted.

Media Management Strategy

The first step in using the media wisely is to decide on a general strategy. Essentially, there are four options available in designing such a strategy. One is to be *reactive* to the media. A second is to be *active* and create media opportunities on a regular basis. Still another is to use a *combination* of the first two. Finally, one can have no systematic strategy and just "wing it."

There is little to recommend the last option and it should be avoided. Using a combination of active and reactive strategies is usually the best bet because it allows a leader to customize the media strategy to the issue, the situation, and his or her personal style. It also allows some flexibility. At the same time, most successful government public relations practitioners believe that their experience indicates a good, active strategy keeps the media busy and focused on the government leader's agenda. Above all, closing the door and hanging out the "no comment" sign sends the media people to your critics, who are always willing to talk.

Ground Rules for Government-Media Dialogue

Before a leader or spokesman can play the media game, he or she must understand the ground rules. These are part of the American culture defining the nature of government-media relationships and don't apply necessarily to other countries, which have their own rules. It should be stressed that there are different interpretations of the rules in different situations, so the official and the reporter must negotiate and agree on which rules apply to each specific case. This negotiation usually takes place before the interview or news conference, and the decision should be repeated prior to the event to avoid any misunderstanding.

Some news organizations refuse to allow their reporters to attend major briefings where officials do not allow direct attribution. Again, officials should understand that those reporters who refuse to attend have not agreed to follow the rules. These excluded reporters may later interview people who were in the briefing and then report the event using secondhand sources and name the official.

To illustrate how such rules can work, Henry Kissinger, as National Security Advisor and later Secretary of State in the Nixon and Ford administrations, developed the habit of talking to reporters on Air Force One (the President's plane). The rules governing the encounter were that the discussions provided "background," with attribution to a "senior administration official" or "senior White House official." After a while, however, everyone in the government and news business knew who was speaking and some news organizations started directly attributing Kissinger, with the explanation that his use of this rule no longer applied since everyone knew the source anyway.

When government public relations officials engage in dialogue with the press, the ground rules usually take one or more of the following forms:

Embargoed Information   Under this rule, information is provided to the media in advance of the official release time and date to allow reporters to study it. The agreement is that reporters must not publish or air reports until the official release time and date. This rule is used when the information is complex or the volume of information is great. For example, the federal government's enormously complex annual budget document is usually given to reporters on an embargoed basis a day or two before it is officially released. This allows time for reporters to digest the material and write accurate stories and to prepare graphic material.

At present, this rule is used less often than in the past because some less-responsible media organizations have broken the embargo to get their stories out first. Once the embargo is publicly broken, even the more responsible media are likely to go public with the information. This situation is frustrating for officials who see the standards of media conduct driven down to the level of the least responsible reporters or media organizations.

Relatively complex rules govern interview or news briefing situations. These include such agreements as on the record, off the record, background, and deep background. The basic requirements can be summarized as follows:

B O X 31–2

Government leaders and their spokespersons who are successful in their public relations tend to use a media management style based on a clear set of assumptions.

1. It is essential to be a media consumer and understand that there is an important "public dialogue" going on in the press between various public players. It is for this reason that most officials spend their first hour at the office reading the news clips prepared overnight by their public relations staff.

2. An important step is to take some type of media training to sharpen skills in interviewing and message presentation.

3. It is a very good practice to make time available to see media people on a regular basis, even though talking to a reporter is a risk.

4. Remember the dictum that: "practice makes perfect." That is, officials must do their homework before all interviews. Especially valuable are "dirty question and answer" drills, where the public relations staff plays the role of the reporter to lessen risks.

5. Sorting out and recognizing which are the good and bad reporters provides an important edge. Since they see reporters regularly, officials learn to call them by their first names and know whom to trust and whom to avoid.

6. Using meetings with press representatives to "interview the reporter" provides opportunities to get fresh, outsider feedback on how the public dialogue is going. Veteran reporters have a lot of contacts and good political insight; the trick is to get them to share it.

7. Each media organization is different, with particular needs. For example, officials must understand varying media deadlines and that television's requirements are different from those of the print media, and so on. When a public relations officer needs a quick response to meet a media deadline, this leader insight is invaluable.

8. It is essential to view reporters as human beings to whom it is possible to relate in friendly terms. If the reporter feels he or she has a positive working relationship with the official, that individual is more likely to give early warning of a negative story. This gives the official a chance to give his or her side rather than just to react after the story is released to the public.

9. Silence may be "golden" at times—that is, necessary on rare occasions. However, this is not usually appropriate because it gives the critics or others a chance to fill the void.

10. "No comment" is a no-win tactic. This invites the public to interpret the situation as "they're hiding something," or worse, "they're guilty of something." Even so, there will be times when the official can't talk to the media and must tell the reporter, "Sorry, I can't talk now."

11. Competent officials understand the principle that bad news is better released sooner than later.

12. There are times when the government should publicly admit a mistake and get on with business.

13. Above all, never lie to the media. Keep in mind, however, not all sensitive questions need to be answered fully.

On the Record As far as both media reporters and government officials are usually concerned, this is the preferred rule. In this situation the person interviewed or giving the briefing is clearly identified by name and government title or position (e.g., "Secretary of Labor Jones said today . . .")

Off the Record Under this rule, the government source and media reporter talk, but the information is not intented for a specific story. Instead, the information is exchanged to place an issue or event in some "context" for the reporter to understand more fully what happened and why. This rule is usually reserved for situations in which the source and reporter have some sort of long-term working relationship.

Background This is sometimes called the "not-for-direct-attribution" rule. Under these conditions, the government source and media reporter talk, but the source's name and specific title or position are not to be disclosed. Instead, a general attribution is agreed on between the source and reporter. The attribution is then used to indicate the source's general expertise or location in the bureaucracy (e.g., "A State Department official, speaking on condition of anonymity, said today . . ." or "A senior government official, with access to the negotiations, said . . .")

One of the great examples of not-for-direct-attribution was in the July 12, 1994, *The New York Times* story written just after the North Korean leader, Kim Il Sung, died. The story included interviews with diplomats for their views on who the new leader of North Korea would be. Reporter Andrew Pollack wrote, "The four diplomats in Pyongyang, all of whom spoke on the condition that neither they nor their countries be identified, said . . ."[17]

Deep Background Under this type of agreement, the government source and media reporter meet and information is given, which the reporter may use for a story, but only if the source appears with no attribution ("It has been learned that . . ."). For example, Bob Woodward, in his book *The Agenda: Inside the Clinton White House*, used this rule. (This was also the agreement with the famous Deep Throat in the Watergate investigation.) He stated his reason for using this rule with officials in the Clinton case was:

> Nearly all the interviews were conducted on "deep background," which means that I agreed not to identify these sources. Without such a stipulation, people often will not discuss their conversations or interactions with the President or other high-level officials frankly—or at all.[18]

These various rules are somewhat flexible. When the source and media reporter are not sure which rules to use, they may agree to do the interview under one, such as background; then, during or after the interview, certain questions and answers can be negotiated under a different rule, such as on-the-record.

Tactics for Dealing with Leaks

During World War II, posters in places where cargo was loaded on vessels bound for the war zone cautioned, "Loose lips can sink ships." Today, loose lips of unnamed and unauthorized government sources talking to reporters can sink, or at least seriously affect, government policy and planning. Because such leaks of confidential information are a serious problem, government leaders and spokespeople must understand how and why they occur. Moreover, in the words of former American cabinet secretary Harold Brown, officials must ". . . view with some equanimity the inevitability of such leaks." In fact, most seats of government are the "leak capitals" of the nation. Passing on confidential information to unauthorized persons is part of the regular discourse in government. Leaks are inevitable, and a number of observations help place them in perspective:

1. Leaks, in this discussion, are defined as involving both classified or unclassified government information. They include nonclassified but politically sensitive information provided in an unauthorized manner to people without current government authorization for access to the information.

2. It takes at least two people to spring a leak—an inside government source and an outside receiver, usually a reporter.

3. Leaks require an outside transmitter, usually a news media outlet, to publicize the information.

4. Leaks of classified or politically sensitive information are widespread throughout government.

5. Leaks usually feed controversy. Therefore, they benefit the vested interests of the source and sometimes the economic or prestige interests of the news media or other transmitter.

6. Generally occurring around key decision milestones, leaks are timed by sources to influence government decision-making.

7. Leaks from inside a bureaucracy may reflect an internal power struggle that the source has an interest in airing publicly.

8. They may have a multiplier effect, with one leak stimulating another countermeasure leak championing the opposite position.

9. Leaks by their nature highlight the more dramatic aspects of an issue and seldom present a balanced view of a complex issue.

10. Once leaked information is put into the public domain, the future course of the issue is not controlled by anyone. In other words, the person who leaks, or who publicizes the leaks, cannot forecast the final effect of such action. This is often called the "myth of the controlled leak or plant." The effects of neither leaked (unauthorized) nor planted (authorized) information can be orchestrated once in the public domain.

11. Finally, the sources of leaks are almost impossible to track down, and while it may be necessary to seek them, investigations aimed at finding such sources seldom succeed and can actually be counterproductive. The result is usually adding to media coverage and keeping an issue alive.[19]

There are a number of specific tactics that can be used in trying to control damage that results from leaks. The challenge is to reply to a leak on the public record, without causing further classified security problems—or in the case of sensitive information, without further fanning the flames of controversy. These tactics assume that government spokespeople are usually on the defensive or reactive in the case of leaks. If that is indeed the case, the following defensive options are possible:

Refuse to confirm or deny. This is, in effect, a "no comment." While the no comment tactic is generally not advisable, this may be the only option if the information is classified. Some spokespeople view this as a neutral response. However, the net effect from the public's point of view may well be, "There must be some truth to it or they would give a better answer."

Demand a retraction, or write a letter to the editor. It is almost impossible to get a retraction. However, a letter keeps the story alive even though it may not get any action from the media outlet and if it is run, the letter will not be presented in the context of the original story. Also, the timing or placement will not be under the government's control. Overall, however, it beats doing nothing.

Issue a public statement or news release. Usually, this is fighting to catch up after the damage is done. Nonetheless, if aggressively pursued, the effort may change the momentum of the story. Furthermore, it does keep the story going.

Hold a news conference. This involves the same problems as the previous option. However, if one wants to take a strong public rebuttal stand, there is nothing like a leader taking charge, who can change the dynamic from reactive to a more active driving of the story. If truth is on your side, this is the best option, with the government spokesperson face-to-face with reporters.

Give a background interview or provide a counterleak. Most reporters want official on-the-record responses, not more anonymous leaks. However, if the topic is hot and reporters feel they will get new angles, or they're worried that the competition is moving in, they will attend a backgrounder and dutifully report a new leak.

Prepare an "answer for query only." This passive tactic is useless if the right question is not asked. Of course, the spokesperson can tell a reporter, "Why don't you ask the news desk this question?"

Prepare a side-by-side or "questions and answers." This is a written document in which each leaked allegation is taken on, issue-by-issue, with points that are (or are likely to be) raised by reporters and the official comments on each. It can be actively marketed or passively held for answer to query.

Use a third-party surrogate expert. This tactic uses an expert from outside the government or a retired government official who attacks the credibility of the leaked information and/or source. Some believe this is the best option because it can cause reporters and/or editors to worry about the credibility of the information used in a news story and, consequently, about their personal professional reputations among peers.

Preemptive leaking. This tactic best meets the needs of reporters, and it takes preventative maintenance measures against being blind-sided by unauthorized leaks. For example, reporter Stephen Rosenfeld, writing in *The Washington Post*, suggests:

> The best way to balk "damaging leaks" of special-interest material, however, is to make a broad range of material available routinely in a context devised not by special interest but by the government itself. Call it preemptive leaking or public information.[20]

Media Crisis Management

Most of the demanding government media relations work comes when handling nonroutine matters. A crisis comes without much warning and is related to events beyond the control of the public affairs office. The events may be triggered by leaks, by an accident, or by some other unfortunate incident. For example, during the late 1980s and early 1990s, the U.S. Navy was confronted with several very challenging situations related to four major accidents or incidents. These can be summarized as follows.

The USS Stark. On May 17, 1987, this ship was attacked by an Iraqi fighter while on patrol in the Persian Gulf (before the Gulf War). Two Exocet missiles hit the ship and 37 sailors were killed. An investigation followed, and the captain of the ship was forced to retire. The investigation revealed inadequate defensive reactions on his part and questions about his crew's combat-readiness.

The USS Samuel B. Roberts. On April 11, 1988, the ship hit a mine in the Persian Gulf. While no serious injuries occurred, the ship almost sank. The investigation that followed revealed that the captain and the crew had taken all appropriate actions to defend and save the ship.

The USS Iowa. On April 19, 1989, an explosion in a gun turret on this battleship killed 47 sailors. Leaks from the initial Navy investigation caused the family of one of the dead sailors to file suits against the Navy and against NBC-TV. Members of Congress got involved, and under Congressional pressure, the Navy's technical investigation had to be reopened. In 1991, the Navy was forced to apologize to the family of a sailor who was implicated in the original official investigation. This incident and the legal actions were still causing headlines in 1994.

Tailhook. On September 7, 1991, during a convention of naval officers in Las Vegas, more than 30 women were sexually assaulted or abused. A lengthy investigation followed. One of the female aviators who claimed that she had been assaulted went to the media because she felt that the Navy wasn't responsive. Congress stepped in and held up Navy promotion lists to force more effective action. While Navy legal actions against the accused lasted from 1991 through 1993, no accused male naval officers were found guilty. As a result of the Tailhook incident, both the Secretary of the Navy and the Chief of Naval Operations were forced out of office. The female naval officer who went public later resigned, saying that she was unable to stay in the Navy due to harassment from other officers. The headlines continued into 1996.

From experiences with crisis management, the lessons learned can be summed up in the following list of basic do's and don'ts. First, among the "do's"

1. Do protect the legal investigative process.
2. Do protect the privacy rights of individuals and their families.
3. Do have a crisis response and coordination team. This team must have all the important players, such as lawyers, legislative affairs, public affairs, investigative and technical experts.
4. Do have a media training team ready to prepare leaders for each major media event with a full dress rehearsal. A tip here is to use news desk officers to play the role of reporters; since they have been handling the hot inquiries, they know the issues and questions to ask.
5. Do stay cool under fire from the media and critics.
6. Do show respect for people who become critics.
7. Do be prepared for the unexpected.

As to the "don'ts," the list is somewhat shorter and perhaps more obvious:

1. Don't be a party to speculation in the media.
2. Don't deal with hypothetical questions.
3. Don't get emotionally involved in a story.

MAKING MEDIA DECISIONS AT THE SPEED OF TV SATELLITES

In these Navy cases, as in other recent government investigations, the speed at which rumor and stories spread via modern communication systems means the response time for government public relations officials has become more critical. There is little time to think about, not to mention effectively plan, a strategy when there is a media deadline every minute, 24 hours a day, seven days a week.

Government public relations personnel must learn how to deal with the new 1990s factor of decision-time compression driven by worldwide satellite television that presents live views of events to the public 24 hours a day. Former Secretary of Defense Dick Cheney spoke to the American Political Science Association shortly after the Gulf War and stated, "As an administrative official, it's gotten increasingly difficult to sort out what we know from intelligence and what we know from CNN." The fact is that from the White House Situation Room to the Pentagon's National Military Command Center (NMCC) and to every other government command center, CNN is the closely monitored unofficial news source of choice. The government's operational and intelligence worldwide reporting systems often can't keep up with CNN.

It is a fact of life that CNN is playing a larger and larger role in crisis management by government. This medium not only drives the timing of decisions and responses by government, but also it may get inside the government's decision cycle—depending on what is on television. In a crisis or fast-breaking event, CNN is not just a passive reporter, it is a major communication's player. In today's world, leaders learn of the event on satellite TV and they must react via the same medium within minutes.[21]

The problem can only get worse with other new worldwide 24-hour news services, such as Microsoft-NBC (MSNBC) or News Corp.'s Fox News Channel (FNC). We now have television- and Internet-converged news connections that add more pressure on the government's public relations organization. For example CNN's web site is at <http://www.cnn.com>, MSNBC's is at <http://www.msnbc.com>, and Fox News is at <http://www.foxnews.com>.

Satellite television, and CNN in particular, has changed the way governments work. Television pictures from sites such as Somalia and Bosnia-Herzegovina to Haiti, and Rwanda, can shape public opinion. Television can cut through the bureaucratic red tape and move presidents, prime ministers, and legislatures to react quickly to events, which used to be out of sight and mind. Today, government leaders use this new global television medium to conduct diplomatic dialogues, as citizens watch in real time. Government leaders and their spokespeople must be able to respond faster to global audiences. Because of services like CNN, citizens are becoming better informed and are demanding more information- and they want it now!

News correspondent Daniel Schorr has commented on the problem of "instant television" driving both government policy makers and news media agendas. Schorr pointed to the recent statement by Secretary of State Warren Christopher before the Senate Foreign Relations Committee. Christopher said, "Television is a wonderful phenomenon and sometimes even an instrument of freedom. But, television images cannot be the North Star of America's foreign policy." Schorr then commented,

> Who says it can't, because I think it is. I think that our constant lurches in policy don't happen for no reason at all. I think that, long before we reach that thing called "the information highway," we are coming to something called an interactive system of policy formulation. The instantaneity of modern television makes it necessary to formulate policy on the run.[22]

Increasing demands for speed put most democracies at a disadvantage in the war of words and images. Our democratic process is one of bureaucratic coordination aimed at getting consensus on a response. Add the international element of United Nations, NATO or EC coordination, and democratic government officials have a response-time disadvantage when dealing with nongovernment groups such as rebels, terrorists, or dictatorship-style governments. Those who have worked in government crisis management also know that the first television reports suffer the problem of all initial reports: they are single-view snapshots. At best, they are usually incomplete and at worst, wrong.

So what does a government information service do? It must, as the military did during the war in the Gulf, adjust to the changing global information environment. The government unit must reengineer the public information process and set up new interactive channels of communication to meet changing public information demands. Special crisis information telephone hotlines and computer networks may have to be established. Obviously, information technology will be a big player as government seeks to provide better information services to its customers in the future.

LOOKING TO THE FUTURE

What will be the nature and function of government public relations in the years ahead? This is an especially important question considering the changes now coming about in the emerging digital information age. Bill Gates, the chairman and CEO of Microsoft Corporation, defines the information age as a time when, "People should have easy access to information of any type, for use in business, information, entertainment or education. Anywhere they go, they should find that easy to do."[23]

Government Public Relations in the Information Age

For the government public relations officer, in many ways that time is already here. With global satellite television and computer networks, many new electronic and print media options reach out to targeted publics. The questions is not, "will we use the old or new media?" It is, "which combination of the growing media channels will we use to reach our target audiences?" The government is now, and increasingly will be, a participant in the world of interactive multimedia. Moreover, audiences will become more fragmented in the 500-channel universe. Thus, the government public relations officer, who had his or her hands full with traditional news media or public inquiries, will now face a growing stack of electronic mail (E-mail) inquiries. The U.S. Congress and executive branch are using Internet World Wide Web sites, like the U.S. Congressional "Thomas" site <http://thomas.loc.gov/> or the White House site <http://www.whitehouse.gov>, as new public relations tools.[24]

The January 17, 1994, issue of *Newsweek,* included an article titled "A Post-Modern President" that raised the question: "How does one establish authority—how does one lead now, given the false sense of intimacy and the very real cynicism that seem natural byproducts of the information age?" The article then focused on President Clinton, saying,

> ... more importantly, Clinton intuitively understands how to send a message in the information age. ... He knew that communication was now two-way, interactive (there is, in fact, a school of marketing experts that believes the era of one-way communication—of old-fashioned advertising—is over; people are now too sophisticated to simply be told to buy).[25]

The thrust of the article was that citizens as information consumers are going to be more in control, or at least active participants in the future government communication process. Thus, technology is empowering citizens in new ways and the government information playing field is getting more complex and time sensitive.

Even the traditional news media are beginning to establish new interactive media partnerships. The media have really begun to listen and give their audiences an interactive voice beyond the letters to the editor or editorial spaces. Consider the following factors:

First, CNN has gone interactive. The company joined forces with CompuServe, the on-line computer service. CNN selected CompuServe as its on-line service for the program "Talk Back Live," which first went on the air on August 23, 1994. The interactive program is broadcast weekdays from 1 to 2 P.M., and the live studio audience discusses the topic of the day with a host. The at-home audience can interact "live" via telephone or with a computer by using CompuServe. CNN also has its Interactive Internet web site <http://www.cnn.com>.[26]

Second, traditional television station news operations are establishing public feedback centers where citizens can talk to reporters via fax and electronic mail. As a regular feature, an issue is raised on a local newscast or national network news magazine program and before the program is over, people are asked to call a telephone number to get almost immediate (and nonscientific) public opinion feedback.

A third factor is that new traditional media partnerships are forming. An example is "The People's Voice," a public opinion project in Boston where three media outlets, *The Boston Globe*, WABU-TV, and WBUR-FM (NPR), coordinated efforts, bringing in citizen focus groups to comment on issues of the day, including election issues for statewide elections.

Fourth, old and new media partnerships are forming such as *The Boston Globe* and New England Cable News (NECN) to allow people to have access to the *Globe* reporters during the day, when stories are being written. In effect, the *Globe* is using cable television to interact with reporters and "leak" what's going to be in the next morning's newspaper. *The Boston Globe* also uses its Internet web site <http://www.boston.com> to interact with the public.

Finally, through the Internet citizens are able to access more government information including news releases and other documents at the same time reporters get such access, or even before. For example, the Massachusetts Internet "Access to Government Network" web site is <http://www.magnet.state.ma.us> and the City of Boston's web site is <http://www.ci.boston.ma.us/>. Also, citizens can watch government live on C-SPAN, CNN, or other public affairs cable channels. We have gone from interpersonal (two-way) communication to mass media (one-way) communication to the new electro-personal (interactive) communication. These types of interactive changes are why Vice President Gore's attempt to "reinvent the government" and provide better citizen access to services via the electronic information superhighway makes good common sense.

As they face these changes, government leaders and public relations officers must decide how to change their relationship with their publics. Given the fact that control of government information will be less in the hands of a few leaders or information officers and more in the faces and at the fingertips of citizen users, everyone will have to learn to deal with this fast-changing situation.

Citizens' Sources of Information

Using existing technology, how do citizens get information about their government? Looking at citizen electronic information capabilities we see some interesting facts, as of November 1996:

1. About 40 percent of U.S. households own personal computers and 20 percent of those have modems for on-line services. (If they have modems and an Internet access provider, they can have Internet connections.)

2. Among U.S households, 94 percent have telephone service (which means that when the telephone companies get into the cable TV and information highway business, most homes are ready to go).

3. Among U.S. households, 96 percent have television sets (which means when digital set-top boxes are available—these homes can have surf the Internet using web-TV).

4. Again, among those TV households, 65 percent subscribe to cable television and 97 percent already have the technical capabilities to be cable-connected.

It seems clear that television will remain as the citizen's main information and entertainment center over the next decade. However, the TV set is likely to change greatly. Raymond W. Smith, chairman and CEO of Bell Atlantic Network Services, described this change, saying,

> . . . the three basic communications appliances in the American home—the telephone, the television, and the personal computer—are merging into one, technically and corporately. . . . I use the word "convergence"—easily the most dreaded term in the communications lexicon since "infrastructure." . . . Before this industry transformation is through, your computer will speak, your TV will listen, and your telephone will show you pictures.[27]

Additional insights into what lies ahead for government can be seen by looking at what has happened in the business world. Blayne Cutler defines electronic digital networks as the "fifth medium," stating,

> . . . consider the fact that digitalization has completely changed the way Americans do business. And it's about to change the way we communicate. . . . The four pillars of modern communication media have been radio, television, newspapers, and magazines. The emergence of on-line interactive information and entertainment will give us a fifth pillar—a fifth medium.[28]

What are the implications of these convergences for government public relations officers? They pose a number of strategic elements that must be considered. A U.S. government report listed seven key strategic elements to be considered when planning electronic delivery of government information and services in the years ahead.[29]

1. Grassroots involvement of local citizens and recipients of services.

2. Community infrastructure development involving schools, libraries, community centers, town halls, and local agencies involved in training, education, and implementation.

3. Encouragement of innovation by government employees, clients, and other participants.

4. Creation of electronic directories of government agency services.

5. Creation of new electronic delivery ideas—matching electronic opportunities with government agency missions.

6. Strategic partnering involving: federal, state, local, voluntary, not-for-profit, philanthropic, and commercial companies.

7. Preoperational testing of electronic systems, with attention to consumer evaluation and policy development.

T A B L E 31–1

Strategies for Government Public Relations Planning

Area	Old Way	Future Way
Strategy creation	A few senior officials	Team effort with citizen input
Key players	Insiders	Public customers
Audience size	National	Global
Audience makeup	Undifferentiated	Niche-fragmented
Transmitting media	Mass (one way)	Converged and interactive
Public access to government information	Limited, with gatekeepers	More open and interactive

In the final analysis, it remains an open question as to how government will respond to the information age. But one thing is clear: incentives must be provided to encourage both government employees and the public to use the new information technologies. What is unclear at this point is whether the push of technology or the pull of consumer demand will control the final outcome of how the government will be reinvented to provide better electronic information services. If history is any guide, the most likely outcome will be some pattern of trade-offs between what technology can provide, what the government can afford, and what citizen-consumers demand. A guiding principle will be that, unlike the traditional media age of one-way communication (government to media to public), the public has now gained a real-time interactive voice (public to government, government to public). The old gatekeepers in the media and government are losing power and this is not a time to do government business as usual.

In looking ahead for ways to plan new government public relations services, the relationships summarized in Table 31–1 provide a point of departure:

In developing plans for new strategies based on the future interactive multimedia market-place, keep in mind four prime providers whose roles must be considered: the providers of *content, hardware, software*, and *network services*. Sometimes, new mergers or partnerships blur these lines. For example, Microsoft (software) teamed up with NBC (content) to form MSNBC cable TV. In the United States, the government has been in the network provider business, but that area has shifted to the private sector as the government reinvents itself.

In the future, the government will provide content to the information superhighway. In 1996, the Internet's 3 million host servers provided information to an estimated 45 million people worldwide.

In addition, government public relations planners must look at new information-sharing partnerships with private and public networks. All over the world groups are working on publicly accessible computer networks for their communities. Some are so-called Free-nets, such as the Cleveland Free-net, which is an electronic city. Another is the Pen System in Santa Monica, which aims to "increase public participation in city government and politics." At a broader level, there is a National Public Telecomputing Network, which in July 1994 represented 38 Free-nets operating in 41 states and 8 countries. In addition, 116 formal organizing committees are involved in creating local Free-nets.

T A B L E   31–2

Numbers of On-Line Subscribers (Nov. 1996)

On-Line Services	Owners	Subscribers (in millions)
1. America Online	Independent	7,000,000
2. CompuServe	H&R Block	5,300,000
3. Prodigy	IBM & Sears	1,500,000
4. Microsoft (MSN)	Microsoft	1,500,000

Source: Company spokespersons.

Some U.S. government agencies have become information partners with the growing number of commercial computer on-line services such as Prodigy, CompuServe, and America Online. Other agencies have gone directly on the Internet. It is estimated these American on-line services, which had about 15 million subscribers in 1996 will continue to grow. The main future challenge in this on-line network provider industry, according to market research analyst Lisa Johnson, is the race for content. According to Johnson, "The different services are now challenging themselves to come up with creative ways to present information and find sources of information."[30] That should sound like an open invitation to government information providers to find new creative ways of getting government information on-line, at very little cost.

Typically, commercial on-line or Internet access providers charge the public a monthly fee of $19.95. In 1996, the top four American commercial on-line services and subscribers were ranked as shown in Table 31-2.

In general, government leaders and public relations officers must adapt their communications strategies and tactics to the new ways of the electronic information marketplace. Changes can and must be made. People working together within and outside government can make sure that the vital flow of accurate and timely information continues to flow in the future.

Already, many government information services are connected to the new electronic information channels that are available worldwide via the Internet. However, in terms of audience size, the commercial on-line services are still relatively small. Doug Houston, chairman of Houston, Effler & Partners, one of the top business advertising agencies in the United States, when asked for his evaluation of the new media-on-line services said:

> If you're looking for a small, well-defined target (audience), the on-line services are pretty terrific. But right now most of our businesses need reach: we want to reach a lot of people, fast. And the on-line services haven't gotten to the point where you can do that. Everyone's watching them, but their time hasn't really come. The big question is: How will they get these services in the hands of a lot of people, not just the computer literates who have laptop computers on their desks?[31]

Electronic means will be the fastest and most economical ways for government to be interactive with citizen customers. Internet, cable television, telephone, and new "wireless" companies are converging on the television set as the central home information and entertainment center. While there are literally dozens of U.S. Government agencies that currently use electronic information channels, these four provide examples of direct interactive contact:

1. Internal Revenue Service (IRS) tax filing and refunds.
2. Department of Agriculture (USDA) Food and Nutrition Service is using electronic benefits transfer for food stamp and WIC (women, infants, and children) recipients.
3. Department of Veteran Affairs (VA) is using electronic kiosks for service delivery.
4. National Science Foundation (NSF) is using pilot electronic program for filing of grant proposals.

Additional Channels for Disseminating Information to Citizens

In addition to the on-line services, there is a wide variety of additional channels that can be utilized by government public affairs offices as media to disseminate government information. These include:

Electronic Bulletin Boards (BBS)   These involve not only government-provided networks, but partnerships with universities and commercial on-line services and networks. For example, the Navy Office of Information has a Navy internal weekly news product (NAVNEWS). The Navy approached a commercial on-line service and got their product, at no additional cost, to be on the commercial service, because the service was looking for quality content. Another example is the government-run BBS and web site FedWorld http://www.fedworld.gov/. Since 1993, the National Technical Information Service (NTIS) has run FedWorld with access to about 100 government BBS.

Journalists are some of the main users of such government electronic information and databases. Computer-assisted reporting is becoming a new specialty. Journalism professional publications, such as the July/August 1994 *Quill* magazine, carry articles on how to navigate the Internet, including: "Beltway access without a bureau: Internet puts government documents in easy reach," "Database dangers," or "Cyberspace in print."[32]

CD-ROMs   Increasingly, government public affairs staffs are looking at how a CD-ROM (read-only memory) product might be used in their particular operations. One CD-ROM disk can store over five billion bits of data, the equivalent of an encyclopedia. This is especially valuable as a means of providing public access to long government documents.

Interactive Multimedia   With new and cheaper software, interactive multimedia products are becoming more feasible. The term multimedia means a digital product in which you can combine the elements of text, sound, computer graphics, photography, and video. These methods of communicating can convey rich combinations of information.

Electronic Kiosks   Kiosks are much like a bank's ATM facility but may include interactive multimedia options. Some governments such as the State of California have used electronic kiosks to provide government services and information. This pilot program indicates 60 percent of the clients used the kiosks after normal business hours.

E-mail   This increasingly popular medium has many practical uses. Those government offices or agencies that have BBSs often have an electronic-mail option. While e-mail has long been an internal information medium in government, as it grows in the public arena external citizen customers, including journalists, will increasingly place their inquiries via this technology. Therefore, public affairs offices need to be able to respond quickly and effectively to such inquiries. One public affairs officer is working on issue papers via e-mail. The concept is to have a file on a BBS that includes a brief statement on an issue and the department's communication points for public access via computer.

On-Line Computer Conferences On January 13, 1994, history was made when the first White House on-line conference was held by Vice President Al Gore. It was broadcast by C-SPAN television and the electronic "hosts" were U.S News Online (an on-line service of *U.S. News & World Report* magazine) and CompuServe. It is not hard to imagine an on-line desktop video conference in the future.

Intranet Some government agencies are using Internet world wide web software to run internal agency computer networks called Intranets. These Intranets can be used to track issues, assign tasks, and disseminate internal information in multimedia formats.

Generally, then, in looking to the future, government public relations officers, like their private business colleagues, must understand, adopt, and use the rich technology that the information age provides for their operations and functions. Specifically, they must be willing to exploit every technology that presents a viable opportunity to interact with the citizens that they serve to provide a free flow of information.

As Lawrence Grossman, the former President of NBC News and former President of the Public Broadcasting System (PBS) said in his 1995 book, *The Electronic Republic,*

> This is the first generation of citizens who can see, hear, and judge their own political leaders simultaneously and instantaneously. It is also the first generation of political leaders who can address the entire population and receive instant feedback about what people think and want. Interactive telecommunication increasingly give ordinary citizens immediate access to the major political decisions that affect their lives and property.[33]

So, we must remember that it is people who are driving faster on the information superhighway and the public affairs officer better get up to speed with them, or get out of the way.

E N D N O T E S

1. In government offices the terms *public relations* and *public affairs* are used to describe the same function.

2. Stephen Hess, *The Government/Press Connection* (Washington, D.C.: Brookings Institution, 1985), p. xiii.

3. Thomas E. Patterson, "Legitimate Beef—The Presidency and a Carnivorous Press," *Media Studies Journal*, 8, no. 2, Spring 1994, p. 23.

4. Ibid., pp. 25–26.

5. Robin Tower, "For Majority Leader, A Quest for Health Care Consensus," *The New York Times*, July 18, 1994, p. A1.

6. Matthew L. Wald, "Energy Chief Expresses Chagrin Over Monitoring Reporters, and editorial, "Energy's Friends and Enemies List," *The New York Times*, Nov 11, 1995, pp. 9 and 22.

7. J. W. Fulbright, *The Pentagon Propaganda Machine* (New York: Liveright, 1970), pp. 21–22.

8. See 38, Part I, U.S. Stat. 212.

9. William D. Montabond, "British Beef Crisis: A Menue for Despair," *Los Angeles Times*, March 31, 1996, p. A1.

10. See U.S. Office of Personnel Management, "Occupations of Federal White-Collar and Blue-Collar Workers Federal Civilian Workforce Statistics as of September 30, 1993," which indicates 4,438 public affairs specialists and 1,940 writers and editors in federal civil service, for a total of 6,378. In addition, the Defense Department's military departments have 3,261 uniformed active duty public affairs officers, and enlisted public affairs specialists, as follows: Army: 47/735; Navy 200/714; Air Force 350/786 and Marine Corps 89/340, as reported by the Directorate of Defense Information on July 25, 1994. In the Transportation Department, the Coast Guard has an additional 91 uniformed enlisted public affairs specialists. So, not counting other administrative support staff, the uniformed public affairs staff totals 3,352. Exact totals are 6,378 civilians and 3,352 uniformed for a federal government reported total public affairs staff of 9,730. The amount of federal funds spent on the public affairs function is almost impossible to find, since many costs are buried in administrative costs. The $1 billion figure is the author's best estimate after talking to officials in the Office of Management and Budget (OMB).

11. These descriptions of public affairs responsibilities are typical for a secretary in an executive department of the U.S. government.

12. The public affairs titles in the U.S. government, by department are as follows:
Assistant Secretary for Public Affairs (for)*
   Health and Human Services
   Housing and Urban Development
   Labor
   State
   Treasury (and Public Liaison)
   Veterans Affairs (and Intergovermental Affairs)

Assistant to the Secretary for Public Affairs (for)†
   Defense
   Transportation
Director of Public Affairs (for)‡
   Agriculture
   Commerce
   Education
   EnergyR   Interior (External Affairs)
   Justice (Information and Privacy)

*political appointee positions, subject to Senate confirmation.
†Usually a political appointee, not subject to Senate confirmation.
‡Usually the directors are career public affairs people.

13. ABC News, "Nightline," February 15, 1993.

14. Bob Woodward, *The Agenda: Inside the Clinton White House* (New York: Simon and Schuster, 1994), p. 254.

15. Melvin Mencher, *News Reporting and Writing* (Madison: Brown and Benchmark, 1994), p. 486.

16. Walter Karp, "All the Congressmen's Men: How Capital Hill Controls the Press," *State of the Art: Issues in Contemporary Mass Communication* (New York: St. Martins Press, 1992), p. 109.

17. Andrew Pollack, "North Korea's Heir Apparent Meets Foreign Diplomats," *The New York Times*, July 12, 1994, p. A3.

18. Woodward, op. cit., p. 12.

19. Brent Baker, "Leakology: The War of Words," U.S. Naval Institute *Proceedings,* Vol. 103/7/893, July 1977, pp. 43–49.

20. Quoted in ibid., p. 49.

21. Brent Baker, "Decisions at the Speed of TV Satellites," *Vital Speeches of the Day,* Vol. 58, no. 19, July 15, 1992, pp. 581–583.

22. Daniel Schorr, "The Theodore H. White Lecture," John F. Kennedy School of Government, Harvard University, Cambridge, MA, November 18, 1993, p. 17.

23. Bill Gates, "The Business and Social Impact of the Electronic Highway," Remarks to the Commonwealth Club of California, San Francisco, CA, October 21, 1993.

24. See Chris Casey, *The Hill On The Net* (New York: Academic Press, 1996) for a history of how members of the U.S. Congress used new technology to reach their audiences.

25. "A Postmodern President," *Newsweek,* January 17, 1994, p. 19.

26. "Plugged In, Technically Speaking," *The Boston Globe,* July 15, 1994, p. 59.

27. Raymond W. Smith, "The Cable and Television Industries In Transition," Los Angeles, CA, December 2, 1993.

28. Blayne Cuter, "The Fifth Medium," *State of the Art Issues in Contemporary Mass Communication* (New York: St. Martins Press, 1992), p. 399.

29. U.S. Congress, Office of Technology Assessment, "Electronic Delivery of Federal Services Report," November 4, 1993, Chapters 2 and 12.

30. Peter H. Lewis, "A Boom for On-line Services," *The New York Times,* July 12, 1994, pp. D1, D14.

31. D. C. Denison, "The Interview," *The Boston Globe,* July 17, 1994, p. 10.

32. See articles in *Quill,* The Magazine for Journalists, July/August 1994, pp. 35–40.

33. Larry K. Grossman, *The Electronic Republic* (New York: Viking Penguin, 1995), p. 4.

Public Relations and Communications for Nonprofit Organizations

Ray Boyer
Associate Vice President, Communications
The John D. and Catherine T. MacArthur Foundation

A STRATEGIC APPROACH

Use of Public Relations and Communications in the Nonprofit Sector

Every organization, whether it realizes it or not, is actively engaged in communications and public relations activities. From the simplest phone call to the most complex presentation, each such contact conveys a message about the organization and its work. Regardless of their position, staff members answering simple questions over the phone are delivering a message about the organization just as surely as the executive director in a formal speech. And there are many more phone calls than speeches.

It would be fairly straightforward to discuss the function of a communications office within a nonprofit organization, but it would be less than useful for two reasons. First, of course, it is perfectly likely that a typical nonprofit group will not have a communications staff. Second, even for those that do, it is important that communications and public relations be considered from an integrated and organizationwide perspective, not as a function that can be neatly sliced off from others.

It is through the process of communications and public relations that an organization systematically identifies the audiences for its various messages and ensures those messages are conveyed and reinforced in an effective way. Communications is integral to an organization's strategic plan and deserves special focus.

For nonprofit groups, there are very useful and inexpensive approaches to this work that can, if designed and implemented wisely, tend to communications issues at every level of the organization.

The Nonprofit Sector

The nonprofit sector of the United States economy includes more than 1.1 million organizations, with an estimated 45,000 new ones established each year. Statistics published by

Independent Sector, the organization representing the entire cross section of philanthropic and nonprofit organizations in the United States, indicate that such groups make up about 4.2 percent of all institutions in the country, employing 6.7 percent of the nation's workforce.[1]

Included under the nonprofit umbrella are many organizations that look and act very much like for-profit businesses. Products are designed and sold. Profits are kept. In very general terms, the main difference in qualifying for nonprofit status, and the tax exemption that goes with it, is that the money raised must be used to advance the mission of the organization, not to enrich its owners. And they must serve a qualifying public service.

While organizations that look and act like traditional for-profit firms, complete with healthy balance sheets from businesslike operations, may find useful guidance in this chapter, they are more likely to find their best guide to public relations and communications strategies in other chapters of this book. Under discussion here will be strategies for nonprofit organizations that are (1) heavily dependent on fund-raising activities for support and (2) typically local or regional in the scope of their work. Annual operating budgets for such groups tend to be from a few hundred thousand dollars to the low millions per year. Salaries are modest and money tight.

Even in this smaller arena, according to Independent Sector, there are approximately 700,000 organizations in the United States. Missions vary widely. There are groups, for example, that provide direct services, while others focus on issues with an emphasis on finding solutions to social problems. Many are advocates for action around various issues. It is such a complex web of activity that Independent Sector, working with a national sampling of tax returns from nonprofit organizations, developed a classification system that is broken down into 10 major categories and 26 major groups. It is a very busy corner of the economy.

KEY AUDIENCES FOR NONPROFIT ORGANIZATIONS

The discussion of communications and public relations for nonprofit organizations can, in general, be considered in terms of two primary sets of audiences.

The first, of course, is composed of those on the receiving end of the nonprofit's work. If it is a service provider, it is those who would receive the service; if an advocacy group, those the organization is attempting to influence.

The second is communications geared toward the people and institutions providing the money and other forms of support a nonprofit organization needs to do its work. There is a very straight line between the amount of money an organization has and the scope of its work. Assuming wise management, more money translates directly into more good work being done. Properly carried out, effective communications strategies can translate into greater financial support just as surely as product advertising translates into increased sales.

Determining the audiences linked to the work of a nonprofit organization is a key component of a communications planning exercise that will be discussed in detail in the "Tactics" section of this chapter. The first step of that exercise is a listing of audiences, followed by a determination of messages appropriate for each and the techniques that might be employed to reach them. While the communications task of a nonprofit organization can be roughly broken down into the two large sets of audiences, there will, of course, be considerable overlap between them.

TRENDS AND DEVELOPMENTS THAT HAVE SHAPED THE NONPROFIT SECTOR IN THE UNITED STATES AND INTERNATIONALLY

The nature of nonprofit organizations varies considerably from nation to nation and culture to culture. From the very earliest days of the United States there has been a tradition of voluntarism that evolved into the nonprofit sector of today. Lester Salamon of the Johns Hopkins University Institute for Policy Studies, has traced the history of nonprofit groups.[2] He notes that in the early days of the nation, despite a great spirit of self-reliance, the colonists formed voluntary associations to provide services that the government could not. As the nation grew, the number and importance of the nonprofit groups grew as well. For a variety of reasons, following the Civil War and continuing through the Depression, the link between nonprofits and the government grew considerably, despite efforts to downplay this relationship for political reasons. During the Great Society era of the 1960s and 1970s, however, this partnership between government and the nonprofit sector grew massively, as the federal government entered the human service field in a major way with the resources necessary to effectively address people's needs, while relying on the nonprofit sector to do the work. Salamon writes that by the late 1970s, "nonprofit organizations were delivering a larger share of government-financed human services than all levels of government combined . . . "

In other nations, the development of the nonprofit sector has followed many different paths. Salamon and his colleagues have found that nonprofit, nongovernmental organizations are present in virtually every country, and their presence has recently been expanding significantly.

International links among nongovernmental organizations attracted considerable notice in the early 1990s because of their impact on the course of major conferences organized by the United Nations in Rio de Janiero (on the environment), Cairo (on the family), and Beijing (on women). Each was marked by a major gathering of international NGOs. Of particular note were the communications techniques employed to mobilize groups from many different nations. International organizing by the NGOs included such traditional means as travel grants and support for publications. But the remarkable success of the NGO gatherings at the United Nations meetings also can be traced, in large part, to the creative use of electronic communications, primarily fax technology, and Internet-based E-mail. As the new technologies become more widely available, national borders will be even less formidable barriers to communications.

KEY INFLUENCES ON THE PRACTICE OF COMMUNICATIONS AND PUBLIC RELATIONS IN THE NONPROFIT SECTOR

Because the nonprofit sector is defined by legislation, there are many rules and regulations governing the work of these organizations. There are clear limits, for example, on the extent to which nonprofits that receive federal funding can engage in lobbying activities. Philanthropic foundations are forbidden to engage in any lobbying activities at all unless it is directly related to the rules governing their operations.

There is, however, one unchanging fact of life confronting virtually all nonprofit organizations: There is never enough money. Reading the annual budget of most nonprofits is a visit to the world of tradeoffs. Choosing one course of action invariably comes at the expense of other work the group would like to do. It is the rare nonprofit manager who can sit back at the end of the day and reflect on how the financial statements never looked better. It is small wonder then that such organizations have traditionally put concern about communications and public relations well down on the list of priorities. With so much that needs to be done, the argument goes, how can one possibly spend scarce resources on self-promotion?

The answer, of course, lies in one's perspective. If viewed as the need to hire a new staff member, retain public relations counsel, or engage in a stream of attention-grabbing special events to hype the organization, building such capacity could easily (and rightly) be seen as a frill. By adopting the perspective that communications and public relations are critical to carrying out the mission of a nonprofit organization and a powerful tool in fund raising, it becomes too important to ignore.

THE RELATIONSHIP OF PUBLIC RELATIONS AND COMMUNICATIONS TO THE ORGANIZATIONAL MISSION AND GOALS OF A NONPROFIT GROUP

When nonprofit organizations approach foundations for financial support, it is unusual to see a request for communications support included. There is frequently a perception both on the part of the groups doing the asking and the groups doing the giving that communications is an add-on, something that can be done when the time is right—if there is something to communicate. The director of a nonprofit group in Chicago described it as "feeling like there are only so many things you can ask of the tooth fairy. You don't want to spend your wish on public relations when there are so many other needs."

The good news in this scenario is that funders are increasingly recognizing the importance of communications in the efforts of those they support. A decade ago, for example, it was only the very largest foundations that had communications specialists as staff members. At the urging of veterans in the field such as Frank Karel, vice president for communications of the Robert Wood Johnson Foundation, the Council on Foundations established an affinity group called the Communications Network in Philanthropy, which currently has almost 200 members. The Robert Wood Johnson Foundation spends $15 to $19 million per year on communications activities in support of the projects it funds. An analysis of the John D. and Catherine T. MacArthur Foundation's 1994 grantmaking indicates that approximately $15 million of its $140 million in grantmaking that year was either expressly for communications activities or for the communications aspects of individual projects.

THE LINK WITH MARKETING

Nonprofit organizations rarely use the term *marketing* in discussing their work, but it does not take much of a conceptual shift to think of the two main areas in which communications and public relations is key—fund raising and service delivery—as marketing efforts. For nonprofit groups, in the absence of advertising budgets, communications and public relations strategies that can be carried out at low or no cost take on special significance.

The link between money and message is a blunt one. With lots of money, it is possible to buy a great deal of awareness of an issue by the public. Consider, for example, the Paramount Pictures movie *Congo*. *The Wall Street Journal* noted that the film was launched with approximately $97 million worth of advertising, publicity, and product tie-ins, an amount that is roughly one-third the annual grant-making budget of the Ford Foundation, the largest philanthropic foundation in the United States.[3] It is tempting to think about the impact advertising budgets approaching $100 million could have on attitudes about issues such as war, peace, racism, and poverty. But that is not the way society has arranged itself, so the nonprofit sector uses strategies that make the greatest possible use of "free media," with very little spent on paid advertising.

INTERNATIONAL CONSIDERATIONS

For U.S.-based organizations doing communications and public relations work in other cultures, it is very important to exercise caution. The worldwide reach of media organizations such as CNN may lead one to think that communications strategies are cross-cultural. They are not. A safe rule of thumb is to simply assume that each time borders are crossed, the rules of the game change. The ways in which public relations people work with newspaper reporters in Mexico, for example, is significantly different from customary techniques in the United States. Asian media climates are vastly different from those of the United States, and in the former Soviet Union many of the rules are written as one goes along.

Along with the importance of understanding and being sensitive to different cultures, it is important, in many nations of the world, to consider security issues as well. If there is even the slightest question about whether calling public attention to a person or organization can lead to physical danger, it is obviously best to err on the side of caution. Communications tools as basic as press releases should not be used unless there is complete confidence that the information in the release is safe for all concerned.

Nonetheless, it is still perfectly possible to do effective communications and public relations work in other nations. A useful step for first-timers is to seek guidance from colleagues or people in organizations already engaged in communications activities within that culture. A great deal of useful information about customary practices and fees can be quickly gathered from a trusted person with firsthand experience. In seeking such advice or in moving to the stage of implementing a communications strategy, it is important to keep values in mind. There may be significant differences in the way this work is done from country to country, but if the approach that is recommended doesn't feel comfortable, it is probably best to avoid it.

It would be impossible to discuss international issues in public relations and communications without mentioning the transforming nature of fax technology, the Internet, Internet-based E-mail, and cell phones on the field. The combined impact of the new technologies on the nonprofit field has been enormous and is growing fast.

An organization named E-Law, for example, with headquarters in Eugene, Oregon, uses Internet-based E-mail links provided through the Institute for Global Communications in San Francisco to connect lawyers throughout the world who work through their nations' legal systems to protect and improve the environment.[4] Legal information and documents that might have taken weeks or longer to make their way around the globe now arrive in minutes. The role of fax and the Internet in providing alternative sources of information about events in the former Soviet Union as the Iron Curtain was collapsing are well known. There were memorable stories during the Gulf War of people keeping in touch with relatives in Kuwait City by cell phone long after official communications were cut off.

Nonprofit organizations throughout the world are finding that they can seek out people and organizations doing similar work and engage in electronic conversations in ways that were simply not possible just a few years ago. What it adds up to is the simple observation that any communications or public relations planning should include strategies for using electronic technology. It is cheap and ever-more-widely accessible.

RULES OF THUMB FOR BUDGETING

As with so many aspects of nonprofit management, it is safe to assume that work in communications or public relations will be done with an eye on keeping costs as low as possible. This generally means minimal advertising budgets, less than glossy publications, the least expensive ways to use the mail, and so on right down the line. Given these constraints, it might be useful to review several considerations that can have an impact on the cost of communications efforts.

Design and Printing Costs   Printing is a highly competitive industry that has been dramatically altered in recent years by computerized design and layout technology. There can be enormous variations in the cost of these services. The advice of colleagues can be invaluable and the importance of competitive bids cannot be overstated.

Consultants   A great deal of valuable information and guidance can be provided by consultants. It is important to have a clear agreement with them about the budget and who covers expenses. It is equally important to have a clear understanding of the task the consultant is asked to do. It should be the organization that drives the consultant, not the other way around.

Freelance Writers   Most freelancers charge by the hour. It is virtually impossible, however, to arrive at a precise number of hours and unwise to simply leave the meter running. It is best to arrive at an overall estimate for a job based on a reasonable estimate of the time involved. Partial payments at the beginning, middle, and end of a project are a good practice, as is agreement on procedures for cancelling a project.

Public Relations Firms   Such firms can be invaluable in carrying out a communications or public relations strategy. They can also be expensive. It is possible, however, to find high quality counsel for affordable prices. As with consultants, it is important to have a clear vision of what is to be accomplished. It can be expensive, and frequently unsatisfying, to depend on a firm to provide vision as well as follow-through. Again, advice from experienced colleagues can be invaluable. In some cities there are nonprofit organizations that provide low-cost communications services. Examples include the Community Media Workshop[5] in Chicago, and the Communications Consortium[6] in Washington, D.C. Also, it may well be worth checking the journalism or communications programs at local colleges or universities as possible sources of help.

Volunteers Excellent counsel can be provided by volunteers serving on boards and committees. Remember that while such advice might be free, the cost of those recommendations may have a very real price tag.

A FEW SUGGESTIONS FOR THE PURCHASE OF PRODUCTS OR SERVICES

It is difficult to state in general what communications services should cost, but it would be quite easy to establish what the nonprofit sector is paying in any one city or region. There will generally be a local group of nonprofit organizations, and those doing the most effective work in communications and public relations can usually be easily identified. People working in the nonprofit sector are, in general, more than willing to share information about resources and expenses. Remember, it is possible to spend a great deal of money and get terrible results. It is equally possible to develop creative, low-cost strategies that will have a substantial impact.

TACTICS

THE COMMUNICATIONS PLAN

There is a tendency to think of communications as an episodic activity carried out through the media. In simplest terms, this means calling a press conference to make an announcement, harvesting a few inches of newspaper space or a moment on the nightly news and feeling like the work has been done. In this scenario, a public relations firm might be hired to work on the project and there will be a lot of activity for a short period of time. The project will end and a quiet status quo returns. It probably cost a lot of money, and that might prompt a diligent board member to wonder out loud if the short burst of media exposure was worth the time and expense.

The key to gaining acceptance of a communications and public relations strategy, both within an organization and by external funders, is to be clear on the ways in which the work will be done and the ways in which communications supports other priorities of the organization.

Such a plan should lay out:

- Each of the audiences for information about the organization and its work.
- What the organization wants each of those audiences to understand—its messages.
- Strategies for delivering those messages.

This communications planning model can be applied to the communications objectives of an entire organization or implemented when a very specific project is under discussion. It provides an excellent framework for thinking about multiple audiences, the ways in which they overlap, and the ways in which specific messages can reach them from multiple sources.

The Communications Grid

A useful and practical approach to developing a communications plan is to set up a communications grid composed of audiences, messages tailored for each audience, and strategies for delivering the messages. The exercise of building the grid lends itself well to a moderated group discussion. The leader need not be a communications professional, just the person within the organization whose job most logically includes concern for such matters. For tens of thousands of small nonprofit organizations this usually means the executive director.

Audiences

Those who develop an organization's communications grid should first identify each of the main audiences important to the group. For a nonprofit organization, this list would typically include two large subcategories: (1) those critical to fund-raising efforts such as foundations, individual donors, and governmental agencies; and (2) those who are the object of the main work of the organization such as those who might receive the group's services, local and state politicians, policymakers, and the general public.

Typical audiences for the work of nonprofit organizations might include:

- The staff of the organization.
- The organization board.
- The people and groups served by the organization.
- The people or groups whose attitudes or behavior the group would like to influence.
- Other organizations doing similar work.
- State and local politicians.
- The general public.
- The media.

The Johns Hopkins School of Public Health, in an issue of its publication *Population Reports,* devoted to media strategies, notes five general stages people go through as they are exposed to new information about an idea or issue: knowledge, persuasion, decision, action, and confirmation and advocacy.[7] Messages should be designed with the level of the audience's understanding in mind.

Messages

When Susan Silk, a Chicago journalist who turned her considerable energy to public relations, was developing her approach to spokesperson training, she focused on the importance of the carefully developed message.[8] She emphasizes that the message is not a recitation of an organization's mission statement but a plain-language, conversational sentence that describes the nature of a group's work. There is often lively debate in her classes as trainees struggle to agree on how to say what it is that they do.

The same lively debate will usually occur during development of the messages that must lie within the communications grid.

The Donor's Forum of Chicago is an organization that includes both the philanthropic community of Chicago and its nonprofit groups.[9] In doing its communications plan, the forum developed the following set of messages for its audiences:

Audience	Message
Members	The forum provides important educational and networking opportunities allowing members to obtain quality information that will enhance their grantmaking efforts.
Nonprofit groups and prospective nonprofit members	The forum provides many opportunities for representatives of nonprofit organizations to develop their professional skills.
Members, media, policymakers, and the public	The forum is the authoritative source of information on philanthropy in the Chicago region.
Media, policymakers, and the public	The voice of philanthropy and nonprofits needs to be heard on important issues that affect the communities they serve.

The list goes on. The plan developed by the Donor's Forum nicely illustrates how messages and audiences overlap, knowledge that can be useful when it comes to agreeing on the best vehicles for reaching selected audiences.

A word of caution. Keep the messages consistent. Touting worldclass facilities to potential users while describing the deplorable state of facilities to potential funders, for example, can be a sure-fire source of embarrassment.

Vehicles

Having agreed on audiences and messages, the planning process moves to the question of delivery. Just as messages overlap, the same will be true of vehicles. Some, like media placement, have the potential to reach every audience. Others can be highly targeted. In the case of the Donor's Forum, for example, vehicles included the more obvious ones such as newsletters, brochures, and the annual report as well as ventures into Internet-based electronic communications.

In thinking about the audiences and the methods for communicating with them, useful considerations to keep in mind would include knowing the attitudes of the audience at the start of the project; their stage of understanding; the appropriate ways of reaching them, including consideration of their culture; and other matters that are competing for their attention.

The process of thinking through communications vehicles is an opportunity to tap into the planning group's ingenuity. It would be a pretty dull plan if, after working through audiences and messages, the vehicles were limited to brochures and press releases. The world of communications and public relations does, after all, include both craft and creativity.

Media Relations and Media Placement

Frank Karel of the Robert Woods Johnson Foundation draws an interesting distinction between media relations and media placement. "The president or the director of an organization should have good media relations skills," says Karel. "He or she should be able to sit dowr with a reporter and speak effectively about the work being done." It is the job of a media placement specialist, on the other hand, to actually sell the story or, when the situation calls for it, try to prevent one. The sales analogy, in which the product is an idea, is a good one.

While the essence of a sound communications plan is a deliberate thought about how to reach all appropriate audiences, it is still important to pay special attention to good old-fashioned media placement work. It is the media, after all, that has the greatest influence in framing the set of issues under consideration by the public at any one time. There is no media conspiracy to manipulate what the public sees and reads; it is simply a matter of journalists involved in the mass media reacting to the same information at the same time. It is an understanding of the agenda-setting role of the media that lies behind the well-known presidential "bully pulpit," in which the president is able to influence the content of the news by simply choosing what to say on any particular day. Savvy communications specialists at the local, national, or international level can accomplish the same by carrying out effective media strategies.

The right kind of media attention at the right time can play an important reinforcing role in a communications effort. If, for example, a story in the local newspaper profiles the work of a nonprofit group at the same time a fund-raising appeal arrives on an executive's desk, the impact can be considerable. So an important consideration in planning a media relations effort is the way more targeted communications focused on selected audience can be carried out simultaneously.

Groups attempting to call attention to an issue will have an easier time if their work is reinforced by a media that has created a general bed of awareness about it.

If circumstances allow, it can often be easier to time an organization's communications efforts to a moment when an issue of interest to the organization is in the news, as opposed to doing the hard work of getting an item on the agenda from scratch. During the 1996 presidential primaries, for example, nonprofit groups advocating workers' rights in the face of widespread corporate downsizing found a marketplace in the media for their ideas once the Republican candidate Patrick Buchanan raised the issue at the national level.

It is, of course, important, to try to bring new issues to the nation's attention through the media, and many nonprofit groups are in business for the purpose of encouraging society to consider one issue or another. But there is no person more grateful than a journalist offered a solid source or idea about a story already underway.

The staff of the *Bulletin of the Atomic Scientists* added a media relations strategy to their efforts surrounding an issue devoted to the 10th anniversary of the nuclear disaster at Chernobyl.[10] The work resulted in significant coverage by ABC, CBS, CNN, and *The New York Times,* among others, and advanced the *Bulletin's* work to stimulate international debate about nuclear issues.

There are few days quite so pleasant for a communications specialist as the day a favorable story about the organization is in the paper or on the air.

A good media specialist can be hard to find, but it is worth the search. As with so much of the communications field, effective media placement blends craft with art, and there can be many approaches that work. Some prefer simply picking up the phone and pitching an idea, others feel strongly about leading with a letter. It is results that count.

In considering whether to work with a particular media relations person, all the usual rules apply about checking references and track record. This is important in establishing a person's capacity for attention to detail and reputation for follow-through, but these steps only provide clues to a person's ability to place a story. One of the best tests of this skill takes place when the candidate is asked how a story that appears fairly dull on the surface might be handled. If creative ideas start to flow about things that might be tried or angles that might work, it is a very good sign. Also, pay attention to how well a person sells their own qualifications for the job. If placing a story is at its heart a sales job, a person who does such work should be able to sell himself or herself as well. Finally, checking a person's reputation with reporters who have worked with the candidate can be very useful.

The Communications Staff

One of the most frequently asked questions about communications in nonprofit organizations is whether to have a staff communications director. The answer depends in part on the nature or size of the organization. The first issue to address, though, is the perception of communications within an organization.

As recently as the mid-1970s there were very few communications specialists holding senior administrative positions in the field of higher education. College or university news bureaus were largely responsible for hometown press releases and announcements for the local papers about college events. The most senior communications person was typically a mid-level manager at best, and it would not be at all unusual for a public relations firm to be hired without the news bureau director even knowing about it, much less being involved in the decision.

How times have changed. When the baby boom generation moved through college, schools that once had more applicants than they could handle suddenly faced a dramatic marketing challenge as competition for applications heated up. The cost of maintaining a first-class educational facility shot up, so the need to reach out to alumni and other donors in new ways became pressing. Higher education in this nation did a remarkable job of meeting the challenge. Colleges and universities recognized that developing increased interest among prospective students and stimulating more financial support was in large measure a communications task. Today it is the rare college or university that doesn't have a seasoned communications specialist holding a senior position in the administration.

What college and university administrators recognized was that communications is not a function that can be neatly relegated to a tidy corner. It is a function that permeates an organization; each person who works there is, in some way, engaged in the communications process.

For some organizations it is perfectly appropriate to have communications as a staff function, for others it may not be feasible. The challenge for the nonprofit organization is to recognize the importance of the work and properly tend to it. For groups that have sufficient resources, having a communications specialist on staff as a member of the senior management team can generate results that justify the investment many times over. This can be particularly true when the communications strategy is linked to fund-raising efforts and the link between a successful message and money in the bank is a direct one.

Outside Consultants

According to Paul Argenti, professor of management and corporate communication at Dartmouth College's Tuck School of Business Administration, communications and public relations is never something that can be simply farmed out. While there are many excellent firms and individual contractors who do fine work, Argenti's view is that at least one person within the organization must understand its communications needs, have an appreciation of their importance, and be responsible for tending to them.

Argenti's view is that there is no substitute for working within an organization to understand both the big picture and the fine points of what needs to be done. It may well be, says Argenti, that such a person would retain communications counsel on a long-term basis, a project basis, or both. But he stresses the importance of someone in-house defining communications needs, being the driver in developing a communications plan, and overseeing its implementation.

Shoestring Strategies

Some of the most cost-effective communications and public relations strategies that can be adopted by a nonprofit organization are advocated by Thom Clark, the founder and president of Chicago's Community Media Workshop.

Established in 1989, the workshop is a nonprofit organization that provides communications training to Chicago's nonprofit community. According to Clark, it is a mistake for cash-strapped organizations to spend scarce resources on special events or other activities that are primarily designed to attract attention.

Using Clark's approach, a nonprofit manager should take a close look at the organization's strategy, with an eye toward the opportunities it offers to advance communications efforts without adding significant new costs. Examples might include:

- Building visits with journalists into travel schedules. A group doing interesting work on an issue in one city may find that the news media in other cities are interested in learning about it. A low-cost but potentially high-impact media relations project can consist of simply arranging media sessions for traveling staff members.

- Taking advantage of conferences or other gatherings of people with whom a group wants to communicate. Somebody is responsible for putting together the agendas for such meetings. An offer to do a workshop may well be eagerly accepted. It is only a short step beyond that to arranging meetings with the trade press covering a conference.

- Writing for the trade press. There are literally thousands of special interest publications serving nonprofit organizations or the people who use their services. Contacting the editor of such publications with an offer to write a column or an article may well be accepted, especially if the offer is based on some prior research about the editorial needs of the publication.

- Staying in touch with key audiences. Thanks to desktop publishing, the cost of producing an attractive, informative newsletter has plummeted. Such a publication can be used to stay in touch with selected audiences on a regular basis.

- Writing letters. Some audiences, especially those most important to an organization, deserve more than a newsletter. For such people, mass-produced but highly personalized letters can be extremely effective. A personal salutation, a signature in ink, a typed envelope as opposed to a label, and a genuine stamp, all give the look and feel of a personal letter and will be treated as such. The information may be the same as in a newsletter, but the difference in the vehicle used can be significant.

Pro-Bono Support

The notion of pro-bono support has a great deal of appeal because of the implication that it is free. Indeed a great deal of excellent communications and public relations advice can be provided by volunteer board members or through other arrangements with communications firms or corporate communications officers. The way such arrangements come about depends largely on the ingenuity of the nonprofit manager. Whatever the case, it is virtually always a good idea for a nonprofit group to include a communications specialist on its board. It signals recognition of the importance of communications to a nonprofit organization and ensures a communications perspective will reach the top level of management.

It should also be understood that pro-bono support has its limits—usually the point at which the support goes beyond advice and involves expenses such as printing, travel, and video production. Marianne Philbin, director of the Chicago Foundation for Women, worked with her colleagues to devise an excellent communications strategy that blends pro-bono communications counsel with a commitment to spending money in a strategic way to advance their overall communications objectives.[11] She and her board set up an arrangement with the marketing staff of the Quaker Oats Company to do focus groups, develop a communications strategy, and prepare an advertising campaign about the Foundation for Women. Philbin concluded that one place to spend money was on advertising time and space, as opposed to depending on the fringes customarily allocated to public service announcements. (The communications strategy developed by the Chicago Foundation for Women is an impressive one. An overview, written by Ms. Philbin, is included with this chapter.) Over a two-year period, the assets of the foundation grew by 30 percent.

Electronic Communications

Revolutionary changes in the technology of communications have brought about vast new opportunities for nonprofits to communicate with one another, with targeted audiences, and with the general public. The centerpiece, of course, is the Internet. While it is far from universally used, nonprofit groups by the thousands around the world have set up E-mail links, and many have set up a home page about themselves. The result is an incredibly rich source of information and contacts that simply did not exist a decade ago.

An important source of electronic networking for the nonprofit community is Handsnet, headquartered in Cupertino, California, whose members are virtually all nonprofit organizations.[12] Handsnet also provides a gateway to the entire Internet.

Advocacy groups have found that electronic communications among motivated activists can be a powerful tool for organization and action. Antismoking groups, for example, working with the Advocacy Institute of Washington, D.C., set up a private electronic network to share information and strategy.[13]

The moment has passed when a nonprofit group should consider whether to have an Internet link. The question now is how to do it. As with every aspect of the communications world, it is possible to spend a great deal of money in very unwise ways to set up electronic communications. Virtually every community will have people or groups who can show how to do it for remarkably little cost. It is just a matter of seeking them out.

MEASUREMENT

Evaluating the success of a communications or public relations strategy should take place at two different levels. First is the strategic level, in which communications is seen as integral to the goals and objectives of the organization. It can be difficult teasing out of a larger strategy the precise impact of the communications efforts. If, however, there is a communications plan that identifies audience, messages, and vehicles for conveying those messages,

B O X   32–1

CASE STUDY: The Chicago Foundation for Women

Marianne Philbin, *Director, Chicago Foundation for Women*

It's tough to convince prospective donors that your organization is the hottest thing in town if they've never heard of you.

For the Chicago Foundation for Women, which raises money it then gives in grants to organizations serving women and girls, a basic shift in overall thinking regarding public relations and marketing led to significant organizational investment in media relations, paid advertising, an upgraded newsletter, upgraded collateral materials, a speakers bureau program, and a full-time communications officer on staff.

Although the foundation had not completely ignored public relations work for its first 10 years, its efforts were modest, and few dollars were spent. A "capacity building" initiative in its 10th year led the foundation to see communications and public relations for what it really is for many nonprofits: a development strategy as important as any other fundraising strategy, as directly tied to getting donations in the door as advertising is to product sales in the corporate world.

In its early years, the Chicago Foundation for Women grew steadily, increasing its budget at an annual rate of 9 percent to 13 percent, a rate of growth most nonprofits would be proud of. But we were not satisfied with continued growth at that level. There was too much to do and we were ambitious for our organization and passionate about our mission.

The board became convinced that just as a for-profit business requires a certain level of reinvestment of its capital if it wants to grow, a nonprofit must invest in its own fundraising if it is to expand its programs and services. In order to grow, we needed a shift in strategies, resources and thinking, and part of that shift meant re-conceptualizing the role of communications.

Once the board agreed to invest a larger percentage of the Foundation's budget in fundraising marketing and communications each year, we decided to seek outside help in order to help determine which of many strategies we were pursuing should be expanded. Through grant support, we retained the Chicago-based firm of Donald A. Campbell and Company to conduct a development assessment and explore a wide range of strategies to reach out to new sources of support.

One word kept surfacing in their conversations with supporters, in focus groups and ultimately in their final report to us: *visibility.* The one investment that would enhance all our fundraising strategies, from mail appeals to special events to major donor cultivation, would be investment in visibility-building efforts such as upgraded publications, focused media relations, product marketing, advertising, and a communitywide image program.

Like many nonprofits, with the exception of a handful of staff and board members, the Foundation tended to see public relations and communications as "optional," as a luxury, a nice thing when you could get it, but not something you should spend a lot of time or money on. Nonprofits working in the social services and social justice sector seem particularly subject to this attitude; believing, perhaps, that spending money on themselves is a *selfish* use of resources.

However, once the Foundation's understanding of communications was recast in light of fundraising, attitudes began to change. Why would we eliminate from our arsenal ANY strategy that could help bring in money, especially when ours was an organization whose very work was about money—raising it and granting it to organizations dealing with such issues as domestic violence, women's health care, teen pregnancy, women's economic development, and day care.

Four components, which have become the basis of our communications strategies, were introduced that first year. Our priorities were (1) to establish our institutional identity and make

CASE STUDY: The Chicago Foundation for Women (Continued)

it more visible; (2) design an advertising campaign and make modest but strategic investments in paid advertising; (3) develop livelier and more sophisticated collateral materials; and (4) create a staff position for a communications professional to oversee all communications and public relations work.

The communications officer reports to the Director of Development, whose own title and responsibilities were eventually expanded to better integrate fundraising and public relations strategies. Although there are countless ways communications and public relations are integral to the smooth functioning of an entire organization, this organization found its best arguments for supporting this work in the increased emphasis placed on development.

We began by overhauling our institutional identity, with help from a professional firm which donated its services, thanks to our relationship with the Quaker Oats Company. Quaker's advertising agency, Berry*Brown Advertising of Dallas, Texas, interviewed staff and board, conducted focus groups, reviewed and analyzed materials including text of speeches, brochures, newsletters, the look of our letterhead, and our logo. The logo and soft colors which 10 years earlier had been described by one of our supporters as "elegant, understated, and Armani-esque" (!) were now being described in focus groups as "tired," "monochromatic," and "too beige." You can imagine our reaction: if there was anything the foundation was NOT, it was "beige." So a bold and modern logo in vivid colors was designed.

Berry*Brown also helped us examine the language we were using to describe our work, testing various words, phrases and concepts in focus groups, and exploring with donors and prospects what motivated their giving. Berry*Brown provided an actual list of words to stop using, and phrases to substitute. For years, for example, we had talked about "funding social change advocacy." Not surprisingly, those words didn't exactly resonate with the average person we were approaching. The consultants encouraged us to "meet people where they were" and stress concepts like the Foundation's track record in helping women to help themselves. The tagline we now use with our logo on all our materials is "Chicago Foundation for Women. Providing Opportunities. Promoting Solutions."

Our newsletter, which goes to a mailing list of 4,000, was redesigned to incorporate the new logo, colors and lessons learned. Although it's not intended to be a significant income-generating vehicle, a remittance envelope is enclosed in two issues per year as a "soft ask." After the overhaul of the newsletter, the income generated by a single issue went from approximately $500 to over $5,000.

Once the institutional identity was established, we focused on developing an advertising campaign to help build and reinforce the image and messages we wanted to convey. As with other materials, we steered clear of industry jargon, and decided that the most important goal was for the ad to make an immediate, emotional connection with the viewer.

We were amazed at the "return" from even a modest investment in advertising. We spent a little under $40,000 on media buys in the first year, increasing the budget to $52,000 in the second year. That may sound like a lot of money, but is in fact less than other kinds of fundraising can entail, and is an amount we felt was appropriate for an organization with an annual budget over $1 million. We spent about 12 percent on radio ads, 45 percent on cable TV, and 43 percent on print. Venues were carefully chosen to reach our target audience, which we had defined through previous research to be women ages 35–55 with household income of $75,000 or more. Production costs were minimal, due to donated services.

We received hundreds of phone calls in just the first few months. A post-advertising awareness study (conducted professionally at a reduced cost) showed that among our target audience, the Foundation had an "awareness level" of 12 percent, much higher than the 3

CASE STUDY: The Chicago Foundation for Women (Concluded)

percent to 4 percent we expected. The study surveyed households that fell into the zip code zones where we had advertised and that met our donor demographics. Results indicated that the timing of when respondents first became aware of the Foundation and the level of awareness itself was directly tied to the advertising and communications campaign. One year later, the awareness level increased to 14 percent.

It is difficult to say precisely which donations came in as a direct result of our upgraded communications program, since the program is an integral part of the larger development strategy. In the two years since we began the program, however, our annual income has gone from $1.3 million to $1.7 million. Perhaps most impressive is the 125 percent increase in gifts from major donors, which we define as individuals giving $1,000 or more. Feedback from donors at all levels underscores the importance of our communications effort in increasing donor interest in Chicago Foundation for Women's work.

Most exciting, perhaps, is the fact that our staff and fundraising volunteers no longer experience those horrible moments when a very "hot prospect" we fully expect to be interested in our work stops us in midsentence and says, "I'm sorry, now . . . what again is your organization, exactly?"

We're much more likely to hear our new friend say, "Oh, I saw your ad!" or "Yes, I just read an article about you somewhere . . ." Fundraising has long been reputed to be about who you know; but in the competitive environment that exists for nonprofits today, it's as much if not more likely to be about who knows you.

---

and if there is some baseline information about the level of awareness before the communications strategy is launched, follow-up survey work can determine if the effort was successful and suggest areas that need more attention.

The narrower the communications task, the more straightforward the process of measuring results. It is also important to keep fairness in mind. A media relations effort, for example, should be launched with the intention of achieving a certain level of coverage in certain media outlets. Measurement of results should be how well it accomplished those objectives, not on a vague larger objective like the impact of media coverage on helping improve public education or reduce poverty. There may be a very direct link to such matters, but there will always be other factors involved as well. It is important to measure results, but also important that the criteria used for such measurement be appropriate.

THE FUTURE

FUTURE TRENDS

As with virtually every institution worldwide, the future will pose enormous challenges for the managers of nonprofit organizations. The shifting political climate in the United States has triggered a questioning of the relationship between governments and the nonprofit sector. The resolution of that debate will have a great impact on government sources of funding for nonprofits. If the sentiment about cutting the size of government that began in the United States in the early 1990s takes root, for example, nonprofit managers may well be faced with the tasks of simultaneously expanding services and developing new and larger sources of funding.

From an international perspective, the dominance of market forces in shaping international relationships is clearly established. As the global economy undergoes this transformation, traditional links between governments and nongovernmental organizations will almost certainly change. The need for their services, however, will only increase. With the end of the Cold War, for example, issues of ethnic and religious rivalry, border disputes, access to resources, and previously overlooked environmental issues all triggered new social needs. As nongovernmental organizations throughout the world grapple with these issues, communications will be important in the success or failure of their efforts.

THE CHALLENGE FOR MANAGERS

Despite the sense of change, the two major sets of audiences—those who provide support and those who are the focus of the organization's work—will remain the same. Nonprofit organizations will need innovative communications strategies designed to reach both.

One of the most significant opportunities, of course, is the greatly expanded marketplace for information. There may be more people and organizations competing for public attention than ever before, but the opening up of societies throughout the world coupled with new techniques for gaining access to them is unprecedented as well.

By the mid-1990s, the pattern of explosive growth of the Internet was clearly established. Nonprofit groups were among the leaders in recognizing the value of electronic communications as a very cost-effective way to reach targeted groups worldwide. It may be that at some point everyone will have access to electronic communications, but a significant challenge for the nonprofit manager is how to make appropriate use of the new technologies without cutting off the access to information for those who do not have computers, cell phones, satellite links, and fax machines. Just as there are haves and have-nots in economic terms, the same goes for information. What a shame it would be if people or groups did not know about resources available to them or could not make their need known because traditional ways of making themselves heard were eliminated.

A great deal has been written about how successful business organizations in the new century will be able to adapt quickly to changing competitive environments. By the same token, nonprofit organizations must adapt to changing economic and social environments. Effective communications and public relations strategies will be central to their success.

E N D N O T E S

1. Hodgkinson, Weitsman, and Noga, *Independent Sector's Nonprofit Almanac* 1992–1993 (San Francisco: Jossey Bass Publishers, 1992). (And conversations with Independent Sector staff.)

2. Lester M. Salamon, "Defining the Nonprofit Sector: The United States," *Working Papers of the Johns Hopkins Comparative Nonprofit Sector Project,* no. 18, edited by Lester M. Salamon and Helmut K. Anheier. Baltimore: The Johns Hopkins Institute for Policy Studies, 1996.

3. Lisa Bannon, "The Hyped and the Hypeless: Fate of Two Films," *The New York Times,* July 5, 1995, sec. B, p. 1.

4. Environmental Law Alliance Worldwide (E-LAW), 1877 Garden Avenue, Eugene, Oregon 97403. (503)687-8454.

5. Thom Clark, executive director, Community Media Workshop 600 S. Michigan Avenue, Chicago, Illinois 60605-1996. (312)663-3223.

6. Communications Consortium, 1200 New York Avenue, N.W., Suite #300, Washington, D.C. 20005. (202)326-8700.

7. B. Robey, and P. Stauffer, "Helping the news media cover family planning," *Population Reports,* Series J, No. 42. Baltimore, Johns Hopkins School of Public Health, Population Information Program, November 1995.

8. Susan Silk, president, Media Strategy, Inc., 343 W. Erie, Chicago, Illinois 60610. (312)944-7398.

9. Donor's Forum, 53 West Jackson, Suite 426, Chicago, Illinois 60606. (312)431-0260.

10. Bulletin of Atomic Scientists, 6042 S. Kimbark Avenue, Chicago, Illinois 60602. (312)702-2555.

11. Marianne Philbin, Chicago Foundation for Women, 230 W. Superior, 4th Floor, Chicago, Illinois 60610-3536. (312)266-1176.

12. HandsNet, 20195 Stevens Creek Blvd., Suite 120, Cupertino, CA 95014. (408)257-4500.

13. Advocacy Institue, 1707 L Street, N.W., Suite 400, Washington, DC 20036. (202)659-8475.

Public Relations and Communications for Associations

Richard L. Hanneman
President
Salt Institute

Changing public attitudes and opinions and motivating others to act can be honored as the essence of human progress and happiness or condemned as deceitful manipulation. This credo stems from one of my early and formative public affairs positions, as assistant to Wisconsin Governor Warren P. Knowles, who lived as he taught: "Good government is good politics." In public relations and communications, our tools can be misused, but, employed in a good cause, they can help us achieve greater human understanding, productivity, and happiness.

A STRATEGIC APPROACH TO ASSOCIATION PR

Associations exist for just these reasons. They are voluntary, not-for-profit organizations formed in recognition of the greater, even synergistic, potential of uniting in common purpose. In some ways, associations act as any business in defining their core purpose or niche, developing and marketing their goods and services. They provide employment, produce goods and services, and pay taxes. But the bottom line is not only the fund balance of their financial statements; for most associations, the goal is achieved along the path traveled, not measured in a financial destination.

In many ways, public relations and communications in associations, mirrors the strategic and tactical decision-making processes in for-profit enterprises. The selling of toothpaste, municipal bonds, or pork bellies shares common principles with providing financial support for kidney research, upgrading worker safety procedures in salt mines, and expanding markets for California raisins, industrial machinery, or computers. Many of the challenges of communications within the for-profit sector are shared by non-profit associations.

Associations have one significant difference, however. It's not that they don't make money, or produce consumer goods and services, or pay taxes; they do. The difference is implicit in the membership concept—many individuals or businesses uniting to support the association. In this complex setting, strategic and even tactical decisions in association public relations and communications must be devised and implemented against the backdrop of internal political decisions that usually are more significant to organizational survival and explicit than those in business and industry.

Associations are almost as varied and unique as people. They come in all sizes and shapes, from the local PTA to the International Red Cross. Associations represent all types of charitable purposes, providing a private-sector response to concerns that would otherwise build into demand for public-sector responsibility. Multinational corporations are common-place, but more and more trade associations and professional organizations are bridging national boundaries when their charters demand attention to broader concerns. America has long recognized this voluntary segment of society, and the U.S. tax code makes specific provision for code section-defined "501(c)(3)" charitable and public interest groups and "501(c)(6)" trade associations. The differences between the two in terms of public policy objectives, strategies, and tactics is, in practice, often indistinguishable.

Many associations provide valuable education. The quality and success of America's public school system may be a current issue, but historically, the K–12 and university teachers on public payrolls always have had not only private-sector counterparts, but also, perhaps more importantly, private-sector supplementation. Employers provide training as do a myriad of specialized-education industry groups. Associations play an important role in fostering professional in-service, lifetime-learning educational experiences and inter- and intraindustry exchanges of expertise to improve productivity, worker safety, environmental protection, and a host of other socially sanctioned services.

Apart from feeding the hungry, promoting the arts, or teaching businesspeople how to cope with their changing work and marketplaces, associations also exist to market ideas, to advance ideological causes, and to promote efficient industrial production or product acceptance through generic marketing of ideas and philosophies. These are the "special interests" so commonly attacked as undermining the public interest, yet reflect the individual opinions of citizens in their multitude of ethical, political, philanthropic, and economic diversity. Our political and social structure rewards effective group action; small wonder, then, that effective groups are formed in response. So, whether the view is that more money needs to be spent for AIDS research, that government is "too big" or "not doing enough," that zoning should protect the integrity of neighborhoods, that bald eagles need protected nesting areas, or that dairy farmers need price supports, citizens vote with their memberships (and their time and money) to advance their special interests through associations. With the extension of governmental concern into detailed questions of medical research sponsorship, marketplace policing, and technology promotion, lawmakers and regulators would be lost and ineffective without the specialized expertise of the "special interests" represented by voluntary associations.

Associations are governed by charters and bylaws that define their general purposes and objectives. Achievement of these objectives—well recognized by sophisticated associa-tion management professionals—requires consideration of the role of public relations and communications in both strategic planning and tactical implementation. Thus, "Save the Whales" and eating "Five a Day" servings of fruits and vegetables elucidate organizational strategies. The core strength of any association is the power of the ideas it espouses to motivate to action either its members or some targeted individual or group. If the motivating idea is the source of power, the communications strategy is the essence of an association's mission.

Members of the Salt Institute have been tutored to distinguish their business—to make and sell salt—from the business of their trade association—to develop and sell ideas on their behalf. This maxim replicates the mission of many associations providing a targeted communications function on behalf of its members, whether advocating humanitarian aid to the Third World or central cities or expanded consumer acceptance of a product or service.

Once associations were essentially local. But the spurt of central government dominance beginning with the New Deal in the 1930s in the United States has led to stronger national associations. The 1980's decentralization of governmental activism from Washington to state capitals resulted in reinvigoration of state-level associations dealing with governmental issues. Growth of global focus has produced international associations.

These shifts, clearly, also reflect the advances in communications technology and infrastructure. *The Wall Street Journal* is downlinked from satellites and printed simultaneously around the world. Television, movies, magazines—popular culture in general is national. People listen to The Beach Boys in Memphis and Randy Travis in Malibu. Ideas flow along this broad information highway . . . and now, the electronic information superhighway. Associations are driven by advancing technology and the communications infrastructure, just like other entities seeking markets for their messages.

Government regulations and communication technologies influence communications strategies adopted by associations. Take meetings, for example. While associations have long held meetings as a primary means of communicating with members and conducting organizational governance, phone and fax technology, video teleconferencing, and E-mail have negated the need for some meetings. Removal of the tax deduction for spouse travel may be the next blow to the traditional meetings of trade associations and professional societies. Classifying association expenditures for lobbying as nondeductible is another example of how government has acted to retard the ability of associations to represent members' views.

Associations are walking a fine line. They have invited governmental scrutiny not only by emerging as effective agents in promoting their members' causes, but by stretching the boundaries of their income-tax-exempt status. Some association activities are performed by for-profit subsidiaries (such as magazine publication and insurance company ownership) and the organizations are becoming increasingly reliant on nondues income. Sales to members and nonmembers alike of various materials, charges for special services, rental of mailing lists—these, and many more creative money-raising initiatives, often blur the line between associations and for-profit ventures. In many associations, the greatest growth in communications is in support of the expanding array of nondues revenue programs.

Associations are characterized by the same sort of merger and spin-off machinations as the corporate for-profit sector. The most specialized of business or ideological interest can be found represented with its own association. New industries or emerging growth segments of an association's membership often choose to establish new organizations to promote the specialized interest not addressed by the original association. Yet mergers driven by cost-conscious boards have resulted in movement in the opposite direction as well. Such shifts imbue the association's internal communications program and its strategic external communications efforts with a critical role.

Even more pronounced than the permanent merger of related associations is the dramatically increased frequency of *ad hoc* alliances and coalitions, some with their own staff apparatus, many without. If the rationale for associations is that there is strength in numbers, association activists recognize that joint action of many associations raises the truism exponentially. Just as "politics makes strange bedfellows," *ad hoc* coalitions exist issue by issue; today's antagonist is tomorrow's valued ally.

Association governance is a key variable distinguishing association public relations and communications in the for-profit sector. Boards of directors, often augmented by standing public relations committees of member volunteers, bring to the table a diverse set of interests and concerns. In some association cultures, the members predominate. Small associations, of course, often lack paid staff and the function is entirely volunteer. But growing associations with fewer than 10 staff members, and often larger ones as well, often remain member-driven, with members moving far beyond policy setting into an active hands-on role. Such instances invite substituting the members' individual, sometimes private interests and views for those of the association in general. The opposite model is the staff-driven organization in which association management professionals are given broad latitude to manage the program. Unfortunately, as in any group of people, there are managers who mismanage their duties or abuse their trusts. The association management profession, obviously, favors a hybrid of the member-driven and staff-driven extremes.

The principles of successful public relations and communications by associations are the same as for other entities. Essentially, success depends on aligning the group's interests with those of the public. Skilled association communicators define the issues. The association either must convince a significant segment, if not a majority, of the public that its perspective is worthy of support or abandon its programs and advocacy objectives. For some associations, addressing gun control is a question of the public insisting on removing criminals' access to weapons, while for other associations, the issue represents an individual's constitutional rights and ability to protect self and family. The salt industry's interest in selling deicing salt becomes transformed into a salt-for-sand substitution strategy in communities with elevated wintertime airborne particulate levels that seek to satisfy the requirements of the Clean Air Act. The public has little sympathy for gun merchants or shooting clubs and cares little whether the salt industry sells more salt, but it certainly endorses preserving public safety, protecting Constitutional rights, and supporting the ability of people to protect themselves and their families while breathing clean, healthful air.

TACTICS THAT IMPLEMENT ASSOCIATION STRATEGIES

The ability to define the issue is usually more important than the tactics chosen. The most effective tactical weapons cannot salvage targeting the wrong objective. Perhaps the best recent example was in government, not associations. The legacy of President Lyndon B. Johnson's Great Society was the establishment of a discussion of the proper role of government which asked the question: Is there a need which is going unmet? President Ronald Reagan's signal domestic achievement was to recast that debate to answer the question: Can we afford to have government respond? This was a more important supply-side policy issue than that of Reagan's tax policy.

Tactics, however, separate the sheep from the goats. Even if the fireman has the ladder leaning against the right house, if he can't climb, aim a hose, or wield an ax, the house will be destroyed. Knowing who needs to be convinced and what they need to be convinced to do—but not knowing how to convince them—is a recipe for communications impotence. Effective public relations practitioners need to understand the big picture, but also master the tools of the trade.

While no tactical plan should be implemented unless anchored in a larger strategic objective, there are times when just knowing the tools can stimulate that strategic objective. When the Ontario Solid Wastes Management Association catalogued problems of Toronto-area trash truck operators, it lamented a specific policy of the regional government. The policy denied access after 3 p.m. by private waste haulers to public transfer stations convenient to their customers. "Too bad, but what can we do about it?" was the waste haulers' lament. Staff knowledgeable about the policy-making process suggested a simple, direct meeting with the agency to outline the problem. The meeting was held and the hours adjusted.

A key strategic need of associations is in the area of internal marketing. This includes not only getting members to renew their dues, but also to buy association-produced books and videos, register for association meetings, raise assessments for special projects, buy insurance from the association's captive company, use the association-sponsored credit card, and place ads in the association's magazine. In short, plans include the use of any number of special services from which the association derives non-dues income. Associations use brochures and fact sheets, internal newsletters, telemarketing, direct mail, broadcast fax, computer bulletin boards and membership meetings, and door-to-door solicitation. For example, the neighbor who collects for the American Heart Association may be a volunteer, but many environmental and consumer groups must pay commissions to their young door-to-door solicitors. Often modeled after business tactics, there is nothing unique about the tools employed to build member and public support.

The second major area in which associations need to communicate is to support the selling of ideas. Here the communications objectives are external, though they often include both member education and grassroots involvement. The tools include the full range of member communications listed above. In addition, the tools are used to leverage the association's special interests by mobilizing potential allies in a temporary alliance or coalition. For example, direct mail to concerned publics, paid advertising in the consumer or trade media, formal legislative and/or regulatory testimony, personal visits with legislators and regulators, third-party endorsements particularly of especially credible individuals or groups or by celebrities, and political action contributions with elected officials are all used.

The Salt Institute's Programs

The selection of strategic objectives and tactical tools benefits when it is part of a systematic process, as it is in the industry-sponsored Salt Institute. Since the late 1980s, the Salt Institute has followed a standard method of evaluating its public relations and communications activities as part of a formal issues management system.

The Salt Institute is the trade association representing North American salt producers. Associate members include similar companies from two dozen countries around the world. Membership is composed of companies which mine sodium chloride from the ground or extract it by dewatering intake from the Great Salt Lake in Utah or other saline bodies such as San Francisco and San Diego Bays. Its basic objectives are to enhance the business operations and market opportunities of its members. There are more than 14,000 known uses for sodium chloride, the principal ones being the raw material for the entire chlor-alkali industry, highway deicing, water softening, use in food processing and preparation, and in feeds for poultry and livestock.

The Salt Institute issues management program has established objectives in each of these areas and in the area of production and distribution issues related to enhancing the productivity of salt production and shipment to customers. Most of the member companies participate in most markets and use all three primary technologies: conventional shaft mining, solution mining/vacuum pan evaporation, and solar evaporation. At board meetings twice a year, the members, each represented by their chief executive officer, examine a detailed book of the association's strategies and tactics. It is updated for each meeting and distributed in advance; each policy issue discussion is printed on its distinctive colored paper facilitating member retention and separating the issues for easy referral in the meetings. Discussion of each issue follows a standard format:

- Statement of goal;
- Listing of priority target audiences;
- A series of short summaries of the strategy for each target audience;
- A listing of the projects which are being used to implement the several target audience strategies;
- A listing of the measures of results and evaluation by which the issues management strategy performance will be evaluated;
- A listing of priority networking contacts, with a subsidiary listing of other networking contacts worth mentioning;
- A similar listing of priority media outlets including both Institute publications or audio-visual materials and outside publications and electronic media; and finally,
- A list of the priority communications vehicles being employed in each strategy. There are about 25 communication vehicles identified, split into two groups, one listing in priority order the vehicles being used, the other serving as a ready reminder of options not chosen.

To illustrate the process, consider the case of the issues management strategy for highway deicing salt. A background scan reveals that the significant barriers to what the Institute terms "sensible salting" (that is, application of the minimum amount of salt to roadways to ensure traffic safety and mobility) are well-documented concerns about (1) salt enhancing the rate of corrosion of vehicles, roads, and bridges; (2) salt damage to plants and animals near the roadway; and (3) salt leaching into drinking water wells sited near the roadway. In 1972, the Institute won a Silver Anvil strategic campaign award from the Public Relations Society of America for its Sensible Salting Program. The program included a series of free, staff-provided training seminars for equipment operators employed by state and local highway agencies and toll road authorities.

A scan of the environment also continues to document several trends and issues:

1. Some agencies have tried, but abandoned, bans on the use of deicing salt.
2. Some jurisdictions have reduced service levels to cut salt usage, both in speed and in amounts applied to arterials, and, in a few cases, abandoned service to less travelled streets.
3. Some communities use a sand/salt mix, sometimes as high as 10–1, to reduce salt use.
4. With the active encouragement of the Federal Highway Administration, a commercially competitive product has been in use for the past 15 years but has been unsuccessful in achieving significant market penetration.
5. Salt companies have developed several proprietary deicing formulas which largely prevent the corrosion-enhancing effects of salt, but these also have been slow to gain acceptance, even though less costly than the non-salt deicer.

6. Finally, salt sales have been relatively flat since 1979, with variations only for the severity of the winter.

The Salt Institute's highway deicing salt issues management plan tracks related issues and manages the association's plan to increase the use of deicing salt. Target audiences include highway users and highway traffic safety groups, elected officials, public works and highway safety employees of transportation agencies, and environmental regulators. There are other potential audiences such as environmental groups, but these are the selected targets in priority order.

It was only a few short years ago that the priority list was basically flip-flopped. The Institute had, until then, provided materials to the direct customers, those buying salt and applying it to the roadways. The strategy emphasized enhancing their operational effectiveness, and recognition by elected officials and the concerned public of their careful use of salt. But these objectives were largely achieved. The new strategy reflects two emerging trends: (1) Budgetary support for winter maintenance activities is frequently in jeopardy with many states facing budget pressures, and (2) the focus is on highway safety and mobility rather than the more controversial salt usage.

Facing similar conditions as the salt industry in North America, German salt producers commissioned an academic study documenting the impact of winter highway maintenance using deicing salt on traffic accident rates and injury accident rates. They found three-fourths of the accidents were prevented with good practices. The Salt Institute commissioned a scientifically similar study by an independent research institution, conducted in five U.S. snowbelt states. The study not only confirmed the German results, but found that U.S. maintenance practices are even better, reducing accidents by 85 percent and injuries by 88 percent.

Armed with this information, the Institute launched a revised strategy aimed at mobilizing highway users and traffic safety advocates and officials to support high levels of winter maintenance service. Existing projects were modified under the revised strategy. An industry seminar program added the results of the study to emphasize to equipment operators the importance of the service they provide. The American Public Works Association (APWA) and the Salt Institute created a booklet entitled "Fight Winter and Win" designed for use by public works managers to educate their locally elected officials and concerned citizens.

New emphasis was also placed on certain networking opportunities. For years, the Salt Institute held memberships in the National Safety Council and the American Highway Users Alliance, but had little involvement in the NSC's Highway Traffic Safety Division or the AHUA-sponsored Roadway Safety Foundation. With its new strategy, the Institute undertook active participation in these latter two groups, making the point that safety performance is largely unmeasured in terms of the safety effectiveness impact of winter maintenance operations. Cooperation with the roadway safety section of the Federal Highway Administration received higher priority, and contacts were initiated with the National Association of Governors' Highway Safety Representatives, particularly in the snowbelt states. Briefings have been conducted for such groups as the American Trucking Associations, American Bus Association, and American Automobile Association, and presentations were made to the National Transportation Public Works Association and the Better Roads and Transportation Council. Three of the past four winters have been particularly severe in the North American snowbelt. Without question, customers have been all too happy to use what salt they needed to keep highways open and safe. Sales increased 70 percent from the previous historic high. Other ongoing activities are summarized in Figure 33–1.

Salt Institute Projects Supporting the Use of Deicing Salt

---

1. Regular exhibits at the annual American Public Works Association and the North American Snow Conference.

2. Production and distribution to highway agencies of training materials *(The Snowfighters Handbook* and the video *Snowfighting from A to Z).*

3. Production of a booklet, "Deicing Salt and Our Environment," documenting the facts on environmental impact of deicing salt.

4. Cooperation with the Transportation Research Board in its Congressionally mandated study comparing salt with its Federal Highway Administration-endorsed competitor, and wide distribution of the resulting report which concluded salt was superior (much to the chagrin, no doubt, of the competitor which had lobbied Congress for the $230,000 study; the company divested itself of that business within six months).

5. Participation with the American Society for Testing and Materials in their periodic standard-setting activities pertaining to deicing salt.

6. Encouraging proper storage of deicing salt by customer public works agencies by means of an awards contest with public relations exposure for the winners (improper storage is estimated to be responsible for 90 percent of the environmental problems in deicing salt use).

7. Encouraging state and federal agencies, through personal contacts, to adopt some system to measure "level of service" performance with regard to winter maintenance.

8. Supporting Traffic Research Board funding and providing data-collection assistance for a compendium of proper winter maintenance operations practices.

9. Working with the U.S. Environmental Protection Agency and several state environmental and transportation agencies to substitute salt for sand as a winter maintenance material in areas experiencing high wintertime particulate levels. All such areas in the state of Utah, for example, have been totally converted to salt.

10. Participate, by invitation, in an advisory capacity to the recently concluded five-year Strategic Highway Research Program and, again by invitation, advise FHA on the continued implementation of the research results.

The success of the program is measured in terms of the acceptance of Institute advocacy positions by the targeted groups, the lessened incidence of attempts to ban the use of salt, improved access and credibility accorded to Institute staff by various target groups, and formal endorsements of the Institute's advocacy of support for quality winter maintenance by these groups. The Institute's board has judged the program successful and authorized a follow-on strategy reflecting its confidence.

The Post-Closure Liability Fund

The success story of the Post-Closure Liability Fund, the brainchild of the National Solid Wastes Management Association (NSWMA), illustrates the crucial importance of sound strategic thinking and of aligning an association's advocacy position with a genuine public concern. The Fund was enacted into law as a minor provision of the massive Superfund (CERCLA) legislation in 1980.

With the enactment of the landmark federal solid waste statute—the Resource Conservation and Recovery Act of 1976 (RCRA)—the Congress created a federal regulatory program to ensure that hazardous chemical wastes were properly treated and disposed of by closing improper sites. Waste technology was evolving but few state-of-the-art facilities existed. Some advanced facilities operated by NSWMA members had difficulty attracting sufficient volumes of waste to be commercially viable because less-costly but less-protective options were still legal. At the same time that the public interest lay in directing wastes to state-of-the-art facilities as quickly as possible, NSWMA members' interests lay in opening as many of these modern-technology facilities as necessary to receive these wastes. Adding to the issue chaos, some environmentalists opposed even the generation of hazardous wastes, which would lead to "constipating the system" by denying approval of any legal disposal facilities. Other environmentalists were intent on punishing anyone responsible for environmental discharges. Finally, some industrial waste generators were concerned with minimizing the costs of waste disposal to control operating costs and maintain their international competitiveness.

The NSWMA had an effective Legislative Planning Committee (LPC) which operated under loose direction from the board of directors. The idea of a Post-Closure Liability Fund, offered by an LPC member, drew quick support. The concept was that the modern treatment and disposal facilities using state-of-the-art technologies would eventually receive EPA permits. A significant concern in bringing these expensive facilities into being was the potentially huge liability for unknowable future failures and resultant environmental contamination. Thus, the reasoning continued, if some insurance mechanism could be provided, the insurance cost could be reflected in prices charged at the time of disposal. The proposed Post-Closure Liability Fund would bear the entire cleanup costs for properly licensed and properly-closed facilities. It would be funded by a special disposal fee levied at the time of disposal and retained in a separate account for the generations to come.

The fund was a novel idea that it addressed the public desire to manage the waste properly since it provided a significant incentive to facility operators to qualify for the fund by properly managing and closing their facilities. It provided otherwise-unavailable insurance for the operators to encourage investment in facilities which would qualify for RCRA permits.

The NSWMA did not have an organized issues management program, but the strategy incorporated concepts of strategic communications and effective public relations tactics. The target was Congress and the concept was new, different, narrowly focused, and likely to be opposed by significant political forces. Environmentalists would likely oppose the measure as encouraging additional disposal capacity and shielding operators from long-term liabilities associated with their activities. Industrial producers of waste materials could be counted on to oppose the new fee that they would be paying.

The NSWMA adopted a two-part strategy. First, the concept would be broadly legitimized through discussion in public forums, articles in environmental and trade journals and one-on-one meetings with EPA staff and a number of key Congressional staff. Then, communications directed through highly credible Congressional staff who were sold on its merits would be used as a means of delivering broader waste service industry support to the Superfund bill moving through the same committee, the Senate's Environment and Public Works Committee, at the same time. When the Post-Closure Liability Fund emerged as part of the final version of the act, it was a "done deal." Environmentalists and industrialists all conceded they were familiar with the idea; they just had no idea it was going to be in the final law.

The postscript to this public relations success story, unfortunately, is not so pleasant, at least for NSWMA. Forces opposed to the Fund mounted efforts to have that portion of the Resource Conservation and Recovery Act repealed. The association, in part due to staff changes, proceeded on to its next challenge instead of recognizing the need to defend what had already been achieved. The Fund legislation was replaced.

Evaluation and Accountability

This leads naturally to the question of evaluation and accountability. How do we know if we've won? Association public relations and communications staffers often learn a harsh lesson at the hands of their boards, particularly if those boards are composed, as they often are, of hard-nosed, successful business executives. And the lesson is equally applicable if the organization is charitable, education-oriented, devoted to some ideological cause, or pursuing the economic interests of its corporate members.

PR practitioners are notorious for quantification of publicity. They collect newspaper and magazine clippings and calculate the number of column inches or the potential combined readership of the distribution. They boast of the number of viewers or listeners. They count business cards collected in a fishbowl at trade shows or the number of people in the audience for key presentations. They miss the point.

Strategic thinking in public relations and communications demands that publicity be only a side indicator, an interim measure at best. The objective is some behavior change on the part of the target audience. That's true whether the audience is a congressional conference committee or 260 million Americans. The board of directors wants to know whether the publicity produced additional membership and dues revenues, whether it resulted in an expanded market for the association members' products or services, whether additional and effective research areas were opened, or whether hungry people were fed or homeless were housed. They want the bottom line. It's never easy and it's sometimes impossible to document all the answers to the right questions. But it is always appropriate to address the right questions; it shows the PR pro is just that, someone who really knows what is important, and what is not.

PR pros deserve a place at the table when strategic planning decisions are discussed. No effective association can operate without input and guidance from a board sensitive to strategic public relations and communications. In associations with paid staff, the public relations or communications director should be at the table, and on the inside. But the status must be earned, not offered because it was recommended in a handbook of proper practice.

TECHNOLOGY'S EFFECT ON THE FUTURE

Communications will remain the central mission of associations as long as there are associations. The tools will change. Association Intranets, Websites, LISTSERVs, E-mail, and other new technologies will characterize the operations of even small association staffs. Gathering information is an even greater challenge. The Internet and the panoply of available commercial databases and information services threaten to overload our circuits, but they offer needed information at the same time.

Members of associations and members of the various publics with which they interact are all facing the prospect of information overload. Communications professionals understand the challenge. And they recognize the opportunity for those who can meet the challenge. The post-industrial society is information based. Those who have it, those who manage it . . . they, and the associations who employ, them have an edge on the future.

## PART FIVE

Special Tactics for Public Relations and Corporate Communications

Changing Your Own Behavior to Enhance Behavioral Results

Kerry D. Tucker
Chief Executive Officer
Nuffer, Smith, Tucker, Inc.

Larry Nuffer
Executive Vice President
Nuffer, Smith, Tucker, Inc.

How many times have you heard or even said: "We've got to tell *our* story to the public. We need to make *them* understand our position. If *they* could just see the 'big picture'." The assumption is that, if we can just get our target public to understand, they will do what we want them to do.

But there's a big flaw in this assumption.

For the most part, people don't care about our organization's problems. They've got enough of their own. And simply communicating information to obtain a desired behavior rarely works. Twenty years of research across a wide range of disciplines and issues have shown that providing information alone on an issue, a product, or service will not significantly change the behaviors of a given public.

We live in a society with excess information. Literally tens of thousands of bits of information bombard us every day. Some we want; some we don't. Some of it we absorb and use; most of it never registers cognitively at all.

As communicators, we have not succeeded in shaping our communications into information the target public wants or needs. We typically organize our information into an understandable and (what we believe to be) creative format and then blurt it out in the public arena and hope for the best. That rarely works.

No matter how motivated the communicator might be, unsolicited information rarely finds as motivated a receiver. Very few members of a given public are prepared or even willing to act to the extent we want them to on the content of a public relations communication. A simple example helps make the point.

"Dick Daniels" opens up his crisis management and media training consulting firm just down the street from you and sends out a tasteful card communicating his new address and phone number. He sent that card trying to elicit action—or behavior. He wants people to call him. Do people automatically call for an appointment? Probably not. People will call him—that is, behave the way he wants them to—only if they perceive the need for counsel on how to handle a crisis or a media interview.

This chapter explores three phases of a behavioral public relations program, two of which occur before a news release is sent or other campaign tools are created: strategy development, packaging, and delivery. They apply to public relations and issues management as well as marketing communication.

Included in the packaging segment of this chapter is a behavioral framework that represents one systematic way practitioners can organize writing and public relations tactics to carry out the public relations plan that taps into our knowledge of human motivation.

STRATEGY DEVELOPMENT

Successful behavioral strategy evolves from a planning process designed to help public relations practitioners carry out their fundamental responsibility: to help their organizations or clients build and maintain a hospitable business climate.[1]

Public relations is best organized when it has systems in place to anticipate issues likely to affect the organization and has plans to address the top-priority issues (both threats and opportunities) at an early stage when they are most manageable. For example, an agricultural trade group might have to face a litany of issues involving the environment and competition for natural resources. A telecommunications firm could face public concern about invasion of privacy. A governmental regulatory agency may face growing skepticism over regulations that don't make common or economic sense. Preparing for anticipated changes can often head off undesirable changes or speed up those that are positive.

One effective public relations planning process, designed by Nuffer, Smith, Tucker, Inc., includes eight steps, as shown in Figure 34–1. Once a system has been set up to anticipate and prioritize issues likely to impact the mission of an organization, plans turn to building and maintaining relationships with others affected by the issues important to your organization.

Clarifying the threat or opportunity and analyzing the other groups affected is part of the second step in this public relations planning process: the situational analysis. Assessing the likely perceptions, positions, and behavioral inclinations of those holding a stake in the issue lays the foundation for publics identified later in the process. The situational analysis also includes an assessment of the forces working both for and against the potential threat or opportunity, and assumptions about which direction the issue appears to be headed.

The situational analysis provides a database to call upon when you begin making behavioral strategy decisions. The first decision lies with the position of the organization. The key question to ask in searching for the strategy with the highest odds for behavioral outcome is: Can you take a position that is mutually beneficial to the organization, to most of the stakeholders you've identified and analyzed in your situation analysis, and to the greater public good? Positions designed for mutual benefit have the most potential for eliciting widespread public support.

Once a position is decided on, the planning process turns to the publics most critical to advancing that position. Once again, the situational analysis provides the database. Of the stakeholders analyzed:

1. Who are the decision makers on the issue?
2. Who has influence on the decision makers?
3. Who is likely to support your position?
4. Who is likely not to support your position?
5. Who can you successfully target to make the biggest difference in advancing your organization's position on the issue?

F I G U R E 34–1

Public Relations Planning Process

Source: Kerry D. Tucker, Doris Derelian, and Donna Rouner, *Public Relations Writing, An Issues–Driven Behavioral Approach*, 2nd ed. (Englewood Cliffs, NJ: Prentice Hall, 1994), p. 9.

The answers to these questions lead to targeted publics. Behavioral goals—the ultimate outcomes and objectives that make possible the measurement of success—represent the next step in the behavioral planning process. *The behavioral strategy then is the route taken to achieve each objective.*

Force field analysis, a situational problem-solving technique developed in the 1940s by Kurt Lewin, is extremely helpful here. The playing field is diagrammed by forces working for and against your behavioral goal(s). The visual impact gives you a sense of the complexity of the issue and the factors that will need to be addressed for behavioral results (see Figure 34–2).

The strategy development process is advanced by asking a series of questions:

- Which factors will make the biggest difference in advancing the desired behavior? Of those, which can we be successful addressing?
- Of these priority issues, how can those that restrain us be eliminated or at least minimized? How can those that support our behavioral goal be strengthened?
- Which new forces can we add to the force field to advance the desired behavior?

The final question says it all:

- Where can we put time and resources to make the biggest difference in advancing our behavioral goal?

F I G U R E   34–2

Force Field Analysis of the Issues and Factors Involved in Reducing Solo Car Trips

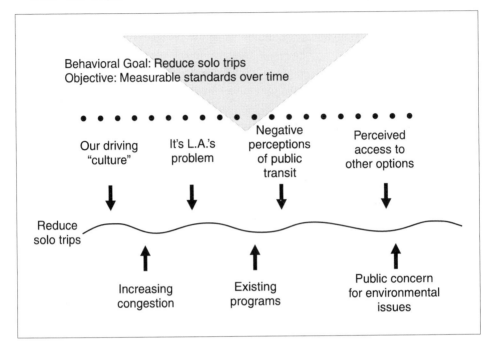

Communication (or education) is only one strategic option. Public relations practitioners tend to draw a line in the sand and limit themselves to the communication option. The truth is that other options often are needed to garner public support for an organization's position or a desired action. Public relations practitioners should recommend strategies beyond communication, even if they aren't the ones who carry them out. Other successful behavioral strategies[2] include:

- Changing rules or laws (for example, restricting smoking areas in restaurants, or mandatory use of seat belts).
- Making social or structural changes (such as physically redesigning campsites to make accidental fires less likely, or redesigning toilets to use less water).
- Creating interpersonal support (for example, organizing support groups like Weight Watchers, or forming neighborhood coalitions to apply peer pressure to those refusing to recycle cans, bottles, and newspapers).

PACKAGING FOR BEHAVIORAL OUTCOMES

Messages are created to advance the behavioral goals and objectives. They are developed as part of communication strategy. A logical question to ask is: What can be said about the position that will facilitate the desired behavior? What can we say to maximize the forces working in our favor and minimize those working against us?

The American Institute of Wine & Food's behavioral goal, to generate public endorsement by the nation's health leadership that all foods (in moderation) fit in a healthful diet, has three priority messages:

1. Restrictive food regimens fail to improve the dietary behavior for most Americans.
2. Taste is the number one motivation for making food selections.
3. There are no good foods or bad foods. Low- and high-fat foods can be balanced over several days to meet dietary recommendations.

Following the settlement of a multi-million-dollar consumer fraud lawsuit, a community garbage collection company targeted city officials and their staff with these two behavioral goals: (1) improve business relationships with city officials and staff; and (2) convince city officials and staff not to add more regulations. Its messages were:

1. We've resolved the problem.
2. We're up-front, responsive, honest, and fair.
3. We're your partners in recycling and committed to your community.

While people naturally resist change, communication strategies and messages (and tactics) can be organized to increase the odds of breaking through the information clutter we all face daily. They can do so by contrasting existing behavior with the desired behavior, facilitating discomfort with existing behavior, and offering help in adopting a new action.

An effective framework to apply in evaluating communications against behavioral principles is organized around four basic sets of questions:

1. Does the communication raise a public need, concern, or interest?
Consistently attracting attention from publics and their opinion leaders demands painting real-life scenarios. While a federal government report on calcium deficiencies in the American diet may be rather boring on its own, it can be made relevant by packaging it to raise a concern among mothers who substitute soda for milk, thereby putting their children— especially young daughters—at serious risk for osteoporosis later in life. Metaphors and analogies help here too, using something familiar to make a new idea relevant.

2. Is your desired behavior clearly and credibly packaged to meet the need, resolve the concern, or satisfy the interest?
The more precise you are in packaging the desired behavior as a resolution to the need, concern, or interest you've raised, the better. The Coalition for Local Control, a group formed to stop the merger between San Diego Gas & Electric Company and Southern California Edison, raised a community concern about the "Los Angelization" of San Diego to the constituents of its far-reaching coalition. The Coalition offered as a solution contacting the state's public utility commission with a plea to stop the merger.

3. Have you clearly presented the benefits of action and the consequences of inaction? Have you made the strongest case you can to create discomfort with existing behavior?
The key to moving past public resistance to change is often creating discomfort with an existing behavior pattern. If those who shape public opinion on health are apathetic about serving children milk, mothers no doubt will be ambivalent. The research presented in a federal government report, if packaged correctly, can cause the discomfort necessary to initiate behavior change. This can be the "trigger," as counselor Patrick Jackson calls it, that motivates a public to opt for a new action.

4. Have you helped the receiver mentally rehearse the desired behavior?
Mental rehearsal is a natural process of thinking about a planned behavior—what you will do, when you will do it, where you will do it, and, most importantly, how you will successfully perform the behavior. It is analogous to a dress rehearsal that all of us run through at some level or another before we try a new behavior.

Most people have difficulty transferring information to behavior without help. Focusing only on sharing information leaves the action up to the receiver. The risks are great that an individual will pass up information, not because it isn't useful, but because you haven't helped create a mental picture of how to use it.

For example, what are the steps to encourage a call or letter to members of the Public Utility Commission on behalf of the Coalition for Local Control? It may be as simple as providing a name, phone number, and address. It may also mean helping individuals think of how they will answer potential questions from the Commission staff. Providing individuals with tips on how to adopt the desired behavior is probably the most common mental rehearsal technique. For example, mothers being encouraged to manage their children's food choices in a less-controlling way may be given the following tips: monitor what your children eat over several days rather than by food or by meal; and have plenty of healthful foods—particularly fruit and vegetable snacks—on hand.

With brochures and pamphlets, cueing phrases such as "think through," "when was the last time you," or "picture yourself" can be particularly helpful. Questions also help an individual think through the desired action. Examples are "What is your best option for taking the action?" or "If that doesn't work, what can you do to make it work?" The key is getting people to begin thinking about incorporating the desired behavior into their own lives.

This four-element framework is helpful in organizing written content for oral presentations, direct mail, collateral materials, publicity angles, public service announcements, and business letters—virtually any public relations tactic. It also can serve as valuable criteria to evaluate communication content for the greatest odds of stimulating supportive behavior.

A real-world example helps communicate the framework components (see Figure 34–3). A news release written for the California Dietetic Association responded to a growing trend of parents exerting too much control over their children's food choices. Keep in mind that the order of the second and third components can be reversed and still achieve the same results, as you'll see.

A *concern was raised* in the lead about parents who expect children to follow dietary guidelines for adults and the fact that they might be putting unnecessary, harmful pressures on their youngsters. In the third paragraph, the *consequence of the undesirable behavior* is articulated in the form of a quote from the organization president. Further into the press release, the *desired behavior* (to resolve the concern)—lightening up on your kids' food choices—is communicated, again in the form of a quote from a credible expert. Lastly, the reader is given three tips to *help him or her mentally rehearse the desired behavior.*

THE TACTICS OF MESSAGE DELIVERY

Tactical decisions on how best to carry out each strategy are next. It's here that you decide what communication vehicles will best contribute to the desired behaviors. How can we best reach the opinion leaders and their publics?

F I G U R E 34–3

Press Release Illustrating the Four-Element
Communications Framework

NEWS– CALIFORNIA DIETETIC ASSOCIATION

For April 8 release:

EXPECTATIONS OF CHILDREN'S EATING HABITS MAY CAUSE UNDUE STRESS

Parents who expect their children to follow dietary guidelines for adults may be heaping unnecessary and potentially harmful pressures on their youngsters.

That's one of the conclusions drawn by the Coalition for Healthy Children, a group of national experts in health, nutrition, education and anthropology assembled recently to address the growing misperceptions about the healthy development of children.

"Children can easily be treated like little adults when it comes to expectations about eating," said Barbara Gaffield, R.D., president of the California Dietetic Association. *The resulting stress can be unhealthy for children and their families.*

A case in point, she said, are the guidelines for children released this week by the National Cholesterol Education Program. They recommend that children and adolescents, like adults, restrict total fat in their diets to 30 percent of all calories consumed and keep saturated fats to less than 10 percent of total calories.

"Parents and caregivers of children can interpret this regimen in a way that may unnecessarily narrow food choices for children and label as "bad" many foods children enjoy eating, such as cake and ice cream at birthday parties or a hot dog at a baseball game, or a small chunk of cheese after school," said Gaffield.

"Eating should not be an area for excessive parental control and food should not be used as a reward or punishment," she said.

Gaffield offered the following suggestions for helping to manage children's food choices.

- Monitor the foods your children eat over several days rather than food by food, meal by meal. Then evaluate the quality of all the foods consumed.

- Encourage your children to eat fruits and vegetables such as oranges and carrot sticks, as well as breads, which are naturally low in fat. Have plenty of these foods on hand. They will help balance their consumption of higher fat foods and ensure that their total food intake is moderate in fat.

- Your children will have more flexibility in food choices if they are active at play one to two hours per day.

The California Dietetic Association, with the help of pediatric dietitians statewide, has developed several other tips to help parents manage their children's food choices and healthy diets. For a copy of the tips, send a self-addressed, stamped envelope to "Children's Tips" 3170 Fourth Ave., Suite 300, San Diego, CA 92103.

Obviously, you need to know where your targeted publics get their information. Of equal importance is which information sources have the most behavioral clout. Which carry the greatest odds of facilitating support for your position on an issue?

Credibility is the primary selection criterion because it has the greatest impact on behavioral goals and objectives. The more personal the communication, the more important the credibility factor. The more credibility, the more likely the targeted public is to receive, accept, and act on your message.

Communication tactics can be segmented for credibility into five categories in order of believability:

1. Individual presentation (one-on-one, small group, large group).
2. Personal communication (telephone, direct mail).
3. Targeted media (specialty magazines, trade and employee media).
4. Mass media coverage.
5. Advertising.[3]

Because advertising is the least credible tactic in the practitioner's quiver—also frequently the least personal—this chapter will not explore it in any further detail but will focus on the four other tactics.

Individual Presentation

One-on-one, eyeball-to-eyeball communication is incredibly powerful, especially if the message is delivered by an opinion leader, an individual whose views on a subject are respected, even sought out. A respected scientist shares new research data with another scientist. The leader of a prestigious community business group shares the impact of a proposed legislative initiative with a business colleague. A physician shares the latest development in preventive treatment with a patient.

Opinion leaders are direct conduits to targeted publics. They already have the relationships you need to facilitate support for your position on an issue. If they buy into and adopt your organization's position, they can help advance it with their own constituencies, both independently and as campaign spokespersons.

One-on-one communication is credible; messages can be personalized to the needs, concerns, and interests of the receiver, and a case can be built for the desired behavior. The dialogue that results from this type of exchange is a powerful technique for changing behavior.

Practically speaking, one-on-one communication, facilitated by a public relations practitioner, is usually reserved for opinion-leader-to-opinion-leader communication. Examples include: a meeting arranged for a leading scientist and decision-making bureaucrats within the Department of Health and Human Services to initiate discussion on a new direction on public policy; a meeting arranged between the "right" constituent and a state senator on a pending legislative vote; and a meeting arranged between chief executives of the two major corporations in town to recruit participation in a fund-raising drive.

Building coalitions is a highly effective mechanism for one-on-one communication with opinion leaders. Coalitions bring together opinion leaders representing various interests who share a common issue. Mutually beneficial positions are facilitated through dialogue. Strategies are crafted together to advance the position.

While coalition-building has long been a tactic in managing regulatory and legislative issues, its use is expanding to other areas of public relations as one-sided communication tactics are increasingly replaced with relationship-building strategies. Building relationships requires dialogue and harmony among those sharing a stake in the issues confronting organizations and industries. Coalition-building is prospering because most companies and industries can no longer afford to exist alone. There is power in numbers. There is power in diversification. The collective influence of many interests is formidable. The credibility of coalition-building can generate support for a desired behavior from the constituencies of opinion leaders and broader publics.

Nearly as important as one-on-one communication is the use of small-group presentations in which individuals are given opportunities to seek answers to their questions, challenge assumptions, and work through the benefits and consequences of embracing the desired behaviors.

Interaction is more difficult with large-group presentations. Organizing presentations using the behavioral framework and providing adequate time for questions and answers are the most effective techniques. Sticking around after the presentation and soliciting questions and answers is also effective. Dialogue is the greatest strategy for creating discomfort with existing behaviors, which is necessary to facilitate change.

Personal Communications

When individuals know and respect one another, personal communication runs a close second to one-on-one, in-person communication. Telephone communication becomes more difficult when the parties do not know one another. It often is used in tandem with the mail to introduce an idea and build momentum for a direction. A letter from a trusted colleague can open the doors for a public relations practitioner to make a coalition recruitment call to a targeted opinion leader. Or, a cold call can be followed up with a letter and package of materials building a case for the importance of getting on board.

Direct mail is probably the most under-utilized technique available to the practitioner. Next to face-to-face communications and the telephone, it is one of the most personal tactics and one of the most effective. Direct mail advertising, driven by marketing communications objectives, is opened by two-thirds of American households. Public relations-driven direct mail, because of its subtlety and use of credible third-party spokespersons, enjoys even better results.

Public relations practitioners use direct mail as a means of facilitating communications not only between an organization and its publics, but also between opinion leaders and opinion leaders, as well as between opinion leaders and their constituencies. A simple letter can be a powerful tool when sent by the right person *to* the right person. Lists of opinion leaders are as important to a practitioner as media lists.

There are a few things to keep in mind when writing direct mail, personal letters, and other communications tools. Public relations writing is more than just sitting down at a word processor and writing beautiful prose or generating a hard-hitting publicity angle. Writing for public relations focuses on advancing messages to create supportive behavior from groups of people who are involved with or affected by the way an organization conducts its business. Consequently, the most effective way to write and organize techniques for public relations writing is to use knowledge about human motivation. In the end, it is not how well you have generated what you, the writer, consider to be an interesting letter or publicity angle, but rather how well you catch the attention of targeted publics and help them work through the steps necessary to generate supportive behavior.

The four-element behavioral framework presented earlier is a guide for organizing all public relations writing. The behavioral framework can be used to package written materials with the greatest odds for reaching and motivating targeted publics to act; to build the case for an issue; and to advance it with employees, opinion leaders, and target publics in oral presentations, direct mail, publications, special events, and publicity.

Targeted Media

Specialty newspapers, magazines, industry trade publications (virtually every industry has at least one and frequently several), and newsletters provide a direct route to the target public. Like specialty sections of newspapers, they are prescreened for the target audience and already address the appropriate needs, concerns, and interests.

Specialty publications often carry more credibility with the reader than mass media because of the in-depth way in which they cover their subject. Their readers also tend to be more active seekers of information than mass media readers and, as such, more receptive to behavioral objectives. Newsletters are among the better-received controlled publications, especially when they're designed to meet targeted public interests or needs. The purpose of newsletters is usually threefold:

- To present special information to a special audience.
- To positively reinforce cognitions and attitudes about the sponsoring organization.[4]
- To generate supportive behavior for an organization's position on issues.

Newsletters should be organized for mutual benefit of the sender and receiver. Formats vary from rapid-fire, three-dot journalism, and "Kiplinger-style" news capsules (see Figure 34–4) to slick, four-color publications with photographs and illustrations (see Figure 34–5).

Mass Media Coverage

Print

Among the first tasks handed to a public relations practitioner is the research and writing of support materials for mass media publicity campaigns. Position papers, backgrounders, biographies and fact sheets, query letters, advisories, and news releases are among the tools researched and written by public relations professionals.

Fact sheets describe quickly and clearly in some variation the basic who, what, when, where, why, and how of an issue or organization. In fact, a simple fact sheet format can reflect those very questions.

A fact sheet may describe an issue, an organization, a special event, or an important change in organization policy. Fact sheets are basic, quick-read information for executives, co-workers, spokespersons, external opinion leaders, and journalists.

The **backgrounder** goes into more detail than the fact sheet. The writing style continues to be brief, direct, concise, and informative. The writing tone is neutral and factual.

Backgrounders are a key mechanism used to report on current issues and trends of importance to the mission of the organization. A backgrounder may be used as part of a report to shareholders or a board of directors. It may be used to train a spokesperson for a media interview. Or, it may stand on its own as a component of a press kit organized to advance a position on an issue.

A **position paper, often referred to as a "white paper,"** evolves from the situation analysis. In fact, it can be considered the public version of the situation analysis. While the situation analysis provided data for management to develop its position on an issue, the position paper describes the organization's position and its rationale for that position. It clearly takes a stand on an issue and provides evidence to support its position.

F I G U R E 34–4

A Newsletter Format Featuring Brief News Capsules

DAIRY COUNCIL OF CALIFORNIA

TRENDS

SPRING 1993

FOOD/NUTRITION ISSUES LIKELY TO IMPACT THE DAIRY INDUSTRY IN THE NEXT 3 TO 5 YEARS

Top 10 Nutrition Trends 92-93

Following is a quick look at the nutrition issues cited most during the last planning year (March 30, 1992 - March 1, 1993) with updates and implications for the future. (The number in parentheses indicates the issue's ranking last year.)

1. Dietary Fat (6)
- It's a given among health professionals that Americans need to lower their fat intake; pressure to make it happen will continue.
- The increasing incidence of heart disease and cancer will continue the trend toward recommendations to limit dietary fat intake to less than 30-percent calories from fat; some are advocating levels as low as 20 to 25 percent.

2. Food safety (4)
- Concerns for the safety of our food supply will continue to be a part of the overall environmental discussion with a big focus on the risks posed to children.
- The new administration will likely change the roles of federal regulatory agencies (USDA, FDA, EPA...) in protecting our food supply.

3. Children's issues (2)
- Spurred by recommendations from the American Academy of Pediatrics (AAP), pressure will increase to lower children's dietary fat intake to less than 30 percent calories from fat.
- Concern for children's welfare will receive increasing attention and drive the dialogue on children's food and nutrition topics.

4. Nutrition legislation (3)
- Education to support the new labeling law will teach consumers how to count grams of fat and allow them to make comparisons among different foods. Such comparisons will put 1-percent and nonfat milk in a positive light.

5. Milk and dairy products (5)
- So-called "consumer advocacy" groups will continue to make claims that certain foods commonly believed to be healthful, including milk, are "bad" for you, despite growing evidence for their role in overall health. Two-percent milk will come under increasing attack as not being "lowfat."

6. Food Groupings (9)
- Application of the USDA Eating Right Pyramid will lead to a continued use of food groups in nutrition education.

7. Food products and processing (7)
- Manufacturers will continue to develop products to meet the growing demand for healthy food choices, including dairy.

8. Calcium (Not in top 10)
- The growing body of knowledge linking calcium consumption with building peak bone mass, reduced bone loss and decreased risk of other diseases (colon cancer, hypertension) will gain increased attention.
- A majority of health professionals will continue to recommend getting calcium from foods rather than supplements.

9. Environment (Not in top 10)
Note: The environment is being tracked separately this year due to increased linkages between environmental issues and food products, including dairy.
- Food and agricultural products will increasingly be tied to discussions on environmental issues in the areas of water use, pesticides, animal rights and drug residues.

10. Supplements (Not in top 10)
- The growing body of research on protective properties of foods (neutraceuticals) will lend support for consumption of vitamin/mineral supplements as well as fortification of existing food products.

Courtesy of Dairy Council of California.

FIGURE 34–5

A Magazine-Style Newsletter Form

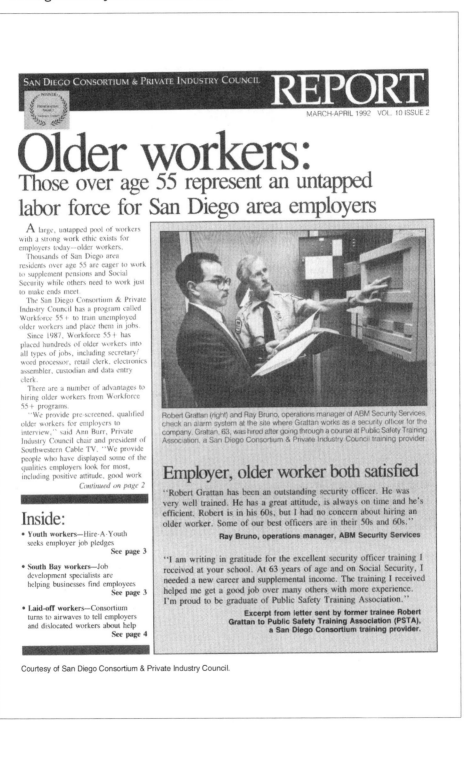

SAN DIEGO CONSORTIUM & PRIVATE INDUSTRY COUNCIL REPORT

MARCH-APRIL 1992   VOL. 10 ISSUE 2

Older workers:
Those over age 55 represent an untapped labor force for San Diego area employers

A large, untapped pool of workers with a strong work ethic exists for employers today—older workers.

Thousands of San Diego area residents over age 55 are eager to work to supplement pensions and Social Security while others need to work just to make ends meet.

The San Diego Consortium & Private Industry Council has a program called Workforce 55+ to train unemployed older workers and place them in jobs.

Since 1987, Workforce 55+ has placed hundreds of older workers into all types of jobs, including secretary/ word processor, retail clerk, electronics assembler, custodian and data entry clerk.

There are a number of advantages to hiring older workers from Workforce 55+ programs.

"We provide pre-screened, qualified older workers for employers to interview," said Ann Burr, Private Industry Council chair and president of Southwestern Cable TV. "We provide people who have displayed some of the qualities employers look for most, including positive attitude, good work

Continued on page 2

Inside:

- **Youth workers**—Hire-A-Youth seeks employer job pledges
  See page 3

- **South Bay workers**—Job development specialists are helping businesses find employees
  See page 3

- **Laid-off workers**—Consortium turns to airwaves to tell employers and dislocated workers about help
  See page 4

Robert Grattan (right) and Ray Bruno, operations manager of ABM Security Services, check an alarm system at the site where Grattan works as a security officer for the company. Grattan, 63, was hired after going through a course at Public Safety Training Association, a San Diego Consortium & Private Industry Council training provider.

Employer, older worker both satisfied

"Robert Grattan has been an outstanding security officer. He was very well trained. He has a great attitude, is always on time and he's efficient. Robert is in his 60s, but I had no concern about hiring an older worker. Some of our best officers are in their 50s and 60s."

Ray Bruno, operations manager, ABM Security Services

"I am writing in gratitude for the excellent security officer training I received at your school. At 63 years of age and on Social Security, I needed a new career and supplemental income. The training I received helped me get a good job over many others with more experience. I'm proud to be graduate of Public Safety Training Association."

Excerpt from letter sent by former trainee Robert Grattan to Public Safety Training Association (PSTA), a San Diego Consortium training provider.

Courtesy of San Diego Consortium & Private Industry Council.

Writing a **news release** provides the practitioner with basic training in what it takes to generate news; it is the training ground for generating publicity. Two additional criteria should be added to the who, what, where, when, why, and how news criteria of a release. First, it is written to advance public relations objectives, and second, the release is organized to capitalize on behavioral principles, using the behavioral framework.

Publicity targeted to stimulate dialogue among opinion leaders, their peers, and their constituencies can be powerful. The following two-paragraph feature lead, published in *The Wall Street Journal*[5], raises a public's interest, provides a solution, and offers some concrete imagery. Note that the spokesperson's direct quotation even uses the word "solution":

> WASHINGTON—Does the air in your office make you nauseous? Try sitting next to a plant. Better yet, sit next to a fan pointed at a plant.
>
> The National Aeronautics and Space Administration says plants can clean up fumes from paint, furniture, and cigarettes that make office workers woozy. B. C. Wolverton, a scientist at NASA's Stennis Space Center in Bay St. Louis, Miss., calls plants a "promising, economical solution to indoor air pollution."

One of the leads used by the Associated Press strengthened the concept:

> Thousands of Americans, attempting to become healthier, may be poisoning their bodies with huge doses of vitamin supplements that can be dangerous in large quantities, a group of scientists said Monday.[6]

The Associated Press lead raised an audience concern (that supplements may be dangerous), and the third and fourth paragraphs delivered the second part of the message verbatim from the news release:

> "We in the scientific community are concerned with the increasing notion that supplements can be used to prevent serious diseases, such as cancer and osteoporosis," said Dr. David Heber, chief of clinical nutrition at the UCLA School of Medicine.
>
> "Americans should get their nutrients from food instead of pills," Heber said. "Large supplement doses of single nutrients won't prevent diseases, but instead will upset absorption of other nutrients."[7]

The lead raises the need/concern/interest. This is followed in the body copy by the desired behavior as a solution, a description of the benefits of acting on the message and the consequences of inaction. Helping the reader think about how to adopt the desired behavior (mental rehearsal) also falls in the body of the copy.

Once the case is adequately made—preferably on one page but no more than two to three pages—the release is complete.

When a news release is completed, the writer should ask the following guiding questions:

1. Have I clearly raised a public need, concern, or interest?
2. Is the desired behavior clearly presented as a believable solution?
3. Have I clearly presented the benefits of acting and the consequences of inaction? Have I made the strongest case I can to create discomfort with existing behavior?
4. Have I helped the individual mentally rehearse the desired behavior?

Electronic Media

Most radio and television publicity opportunities come from interview placements on talk and news shows, secured through the **query letter.** As in news releases, content for the query letter starts with brainstorming ideas to advance your behavioral framework.

The query letter is usually a one-page description of the news angle. It forces the practitioner to organize his or her thoughts, to crystallize the most salient news angle. Reasons are presented to pique the interest of the reporter in a story idea.

When dealing in television there is the added need for visual ideas. The query letter to television news assignment editors or talk show producers must provide suggestions for bringing the story alive for the eye. Ask yourself: What action do we want the audience to take? How can we expand the message with visuals? What visual best demonstrates our message? How can we best transfer the message to the viewer's own real-life experiences? The first paragraph of the query letter is as important as the lead in a news release. It must grab the reader's interest. To illustrate, the following was the first paragraph of a query letter from US WEST Cellular to local newspapers:

> The stage is set. The gloves are off. The battle lines drawn. To the victor goes dominance in Seattle's growing cellular telephone service.

Thus, you lead the query letter with a strong appeal to the needs, concerns, or interests of the journalist who is charged with determining public interests.

The lead paragraph should be followed up with a series of tightly written, brief paragraphs or bulleted facts describing the news angle and why it is important to readers, listeners, and/or viewers.

Advisories, like query letters, are designed to quickly pique the interest of the media gatekeeper. A mental picture of a special event such as a news conference is painted for those who make decisions regarding who gets in the newspaper or on a broadcast news or talk show.

Successful media advisories have common characteristics. First, they get attention with a hard-hitting paragraph about the nature of the event and why it should be covered. Second, they read fast (short words and sentences). Third, they are contained in one (or two) pages. And fourth, they are sent to the right person.

In a media advisory for Bumble Bee Seafoods, the what, when, and where were outlined in bullet points with additional information raising the need, concern, and interest at the top (see Figure 34–6).

Writing **public service announcements** (PSAs) is another story. Public relations practitioners are called on to capitalize on time given free by radio and television stations to messages in the public interest. Quality, time-intensive, but conversational writing can be the difference for successful public service announcements.

Keep the PSA simple, trying to motivate the listener or viewer to one basic action step. Straightforward, clean action steps work the best.

All of these tactics are strengthened when using the behavioral packaging discussed earlier. All are strengthened when speaking through those who shape the opinions of the publics targeted: their opinion leaders.

FUTURE PUBLIC RELATIONS BEHAVIOR

Information alone rarely obtains a desired public behavior. Decades of research bear it out. Practitioners, in their guts know it too.

As communicators, we have to do a better job of shaping our communication into information that targets publics' wants or needs. Public relations campaigns that are systematically strategized, packaged, and delivered to target publics with specific, suppor-

F I G U R E 34–6

A MEDIA ADVISORY

The Omega 3 Connection

Bumble Bee Seafoods, Inc.
P.O. Box 25508
San Diego, CA 92123
(619) 560-4404

NEWS

Contact: Valerie Lemke or
Gretchen Griswold
(212) 883-1234
July 25 - 29
or (619) 296-0605
After July 30

MEDIA ADVISORY

New research from Massachusetts Institute of Technology (MIT) disproves widespread speculation that cooking and processing fish destroys beneficial omega-3 fatty acids, thought to prevent heart disease.

The MIT Sea Grant program tested five of the most commonly consumed fish to measure levels of omega-3 fatty acids, including canned tuna and breaded fish filets. The results point to inexpensive and more practical alternatives to fish oil capsules.

The MIT officer in charge of this study will be available to discuss the findings. Also available will be a UCLA lipid researcher who can sift through the health claims and outline the best omega-3 sources. Visuals provided.

EVENT: Presentation of MIT findings of Omega 3 levels of commonly consumed cooked fish

WHERE/WHEN: Monday, July 27, 1987, 10 a.m. to 11 a.m.
Room 1428, Grand Hyatt Hotel
Park Avenue at Grand Central Station

PARTICIPANTS: Arthur Clifton, project director
MIT Sea Grant Program

Judith Ashley, M.S.P.H., R.D., research associate
UCLA School of Medicine

# # #

Courtesy of Bumble Bee Seafood, Inc.

tive behavioral outcomes at the core stand a much better chance of breaking through today's information clutter and demonstrating to the CEO that public relations *can* generate measurable, supportive behaviors, *can* make an impact, *can* move the needle.

ENDNOTES

1. "A Challenge to the Calling: Public Relations Colloquium," sponsored by San Diego State University, Northwestern University, and Nuffer, Smith, Tucker, Inc., 1992.

2. *pr reporter* 26, no. 5 (January 31, 1983).

3. Center, Allen H., and Frank E. Walsh, *Public Relations Practices: Managerial Case Studies and Problems* (Englewood Cliffs, NJ: Prentice Hall, 1985), p. 17.

4. Grunig and Hunt, *Managing Public Relations*, p. 455.

5. *The Wall Street Journal*, September 27, 1989, p. 1.

6. Associated Press, *Arizona Daily Star*, May 6, 1986, p. 1.

7. Ibid.

CHAPTER 35

The Value of Effective Speechwriting

Lee W. Huebner, Ph.D.
Professor, Communications Studies and Journalism
Medill School of Journalism
Northwestern University

Speechwriters like to share the story about a somewhat overbearing politician who not only made enormous demands on his staff but was notoriously unappreciative of even their finest efforts. Nonetheless, his power and influence helped him attract a wide array of talented aides, one of whom prepared a particularly eloquent text for him on a particularly important occasion. "Ladies and gentlemen," the Senator began to read as his distinguished audience gave him their rapt attention. "It has been said again and again through the years that you can't have a full employment economy and still have enduring price stability. Well, I say you can have both—and tonight I'm going to tell you how to do it. And they say," he continued, "that you can't invest in a stronger national defense, while at the same time cutting taxes and balancing the budget. Well, tonight I'm going to tell you how to do that, as well. And, finally, the experts are also fond of saying that you can't address this country's pressing social problems, and still cut back on the size of government bureaucracy. Well I say you can, and tonight, once again, I'm going to tell you how."

And then he turned to the next page of his manuscript, and looked down to see the following handwritten words: "All right, old timer, you're on your own. I quit."

A STRATEGIC APPROACH TO SPEECHWRITING

Descriptions and Definitions

Whatever this story may say about the frustrations of unsung and anonymous staff assistants, it can also be seen as a pointed reflection of the growing importance of the speechwriter in contemporary society. For increasingly, in both the public and the private sectors, the person who speaks is not the person who writes the speech, and the person who actually has all the answers is not necessarily the person who brings those answers into public view.

And the public knows it. The existence of that invisible agent who was once called a ghostwriter is no longer a secret. Anyone who speaks from a manuscript these days risks the charge that he or she is reading someone else's rhetoric, and perhaps even relaying someone else's views.

One response to this development has been a massive rush to the use of an extemporaneous style of speaking which is clearly, and sometimes even ostentatiously, unscripted. We are encouraged from our early years to "say it in your own words," to speak conversationally. And the rise of the talk-show culture has fed even further our expectation that we will get to know public figures initially and primarily as conversationalists rather than as orators.

To be sure, the admonition to speak without a script is often very good advice; there are countless speaking situations in which communication is dramatically enhanced when the speaker tosses away his or her manuscript—figuratively, or even literally. Richard Nixon, who criticized the fact that John Kennedy used notes in the first presidential campaign debates in 1960, later made it a trademark to speak whenever possible without a lectern, using only a stand-alone microphone to dramatize the fact that he was speaking entirely from memory, and therefore, presumably, from personal conviction rather than from a prefabricated text. President Bill Clinton has even extemporized a part of his State of the Union Address to the Congress, a striking expression of our growing social inclination—bred perhaps by the informality of television—to give a higher value to spontaneity than to precision, to value sincerity more than eloquence.

For many speakers and in many situations, the extemporaneous form—using notes perhaps but not a full speaking text—is often the best choice, if only because so many of the worst speeches we hear are full-text offerings which are not only poorly written but are also poorly read. Think of the many times we all leave a speech with the observation: "He was much better in the question-and-answer period." Or "It was only after she got away from her text that the program really came alive." Audiences are often right to prefer the warmth and directness of a conversational talk (however much it may ramble or repeat) to the chilling, numbing ordeal of having to sit patiently while a lifeless reader stands stiffly and remotely at the front of the room, droning through a dry document which could have been comprehended much more easily (and much more speedily) if it had simply been passed out for everyone to read.

And yet, for a variety of reasons, the scripted speech still holds a valued place in our society, especially in the corporate world. The answer to the ubiquitous problem of the deadly full-text speech is not only to use texts less, but also to use texts better.

This means, of course, that we must learn the art of delivering a pre-written presentation in a graceful and engaging manner (Ronald Reagan built a dazzling political career around this special competence). But it also means, perhaps even more importantly, that we must learn to write speeches in ways which will appeal to the ear of the listener who hears them in person and not only to the eye of the reader who sees them on a page. It was when the delivery skills of Ronald Reagan (well honed over many years spent mastering scripts for films) were matched with the writing skills of Peggy Noonan (well honed in the daily grind of writing for CBS radio audiences) that the Reagan presidency reached many of its rhetorical heights.

Trends and Developments

Why should we make such an effort to hang onto the fully written speech as a central weapon in our communications arsenal? Why not simply abandon the form—as most political campaigners seem to have done? Are there any particular advantages to the scripted speech which explain its continued use and which validate any time and attention we give to improving the way the form is handled?

There are good and persuasive answers to all of these questions. For one thing, a manuscript speech fosters a level of precision which extemporaneous speaking cannot match—and which can be essential in the discussion of sensitive topics. Working with a text can also be an extremely effective way to institutionalize a speech, to use the writing and vetting process as a way both to formulate policy and to achieve consensus within the organization which the speaker represents. Using a manuscript can also ensure the most efficient and effective use of time; only when phrases are carefully chosen and chiseled and polished in advance of the speaking situation can one be sure of packing the most meaning into what is often (in our busy world) a sharply restricted time frame.

If it is well done, moreover, a written manuscript can aspire to rhetorical and persuasive heights which the extemporaneous speech normally writes off, or, at best, leaves to the inspiration of the moment. The mere existence of a manuscript can also have its own persuasive impact: in some situations it can be an eloquent symbol in its own right, saying to the audience, "I consider this occasion so important that I wanted to choose my words in advance. And you would do well to listen to this speech as carefully as I have prepared it." (The risk, of course, is not delivering on that ambitious promise.)

Another advantage is that a manuscript speech can be easily circulated after the event at which it was presented, vastly broadening its audience. There are, in fact, any number of speaking occasions which are created primarily to legitimize the preparation and circulation of what was intended from the start to be a written document. For decades, politicians have treated local stump speeches in this fashion, releasing texts to the press with an indication that they were "prepared for delivery at the XYZ dinner." The practice has now even developed to the point at which preparing and labeling such a text can sometimes be enough—and no one really seems too bothered if the XYZ dinner never hears the words which will be in the news the next morning.

On the other hand, when Adlai Stevenson ran for the Presidency of the United States in 1952, he was widely criticized for making the opposite mistake, polishing his language until the last possible second (even while waiting to be introduced on stage). It was as if the only audience that mattered to him was the one that was in the room. The result was that the full impact of the speech was often lost on the wider public since the press corps—deprived of an advance text—had to miss important deadlines or report the speech from notes which often failed to capture the candidate's most effective phrases.

There are, then, a wide range of substantive reasons why a manuscript speech, whatever its communicative disadvantages, is still a part of the strategic arsenal for many speakers, especially in the corporate world. In addition, however, there are also a variety of social developments which have not only been helping to keep the craft of speechwriting alive, but have also been turning it into a specialized pursuit in its own right, performed increasingly by a specialized guild of skilled practitioners.

The natural persistence of simple stage fright is one such factor. Even the most confident of business executives can turn uncertain and anxious at the thought of wandering into the public arena without the security blanket of a clearly worded text. The sheer complexity of modern life further contributes to this phenomenon. For one thing, it takes more time and greater expertise to get one's arms around many of the subjects one is called to speak upon these days, even when the subject involves one's own company. Consider, for example, how much time even the most astute chairman will spend preparing for an annual shareholders' meeting.

In addition, the growing realization that most businesses are inextricably linked to a wide range of issues and constituencies—going well beyond the traditional and immediate concerns of the company—multiplies dramatically the range of occasions, audiences, and topics which any corporate speaker is asked to address. As a company's perception of its stakeholders becomes more wide-ranging and sophisticated, the ability of any spokesperson to address those stakeholders in a thoughtful and competent manner inevitably becomes less certain.

But at the same time that the speaker must understand more and more about a wider range of issues, the growing complexity of business life provides less time and fewer occasions for the typical executive to think and to train outside his or her own highly specialized areas of expertise. People come up through the ranks in their companies as specialists these days, in finance, perhaps, or in law or marketing or manufacturing or human resource matters, and even those who are most inclined to think of themselves as generalists are usually frustrated by their limited ability to attend to a fuller range of relevant issues.

And if all of this isn't enough, remember, too, that the audiences we speak to these days are far more demanding than may once have been the case. They, too, live ever-busier lives and are more protective of their time. They come to a speech with higher expectations and less patience than their counterparts did a generation or a century ago. One suspects that even Lincoln and Douglas would have more trouble holding the attention of a standing throng for hour after hour in the 1990s than they did in the 1850s. What time and patience a modern audience does possess, moreover, is constantly subjected to conflicting claims as a growing array of voices competes vigorously for public attention. Constant exposure to the most sophisticated, compelling, and entertaining messages that Madison Avenue and Hollywood can fashion must surely have a long-term impact on the expectations that any public brings to any speech.

It is also worth noting that speeches wear out more quickly these days. Media exposure and public mobility mean that the best lines and thoughts and jokes and stories—and even the best speeches—travel more quickly to more ears in more places than was the case in a simpler time. Gone are the preelectronic days when a great orator could build a career around one or two glittering gems of rhetoric, repeated thousands of times for thousands of audiences. Today's public speaker is, at the very least, under greater pressure to be original.

There is also less time for trial and error in modern life, less room, as it were, for out-of-town tryouts. Getting it right the first time has become a credo for ambitious managers—especially when it comes to public appearances.

On every side, then, the trends of our time are raising the stakes for public speakers, complicating their tasks, amplifying what is expected of them, and intensifying their competition. And all of this is happening at a time when writing skills are generally in decline, when there is less time, less need, and less inclination for most of us even to write letters, for example, or to read well-written books.

It is little wonder then that even the most self-reliant of corporate executives will turn more often to their wordsmiths—or even to a stable of wordsmiths—who can then turn their full talents and attention to meeting the challenges of an executive speech.

Even these corporate leaders who are most articulate in an extemporaneous settings, and who thus prefer the advantages of speaking conversationally from notes rather than relying upon texts, will still—for all of the reasons mentioned above—make use of writers who can assemble relevant information, pull together useful materials, and create appropriate language which a good speaker can then weave effectively into what may otherwise seem to be an entirely extemporaneous speech. Richard Nixon's writing staff spent much of its time preparing what were called "suggested remarks" for the president's public appearances—not full texts, but rather a loosely presented potpourri of supporting materials, illustrations, rhetorical suggestions, humorous or historical references—in short, a menu of suggested verbal ornaments from which the president could pick and choose appropriate and appealing items to dress up his informal talk.

The two forms, in other words, can often be blended; one can enjoy at least some of the spontaneity of the extemporaneous style without completely sacrificing the control and precision of the formal text. Mark Twain recognized this possibility when he remarked that "it takes about three weeks to prepare a really good extemporaneous speech," an observation which describes the technique of many accomplished "impromptu" speakers, including, as his biographers now tell us, Sir Winston Churchill.

Speechwriting and the Corporate Mission

Someone (with tongue perhaps at least partly in cheek) has compared the emergence of the speechwriting profession to the separation of writing and performance in other fields. We do not, for example, expect even the best musicians to play only their own compositions, the argument runs. Everyone knows that the actors in a play have not created their own dialogue. Why should speakers have to pretend that their speeches are all self-written?

However one answers that question, it seems clear that the task of speechwriting is now a fairly well-established discipline in many corporations. Those who perform it, to be sure, may carry a variety of titles and can perform a variety of other duties. Sometimes, indeed, the speechwriting task will even be farmed out to agencies or independent consultants or (even less formally) to friends and acquaintances ("Could you take a couple minutes to run through this draft and see if you can put a little life into it?"). But it is an unusual corporate office that does not turn to some sort of designated writer at fairly regular intervals. Not only are the days of the silent and mysterious corporate executive clearly over, but so are the days when a corporate spokesman could rely on personal instincts and the inspiration of the moment in articulating a company's point of view.

The strategic contribution of the speechwriter can, of course, be as varied as life itself. For the spoken word—especially from the mouth of a senior corporate representative—can be one of a company's most effective tools in the pursuit of almost any strategic objective. The recent popularity of the stakeholder concept in analyzing corporate constituencies helps demonstrate the manifold ways in which speechwriting can advance the corporate mission. Anyone and everyone listed on a well-drawn stakeholder map is a likely target audience for the corporate speaker and speechwriter.

A marketing speech to potential customers is an obvious and important possibility, of course. But so is testimony before a planning board or a legislative committee, a briefing for Wall Street analysts, a pep talk at a management retreat, an awards presentation at a community dinner, a toast at a retirement luncheon, or an address to a professional convention. On all these occasions—and a thousand others—any speaker who is known to be coming from a particular company is also—and almost inevitably—seen as speaking for that company, helping in direct and indirect ways to shape some public picture of the company's personality and character.

In an organization where long-range questions of public image do not seem especially important, then speechwriting will surely have a less-important place. But for that rapidly growing array of institutions which see their destiny being shaped by a growing array of stakeholders—and who realize that modern media have increased the transparency of all their transactions and have raised the audibility of all their communications—then the way that company introduces and explains itself and its views is an ever-more-critical part of its strategic planning.

It also goes almost without saying that such communications are increasingly global in their impact. At one level, a company doing business in many cultures must be ready to address those cultures on their terms and, whenever possible, in their language. But it is also important to remember another implication of global impact is the fact that any corporate communication, to any single stakeholder, is likely to be heard as well by many other stakeholders in many other places. The age of universal and fairly instantaneous communication is also an age that penalizes those who have a different line for each audience. While the style and emphasis of our various communications must be carefully adapted to each distinctive constituency, we must also pay more attention than ever before to the internal consistency of our messages. The whole world is listening, and the smart corporation no longer says anything to any one of its publics that it is not prepared to defend in front of all of its publics.

What it all boils down to is simply this: We must all pay increasing attention to what we are saying and how we are saying it. This communications requirement, in turn, gives a distinct competitive advantage to companies which have refined their sense of corporate mission and consolidated their sense of corporate strategy. And for companies which have achieved a strong sense of internal coherence and corporate consistency, good speechwriting can be looked upon as a particularly powerful way to leverage that accomplishment.

Seen in this strategic context, the speechwriter's role becomes much more than a passive and largely reactive exercise. It develops, instead, into an exhilarating, creative, proactive function. In this context, the writer no longer simply applies the last coat of rhetorical paint to policies that are formulated by others; he or she no longer is seen primarily as one who whips up a few risk-free phrases to keep the press at bay or to get the boss through the potential booby traps of yet another speaking situation. For the proactive, creative speechwriter—for the strategic speechwriter—understanding the company's mission and strategy is an essential first step to true effectiveness. And the second step is to use the speaking text and the speaking situation as a well-honed instrument for pursuing those strategic objectives.

Working with a range of corporate leaders, the strategic speechwriter will invest a good deal of time in an ongoing search for the theme that must be sounded, the idea that must be explored, the public that must be addressed, the criticism that must be answered. Looking and listening will be as important as writing for such a professional, for the key to a truly effective speech is finding the right match of speaker, topic, occasion, and audience. By proposing an interesting and appropriate range of topics and venues, and by contributing to the process by which the right selection of topics and venues is made, the proactive speechwriter can make an enormous contribution.

If audiences and topics are actively chosen to advance a clear corporate agenda, the task of writing a speech becomes much more interesting—and much more likely to end in triumph. The point of virtually any speech is to take an audience from where they were before the speech began to where you want them to be afterward. And how much more satisfying it is to accomplish this goal on behalf of some larger corporate mission!

SPEECHWRITING: SOME TACTICAL CONSIDERATIONS

Once the audience, the goal of the speech, and the identity of the speaker are clear, the task remaining is essentially one of finding the right words to bind these three elements together. This is essentially a tactical challenge, and the techniques involved have been the subject of many centuries of study and many volumes of counsel. New studies still appear regularly in the field, joined recently by a spate of speechwriting newsletters and manuals, many of which provide a rich sampling of those raw materials or building blocks (quotations, statistics, anecdotes, historical references, slogans, punch-lines, and so on) that, can do so much to bring a speech alive. Rather than trying to provide a comprehensive overview of the tactics of good speechwriting, the comments that follow will point to a few tactical considerations which seem to deserve special emphasis, especially in the current social context.

Understanding the Audience

Common sense would seem to dictate that if a speech is going to connect with an audience and change its thinking, then it has to be written with a specific audience in mind. Yet more speeches probably go wrong because they fail this test than for any other reason. For understanding diverse and scattered audiences in our day often requires a much greater commitment to research and a much finer capacity for empathy than was the case in more intimate societies and in simpler times. Knowing an audience means knowing what its background is and where its values lie. It means comprehending those areas in which the speaker can most easily achieve a ready rapport with the audience, and it means locating those preexisting hooks of emotion and belief to which the speaker can connect new propositions.

But understanding audiences involves not only a knowledge of how they think but also a feeling for how they themselves communicate. It means being able to speak their language—and doing so in a full and complete sense. This not only means appealing to their motives and values, but also using images that have power in their subculture, employing vocabulary and adopting rhythms that will give added richness and power to what is said. Like a good novelist or screenwriter, a good speechwriter will develop an ear for dialogue, an ability "to talk the talk," to appropriate the jargon, to use the rhetorical style of the audience whenever possible as a means of identifying the speaker with them.

All of this can be overdone, of course. The objective is to link the speaker and the audience, not to subsume or obliterate the speaker's own identity. But most speakers can retain their own personalities and still adapt their language and anecdotes, their sense of drama, and their sense of humor to what will work best with a particular group of listeners. The speaker who describes the process of downsizing or "making redundant" in one forum might communicate more effectively in other forums by changing the terminology to firing, or sacking, or even "tossing on the scrap heap." When presidential candidate Pat Buchanan used the rifleman's phrase "Lock and load!" as a metaphor to rally his followers against the perceived threats of foreign imports and illegal immigrants, he clearly and powerfully identified himself with what some have called "the warrior subculture" in modern America (though at the risk, perhaps, of bewildering if not offending other potential constituencies).

Adapting well to an audience means understanding not only its demographic composition but also what analysts now call its sociographic and psychographic nature. Even if one is presenting the same essential argument—the case for a particular educational reform, for example—one would make different appeals and use different words if one were speaking to an audience of secondary school principles in Wisconsin than one would use for a group of California college professors, or a parent-teachers association in Texas, or a local school board in the Bronx.

Understanding an audience in such depth is not an easy thing. It requires an unusual ability to stand on the other person's porch, to view the world from a variety of perspectives, to walk around, as the old proverb puts it, "in another man's moccasins," to fashion a speech by thinking not from the inside out but from the outside in.

Understanding an audience also means understanding the particularities of the occasion on which one speaks. It requires some knowledge as to how well the audience knows both the topic and the speaker, and how effectively both are to be introduced at the time the speech is given. It means being sensitive to the receptivity of the audience—whether it will, in a burst of early morning energy, be ready to chew heartily on a meaty subject or whether it will instead be supersaturated before the speaker is introduced at the end of a long day of speeches or after an elaborate dinner. A brilliant address for one audience and occasion may well fall flat before another audience or on another occasion, and there is as little consolation in being able to say "Well, the speech worked well last week!" as a doctor might find in saying "Well, the treatment worked well on another disease!"

Oscar Wilde is said to have responded, when someone asked him how opening night at the theater had gone, "The play was a great success, but the audience was a failure!" Unfortunately, the effective speechwriter can rarely find consolation in such a rationalization. If the speech did not work with the immediate audience, then it is the speech that needed repair. Just as a humorist is judged by whether the audience laughs or not, just as good teaching is tested by whether the student learns or not, just as good marketing is tested by whether the product sells or not, so good speechwriting is tested by how a particular audience responds at a particular moment, not by what the writer or the speaker or their friends and their families thought when they read through the text.

To paraphrase the in-house slogan of the 1992 Clinton campaign: "It's the audience, stupid!"

Pacing for the Ear

The simplest difference between writing speeches and writing other texts is that other texts enter the brain through the eye, while a speech goes in through the ear. It is a simple distinction with profound implications. For the process by which the brain absorbs oral communication is very different from that through which it apprehends visual stimuli. So different are the two processes—writing for the ear as opposed to writing for the eye—that they can usefully be described as writing in two different languages. And one of the most useful exercises that can be used to teach good speechwriting is to ask the student quite literally to translate a piece of conventional written prose into language that works as effectively when spoken to a group aloud.

It also follows from what has just been said that the best way to judge a speech text is not to read it over silently but actually to read it aloud, or, better yet, to have someone read it to you while you sit back and put yourself into the mind-set of the eventual audience. Again, a useful classroom technique for conveying this sensibility is to have students write speeches that someone else then delivers, while the writer is required to listen to something that invariably sounds a bit different when witnessed from the point of view of the audience.

One of the central contrasts between effective writing for the ear and for the eye is the matter of pacing—how much information is relayed over how long a period of time. The simple truth is that the eye absorbs written information at an incredibly faster pace than the ear absorbs oral communication. Squiggly lines on pieces of paper are a far more efficient way to relay information than sound waves traveling through the air. A half hour of evening television news copy would fit easily onto a single page of a broadsheet newspaper. And the lecture that takes almost an hour to present in the classroom can probably be read in about 10 or 12 minutes if a printed copy is simply handed to the class.

The implication of this distinction is that a speechwriter has to be particularly selective about the number of points the speech should make, the complexity of the arguments to be presented, and the methods of support that can be used. Above all, he or she must be attentive to the rate at which information will soak into the memory of the listener, finding ways to shift the speech into neutral gear from time to time while the ear catches up with the speaker's mouth and the audience wraps its mind around the full meaning of what it has heard.

Writer Jeff Scott Cook has described this requirement as the need to use "more words per square thought." Good speechwriters accomplish it in a variety of ways. One example would be the padding out of paragraphs with sentences that reinforce or even repeat the major point, but do so without requiring the listener to process significant new information. A so-called applause line such as "Let there be no mistake about that," or a rhetorical question such as "What does all of this really add up to?" or a reinforcing statement such as "Now doesn't that sound pretty appealing to you?"—all such phrases are essentially little more than verbal padding, the equivalent of what musicians call vamping, a way stylishly to pass a little time before moving along to another theme.

Producing more words per square thought requires a reflex quite the opposite of that which print journalists and other writers for the eye are encouraged to develop. A tight, clean, hard, telegraphic writing style can be useful for a speechwriter, to be sure, but it should ideally be accompanied by the ability to sense the pace at which a speech works best for a listening audience. A background in scriptwriting (like that of Robert Sherwood, for example, who became one of Franklin Roosevelt's most effective speechwriters) or in radio or television writing can often be more helpful to a writer of speeches than experience which is confined to producing the printed word. One of the most familiar figures in the speech-writing world is the accomplished print journalist struggling (often unsuccessfully) with the unexpected challenge of learning to write effective spoken prose.

Repetition, Repetition, Repetition

Closely related to the important role of realistic pacing in a speech is the need for frequent repetition—not only of central concepts but even of critical language. Again, the relative inferiority of the ear to the eye as an avenue for receiving information is at the heart of the matter. "The ear has a lousy memory," is how one writer puts it—a fact echoed by the familiar expression: "In one ear and out the other." It is interesting—and important—to note that the phrase "in one eye and out the other" is not one we commonly hear. The eye has great powers of recall, but the ear does not.

Reinforcing this advantage is the fact that the reader can control the pace at which he or she absorbs information—scanning at times, slowing to ponder each word at other times, and even rereading crucial phrases or passages if their meaning is not readily apparent. More than that, the mind of the reader can wander—as the mind of any audience will inevitably wander—without compromising the effectiveness with which information is received. The eye compensates for the wandering mind by simply stopping for a moment or moving back to an earlier point in the document.

For the listening audience, however, there is no "rewind button," no opportunity to attend again to critical material, no way whatsoever to compensate if the mind wanders or if comprehension slows down. All the listener can do is "hang on for the duration of the ride" and hope that the speaker will be sufficiently clear and sufficiently repetitive so that even an overloaded and sporadically attentive ear will get the help it needs to comprehend the essential message.

And when the speech is over and the audience scatters and someone asks one of its members, "What did the speaker have to say?" the chances of a coherent and accurate response will be much enhanced if a single line or two has been repeated often enough so that even the feeble ear has managed to retain the gist of the story.

Good Architecture: Making the Bones Stick Out

Given all the handicaps which accompany oral as compared to visual communication, the speechwriter must use every possible device to make the text as user-friendly as possible. One of the most important is to organize the material into appropriate sections and subsections and sub-subsections, constantly breaking larger chunks down into digestible, bite-sized smaller chunks, and thus developing a clear sense of the structure of the speech which can help the listener both in understanding its message and in retaining it.

The mind naturally remembers far more vividly when it can compartmentalize. When asked to name their household possessions, most people will automatically start thinking of them room by room. If you are told to memorize a list of the people who work in your company, you will probably create a mental organization chart, and then tick off the names division by division, department by department, working group by working group. A strong outline is to a speech what an organization chart is to a company. It helps us make sense of what might otherwise seem a random and inexplicable body of unrelated details.

The architect I. M. Pei has described the challenge of designing comfortable public buildings as one of making them "user-friendly," by which he means (in part) enabling users to relate the place within the building where they are standing to the building as a whole. A family meandering through a museum, for example, should have a comfortable sense of how much they have seen and how much is still to be seen so that the time they spend in the museum can be planned and continually adjusted in the most effective manner.

Good speech architecture should similarly give the listener a clear sense of how the passage of the moment relates to the overall message, an appreciation at every moment of where the speaker has come from and where the speaker is going. Ideally, the listener should even have a rough notion of how much more is coming before the speaker stops!

Again, a reader can at any moment look forward and backward in a text, determining (as most of us do habitually) just how far he or she has come in the document and just how much still remains. But the listener, trapped in the immediate moment, can only hope that the speaker will provide a clear, overall road map early in the address, and will then send frequent signals to the audience as to their current location.

All of this means not only that the structure of a speech should be made clear at the outset, but also that transitions from section to section should normally be highlighted with special clarity. Subtlety in creating bridges between one block of material and another can often prove counterproductive when one is depending upon the ears of the audience to pick up these signposts.

Also worth emphasizing is the fact that detail—even highly important and well-researched detail—which is not firmly anchored in crystal-clear architecture is easily lost and forgotten when communication is oral and there is no opportunity to "rewind" a passage or reread a page. Only when there are larger categories into which details can fit—mental file folders, as it were—can the speaker have some hope that an audience will remember not only the detail but the point it was used to support. Just as a book in a library can be lost forever if it is not carefully placed at just the right place on just the right shelf, so even the most careful research or most creative argument can be wasted if it is not linked in easily remembered ways to a clear and compelling pattern.

Someone said that the normal speech has three parts: A beginning, a *muddle,* and an end. No, that is not a typographical error in the preceding sentence. The "muddle in the middle" is probably the most important weakness one can point to in the typical speaking text. And it often exists despite the speaker's own impressions to the contrary. What a skilled speechwriter can do is take what is clear and cogent when it leaves the mind of the speaker and ensure that it will still be clear and cogent when it enters the mind of the listener. A strong sense of structure is an indispensable tool for accomplishing that task.

Language That Sticks in the Mind

If there is a single tactic that can be applied more readily and have more immediate impact than any other in the translation of competent prose for the eye into effective speech for the ear, it is the use of language which has a high visual impact. And if there is any one technique that distinguishes good speechwriters, it is probably their ability to paint verbal pictures which can then be remembered by the "inner eye."

Test after test, study after study shows that what audiences remember from a speech long after it has ended are the images which created visual effects, the words which pointed to things concrete, the names of specific places and people and objects. Visual language uses the ear as a means of getting into the brain, but then sticks there rather than going "out the other ear." And the reason it "sticks" is because it can be so easily translated into a compelling mental picture which can be readily and vividly remembered long after more abstract concepts have dimmed and disappeared.

Language that "glows in the dark," as someone has described the phenomenon, or "Velcro" language, to use yet another appropriate term, is language that constantly illustrates and exemplifies and compares, language that communicates the abstract by citing the particular. It is normally metaphorical, and sometimes metaphorical to a fault. A particularly effective speechwriting technique, for example, is to organize an entire speech around a single controlling metaphor, an image which is easily recalled and which, once recalled, becomes a key for unlocking the entire meaning of the discourse. Churchill's "Iron Curtain" speech in March of 1946 exemplified the power of this approach. This year, the 50th anniversary of that address, was being celebrated in Fulton, Missouri, where it was originally delivered. But one doubts whether the same message, however eloquently expressed, would have had the same lasting impact had the central metaphor not been such a felicitous one.

A similar case is that of the student who, when asked to recall any address heard in childhood, remembered best an Easter sermon built around the notion that the dandelion, not the lily, should be the symbolic flower of the day. More than that, she still remembered the precise arguments that grew out of that vivid, visual image. Or, to take a very different example, consider the business leader who organized a research-laden talk about high employee turnover around the continuing metaphor of a leaky fuel pipe, virtually forcing his mechanically oriented audience to see and to remember the wasteful oozing away of something that was absolutely indispensable if their "machinery" was to operate.

As any of us looks back over an experience—or back over a lifetime of experiences—what we tend to remember best are "scenes." When we try to tell someone about a film we have attended, for example, we normally picture and then describe a sequence of scenes we see in our mind's eye rather than replaying the dialogue in our mind's ear. When we do remember the sound of a film, it is often the music that comes evocatively back to us—a phenomenon which ought to suggest to any speechwriter the importance of using sounds and rhythms to create what are essentially musical effects. Pat Buchanan (who was a presidential speechwriter before he became a presidential candidate) has described this process as "going iambic," the equivalent of writing poetry. "They are honed," he said of his most memorable lines. "You work on it and you work on it and then you get the cheer line."

But even the less poetic writer can learn, at the very least, to employ concrete language and to paint verbal pictures—to talk about Ken, who got his wrench handed to him in Hoboken last Tuesday, rather than dwelling intently on the "rising unemployment rate among skilled and semiskilled workers."

Ernest Hemingway made a closely related point when he wrote, in *A Farewell to Arms,* of the embarrassment his narrator felt in hearing "the words sacred, glorious, and sacrifice and the expression in vain." These abstractions had been so abused, so misused, he explained, that you could not stand to hear them any more and "finally only the names of places had dignity. Certain numbers were the same way and certain dates and these with the names of the places were all you could say and have them mean anything."

The wearing out of traditional public language is a central theme in the cultural history of the 20th century, and one that reinforces the argument that effective writing in our time will lean heavily on words which are simple and direct and concrete. When T. S. Eliot wrote earlier in the century about what he called the "objective correlative," he was making a closely related point. The modern artist, he argued, can create an emotion for an audience not by describing or naming the emotion but rather by "finding an objective correlative, . . . a set of objects, a chain of events, which shall be the formula of that particular emotion, such that: when the external facts are given . . . the emotion is immediately evoked."

"Objective" language, then, is not only memorable language. It is also credible language—language that has at least a reasonable chance of evoking and harnessing the emotions of those who attend to it. Another quintessential 20th century writer, Franz Kafka, once said that "Words are like ice picks we use to break up the frozen seas within us." A good speechwriter is one who can find those "ice pick" words and use them to make a lasting impact on how an audience thinks and feels.

THE FUTURE OF SPEECHWRITING

This list of tactical considerations is intended to be neither exhaustive nor infallible. Most rules for writers are made to be broken, and the best test for any speech is not "Did it follow the rules?" but rather "Did it work?" On the other hand, the tools described above are, at the very least, techniques of proven value, approaches to writing which have helped many speakers overcome the special challenge of reaching audiences through their ears rather than their eyes. Used well, they can help create that magical moment when a speaker discovers that the heads before him are nodding in assent, that eyes are brightening and that faces are smiling, that hearts are beating and that brain cells are snapping, and that all of this is happening because he has sent out the right sound waves and his message has gotten through.

And if a speechwriter is technically adroit and tactically accomplished, then he or she will be well positioned to play an important strategic role, as well. For the simple truth of the matter is that there are many more good writers for the eye than there are for the ear. Good speechwriters are not easily made—or found. And when one comes along, he or she can often have an impact far beyond most normal expectations.

The ability to write good speeches can be a particularly valuable tool for any public relations professional, giving that person not only an important competitive advantage, but also providing ready access to the most important corporate decision makers and even a seat at the table when the most important decisions are discussed.

Strategic speechwriters will, in short, be able to build upon the access which their tactical skills have earned for them, using their roles in proactive ways which can directly influence the strategies of their companies.

Few corporate leaders will be as dependent on their writers as was the senator whose futility was described at the beginning of this chapter. Nor will their attitudes be as cavalier as those of one legendary CEO who asked his speechwriter one day to put together a speech for an upcoming company dinner. When the writer naturally responded by asking, "What about?" the CEO is said to have simply responded, "About 30 minutes."

Most leaders, in the business world or in other sectors of society, will have at least a somewhat stronger sense than did that CEO of what their speeches should be about. But they will rarely have the time or the information or the inclination or even the ability to determine for themselves all the things that should be said, and on what occasions and to what audiences, and in what manner. It will be the expanding function of the proactive speechwriter to help address all of these important questions and, in the process of doing so, to play a central role in determining and advancing the organization's strategic objectives.

## CHAPTER 36

Clear Writing for Public Relations Practitioners

George Harmon
Associate Professor
Medill School of Journalism
Northwestern University

He advocated the preservation of choices among oleochemical and petrochemical surfactants for detergent formulations through sound scientific evaluation of broad environmental impacts.

—Press release, Texas chemical company

Once your package is ready for design, show it to key staff for a final look. If possible, have an experienced direct mail specialist critique your work. Ask he or she to point out the major flaws . . . .

—Newsletter for managers

Funds that were used to pay interest can now be applied to growing our divisions.

—Annual report, Fortune 500 corporation

Management has become cognizant of the necessity of eliminating undesirable vegetation surrounding the periphery of our facility.

—A memo on killing the weeds around the building.

We're surrounded by unclear writing, aren't we? Industrial jargon, business slang, odd grammar. Over the airwaves, on street signs, in the mail, on the sides of buildings. Yes, even in press releases. As James Thurber said, "A word to the wise is not sufficient if it doesn't make sense."

Our factory is a facility. This is a nonsmoking building. We don't help solve problems here; we facilitate. Outside on the parkway a sign says, "slow children," and we don't see why anyone thinks that's an insult. On the street are cars (not used, but predriven or preenjoyed) with automotive inflatable restraint systems, not airbags.

Such messages may be convoluted and unintelligible. But somehow they sound authoritative. Businesslike. Educated. Professional.

More than half a century ago, writer George Orwell warned in a famous essay called "Politics and the English Language" that bureaucratic language was either a lazy or a false way of presenting truth. The situation is little better today. Corporations, unconsciously or even deliberately, obscure their messages.

Four Barriers to Clear Writing

If Orwellian lingo is worsening in the late 1990s, the blame might lie at the feet of four huge trends:

1. Industrial Tribalism

Each discipline—management, accounting, science, education, government—has its own terminology. Within those disciplines are subsets. The jargon of a professional discipline has its pluses. For instance, it's shorthand that enables the cognoscenti to communicate quickly. It's permissible at a so-called "trade" magazine that goes to a single industry. But jargon is also partly a badge of admission, and partly it's a code made difficult for outsiders to break. As the end of the Cold War gave rise to a new tribalism in Eastern Europe, where people huddled with the familiar, so did bleaker job prospects cause American workers to throw up defenses. Part of tribal language in industry is an effort to protect turf. Stating an idea in plain language might leave it revealed in all its simplicity. It could lose its mystique and any profit therefrom.

Corporate writing gets into trouble when it forgets the audience. It tends to mingle accounting language with management buzzwords with scientific terms in an annual report that goes out to stockholders who are a cross section of America. They constitute a general readership. Despite having jargons at their own workplaces, the readers can enter another profession's message only through plain language. Stockholders (and editors and customers) are a mass audience. They need back-fence, plain-language explanations. If they live overseas or use English as a second language, they need it even plainer. If you insist on calling a staple a resin-coated power fastener, you guarantee a small audience.

2. Speed

We have voice mail, fax mail, E-mail, beeper mail, overnight mail, car phones, in-house computer networks, Web pages. Each of them delivers messages immediately. They sever the connection between geography and community.

Fewer eyes are on each bit of writing because it goes out faster. Even the time one takes to walk to the printer in the next room results occasionally in a writer deciding to rewrite. Columnist Bob Greene called the phenomenon the Twitching of America, a national speeding-up: "With instant communication so readily available, people seem addicted to their own adrenaline. For several years now the country's psyche has seemed to be in a constant state of overdrive."

More speed equals more information, equals more messages, equals more errors, equals more frustration. Why else is it so difficult for a company to tell the public what it's doing?

3. More Choices

There's been an explosion in the numbers of publications and ways to use one's time.

People aren't always hungrier for information than ever before. If so, the parking lot would be full at the library. They need wisdom and common sense. As John Naisbitt *(Megatrends)* said, we're drowning in information but starved for knowledge. Perhaps that's one reason why book sales now are rising faster than population growth.

As many as 1,500 messages a day bombard the average person. Many of these are nonsense: Please wait for the waitress to be seated. Inadvertent flag. Viewer discretion is advised.

An idea can lose 80 percent of its meaning as it passes through a chain of command, written and rewritten, put into jargon. Even the sensible ideas sometimes miss the mark because a reader is distracted, busy, fatigued.

4. Teams

Corporations today make better and better use of teamwork. But writing doesn't always. The best writing happens alone, with a single person responsible for the content and the style. How many best-sellers are by six authors? Yet corporations seem to be doing even more writing by committee and editing by lawyer. The result sometimes is corporate gibberish. Thomas Paine's "these are the times that try men's souls" might be "it is times like these which impact the psyches of all persons" if it came out of a modern corporation. Just because you work for an institution doesn't mean you have to sound like one.

So a world of jargon, speed, shrinking time, and overwriting runs the risk of bringing us more corporate gibberish. While working with a company on some of its external communication, I came on the following phrases in a single publication intended for customers and shareholders:

- Major market share position
- Marketing-sensitive products
- Common distribution channels
- Maximize long-term stockholder value
- Consumer personal products
- Increase corporate returns
- Low-cost producer programs
- Leveraging strong brand names
- Cross-channel distribution opportunities
- Introducing value-added new products
- Competitive leadership in key markets
- Rollout in selective markets
- Implement safe processing practices
- Downsizing of administrative staff
- Steps were initiated to improve production efficiencies
- Progress was achieved
- Efforts continued to better utilize existing plants through modernization and expansion programs
- Consumers increased interest in value

■ Initiated the construction of a production facility.

The company was committing nearly all of the sins of "businessese."

The 15 Sins of "Businessese"

1. Ignoring the audience, or writing in one's own terms instead of the reader's. A *Time* editor once said: "The most difficult task is to make them read what they ought to read." George Orwell added, "Good prose is like a windowpane," meaning that the writing ought not come between the reader and the information.

A writer ought to weigh questions about the members of the audience. How literate are they? What do they already know about the topic? What things do they find useful? What do they ignore? What is the threshold for pain, considering the subject matter? What do they need to know or want to know?

We often overestimate the stock of readers' information while we underestimate their intelligence. Readers may be poorly informed about current events (surveys keep telling us things such as 40 percent of Americans don't know that the United States must import oil), but they are not stupid. They don't mind being reminded of simple facts and they don't mind something that is easy to read.

2. Oxymoron, or self-contradiction. Legal brief, nondairy creamer, working vacation, exact estimate, limited obligation, corporate family, managed competition, negative income, jumbo shrimp, truth in advertising.

3. Euphemisms, or substitute words. They avoid giving offense, they disguise fear, they use tact. They're overused in business, either as camouflage or in laziness. It's OK to avoid mentioning the word "death" in a letter of condolence, but we don't write, "Hamlet passed on." Business terminology often has an aversion to saying what it means. In business, bug killer = pest control = crop protection; increasing taxes = revenue enhancement; brokers = financial consultants = account executives = investment executives; stock market slide = equity retreat; black-and-white TV = television with nonmulticolor capability; death = negative patient care outcome; explosion in a nuclear power plant = energetic disassembly; billboard = outdoor advertising; suicide on train tracks = pedestrian involvement; rich people = advantaged = high net worth.

No one is fired, laid off, pink-slipped, or canned. Big executives resign "for personal reasons." When you're unemployed, you're in an orderly transition between careers. Or it's a case of restructuring, downsizing, separation, corporate leaning, slimming down, rightsizing, demassing, sending people off for opportunities to find the right fit, delayering, eliminating jobs, workforce readjustments, headcount reductions, negative employee retention, being asked to take early retirement, furloughed, requested departures, streamlining, managing our staff resources, surplussing, volume-related schedule adjustment, initiating a career alternative enhancement program, hiring permanent replacements, given freedom to pursue new career opportunities, employee transition program, buyout, on special assignment, MIA'd (or management-initiated attrition), terminated. (The last term—terminated— changes fast. In the spy lingo of little more than a decade before businesses began using it, to assassinate was to "terminate with extreme prejudice.")

The so-called "political correctness" of the 1980s and 1990s was a delight to linguists because of the ingenuity of its euphemisms. Short people became height-disadvantaged, bald men became hair-disadvantaged (or "follically challenged," according to comedians), a commune became an intentional community. A pet became a companion animal, with its owner or master being caretaker, guardian, steward, or human companion of the nonhuman companion. Terrorists who fought on our side are freedom fighters waging wars of liberation for self-determination and human rights.

Many linguistic scholars oppose such renaming, for research shows them that language is separate from thought. In other words, in Orwellian terms, removing the word freedom from the language still leaves people who want to be free, whether or not they use the term. Dehiring someone won't convince her that she's not been fired.

4. Inflated labels and titles. Sanitary engineer, motorized module attendant, executive assistant, maintenance engineer, outside aerial technicians (utility linemen), delivery ambassadors (Domino's pizza drivers), maintenance engineer, behavior transition corridors (school hallway), early learning center (a nursery school), combustion indicator (fire-alarm bell), movable partition (a door), decorative fixture (a window), equipment access (a manhole). *New Yorker* magazine, which delightedly publishes cartoons that lampoon businessese, ran a drawing of galley slaves rowing while their boss, bullwhip in hand, answered a cellular phone: "Human Resources."

5. Redundancies. Sum total, most unique, foreign imports, IRA account, HIV virus, plans for the future, first priority, active participant, located at, mutual agreement, preboarding, preexisting mutual agreement, tiny paper clip, past history, most unique, untimely death, new innovation, decide one way or another, look forward.

6. Pomposity. The title of a paper delivered at an American Economics Association meeting was "Stylometrics: Statistical Evidence on the Decline in the Quality of Writing in the Economics Profession." How would a lawsuit say, "Give us this day our daily bread"? Communications professors lecture on "Cognitive Moderators of Negative Emotions: Implications for Understanding Media-Context Effects."

7. Slang. We all want to come across as being part of the inner circle. So we say bottom line, deplane, prioritize, finalize, optimize, ongoing, colorization, parameter. We no longer find information; we access it. We speak of easibility, cost-effectiveness, funding, conferencing, partnering, we'll dimension this project, viable, oriented, parameter, ongoing, interface, impact, optimize, commitment to quality.

"The patient did not fulfill his wellness potential," wrote a medic, muddying the fact that the patient died and placing blame firmly on the deceased.

8. Verbs from nouns, and vice versa. We add "ize" to a noun and turn it into a verb or a longer noun. We add "ing" to create a new gerund. Positivize, incentivize, corporatize, multitasking, and multiwindowing, "Peter Power of the Dealer Services Department will now also be officing at this address." An Army commander wrote a private's parents: "I am pleased to inform you that Michael has arrived safely at Fort Bliss and has begun the soldierization process."

9. Misused or mixed metaphors. A metaphor is figure of speech applying a term to something it doesn't literally apply to in order to suggest a resemblance, and it's a grand way of putting the abstract into human terms. Referring to child-worshippers and child-haters, one writer said that "the opposing emotions seem to be stitched together something like the two skins of a baseball."

A tidal wave can't be of avalanche proportions, and the leader can't put the ship of state on its feet.

A Tennessee securities firm once began an analysis of Wometco Enterprises, Inc., by stating that "with the recent passing of Chairman Mitchell Wolfson, 82, founder and 15 percent owner of this Miami-headquartered company, we believe the future of Wometco will lie in different hands."

Often we can't sustain an image throughout an expression. U.S. budget czar David Stockman, in a book about the Reagan years, blamed "the false belief that in a capitalist democracy we can peer deep into the veil of the future and chain the ship of state to an exacting blueprint." An executive once told *American Banker* newspaper : "This is probably a watershed in our central bank policy. We've got a whole new ball of wax in monetary policy. The channels are different and we're seeing central bank policy in full light." The dean of a law school told the *New York Times:* "That fly-by-night stuff is nothing but a smoke screen, which they have used to feather the nests of the professoriate which has captured the accreditation process."

10. Overcapitalization. "In charge of the project is Executive Vice President and Director of Planning T. Bradford Hutchins III." Communications people roll their eyes in agreement when you ask whether their companies' top executives spend too much time agonizing over what to capitalize.

The solution is simple. Many companies are adopting the Associated Press stylebook, and then supplementing it with a short stylebook where the company's style differs.

11. Convoluted grammar. "Richard Dombrowski on the Midwest Stock Exchange floor married Jennifer Smith on September 19." The New York Stock Exchange put out this message to the staff: "The following are the 1988 holiday closings as per the Secretary of the NYSE." An ad sought to find a Freeze Dried Pharmaceuticals Manager. A letter sent out by an executive search company: "Our firm has recently undertaken a search for the Provost of George Mason University." Had they tried a missing persons bulletin?

12. Reliance on **passive voice** and dead constructions. "Priorities were established," "mistakes were made," "there will be a meeting," "viewer discretion is advised." The inference is that no human did these things. They just happened. Is passive voice part of a late-century American timidity, a way of sliding off the hook? If "mistakes were made," who can come around later and say, "*You* blew it, *you* goofed?" "The girl walked the dog" is always shorter and more direct than "the dog was walked by the girl."

Dead constructions (or "expletives") perform no function in a sentence. They add clutter and rob a sentence of its power by placing emphasis on a weaker verb. Example: "It was their aim to stretch out the time required to take over the market." How much more direct to write: "They hoped to stretch out the time required to take over the market."

13. Unconventional punctuation. Corporate writing teems with misused semicolons, hyphens, colons, and em dashes.

14. Piling on adjectives. Strings of modifiers before a noun, such as "emerging object-oriented client/server development market," make the eye hunt for meaning.

15. False warmth. Corporations sometimes torture us with efforts to sound friendly. The airlines invite us to "please join us in the boarding process" or to "kindly extinguish smoking materials." If a corporation actually does manage to sound like family, it often quickly undoes the achievement by using businessese: "before you deplane," "please refrain from smoking until you are inside a designated smoking area inside the terminal," "this ends the audio portion of your flight," "ask a flight attendant to receipt you."

What the Best Have Said About Writing

Writing is man's greatest invention. It enables us to converse with the dead, the absent, and the unborn, all at great distances of time and space. To it we owe everything which distinguishes us from savages. Take it from us and the Bible, all history, all sciences, all government, and nearly all social intercourse go with it.

Abraham Lincoln

Be careful that you write accurately rather than much.

Erasmus

Thanks to words, we have been able to rise above the brutes; and thanks to words, we have often sunk to the level of the demons.

Aldous Huxley

Education doesn't change life much. It just lifts trouble to a higher plane of regard.

Robert Frost

Writing is something that you can never do as well as it can be done. It is a perpetual challenge and it is more difficult than anything else that I have ever done . . . so I do it. And it makes me happy when I do it well.

Ernest Hemingway

A STRATEGY FOR WRITING

Clear writing is hard work. It's as difficult as inventing and painting and many other skills. Michelangelo said: "If people only knew how hard I work to gain my mastery, it wouldn't seem too wonderful at all." Thomas Edison's version of that belief was: "Genius is one percent inspiration and ninety-nine percent perspiration." William Zinsser *(On Writing Well)* a former *Life* magazine writer who went into training business executives in communication, once told the *Chicago Tribune:* "Executives at every level are prisoners of the notion that a simple style reflects a simple mind. Actually, a simple story is the result of hard work and hard thinking."

A former managing editor of *Business Week* used to relate how the magazine once did a cover story on a nationwide trucking company. After the story hit the newsstands, the directors fired the company's president because they hadn't understood his strategy until they read the story. His view, translated into everyday English by *Business Week,* wasn't what they had in mind for the company.

Since the mid-1980s, many mid-career writers have adopted the writing process. They used it to break writing into five steps: idea, research, organization, rough draft, and clarifying draft. Their objectives are accuracy and speed. The idea for the article—what this is all about—actually appears in the text in plain language. Their organization stage is a quick diagram that puts all the ideas onto a single page. When they run into trouble at any step in the process, they move back one step. That's where the problem lies. Can't organize it? Do more research. Can't write it? Reorganize it. Can't research it? Change the idea.

Use the writing process, straighten your own steps, and you can improve your writing quickly.

Can clear, concise writing help a business career? Judge for yourself.

A study showed that Fortune 500 CEOs were exceptionally clear writers and speakers. Dow Chemical once stated: "Our whole philosophy is that the articulate individual is promotable." Some CEOs won't read a memo longer than a page. A vice president of a large advertising firm said: "We look at how much attention a person pays to detail. Things like grammar, spelling, and mechanics mean a lot to us. We figure, if the person can't accomplish these things, how can we expect him or her to move on to the bigger job?"

Joel Raphaelson, once creative head of Ogilvy & Mather, said: "As people advance in their careers, they have to make recommendations. The recommendation may be a good idea, but if it isn't made in writing in a way that's clear, it's less likely to get acted on. There is a connection between expressing ideas well, forcibly, and clearly in writing and getting ahead."

But clear writing is easier said than done. Writing takes practice, practice, practice. It takes trips to the dictionary and to usage books. The supersalesman Dale Carnegie, author of *How to Win Friends and Influence People,* exaggerated only slightly when he said, "It was easier to make a million dollars than to put a phrase into the English language."

TACTICS FOR CLEAR WRITING

Editing Yourself

Our communication is based on shared understandings and common conventions. To convey meaning accurately, we frame language according to accepted rules: grammar. To show our ability to use language in a correct and creative way, we employ another component: style.

When editing your own writing, you face the dilemma of reading across four dimensions at the same time:

- Structure and sense of the article.
- Facts.
- Grammar and punctuation.
- Associated Press stylebook (or any other manual you follow).

So, if you're trying to edit for all those rules at once, your mind constantly must switch gears. Maybe you need to edit the story four separate times, reading for each category and nothing else.

Experienced writers become so adept at grammar and style that they "automate" the last two functions as they are writing. They execute basic Associated Press style and they "write around" grammatical difficulties. Then, when they edit their own copy, they worry primarily about facts and structure. It follows that they turn out copy with few errors.

Writing an article may be the easiest part of all. The tough part comes in the self-editing, when we become serious about how we're delivering a story to readers.

So the final review is one that has the audience in mind. If grammar and punctuation are correct, if AP style is in place, if the facts double check, if the structure is logical, then the piece must face an "audience test" before it goes to an editor. Here are some questions designed to filter out problems that may cause trouble for your readers:

Have I told the story to the reader, rather than to myself or to my editor?

B O X   36–1

A CHECKLIST FOR EDITING YOURSELF

1. Spelling of proper names. Start at the bottom and work upward, looking at words with capital letters.

2. Clarity. Make sure that the identifications are correct for each difficult term.

3. Message. Does the piece stick to a single unifying point?

4. Sound. Find a corner to yourself and read the piece aloud.

5. Spell check, 19th century version. Read sentences back to front. Or run your cursor from bottom to top. This will cause you to examine each word.

6. Fat. Find out how to use the word count function on your computer's word-processing program. Measure the piece, then cut 10 percent. If you can't, give it to a colleague to cut.

7. Directness. Search for the passive voice and remove it.

8. Distance. Remove yourself from ownership. Walk away from the piece for a while. When you come back to it, try to look at it as a reader would.

Is the first sentence intriguing, interesting, accurate, and appropriate?

Have I put the facts in logical and readable order?

Do my transitions eliminate jolts as the story shifts from one topic to another?

Do any paragraphs need separating? Combining?

Do the sounds of the sentences vary? Is the voice of the writer consistent?

Have I slipped unnecessarily into jargon or cliché?

Can I trim any fat?

What's the headline?

William Blundell, who had a long career as a feature writer for *The Wall Street Journal* said that the key to editing oneself is the discipline of walking away from a story for a while: "A piece still warm from the typewriter is one too close to the writer's heart. The writer who doesn't spend at least a half day editing such a piece is either a supreme craftsman or a masochist begging to see his work truncated and altered by others."

Using a checklist such as the one shown in Box 36–1 should help eliminate problems of the sort that appeared in an advertisement in a Boston newspaper: "We are looking for a highly motivated professional Telemarketing Director, with excellent communication skills, having the ability to analyze statistical data and develop strategies to minimize efficiency."

Writing Directly by Removing Empty Words

When you've finished a piece of writing, look for the so-called "empty" words that creep into business prose. When you find one, slice it out. One thumb rule is to take anything you've written, do the word count function on your word processor, and then remove 10 percent of the words. Most of the time, it will read more clearly. The following phrases should raise suspicions when you see them:

We take the position that (it is our opinion that)

A substantial majority of employees

We held a meeting for the purpose of

During the course of our conversation

In the event that we find ourselves in disagreement

At a later date

Plans for the future

Located at

By virtue of the fact that

At the present time, at this point in time

This policy has been in full force and effect for the period of a year.

She is currently working on

Take under advisement

A substantial segment of the population

Ascertain

Are fully cognizant of

Effect the destruction of

We limited our discussion to the basic fundamentals.

In this connection, the writer would like to point out the discrepancy that exists.

She is a person who does an excellent job as a programmer.

The main consideration is a matter of time.

Please plan in advance to present your recommendations when the next meeting is held.

Price enhancement, price reduction

Reduced demand for product

Period of accelerated negative growth

Shortfall

Planned staff reductions

Workshop sessions

Public opinion survey

Petroleum hydrocarbons

Attached hereto

Loan obligation

Budget forecast

Dollar amounts

Prompt and speedy

True facts

Vitally essential

Assemble together

Consensus of opinion

Endorse on the back

Follows after

Revert back

Free and gratis

New beginning

What the Research Tells Us About Writing

- Money managers often view unclear writing as a corporate cover-up.
- Many corporations value writing as the most important skill for business.
- For a century, novels have been growing easier to read while newspapers have been growing more difficult to read. We can assume that business communication parallels the problems of newspapers.
- If sentences average 17 words or less, comprehension is about 85 percent.

- Readership measures such as the fog index have some value. The index, or Gunning readability formula, measures the reading level, by grade. Some fog index levels: Michigan official driver's manual, 6.7; King James version of 23d Psalm, 9.3; federal income tax instructions, 9.3; instructions on a frozen turkey dinner, 10.3; *Time* magazine, lead article, 12; a computer manufacturer's press release, 21.6.

- The passive-nominal sentence ("It has been found by researchers that more and more Americans are running for the achievement of physical fitness") is a no-no.

- So is the acronym. Readers simply don't recognize universally what those initials stand for, even common ones such as FDA and FCC.

The Virtue of Translation

Today it's simply impossible for managers to keep up with the buzzwords of the management tribe along with the jargon of their own industries and the slang of the industries of key customers.

They need translators. The only way that ideas will transfer in the year 2000, when we're all dealing with global communication and second languages, is through clear writing by the translators. The principle of business is simple: money in, money out, reinvest what's left over. We don't want basic ideas obscured.

It's up to communicators to grab only the best of standard language and discard the rest. When trying to float a *new* idea, such as business process controls, the communicator needs to rely on *old* ideas. Then the reader or listener only has to wrestle with understanding the new idea.

In *Field of Dreams,* the slogan went something like, "If you build it, they'll come." In business, if they understand why it's useful, they'll buy it.

We don't need to jumble together "focused market segments" with "best practices" with "corporate-wide management restructuring" with etc. in short order. Most of these terms were nowhere just five years ago. We don't need to overcapitalize, we don't need alphabet soup, we don't need multiple verbs in sentences, we don't need passive voice. We don't need barriers between messenger and audience. Watch out for words that trigger spell-check in the computer dictionary, which is 100,000 words or more. (The average person has a working usage of just 1,000 words; an accomplished writer uses 10,000; Shakespeare supposedly had a working vocabulary of 20,000.) Why try to create new words when we already have 100,000 good ones to use?

So we need to follow a communications strategy. We need to try to communicate concepts primarily as *people* rather than as businesspeople. The readers may all be businesspeople, but they haven't all attended the same seminars.

The Powerlessness of Businessese

The prose of President Warren G. Harding had touches of the modern bureaucrat's lingo. So far, he hasn't gone down in history as one of our more successful presidents. Said a political opponent: "His speeches leave the impression of an army of pompous phrases moving over the landscape in search of an idea. Sometimes these meandering words would actually capture a straggling thought and bear it triumphantly, a prisoner in their midst, until it died of servitude and overwork."

B O X   36–2

SIX TIPS TO REMEMBER

- Watch out for piling adjectives before the noun, because the reader has to slow down in order to avoid losing the noun.

- Avoid using the same word twice in a sentence or a paragraph.

- Look for new action verbs for the beginning sentence. Having your company's press releases "announce" this and "announce" that makes it seem almost as if the company doesn't do anything but proclaim.

- Try to cut down on the passive voice. "The product engineering department has also been restructured" could be "the product engineering department also has a new structure."

- Police the jargon. "Growing" sales and "market share" is jargon that ought to stay inside a company.

- Avoid acronyms, overcapitalization and all-cap headlines. Many corporations are settling arguments over trivial matters by adopting the Associated Press stylebook. Their rationale: It's logical and it's widely accepted.

So pomposity can obscure meaning. As illustration, we leave you with business translations of two of our most important phrases.

Give us this day our daily bread: "We respectfully petition, request, and entreat that due and adequate provision be made, this day and date first above inscribed, for satisfying of petitioner's nutritional requirements and for the organizing of such methods of allocation and distribution as may be deemed necessary and proper to assure the reception by and for said petitioner of such quantity of cereal products (hereinafter called bread) as shall, in the judgment of the aforesaid petitioner, constitute a sufficient dietary quotient."

I love you: "The emotional intensity factors of my cognitive areas have been evaluated and the data permit the conclusion that your personality structure, and its continued proximity to my own, are of high quantitative value to my sustained happiness level rate."

And, finally, the job description for a homemaker: "Responsible for logistic support of my group, established work-flow priorities, performed duties with fiscal responsibility, supervised transportation, trained my unit, administered a nutritional program."

Now, was that any way to bring up babies, to court, or to worship?

B I B L I O G R A P H Y

Associated Press, *The Associated Press Stylebook and Libel Manual: The Journalist's Bible* (Reading, MA: Addison-Wesley Publishing). It contains all the answers you'll need, briefly. (Sample entry: "adviser. Not *advisor.*") Also included are a punctuation guide, a libel manual, and proofreaders' marks.

Baird, Russell N., et al., *The Graphics of Communication* (New York: Harcourt Brace, 1993). Practical advice on putting concepts, words, and data into visual treatments.

Berner, Thomas, *The Process of Writing News* (Boston: Allyn & Bacon, 1990). Most textbooks for beginning journalists offer industry models, the finished products, but this author tries to let writers concentrate on their process of writing the news.

Brooks, Terri, *Words' Worth* (New York: St. Martin's Press, 1989). The idea throughout is to publish, publish, publish. Especially useful are the sections on voice, the "weave," and selling one's writing.

Bruce, Harry J., Russel K. Hirst, and Michael L. Keene, *A Short Guide to Business Writing* (Englewood Cliffs, NJ: Prentice Hall, 1995). An excellent guide to writing memos, reports, and speeches.

Brusaw, Charles, Gerald Alred, and Walter Oliu, *The Business Writers' Handbook* (New York: St. Martin's Press, 1993). Entries such as "comprise/compose" and "who's/whose" are short, while lengthy treatment goes to thornier problems such as "conciseness," "formal reports," and "proofreading."

Clark, Roy Peter, and Don Fry, *Coaching Writers: Editors and Reporters Working Together* (New York: St. Martin's Press, 1992). "Coaching writers is the human side of editing," the authors say. Their mission is to help a person edit the work of both colleagues and underlings.

Collins, Maryclaire, *How to Make Money Writing Corporate Communications* (Perigee, 1995). Plain-spoken advice for writers who hope for freelance assignments from major corporations.

Corbett, Edward P. J., *The Little English Handbook* (New York: HarperCollins Publishers).

Fisher, Lionel L., *The Craft of Corporate Journalism* (Chicago: Nelson-Hall Publishers, 1992). Tips on being creative when writing and editing corporate publications. No visual tips here.

Flower, Linda, *Problem Solving Strategies for Writing* (New York: Harcourt Brace, 1989). The author tries to help writers break down their work into stages and be more aware of how context shapes writing.

Goldberg, Natalie, *Writing Down the Bones* (Boston: Shambhala, 1986). Useful tricks for fighting writer's block.

Kennedy, George, Daryl R. Moen, and Don Ranly, *Beyond the Inverted Pyramid* (New York: St. Martin's Press, 1993). The members of the so-called "Missouri Group" have another useful guide for the practitioner. This one targets feature writers for newspapers, magazines, and specialty publications.

_____, *The Writing Book* (Englewood Cliffs, NJ: Prentice Hall, 1984). The group provides practical tips for improving your writing, sprinkled liberally with examples from journalism.

Kessler, Lauren, and Duncan McDonald, *When Words Collide: A Media Writer's Guide to Grammar and Style* (Belmont, CA: Wadsworth, 1996). The authors provide a grammarian's bible, well indexed, with self-tests and lists of worrisome notions such as the words most commonly misspelled by journalists.

Lutz, William, *Doublespeak* (New York: Harper & Row, 1989). Springing from the seeds planted half a century ago by Orwell, this Rutgers professor skewers the masters of the obtuse phrase: educators, bureaucrats, and business executives.

McAdams, Katherine, and Jan Johnson Elliott, *Reaching Audiences* (Boston: Allyn & Bacon, 1996). Puts the emphasis where it belongs and provides a resource for those who must write constantly for different bodies of readers.

Maggie, Rosalie, *The Bias-Free Word Finder* (Boston: Beacon Press, 1991). See Miller and Swift's *The Handbook of Nonsexist Writing*.

_____, *How to Say It* (Englewood Cliffs, NJ: Prentice Hall). Chooses the right word, phrase, sentence, paragraph, or sample letter for 40 types of correspondence, from fund-raisers to thank-yous.

Miller, Casey, and Kate Swift, *The Handbook of Nonsexist Writing* (New York: Harper & Row, 1988). Helps remove sexist language in ways beyond the stilted "he or she."

Murray, Donald, *Writing for Your Readers: Notes on the Writer's Craft from the Boston Globe* (Old Saybrook, CT: Globe Pequot Press, 1983). Tips and more tips on how to add "vigor, clarity, and grace" to writing.

Plimpton, George, *The Writer's Chapbook* (New York: Viking Press, 1989). Advice and opinion from the greatest writers of the 20th century.

Rayfield, Robert E., et al., *Public Relations Writing: Strategies and Skills* (Dubuque, IA: Wm. C. Brown, 1991). Designed as a textbook, it provides an overview of the public relations practitioner's duties. Many practical examples. The writing chapters are solid, augmented by a grammar section.

Sabin, William, *Gregg Reference Manual* (New York: McGraw-Hill, 1985). A grammar and usage bible.

Strunk, Jr., William, and E. B. White, *The Elements of Style* (New York: Macmillan, 1979). This old favorite, in print and popular for decades, is the benchmark for books on writing. Prof. Strunk's one-time student was White, famous for writing *Charlotte's Web.*

Sweetnam, Sherry, *The Executive Memo* (New York: John Wiley & Sons, 1992). Offers prototypes of business communication such as information memos and sales letters.

Tibbetts, A. M., *To the Point* (Glenview, IL: Scott, Foresman, 1983). Everything you wanted to know about English, digested to its absolute basics.

Williams, Joseph, *Style: 10 Lessons in Clarity and Grace* (Glenview, IL: Scott, Foresman). The author wants the reader to work through a series of exercises.

Yudkin, Marcia, *Persuading on Paper: The Complete Guide to Copy That Pulls In Business* (New York: Penguin Books, 1996). Helps writers of sales letters, ads, and press releases.

Zinsser, William, *On Writing Well,* 4th ed. (New York: Harper & Row, 1994). A hot seller, this guide to writing nonfiction covers business, technical, science, criticism, and sports writing as well as general principles. Lively and entertaining, Zinsser issues pithy guidelines such as "Clutter is the disease of American writing" and "There's not much to be said about the period except most writers don't reach it soon enough."

_____, *Writing to Learn* (New York: Harper & Row, 1988). Writing is thinking. Pascal: The last thing one knows in constructing a work is what to put first.

## CHAPTER 37

The Big Idea: Creativity in Public Relations

Sandra E. Moriarty, Ph.D.
Professor
School of Journalism and Mass Communication
University of Colorado–Boulder

Behind every good public relations campaign is a Big Idea, the creative concept that make the message attention-getting and memorable. Creative thinking that produces Big Ideas is important in public relations because PR messages have to break through the clutter of a busy media environment and have impact on their target audience's opinions and attitudes. These creative concepts have to solve communication problems in an original way and be interesting enough that they captivate the minds of the target audience.

An example of a Big Idea that captivated its audience was Snapple's Letters campaign, created by the PR department at Kirschenbaum & Bond. The phenomenon behind this Big Idea was that people were willing to write to the company about their relationship with this drink. The first unsolicited letters related how the writers felt—that they discovered the drink, and they were driven to share the news with others.

The letters gave the agency an idea for a campaign based on a Snapple employee named Wendy who receives the letters, reads them, and responds. The campaign featured real letters from real people who tried the beverage and loved it. Television production crews traveled to these people's home towns and filmed them there—a technique which could backfire when you put untrained performers on camera, or could be a stroke of genius if they project an infectious enthusiasm—as happened. The filming also became a publicity event at the local level because the company involved the community in the release of the commercials. This incredible relationship evolved to the point that Snapple eventually was receiving some 20 boxes of letters a month.

BIG IDEAS: A STRATEGIC APPROACH

Big Ideas are designed to solve communication problems. If they are not strategic then they are not Big Ideas, but rather just random thoughts or tactics. There are two keys to effective public relations ideas: the first, is that they must be inherently interesting, and the second is that there must be some logical connection between the great idea and the organization's communication objectives. PRSA's Silver Anvil awards and *inside PR's* CIPRA (Creativity in Public Relations Award) are given to public relations programs that have successfully addressed some issue both strategically and creatively.

Mission: Excitement!

The communicator's mission is to stage the Big Idea, to find an exciting new way to present an idea in order to communicate a persuasive message that, in its strategic language, may sound like a dull piece of business writing. Finding the brilliant creative concept involves what some experts have called the Creative Leap. The difference between the dull business language and the Big Idea represents the leap. Strategy statements are often outlines or platforms for in-house discussion and agreement—not messages that will persuade people about something and captivate their minds.

An example of a Big Idea is the PRSA Silver Anvil award-winning celebration of the 30th anniversary of the Oscar Mayer Wiener Jingle. Oscar Mayer and Ketchum Public Relations/Chicago threw a party for the song. Strategically, the objective was to celebrate the jingle's position in American popular culture and strengthen the company's position as the favorite U.S. hot dog producer. Consumers, stopped on the street for an informal survey, were asked to sing the jingle, and the tremendous level of response and recognition was the basis for the celebration.

A musical media kit included a chip with a recording of the jingle along with biographical information on the jingle's composer and his small daughter, who sang the jingle in the first commercial in 1963. A company-wide employee party was held, along with a satellite media tour with the jingle's composer for TV stations in key markets. Generic sound bites taped at the party were added to a short videotape featuring people on the street singing the jingle and a selection of memorable commercials featuring the jingle. The effort gained almost 29 million media impressions through more than 550 television and radio placements. But more importantly, each one reinforced Oscar Mayer's position as the leader in hot dogs.

What Makes an Idea Creative?

To come up with a Bid Idea, communicators have to move beyond the safety of strategy statements and the traditional way of doing things, and leap into the world of the untried and unknown. Once the Big Idea has been captured and successfully executed, it often appears simple—the obvious solution to the communication problem. But that's afterwards. New ideas are always risky.

Risk

Crayola faced up to the risk of modifying a cultural icon when it "retired" eight of its traditional colors and replaced them with vivid contemporary colors that children liked better. To avoid an Old Coke/New Coke disaster, the Binney & Smith PR team established a Crayola Hall of Fame and inducted the old colors in a heavily publicized ceremony. The event generated an average of 300 calls and letters concerning the "Crayola 8" each month from the media as well as Crayola aficionados. The handling of the retirement party and the launch of the new colors won a CIPRA award in 1991.

In an attempt to leverage the visibility, Binney & Smith decided to "unretire" the colors a year later and released them in a nostalgic "collectors series" tin. The relaunch of the colors was announced at a press conference, and the media coverage generated almost 10,000 calls from consumers who wanted to buy the commemorative tin. The low-budget, $35,000 campaign not only won a second CIPRA award, it eclipsed the previous year's efforts which had impacted on sales more dramatically than any other promotion effort in Crayola's 88 colorful years.

Relevance

Most public relations programs attempt to deliver the right message to the right person at the right time. The goal is persuasion that results in some kind of impact on opinions. To have impact on attitudes, however, ideas have to have relevance; in other words, they have to mean something to the target audience. So relevance is an important part of the Big Idea in public relations.

Visa U.S.A., working with Lucas Arts Entertainment Company, developed a high-tech learning module for students called "Choices and Decisions: Taking Charge of Your Life." This highly relevant effort to help students learn fundamental financial management skills was designed with the consultation of respected educators. It involves interactive video-type games in which students help on-screen characters make tough financial choices. The company held demonstrations and training sessions for educators, consumer groups, and member financial institutions so that they could introduce the program locally. At the time it won the PRSA award, the program was in use in nearly 10,000 U.S. high schools.

The "New Presidential Snack" campaign, a really creative PRSA award-winning program, was designed for the Almond Board of California by Ketchum Public Relations, San Francisco. Ketchum found out in 1992 that then President Bill Clinton's personal chef had ordered more than 1,600 pounds of cinnamon-glazed almonds, a Clinton favorite, to be served at the official inaugural balls and special events. Ketchum quickly seized the opportunity to position almonds as the new presidential snack. A "First Snack" press release and media kit were distributed, along with samples of the cinnamon-glazed almonds in a specially designed inaugural jar. KPR also produced a 90-second video news release featuring stories about favorite snack foods of Presidents Bush, Reagan, Carter, and Clinton. California almonds received wide exposure, reaching an estimated audience of 56.3 million with coverage on *NBC Nightly News*, CNN's *Headline News,* and the *Today Show.*

Impact

To be creative, a relevant idea must also have impact. Many mass communication messages just wash over the audience because they are so common, so obvious, or so expected. A message with impact can break through the screen of indifference and focus the audience's attention on the message. It has the stopping power that comes from an intriguing idea; it stops you because it is something you have never thought of before. News is particularly good at stopping people, as are messages with high emotional power.

The "Shot of Love" program sponsored by the Carter Center's Atlanta Project inspired low-income parents to have their preschool children vaccinated. Begun by former President Jimmy Carter to address the problems facing Atlanta's poorest communities, the initiative included a neighbor-to-neighbor walk-through, visiting every household in the targeted areas to identify children under age five. Tools to inform the community included pro bono ads in local newspapers and minority publications, as well as special inserts in telephone bills, posters, billboards, and educational materials featuring the "Give Your Kids a Shot of Love" theme. The initiative was hailed by the Center for Disease Control and national health experts as the most successful U.S. immunization program in history, and much of the success has to do with the emotional power of the message.

Originality

But most of all, in order to have impact the Big Idea has to be original, novel, fresh, or unexpected. Original means one of a kind. Any idea can seem creative if you have never thought of it before, but the essence of a really creative idea is that no one else has thought of it either. In classes on creative thinking, a teacher will typically ask students to come up with ideas about, for example, what you can buy with ten pennies. Some ideas—like penny candy—will appear on many people's lists. Those are the obvious and expected ideas. Original ideas are those that only one person thinks of—like a pay phone call in a small town that has its own phone system.

TACTICS AND PROCEDURES

Supporting the Big Idea is the execution with tactics that must be handled creatively. The execution involves message design—how the idea is spun out into specific promotional materials such as press releases, brochures, posters, and special events. Every message is an opportunity for the Big Idea to be showcased or fumbled. For Swiss Army Knives, the Big Idea was that the knife was the survival tool of the 90s. Madeline de Vries, president of New York-based De Vries PR, explained that "once we had the concept, that was the standard we applied to everything we did." The "survival tool" angle became the hallmark of the knife.

Another well executed Big Idea is the PRSA Silver Anvil award-winning special event by The Peanut Butter Advisory Board. The Peanut Butter Board found the small unincorporated town of Peanut, Pennsylvania, and convinced the entire town to help stage and support a Peanut Butter Lovers' Festival. The Festival featured the creation of the world's largest peanut butter and jelly sandwich, assembled by the town's 140 residents. As a goodwill gesture, the $2 admission fee raised $1,800 for the local library. In a related school food drive the week before the event, more than 1,000 pounds of peanut butter were collected and donated to the local food bank. Every element of the execution reinforced the theme.

Visual/Verbal Synergy

The Big Idea may come to mind as a visual, a phrase, or a thought that uses both visual and verbal expression. If it begins as a phrase, the next step is to try to visualize the concept. If it begins as an image, the next step is to come up with words that express and reinforce the visual. The ideal concept is expressed simultaneously through both the visual and verbal elements. Stephen Baker explains this synergy in noting the need in advertising for "writers who doodle and designers who scribble." [1]

Using the tall ship *Rose* as the focus of a special event to call attention to recycled plastics illustrates the powerful use of visual symbols. This campaign, planned by the American Plastics Council with Fleishman-Hillard in Washington, D.C., was another Silver Anvil award winner. The *Rose* is outfitted with 13,000 square feet of sails woven from 126,000 recycled plastic soft drink bottles. To disseminate the message to legislators and the general public that plastics can be recycled and that the plastics industry supports recycling, the *Rose* sailed up the Potomac River and docked for a week of special events in Washington. On board were educational displays explaining the recycling process and the industry's commitment to recycling, as well as additional items made from recycled plastics. Two Connecticut legislators cosponsored a reception aboard the ship for members of

Congress. Pirate maps distributed in recycled plastic bottles invited guests to the events, with the suggestion that they bring the bottles back for recycling. Evaluation against baseline surveys showed that almost 60 percent of the influentials visiting the *Rose* changed their opinions in a positive way about the plastic industry's commitment to recycling.

Getting Ideas

How do people get big new ideas? There is a myth that certain people are naturally creative and they get Big Ideas by the bushelfull. Actually, creativity is a special form of problem solving; everyone is born with some talent and everyone can develop and improve their personal creative skills if they know what to think about and how to do it. James Adams' book, *Conceptual Blockbusting*, is a particularly good guide to this process.[2]

Consider the concept of an idea. An idea is a new combination of thoughts. As James Webb Young explained in his book, *A Technique for Producing Ideas*, "the ability to make new combinations is heightened by an ability to see relationships."[3] An idea, in other words, is a thought that places two previously unrelated concepts together. The juxtaposition sets up new patterns and new relationships and creates a new way of looking at things. This phenomenon has been described as making the familiar strange and the strange familiar. A creative idea involves a "mind shift." Instead of seeing the obvious, a creative approach looks at something from a different angle. The idea of "Whack Packs," decks of cards designed to jolt people out of their habitual thought patterns and into these mind shifts, was developed by Laurie Kretchmar.[4]

An example of how this juxtaposition works is "Green Speed," a program of the California Office of Traffic Safety created by Manning, Selvage & Lee, Los Angeles, which combined public concerns for speeding and ecology. The effort was directed at the 74 percent of surveyed motorists who indicated that they sometimes speed but would moderate their fast driving if they had sound reasons to do so. "Green Speed" was coined by MSL to serve as the theme of a campaign that gave sound reasons—a combination of safety, environmental, fuel efficiency, and monetary benefits—to these "sometime speeders." The campaign, which won a PRSA Silver Anvil, was launched with a news conference at the state capitol reporting on the survey. PSAs were distributed to TV and radio stations. A nonprofit entity called Californians for Green Speed was created to gain corporate and organizational support.

An unexpected idea can begin with a twist on an old thought, an unusual association or juxtaposition, or catchy phrasing that sticks in the mind. A familiar phrase, like a cliché, can become the raw material of a new idea if it is presented in some unusual way or unexpected situation. A play on words is also a good way to develop something unexpected.

Creative Thinking

According to James Sowrey creative thinking is based on two approaches: association and analysis.[5] Associative thinking is in line with Young's definition of a new idea which calls for the juxtaposition of two seemingly unrelated thoughts. Developing free association skills is one step toward becoming more creative. In free association, you think of a word and then list everything that comes to mind when you imagine that word. Associative thinking can be visual as well as verbal; you can start with a picture. Likewise, you can associate by thinking of either pictures or words.

In contrast, an analytical approach uses information such as that gathered by opinion research and focus group sessions. The raw information is combed for new ideas and unexpected findings which could be the basis for a Big Idea. Associational techniques generate more new ideas than analytical approaches; however, both are needed to stimulate ideas that are both original and strategic.

Creative thinking is also different from the deductive/inductive logical models that are based on a linear logic—one point follows from another, leading to a conclusion. Creative thinking uses an entirely different process. Cognitive psychologist J.P. Guilford distinguishes between convergent thinking, which uses linear logic to arrive at the "right" conclusion, and divergent thinking, which uses associational thinking to search for all possible alternatives rather than a "right" one.[6]

Lateral thinking, an approach developed by Edward de Bono, focuses on an "attitude of the mind" that breaks away from expected ways of thinking. He compares lateral thinking to a dog digging for a bone, or even better, a driller drilling for oil—there's some conscious notion of what you are looking for, but the location process is not as structured as following a map.[7] Attitude, as explained by Michalko in his book *Tinkertoys*, is definitely a part of creativity and the primary personality difference between those who are creative and those who aren't; creative people believe in their creativity.[8]

Another type of divergent thinking, called synectics, uses comparisons such as analogies and metaphors to stimulate associations. Developed by George M. Prince and described by William J. J. Gordon in his book *The Metaphorical Way of Learning and Knowing*, synectics asks participants to solve problems by thinking in analogies—to identify ways in which one pattern or situation is like or similar to another totally unrelated pattern or situation.[9]

APPROACHES TO CREATIVE THINKING

1. Develop free association skills (visual or verbal)
2. Follow an analytical approach (search raw information for new ideas and unexpected findings)
3. Use divergent thinking (search for alternatives)
4. Use lateral thinking (approach data with an altered attitude)
5. Use synetics (analogies and metaphors) to stimulate associations

In current neurophysiology, these two types of thinking also have been identified with different hemispheres of the brain. Left-brain thinking is generally logical and controls speech and writing; right-brain thinking is more intuitive, nonverbal, and emotional. Most people use both sides of their brains, depending on the task. An artist is generally more oriented to right-brain thinking, whereas an accountant is more left-brained. Betty Edwards explains these differences in her book, *Drawing on the Right Side of the Brain*.[10]

The Ideation Process

There is a tendency to stereotype a creative person as someone who sits around waiting like a lightning rod for that one Big Idea to strike. People who are particularly adept at getting Big Ideas, however, know that good ideas are more often developed by diligent effort than they are by a random thought occurring like the proverbial light bulb. People who are creative read, study, analyze, test and retest, observe, sweat, curse, worry, and sometimes give up. Major breakthroughs in science and medicine may take years, even decades. The original thought that qualifies as a Big Idea in any field doesn't come easily.

There is a great deal of agreement among the different theoretical descriptions of the creative process. It is usually portrayed as a series of sequential steps. As long ago as 1926, an English sociologist named Graham Wallas put names to these steps. He called them preparation, incubation, illumination and verification.[11] More recently Alex Osborn, former head of the BBDO advertising agency, founder of the Creative Education Foundation, and author of one of the most important books on creativity, *Applied Imagination*, suggested a more comprehensive process:

1. Orientation: pointing up the problem.
2. Preparation: gathering pertinent data.
3. Analysis: breaking down the relevant material.
4. Ideation: piling up alternative ideas.
5. Incubation: letting up, inviting illumination.
6. Synthesis: putting the pieces together.
7. Evaluation: judging the resulting ideas.[12]

Although the steps vary somewhat and the names differ, all descriptions of the creative process have found that ideas come after the person has immersed himself or herself in the problem and worked at it to the point of giving it up.

The process of creative thinking used in a group situation to get Big Ideas is called brainstorming. Developed in the early 1950s by Osborn, brainstorming uses associative thinking with a group of six to ten people. The idea is that one person's ideas will stimulate someone else, and the combined power of the group associations will stimulate far more ideas than any one person can think of alone. The secret to effective brainstorming is for the group to remain positive and defer evaluation. Negative thinking during a brainstorming session can destroy the trusting atmosphere necessary to stimulate the new risky ideas which often appear at first glance to be zany and off the wall. Judgmental habits can inhibit the creative flow and squelch new ideas.

In reality, most people get ideas all the time and any individual is capable of coming up with an idea or two. The difference between this level of ideation and truly creative thinking is that many random ideas lack originality, are impractical, or stray from the desired strategy. Random ideas come mainly by chance but, as Figure 37–1 illustrates, creative ideas are best generated through a disciplined procedure that stimulates a tremendous quantity of ideas in order to find the diamond. Rarely do Big Ideas just come out-of-the-blue.

The creative mind searches for the positives in a potentially negative situation. Stevens Aviation, a small company that serviced private and corporate aircraft on a largely regional basis, discovered that Southwest Airlines was using a new advertising slogan, "Just Plane-Smart," that mirrored Stevens' slogan, "Plane Smart." Rather than take Southwest to court, Stevens' agency, Earle Palmer Brown, and company president Kurt Herwald decided to challenge Southwest's colorful chairman Herb Kelleher to a winner-take-all arm wrestling contest to determine the rights to the slogan. In addition to creating tremendous publicity, the CIPRA-winning David-and-Goliath battle, dubbed "Malice in Dallas," also let Herwald promote his fervent anti-litigation stance.

The Creative Personality

Creative thinkers are found in every field. Henry Ford (who created and then promoted his Model T), Steven Jobs (the inventor of Apple Computers), and Anita Roddick (who built

F I G U R E 37–1

The Creative Process

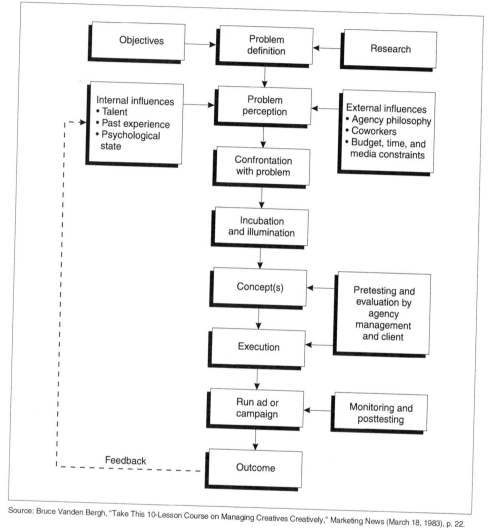

Source: Bruce Vanden Bergh, "Take This 10-Lesson Course on Managing Creatives Creatively," Marketing News (March 18, 1983), p. 22.

Body Shop into an international skin care and cosmetics retail phenomenon) are highly creative. They are idea people, creative problem solvers, and highly original thinkers. Creative people are found in business, in science, in engineering . . . and in public relations.

Are people who come up with Big Ideas born with the talent or have they developed or learned a set of creative skills? Researchers who have studied this question believe that everyone is born with some creative potential—the ability to solve problems by combining complex and sometimes unrelated ideas. Some people, however, have more natural creative skills, just as some people have more natural musical talent. People with more creative skills may start off with an advantage, but that's where it ends. Such talent can even be a disadvantage if the person is too mentally hyperactive to focus on a business situation.

Research by the Center for Studies in Creativity and Creative Education Foundation has found that most people can sharpen their skills if they know the characteristics of creative people. The first characteristic is that creative individuals soak up experiences like sponges. Like Sherlock Holmes, they have a huge personal reservoir of material to work with—things they have read, watched, or listened to, places they have been and worked in, and people they have known. Research has also found that creative people tend to be independent, self-assertive, self-sufficient, and persistent, with a high tolerance for ambiguity. They are risk-takers. They also have powerful egos. In other words, they are internally driven and don't care much about group standards and opinions. They reach conclusions through intuition rather than through logic. They also have a mental playfulness that allows them to make the novel associations that are critical to creative thinking.

Creative people in business are often characterized as zany, weird, off the wall, and unconventional. George Lois, who wrote *What's the Big Idea?*, is an advertising executive who cultivates an outrageous image. The subtitle of his book, however, is *How to Win with Outrageous Ideas (That Sell!)*[13] In other words, creative people in business, even the zany ones like Lois, are still focused on doing effective, strategic work. In public relations, creative people also have to be disciplined because they have to live with deadlines, strategies, and client demands. Some creative people say it is this pressure that makes them perform; the more pressure, the better their work.

Michael Ray and Rochelle Myers, in their book *Creativity in Business*, explore such factors as curiosity, stress, and inspiration in solving business problems. They believe that we all have creative ability, but we have allowed negative thinking, fear, and the right-brained "chattering of our minds" to get in the way of our creativity.[14]

Creativity is complex and involves more than just individuals and their personal characteristics. Creative thinking usually occurs in a social environment and the family, school, and workplace are all important in stimulating or inhibiting Big Ideas. *Theories of Creativity*, a book edited by Mark Runco and Robert Albert, explores these other social and cultural factors from an academic viewpoint.[15]

FORWARD THINKING: THE FUTURE

One trend that both complicates and leverages the creative dimension of public relations is integrated communication or integrated marketing communication (IMC). In zero-based communication planning, which is a foundation concept in IMC, the various functional areas are compared in terms of their abilities to meet the communication objective. If awareness is a problem, for example, then advertising will probably lead the campaign; if credibility is a problem, then public relations will probably lead the effort.

Then the brainstorming begins. Because the Big Idea should come from the functional area that can contribute

Coors looked to its community and came up with a large multifaceted program, "Literacy! Pass it on," that has won a number of CIPRA awards. To bring the impact of illiteracy to life, Coors and its Denver-based agency, Schenkein Sherman, created an event called Wordless USA. A traveling 4,250 sq. ft. town resembling a Broadway set was constructed with signage written in Ameruss—English written in Russian characters—to help literate people experience what it is like to be unable to read. Coors' multiyear, multimillion-dollar commitment to educating the public about literacy has established it as the company most concerned with this issue.

the most to the problem solution, that area may be on the spot. In a boundary-spanning organization in which people are working across disciplines, public relations people will need to be able to hold their own with the creative people from other areas such as advertising, sales promotion, and event marketing. That's why it is important that the creative dimensions of public relations be recognized and encouraged.

Communication managers know that public relations messages are up against a very cluttered environment and an often-indifferent audience. Captivating Big Ideas are needed to grab attention and anchor a thought in the target audience's memory. The only way to break through the clutter and create impact is by expressing the persuasive message in an original way with a Big Idea. Breakthrough ideas, in order to be effective, have to be both creative as well as persuasive. The "Aha" moment represented by that elusive lightbulb is as much a product of perspiration as it is of inspiration. Getting high-level Big Ideas is hard work. This hard work will be even more important in the 21st century as the communication industry reengineers itself to be more effective, more efficient, and more integrated.

E N D N O T E S

1. Baker, Stephen, *A Systematic Approach to Advertising Creativity* (New York: McGraw Hill, 1979).

2. Adams, James L., *Conceptual Blockbusting: A Guide to Better Ideas* (New York: W. W. Norton, 1980).

3. Young, James Webb, *A Technique for Producing Ideas,* 3rd ed. (Chicago: Crain Books, 1975).

4. Kretchmar, Laurie, "How to Think Differently," *Fortune* (January 15, 1990), pp. 11–12.

5. Sowrey, Trevor, "Idea Generation: Identifying the Most Useful Techniques," *European Journal of Marketing* 24, no. 5, pp. 20–29.

6. Guilford, J. P., "Traits of Personality," in *Creativity and Its Cultivation*, H. H. Anderson, ed. (New York: Harper & Brothers, 1959).

7. De Bono, Edward, *Lateral Thinking: Creativity Step by Step* (New York: Harper & Row, 1970).

8. Michalko, Michael, *Tinkertoys* (Berkeley, CA: Ten Speed Press, 1991).

9. Gordon, William J. J. *The Metaphorical Way of Learning and Knowing* (New York: Penguin Books, 1971).

10. Edwards, Betty, *Drawing on the Right Side of the Brain* (Los Angeles: Tarcher, 1979).

11. Wallas, Graham, *The Art of Thought* (New York: Harcourt Brace & Co., 1926).

12. Osborn, Alex F., *Applied Imagination,* 3rd ed. (New York: Charles Scribner's Sons, 1963).

13. Lois, George, *What's the Big Idea? How to Win with Outrageous Ideas (That Sell!)* (New York: Penguin Books, 1991).

14. Ray, Michael, and Rochelle Myers, *Creativity in Business* (Garden City, NY: Doubleday Publishing, 1986).

15. Runco, Mark A., and Robert S. Albert, *Theories of Creativity* (Newbury Park, CA: Sage Publications, 1990).

The Future of Integrated Communications and Public Relations

Clarke L. Caywood, Ph.D.
Chairman
Department of Integrated Marketing
and Communications
Medill School of Journalism
Northwestern University

The best advice in business today is "under promise and over deliver." I hope, if you read the book from cover to cover (or even sections), that you found more than useful its contribution to your thinking about public relations, integrated communications, stakeholders, and specific industries.

A primary objective of this book is to document how no significant field of management can be practiced without being integrated through the efforts of public relations. It is my prediction, based upon over 20 years of business, marketing, and public relations education in a concurrent career in government and business consulting, that there will be no patience for men and women who want to practice their profession or craft isolated from other business or organizational functions.

In short, the future managers must be very much like the authors of this book who compiled knowledge on the best practices in their areas of business and other organizational specializations. The chapter authors were "cross nominated" by other professionals in the field as leaders in their industry, as excellent writers, and as dedicated professionals willing to share their knowledge with their contemporaries and with a new generation of public relations professionals and other managers. Most of the authors were personal and professional associates from my work in the Arthur W. Page Society, the Public Relations Society of America, and my work at Northwestern University as director of the Graduate Program in Corporate Public Relations beginning in 1989.

While I have practiced and taught public relations all my professional life, the experience gained at Northwestern's Medill School has been unmatched for the richness of opportunity to work closely with the top professionals in the field. My earliest start in public relations was inspired by Harry Backer who served for many years as director and then vice-president of Oscar Mayer & Co. and by Professors Scott Cutlip and Doug Jones at the University of Wisconsin-Madison School of Journalism and Mass Communications.

Even then my interests in communications as a field of study coincided with my professional interest in the management of complex organizations. By persuading an understanding assistant dean of the School of Commerce that communications coursework in the School of Journalism would enhance my education, I set in motion the idea in my mind that management, marketing, public relations, and advertising should be integrated through communications, and research-based decision making.

Nearly ten years later I returned to both schools and persuaded their separate graduate faculties and deans that a joint degree at the doctoral level would make sense. I based my argument on a lengthy proposal citing their writing and my recent experience working with business closely as an assistant for a governor and later as a lobbyist for an attorney general of Wisconsin. My educational experience was reinforced in practice seeing the power and value of communication in the election process (perhaps the most vivid example of the integrated communications process described in the Introduction) and in the management of government and business relations.

It seemed to me at that time, and it still seems to me, that the field of public relations as a professional education degree offers the student and participant both the widest and deepest use of his or her mind and the challenge of applying ideas into action. In the 1996–97, *Journal of Corporate Public Relations* (renamed *The Journal of Integrated Communications* in 1997), I wrote about the "Renaissance" quality of the men and women in public relations. The intellectual and practical demands made on public relations professionals requires the widest knowledge of contemporary issues represented in this book, qualitative and quantitative problem solving and analysis. In short, the demands on public relations represented in this book suggests the range of the authors' intellect and skill as well as their depth of knowledge of specific issues.

The promise of public relations is the delivery of a sharper focus on the needs and interests of one or many stakeholders with relevant, important, and useful messages. The promise of public relations is reflected in the work of the many co-authors of this book as they tell the reader how to more strategically develop efficient, effective, and equitable integrated communications and management programs to accomplish the mutual goals of the organization and society.

The challenge facing the men and women who run our institutions at the turn of the new century will be to use all the knowledge available to them to manage their organizations' responses to their customers, their employees, and other stakeholders.

It seems permissible to predict some developments in the field of public relations based upon experience. The challenge facing the reader will be to keep an old copy of this book on a back shelf over the years so that it might be possible to validate these predictions.

- Organizations will be restructured nearly continuously at different levels based upon the demands of the market, stakeholders, and society.

- Greater and greater amounts of managed information will be used for public relations and management decision making from syndicated and proprietary databases built from integrated communications programs.

- Organizations will use more "zero-based" thinking and planning to move away from incremental budgeting and implementation.

- Organizations will track external trends and events with greater rigor and precision to anticipate changes relevant to their products, services, and stakeholders.

- In general, organizations will be managed increasingly from the outside-in rather than the inside-out with the benefit of issues management and other PR practices.

- Organizations will be managed by modern "renaissance men and women" with both qualitative and quantitative skills and the hearts and minds to use the skills.

- Corporate and organizational values and will align more precisely with ethical standards.
- Organizations will use more precise and fiscally measurable methods to evaluate and judge the results of integrated management and communications programs.
- The growth of new and more effective media will increase the value of public relations as a communications-based field.
- Global relationship building will contribute to a more significant role for public relations using advanced communications technologies and knowledge.
- Public relations thinking and practice will permeate all levels of organizations with both the ability to contribute to the long- and short-run objectives.
- Career opportunities will increase for public relations and PR-related areas of professional practice.
- Organizations will rely increasingly on stronger alliances with customers, suppliers, and other stakeholders. In some cases organizations will work more closely with their historical competition.

In short, the organization of the future will be fully integrated.

As a professor in a professional field of study, I often conclude my classroom courses with my graduate students and my speeches and presentations to industry with career advice.

It is clear to me that while the level of professional performance will continuously improve and challenge the public relations professional's ability to produce high quality research and communications, improvement in areas of skill will not be enough. The success of managers will be determined by their specific and accurate knowledge of stakeholder and customer segments relevant to their organization. Young and older professionals must develop a detailed knowledge of specific customer, consumer, and other stakeholder groups. The level of knowledge and insight should be so great that the organization cannot hold meetings, plan for the future or make decisions on issues related to the customer or stakeholder without the contribution of the PR professional in person, electronically, or even virtually. Such expertise will make the PR professional crucial to the success of the organization. And the success of the organization using the advanced and integrated practices of public relations will ensure the success of the field and of the professionals who lead it.